The Best Bed & Breakfast
in England, Scotland & Wales
1998–99

Sigourney We

Jill Darbey

Joanna Mortir

The finest Bed & Breakfast accommodations in the
British Isles
from the Scottish Hebrides to
London's Belgravia

Country Houses, Town Houses, City Apartments, Manor
Houses, Village Cottages, Farmhouses, Castles

U.K.H.M. Publishing, London, U.K.

The Globe Pequot Press, Old Saybrook, Connecticut, U.S.A.

Library of Congress Catalog Card Number: 91-074158

U.S. ISBN 0-7627-0142-0

Typeset by U.K.H.M. Publishing Ltd., London.
Printed in Hong Kong.

U.K.H.M. Publishing Ltd., P.O. Box 2070, London W12 8QW, England.

Contents

Foreword

Bed & Breakfast has suddenly become the fashionable way to travel. The secret has escaped & thousands of people are discovering for themselves that it is possible to combine high quality accommodation with friendly, personal attention at very reasonable prices. The New York Times said about us that "...after an unannounced inspection of rooms booked through The Worldwide Bed & Breakfast Association it is clear that the standards of comfort & cleanliness are exemplary ...at least as good as in a five star hotel & in most cases, better, reflecting the difference between sensitive hosts taking pride in their homes & itinerant hotel staff doing as little as they can get away with..."

Discerning travellers are turning away from the impersonal hotels with the expensive little refridgerators & microwave breakfasts in each room. How much nicer to have a real English breakfast to begin the day, enough to keep you going until evening. Many of our houses will provide dinner too - often the hostess will be a Cordon Bleu cook & the price will be within your range. We try to provide the best accommodation possible within a wide range of prices, some as little as £15.00 per person per night, whilst others will be up to £55.00 per person per night. The choice is yours, but you can be certain that each will be the best available in that particular area of the country at that price.

Our inspectors are out & about visiting our homes to ensure that standards are maintained. We encourage everyone to use the recommendations & complaints page at the back of the book. Let us know your opinion of the accommodation or inform us of any delightful homes you may have come across & would like to recommend for future inclusion.

In order to avoid the classification trap, which we feel is invidious, we encourage you to read about each home, what they offer & their respective price range, so that you find the one that best suits your expectations. Our hosts in turn offer hospitality in their own unique style, so each home naturally retains its individuality & interest. We have found this to be a very successful recipe which has often led to firm friendships with invitations being extended to visit each other again.

Bed & Breakfast really is a marvellous way to travel, meeting a delightful cross section of fellow travellers with whom to exchange information & maybe the address of... that lovely little place which was discovered by chance and which serves the most delicious dinner or... the best route to take to a particular farmhouse but make sure you get there by 5 o'clock so that you're in time to watch the evening milking.

This is the fun & real pleasure that is part of Bed & Breakfasting. Once you've tried it you will be a dedicated Best Bed & Breakfaster.

How to use this Guide

To get the full benefits of staying at our Bed & Breakfast homes it is important to appreciate how they differ from hotels, so both hosts & guests know what to expect.

Arrival & Departure

These times are more important to a family than to hotel desk clerks, so your time of arrival (E.T.A.) is vital information when making a reservation either with the home directly or with one of our agencies. This becomes even more important to your reception if you intend travelling overnight & will be arriving in the early morning. So please have this information & your flight number ready when you book your rooms. At most B & Bs the usual check-in time is 6 p.m. & you will be expected to check out by 10 a.m. on the morning of departure. These arrangements do vary from home to home so the secret to an enjoyable visit is to let your hosts know as much about your plans as possible & they will do their best to meet your requirements.

Other personal requests

There are a few other details that you should let your hosts know when planning your Bed & Breakfast trip that will make everyone much happier during your visit.

*Do you smoke? Would you prefer to be in a non-smoking home?
*Do you suffer from any allergies? Some families have cats, dogs, birds & other pets in the house.
*Can you make it up a flight of stairs? Would you prefer the ground floor?
*Do you have any special dietary requirements? Will you be staying for dinner?

*Do you prefer a private bathroom or are you prepared to share facilities?
*Do you prefer a shower instead of a bath?
*The ages of any children travelling.
In all these cases let your host know what you need & the details can be arranged before you arrive rather than presenting a problem when you are shown to your rooms.

Prices

The prices quoted throughout the guide are the *minimum* per person per night for two sharing. Single occupancy usually attracts a supplement. Prices will increase during busy seasons. You should always confirm the prevailing rate when you make a reservation.

Facilities

The bathroom & toilet facilities affect the prices. Sharing is the cheapest, private is a little more costly & en-suite carries a premium.

Descriptions

Rooms are described as follows:
Single: 1 bed (often quite small).
Double: 1 large bed (sometimes King or Queen size).
Twin: 2 separate single beds.
Four-poster: a King or Queen size bed with a canopy above supported by four corner posts.
Bathrooms and toilets are described as follows;
Shared : these facilities are shared with some other guests or perhaps the hosts.
Private : for your use only, however they may occasionally be in an adjacent room.
En-suite: private facilities within your bedroom suite.

Making a Reservation

Once you have chosen where you want to stay, have all the following information ready & your reservation will go smoothly without having to run & find more travel documents or ask someone else what they think you should do. Here is a brief check list of what you will probably be asked & examples to illustrate answers:

* Dates & number of nights .... August 14-19 (6 nights).
* Estimated time of arrival at the home ...7 p.m. (evening) & flight number.
* Type & number of rooms.... 1 Double & 2 Singles.
* Toilet & Bathroom facilities ...1 Double en-suite) & 2 singles (shared)
* Smoking or Non-smoking?
* Any allergies?
* Special dietary requests?
* Children in the party & their ages?
* Any other preferences… Is a shower preferred to a bath?
* Maximum budget per person per night based on all the above details.

The London Reservation Agency

There is a minimum two night consecutive stay at our London Homes.

Reservations for London homes can only be made through one of our Worldwide Bed & Breakfast Agencies. They can be contacted by 'phone, fax or e-mail. Why not visit our website at www.bestbandb.co.uk

All reservations must be confirmed with advance payments which are non-refundable in the event of cancellation. You simply pay the balance due after you arrive at the home. The advance payment can be made with major credit & charge cards or by cheque. Cash is the preferred method of paying the balance & always in pounds sterling.

The advance payments confirm each night of your visit - **not just the first one**. When arriving at a later date or departing at an earlier date than those confirmed, the guest will be liable to pay only the appropriate proportion of the stated balance that is due. For example, staying three nights out of four booked means paying 3/4 of the stated balance due. The advance payment is non-refundable. A minimum of 2 nights will always apply.

Outside London

We encourage you to make use of the information in this guide & contact the homes directly. The hosts may require varying amounts of advance payments & may or may not accept credit & charge cards. Remember, many B&Bs are small, family-run establishments and are unable to accept payment by credit card. The confirmed prices shall be those prevailing on the dates required… as previously mentioned, *the prices shown in this guide are the minimum & will increase during the busy seasons.*

Alterations .

If you wish to alter or change a previously confirmed booking through one of the agencies there will be a further fee of £15 per alteration.

Cancellations

All advance payments for London are non-refundable.

All booking fees outside London are non-refundable.

Notice of cancellation must be given as soon as possible & the following suggested rates shall apply outside London only;

30-49 days notice - 80% refund.
10-29 days notice - 50% refund.
0-9 days notice - No refund.
The Worldwide Bed & Breakfast Agencies reserve the right to alter your accommodation should it be necessary & will inform you of any alteration as soon as possible.

The Best Bed & Breakfast London Reservation Agency

Visit our website at: www.bestbandb.co.uk

We have an outstanding selection of accommodation in London. As with all our accommodation each one has been personally inspected so you can be sure of the highest standards. We offer an immensely wide range of accommodation. We have a type, style and location to suit everyone. From city apartments close to shops, museums and galleries to spacious homes in leafy residential suburbs near the river, parks and restaurants. No matter what your reason for visiting London we can accommodate you. Whether business or vacation Best Bed & Breakfast provides great accommodation together with a fast, efficient reservation service. Our helpful staff are always happy to advise you on all your accommodation requirements. We know London, we are located in London and we know all our hosts. We know how to provide an enjoyable, affordable, hassle free trip to London. There are plenty of ways to contact us. To make a reservation simply do one of the following;

Call us on: Tel: 44 181 742 9123 (24Hrs.)

Fax us on: Fax: 44 181 749 7084

E-mail us: E-mail:bestbandb@atlas.co.uk

U.S.A., Canada & Australia call:
Toll Free: 0 800 852 26320

The Discount Offer

This offer is made to people who have bought this book & wish to make reservations for Bed & Breakfast in London through our London Reservation Agency. The offer only applies to a minimum stay of three consecutive nights at one of our London homes between the following; January 1. 1998 & April 15. 1998 then from September 15 .1998 to December 1. 1998. Only one discount per booking is allowed. Call the reservation office to make your booking in the normal way & tell the clerk that you have bought the book & wish to have the discount. After a couple of questions the discount will be deducted from the advance payment required to confirm the reservation.

Regions

To assist tourists with information during their travels, counties have been grouped together under Regional Tourist Boards that co-ordinate the various efforts of each county.

The British Tourist Authority has designated these areas in consultation with the English, Scottish & Wales Tourist Boards & we have largely adopted these areas for use in this guide

Counties are listed alphabetically throughout our guide & then have a sub-heading indicating which Tourist Region they belong to.

ENGLAND
Cumbria
County of Cumbria
Northumbria.
Counties of Cleveland, Durham, Northumberland, Tyne & Wear.
North West
Counties of Cheshire, Greater Manchester, Lancashire, Merseyside, High Peaks of Derbyshire.
Yorkshire & Humberside
Counties of North Yorkshire, South Yorkshire, West Yorkshire, Humberside.
Heart of England
Counties of Gloucestershire, Herefordshire & Worcestershire, Shropshire, Staffordshire, Warwickshire, West Midlands.
East Midlands
Counties of Derbyshire, Leicestershire, Nottinghamshire, Rutland, Lincolnshire & Northamptonshire,
East Anglia
Counties of Cambridgeshire, Essex, Norfolk, Suffolk.
West Country
Counties of Cornwall, Devon, Dorset (parts of), Somerset, Wiltshire, Isles of Scilly.
Southern
Counties of Hampshire, Dorset (East & North), Isle of Wight.
South East
Counties of East Sussex, Kent, Surrey, West Sussex.

SCOTLAND
The subdivisions of Scottish Regions in this guide differ slightly from the current Marketing Regions of the Scottish Tourist Board.

The Borders, Dumfries & Galloway
Districts & counties of Scottish Borders, Dumfries & Galloway.
Lothian & Strathclyde
City of Edinburgh, Forth Valley, East Lothian, Kirkaldy, St. Andrews & North-East Fife, Greater Glasgow, Clyde Valley, Ayrshire & Clyde Coast, Burns Country.
Argyll & The Isles
Districts & counties of Oban & Mull, Mid Argyll, Kintyre & Islay, Dunoon, Cowal, Rothesay & Isle of Bute, Isle of Arran.
Perthshire, Loch Lommond & The Trossachs.
Districts & counties of Perthshire, Loch Lomond, Stirling & Trossachs.
The Grampians
Districts & counties of Banff & Buchan, Moray, Gordon, Angus, City of Aberdeen, Kincardine & Deeside, City of Dundee.
The Highlands & Islands
Districts & counties of Shetland, Orkney, Caithness, Sutherland, Ross & Cromarty, Western Isles, South West Ross & Isle of Skye, Inverness, Loch Ness & Nairn, Aviemore & Spey Valley, Fort William & Lochaber.

WALES
The regions are defined as follows:
North Wales
Counties of Anglesey, Conwy, Denbighshire, Flintshire & Gwynedd.
Mid Wales
Counties of Ceredigion & Powys.
South Wales
Counties of Carmarthenshire, Glamorgan, Monmouthshire, Newport, Pembrokeshire & Swansea.

The photographs appearing in the Introductions & Gazeteers are by courtesy of the appropriate Tourist Board for each county or W.W.B.B.A.

Counties map

Each county has been assigned a page number where a more detailed map can be found. These maps include principal towns, major roads & the location of each Bed & Breakfast establishment.

SCOTLAND
508

1 INVERCLYDE
2 DUNBARTON & CLYDEBANK
3 RENFREWSHIRE
4 EAST RENFREWSHIRE
5 GLASGOW
6 EAST DUNBARTONSHIRE
7 NORTH LANARKSHIRE
8 FALKIRK
9 CLACKMANNAN
10 WEST LOTHIAN
11 EDINBURGH
12 MID LOTHAIN

OUTER HEBRIDES
WESTERN ISLES
INNER HEBRIDES
H I G H L A N D S
MORAY
ABERDEENSHIRE
ABERDEEN
PERTHSHIRE & KINROSS
ANGUS
DUNDEE
ARGYLL & BUTE
STIRLING
FIFE
EAST LOTHIAN
NORTH AYRSHIRE
SOUTH LANARK-SHIRE
BORDERS
EAST AYRSHIRE
SOUTH AYRSHIRE
DUMFRIES & GALLOWAY
NORTHUMBERLAND

North Sea

TYNE AND WEAR
291
DURHAM
CLEVELAND

CUMBRIA
86

YORKSHIRE

467 HUMBERSIDE

LANCASHIRE
51

Irish Sea

MANCHESTER
MERSEYSIDE

ENGLAND

FLINTSHIRE
DENBIGHSHIRE
ANGLESEY
CONWY
CHESHIRE **51**
DERBYSHIRE & STAFFORD-SHIRE **118**
NOTTINGHAM-SHIRE, LEICESTERSHIRE & RUTLAND **266**
LINCOLNSHIRE **273**
WREXHAM
GWYNEDD
NORFOLK **280**

WALES
564

SHROP-SHIRE **322**
CEREDIGION
POWYS
HEREFORD & WORCESTER **231**
WARWICK-SHIRE **427**
CAMBRIDGE-SHIRE & NORTHAMPTON-SHIRE **42**
SUFFOLK **387**

CARMARTHENSHIRE
PEMBROKESHIRE
MONMOUTH-SHIRE **185**
GLOUCESTER-SHIRE **303**
OXFORD-SHIRE **30**
BEDFORDSHIRE, BERKSHIRE, BUCKINGHAMSHIRE, & HERTFORDSHIRE
ESSEX **179**

SWANSEA
NEWPORT
CARDIFF
VALE OF GLAMORGAN
NEATH & PORT TALBOT
LONDON
18
KENT **244**

1 BRIDGEND
2 RHONDA CYNON TAFF
3 MERTHYR TYDFIL
4 CAERPHILLY
5 BLAENAU GWENT
6 TORFAEN

WILTSHIRE **453**
SOMERSET **339**
HAMPSHIRE **216**
SURREY **399**
SUSSEX **407**

DEVON **131**
DORSET **162**

CORNWALL **63**

English Channel

General Information

To help overseas visitors with planning their trip to Britain, we have compiled the next few pages explaining the basic requirements & customs you will find here.

Before you arrive

Documents you will have to obtain before you arrive;

Valid passports & visas. Citizens of Commonwealth countries or the U.S.A. don't need visas to enter the U.K. Bring your local Driving Licence.

Medical Insurance.

This is strongly recommended although visitors will be able to receive free emergency treatment. If you have to stay in hospital in the U.K. you will be asked to pay unless you are a citizen of European Community Countries.

Restrictions on arrival

Immigration procedures can be lengthy & bothersome, be prepared for questions like:

a) where are you staying in the U.K.?
b) do you have a round trip ticket?
c) how long do you intend to stay?
d) how much money are you bringing in?
e) do you have a credit card?

Do not bring any animals with you as they are subject to 6 months quarantine & there are severe penalties for bringing in pets without appropriate licences. Do not bring any firearms, prohibited drugs or carry these things for anyone else. If you are in doubt about items in your possession, declare them by entering the Red Channel at Customs & seek the advice of an officer.

After you have arrived

You can bring in as much currency as you like. You can change your own currency or travellers cheques at many places at varying rates.

Airports tend to be the most expensive places to change money & the 'Bureau de Change" are often closed at nights. So bring enough Sterling to last you at least 2 or 3 days. Banks often charge commission for changing money. Some Cashcard machines (or A.T.M.'s) will dispense local currency using your charge card, if they are affiliated systems, & don't charge commissions to your account. Major credit cards/charge cards are widely accepted & you may only need to carry small amounts of cash for "pocket money".

Driving

Don't forget to drive on the Left... especially the first time you get into a car... at the airport car hire parking lot... or from the front of a railway station... or straight after breakfast... old habits are hard to shake off. If you need to know the rules, get a copy of the Highway Code. You must wear a seat belt & so must any other front seat passenger. The speed limits are clearly shown in most areas - generally 30 mph. in residential areas (48 kph) & 70 mph on motorways (113 kph.). Traffic lights are at the side of the road & not hanging overhead. Car hire is relatively expensive in the U.K. & it is often a good idea to arrange this before you arrive. Mileage charges, V.A.T. (Sales Tax) & insurance are usually charged extra & you will need to be over 21 to hire a car in the U.K. Petrol (gas) is also relatively expensive & you may find petrol stations hard to find or closed at night in rural areas... so fill up often. Driving in London is not a recommended experience for newcomers & parking is also a very complex arrangement which can become a nightmare if the car gets "clamped" (immobilised) or towed away.

General Information

Buses & Coaches

If you are not driving & only want to travel 5-10 miles there are good bus services within most towns & cities, however, rural routes have seriously declined over the last few years. There are regular & fast coach services between the major towns which are very popular - so book ahead to be sure of a seat.

Trains

There is an extensive railway system throughout the U.K. which serves the major towns on a fast & frequent basis. British Rail is a relatively expensive service & like most railway systems subject to delays.

However, if you plan to do lots of rail travel the best deal is to buy a Britrail Pass before you leave home (you can't buy these once in the U.K.)

Tubes (Subways)

London is the only city with an extensive subway system although some other towns do have "Metro" trains of linked under & overground systems.

The "tube" is a very popular means of getting around London, but it can get very crowded & unpleasant at "rush hours". It is often the preferred way to get into London from say Heathrow Airport in the early morning, when there are long delays on the roads that hold up both buses & taxis with increasingly expensive rides into the city centre, £35 is not unusual for this cab fare, compared with a few pounds on the "tube". The "tube" in London is operated by London Transport which also operates the London bus service ... the famous red buses. They sell tickets which allow you to travel all over London on tubes, buses & trains at very good rates, called Travelcards... a transfer system. Ask your local travel agent about these & other travel passes throughout the U.K.

Telephones

When calling the U.K. from abroad always drop the 0 from the area code. In the U.K. the only free calls are the operator - 100, enquiries - 192 (international 153) & emergencies - 999.

You may use your calling card to call home which is billed to your account or call collect, ask the operator to "reverse charge" the call. The famous red telephone kiosks are slowly being replaced with new glass booths & they differ in that the old boxes only take 10 & 50 pence pieces & don't give any change, whereas the new ones take many combinations of coins & do give change. Phonecards are becoming more popular as the number of boxes that only accept these cards increases. Cards can be bought at Post Offices & many newsagents & shops.

Doctors/Chemists

All local police stations have lists of chemists & doctors should you need one, at night, for instance.

Voltage

The standard voltage throughout the country is 240v AC.50Hz. If you bring small electrical appliances with you, a converter will be required.

Tipping

Is not obligatory anywhere but a general guide if you wish to leave a tip for service is between 10%-15%.

Pubs

Most open between 11 a.m. & 11 p.m. every day.
You must be over 18 years old to buy & drink alcohol in pubs .

11

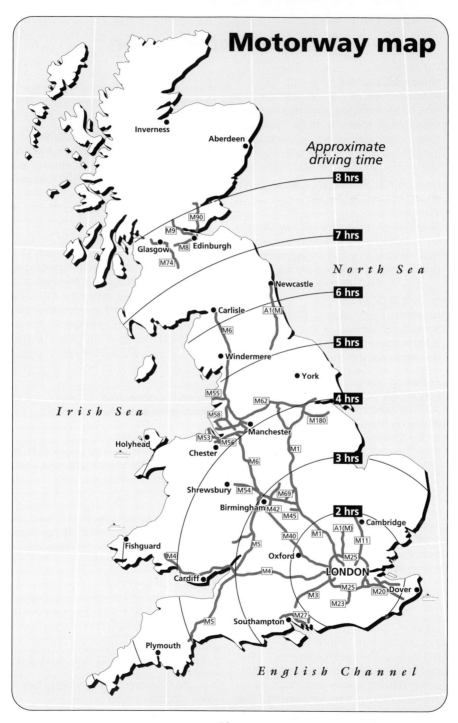

Motorway map

Approximate driving time

8 hrs

7 hrs

6 hrs

5 hrs

4 hrs

3 hrs

2 hrs

North Sea

Irish Sea

English Channel

Inverness

Aberdeen

M90
M9
M8 Edinburgh
Glasgow
M74

Newcastle

Carlisle   A1(M)
M6

Windermere

York

M55
M62
M58   M180
M53
M56 Manchester
Chester   M1
Holyhead   M6

Shrewsbury   M54   M69
Birmingham M42
M45
M40   M1   A1(M)   Cambridge
M5   M11
M25
Oxford
LONDON
M4
Cardiff
M5   M25   M20 Dover
M3   M23
Fishguard
M4
M27
M5   Southampton

Plymouth

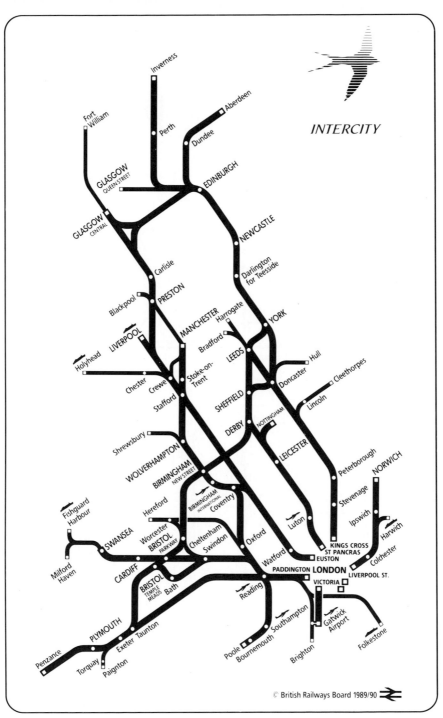

INTERCITY

TLB/90/1008

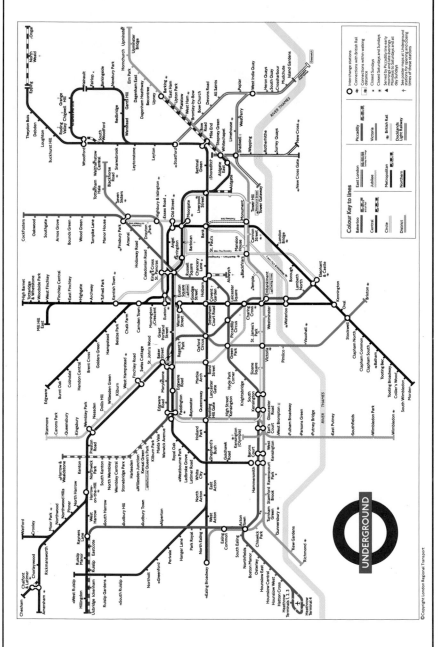

UNDERGROUND

© Copyright London Regional Transport

91/1258

LONDON MAP

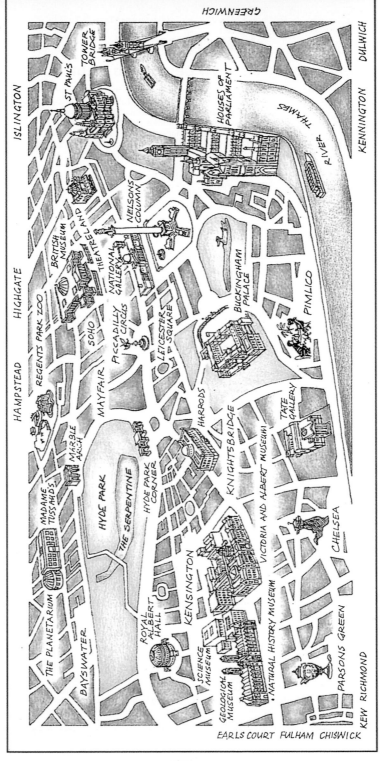

London

		rate from £ per person	children taken	evening meals	animals taken
Home No. 01 **W.W.B.B.A.** **London** **Tel: 0181-742-9123 (24hrs.)** **Fax: 0181-749-7084** **U.S., Canada & Australia** **Toll Free 0-800-852-26320** E-mail:bestbandb@atlas.co.uk	Nearest Tube: Putney Bridge An attractive Victorian terraced house, situated in a quiet residential street, yet only 3 mins walk from the station. 1 spacious double-bedded room with an en-suite bathroom & a twin-bedded room with a private bathroom. Each room is attractive & tastefully furnished & has tea/coffee facilities. (T.V. available.) Breakfast is served in the pleasant kitchen/dining room. Many good pubs, restaurants & shops locally. An excellent location from which to explore London. Parking. Children over 12.	£28.00	Y	N	N
Home No. 03 **W.W.B.B.A.** **London** **Tel: 0181-742-9123 (24hrs.)** **Fax: 0181-749-7084** **U.S., Canada & Australia** **Toll Free 0-800-852-26320** E-mail: bestbandb@atlas.co.uk	Nearest Tube: Parsons Green Located less than two minutes walk from the underground, in a quiet & leafy street in Parsons Green. A comfortable Victorian terraced house which is delightfully furnished & decorated to a high standard. The charming hosts offer two twin-bedded rooms, 1 with access to own garden, both have en-suite bathroom, colour T.V. & hairdryer. The enjoyment of your stay is the first consideration of the hosts. Only 20 minutes from Piccadilly, Knightsbridge & Buckingham Palace.	£28.00	N	N	N
Home No. 05 **W.W.B.B.A.** **London** **Tel: 0181-742-9123 (24hrs.)** **Fax: 0181-749-7084** **U.S., Canada & Australia** **Toll Free 0-800-852-26320** E-mail: bestbandb@atlas.co.uk	Nearest Tube: South Kensington Located in the heart of Chelsea with its' many fashionable shops & restaurants, yet set in a very quiet street. This delightful Victorian terraced townhouse is attractively decorated throughout & tastefully furnished with antiques. The charming host offers 1 spacious & beautifully furnished double-bedded room with T.V. & a superb private bathroom with jacuzzi bath, power shower etc. A delicious breakfast is served. Within easy walking distance are the museums at South Kensington, the V & A, Knightsbridge & Harrods.	£33.00	N	N	N
Home No. 06 **W.W.B.B.A.** **London** **Tel: 0181-742-9123 (24hrs.)** **Fax: 0181-749-7084** **U.S., Canada & Australia** **Toll Free 0-800-852-26320** E-mail: bestbandb@atlas.co.uk	Nearest Tube: East Putney A Victorian terraced house with a traditional family atmosphere & set in a quiet residential street. The friendly hosts offer 1 comfortable twin-bedded room with T.V., overlooking the rear garden, & with an adjacent private bathroom. A large Continental or Full English breakfast is served. Putney is a delightful area with many good shops & restaurants. Excellent tube service to central London & the sights.	£26.00	Y	N	N
Home No. 09 **W.W.B.B.A.** **London** **Tel: 0181-742-9123 (24hrs.)** **Fax: 0181-749-7084** **U.S., Canada & Australia** **Toll Free 0-800-852-26320** E-mail: bestbandb@atlas.co.uk	Nearest Tube: Earls Court This is a beautiful apartment set within a Victorian townhouse. The charming host, who is an interior designer, has stylishly decorated & furnished this home throughout. A stunning en-suite double-bedded room is available which is extremely comfortable & has a T.V. & video. Guests have access to a small patio from their room. Breakfast is served in the attractive kitchen/diner which overlooks the pretty terraced garden. Easy access to Londons' many attractions & Heathrow by tube.	£31.00	N	N	N

London

Visit our website at: www.bestbandb.co.uk

	rate from £ per person	children taken	evening meals	animals taken
Home No. 13 **W.W.B.B.A.** **London** **Tel: 0181-742-9123 (24hrs.)** **Fax: 0181-749-7084** **U.S., Canada & Australia** **Toll Free 0-800-852-26320** **E-mail: bestbandb@atlas.co.uk** Nearest Tube: Marble Arch An attractive apartment situated in a square of period houses, less than 10 mins walk from Marble Arch. The friendly & well-travelled host offers 1 cosy & very comfortable single-bedded room which is tastefully furnished & has a T.V. etc. There is an excellent private shower room adjacent. A large Continental breakfast is served. A superb location for sight-seeing; theatreland & the West End are just a short walk away.	£46.00	N	N	N
Home No. 17 **W.W.B.B.A.** **London** **Tel: 0181-742-9123 (24hrs.)** **Fax: 0181-749-7084** **U.S., Canada & Australia** **Toll Free 0-800-852-26320** **E-mail: bestbandb@atlas.co.uk** Nearest Tube: Richmond Situated in an exclusive 17th-century terrace this is an outstanding home, elegantly furnished throughout with antiques. 2 guest rooms, each with a private bathroom. The Florentine with romantic 4-poster bed & the Venetian which is twin-bedded are both beautifully decorated. From each room French windows open out onto a private & very pretty patio garden, where breakfast can be served (weather permitting.). Fashionable shops, pubs & restaurants are a few mins walk & central London is only 25 mins away by tube.	£39.00	N	N	N
Home No. 18 **W.W.B.B.A.** **London** **Tel: 0181-742-9123 (24hrs.)** **Fax: 0181-749-7084** **U.S., Canada & Australia** **Toll Free 0-800-852-26320** **E-mail: bestbandb@atlas.co.uk** Nearest Tube: High St. Ken. A beautiful house, furnished with many interesting paintings & situated in the heart of Kensington. The charming host offers 1 light & airy, twin-bedded room with a good private bathroom. There is also another, equally attractive twin-bedded room, across the hall, which is ideal for a third or fourth member of the party. Each bedroom is well-furnished & a T.V. is available. Only a short walk from the High Street with its many shops & restaurants & within easy reach of Kensington Palace & gardens, Knightsbridge & the museums.	£29.00	N	N	N
Home No. 19 **W.W.B.B.A.** **London** **Tel: 0181-742-9123 (24hrs.)** **Fax: 0181-749-7084** **U.S., Canada & Australia** **Toll Free 0-800-852-26320** **E-mail: bestbandb@atlas.co.uk** Nearest Tube: Parsons Green Located in the quiet Parsons Green area of Fulham. This superb house offers accommodation in 1 king-size double-bedded room with private facilities & 2 doubles which share a bathroom. Each room is beautifully decorated & very comfortably furnished. This is a delightful home & the ideal base for visitors to London. Many of the attractions including Buckingham Palace & Knightsbridge are only 15 mins away by tube.	£28.00	N	N	N
Home No. 21 **W.W.B.B.A.** **London** **Tel: 0181-742-9123 (24hrs.)** **Fax: 0181-749-7084** **U.S., Canada & Australia** **Toll Free 0-800-852-26320** **E-mail: bestbandb@atlas.co.uk** Nearest Tube: Hammersmith This is a charming Victorian terraced house, where the welcoming hosts offer 1 spacious & comfortably furnished twin-bedded room with sitting area & 1 attractive king-size double/twin room. Each with private facilities, T.V. & tea/coffee. Breakfast is served in the elegant dining room. A delightful family home set in a quiet street, yet only 8 mins walk from Hammersmith with its many restaurants etc. Easy access to Heathrow, central London & the sights by tube.	£26.00	Y	N	N

London

Visit our website at: www.bestbandb.co.uk

	rate from £ per person	children taken	evening meals	animals taken

Home No. 24
W.W.B.B.A.
London
Tel: 0181-742-9123 (24hrs.)
Fax: 0181-749-7084
U.S., Canada & Australia
Toll Free 0-800-852-26320
E-mail: bestbandb@atlas.co.uk

Nearest Tube: Parsons Green
An elegantly furnished Victorian terraced house, situated in a quiet street yet only 5 mins walk from all transport facilities. The most charming hosts offer 1 delightful double-bedded room which overlooks the rear garden & an attractive king-size double/twin-bedded room. Each has a private bathroom & every comfort including T.V. & tea/coffee-making facilities. Parsons Green is an ideal base from which to explore the delights of London & has many excellent restaurants & shops. Non-smokers preferred.

£28.00 | N | N | N

Home No. 29
W.W.B.B.A.
London
Tel: 0181-742-9123 (24hrs.)
Fax: 0181-749-7084
U.S., Canada & Australia
Toll Free 0-800-852-26320
E-mail: bestbandb@atlas.co.uk

Nearest Tube: East Putney
Located in the residential area of Putney, this is a lovely Victorian house set in a quiet street - yet only 20 mins. to central London by tube. The charming & helpful host offers 2 beautiful guest rooms, 1 a spacious double/twin & a double overlooking the rear garden; ideal for parties of 2 or more. Guests have their own private bathroom. A delicious & varied breakfast is served. Many good local pubs & restaurants. Host can arrange taxi from Gatwick/Heathrow. Children over 8.

£28.00 | Y | N | N

Home No. 31
W.W.B.B.A.
London
Tel: 0181-742-9123 (24hrs.)
Fax: 0181-749-7084
U.S., Canada & Australia
Toll Free 0-800-852-26320
E-mail: bestbandb@atlas.co.uk

Nearest Tube: Parsons Green
A charming Victorian terraced house, situated only minutes from many excellent shops & restaurants in Fulham. The welcoming host, who is an antiques dealer, has elegantly furnished this property throughout. 1 attractive king-size double/twin-bedded room with a good private bathroom. There is also a cosy single room for a third member of the party. A large Continental breakfast is served. This is an excellent base from which to explore London. Children over 12 years.

£29.00 | Y | N | N

Home No. 34
W.W.B.B.A.
London
Tel: 0181-742-9123 (24hrs.)
Fax: 0181-749-7084
U.S., Canada & Australia
Toll Free 0-800-852-26320
E-mail: bestbandb@atlas.co.uk

Nearest Tube: Earls Court
A beautifully furnished apartment situated in a quiet garden square of period houses, with many local restaurants. Only 4 minutes walk from the tube station (direct to Heathrow) & within 20 mins' Harrods, Victoria & the museums of South Kensington. 1 very attractive double/twin bedroom beautifully furnished with interesting pictures & curios, tea/coffee & opening onto a patio garden. A private bathroom with power shower. Host is in the travel business & has an in-depth knowledge of London & the countryside. Children over 12.

£34.00 | Y | N | N

Home No. 35
W.W.B.B.A.
London
Tel: 0181-742-9123 (24hrs)
Fax: 0181-749-7084
U.S., Canada & Australia
Toll Free 0-800-852-26320
E-mail: bestbandb@atlas.co.uk

Nearest Tube: Fulham Broadway
Located in Fulham, this modern townhouse is set in a quiet street & yet is only 5 mins walk from the station. The friendly & helpful host offers 1 twin-bedded room with an adjacent private bathroom. Also, 1 double room is available for another member of the party. Each room is tastefully furnished & well-appointed with T.V. & tea/coffee facilities. A large Continental breakfast is served. A variety of restaurants locally, offering a wide choice of international cuisine. Children over 12.

£28.00 | Y | N | N

London

Visit our website at: www.bestbandb.co.uk

			rate from £ per person	children taken	evening meals	animals taken
Home No. 38 **W.W.B.B.A.** **London** **Tel: 0181-742-9123 (24hrs.)** **Fax: 0181-749-7084** **U.S., Canada & Australia** **Toll Free 0-800-852-26320** E-mail: bestbandb@atlas.co.uk	Nearest Tube: Earls Court A lovely apartment situated on the top floor of a Victorian mansion block (with lift access) & only 3 mins walk from Earls Court station. The charming host offers 1 spacious & attractively furnished double bedded room with an en-suite bathroom & T.V. Breakfast is served in the attractive dining area. Easy access to Knightsbridge, South Kensington & the museums & Heathrow. Many good local restaurants.		£29.00	Y	N	N
Home No. 39 **W.W.B.B.A.** **London** **Tel: 0181-742-9123 (24hrs.)** **Fax: 0181-749-7084** **U.S., Canada & Australia** **Toll Free 0-800-852-26320** E-mail: bestbandb@atlas.co.uk	Nearest Tube: Earls Court A superb home, designer decorated & furnished to the highest standard with antiques throughout. 2 double & 1 twin bedded rooms. Each beautiful bedroom is large & airy with a lovely bathroom en-suite, T.V. & tea/coffee facilities. A large dining room. A delightful garden where breakfast can be served if the weather is good. Guests have their own private entrance. Only 10 mins. to Harrods. Children over 12 years. Parking.	*see PHOTO over*	£41.00	Y	N	N
Home No. 40 **W.W.B.B.A.** **London** **Tel: 0181-742-9123 (24hrs.)** **Fax: 0181-749-7084** **U.S., Canada & Australia** **Toll Free 0-800-852-26320** E-mail: bestbandb@atlas.co.uk	Nearest Tube: Gunnersbury A large Victorian residence, with garden, only a few minutes walk from the tube station, with easy access to Heathrow, central London, Richmond & beautiful Kew Gardens. The charming host offers 2 spacious guest rooms suitable for doubles or twins & ideal for families. Each room has an en-suite bathroom, T.V., tea/coffee-making facilities & is decorated in natural tones with stripped pine. Children are especially welcome.		£27.00	Y	N	N
Home No. 41 **W.W.B.B.A.** **London** **Tel: 0181-742-9123 (24hrs.)** **Fax: 0181-749-7084** **U.S., Canada & Australia** **Toll Free 0-800-852-26320** E-mail: bestbandb@atlas.co.uk	Nearest Tube: Parsons Green A charming Victorian terraced house in the fashionable area of Parsons Green. Accommodation is in 1 light & airy twin-bedded room with an excellent private bathroom. There is also an equally attractive double-bedded room for a third or fourth member of the party. Each bedroom is tastefully furnished & well-appointed. A delicious breakfast is served in the attractive kitchen/diner. A delightful home, only a short walk from the tube station providing easy access to the main attractions. Many good local restaurants.		£26.00	Y	N	N
Home No. 44 **W.W.B.B.A.** **London** **Tel: 0181-742-9123 (24hrs.)** **Fax: 0181-749-7084** **U.S., Canada & Australia** **Toll Free 0-800-852-26320** E-mail: bestbandb@atlas.co.uk	Nearest Tube: Richmond Situated in the heart of delightful Richmond this really is the perfect location for a relaxing break in London. The charming hosts have beautifully refurbished their Victorian home & offer 1 gorgeous double-bedded room which has a superb private bathroom adjacent. Delicious breakfasts are served in the lovely kitchen/diner which overlooks a pretty landscaped garden. Richmond abounds with fashionable shops, restaurants & traditional pubs. Transport facilities are excellent & central London is only 25 mins away.		£28.00	N	N	N

Home No. 39. London.

London

		rate from £ per person	children taken	evening meals	animals taken

Home No. 48
W.W.B.B.A.
London
Tel: 0181-742-9123 (24hrs.)
Fax: 0181-749-7084
U.S., Canada & Australia
Toll Free 0-800-852-26320
E-mail: bestbandb@atlas.co.uk

Nearest Tube: Parsons Green
A beautifully decorated, very stylish early Victorian house, situated in leafy Parsons Green & only 10 mins. from Harrods by tube. Accommodation is in 3 twin & 1 double room, all with en-suite showers & furnished to the highest standards of comfort. Guests are welcomed with a glass of sherry. A delicious country house breakfast is served. There are many excellent local restaurants & antique shops etc.. This is a no smoking house.

£34.00 — N — N — N (no smoking)

Home No. 51
W.W.B.B.A.
London
Tel: 0181-742-9123 (24hrs.)
Fax: 0181-749-7084
U.S., Canada & Australia
Toll Free 0-800-852-26320
E-mail: bestbandb@atlas.co.uk

Nearest Tube: Holland Park
Set in a quiet, secluded street, this is an elegant modern mews house situated only a few minutes walk from fashionable restaurants, antique shops & beautiful Holland Park. It has been attractively furnished throughout by the host who is an interior designer. There is 1 delightful & spacious double-bedded room which is well-appointed with T.V. etc. & has a super en-suite bathroom. A large Continental breakfast is served. Easy access to many of London's attractions. A charming home.

£31.00 — N — N — N (no smoking)

Home No. 52
W.W.B.B.A.
London
Tel: 0181-742-9123 (24hrs.)
Fax: 0181-749-7084
U.S., Canada & Australia
Toll Free 0-800-852-26320
E-mail: bestbandb@atlas.co.uk

Nearest Tube: South Kensington
Located in Chelsea, in a quiet residential street yet, only a short walk from many fashionable shops & restaurants. A charming Victorian terraced house which has been attractively decorated throughout with many interesting prints & artifacts. The friendly hosts offer 1 spacious double-bedded room & a lovely twin-bedded room. Each has an en-suite shower room, T.V. & tea/coffee facilities. A delightful home with easy access to the museums, Knightsbridge & Harrods.

£31.00 — Y — N — N

Home No. 55
W.W.B.B.A.
London
Tel: 0181-742-9123
(24hrs.)
Fax: 0181-749-7084
U.S., Canada & Australia
Toll Free 0-800-852-26320
E-mail: bestbandb@atlas.co.uk

Nearest Tube: Sloane Square
Centrally situated only 5 mins walk from Sloane Square & 7 mins from Harrods, this really is a marvellous spot from which to explore London. Set in an elegantly furnished apartment, the charming host offers 1 beautifully decorated double-bedded room with an excellent en-suite shower room, T.V. & access to patio. A large Continental breakfast is served in the attractive dining area. Many good restaurants & chic stores abound & Buckingham Palace, the V & A & the West End are all within easy reach.

£33.00 — N — N — N (no smoking)

Home No. 56
W.W.B.B.A.
London
Tel: 0181-742-9123
(24hrs.)
Fax: 0181-749-7084
U.S., Canada & Australia
Toll Free 0-800-852-26320
E-mail: bestbandb@atlas.co.uk

Nearest Tube: Hammersmith
A lovely house, pleasantly situated in leafy Brook Green mid-way between Hammersmith & Kensington. Offering a spacious & comfortably furnished double bedded room with private bathroom & tea/coffee facilities. Also, an attractive single room, ideal for a third member of the party. Each room overlooks the rear garden. A pretty lounge with T.V. is often available & in which guests may choose to relax. An ideal base, with good access to Heathrow & central London.

£28.00 — Y — N — N (no smoking)

London

Visit our website at: www.bestbandb.co.uk

		rate from £ per person	children taken	evening meals	animals taken

Home No. 60 **W.W.B.B.A.** **London** **Tel: 0181-742-9123 (24hrs.)** **Fax: 0181-749-7084** **U.S., Canada & Australia** **Toll Free 0- 800-852-26320** **E-mail: bestbandb@atlas.co.uk**	Nearest Tube: High St. Ken. A beautifully appointed home located in a quiet cul-de-sac, close to Kensington Palace. A lift will take you to the 2nd floor accommodation. A delightful, spacious & elegantly furnished double room with brass bed & en-suite shower. T.V., tea/coffee-making facilities & biscuits are also provided. A delicious varied breakfast is served. Knightsbridge, Kensington & Hyde Park are all just a short walk from here.	£33.00	N	N	N
Home No. 61 **W.W.B.B.A.** **London** **Tel: 0181-742-9123 (24hrs.)** **Fax: 0181-749-7084** **U.S., Canada & Australia** **Toll Free 0-800-852-26320** **E-mail: bestbandb@atlas.co.uk**	Nearest Tube: Holland Park A lovely apartment situated on the 7th floor of an Edwardian mansion block with lift access. Offering 1 spacious & attractive double bedded room with a private bathroom, T.V. & a small balcony with rooftop views. A large Continental breakfast is served. The charming hosts have an extensive knowledge of London & are happy to give advice on what to see do. Their home is ideally situated & has easy access to central London & the sights, beautiful Holland Park & many good shops & restaurants. Heathrow Airbus stops nearby.	£31.00	N	N	N
Home No. 63 **W.W.B.B.A.** **London** **Tel: 0181-742-9123 (24hrs.)** **Fax: 0181-749-7084** **U.S., Canada & Australia** **Toll Free 0-800-852-26320** **E-mail: bestbandb@atlas.co.uk**	Nearest Tube: Sloane Square An attractive 2-storey penthouse apartment with prize-winning roof garden, situated in the heart of fashionable Chelsea & only minutes from the River Thames & the trendy shops & restaurants of the King's Road. The delightful host, who is an artist, is always happy to advise guests on what to see & do. 1 comfortable en-suite double-bedded room. A large Continental breakfast is served in the attractive dining room which is adorned with many of the hosts interesting pictures.	£31.00	N	N	N
Home No. 64 **W.W.B.B.A.** **London** **Tel: 0181-742-9123 (24hrs.)** **Fax: 0181-749-7084** **U.S., Canada & Australia** **Toll Free 0-800-852-26320** **E-mail: bestbandb@atlas.co.uk**	Nearest Tube: Camden Town A unique timber & glass house (designed by the host who is an architect), only mins. from the bustling market, shops & restaurants. 1 attractive double-bedded room with T.V. & tea/coffee facilities & a single room for a third member of the party. Each room is light & airy, very comfortable & modern in design. An excellent private bathroom. Breakfast is served in the lovely open-plan kitchen/dining area which overlooks the garden. Easy access to the West End & theatreland.	£31.00	Y	N	N
Home No. 65 **W.W.B.B.A.** **London** **Tel: 0181-742-9123 (24hrs.)** **Fax: 0181-749-7084** **U.S., Canada & Australia** **Toll Free 0-800-852-26320** **E-mail: bestbandb@atlas.co.uk**	Nearest Tube: Baker Street An elegant Georgian townhouse, situated only a 2 min. walk from Baker Street in the heart of central London. It is beautifully furnished & well-appointed throughout & there are 3 charming guest rooms. (1 double en-suite, 1 single en-suite & 1 triple with a private bathroom.) Each bedroom is spacious, attractively decorated & very comfortable. An elegant lounge in which guests may relax where tea/coffee are available. A large Continental breakfast is served. A marvellous location only minutes from the West End.	£33.00	N	N	N

London

		rate from £ per person	children taken	evening meals	animals taken
Home No. 66 **W.W.B.B.A.** **London** **Tel: 0181-742-9123 (24hrs.)** **Fax: 0181-749-7084** **U.S., Canada & Australia** **Toll Free 0-800-852-26320** E-mail: bestbandb@atlas.co.uk	Nearest Tube: Earls Court A spacious apartment located at garden level offering attractive accommodation in 1 double bedded room with en-suite facilities & T.V. The friendly host (a fashion designer) has tastefully furnished & pleasantly decorated this apartment with many interesting paintings. Guests may relax in the garden which is accessible from their room. Situated only a few minutes walk from the underground station, this home is within easy reach of museums, galleries, shops & theatres.	£28.00	N	N	N
Home No. 68 **W.W.B.B.A.** **London** **Tel: 0181-742-9123 (24hrs.)** **Fax: 0181-749-7084** **U.S., Canada & Australia** **Toll Free 0-800-852-26320** E-mail: bestbandb@atlas.co.uk	Nearest Tube: South Kensington A super home from which to explore London, situated only a very short walk from the Natural History & Science Museums & the station. An attractively furnished apartment, located on the 3rd floor of an Edwardian conversion (elevator access), where the friendly host offers 1 light & airy double-bedded room with full en-suite bathroom & T.V. A large Continental breakfast is served. Many good local restaurants.	£31.00	N	N	N
Home No. 70 **W.W.B.B.A.** **London** **Tel: 0181-742-9123 (24hrs.)** **Fax: 0181-749-7084** **U.S., Canada & Australia** **Toll Free 0-800-852-26320** E-mail: bestbandb@atlas.co.uk	Nearest Tube: Earls Court A lovely home with a traditional family atmosphere situated in Kensington. The very friendly & helpful hosts offer 1 ground-floor double-bedded room with a private shower room & 1 double/twin bedded room located on the 2nd floor, with private bathroom. Also, 1 twin & 1 single room are available for other members of the party. Delicious breakfasts are served in the kitchen/dining area with Aga. Easy access to Heathrow, Knightsbridge, South Kensington & the museums. Parking available by arrangement.	£28.00	Y	N	N
Home No. 72 **W.W.B.B.A.** **London** **Tel: 0181-742-9123 (24hrs.)** **Fax: 0181-749-7084** **U.S., Canada & Australia** **Toll Free 0-800-852-26320** E-mail: bestbandb@atlas.co.uk	Nearest Tube: Baker Street A traditional 4-storey Victorian townhouse in a marvellous location, mins. from the Sherlock Holmes museum, Lord's Cricket Ground & Regents Park. The charming hosts, who are artists, offer 2 spacious & comfortably furnished en-suite double-bedded rooms (1 with low-beamed ceilings), with T.V., tea/coffee facilities & views towards Regents Park. A wonderful base for discovering London, galleries & museums, the West End & theatreland are only 10 mins away.	£36.00	Y	N	N
Home No. 73 **W.W.B.B.A.** **London** **Tel: 0181-742-9123 (24hrs.)** **Fax: 0181-749-7084** **U.S., Canada & Australia** **Toll Free 0-800-852-26320** E-mail: bestbandb@atlas.co.uk	Nearest Tube: Sloane Square A delightful Victorian townhouse in fashionable Chelsea, & very close to Harrods, stylishly decorated throughout & offering 2 lovely guest rooms. 1 a king-size double/twin-bedded room with en-suite shower room & the other a double with an en-suite bathroom & access to a pretty garden. Each is comfortably furnished & has T.V. & tea/coffee facilities. A wonderful location & only a short walk from Sloane Square, Knightsbridge, the museums at South Kensington, superb restaurants & many tourist attractions.	£36.00	Y	N	N

Home No. 77 . London.

London

Visit our website at: www.bestbandb.co.uk

		rate from £ per person	children taken	evening meals	animals taken
Home No. 76 W.W.B.B.A. London Tel: 0181-742-9123 (24hrs.) Fax: 0181-749-7084 U.S., Canada & Australia Toll Free 0-800-852-26320 E-mail: bestbandb@atlas.co.uk	Nearest Tube: Earls Court One king-size double or twin-bedded room with very large en-suite bath & separate shower & 1 king-size double with adjacent private bath & shower. Each room has a colour T.V. & clock/radio & have been beautifully decorated & furnished by this most helpful host. Very close to all the best places for shopping, museums, sight-seeing & within walking distance of many excellent restaurants. A delightful home.	£28.00	N	N	N
Home No. 77 W.W.B.B.A. London Tel: 0181-742-9123 (24hrs.) Fax: 0181-749-7084 U.S., Canada & Australia Toll Free 0-800-852-26320 E-mail: bestbandb@atlas.co.uk	Nearest Tube:Clapham Jt.(B.R.) A large Edwardian house built for Earl Spencer backing onto a private park. Breakfast may be served in the dining room or large conservatory. There is 1 double en-suite room, 1 family room en-suite, 1 twin bedded room with private facilities, also, 1 double room with shared bathroom. Plenty of car parking space. There are two cats & a friendly dog. A charming & most friendly host. Smoking permitted on the ground floor.	£30.00 *see PHOTO over*	N	N	N
Home No. 78 W.W.B.B.A. London Tel: 0181-742-9123 (24hrs.) Fax: 0181-749-7084 U.S., Canada & Australia Toll Free 0-800-852-26320 E-mail: bestbandb@atlas.co.uk	Nearest Tube: Parsons Green An impressive Victorian house with pretty garden in a fashionable area facing a park with a public tennis court. Easy access to central London & excellent shops & restaurants nearby. The charming host is an author, with 1 cat. There are 2 bedrooms, each with a double bed, completely private facilities, T.V. & hairdryer. A full English breakfast is served. Charming guest sitting-room (rare in a private home). No business facilities.	£30.00	N	N	N
Home No. 79 W.W.B.B.A. London Tel: 0181-742-9123 (24hrs.) Fax: 0181-749-7084 U.S., Canada & Australia Toll Free 0-800-852-26320 E-mail: bestbandb@atlas.co.uk	Nearest Tube: East Putney An elegant Victorian house with a pretty garden located in the residential area of Putney. The charming hosts offer 2 stylishly decorated guest rooms, located on the 3rd floor. An attractive & spacious twin room with a lovely private bathroom & one large, sunny double bedroom with shower room en-suite. Each room has colour T.V. Only 25 minutes to central London by tube or 35 mins' to Windsor by train. River trips to Hampton Court & Kew go from Putney Bridge just 10 minutes walk away. Many excellent local restaurants.	£28.00	Y	N	N
Home No. 81 W.W.B.B.A. London Tel: 0181-742-9123 (24hrs.) Fax: 0181-749-7084 U.S., Canada & Australia Toll Free 0-800-852-26320 E-mail: bestbandb@atlas.co.uk	Nearest Tube: Fulham Broadway Situated in Fulham, with many good restaurants, pubs & antique shops nearby. This is a charming Victorian house, standing in a quiet street. The delightful hosts offer 1 spacious King-size double/twin-bedded room with an exquisite en-suite bathroom & another lovely, light & airy twin-bedded room with a beautiful private bathroom adjacent. Each bedroom is well-furnished & has colour T.V., hairdryer & tea/coffee-making facilities. Very good access to central London & the sights by bus or tube.	£27.00	Y	N	N

Beds:Berks:Bucks:Herts.

Bedfordshire
(Thames & Chilterns)

The county of Bedfordshire is an area of great natural beauty from the Dunstable Downs in the south to the great River Ouse in the north, along with many country parks & historic houses & gardens.

Two famous wildlife parks are to be found, at Woburn &Whipsnade. The Woburn Wild Animal Kingdom is Britain's largest drive-through safari park, with entrance to an exciting leisure park all included in one admission ticket.

Whipsnade Zoo came into existence in the 1930's as a country retreat for the animals of London Zoo, but is now very much a zoo in its own right & renowned for conservation work.

Woburn Abbey, home of the Dukes of Bedford for three centuries, is often described as one of England's finest showplaces. Rebuilt in the 8th century the Abbey houses an important art collection & is surrounded by a magnificent 3,000 acre deer park.

John Bunyan drew on local Bedfordshire features when writing the Pilgrims Progress, & the ruins of Houghton House, his "House Beautiful" still remain.

Buckinghamshire
(Thames & Chilterns)

Buckinghamshire can be divided into two distinct geographical regions: The high Chilterns with their majestic beechwoods & the Vale of Aylesbury chosen by many over the centuries as a beautiful & accessible place to build their historical homes.

The beechwoods of the Chilterns to the south of the county are crisscrossed with quiet lanes & footpaths., Ancient towns & villages like Amersham & Chesham lie tucked away in the

Rose gardens. St.Albans. Herts.

folds of the hills & a prehistoric track; the Ichnield Way winds on its 85 mile journey through the countryside.

The Rothschild family chose the Vale of Aylesbury to create several impressive homes, & Waddesdon House & Ascott House are both open to the public. Benjamin Disraeli lived at Hughenden Manor, & Florence Nightingale, "the Lady with the Lamp", at Claydon House. Sir Francis Dashwood, the 18th century eccentric founded the bizarre Hellfire Club, which met in the man-made caves near West Wycombe House.

Berkshire
(Thames & Chilterns)

Berkshire is a compact county but one of great variety & beauty.

In the East is Windsor where the largest inhabited castle in the world stands in its majestic hilltop setting. Nine centuries of English monarchy have lived here, & it is home to the present Queen. The surrounding parkland, enormous yards, vast interior & splendour of the State Apartments make a trip to Windsor Castle an unforgettable experience.

To the West are the gently rolling Berkshire Downs where many a champion racehorse has been trained.

Beds:Berks:Bucks:Herts.

To the north of the county, the River Thames dominates the landscape - an opportunity for a river-bank stroll & a drink at a country pub.

In the south is the Kennet & Avon Canal, a peaceful waterway with horse-drawn barges.

Historically, Berkshire has occupied an important place due to its strategic position commanding roads to & from Oxford & the north, & Bath & the west. Roundheads & Cavaliers clashed twice near Newbury during the 17th century English Civil Wars. Their battles are colourfully recreated by historic societies like the Sealed Knot.

The Tudor period brought great wealth from wool-weaving. Merchants built wonderful houses & some built churches but curiously, there is no cathedral in Berkshire.

Hertfordshire
(Thames & Chilterns)

Old & new exist side by side in Hertfordshire. This attractive county includes historic sites, like the unique Roman theatre in St. Albans, as well as new additions to the landscape such as England's first Garden City at Letchworth.

The countryside varies from the chalk hills & rolling downlands of the Chilterns to rivers, lakes, canals & pretty villages. The county remains largely rural despite many large towns & cities. The Grand Union Canal, built at the end of the 18th century to link the Midlands to London, passes through some glorious scenery, particularly at Cassiobury Park in Watford.

Verulamium was a newly-built town of the Roman Empire. It was the first name of Alban, himself a Roman, who became the first Christian to be martyred for his faith in England. The great Abbey church was built by the Normans around his original church, & it was re-established under the Rule of St. Benedict & named St. Albans some 600 years after his death.

Windsor Castle.

Beds:Berks:Bucks:Herts.

Bedfordshire
Gazeteer
Area of outstanding natural beauty.
Dunstable Downs, Ivinghoe Beacon.

Historic Houses
Woburn Abbey - house & gardens, extensive art collection, deer park, antiques centre.
Luton Hoo - the Wernher collection of Old Masters, tapestries, furniture, ivories & porcelain, unique collection of Russian Faberge jewellry. Parkland landscaped by Capability Brown.

Other Things to see & do
Woburn Wildlife Park
Whipsnade Zoo-Whipsnade
Old Warden - the village houses a collection of working vintage aeroplanes with flying displays each month from April to October.

Berkshire
Gazeteer
Areas of outstanding natural beauty.
North West Downs.

Historic Houses & Castles
Windsor Castle - Royal Residence at Windsor
State apartments, house, historic treasures. The Cloisters, Windsor Chapel. Mediaeval house.
Basildon Park - Nr. Pangbourne
Overlooking the Thames. 18th century Bath stone building, massive portico & linked pavilions. Painted ceiling in Octagon Room, gilded pier glasses. Garden & wooded walks.
Cliveden - Nr. Taplow
Once the home of Nancy Astor.

Churches
Lambourn (St. Michael & All Saints)
Norman with 15th century chapel. 16th century brasses, glass & tombs.
Padworth (St. John the Baptist)
12th century Norman with plastered exterior, remains of wall paintings, 18th century monuments.
Warfield (St. Michael & All Angels)
14th century decorated style. 15th century wood screen & loft.

Museums
Newbury Museum - Newbury
Natural History & Archaeology - Paleolithic to Saxon & Mediaeval times.
Household Cavalry Museum - Windsor

Other Things to see & do
Racing - at Newbury, Ascot & Windsor
Highlight of the racing year is the Royal Meeting at Ascot each June, attended by the Queen & other members of the Royal Family.
Antiques - Hungerford is a famous centre for antiques.

Buckinghamshire
Gazeteer
Area of outstanding natural beauty.
Burnham Beeches - 70 acres of unspoilt woodlands, inspiration to poet Thomas Gray.

Historic Houses
Waddesdon Manor & Ascott House - homes of the Rothschilds.
Chalfont St. Giles - cottage home of great English poet John Milton.
Old Jordans & the Meeting House - 17th century buildings associated with William Penn, the founder of Pennsylvania & with the Society of Friends, often called the Quakers.

Things to see & do
Buckinghamshire Railway Centre - at Quainton
Vintage steam train rides & largest private railway collection in Britain.
Chalfont Shire Horse Centre - home of the gentle giants of the horse world.

Beds:Berks:Bucks:Herts.

Hertfordshire

Gazeteer

Areas of outstanding natural beauty.
Parts of the Chilterns.

Historic Houses & Castles

Hatfield House - Hatfield
Home of the Marquess of Salisbury.
Jacobean House & Tudor Palace -
childhood home of Queen Elizabeth I.
Knebworth House - Knebworth
Family home of the Lyttons. 16th century
house transformed into Victorian High
Gothic. Furniture, portraits. Formal
gardens & unique Gertrude Jekyll herb
garden.
Shaw's Corner - Ayot St. Lawrence
Home of George Bernard Shaw.

Cathedrals & Churches

St. Albans Cathedral - St. Albans
9th century foundation, murals, painted
roof over choir, 15th century reredos,
stone rood screen.

Stanstead St. Abbots (St. James)12th
century nave, 13th century chancel, 15th
century tower & porch, 16th century
North chapel, 18th century box pews
& 3-decker pulpit.
Watford (St. Mary)
13 - 15th century. Essex chapel.
Tuscan arcade. Morryson tombs.

Museums

**Rhodes Memorial Museum &
Commonwealth Centre** - at Bishop
Stortford
Zoological Museum - Tring
Gardens
Gardens of the Rose - Chiswell Green
Nr. St Albans
Showgrounds of the Royal National Rose
Society
Capel Manor
Extensive grounds of horticultural
college.
Many fine trees, including the largest
copper beech in the country.

Bledlow Village; Bucks.

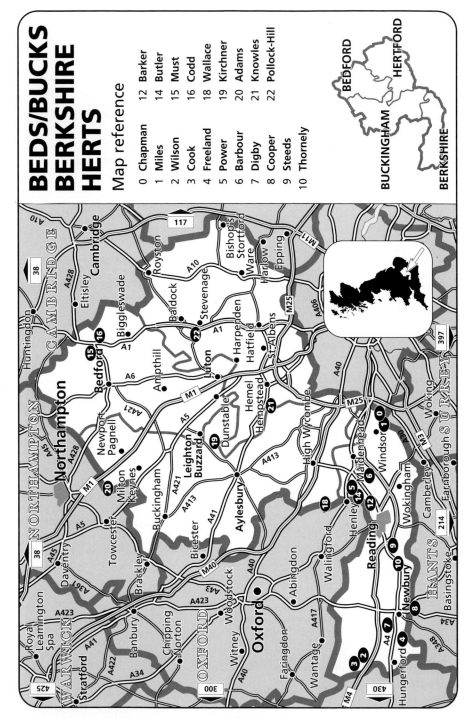

BEDS/BUCKS
BERKSHIRE
HERTS

Map reference

0	Chapman	12	Barker
1	Miles	14	Butler
2	Wilson	15	Must
3	Cook	16	Codd
4	Freeland	18	Wallace
5	Power	19	Kirchner
6	Barbour	20	Adams
7	Digby	21	Knowles
8	Cooper	22	Pollock-Hill
9	Steeds		
10	Thornely		

Berkshire

		rate from £ per person	children taken	evening meals	animals taken
John & Sieglinde Miles **Ennis Lodge Private** **Guest House** **Winkfield Road** **Ascot SL5 7EX** **Tel/Fax: (01344) 21009** **Open: ALL YEAR** **Map Ref No. 01**	Nearest Road: A.329, A.330 Ennis Lodge is situated in central Ascot, adjacent to the racecourse. There are 5 tastefully furnished twin-bedded rooms & 1 single, each en-suite with T.V., tea/coffee-making facilities, trouser press, hairdryer & radio alarm. Conveniently located within walking distance of the mainline station. London only 45 mins by rail. Also within easy reach of Windsor (10 mins), Heathrow Airport (25 mins), Legoland (10 mins). M.3, M.4 & M.25 close by. German spoken. Single room supplement. CREDIT CARD VISA M'CARD	£22.50	Y	N	N
Mrs Mary Wilson **Fishers Farm** **Shefford Woodlands** **Hungerford RG17 7AB** **Tel: (01488) 648466** **Fax 01488 648706** **Open: ALL YEAR** **Map Ref No. 02**	Nearest Road: A.338, M.4 Jt.14 A traditional farmhouse on a working arable & livestock farm with all modern comforts & a beautiful large garden in a secluded & peaceful location, yet only 1 mile from Jt. 14 of the M.4 motorway. 3 large bedrooms with en-suite/private bathrooms. An ideal base for exploring southern England, & within easy reach of Heathrow & Gatwick Airports. A heated indoor swimming pool. Excellent cooking using many home-grown ingredients. (Dinner & animals by arrangement.)	£25.00	Y	Y	Y
John & Sally Cook **Lodge Down** **Lambourn** **Hungerford RG17 7BJ** **Tel: (01672) 540304** **Fax 01672 540304** **Open: ALL YEAR** **Map Ref No. 03**	Nearest Road: B.4000, M.4 A warm welcome is assured at Lodge Down, a country house with superb accommodation & en-suite bathrooms, set in lovely grounds. Excellent & varied dining in surrounding villages. Easy access to the M.4 motorway at Jts 14 & 15. 1 hour or less for Heathrow (60 miles), Bath (43 miles) & Oxford (26 miles). This location provides a central base for excursions to Stonehenge, Salisbury & the Cotswolds, etc., or an easy drive to Heathrow & London. A charming home.	£21.00	Y	N	N
		see PHOTO over			
Mrs Beroe Freeland **Holt Lodge** **Kintbury** **Hungerford RG17 9SX** **Tel:(01488) 668244** **Fax (01488) 668244** **Open: ALL YEAR** **Map Ref No. 04**	Nearest Road: A.4 An attractive 18th-century family house set in large, mature gardens surrounded by parkland. Situated south of Kintbury, halfway between the River Kennet & the Hampshire Downs. A friendly welcome is assured for visitors who appreciate informality & the seclusion & comforts of a family home. A chioce of double, twin or single rooms, all with modern facilities. Conveniently sited for Berkshire, Hampshire, Wiltshire or Oxfordshire.	£20.00	Y	Y	Y
Michael & Joanna Power **Woodpecker Cottage** **Warren Row** **Nr. Maidenhead** **RG10 8QS** **Tel: (01628) 822772** **Fax 01628 822125** **Open: ALL YEAR (Excl. Xmas)** **Map Ref No. 05**	Nearest Road: A.4 Idyllic woodland setting near rural village & yet with easy access to motorways & Heathrow Airport. River Thames & Henley 5 minutes; Windsor 15 minutes; frequent trains (35 minutes into London) from nearby Maidenhead. 3 ground-floor rooms - a large double & spacious single, both en-suite, & a twin-bedded room with a private bathroom. All rooms have T.V., radio & hot drinks tray. Breakfast includes delicious home-made bread & jams. Children over 8. Barbecue area. **E-mail: woodcot@masterkey.co.uk**	£20.00	Y	N	N

Lodge Down. Lambourn.

Berkshire

		rate from £ per person	children taken	evening meals	animals taken
Mrs Charlotte Digby **Rookwood Farmhouse** **Stockcross** **Newbury RG20 8JX** **Tel: (01488) 608676** **Fax 01488 608676** **Open: ALL YEAR** **Map Ref No. 07**	Nearest Road: A.4 This charming & comfortable former farmhouse combines ease of access with rural views & a large garden. The guest bedrooms are in a newly converted coach house which is traditionally furnished & yet affords all modern facilities. In winter, there is a welcoming log fire in the guests' sitting room, while in summer, breakfast is served in the conservatory overlooking the swimming pool. An ideal base for a relaxing break.	£27.50	Y	N	N
Sarah Cooper **Adbury Holt House** **Burghclere** **Newbury RG20 9BW** **Tel: (01635) 42846** **Open: ALL YEAR** **Map Ref No. 08**	Nearest Road: A.34 A delightful, secluded Victorian mansion set in its own grounds of 12 acres: of particular interest to gardening enthusiasts, for there are over 100 varieties of trees & many unusual shrubs & plants. The accommodation is very attractive, in 5 lovely, well-appointed bedrooms, 4 with own bathroom, & each with radio, T.V., & tea/coffee-making facilities. Parking. Non-smokers preferred.	£19.50	Y	N	N
Mrs Jane Steeds **Highwoods** **Burghfield Common** **Reading RG7 3BG** **Tel: (0118) 9832320** **Fax 0118 9831070** **Open: ALL YEAR (Excl. Xmas)** **Map Ref No. 09**	Nearest Road: A.4, M.4 A friendly & relaxing atmosphere at this fine Victorian country house set in 4 acres of attractive grounds, with unspoilt, far-reaching views. 2 spacious, comfortable, attractively furnished rooms (1 en-suite) with all modern amenities, including colour T.V.. Guests are welcome to use the garden & hard tennis court. Also, a gallery specialising in English watercolours & prints. Easy access to London, Heathrow Airport, Windsor, Oxford & Bath. Non-smokers preferred.	£20.00	Y	N	N
Mrs Jill Thornely **Bridge Cottage** **Station Road** **Woolhampton** **Reading RG7 5SF** **Tel: (01189) 713138** **Fax 01189 714331** **Open: ALL YEAR (Excl. Xmas)** **Map Ref No. 10**	Nearest Road: A.4, M.4 A warm welcome awaits the visitor to this delightful 300-year-old riverside cottage, offering 5 attractive & comfortably furnished bedrooms with beamed ceilings, including 2 twin-bedded rooms with en-suite facilities. Breakfast is served in a lovely conservatory overlooking the River Kennet, where old narrow boats pass by. It is surrounded by lovely countryside. Close by is the local pub which serves excellent home-cooked suppers. London 1 hour away. Ideal for Heathrow & rail/air connections to Reading & London, etc.	£20.00	Y	N	N
Wynyard & Julia Wallace **Little Parmoor** **Parmoor Lane, Frieth** **Henley-on-Thames** **RG9 6NL** **Tel: (01494) 881447** **Fax 01494 883012** **Open: ALL YEAR** **Map Ref No. 18**	Nearest Road: A.40 M., M.4 A pretty Georgian country house surrounded by farmland, situated in the beautiful Chiltern Hills between Henley & Marlow. Within easy reach of Oxford & Windsor, & 40 mins from Heathrow - a perfect & peaceful spot to begin or end a holiday. 2 spacious & attractively furnished double/twin rooms with en-suite facilities & 1 small double with a private bathroom. All rooms have colour T.V. & tea-making facilities. A pretty, panelled drawing room. Ample parking. Evening meals served if ordered in advance. Children over 5 yrs.	£20.00	Y	Y	N

Berkshire & Bedfordshire

		rate from £ per person	children taken	evening meals	animals taken
Mrs Carel Barker **The Hermitage** **63 London Road** **Twyford** **RG10 9EJ** **Tel: (01189) 340004** **Fax 01189 340004** **Open: ALL YEAR (Excl. Xmas)** **Map Ref No. 12**	Nearest Road: A.4, M.4 A large, elegant Georgian house with unique Victorian additions. A central village location. An ideal base for exploring the Thames Valley (including Henley, Oxford & Windsor). Convenient for Heathrow. A short walk to the mainline station (London 40 mins). A choice of 5 bedrooms (3 en-suite, including 2 in the recently converted coach house), all with colour T.V. & tea/coffee-making facilities. A spacious dining room overlooking a large established garden, which guests are welcome to use. Children over 10.	£25.00	Y	N	N
Mrs Lis Butler **Martens House** **Willow Lane** **Wargrave RG10 8LH** **Tel: (0118) 9403707** **Fax 0118 9403707** **Open: ALL YEAR** **Map Ref No. 14**	Nearest Road: A.321 This a comfortable, friendly Edwardian house, with lawns down to the Thames & views across meadowland. Accommodation is in 2 spacious & attractive twin bedrooms, 1 en-suite & 1 with private bath & 1 single room. There are also tea/coffee-making facilities. Wargrave has several places to eat, & 3 miles away is Henley-on-Thames, known for its Royal Regatta & Festival. Easy access to the M.4, M.40, M.25 & Heathrow. A perfect spot for a relaxing break	£22.50 *see PHOTO over*	N	N	Y

Bedfordshire

		rate from £ per person	children taken	evening meals	animals taken
Mrs Janet Must **Church Farm** **41 High Street** **Roxton MK44 3EB** **Tel: (01234) 870234** **Fax 01234 871576** **Open: ALL YEAR** **Map Ref No. 15**	Nearest Road: A.1, A.421 Church Farm is a lovely 17th-century farmhouse with Georgian frontage, set in a secluded village. Furnished with a pleasant mixture of family antiques, the comfortable guest accommodation has its own staircase & bathroom, with tea/coffee-making facilities in the rooms. Breakfast is served in the beamed dining room, & a lounge is available with open fire & colour T.V.. Whether on business or on a short break, a warm welcome awaits you.	£18.00	Y	N	Y
Mrs Margaret Codd **Highfield Farm** **Great North Road** **Sandy SG19 2AQ** **Tel: (01767) 682332** **Fax 01767 692503** **Open: ALL YEAR** **Map Ref No. 16**	Nearest Road: A.1, A.428, A.14 A tranquil & very welcoming house with comfort, warmth & a friendly atmosphere in a lovely setting on an arable farm. There are 6 attractive bedrooms, 4 en-suite, including 3 ground-floor rooms in tastefully converted stables. Highfield Farm is set back off the A.1, giving peaceful seclusion & yet easy access to London, Cambridge, Bedford, the Shuttleworth Collection, the R.S.P.B. & the east-coast ports. Ample parking. Most guests return.	£20.00	Y	N	Y
Bar Barbour & Sue Lemin **Beehive Manor** **Cox Green Lane** **Maidenhead SL6 3ET** **Tel: (01628) 620980** **Fax 01628 621840** **Open: ALL YEAR** **Map Ref No. 06**	Nearest Road: A.404 (M) Beehive Manor offers all the charm & country-house atmosphere of a Tudor home set in a traditional English garden. Yet, amongst the massive oak beams, latticed windows & linenfold panelling are also all the comforts of the 20th century. Within its wisteria-clad walls, 3 superb bedrooms are available to guests, as well as a sunny drawing & a delightful dining room. London is just 35 mins away by train. Children over 12.	£29.00	Y	N	N

Martens House. Wargrave.

Buckinghamshire & Hertfordshire

			rate from £ per person	children taken	evening meals	animals taken

Charles & Susie Kirchner **The Old Vicarage** **Mentmore** **LU7 0QG** **Tel: (01296) 661227** **Fax 01296 661227** **Open: ALL YEAR** **Map Ref No. 19**	Nearest Road: A.418 Only 45 mins from central London, this imposing Gothic house is set in mature gardens in a picturesque Rothschild estate village. Mentmore boasts a good pub in addition to architectural interest & a fine setting. It is very much a family home with plenty of activity. The guest rooms are spacious with en-suite bathrooms, enjoying uninterrupted views over rolling countryside. Meals are served in the 'William Morris' dining room using garden produce when available.		£25.00	Y	Y	Y
Wake & Chuff Adams **Chantry Farm** **Pindon End** **Hanslope** **Milton Keynes MK19 7HL** **Tel: (01908) 510269** **Open: ALL YEAR** **Map Ref No. 20**	Nearest Road: A.508 Chantry Farm, built in 1650, is a delightful farmhouse & mixed working farm, overlooking a private trout lake & surrounded by glorious open countryside. 3 attractively furnished guest rooms, each with T.V. & tea/coffee-making facilities (1 en-suite). Guests may enjoy the swimming pool, table tennis & croquet lawn or relax in the elegant sitting room with inglenook fireplace. It is the ideal place for a relaxing break, yet is only 15 mins from Milton Keynes. London 50 mins by train.		£18.00	Y	N	Y

Hertfordshire

Mrs Alison Knowles **Broadway Farm** **Berkhamsted** **HP4 2RR** **Tel: (01442) 866541** **Fax 01442 866541** **Open: ALL YEAR (Excl. Xmas)** **Map Ref No. 21**	Nearest Road: A.4251 A warm welcome is guaranteed at Broadway, a working arable farm with its own fishing lake. There are 3 comfortable en-suite rooms in a recently converted building adjacent to the farmhouse. Each has tea/coffee-making facilities & colour T.V. Everything for the leisure or business guest: the relaxation of farm life in an attractive rural setting, yet easy access to London, airports, motorways & mainline rail services. **E-mail: a.knowles@broadway.nildram.co.uk**		£20.00	Y	N	N
Mrs Samantha Pollock-Hill **Homewood** **Park Lane** **Knebworth,** **Stevenage** **SG3 6PP** **Tel: (01438) 812105** **Open: ALL YEAR** **Map Ref No. 22**	Nearest Road: A.1 M Homewood is a classic blend of comfort & style: an Edwardian country house which is also a well-equipped family home. It has been used as a location for period drama by the B.B.C., & is often sought out by admirers of its designer, the distinguished architect Edwin Lutyens. You will be treated as a member of the family, or your privacy will be respected - whichever you prefer. Additional meals can be arranged, incl. dinner. 2 lovely bedrooms, each with private bathroom.		£30.00 *see PHOTO over*	Y	Y	N

Homewood. Knebworth.

Cambridge & Northants

Cambridgeshire
(East Anglia)

A county very different from any other, this is flat, mysterious, low-lying Fenland crisscrossed by a network of waterways both natural & man-made.

The Fens were once waterlogged, misty marshes but today the rich black peat is drained & grows carrots, sugar beet, celery & the best asparagus in the world.

Drive north across the Fens & slowly you become aware of a great presence dominating the horizon. Ely cathedral, the "ship of the Fens", sails closer. The cathedral is a masterpiece with its graceful form & delicate tracery towers. Begun before the Domesday Book was written, it took the work of a full century before it was ready to have the timbered roof raised up. Norman stonemasons worked with great skill & the majestic nave is glorious in its simplicity. Their work was crowned by the addition of the Octagon in the 14th century. Despite the ravages of the Reformation, the lovely Lady Chapel survives as one of the finest examples of decorated architecture in Britain with its exquisitely fine stone carving.

To the south, the Fens give way to rolling chalk hills & fields of barley, wheat & rye, & Cambridge. Punts gliding through the broad river, between smooth, lawned banks, under willow trees, past college buildings as extravagant as wedding cakes. The names of the colleges resound through the ages - Peterhouse, Corpus Christi, Kings, Queens, Trinity, Emmanuel. A city of learning & progress, & a city of great tradition where cows graze in open spaces, just 500 yards from the market square.

Northamptonshire
(East Midlands)

Northamptonshire has many features to attract & interest the visitor, from the town of Brackley in the south with its charming buildings of mellow stone, to ancient Rockingham Forest in the north. There are lovely churches, splendid historic houses & peaceful waterways.

The Waterways Museum at Stoke Bruerne makes a popular outing, with boat trips available on the Grand Union Canal beside the museum. Horse-racing at Towcester & motor-racing at Silverstone draws the crowds, but there are quieter pleasures in visits to Canons Ashby, or to Sulgrave Manor, home of George Washington's ancestors.

In the pleasantly wooded Rockingham Forest area are delightful villages, one of which is Ashton with its thatched cottages, the scene of the World Conker Championships each October. Mary Queen of Scots was executed at Fotheringay, in the castle of which only the mound remains.

Rockingham Castle has a solid Norman gateway & an Elizabethan hall; Deene Park has family connections with the Earl of Cardigan who led the Charge of the Light Brigade & Kirby Hall is a dramatic Elizabethan ruin.

The county is noted for its parish churches, with fine Saxon examples at Brixworth & at Earl's Barton, as well as the round Church of the Holy Sepulchre in the county town itself.

Northampton has a fine tradition of shoemaking, so it is hardly surprising that boots & shoes & other leather-goods take pride of place in the town';s museums. The town has one of the country's biggest market squares, an historic Royal Theatre & a mighty Wurlitzer Organ to dance to at Turner's Musical Merry-go-round ! !

Cambridge & Northants

Cambridgeshire Gazeteer

Areas of outstanding natural beauty
The Nene Valley

Historic Houses & Castles

Anglesy Abbey - Nr. Cambridge
Origins in the reign of Henry I. Was redesigned into Elizabethan Manor by Fokes family. Houses the Fairhaven collection of Art treasures - stands in 100 acres of Ground.

Hinchingbrooke House - Huntingdon
13th century nunnery converted mid-16th century into Tudor house. Later additions in 17th & 19th centuries.

King's School - Ely
12th & 14th centuries - original stonework & vaulting in the undercroft, original timbering 14th century gateway & monastic barn.

Kimbolton Castle - Kimbolton
Tudor Manor house - has associations with Katherine of Aragon. Remodelled by Vanbrugh 1700's - gatehouse by Robert Adam.

Longthorpe Tower - Nr. Peterborough
13th & 14th century fortification - rare wall paintings.

Peckover House - Wisbech
18th century domestic architecture - charming Victorian garden.

University of Cambridge Colleges

Peterhouse	1284
Clare	1326
Pembroke	1347
Gonville & Caius	1348
Trinity Hall	1350
Corpus Christi	1352
King's	1441
Queen's	1448
St. Catherine's	1473
Jesus	1496
Christ's	1505
St. John's	1511
Magadalene	1542
Trinity	1546
Emmanuel	1584
Sidney Sussex	1596
Downing	1800

Wimpole Hall - Nr. Cambridge
18th & 19th century - beautiful staterooms - aristocratic house.

Cathedrals & Churches

Alconbury (St. Peter & St. Paul)
13th century chancel & 15th century roof. Broach spire.

Babraham (St. Peter)
13th century tower - 17th century monument.

Ely Cathedral
Rich arcading - west front incomplete. Remarkable interior with Octagon - unique in Gothic architecture.

Great Paxton (Holy Trinity)
12th century.

Harlton (Blessed Virgin Mary)
Perpendicular - decorated transition. 17th century monuments

Hildersham (Holy Trinity)
13th century - effigies, brasses & glass.

Lanwade (St. Nicholas)
15th century - mediaeval fittings

Peterborough Cathedral
Great Norman church fine example - little altered. Painted wooden roof to nave - remarkable west front - Galilee Porch & spires later additions.

Ramsey (St. Thomas of Canterbury)
12th century arcades - perpendicular nave. Late Norman chancel with Angevin vault.

St. Neots (St. Mary)
15th century

Sutton (St. Andrew)
14th century

Trumpington (St. Mary & St. Nicholas)
14th century. Framed brass of 1289 of Sir Roger de Trumpington.

Westley Waterless (St. Mary the Less)
Decorated. 14th century brass of Sir John & Lady Creke.

Wimpole (St. Andrew)
14th century rebuilt 1749 - splendid heraldic glass.

Yaxley (St. Peter)
15th century chancel screen, wall paintings, fine steeple.

Museums & Galleries

Cromwell Museum - Huntingdon
Exhibiting portraits, documents, etc. of the Cromwellian period.

Fitzwilliam Museum - Cambridge
Gallery of masters, old & modern, ceramics, applied arts, prints & drawing, mediaeval manuscripts, music & art library.

Cambridge & Northants

Scott Polar Research Institute - Cambridge
Relics of expeditions & the equipment used. Current scientific work in Arctic & Antarctic.
University Archives - Cambridge
13th century manuscripts, Charters, Statutes, Royal letters & mandates. Wide variety of records of the University.
University Museum of Archaeology & Anthropology - Cambridge
Collections illustrative of Stone Age in Europe, Africa & Asia.
Britain prehistoric to mediaeval times. Prehistoric America.

Ethnographic material from South-east Asia, Africa & America.
University Museum of Classical Archaeology - Cambridge
Casts of Greek & Roman Sculpture - representative collection.
Whipple Museum of the History of Science - Cambridge 16th, 17th & 18th century scientific instruments - historic collection.

Other Things to see & do
Nene Valley Railway
Steam railway with locomotives & carriages from many countries.

Caius College; Cambridge.

Cambridge & Northants

Northamptonshire
Gazeteer
Historic Houses & Castles

Althorp - Nr. Northampton
Family home of the Princess of Wales, with fine pictures & porcelain.

Boughton House - Nr. Kettering
Furniture, tapestries & pictures in late 17th century building modelled on Versailles, in beautiful parkland.

Canons Ashby House - Nr. Daventry
Small 16th century manor house with gardens & church.

Deene Park - Nr. Corby
Family home for over 4 centuries, surrounded by park, extensive gardens & lake.

Holdenby House - Nr. Northampton
Gardens include part of Elizabethan garden, with original entrance arches, terraces & ponds. Falconry centre. Rare breeds.

Kirby Hall - Nr. Corby
Large Elizabethan mansion with fine gardens.

Lamport Hall - Nr. Northampton
17th & 18th century house with paintings, furniture & china. One of the first garden rockeries in Britain. Programme of concerts & other special events.

Rockingham Castle - Rockingham, Nr. Market Harborough
Norman gateway & walls surrounding mainly Elizabethan house, with pictures & Rockingham china. Extensive gardens with 16th century yew hedge.

Rushton Triangular Lodge - Nr. Kettering
Symbolic of the Trinity, with 3 sides, 3 floors, trefoil windows.

Sulgrave Manor - Nr. Banbury
Early English Manor, home of George Washington's ancestors.

Museums

Abington Museum - Northampton
Domestic & social life collections in former manor house.

Museum of Leathercraft - Northampton
History of leather use, with Queen Victoria's saddle, & Samuel Pepys' wallet.

Waterways Museum - Stoke Bruerne Nr. Towcester
200 years of canal & waterway life, displayed beside the Grand Union Canal.

Cathedrals & Churches

Brixworth Church - Nr. Northampton
One of the finest Anglo-Saxon churches in the country, mostly 7th century.

Earls Barton Church - Nr. Northampton
Fine Anglo-Saxon tower & Norman arch & arcading.

Church of the Holy Sepulchre - Northampton
Largest & best preserved of four remaining round churches in England, dating from 1100.

Other Things to see & do

Billing Aquadrome - Nr. Northampton
Boating, fishing, swimming & amusements.

Wicksteed Park - Kettering
Large playground & variety of amusements for families.

Lilford Park - Nr. Oundle
Birds & farm animals in parkland setting where many special events are held.

Rushton Triangular Lodge.

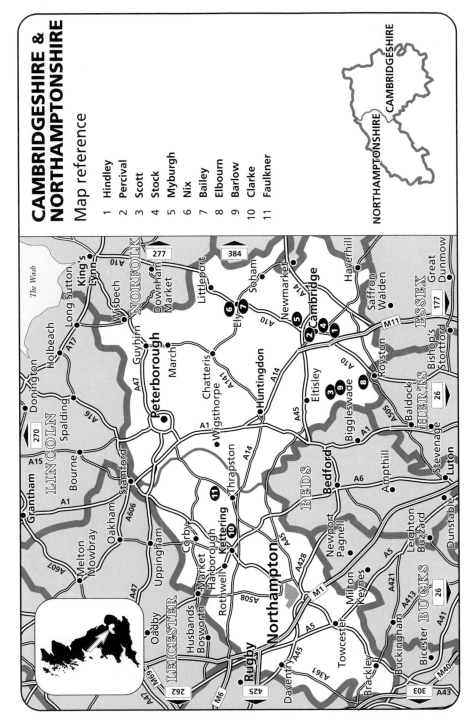

CAMBRIDGESHIRE & NORTHAMPTONSHIRE

Map reference

1 Hindley
2 Percival
3 Scott
4 Stock
5 Myburgh
6 Nix
7 Bailey
8 Elbourn
9 Barlow
10 Clarke
11 Faulkner

NORTHAMPTONSHIRE
CAMBRIDGESHIRE

Cambridgeshire

		rate from £ per person	children taken	evening meals	animals taken
Olga & David Hindley **Purlins** **12 High Street** **Little Shelford** **Cambridge CB2 5ES** **Tel/Fax: (01223) 842643** **Open: FEB - DEC** **Map Ref No. 01**	Nearest Road: A.10, M.11 Lovely, individually designed family home, with 2 acres of parkland, situated in a quiet, pretty village on the Cam, 4 miles south of Cambridge. An ideal centre for Colleges, Audley End House, the Imperial War Museum & bird watching. There are 3 well-appointed double bedrooms (2 ground-floor), all with en-suite bathrooms, colour T.V. & tea/coffee facilities. Varied breakfasts (special diets by arrangement). Restaurants nearby. Children over 8 welcome.	£21.00	Y	N	N
Mrs Alice Percival **136 Huntingdon Road** **Cambridge CB3 0HL** **Tel: (01223) 365285** **Tel: (01223) 568305** **Fax 01223 461142** **Open: ALL YEAR** **Map Ref No. 02**	Nearest Road: A.14, M.11 A large & attractive Edwardian family house, with a secluded garden & private parking, situated within walking distance of Magdalene College & the centre of Cambridge. Accommodation is in 3 charming bedrooms each with either en-suite or private facilities. All are well-equipped. Much thought has been put into the comfort & well-being of guests in this delightful home. Children over 8 years welcome.	£28.00 CREDIT CARD VISA M'CARD	Y	N	N
Peter & Maggie Scott **Church Farm** **Gransden Road, Caxton** **Cambridge CB3 8PL** **Tel: (01954) 719543** **Fax 01954 718999** **Open: ALL YEAR** **Map Ref No. 03**	Nearest Road: A.1198 This elegant & spacious listed farmhouse, which retains original 16th- & 17th-century features with 19th-century additions, is set in over 3 acres of rural peace. A wealth of oak beams, antiques, English watercolours, open log fires, comfortable beds & imaginative country-house cooking make for a relaxing stay. Ely Cathedral, Wimpole Hall, Kings College Chapel, Audley End & the Fitzwilliam Museum are all within easy reach. A delightful home. Children by arrangement.	£27.00 CREDIT CARD VISA M'CARD	Y	Y	N
Roger Stock **Number 55** **55 Montague Road** **Cambridge CB4 1BU** **Tel/Fax: (01223) 327663** **Open: MAR - NOV** **Map Ref No. 04**	Nearest Road: A.14 Number 55 is an attractive Victorian house which retains many period features & is decorated & furnished to a high standard. Accommodation is in 2 comfortable bedrooms with tea/coffee-making facilities. Guests may relax in the attractive lounge with T.V.. An excellent base from which to explore Cambridge: only 15 mins walk from the colleges & historic town centre. A warm & friendly welcome awaits you. Children over 12 years.	£25.00	Y	N	N
Phil & Sally Myburgh **Berry House** **High Street** **Waterbeach** **Cambridge CB5 9JU** **Tel: (01223) 860702** **Fax 01223 570588** **Open: ALL YEAR** **Map Ref No. 05**	Nearest Road: A.14, M.11 Berry House is a Grade II listed building built around 1820. The garden still contains a number of fruit trees from the original orchards. The elegant bedrooms have mahogany double beds, Edwardian & Georgian furniture & modern en-suite facilities, including powerful Victorian-style showers. Tea/coffee-making facilities, radio/alarms & electric blankets are provided in the rooms, which have a warm, period, cottage style. A beautiful home, perfect for visiting Cambridge & Ely, or for exploring this delightful county.	£27.50	Y	Y	N

Cambridgeshire

	rate from £ per person	children taken	evening meals	animals taken
Mrs Hilary Nix **Hill House Farm** **9 Main Street** **Coveney** **Ely** **CB6 2DJ** **Tel: (01353) 778369** **Open: ALL YEAR (Excl. Xmas)** **Map Ref No. 06** Nearest Road: A.142, A.10 A warm welcome awaits you at this spacious Victorian farmhouse, situated in the quiet village of Coveney, 3 miles west of the historic cathedral city of Ely. Open views of the surrounding countryside & easy access to Cambridge, Newmarket & Huntingdon. It is ideally placed for touring Cambridgeshire, Norfolk & Suffolk. Wicken Fen & Welney wildfowl refuge are nearby. 3 tastefully furnished bedrooms, 1 twin & 2 double en-suite rooms, 1 ground floor. All have their own entrance, T.V., clock/radio & tea/coffee. A lounge & garden for guests' use. Children over 12.	£19.00	Y	N	N
Mr & Mrs Derek Bailey **Springfields** **Ely Road, Little Thetford** **Ely CB6 3HJ** **Tel: (01353) 663637** **Fax 01353 663130** **Open: JAN - NOV** **Map Ref No. 07** Nearest Road: A.10 Located in a quiet area, yet only 2 miles from the historic Ely Cathedral & city centre. Springfields is a lovely home set in an acre of beautiful garden. Offering 3 delightful bedrooms, 1 en-suite. All rooms have modern amenities, tea/coffee makers & T.V.. A full English breakfast is served. A warm & friendly welcome awaits you at Springfields, where the accent is on hospitality. Stay a while, & smell the roses. A perfect base from which to explore the changeless beauty of the Fens.	£22.50	N	N	N
Bernice & John Elbourn **Chiswick House** **Chiswick End** **Meldreth** **Royston SG8 6LZ** **Tel: (01763) 260242** **Open: ALL YEAR** **Map Ref No. 08** Nearest Road: A.10 A beautiful timber-framed farmhouse dating from the 16th century. The royal crest of King James I is found above the fireplace, suggesting this was his hunting lodge in the early 1600s. Jacobean panelling, oak beams & open fireplaces create a wonderful atmosphere. 6 en-suite rooms, with tea/coffee-making facilities. T.V. is available. Many excellent inns nearby. An ideal base for touring Cambridge, Suffolk & Hertfordshire. *see PHOTO over*	£21.00	Y	N	Y
Mrs Sue Barlow **Model Farm** **Little Gransden** **Sandy SG19 3EA** **Tel: (01767) 677361** **Fax 01767 677361** **Open: ALL YEAR** **Map Ref No. 09** Nearest Road: A.1198 A warm & friendly welcome awaits visitors to this traditional 1870s farmhouse situated on a working family farm. The house, providing comfortable accommodation & lovely views, is set in open countryside between the villages of Little Gransden & Longstowe. Guests are welcome to walk around the farm & garden. Cambridge can be reached in 20 mins via the B.1046 which takes the motorist on a picturesque drive through villages. E-mail: modelfm@globalnet.co.uk	£18.00	Y	N	Y

When booking your accommodation please mention
The Best Bed & Breakfast

Chiswick House, Royston

Northamptonshire

		rate from £ per person	children taken	evening meals	animals taken
Mrs Audrey Clarke **Dairy Farm** **Cranford St. Andrew** **Kettering** **NN14 4AQ** **Tel: (01536) 330273** **Open: ALL YEAR (Excl. Xmas)** **Map Ref No. 10**	Nearest Road: A.14 Situated in an idyllic Northamptonshire village, Dairy Farm is a charming 17th-century farmhouse, featuring oak beams & inglenook fireplaces. 4 comfortable bedrooms, each with en-suite/private bathroom. Families are well catered for. There is a delightful garden, containing an ancient circular dovecote, for guests to enjoy in a relaxed & friendly atmosphere. Delicious meals, using farmhouse produce. Animals by arrangement.	£22.00 🚭	Y	Y	Y
Mrs Margaret Faulkner **The Maltings** **96 Main Street** **Aldwincle** **Oundle NN14 3EP** **Tel: (01832) 720233** **Fax 01832 720326** **Open: ALL YEAR** **Map Ref No. 11**	Nearest Road: A.605, A.14 There is a warm & friendly welcome with personal attention at this former 16th century maltings - the Faulkner family home for 25 years. A lovely stone house & charming conversion of a small granary, all bordering a plant lover's garden, in a quiet village setting. Exposed beams, inglenooks & antique furniture complete this period home. 3 cosy bedrooms - all with bathrooms - 24-hour heating & good eating places nearby. Children over 10 please. Local attractions: Burghley House, Rockingham Castle & Rutland Water.	£23.50 🚭 CREDIT CARD VISA M'CARD	Y	N	N

All the establishments mentioned in this guide
are members of
The Worldwide Bed & Breakfast Association

When booking your accommodation please
mention
The Best Bed & Breakfast

Cheshire & Lancashire

Cheshire
(North West)

Cheshire is located between the Peak District & the mountains of North Wales & is easily accessible from three major motorways. It has much to attract long visits but is also an ideal stopping-off point for travellers to the Lake District & Scotland, or to North Wales or Ireland. There is good access eastwards to York & the east coast & to the south to Stratford-upon-Avon & to London.

Cheshire can boast seven magnificent stately homes, the most visited zoo outside London, four of Europe's largest garden centres & many popular venues which feature distinctive Cheshire themes such as silk, salt, cheese, antiques & country crafts.

The Cheshire plain with Chester, its fine county town, & its pretty villages, rises up to Alderley Edge in the east from where there are panoramic views, & then climbs dramatically to meet the heights of the Peaks.

To the west is the coastline of the Wirral Peninsula with miles of sandy beaches & dunes &, of course, Liverpool.

The countryside shelters very beautiful houses. Little Moreton Hall near Congleton, is one of the most perfect imaginable. It is a black & white "magpie" house & not one of its walls is perpendicular, yet it has withstood time & weather for nearly four centuries, standing on the waterside gazing at its own reflection.

Tatton Hall is large & imposing & is splendidly furnished with many fine objects on display. The park & gardens are a delight & especially renowned for the azaleas & rhododendrons. In complete contrast is the enormous radio telescope at Jodrell Bank where visitors can be introduced to planetary astronomy in the planetarium.

Chester is a joy; a walk through its streets is like walking through living history. The old city is encircled by city walls enclosing arcaded streets with handsome black & white galleried buildings that blend well with modern life. There are many excellent shops along these "Rows". Chester Cathedral is a fine building of monastic foundation, with a peaceful cloister & outstanding wood carving in the choir stalls. Boat rides can be taken along the River Dee which flows through the city.

Manchester has first rate shopping, restaurants, sporting facilities, theatres & many museums ranging from an excellent costume museum to the fascinating Museum of Science & Industry.

Little Moreton Hall.

Liverpool grew from a tiny fishing village on the northern shores of the Mersey River, receiving its charter from King John in 1207. Commercial & slave trading with the West Indies led to massive expansion in the 17th & 18th centuries. The Liverpool of today owes much to the introduction of the steam ship in the mid 1900s, which enabled thousands of Irish to emigrate when the potatoe famine was at its height in Ireland. This is a city with a reputation for patronage of art, music & sport.

Cheshire & Lancashire

Lancashire
(North West)

Lancashire can prove a surprisingly beautiful county. Despite its industrial history of cotton production, there is magnificent scenery & there are many fine towns & villages. Connections with the Crown & the clashes of the Houses of Lancaster & York have left a rich heritage of buildings with a variety of architecture. There are old stone cottages & farmhouses, as well as manor houses from many centuries.

For lovers of the countryside, Lancashire has the sweeping hills of Bowland, the lovely Ribble Valley, the moors of Rossendale & one mountain, mysterious Pendle Hill.

The Royal Forest of Bowland is a forest without trees, which has provided rich hunting grounds over the centuries. An old windswept pass runs over the heights of Salter Fell & High Cross Fell from Slaidburn, where the Inn, the "Hark to Bounty", was named after the noisiest hound in the squire's pack & used to be the courtroom where strict forest laws were enforced.

Further south, the Trough of Bowland provides an easier route through the hills, & here is the beautiful village of Abbeystead in Wynesdale where monks once farmed the land. The church has stained glass windows portraying shepherds & their flocks & there are pegs in the porch where shepherds hung their crooks.

Below the dramatic hills of Bowland, the green valley of the Ribble climbs from Preston to the Yorkshire Dales. Hangridge Fell, where the tales of witches are almost as numerous as those of Pendle Hill, lies at the beginning of the valley.

Pendle Hill can be reached from the pretty village of Downham which has Tudor, Jacobean & Georgian houses, village stocks & an old inn. Old Pendle rises abruptly to 1831 feet & is a strange land formation. It is shrouded in legend & stories of witchcraft.

Between Pendle Hill & the moors of Rossendale are the textile towns of Nelson, Colne, Burnley, Accrington & Blackburn. The textile industry was well established in Tudor times & the towns grew up as markets for the trading of the cloth woven in the Piece Halls.

The moors which descend to the very edges of the textile towns are wild & beautiful & have many prehistoric tumuli & earthworks. Through the towns & the countryside, winds the Liverpool & Leeds canal, providing an excellent towpath route to see the area.

Lancaster is an historic city boasting the largest castle in England, dating back to Norman times.

Lancashire's coastal resorts are legendary, & Blackpool is Queen of them all with her miles of illuminations & millions of visitors.

Downham Village.

Cheshire & Lancashire

Lancashire Gazeteer

Areas of outstanding natural beauty.
The Forest of Bowland, Parts of Arnside & Silverdale.

Historic Houses & Castles

Rufford Old Hall - Rufford
15th century screen in half-timbered hall of note. Collection of relics of Lancashire life.
Chingle Hall - Nr. Preston
13th century - small manor house with moat. Rose gardens. Haunted!
Astley Hall - Chorley
Elizabethan house reconstructed in 17th century. Houses pictures, tapestries, pottery & furniture.
Gawthorpe Hall - Padiham
17th century manor house with 19th century restoration. Moulded ceilings & some fine panelling. A collection of lace & embroidery.
Bramall Hall - Bramall
Fine example of half-timbered (black & white) manor house built in 14th century & added to in Elizabethan times. .
Lancaster Castle - Lancaster
Largest of English castles - dates back to Norman era.
Astley Hall - Chorley
16th century half-timbered grouped around central court. Rebuilt in the Jacobean manner with long gallery. Unique furniture.
Hoghton Tower - Nr. Preston
16th century - fortified hill-top mansion - magnificent banquet hall. Dramatic building - walled gardens & rose gardens.
Thurnham Hall - Lancaster
13th century origins. 16th century additions & 19th century facade. Beautiful plasterwork of Elizabethan period. Jacobean staircase.

Cathedrals & Churches

Lancaster (St. Mary)
15th century with 18th century tower. Restored chapel - fine stalls.
Whalley (St. Mary)
13th century with 15th century tower, clerestory & aisle windows. Fine wood carving of 15th century canopied stalls.
Halsall (St. Cuthbert)
14th century chancel, 15th century perpendicular spire. 14th century tomb. Original doors, brasses & effigies. 19th century restoration.
Tarleton (St. Mary)
18th century, part 19th century.
Great Mitton (All Hallows)
15th century rood screen, 16th century font cover, 17th century pulpit.

Museums & Galleries

Blackburn Museum - Blackburn
Extensive collections relating to local history archeology, ceramics, geology & natural history. One of the finest collection of coins & fine collection of mediaeval illuminated manuscripts & early printed books.
Bury Museum & Art Gallery - Bury
Houses fine Victorian oil & watercolours. Turner, Constable, Landseer, de Wint.
City Gallery - Manchester
Pre-Raphaelites, Old Masters, Impressionists, modern painters all represented in this fine gallery; also silver & pottery collections.
Higher Mill Museum - Helmshaw
One of the oldest wool textile finishing mills left in Lancashire. Spinning wheels, Hargreave's Spinning Jenny, several of Arkwrights machines, 20 foot water wheel.
Townley Hall Art Gallery & Museum, & Museum of Local Crafts & Industries - Burnley.

Cheshire Gazeteer

Area of outstanding natural beauty
Part of the Peaks National Park
Addington Hall - Macclesfield
15th century Elizabethan Black & White half timbered house.
Bishop Lloyd's House - Chester
17th century half timbered house (restored). Fine carvings. Has associations with Yale University & New Haven, USA.
Chorley Old Hall - Alderley Edge
14th century hall with 16th century Elizabethan wing.
Forfold Hall - Nantwich
17th century Jacobean country house, with fine panelling.

Cheshire & Lancashire

Gawsworth Hall - Macclesfield
Fine Tudor Half timbered Manor House.
Tilting ground. Pictures, furniture,
sculptures, etc.
Lyme Park - Disley
Elizabethan with Palladian exterior by
Leoni. Gibbons carvings. Beautiful park
with herd of red deer.
Peover Hall - Over Peover, Knutsford
16th century- stables of Tudor period;
has the famous magpie ceiling.
Tatton Park - Knutsford
Beautifully decorated & furnished
Georgian House with a fine collection of
glass, china & paintings including Van
Dyke & Canaletto. Landscaping by
Humphrey Repton.
Little Moreton Hall - Nr. Congleton
15th century timbered, moated house
with 16th century wall-paintings.

Cathedrals & Churches
Acton (St. Mary)
13th century with stone seating around
walls. 17th century effigies.
Bunbury (St. Boniface)
14th century collegiate church -
alabaster effigy.
Congleton (St. Peter)
18th century - box pews, brass
candelabrum, 18th century glass.
Chester Cathedral - Chester
Subjected to restoration by Victorians -
14th century choir stalls.
Malpas (St. Oswalds)
15th century - fine screens, some old
stalls, two family chapels.
Mobberley (St. Wilfred)
Mediaeval - 15th century rood screen,
wall paintings, very old glass.
Shotwick (St. Michael)
Twin nave - box pews, 14th century
quatre - foil lights, 3 deck pulpit.
Winwick (St. Oswald)
14th century - splendid roof. Pugin
chancel.
Wrenbury (St. Margaret)
16th century - west gallery, monuments
& hatchments. Box pews.
Liverpool Cathedral - the Anglican
Cathedral was completed in 1980 after
76 years of work. It is of massive
proportions, the largest in the U.K. with
much delicate detailed work.

Museums & Galleries
Grosvenor Museum - Chester
Art, folk history, natural history, Roman
antiquities including a special display of
information about the Roman army.
Chester Heritage Centre - Chester
Interesting exhibition of the architectural
heritage of Chester.
Cheshire Military Museum - Chester
The three local Regiments are
commemorated here.
King Charles Tower - Chester
Chester at the time of the Civil War
illustrated by dioramas.
Museum & Art Gallery - Warrington
Anthropology, geology, ethnology, botany
& natural history. Pottery, porcelain,
glass, collection of early English
watercolours.
West Park Museum & Art Gallery -
Macclesfield
Egyptian collection, oil paintings,
watercolours, sketches by Landseer &
Tunnicliffe.
Norton Priory Museum - Runcorn
Remains of excavated mediaeval priory.
Also wildlife display.
Quarry Bank Mill - Styal
The Mill is a fine example of industrial
building & houses an exhibition of the
cotton industry: the various offices retain
their original furnishing, & the turbine
room has the transmission systems &
two turbines of 1903.
Nether Alderley Mill - Nether Alderley
15th century corn mill which was still
used in 1929. Now restored.
The Albert Dock & Maritime Museum
- Liverpool
Housing the Liverpool Tate Gallery, the
Tate of the North.
Walker Art Gallery - Liverpool
Jodrell Bank - radio telescope &
planetarium.

Historic Monuments
Chester Castle - Chester
Huge square tower remaining.
Roman Amphitheatre - Chester
12th legion site - half excavated.
Beeston Castle - Beeston
Remains of a 13th century fort.
Sandbach Crosses - Sandbach
Carved stone crosses date from the 9th C.

CHESHIRE, LANCASHIRE, MERSEYSIDE & MANCHESTER

Map reference

1 **Taylor**	5 **McGinn**	11 **Butler**
2 **Ikin**	6 **Few**	12 **Rothwell**
3 **West**	7 **Sutcliffe**	14 **Townend**
4 **Read**	10 **Lawrence**	15 **Smith**

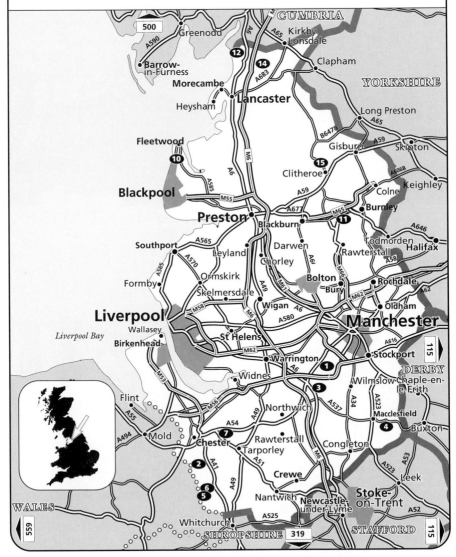

Longview Hotel. Knutsford.

		rate from £ per person	children taken	evening meals	animals taken
David Taylor **Ash Farm Country Guest** **House, Park Lane** **Little Bollington** **Altrincham WA14 4TJ** **Tel: (0161) 9299290** **Open: ALL YEAR** **Map Ref No. 01**	Nearest Road: A.53 Set in beautiful N.T. countryside. David & Janice have renovated this 18th-century farmhouse to a very high standard. Bedrooms are en-suite & have many features to delight the discerning traveller. The residents' lounge & dining area is furnished with an antique oak dining suite & open log fire & is the setting for excellent farmhouse food. 5 mins' walk to Dunham Deer Park; 2 miles M.56, M.6 less than 6 miles. Manchester Airport 10 mins. Easy access to Manchester & Chester. CREDIT CARD VISA M'CARD AMEX	£26.00	N	Y	N
Mrs Ann Ikin **Golborne Manor** **Platts Lane, Hatton Heath** **Chester CH3 9AN** **Tel: (01829) 770310** **Fax 01244 318084** **Open: ALL YEAR** **Map Ref No. 02**	Nearest Road: A.41 Golborne Manor is an elegant 19th century country residence, with glorious views, renovated to a high standard & set in 3 1/2 acres of gardens & grounds. Beautifully decorated with spacious en-suite bedrooms, colour T.V., tea/coffee & clock/radio. Farmhouse breakfasts. Fishing, golfing nearby. Snooker table, piano & croquet set available for guests' use. Large car park. Easy access for motorways. 10 mins' drive south from Chester on the A.41. (Mobile: 0374 695268.)	£25.00	Y	N	N
Pauline & Stephen West **The Longview Hotel &** **Restaurant** **51 - 55 Manchester Road** **Knutsford WA16 0LX** **Tel: (01565) 632119** **Fax 01565 652402** **Open: ALL YEAR (Excl. Xmas)** **Map Ref No. 03**	Nearest Road: M.6, A.50 Set in this pleasant Cheshire market town overlooking the common is this lovely, friendly hotel, furnished with many antiques that reflect the elegance of this Victorian building. Care has been taken to retain its character, while also providing all required comforts for the discerning traveller. All of the 23 en-suite bedrooms are prettily decorated, giving them that cared-for feeling which is echoed throughout the hotel. You are assured of a warm friendly welcome as soon as you step into reception. *see PHOTO over* CREDIT CARD VISA M'CARD AMEX	£30.00	Y	Y	Y
Mrs Anne Read **Hardingland Farm** **Macclesfield Forest** **Macclesfield SK11 0ND** **Tel: (01625) 425759** **Open: MAR - NOV** **Map Ref No. 04**	Nearest Road: A.537 Enjoy yourself in this early-Georgian farmhouse, lovingly restored & furnished with antiques. In a beautiful position in the Peak National Park, with superb views over the Cheshire Plain. Relax in the delightful lounge, & enjoy delicious meals prepared by Anne, who is renowned for her cooking. There are 3 bedrooms, 2 en-suite & all individually decorated. Ideally situated for the Peak District & Cheshire.	£19.00	N	Y	N
Valerie & John McGinn **Broughton House** **Threapwood** **Malpas** **SY14 7AN** **Tel: (01948) 770610** **Fax 01948 770472** **Open: ALL YEAR** **Map Ref No. 05**	Nearest Road: A.41 A friendly welcome to a warm & comfortable home, part of the elegant Georgian stables built for a former 17th-century mansion. Breakfasts are served in the conservatory overlooking parkland & the Welsh hills. Luxurious bedrooms, some with king-size 4-poster beds, have T.V.s & are all en-suite & ground-floor. 1 hour from Manchester & convenient for Chester & North Wales. Many charming pubs & restaurants in the area that serve dinner. Children over 10. **E-mail: mcginn@broughtn.u-net.com** *see PHOTO over* CREDIT CARD VISA M'CARD	£27.00	Y	N	N

Broughton House. Threapwood.

Laurel Farm. Malpas.

Cheshire & Lancashire

		rate from £ per person	children taken	evening meals	animals taken

Mrs Anthea Few
Laurel Farm
Chorlton Lane
Malpas
SY14 7ES
Tel: (01948) 860291
Fax 01948 860291
Open: ALL YEAR
Map Ref No. 06

Nearest Road: A.41
In an outstanding, peaceful situation surrounded by acres of glorious countryside, yet only mins from a market village & set off by a large landscaped duck pond (some cheeky ducks may greet you). This delightful 17th-century farmhouse belies an interior of great warmth & comfort. Sympathetically restored, it retains its original character - beams, old doors, Welsh quarry tiled floor etc. Elegantly furnished with antiques, it is an ideal base for exploring this area. Every room has stunning views, en-suite bedrooms are well-equipped. The hosts are friendly, helpful & have a good knowledge of the area. Children over 12.

£27.00 — Y Y N

see PHOTO over

Mrs Sally Sutcliffe
Roughlow Farm
Chapel Lane
Willington
Tarporley
CW6 0PG
Tel: (01829) 751199
Fax 01829 751199
Open: ALL YEAR
Map Ref No. 07

Nearest Road: A.51, A.54
An 18th-century sandstone farmhouse set in a magnificent position with wonderful views to Shropshire & Wales. A friendly family home elegantly furnished & decorated to a very high standard. 3 well-equipped comfortable bedrooms (all en-suite), 1 with its own private sitting room. An attractive garden encloses the cobbled courtyard. Use of tennis court. Dinner by prior arrangement (min. 4 persons). A superb home in a very peaceful, rural situation only 15 mins east of Chester. An ideal location for exploring Cheshire, the Potteries & N. Wales. Children over 6 years welcome.

£20.00 — Y Y N

see PHOTO over

Lancashire

Mr & Mrs M. Lawrence
Burlees Hotel
40 Knowle Avenue
North Shore
Blackpool FY2 9TQ
Tel/Fax: (01253) 354535
Open: FEB - NOV
Map Ref No. 10

Nearest Road: A.586
Traditionally built as a guest house, Burlees provides quality accommodation with 9 well-equipped & very comfortable en-suite bedrooms. A guest lounge & separate bar ensure a relaxed atmosphere. Excellent breakfast & dinner menus offer variety & choice. Families welcome, & baby listening is provided. The location is ideal for inland exploration of Lancashire, combined with the excitement of Britain's premier fun resort.

£22.00 — Y Y N

CREDIT CARD
VISA
M'CARD

Mrs Mavis Butler
Eaves Barn Farm
Hapton
Burnley
BB12 7LP
Tel: (01282) 771591
Fax 01282 771591
Open: ALL YEAR (Excl. Xmas & New Year)
Map Ref No. 11

Nearest Road: M.65, A.679
Eaves Barn Farm is a mixed working farm situated in a semi-rural location. The award-winning accommodation comprises a spacious cottage attached to the main house, furnished to a high standard & offering superb facilities designed with your comfort in mind. All bedrooms are individually styled, tastefully furnished & very comfortable. Each has en-suite or private facilities. A traditional full English breakfast is served in the conservatory. Easy access to Lancashire's tourist attractions & Manchester Airport by using the extensive motorway network. Children over 10.

£22.00 — Y Y N

Roughlow Farm. Willington.

Lancashire

		rate from £ per person	children taken	evening meals	animals taken
Mrs S. A. Rothwell **The Bower** **Yealand Road** **Yealand Conyers** **Carnforth** **LA5 9SF** **Tel: (01524) 734585** **Open: ALL YEAR** **Map Ref No. 12**	Nearest Road: A.6, M.6 A beautiful, small Georgian country house, set in an Area of Outstanding Natural Beauty. Superb walks right from the door, including to Leighton Moss RSPB reserve. There are 2 lovely bedrooms, 1 with a double & single bed & en-suite bathroom, & 1 with double bed & private bathroom. Both have colour T.V., clock radio, hairdryer, electric blankets & tea/coffee-making facilities. Delicious home-cooked, 4-course dinners. Perfect for exploring the Lake District & Yorkshire Dales. 10 mins from M.6. Very peaceful & ideal for stop-overs to or from Scotland. Children over 12 yrs.	£25.00	Y	Y	Y
Mrs Sally Townend **New Capernwray** **Farmhouse** **Capernwray** **Carnforth** **LA6 1AD** **Tel: (01524) 734284** **Fax 01524 734284** **Open: ALL YEAR** **Map Ref No. 14**	Nearest Road: A.6, M.6 Ex. 35 Ideal stop for London-Scotland, 3 miles from Exit 35, M.6. Set in beautiful countryside. Peaceful & quiet. Ideal for touring the Lake District & Yorkshire Dales. High-quality accommodation in 17th-century former farmhouse. Renowned for warm hospitality, comfort & excellent candle-lit dinners. Superb, non-smoking, fully-equipped king, queen & twin bedrooms with en-suite or private facilities. By arrangement pick-up at Manchester Airport & tours through Lake District, Yorkshire Dales & to Hadrian's Wall. Winner of the Best Bed & Breakfast Award for the North-West. Children over 10. *see PHOTO over* CREDIT CARD VISA M'CARD	£28.00	Y	Y	Y
Gordon & Jean Smith **Peter Barn Country** **House** **Cross Lane** **Waddington** **Clitheroe BB7 3JH** **Tel: (01200) 428585** **Open: ALL YEAR** **Map Ref No. 15**	Nearest Road: A.59 Nestling on the edge of the Forest of Bowland, surrounded by a beautiful garden with stream & ponds is the award-winning Peter Barn. Superb accommodation, oak beams & log fires in the 1st floor sitting room with panoramic views of glorious Ribble Valley. All of the 3 bedrooms are most attractive & each has an en-suite or private bathroom & tea/coffee-making facilities. The homemade marmalade is delicious. Good walking & exploring - Browsholme Hall, Whalley Abbey... or just relaxing.	£19.50	Y	N	N

When booking your accommodation please mention
The Best Bed & Breakfast

New Capernwray Farm. Carnforth.

Cornwall

Cornwall
(West Country)

Cornwall is an ancient Celtic land, a narrow granite peninsula with a magnificent coastline of over 300 miles & wild stretches of moorland.

The north coast, washed by Atlantic breakers, has firm golden sands & soaring cliffs. The magnificent beaches at Bude offer excellent surfing & a few miles to the south you can visit the picturesque harbour at Boscastle & the cliff-top castle at Tintagel with its legends of King Arthur. Newquay, with its beaches stretching for over seven miles, sheltered coves & modern hotels & shops, is the premier resort on Cornwall's Atlantic coast. St. Ives, another surfing resort, has great charm which has attracted artists for so long & is an ideal place from which to explore the Land's End peninsula.

The south coast is a complete contrast - wooded estuaries, sheltered coves, little fishing ports, & popular resorts. Penzance, with its warmth & vivid colours, is an all-the-year-round resort & has wonderful views across the bay to St. Michael's Mount. Here are excellent facilities for sailing & deep-sea fishing, as there are at Falmouth & Fowey with their superb harbours. Mevagissey, Polperro & Looe are fine examples of traditional Cornish fishing villages.

In the far west of Cornwall, you can hear about a fascinating legend: the lost land of Lyonesse - a whole country that was drowned by the sea. The legend goes that the waters cover a rich & fertile country, which had 140 parish churches. The Anglo-Saxon Chronicle records two great storms within a hundred years, which drowned many towns & innumerate people. Submerged forests are known to lie around these coasts - & in Mount's Bay beech trees have been found with the nuts still hanging on the branches, so suddenly were they swamped.

Today, St Michael's Mount & the Isles of Scilly are said to be all that remains of the vanished land. St. Michael's Mount, with its tiny fishing village & dramatic castle, can be visited on foot at low tide or by boat at high water. The Isles of Scilly, 28 miles beyond Land's End, have five inhabited islands, including Tresco with its sub-tropical gardens. Day trips to the numerous uninhabited islands are a special feature of a Scilly holiday.

Inland Cornwall also has its attractions. To the east of Bodmin, the county town, are the open uplands of Bodmin Moor, with the county's highest peaks at Rough Tor & Brown Willy. "Jamaica Inn", immortalised in the novel by Daphne du Maurier, stands on the lonely road across the moor, & "Frenchman's Creek" is on a hidden inlet of the Helford River.

There is a seemingly endless number & variety of Cornish villages in estuaries, wooded, pastoral or moorland settings, & here customs & traditions are maintained. In Helston the famous "Fleury Dance" is still performed, & at the ancient port of Padstow, May Day celebrating involves decorating the houses with green boughs & parading the Hobby Horse through the street to the tune of St. George's Song.

Helford Creek

Cornwall

Cornwall Gazeteer

Areas of outstanding natural beauty.
Almost the entire county.

Historic Houses & Castles

Anthony House - Torpoint
18th century - beautiful & quite unspoiled Queen Anne house, excellent panelling & fine period furnishings.

Cotehele House - Calstock
15th & 16th century house, still contains the original furniture, tapestry, armour, etc.

Ebbingford Manor - Bude
12th century Cornish manor house, with walled garden.

Godolphin House - Helston
Tudor - 17th century colonnaded front.

Lanhydrock - Bodmin
17th century - splendid plaster ceilings, picture gallery with family portraits 17th/ 20th centuries.

Mount Edgcumbe House - Plymouth
Tudor style mansion - restored after destruction in 1949. Hepplewhite furniture & portrait by Joshua Reynolds.

St. Michael's Mount - Penzance
Mediaeval castle & 17th century with 18th & 19th century additions.

Pencarrow House & Gardens - Bodmin
18th century Georgian Mansion - collection of paintings, china & furniture - mile long drive through fine woodlands & gardens.

Old Post Office - Tintagel
14th century manor house in miniature - large hall used as Post Office for a period, hence the name.

Trewithen - Probus Nr. Truro
Early Georgian house with lovely gardens.

Trerice - St. Newlyn East
16th century Elizabethan house, small with elaborate facade. Excellent fireplaces, plaster ceilings, miniature gallery & minstrels' gallery.

Cathedral & Churches

Altarnun (St. Nonna)
15th century, Norman font, 16th century bench ends, fine rood screen.

Bisland (St. Protus & St. Hyacinth)
15th century granite tower - carved wagon roofs, slate floor. Georgian wine - glass pulpit, fine screen.

Kilkhampton (St. James)
16th century with fine Norman doorway, arcades & wagon roofs.

Laneast (St. Michael or St. Sedwell)
13th century, 15th century enlargement, 16th century pulpit, some painted glass.

Lanteglos-by-Fowley (St. Willow)
14th century, refashioned 15th century, 13th century font, 15th century brasses & altar tomb, 16th century bench ends.

Launcells (St. Andrew)
Interior unrestored - old plaster & ancient roofs remaining, fine Norman font with 17th century cover, box pews, pulpit, reredos, 3 sided alter rails.

Probus (St. Probus & St. Gren)
16th century tower, splendid arcades, three great East windows.

St. Keverne (St. Keverne)
Fine tower & spire. Wall painting in 15th century interior.

St. Neot (St. Neot)
Decorated tower - 16th century exterior, buttressed & double-aisled. Many windows of mediaeval glass renewed in 19th century.

Museums & Galleries

Museum of Witchcraft - Boscastle
Relating to witches, implements & customs.

Military Museum - Bodmin
History of Duke of Cornwall's Light Infantry.

Public Library & Museum - Cambourne
Collections of mineralogy, archaeology, local antiquities & history.

Cornish Museum - East Looe
Collection of relics relating to witchcraft customs & superstitions. Folk life & culture of district.

Helston Borough Museum - Helston
Folk life & culture of area around Lizard.

Museum of Nautical Art - Penzance
Exhibition of salvaged gold & silver treasures from underwater wreck of 1700's.

Museum of Smuggling - Polperro
Activities of smugglers, past & present.

Cornwall

Penlee House Museum - Penlee, Penzance
Archaeology & local history & tin mining exhibits.
Barbara Hepworth Museum - St. Ives
Sculpture, letters, documents, photographs, etc., exhibited in house where Barbara Hepworth lived.
Old Mariners Church - St. Ives
St. Ives Society of Artists hold exhibitions here.
County Museum & Art Gallery - Truro
Ceramics, art local history & antiquities, Cornish mineralogy.

Historic Monuments

Cromwell's Castle - Tresco (Scilly Isles)
17th century castle.
King Charles' Fort - Tresco (Scilly Isles)
16th century fort.
Old Blockhouse - Tresco (Scilly Isles)
16th century coastal battery.
Harry's Wall - St. Mary's (Scilly Isles)
Tudor Coastal battery
Ballowall Barrow - St. Just
Prehistoric barrow.
Pendennis Castle - Falmouth
Fort from time of Henry VII.

Restormel Castle - Lostwithiel
13th century ruins.
St. Mawes Castle - St. Mawes
16th century fortified castle.
Tintagel Castle - Tintagel
Mediaeval ruin on wild coast, King Arthur's legendary castle.

Things to see & do

Camel trail - Padstow to Bodmin
12 miles of recreation path along scenic route, suitable for walkers, cyclists & horse-riders.
Tresco Abbey Gardens - Tresco
Collection of sub-tropical flora
Trethorne Leisure Farm - Launceston
Visitors are encouraged to feed & stroke the farm animals
Seal sanctuary - Gweek Nr. Helston
Seals, exhibition hall, nature walk, aquarium, seal hospital, donkey paddock.
Dobwalls Theme Park - Nr. Liskeard
2 miles of scenically dramatic miniature railway based on the American railroad.
Padstow tropical bird gardens - Padstow
Mynack Theatre - Porthcurno

Lands End.

CORNWALL
Map reference

1	Purslow	24	Rowe
1	Thompson	25	Epperson
2	Knight	26	Studley
2	Ruff	28	Jackson
2	Sibley	29	Westmacott
3	Tremayne	30	Nancarrow
4	Ford	31	Batty
5	Phillips	31	Mason
6	Griffin	31	Sykes
7	Rowe	32	Rayner
8	Stanley	32	Devlin
12	Low	33	Fry
13	Norman	34	Heasman
14	Spring	35	Henderson
14	Tuckett	36	Croggon
15	Wynn	37	Dymond
16	Mackenzie		
17	Woodley		
18	Walker		
19	Martin		
20	Hilder		
21	Lee		
21	Mercer		
22	Taylor		
23	Wooldridge		

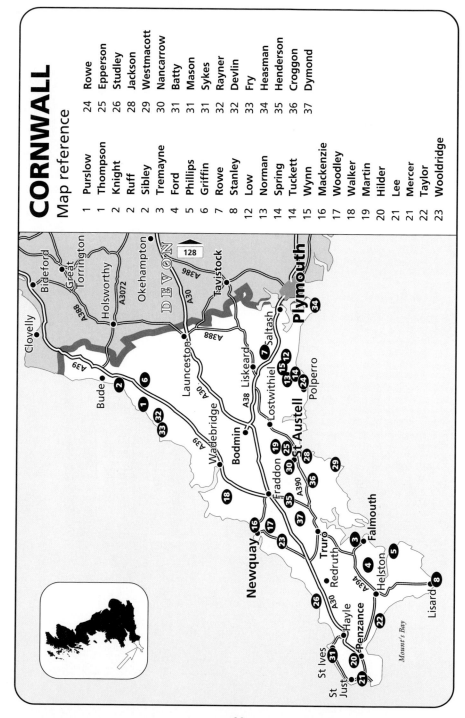

Manor Farm. Crackington Haven

	rate from £ per person	children taken	evening meals	animals taken
Mrs Eileen Purslow **Orchard Lodge** **Gunpool Lane** **Boscastle** **PL35 0AT** **Tel: (01840) 250418** **Open: APR - JAN** **Map Ref No. 01** Nearest Road: A.39, B.3266 Orchard Lodge, set in its own attractive gardens, is a large, delightful base for a relaxing holiday. Offering 6 very pleasant guest rooms, decorated & furnished to a high standard, with modern facilities. A delicious full English or Continental breakfast is served in the pretty dining room, with pine furnishings, which overlooks the garden. Ample parking. An ideal base for touring Cornwall. A warm & friendly welcome awaits you.	£18.00 (non-smoking)	N	N	N
Brenda & Brian Thompson **St. Christopher's Hotel** **High Street** **Boscastle** **PL35 0BD** **Tel: (01840) 250412** **Open: MAR - OCT** **Map Ref No. 01** Nearest Road: A.39 A superb Georgian house retaining its original character while providing excellent, comfortable accommodation in 9 charming rooms, 8 en-suite & all with modern facilities. Here, the welcome & standards are marvellous. The lovely harbour village is unspoilt. There is a wealth of history all around, with plenty of interesting places to visit. Meals are well-prepared, delicious & personally supervised. Children over 12 years.	£19.00 CREDIT CARD VISA M'CARD	Y	Y	Y
Mrs Muriel Knight **Manor Farm** **Crackington Haven** **Bude** **EX23 0JW** **Tel: (01840) 230304** **Open: ALL YEAR (Excl. Xmas Day)** **Map Ref No. 02** Nearest Road: A.39 A really super 11th-century manor house, retaining all its former charm & elegance. Mentioned in the 1086 Domesday book, it belonged to the Earl of Mortain, half-brother to William the Conqueror. Delightfully located in a beautiful & secluded position, & surrounded by both attractive gardens & 40 acres of farmland. Guest rooms have private facilities. Dining at Manor Farm is considered the highlight of the day. Only 1 mile from the beach. Non-smokers only. West Country winner of the Best Bed & Breakfast award.	£30.00 (non-smoking) *see PHOTO over*	N	Y	N
Mrs Lorraine Ruff **Nancemellan** **Crackington Haven** **Bude EX23 0NN** **Tel/Fax: (01840) 230283** **Open: APR - OCT** **Map Ref No. 02** Nearest Road: A.39 A beautiful Grade II listed Victorian country home set in 9 acres of grounds with stunning views towards the sea. The 3 guest rooms are delightfully furnished, all with en-suite or private bathrooms. The atmosphere is warm & informal, & open log fires make for a cosy winter stay. Breakfast is taken in the large family kitchen. A charming home from which to explore beautiful Cornwall.	£22.00 *see PHOTO over*	N	N	N
Brian Sibley **Cliff Hotel** **Crooklets Beach** **Bude** **EX23 8NG** **Tel: (01288) 353110** **Fax 01288 353110** **Open: APR - OCT** **Map Ref No. 02** Nearest Road: A.39 A small, quiet family hotel with an indoor swimming pool, all-weather tennis court & bowls. All rooms are en-suite & have colour T.V.s, telephone, radio & drinks. The hotel is located adjacent to cliff walks, a designated Area of Outstanding Natural Beauty. 200 yds west: Crooklets Beach, 200 yds south: a golf course, 200 yds east: Maer Lake Reserve, where peregrines hunt. The excellent cuisine is freshly cooked & includes local fish, French & traditional dishes.	£25.00 CREDIT CARD VISA M'CARD	Y	Y	Y

Nancemellan. Crackington Haven.

Cornwall

		rate from £ per person	children taken	evening meals	animals taken
Mr & Mrs T. P. Tremayne 'The Home' Country House Hotel, Penjerrick Budock Water Falmouth TR11 5EE Tel: (01326) 250427 Fax 01326 250143 Open: Easter - OCT Map Ref No. 03	Nearest Road: A.39 A quiet & charming country house, with views over Maenporth & Falmouth Bay. Accommodation is in 17 comfortable rooms, 13 with a private/en-suite bath/shower. All have tea/coffee-making facilities. A colour T.V. lounge & bar are available, & guests may relax in the beautiful sheltered garden. A golf course & boating facilities nearby. A friendly host, who prepares delicious meals using local produce. Special diets provided by arrangement. Children over 6 years welcome.	£21.00	Y	Y	Y
Mrs Judy Ford Treviades Barton High Cross Constantine Falmouth TR11 5RG Tel/Fax: (01326) 340524 Open: ALL YEAR Map Ref No. 04	Nearest Road: A.39 This charming, 16th-century, listed farmhouse stands in beautiful gardens close to the Helford River. Offering 3 comfortable double bedrooms with radio & tea/coffee makers; 2 with en-suite facilities. Guests stay in a family atmosphere. A wide range of relaxing or energetic holiday opportunities available locally throughout the year. Evening meals by arrangement. A delightful home & an ideal base for touring Cornwall.	£19.00 CREDIT CARD VISA M'CARD	Y	Y	Y
Huw & Lynne Phillips Tregildry Hotel Gillan, Manaccan Helston TR12 6HG Tel: (01326) 231378 Fax 01326 231561 Open: MAR - OCT Map Ref No. 05	Nearest Road: A.3083 The seaviews are stunning, the location unspoilt & peaceful. The home of Huw & Lynne Phillips, Tregildry is a rather special place to stay in this unique corner of Cornwall. Elegance merges into comfort, there are books, magazines, fresh flowers & a welcoming relaxed atmosphere. The 10 bedrooms are all en-suite & the small stylish restaurant has won awards for Huw's modern British style cuisine.	£35.00 CREDIT CARD VISA M'CARD	Y	Y	Y
Mrs V. Griffin Wheatley Farm Maxworthy Launceston PL15 8LY Tel: (01566) 781232 Fax 01566 781232 Open: MAR - NOV Map Ref No. 06	Nearest Road: A.39 You will be made very welcome at Wheatley, a spacious farmhouse, built by the Duke of Bedford in 1871, which stands in landscaped gardens on a working family farm in the peaceful Cornish countryside. Excellent touring base for exploring Cornwall/Devon. Spectacular coastline nearby. Beautiful accommodation, en-suite bedrooms, 1 with romantic 4-poster; each with T.V. & tea/coffee facilities. Splendid food using local produce. Log fires. Special breaks April, May, Sept.	£20.00	Y	Y	N
Stephanie Rowe Tregondale Farm Menheniot Liskeard PL14 3RG Tel: (01579) 342407 Fax 01579 342407 Open: ALL YEAR Map Ref No. 07	Nearest Road: A.390 Feeling like a break? Relax in style in this charming, elegant farmhouse, beautifully set in an original walled garden. 3 delightful bedrooms, 2 en-suite & 1 with private bathroom, all with T.V., radio & tea/coffee. Log fires for chilly evenings. Home produce a speciality. Play tennis, explore the woodland trail, through a 200-acre mixed farm. Find award-winning pedigree cattle, lambs in spring. Special rates for golf, cycling, fishing from the pond. A warm welcome awaits you.	£19.00	Y	Y	N

Coombe Farm. Widegates

Cornwall

Listing	Description	rate from £ per person	children taken	evening meals	animals taken
Mr & Mrs P. Stanley **Landewednack House** **Church Cove** **The Lizard** **TR12 7PQ** **Tel: (01326) 290909** **Fax 01326 290192** **Open: FEB - DEC** **Map Ref No. 08**	Nearest Road: A.3083 An elegant Grade II listed restored Georgian country house, idyllically positioned overlooking the sea, offering absolute peace & comfort. Delightful sea-view bedrooms, furnished with antiques; 4-poster & half-tester beds with private luxury bathrooms (1 with jacuzzi). Relax in front of log fires, laze in the secluded walled garden, play boules or croquet or just step onto the Heritage coastal footpath of the outstandingly beautiful Lizard Peninsula. Be utterly spoilt in this delightful home at England's most southerly point. CREDIT CARD VISA M'CARD	£36.00	N	Y	N
Alexander & Sally Low **Coombe Farm** **Widegates** **Looe** **PL13 1QN** **Tel: (01503) 240223** **Fax 01503 240895** **Open: MAR - NOV** **Map Ref No. 12**	Nearest Road: B.3253, A.38 A lovely country house, beautifully furnished with antiques, set in 10 acres of lawns, meadows, woods, streams & ponds, with superb views down a wooded valley to the sea. The atmosphere is delightful, with open log fires, a candlelit dining room (in which to enjoy delicious home-cooking) & an informal, licensed bar. An old barn has been converted for indoor games, including snooker & table tennis. Croquet lawn, a swimming pool & many birds & animals, including peacocks & horses. All bedrooms en-suite. Children over 5. *see PHOTO over* CREDIT CARD VISA M'CARD AMEX	£23.00	Y	Y	N
Pat & Bryan Norman **Fieldhead Hotel** **Portuan Road** **Looe** **PL13 2DR** **Tel: (01503) 262689** **Fax 01503 264114** **Open: FEB - DEC** **Map Ref No. 13**	Nearest Road: A.387 A delightful hotel with a fine reputation: guests return year after year. Set in its own grounds, with panoramic views of the sea, & within 200 yds of the beach. 14 most attractive & comfortable rooms, with en-suite facilities. All have radio, T.V. & tea/coffee makers. An attractive residents' lounge, games room, a heated outdoor pool & lovely garden. The area is wonderful for all sports - riding, walking, fishing, sailing, golfing - & the beaches are great. The Norman family make all visitors most welcome. Children over 5 yrs. CREDIT CARD VISA M'CARD AMEX	£30.00	Y	Y	N
Brian & Lynda Spring **Allhays Country House** **Talland Bay** **Looe** **PL13 2JB** **Tel: (01503) 272434** **Fax 01503 272929** **Open: ALL YEAR (Excl. Xmas)** **Map Ref No. 14**	Nearest Road: A.387 Overlooking the beautiful smugglers cove of Talland Bay. House guests enjoy all the warmth & comfort of a family home, complete with magnificent fireplaces & log fires. All 7 bedrooms have satellite-link colour T.V., telephone & tea/coffee makers. Most are en-suite, including 2 ground-floor rooms. Enjoy award-winning food & wine in the candlelit dining room, or amidst the beautiful 'outdoor' surroundings of the Victorian-style conservatory. Children over 10 yrs. E-mail: allhayscountryhouse@btinternet.com *see PHOTO over* CREDIT CARD VISA M'CARD AMEX	£28.00	Y	Y	Y
Mr B. C. Wynn **Harescombe Lodge** **Watergate** **Looe PL13 2NE** **Tel: (01503) 263158** **Open: ALL YEAR** **Map Ref No. 15**	Nearest Road: A.387 Once the shooting lodge of the Trelawne Estate, Harescombe Lodge is situated twixt Looe & Polperro, in the picturesque hamlet of Watergate, overlooking the West Looe River. An idyllic location with interesting walks & wildlife. Peaceful surroundings will appeal to the discerning visitor to south-east Cornwall. Accommodation is in 3 very attractive en-suite bedrooms.	£17.00	N	N	N

Allhays Country House. Looe.

The Old Mill. Little Petherick.

Cornwall

		rate from £ per person	children taken	evening meals	animals taken
Mac & Jennie Mackenzie **Trenance Lodge** **Restaurant & Hotel** **83 Trenance Road** **Newquay TR7 2HW** **Tel/Fax: (01637) 876702** **Open: ALL YEAR** **Map Ref No. 16**	Nearest Road: A.3075 An attractive house standing in its own grounds, overlooking lakes & gardens of Trenance Valley leading to the Gannel Estuary. The restaurant has a reputation for serving the finest fresh local food in elegant surroundings. Adjoining the restaurant is a spacious, relaxing bar lounge. Accommodation is in 5 comfortable bedrooms, en-suite, with colour T.V., radio & tea/coffee facilities. An excellent base for touring, with a warm welcome assured.	£24.00 CREDIT CARD VISA M'CARD	N	Y	N
Mrs Kathy Woodley **Degembris Farmhouse** **St. Newlyn East** **Newquay TR8 5HY** **Tel: (01872) 510555** **Fax 01872 510230** **Open: ALL YEAR (Excl. Xmas)** **Map Ref No. 17**	Nearest Road: A.3058 The original manor house of Degembris was built in the 16th century & is now used as a barn. The present-day house, surrounded by attractive gardens, was built 200 years ago, & its slate-hung exterior blends well with the rolling countryside. 5 bedrooms, 3 en-suite, each decorated in a coordinating theme, with dried flowers & stripped pine promoting the country atmosphere. Centrally situated in superb countryside, yet close to the sea, this is the perfect holiday base.	£18.00 CREDIT CARD VISA M'CARD	Y	Y	N
Michael & Pat Walker **The Old Mill Country** **House** **Little Petherick** **Padstow PL27 7QT** **Tel: (01841) 540388** **Open: MAR - OCT** **Map Ref No. 18**	Nearest Road: A.389 This delightful, 16th-century, converted corn mill, complete with water wheel, stands in its own grounds at the head of Little Petherick Creek. The house & bedrooms are furnished with antiques & collections of genuine artifacts, & each bedroom has an en-suite/private bathroom & tea/coffee-making facilities. Licensed, with a colour T.V. available for the guests' use. Also, a terraced sun garden. Light supper available on request.	£25.50 *see PHOTO over* CREDIT CARD VISA M'CARD AMEX	N	N	N
Keith & Janet Martin **Nanscawen House** **Prideaux Road** **St. Blazey** **Par PL24 2SR** **Tel: (01726) 814488** **Fax 01726 814488** **Open: ALL YEAR** **Map Ref No. 19**	Nearest Road: A.390 Nanscawen is a delightful country house set in an idyllic location. It stands in 5 acres of grounds & gardens in a nature-conservation area. Guests have a choice of 3 luxury en-suite rooms with spa baths. The elegantly furnished drawing room leads into the conservatory, where breakfast is enjoyed. Many good restaurants within easy reach. An ideal base for touring all of Cornwall. Guests may like to use the heated swimming pool & whirlpool hot tub. Children over 12 yrs. **E-mail: 101756.2120@compuserve.com**	£34.00 *see PHOTO over* CREDIT CARD VISA M'CARD	Y	N	N
Trish & Richard Hilder **Carnson House** **East Terrace** **Penzance** **TR18 2TD** **Tel: (01736) 365589** **Open: ALL YEAR** **Map Ref No. 20**	Nearest Road: A.30 Carnson offers you a Cornish welcome & a friendly atmosphere. 8 modern bedrooms, with heating, T.V. & tea/coffee makers. Some en-suite. Licensed, with a pleasant lounge. Enjoying one of Penzance's most central positions close to the railway & bus stations. Coach & boat trips, car hire & bus tours are available all year round, & can be arranged by the hotel. Add international recommendations for food, & it all makes for a happy & memorable visit. Children over 12. **E-mail: rhilder@netcomuk.co.uk**	£16.00 CREDIT CARD VISA M'CARD AMEX	Y	Y	N

Nanscawen House. St. Blazey.

		rate from £ per person	children taken	evening meals	animals taken
Mr & Mrs R. J. Lee **Boscean Country Hotel** **Boswedden Road** **St. Just-in-Penwith** **Penzance TR19 7QP** **Tel/Fax: (01736) 788748** **Open: APR - OCT** **Map Ref No. 21**	Nearest Road: A.30, A.3071 A warm & hospitable welcome awaits you at Boscean, a beautiful country house standing in 3 acres of walled grounds overlooking the sea & open countryside. There are 12 en-suite bedrooms, all with tea/coffee-making facilities. A guest lounge & bar. Delicious meals made with fresh, local or home-grown produce. Situated in an area of natural charm & beauty. An ideal place for touring the many interesting places in the Land's End peninsula. Animals by arrangement.	£22.00 CREDIT CARD VISA M'CARD	Y	Y	Y
M. J. & C. J. Mercer **Roseudian** **Crippas Hill** **St. Just** **Penzance TR19 7RE** **Tel: (01736) 788556** **Open: MAR - OCT** **Map Ref No. 21**	Nearest Road: A.3071, A.30 A small guest house in a quiet rural setting. An ideal centre for exploring the Land's End area. A traditional Cornish cottage, now comfortably modernised, standing in a 3/4-acre terraced garden for guests to enjoy. 3 attractive en-suite rooms, with tea/coffee-making facilities, delicious home-cooked meals, using seasonal garden produce, a lounge with T.V. & the warmest of welcomes all ensure a friendly, relaxed stay. Children over 7. Dogs by prior arrangement.	£18.00	Y	Y	Y
Mrs Christine Taylor **Ednovean Farm** **Perranuthnoe** **Penzance** **TR20 9LZ** **Tel: (01736) 711883** **Open: ALL YEAR** **Map Ref No. 22**	Nearest Road: A.394 A small working farm nestling above the peaceful village of Perranuthnoe, with stunning views over Mounts Bay & St. Michael's Mount. A unique 17th-century barn, lovingly renovated, now offers guests the choice of 3 elegant, country-style bedrooms, with en-suite facilities & charmingly decorated with fresh flowers, pretty chintz & stylish bed linen. Stroll across the fields to the village pub, sandy beach, cliff-top paths & secluded coves. Perfect peace!	£20.00	N	N	N
Mr & Mrs K. Wooldridge **Beach Dunes Hotel** **Ramoth Way** **Perranporth** **TR6 0BY** **Tel: (01872) 572263** **Fax 01872 573824** **Open: JAN - OCT incl.** **Map Ref No. 23**	Nearest Road: A.30, B.3285 A small friendly hotel pleasantly situated in almost an acre of grounds amidst the sand dunes adjoining the golf course, & overlooking Perran Bay with its 3 miles of golden sands & Atlantic beach. 9 bedrooms, 7 en-suite, each with tea/coffee, television/radio & private telephone. Also, 1 with private facilities. Excellent food is freshly prepared. Facilities include an indoor pool, a squash court, a cosy bar & a residents' lounge. An excellent touring centre. Children over 4 yrs. **E-mail: beachdunes@thenet.co.uk**	£26.50 CREDIT CARD VISA M'CARD AMEX	Y	Y	Y
Lynne & Anthony Tuckett **Trenderway Farm** **Pelynt** **Polperro PL13 2LY** **Tel: (01503) 272214** **Fax 01503 272991** **Open:** ALL YEAR (Excl. Xmas) **Map Ref No. 14**	Nearest Road: A.387 Built in the late 16th century, this mixed working farm is set in peaceful, beautiful countryside at the head of the Polperro Valley. Bedrooms here are truly superb, with bathrooms as big as some hotel bedrooms, & are decorated with the flair of a professional interior designer. A hearty farmhouse breakfast is served in the sunny conservatory, using local produce. Although an evening meal is not provided, an excellent range of nearby restaurants can be recommended.	£28.00 *see PHOTO over*	N	N	N

Trenderway Farm. Pelynt.

Landaviddy Manor. Polperro.

		rate from £ per person	children taken	evening meals	animals taken
Eric & Meryl Rowe **Landaviddy Manor** **Landaviddy Lane** **Polperro** **PL13 2RT** Tel: (01503) 272210 Fax 01503 272210 Open: Mid MAR - Mid OCT Map Ref No. 24	Nearest Road: A.387 A beautiful, licensed, 18th-century, small manor house built of traditional Cornish stone. Situated in lovely grounds on a hillside above the picturesque fishing village of Polperro, commanding charming views of the bay & surrounding N.T. countryside. Retaining its former character while incorporating modern comforts. Many of the charming bedrooms feature antique furniture incl. 4-poster & Victorian beds. All have private facilities, most are en-suite. Restaurants within 10 mins walk. Children over 14 years.	£23.00 (no smoking) **see PHOTO over** CREDIT CARD VISA M'CARD	Y	N	N
The Studley Family **Aviary Court** **Mary's Well, Illogan** **Redruth TR16 4QZ** Tel: (01209) 842256 Fax 01209 843744 Open: ALL YEAR Map Ref No. 26	Nearest Road: A.30 Aviary Court stands in 2 1/2 acres of ground on the edge of Illogan Woods. This part 300-year-old house offers guests a choice of 6 comfortable bedrooms, all with en-suite facilities, overlooking the gardens. Each has radio, colour T.V., tea/coffee-making facilities & 'phone. The comfortable lounge has a bar &, in winter, a log fire. The restaurant serves delicious food with a selection of wine. Children over 3 yrs welcome. E-mail: aviarycourt@connexions.co.uk	£30.00 CREDIT CARD VISA M'CARD AMEX	Y	Y	N
Jane & Steven Epperson **Anchorage House Guest** **Lodge, Nettles Corner** **Boscundle, Tregrehan** **St. Austell PL25 3RH** Tel: (01726) 814071 Open: ALL YEAR Map Ref No. 25	Nearest Road: A.390 Every attention has been paid to the smallest detail in this beautiful antique-filled house. The richly furnished en-suite rooms are supremely comfortable with antique king-size beds, satellite T.V. & many thoughtful touches, making your visit thoroughly special. Steven & Jane combine superb cooking, wonderful hospitality & pleasing informality for a stay to remember. Perfect for visiting N.T. gardens, Heligan, Carlyon Bay beach & golf. Children over 15 years.	£24.00 (no smoking) **see PHOTO over**	N	Y	N
Mrs J. Jackson **Polrudden Farm** **Pentewan** **Mevagissey** **St. Austell PL26 6BJ** Tel: (01726) 843213 Tel/Fax 01726 842051 Open: MAR - OCT Map Ref No. 28	Nearest Road: B.3273 Polrudden is a small working farm set in 74 acres of unspoilt coastal farmland with breathtaking views over the bay. A stone's throw from the sea, it is situated centrally between Penzance & Plymouth. 4 well-appointed bedrooms, each with an en-suite/private bathroom, T.V. & tea/coffee-making facilities. A friendly, relaxed atmosphere prevails. Polrudden has a small, secluded private beach & is within 5 mins walk from Pentewan Sands, where there is safe bathing, water skiing, sailing & other beach activities. Children over 8.	£18.00 (no smoking)	Y	N	Y
Mrs G. Westmacott **Mevagissey House** **Vicarage Hill, Mevagissey** **St. Austell PL26 6SZ** Tel: (01726) 842427 Fax 01726 844327 Open: MAR - OCT Map Ref No. 29	Nearest Road: A.390 An elegant Georgian rectory standing in 4 acres of woodland, overlooking the beautiful woodland & valley leading to the harbour & sea beyond. Here, guests can unwind & relax in pleasant, comfortable surroundings. There are 4 rooms, 3 en-suite, all with modern amenities, T.V. & tea/coffee-making facilities. Snacks, morning coffee & Cornish cream teas are available on request. Close by are fishing, beaches & golf courses. Children over 7 years welcome.	£20.00 CREDIT CARD VISA M'CARD	Y	N	N

Anchorage House. Boscundle.

Cornwall

		rate from £ per person	children taken	evening meals	animals taken
Mrs Judith Nancarrow **Poltarrow Farm** **St. Mewan** **St. Austell** **PL26 7DR** **Tel: (01726) 67111** Fax 01726 67111 **Open:** ALL YEAR (Excl. Xmas) **Map Ref No. 30**	Nearest Road: A.390 Set in 45 acres of pastoral farmland, this wisteria-clad farmhouse holds a commanding position, with views across rolling pastures. 5 individually decorated & attractively furnished bedrooms with en-suite/private bathroom, T.V. & tea/coffee. The dining room offers traditional farmhouse fare, with a full English breakfast made using fresh local produce & served in generous Cornish portions. A quiet & comfortable sitting room. Log fire. Close to the south coast of Cornwall, yet centrally situated between Plymouth & Penzance.	£20.00 CREDIT CARD VISA M'CARD	Y	N	N
Moira & Wally Batty **The Grey Mullet** **2 Bunkers Hill** **St. Ives** **TR26 1LJ** **Tel: (01736) 796635** Fax 01736 796635 **Open: ALL YEAR** **Map Ref No. 31**	Nearest Road: A.3074 The Grey Mullet, an 18th-century, Grade II listed building with oak beams & exposed granite walls which are hung with paintings, sketches & old photographs, is situated in the old fishing & artists' quarter of St. Ives & is a 2 min. walk from the Tate Gallery. Visitors are given a warm welcome in relaxed & homely surroundings. There are comfortable en-suite bedrooms with T.V. & tea/coffee-making facilities, some with 4-poster beds, & a sitting room with an open fire. Vegetarian & low-calorie diets catered for.	£20.00	Y	N	N
Diana & Derek Mason **Kandahar** **11 The Warren** **St. Ives TR26 2EA** **Tel: (01736) 796183** **Open:** Mid FEB - Mid NOV **Map Ref No. 31**	Nearest Road: A.3074 Kandahar has a unique water's-edge location, lapped by the Atlantic & overlooking the harbour. The town centre, beaches, coach & railway station are all within 150 yds. All 5 rooms have superb sea views, colour T.V., tea/coffee-making facilities & full central heating. There are 2 en-suite bedrooms. English & vegetarian breakfasts served. There are many restaurants close by. Children over 5 years.	£18.00 CREDIT CARD VISA M'CARD	Y	N	N
Irene & Jack Sykes **The Old Vicarage Hotel** **Parc-an-Creet** **St. Ives TR26 2ET** **Tel/Fax: (01736) 796124** **Open: APR - OCT** **Map Ref No. 31**	Nearest Road: A.30 The Old Vicarage Hotel, set in its own wooded grounds, secluded & peaceful, on the edge of the moorlands to the west of St. Ives. Offering 8 bedrooms, 6 with a private bath/shower, all with colour T.V. All rooms have tea/coffee makers. Families well catered for. A delightful large garden for guests to relax in, & a safe recreation area for children. Convenient for beach & places of interest.	£19.00 CREDIT CARD VISA M'CARD AMEX	Y	N	Y
John & Christina Rayner **The Old Borough House** **Bossiney Road** **Bossiney** **Tintagel PL34 0AY** **Tel: (01840) 770475** **Open: ALL YEAR** **Map Ref No. 32**	Nearest Road: A.39, B.3263 A delightful 17th-century Cornish stone house, formerly the home of J. B. Priestley. It is located between Tintagel & Boscastle in an Area of Outstanding Natural Beauty with N.T. property nearby. The 6 comfortable bedrooms, (3 en-suite/private) have modern amenities & tea/coffee makers. A colour-T.V. lounge & garden are also available for guests. Close by are safe bathing coves, caves & coastal walks. Delicious food & wine available. Children over 4 years.	£17.00	Y	Y	N

Cornwall

		rate from £ per person	children taken	evening meals	animals taken
Mrs J. A. Fry **Polkerr Guest House** **Molesworth Street** **Tintagel PL34 0BY** **Tel: (01840) 770382** **Tel: (01840) 770132** **Open: ALL YEAR** **Map Ref No. 33**	Nearest Road: A.39 Polkerr has been converted from a farmhouse to a refurbished guest house of a very high standard. All rooms are en-suite with T.V. & tea-making facilities. A recent addition has been a beautifully appointed sun lounge where guests can relax after viewing some of the most impressive coastal views of north Cornwall. Within easy reach of Tintagel village is the King Arthur Castle & other amenities such as golf, gardens, horse riding & much more. A charming home.	£18.00	Y	Y	N
John Charlick & **Sean Devlin** **Trebrea Lodge, Trenale** **Tintagel PL34 0HR** **Tel: (01840) 770410** **Fax 01840 770092** **Open: MAR - DEC** **Map Ref No. 32**	Nearest Road: A.39 This lovely Grade II listed Georgian house, set in 4 1/2 acres of wooded hillside, has outstanding views of the north Cornish coast. The land was originally granted by the Black Prince to the Bray family, who lived here for 600 years. The beautiful bedrooms are individually decorated with antique furniture, & all have en-suite bathrooms. Award-winning, high-quality cooking, log fires & a relaxed atmosphere. Trebrea Lodge is a truly delightful home. Children over 12 years.	£39.00 *see PHOTO over* CREDIT CARD VISA M'CARD AMEX	Y	Y	Y
Ann Heasman **Cliff House** **Devonport Hill** **Kingsand** **Torpoint** **PL10 1NJ** **Tel: (01752) 823110** **Open: ALL YEAR** **Map Ref No. 34**	Nearest Road: A.374 Cliff House is a Grade II listed 17th-century building, converted from 2 cottages into 1 house around 150 years ago. Although modernised to include en-suite facilities, it still retains many of its' original features. A drawing room with wonderful views, log fires, T.V. etc. for guests' use. It has a large balcony through French windows overlooking Plymouth Sound, Cawsand Bay & the village. Ann is an enthusiastic wholefood cook, & meals (by arrangement) include homemade soups, mousses, ice cream & freshly baked bread.	£20.00 🚭	Y	Y	N
Elizabeth & Keith Henderson **Bissick Old Mill, Ladock** **Truro TR2 4PG** **Tel: (01726) 882557** **Fax 01726 884057** **Open: ALL YEAR (Excl.** **Xmas & New Year)** **Map Ref No. 35**	Nearest Road: A.30, A.390 Bissick Old Mill, formerly a working corn mill, is conveniently situated in the village of Ladock (10 mins' drive from Truro), & provides exceptional standards of comfort, cuisine & hospitality. Its central position makes it an ideal base from which to visit all areas of Cornwall, whether it be on business or purely for pleasure. A chef proprietor (mostly English/French dishes). A residential licence. Animals by arrangement.	£27.00 CREDIT CARD VISA M'CARD	N	Y	Y
Mr & Mrs Croggon **Creed House** **Creed** **Grampound** **Truro TR2 4SL** **Tel: (01872) 530372** **Open: ALL YEAR** **Map Ref No. 36**	Nearest Road: A.390 Creed House is a Grade II listed spacious rectory built around 1730, set in 7 acres of garden, occasionally open to the public. Across the lawns are an ancient church & the River Fal which flows through tranquil meadows. Creed is at the head of the Roseland Peninsular, renowned for its heritage coastline, coastal walks & many of the famous Cornish gardens nearby. Guests are warmly welcomed. Children over 8.	£27.50 🚭	Y	N	N

Trebrea Lodge. Trenale.

Cornwall

		rate from £ per person	children taken	evening meals	animals taken
Bridget Dymond **Trevispian-Vean Farm** **Guest House** Trevispian-Vean, St. Erme **Truro TR4 9BL** **Tel: (01872) 279514** **Fax 01872 263730** **Open: APR - SEPT** **Map Ref No. 37**	Nearest Road: A.39 A delightful farmhouse, dating back over 300 years, offering a very warm welcome & good accommodation in 12 pleasant & comfortably furnished guest rooms, 10 with en-suite facilities. Only 7 miles from the coast, & surrounded by beautiful countryside, it is a perfect base for everyone. Families will particularly enjoy it here, as children can look around the farm, & there are plenty of places to visit & things to do. There's even a donkey for the children.	£18.00	Y	Y	N

All the establishments mentioned in this guide are members of
The Worldwide Bed & Breakfast Association

When booking your accommodation please mention
The Best Bed & Breakfast

Cumbria

Cumbria

The Lake District National Park is deservedly famous for its magnificent scenery. Here, England's highest mountains & rugged fells surround shimmering lakes & green valleys. But there is more to Cumbria than the beauty of the Lake District. It also has a splendid coastline, easily accessible from the main lakeland centres, as well as a border region where the Pennines, the backbone of England, reach their highest point, towering over the Eden valley.

Formation of the dramatic Lakeland scenery began in the Caledonian period when earth movements raised & folded the already ancient rocks, submerging the whole mass underseas & covering it with limestone. During the ice age great glaciers ground out the lake beds & dales of todays landscape. There is tremendous variety, from the craggy outcrops of the Borrowdale Volcanics with Skiddaw at 3054 feet, to the gentle dales, the open moorlands & the lakes themselves. Each lake is distinctive, some with steep mountain sides sliding straight to the water's edge, others more open with sloping wooded hillsides. Ellerwater, the enchanting "lake of swans" is surrounded by reed & willows at the foot of Langdale. The charm of Ullswater inspired Wordsworth's famous poem "Daffodils". Whilst many lakes are deliberately left undisturbed for those seeking peace, there are others - notably Windermere - where a variety of water sports can be enjoyed. The changeable weather of the mountainous region can produce a sudden transformation in the character of a tranquil lake, raising choppy waves across the darkened surface to break along the shoreline. It is all part of the fascination of Lakeland.

Fell walking is the best way to appreciate the full beauty of the area. There are gentle walks along the dales, & the tops of the ridges are accessible to walkers with suitable footwear & an eye to the weather.

Ponytrekking is another popular way to explore the countryside & there are many centres catering even for inexperienced riders.

There are steamboats on lakes such as Coniston & Ullswater, where you can appreciate the scenery. On Windermere there are a variety of boats for hire, & facilities for water-skiing.

Traditional crafts & skills are on display widely. Craft centres at Keswick, Ambleside & Grasmere, & the annual exhibition of the Guild of Lakeland Craftsmen held in Windermere from mid-July to early September represent the widest variety of craft artistry.

Fairs & festivals flourish in Lakeland. The famous Appleby Horse Fair, held in June is the largest fair of its kind in the world & attracts a huge gypsy gathering. Traditional agriculture shows, sheep dog trials & local sporting events abound. The Grasmere Sports, held each August include gruelling fell races, Cumberland & Westmoreland wrestling, hound trails & pole-leaping.

The traditional custom of "Rush-bearing" when the earth floors of the churches were strewn with rushes still survives as a procession in Ambleside & Grasmere & many other villages in the summer months

The coast of Cumbria stretches from the estuaries of Grange-over-Sands & Burrow-in-Furness by way of the beautiful beaches between Bootle & Cardurnock, to the mouth of the Solway Firth. The coastal areas, especially the estuaries, are excellent for bird-watching. The sand dunes north of the Esk are famous for the colony of black-headed gulls which can be visited by arrangement, & the colony of seabirds at St. Bees Head is the largest in Britain.

Cumbria

Cumbria

Gazeteer

Area of outstanding natural beauty.
The Lake District National Park.

House & Castles

Carlisle Castle - Carlisle
12th century. Massive Norman keep -
half-moon battery - ramparts, portcullis &
gatehouse.
Brough Castle - Kirby Stephen
13th century - on site of Roman Station
between York & Carlisle.
Dacre Castle - Penrith
14th century - massive pele tower.
Sizergh Castle - Kendal
14th century - pele tower - 15th century
great hall. English & French furniture,
silver & china - Jacobean relics. 18th
century gardens.
Belle Island - Boweness-on-Windermere
18th century - interior by Adams Brothers,
portraits by Romney.
Swarthmoor Hall - Ulverston
Elizabethan house, mullioned windows,
oak staircase, panelled rooms. Home of
George Fox - birthplace of Quakerism -
belongs to Society of Friends.
Lorton Hall - Cockermouth
15th century pele tower, priest holes, oak
panelling, Jacobean furniture.
Muncaster Castle - Ravenglass
14th century with 15th & 19th century
additions - site of Roman tower.
Rusland Hall - Ulveston
Georgian mansion with period panelling,
sculpture, furniture, paintings.
Levens Hall - Kendal
Elizabethan - very fine panelling &
plasterwork - famous topiary garden.
Hill Top - Sawrey
17th century farmhouse home of Beatrix
Potter - contains her furniture, china &
some of original drawings for her
children's books.
Dove Cottage - Town End, Grasmere
William Wordsworth's cottage - still
contains his furnishing & his personal
effects as in his lifetime.
Brantwood
The Coniston home of John Ruskin, said
to be the most beautifully situated house
in the Lake District. Exhibition, gardens,
bookshops & tearooms.

Cathedrals & Churches

Carlisle Cathedral - Carlisle
1130. 15th century choir stalls with
painted backs - carved misericords, 16th
century screen, painted roof.
Cartmel Priory (St. Mary Virgin)
15th century stalls, 17th century screen,
large east window, curious central tower.
Lanercost Priory (St. Mary Magdalene)
12th century - Augustinian - north aisle
now forms Parish church.
Greystoke (St. Andrew)
14th/15th century. 19th century
misericords. Lovely glass in chancel.
Brougham (St. Wilfred)
15th century carved altarpiece.
Furness Abbey
12th century monastery beautiful setting.
Shap Abbey
12th century with 16th century tower.

Museums & Galleries

Abbot Hall - Kendal
18th century, Georgian house with period
furniture, porcelain, silver, pictures, etc.
Also contains modern galleries with
contemporary paintings, sculptures &
ceramics. Changing exhibitions on show.
Carlisle Museum & Art Gallery - Carlisle
Archaeological & natural history
collections. National centre of studies of
Roman Britain. Art gallery principally
exhibiting paintings & porcelain.
Hawkshead Courthouse - Kendal
Exhibition of domestic & working life
housed in mediaeval building.
Helena Thompson Museum - Workington
displays Victorian family life & objects of
the period.
Lakeland Motor Museum - Holker Hall -
Grange-over-Sands
Exhibits cars, bicycles, tricycles, motor
cycles, etc., & model cars.
Millom Folk Museum - St. George's
Road, Millom
Reconstructions of drift in iron ore mine,
miner's cottage kitchen, blacksmith's forge
& agricultural relics.
Ravenglass Railway Museum -
Ravenglass
History of railways
relics, models, etc.

Cumbria

Wordsworth Museum - Town End, Grasmere
Personal effects, first editions, manuscripts, & general exhibits from the time of William Wordsworth.

Border Regiment Museum - The Castle, Carlisle.
Collection of uniforms, weapons, trophies, documents, medals from 1702, to the present time.

Whitehaven Museum - Whitehaven
History & development of area show in geology, paleontology, archaeology, natural history, etc. Interesting maritime past.

Fitz Park Museum & Art Gallery - Keswick.
Collection of manuscripts - Wordsworth, Walpole, Coleridge, Southey.

The Beatrix Potter Gallery - Hawkshead

Things to see & do

Fell Walking - there is good walking throughout Cumbria, but check weather reports, clothing & footwear before tackling the heights.

Pony-trekking - opportunities for novice & experienced riders.

Watersports - Windermere is the ideal centre for sailing, waterskiing, windsurfing, scuba-diving.

Golf - championship course to the north at Silloth.

Grasmere.

CUMBRIA
Map reference

1	Seedhouse	24	Wightman
2	Kirby	25	Knowles
3	Hart	26	Briggs
4	Butcher	27	Lowe
5	Hood	28	Lowrey
7	Stobbart	29	Bryant
8	Vickers	30	McCrickard
9	D. Edwards	31	Sanders
10	Sisson	32	White
12	Hodge	33	M. Smith
13	Hatch	34	Weightman
14	Murray	35	Whittam
15	Wilkinson	36	Greenhalgh
16	Danson	36	Holcroft
17	Cervetti	36	Casey
18	Clark	36	Cox
19	J. Edwards	36	Reed
20	Tylor	36	Fishman
21	Savasi	36	Tyson
22	Craig	36	Thomas
23	Midwinter	36	Sanderson
		36	Butterworth
		36	Garside

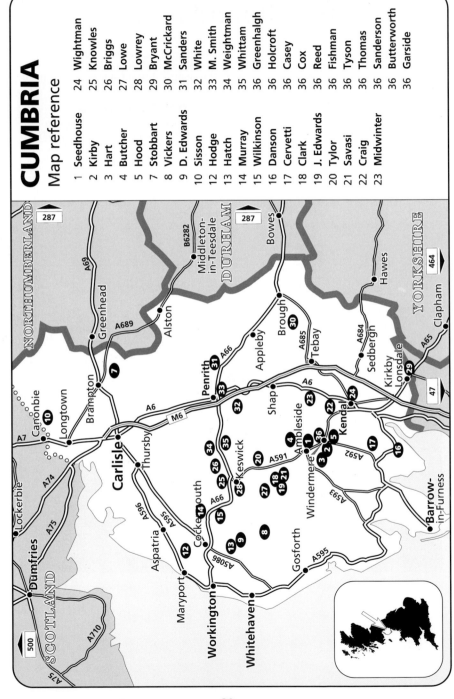

Laurel Villa. Ambleside.

	rate from £ per person	children taken	evening meals	animals taken
Brian Seedhouse Laurel Villa Lake Road Ambleside LA22 0DB Tel: (015394) 33240 Open: ALL YEAR Map Ref No. 01	Nearest Road: A.591 Visited by Beatrix Potter, this charming Victorian residence, now sympathetically restored & refurbished to a very high standard, offers 8 comfortable en-suite bedrooms; 2 of which boast 4-poster beds whilst some at the rear have splendid views over the village & surrounding fells. A residents' lounge in which to relax & an attractive dining room. All major outdoor activities are catered for nearby, including watersports, pony trekking &, of course, fell walking. Car park.	£30.00 *see PHOTO over* CREDIT CARD VISA M'CARD AMEX	N	Y	N
Robert & Helen Kirby Buckle Yeat Guest House Sawrey, Hawkshead Ambleside LA22 0LF Tel: (015394) 36538 Tel/Fax: 015394 36446 Open: ALL YEAR Map Ref No. 02	Nearest Road: B.5285, A.590 Buckle Yeat is famous for its connections with Beatrix Potter. Although over 200 years old, it has been sympathetically & tastefully refurbished. There is a large lounge with log fire & an attractive dining room which also serves morning coffee & afternoon teas. There are 7 comfortable en-suite bedrooms. Many good local pubs & restaurants offer excellent meals. Buckle Yeat is in an ideal position for touring Lakeland, with walks, fishing & birdwatching all nearby.	£22.50 CREDIT CARD VISA M'CARD AMEX	Y	N	Y
Peter & Anne Hart Bracken Fell Outgate Ambleside LA22 0NH Tel: (015394) 36289 Open: ALL YEAR Map Ref No. 03	Nearest Road: B.5286 Bracken Fell is situated in beautiful open countryside in the picturesque hamlet of Outgate. Located between Ambleside & Hawkshead, this makes an ideal base for exploring the Lake District. 7 comfortable rooms, all with tea/coffee-making facilities, outstanding views & either en-suite or private facilities. There is also a comfortable lounge & dining room. All major outdoor activities are catered for nearby, including sailing, fishing, windsurfing & pony trekking. Children over 9.	£20.00	Y	N	N
Philip & Jane Butcher Rowanfield Country House Kirkstone Road Ambleside LA22 9ET Tel: (015394) 33686 Fax 015394 31569 Open: Mid MAR - DEC Map Ref No. 04	Nearest Road: A.591 Set in quiet countryside 3/4 of a mile outside Ambleside, with fabulous lake & mountain views. A beautiful period house, with Laura Ashley-style decor. A warm welcome assured, & a homely atmosphere. All bedrooms are en-suite, & individually & tastefully furnished. Tea/coffee-making facilities, colour T.V., radio/alarm & hairdryer in all rooms. A top professional chef/patron creates exciting evening meals from the finest fresh produce. Unlicensed, but own wine welcome. Children over 5 yrs.	£27.00 *see PHOTO over* CREDIT CARD VISA M'CARD	Y	Y	N
Ray & Barbara Hood Fairfield Country House Hotel Brantfell Rd Bowness-on-Windermere LA23 3AE Tel/Fax: (015394) 46565 Open: ALL YEAR (Excl. Xmas) Map Ref No. 05	Nearest Road: A.591 Fairfield is a small, friendly, 200-year-old Lakeland hotel in a peaceful garden setting, 200 metres from Bowness village, 400 metres from the shores of Lake Windermere & at the end of the Dales Way (an 81-mile walk from Ilkley to Bowness). The Beatrix Potter Exhibition is within easy walking distance. 9 well-appointed & tastefully furnished bedrooms with T.V., welcome tray & private showers/bathrooms. Breakfasts are a speciality. Leisure facilities available. E-mail: ray&barb@fairfield.dial.lakesnet.co.uk	£23.00 *see PHOTO over* CREDIT CARD VISA M'CARD	Y	N	N

Rowanfield Country House. Ambleside.

Fairfield Country House. Bowness-on-Windermere

Fayrer Garden House. Bowness-on-Windermere.

Cumbria

	rate from £ per person	children taken	evening meals	animals taken
Iain & Jackie Garside **Fayrer Garden House** **Hotel, Lyth Valley Road** **Bowness-on-Windermere** **LA23 3JP** **Tel: (015394) 88195** **Fax 015394 45986** **Open: ALL YEAR** **Map Ref No. 36**	Nearest Road: A.5074 Beautiful country house hotel, in 5 acres of grounds overlooking Lake Windermere. Award-winning cuisine served in the air-conditioned conservatory restaurant. All of the delightful & comfortably furnished bedrooms are en-suite with colour T.V., hairdryers etc. Some have 4-poster beds, whirlpool baths & lake views at a supplement. Special breaks, interest weekends & free use of local leisure centre. An ideal spot for a relaxing break. A colour brochure is available on request.	£29.90 *see PHOTO over* CREDIT CARD VISA M'CARD AMEX	Y	Y	Y
Mrs Sheila Stobbart **'Hullerbank'** **Talkin** **Brampton** **CA8 1LB** **Tel: (016977) 46668** **Open: ALL YEAR (Excl. Xmas & New Year)** **Map Ref No. 07**	Nearest Road: A.69, M.6 A Georgian farmhouse, dated 1635-1751, standing in its own grounds near the picturesque village of Talkin, 2 1/2 miles from Brampton. Superb walking country, central for visiting Hadrian's Wall, the Lake District & the borders. A warm, friendly, relaxed atmosphere awaits. 3 comfortable bedrooms, with private facilities, electric underblankets & tea makers. A comfortable T.V. lounge & dining room with excellent home cooking, including home-produced lamb & fresh produce. Children over 12 welcome.	£20.00 (no smoking) CREDIT CARD VISA M'CARD	Y	Y	N
M. Vickers & J. McKenzie **Wood House** **Buttermere** **CA13 9XA** **Tel: (017687) 70208** **Open: Mid FEB - NOV** **Map Ref No. 08**	Nearest Road: A.66, B.5289 Wood House, near Buttermere village overlooking Crummock Water, stands on one of the outstanding sites in the Lake District. The drawing room, with high-quality furnishings & antiques, spanning the front of the house, has a spellbinding view over the lake, as do each of the 3 spacious & attractively furnished en-suite bedrooms. Freshly prepared food is served in the traditional surroundings of a charming dining room.	£29.00 (no smoking)	N	Y	N
David & Dani Edwards **Pickett Howe** **Buttermere Valley** **CA13 9UY** **Tel: (01900) 85444** **Fax 01900 85209** **Open: MAR - NOV** **Map Ref No. 09**	Nearest Road: A.66 Award-winning Pickett Howe is peacefully set amidst stunning mountain scenery. This 17th-century longhouse offers caring, relaxing hospitality. The cosy bedrooms have Victorian bedsteads, whirlpool baths, 'phones & many extras. Quality furnishings & antiques enhance the slate floors & oak beams. Dani's dinners are a treat for both eyes & palate. The breakfast menu is outstanding, always including vegetarian dishes. Children over 10.	£37.00 (no smoking) *see PHOTO over* CREDIT CARD VISA M'CARD	Y	Y	N
Jack & Margaret Sisson **Bessiestown Farm** **Country Guesthouse** **Catlowdy** **Longtown** **Carlisle CA6 5QP** **Tel/Fax: (01228) 577219** **Open: ALL YEAR** **Map Ref No. 10**	Nearest Road: A.7 An award-winning farm guest house, overlooking the Scottish borders, where a friendly, relaxing atmosphere is assured. 4 pretty, en-suite rooms with radio, T.V. & tea/coffee-making facilities. Delightfully decorated public rooms & conservatory. Also, ground-floor accommodation in extremely comfortable courtyard cottages. Delicious home cooking. Residential drinks licence. Guests may use the indoor heated swimming pool (May - Sept). Stop-off to/from Scotland & N. Ireland.	£21.00 *see PHOTO over* CREDIT CARD VISA M'CARD	Y	Y	N

Pickett Howe. Brackenthwaite.

Bessiestown Farm.   Catlowdy.

New House Farm. Lorton.

Cumbria

	Nearest Road	rate from £ per person	children taken	evening meals	animals taken

Pauline Hodge
Sundawn
Carlisle Road, Brideikirk
Cockermouth CA13 0PA
Tel: (01900) 822384
Open: Mid JAN - Mid DEC
Map Ref No. 12

Nearest Road: A.595
Bob & Pauline offer you a warm & friendly welcome. The emphasis here is on comfort, relaxation, personal service & imaginative home cooking. From the sunlounge, view the panorama of the Lakeland Fells & the historic market town of Cockermouth, birthplace of William Wordsworth. Accommodation is in 4 tastefully decorated rooms, 2 en-suite, all with modern amenities & tea/coffee makers. A charming home.

£16.00 | Y | Y | N

John Hatch
New House Farm
Lorton
Cockermouth CA13 9UU
Tel/Fax: (01900) 85404
Open: ALL YEAR
Map Ref No. 13

Nearest Road: A.66
New House Farm is set superbly in the Lorton Vale, has its own 15 acres of fields, ponds, stream & woods & easy access to nearby fells & lakes. All bedrooms are tastefully furnished & en-suite, there is a comfortable sitting room with open fire & a cosy dining room. Lots of personal attention is offered by the hosts. The cooking is fine traditional fare with a Cumbrian flavour. Children over 12. Animals by arrangement.

£30.00 | Y | Y | Y

see PHOTO over

CREDIT CARD
VISA
M'CARD

Mrs Joan Murray
Lakeside
Bassenthwaite Lake
Cockermouth
CA13 9YD
Tel: (017687) 76358
Open: JAN - NOV
Map Ref No. 14

Nearest Road: A.66
An elegant country house offering friendly & relaxing hospitality, with superb views across Bassenthwaite Lake to Skiddaw & the surrounding fells. Keswick is only a short drive away. Also, the peaceful western fells & lakes of Buttermere & Crummock Water. 8 tastefully furnished bedrooms, 7 en-suite, each with T.V., radio & tea/coffee-making facilities. Oak floors & a panelled hall. A pleasant lounge in which to relax, & delicious home cooking - with a 5-course evening meal & wine if required.

£20.00 | Y | Y | N

see PHOTO over

Fred & Hazel Wilkinson
Riggs Cottage
Routenbeck
Bassenthwaite Lake
Cockermouth CA13 9YN
Tel: (017687) 76580
Fax 017687 76580
Open: ALL YEAR
Map Ref No. 15

Nearest Road: A.66
Riggs Cottage is a super 17th-century cottage of great character & charm, with many exposed oak beams, a log-burning inglenook fireplace & period furniture. 3 comfortable & tastefully furnished bedrooms with modern amenities. The cosy lounge is available throughout the day. In the nicely furnished dining room, tasty home-cooked meals are served, using only the best ingredients. Oven-fresh bread & home-made preserves a speciality. Situated 'off the beaten track', an ideal base for a Lakeland holiday. Children over 5.

£19.00 | Y | Y | N

see PHOTO over

Joe & Anne Danson
Greenacres, Lindale
Grange-over-Sands
LA11 6LP
Tel/Fax: (015395) 34578
Open: ALL YEAR (Excl. Xmas & New Year)
Map Ref No. 16

Nearest Road: A.590
Greenacres is a charming 19th-century cottage ideally located for exploring the lakes & dales. Situated in the National Park, in the small village of Lindale at the foot of the beautiful Winster Valley, where you can walk in unspoilt countryside. All bedrooms are luxury en-suite. There is a lovely lounge & conservatory, & cosy dining room where excellent home-cooking is served. Friendly & relaxed atmosphere.

£25.00 | Y | Y | N

CREDIT CARD
VISA
M'CARD

96

Riggs Cottage. Bassenthwaite Lake

Lakeside. Bassenthwaite.

Cumbria

		rate from £ per person	children taken	evening meals	animals taken
Mrs Evelyn Cervetti **Lightwood Country** **Guest House** **Cartmell Fell** **Grange-over-Sands** **LA11 6NP** **Tel: (015395) 31454** **Open: FEB - NOV** **Map Ref No. 17**	Nearest Road: A.592 Lightwood is a 17th-century farmhouse built in approx. 1650. It possesses all modern amenities whilst retaining the charm of original oak beams & staircase. 2 acres of lovely gardens, with streams running through. Individually decorated rooms, with countryside views. 6 bedrooms have en-suite bathrooms. A cosy lounge with T.V. & log fire. A charming dining room facing the early morning sun. Only 2 miles from the southern end of Lake Windermere. Good English breakfast, with free-range eggs.	£22.00 CREDIT CARD VISA M'CARD	Y	Y	N
Martin & Angela Clark **Banerigg House** **Lake Road** **Grasmere** **LA22 9PW** **Tel: (015394) 35204** **Open: ALL YEAR** **Map Ref No. 18**	Nearest Road: A.591 Delightfully situated overlooking Grasmere Lake is this small, friendly guest house. The informal hospitality & relaxing atmosphere make this a super base for a holiday. All 7 comfortable rooms have modern amenities. A pleasant lounge with a cosy log fire. A delicious & plentiful breakfast is served. Ideally located for fell walking, sailing, canoeing & fishing. Angela & Martin ensure that guests have a memorable Lakeland holiday.	£22.00 *see PHOTO over*	Y	N	N
Mrs Joyce Edwards **Riversdale** **Grasmere** **LA22 9RQ** **Tel: (015394) 35619** **Open: ALL YEAR** **Map Ref No. 19**	Nearest Road: A.591 A traditional 6 bedroomed Lakeland stone house of character & charm. Built in 1830, fully centrally heated with decor & furnishings of the highest quality. Quiet riverside setting with fine views. Private parking. Of the 3 guest bedrooms - all very different - 2 are en-suite & 1 has its own private bathroom. Refreshment trays, hairdryers & toiletries are provided. Comfortable lounge. Exceptional breakfast. A friendly relaxed atmosphere & a very warm of welcome is assured.	£21.00	N	N	N
John & Ann Taylor **Woodland Crag** **How Head Lane** **Grasmere** **LA22 9SG** **Tel: (015394) 35351** **Open: ALL YEAR** **Map Ref No. 20**	Nearest Road: A.591 A warm welcome & an informal atmosphere are found in this delightful house, situated on the edge of Grasmere near Dove Cottage. Secluded but with easy access to all facilities, the accommodation has 5 fine, tastefully decorated bedrooms, all with individual character & wonderful views of the lake, fells or garden. Ideal for walking, & centrally placed for the motorist. Enclosed parking. Totally non-smoking.	£25.00	Y	N	N
Mr & Mrs A. L. Savasi **Oak Bank Hotel** **Broadgate** **Grasmere LA22 9TA** **Tel: (015394) 35217** **Fax 015394 35685** **Open: FEB - DEC** **Map Ref No. 21**	Nearest Road: A.591 The Oak Bank Hotel is a little gem one stumbles upon all too rarely, with a new conservatory dining room overlooking the garden, by which the river Rothay flows. An award-winning hotel for Cordon Bleu cuisine, hospitality & comfort. Log fires in the lounge/bar & delightful Victorian-style bedrooms complete this restful, owner-run hotel. The Oak Bank Hotel is the perfect spot for a relaxing break or for touring the Lake District.	£30.00 CREDIT CARD VISA M'CARD	Y	Y	Y

Banerigg House. Grasmere.

		rate from £ per person	children taken	evening meals	animals taken

Maureen & Jack Craig
Burrow Hall
Plantation Bridge
Kendal
LA8 9JR
Tel: (01539) 821711
Open: ALL YEAR
Map Ref No. 22

Nearest Road: A.591
Although built in 1648, this delightful guest house offers modern-day comforts. It is situated amidst open countryside, midway between Kendal & Windermere on the A.591, yet only 10 miles from M.6 Jt.36. All 3 en-suite bedrooms are centrally heated, have colour T.V., tea/coffee-making facilities, radio/alarms & hairdryer & are all tastefully decorated. A well-furnished guest lounge. A warm & friendly welcome is assured.

£20.00   N   N   N
(non-smoking)
CREDIT CARD
VISA
M'CARD

Alison & Philip Midwinter
Low Jock Scar Country
Guest House
Selside
Kendal LA8 9LE
Tel/Fax: (01539) 823259
Open: MAR - OCT
Map Ref No. 23

Nearest Road: A.6
A charming country guest house. A relaxing & friendly atmosphere with genuine warmth. In an idyllic setting with 6 acres of garden & woodland, it is a peaceful base from which to explore the Lakes & Yorkshire Dales. There are 5 comfortable bedrooms (3 en-suite, 2 on the ground floor) & a lounge well-stocked with books & maps. Excellent freshly prepared dinners - vegetarians catered for. Residential licence.

£22.00   N   Y   Y
(non-smoking)

see PHOTO over

Mrs Ada Wightman
The Glen
Oxenholme
Kendal LA9 7RF
Tel: (01539) 726386
Open: JAN - NOV
Map Ref No. 24

Nearest Road: A.65
A large detached house standing in its own grounds. Offering 3 rooms, all with private facilities & modern amenities including radio, colour T.V. & tea/coffee-making facilities. A delicious full English breakfast is served, & there is a lounge for guests to relax in. Situated only minutes from Oxenholme railway station, 'The Glen' is an excellent base for touring the idyllic Lake District. Children over 12.

£20.00   Y   Y   N

John & Ruth Knowles
Blease Farm
Blease Road
Threlkeld
Keswick CA12 4SF
Tel: (017687) 79087
Fax 017687 79087
Open: ALL YEAR
Map Ref No. 25

Nearest Road: A.66
Come & be spoilt at this comfortably renovated 250-year-old Cumbrian farmhouse. Set on the south-facing slopes of the 2800 ft Blencathra, all rooms in the house have stunning mountain views & all bedrooms are en-suite, with quality furnishings, T.V. & drinks tray. Log fires, sun room, smashing evening meals, gardens, trout pond & hosts who offer a genuine, friendly welcome come as standard. Over 200 local walk & drive sheets are available for guests' use. Children over 12 years welcome.

£25.00   N   Y   N
(non-smoking)

Chris & Caroline Briggs
Scales Farm Country
Guest House
Threlkeld
Keswick CA12 4SY
Tel: (017687) 79660
017687 79660
Open: ALL YEAR
Map Ref No. 26

Nearest Road: A.66
Stunning open views & a warm friendly welcome await you at Scales Farm, a traditional 17th-century fells farmhouse sensitively modernised to provide accommodation of the highest standard. All bedrooms are en-suite, centrally heated, with tea/coffee facilities, colour T.V. & fridges. Separate entrance from private car park allows guests access to rooms & traditional lounge. Lakeland Inn/Restaurant next door. A lovely base for touring or walking.
E-mail: scalesfarm@scalesfarm.demon.co.uk

£23.00   Y   N   Y
(non-smoking)

Low Jock Scar. Selside

Dale Head Hall. Lake Thirlmere

Cumbria

		rate from £ per person	children taken	evening meals	animals taken
Alan & Shirley Lowe **Dale Head Hall Lakeside** **Hotel** **Lake Thirlmere** **Keswick CA12 4TN** **Tel: (017687) 72478** **Fax 017687 71070** **Open: ALL YEAR** **Map Ref No. 27**	Nearest Road: A.591, A.66 Lose yourself in the ancient woodlands & mature gardens of an Elizabethan country manor, set serenely on the shores of Lake Thirlmere. Delicious dinners prepared by mother & daughter, using fresh produce from the Victorian kitchen garden, served with fine wines in the oak-beamed dining room. 9 individually decorated bedrooms, some with 4-posters, each with bath/shower rooms. Together with the lounge & bar, there are unspoilt views across lawns, lakes & fells. U.K. Freephone 0800 454166. **E-mail: daleheadho@aol.com** *see PHOTO over* CREDIT CARD VISA M'CARD AMEX	£27.50	Y	Y	N
John & Linda Lowrey **Ravensworth Hotel** **29 Station Street** **Keswick-on-Derwentwater** **CA12 5HH** **Tel/Fax: (017687) 72476** **Open: FEB - NOV** **Map Ref No. 28**	Nearest Road: A.591 Ideally situated near the town centre & its amenities, the lake & lower fells are just a short walk away. Tastefully furnished bedrooms have en-suite bathroom, beverage tray & colour T.V.. Start your morning with a hearty breakfast, before enjoying the Lake District scenery by day, while away the evening in the Herdwick Bar or relax in the spacious lounge. Personally-run for over 12 years welcome. CREDIT CARD VISA M'CARD	£16.00	Y	N	N
Ian & Jocelyn Bryant **Hipping Hall** **Cowan Bridge** **Kirkby Lonsdale** **LA6 2JJ** **Tel: (015242) 71187** **Fax 015242 72452** **Open: MAR - NOV** **Map Ref No. 29**	Nearest Road: A.65 Hipping Hall is a 17th-century country house set in 4 acres of walled gardens on the edge of the Yorkshire Dales National Park, 3 miles from pretty Kirkby Lonsdale & only half an hour from Windermere. The 5 bedrooms (all en-suite) & 2 apartments are attractively furnished & fully equipped. Guests dine together in the beautiful Great Hall with a Minstrel's Gallery. All dishes are freshly prepared by Jos Bryant from home & local produce. Children over 12. Reduced half-board rates throughout year for 2 nights. *see PHOTO over* CREDIT CARD VISA M'CARD AMEX	£38.00	Y	Y	Y
Anne McCrickard **The Old Rectory** **Crosby Garrett** **Kirkby Stephen CA17 4PW** **Tel: (017683) 72074** **Open: ALL YEAR (Excl. Xmas)** **Map Ref No. 30**	Nearest Road: A.685 Little has changed at The Old Rectory since successive Rectors etched their names in the glass window panes in the 18th century. This historic Grade II listed home is set in a secluded rural village. Relax in front of a log fire. Enjoy superb Aga cooking after a day walking or exploring Eden, Lakes or Dales. There are 3 attractive bedrooms. 2 are en-suite, & all are individually decorated & furnished with antiques.	£21.00	Y	Y	Y
Ros Sanders **Hornby Hall Country** **Guest House** **Brougham** **Penrith CA10 2AR** **Tel/Fax: (01768) 891114** **Open: ALL YEAR** **Map Ref No. 31**	Nearest Road: A.66 Hornby Hall is a 16th-century farmhouse situated in quiet countryside near the River Eamont. There are 7 tastefully furnished & comfortable guest rooms, with beverage facilities. 2 are en-suite. Dinner is served in the original sandstone-floored dining hall. Advance bookings are essential, as only the freshest local ingredients are used. Special diets catered for. Licensed. An ideal base for touring the Lake District, Dales, North Pennines & Hadrian's Wall. CREDIT CARD VISA M'CARD	£25.00	Y	Y	Y

Hipping Hall. Kirkby Lonsdale

Cumbria

		rate from £ per person	children taken	evening meals	animals taken
Lesley & David White **Beckfoot Country** **House Hotel, Helton** **Penrith CA10 2QB** **Tel: (01931) 713241** **Fax 01931 713391** **Open: MAR - NOV** **Map Ref No. 32**	Nearest Road: A.66 A fine old residence featuring a half-panelled hall, staircase & attractive panelled dining room. Set in 3 acres of grounds in the delightful Lake District, it is a quiet, peaceful retreat for a holiday base, & is within easy reach of the many pleasure spots in the area. Offering 6 rooms, all with private shower/bathroom & tea/coffee-making facilities. A dining room, drawing & reading room. This is a delightful base for a touring holiday.	£26.00 CREDIT CARD VISA M'CARD AMEX	Y	Y	Y
Mr B. & Mrs M. Smith **Hill Top House** **Morland** **Penrith** **CA10 3AX** **Tel: (01931) 714561** **Open: ALL YEAR** **Map Ref No. 33**	Nearest Road: A.6 Hill Top House stands in an elevated position in the ancient, picturesque & peaceful village of Morland; within easy reach of Lakeland, Scotland & the Yorkshire Dales, & with easy access to Jts 39 & 40 of the M.6 motorway. Brian & May will give you a warm welcome to their friendly Georgian house & secluded garden. 3 rooms - 2 en-suite & a single with private bathroom. You can dine at Hill Top or walk to the village inn. Come & relax at this beautiful home. Children over 7.	£19.00	Y	Y	N
Mrs C. A. Weightman **Near Howe Hotel** **Mungrisdale** **Penrith CA11 0SH** **Tel: (017687) 79678** **Fax 017687 79678** **Open: MAR - DEC** **Map Ref No. 34**	Nearest Road: A.66 A comfortable traditional Cumbrian family house, where guests receive a warm, friendly welcome. Standing in 300 acres of rolling moorland, it offers a choice of 7 nice bedrooms (most with en-suite facilities), a colour-T.V. lounge, a games room & a smaller lounge with a well-stocked bar with log fire. In the pleasant, homely dining room, freshly prepared meals are served, using local produce when possible. Close by are golf, fishing, pony trekking, boating & walking.	£17.00	Y	Y	Y
Mrs Marjorie Whittam **Netherdene Guest** **House** **Troutbeck** **Penrith CA11 0SJ** **Tel: (017684) 83475** **Open: ALL YEAR** **Map Ref No. 35**	Nearest Road: A.66, M.6 A traditional Lakeland house set in its own grounds, with extensive mountain views. Offering a warm welcome & personal attention. Accommodation is in 5 attractively furnished bedrooms, all en-suite, each with central heating, colour T.V. & tea/coffee-making facilities. A cosy lounge with log fire & T.V. is available throughout the day, & a dining room with excellent home cooking. Private parking. An ideal location from which to explore the Lake District. Children over 10 yrs.	£17.50 (no smoking)	Y	Y	N
Anthony & Aurea **Greenhalgh** **The Archway** **13 College Road** **Windermere LA23 1BU** **Tel: (015394) 45613** **Fax 015394 45328** **Open: ALL YEAR** **Map Ref No. 36**	Nearest Road: A.591 Impeccable small Victorian guest house, quietly situated a stone's throw from Windermere village centre, yet with marvellous, open mountain views. Beautifully furnished throughout: antiques, interesting paintings & prints, good books, fresh flowers. 4 individually decorated bedrooms, all en-suite, all with 'phone, colour T.V., tea/coffee trays & Victorian patchwork quilts. Renowned for gourmet home-cooking using fresh local produce. Home-baked bread. Excellent wine list. **E-mail: Anthony.Greenhalgh@btinternet.com**	£22.00 (no smoking) *see PHOTO over* CREDIT CARD VISA M'CARD	N	Y	N

The Archway. Windermere.

Beaumont Hotel. Windermere.

Cumbria

		rate from £ per person	children taken	evening meals	animals taken
Frances & Brian Holcroft **Lynwood Guest House** **Broad Street** **Windermere LA23 2AB** **Tel: (015394) 42550** **Fax 015394 42550** **Open: ALL YEAR** **Map Ref No. 36**	Nearest Road: A.591 A Victorian Lakeland stone house built in 1865, offering 9 centrally heated bedrooms, each with en-suite bathrooms, all with modern amenities including colour T.V. & tea/coffee-making facilities. Guests may relax in the T.V. lounge available throughout the day. Centrally located, only 150 yards from village shops & restaurants, & only 5 mins from the bus & railway station. The host is a Lakeland tour guide, & is happy to assist in planning your stay. Children over 5 years.	£15.00	Y	N	N
Jim & Barbara Casey **The Beaumont Hotel** **Holly Road** **Windermere** **LA23 2AF** **Tel: (015394) 47075** **Fax 015394 47075** **Open: ALL YEAR** **Map Ref No. 36**	Nearest Road: A.591 This elegant Victorian house hotel combines all the grace & charm of its time with all the comforts of today. Ideal for Windermere & Bowness, & perfect for touring the lakes. 10 attractive en-suite bedrooms with tea-making facilities, T.V. & hairdryers. Two 4-poster bedrooms are available for that special occasion, & a 'Romantic Presentation' of wine, chocolates, fruit & flowers may be ordered. The standards are high, breakfasts are hearty & the hospitality is warm & sincere. Private parking. Children over 10 years.	£24.00 *see PHOTO over* CREDIT CARD VISA M'CARD	Y	N	N
Neil & Carol Cox **Kirkwood** **Prince's Road** **Windermere LA23 2DD** **Tel/Fax: (015394) 43907** **Open: ALL YEAR** **Map Ref No. 36**	Nearest Road: A.591 Kirkwood occupies a quiet spot between Windermere and Bowness, offering guests a warm and friendly atmosphere with an individual, personal service. The 7 rooms are large, & all are en-suite. Some have 4-poster beds, all have T.V. and tea/coffee facilities. Your hosts will be pleased to help plan tours or walks, with maps provided. Drying facilities. Packed lunches available.	£21.00 CREDIT CARD VISA M'CARD	Y	N	Y
Peter & Chris Reed **The Chestnuts** **Princes Road** **Windermere LA23 2EF** **Tel: (015394) 46999** **Open: ALL YEAR** **Map Ref No. 36**	Nearest Road: A.591 The Chestnuts offers a delightful home-from-home & a distinctly high standard of comfort & service. The house itself is a century old, enjoying both lovely gardens & private parking. There is a choice of 6 elegantly furnished, comfortable bedrooms, each adorned in striking pine. With sumptuous king-size beds, all with en-suite showers, baths or even corner baths, this is a perfect base for a relaxing break.	£22.00 CREDIT CARD VISA M'CARD	Y	N	Y
Mr & Mrs I Fishman **Fir Trees Guest House** **Lake Road** **Windermere LA23 2EQ** **Tel: (015394) 42272** **Fax 015394 42272** **Open: ALL YEAR** **Map Ref No. 36**	Nearest Road: A.591 Ideally situated midway between Windermere & Bowness villages, Fir Trees offers superb bed & breakfast in a Victorian guest house of considerable charm & character. Antiques & beautiful prints abound in the public areas, while the bedrooms, all having private bath or shower rooms, are truly lovely. The proprietors have achieved an enviable reputation for their scrumptious breakfasts & extending old-fashioned hospitality. An excellent choice in all ways.	£23.00 *see PHOTO over* CREDIT CARD VISA M'CARD AMEX	Y	N	N

Fir Trees. Windermere.

Hawksmoor Guest House.   Windermere.

Blenheim Lodge Hotel. Bowness-on-Windermere.

		rate from £ per person	children taken	evening meals	animals taken
Barbara & Bob Tyson **Hawksmoor** **Lake Road** **Windermere** **LA23 2EQ** **Tel: (015394) 42110** **Open: FEB - NOV** **Map Ref No. 36**	Nearest Road: A.591 Hawksmoor is situated halfway between the centres of Windermere & Bowness, just 10 mins' walk from the lake. Standing in lovely grounds, this creeper-clad house has 10 charming rooms, all en-suite & with garden views; some, also, with 4-poster beds & some strictly no smoking. A comfortable residents' lounge with colour T.V., & a garden for guests' enjoyment. Residential licence. Boating, golf, tennis, swimming, fishing & pony trekking all nearby. Phone for availability before booking. Children over 6.	£25.00 *see PHOTO over* CREDIT CARD VISA M'CARD	Y	Y	N
Mr S. Thomas & Family **Rosemount** **Lake Road** **Windermere LA23 2EQ** **Tel: (015394) 43739** **Fax 015394 48978** **Open: FEB - NOV** **Map Ref No. 36**	Nearest Road: A.591 Rosemount is an attractive Victorian house halfway between Windermere & the lake. Accommodation is in 8 attractively furnished bedrooms (including 2 singles & a spacious family room), each with an en-suite/private bathroom, colour T.V. & tea/coffee-making facilities. An excellent breakfast is served. Rosemount is the perfect base for a relaxing break & affords first-class accommodation in elegant surroundings.	£19.00 CREDIT CARD VISA M'CARD	Y	N	N
Jackie & Frank Sanderson **Blenheim Lodge Hotel** **Brantfell Road** **Bowness-on-Windermere** **Windermere LA23 3AE** **Tel/Fax: (015394) 43440** **Open: ALL YEAR** **Map Ref No. 36**	Nearest Road: A.592 A beautiful Lakeland guest house, overlooking Lake Windermere, offering peace & quiet & yet close to the lake & shops. Jaqueline Sanderson is an expert in traditional English cuisine, & guests' admiration for the food has resulted in their own award-winning cookbook. Fresh local produce. A delightful home & the perfect place for a Lakeland holiday. Please 'phone for booking. Children over 6 yrs welcome. **E-mail: geoff@twicom.demon.co.uk**	£25.00 *see PHOTO over* CREDIT CARD VISA M'CARD AMEX	Y	Y	N
Brenda Butterworth **Orrest Head House** **Kendal Road** **Windermere LA23 IJG** **Tel: (015394) 44315** **Open: FEB - DEC** **Map Ref No. 36**	Nearest Road: A.591 Orrest Head House, Windermere, is a charming country house dating back to the 16th century. All of the comfortable bedrooms are en-suite & have colour T.V. & tea/coffee-making facilities. It is set in 3 acres of garden & woodland & has distant views to mountains & lakes. Close to the station & village with a very homely atmosphere. Children over 6 years welcome.	£20.00 *see PHOTO over*	Y	N	N

When booking your accommodation please mention
The Best Bed & Breakfast

Orrest Head House. Windermere.

Derbyshire & Staffordshire

Derbyshire
(East Midlands)

A county with everything but the sea, this was Lord Byron's opinion of Derbyshire, & the special beauty of the Peak District was recognised by its designation as Britain's first National Park.

Purple heather moors surround craggy limestone outcrops & green hills drop to sheltered meadows or to deep gorges & tumbling rivers.

Derbyshire's lovely dales have delightful names too - Dove Dale, Monk's Dale, Raven's Dale, Water-cum-Jolly-Dale, & they are perfect for walking. The more adventurous can take up the challenge of the Pennine Way, a 270 mile pathway from Edale to the Scottish border.

The grit rock faces offer good climbing, particularly at High Tor above the River Derwent, & underground there are extensive & spectacular caverns. There are show caves at the Heights of Abraham, which you reach by cable-car, & at Castleton, source of the rare Blue John mineral, & at Pole's Cavern in Buxton where there are remarkable stalactites & stalagmites.

Buxton's splendid Crescent reflects the town's spa heritage, & the Opera House is host to an International Festival each summer.

The waters at Matlock too were prized for their curative properties & a great Hydro was built there in the last century, to give treatment to the hundreds of people who came to "take the waters".

Bakewell is a lovely small town with a fascinating market, some fine buildings & the genuine Bakewell Pudding, (known elsewhere as Bakewell tart).

Well-dressing is a custom carried on throughout the summer in the villages & towns. It is a thanksgiving for the water, that predates the arrival of Christianity in Britain. Flower-petals, leaves, moss & bark are pressed in

Haddon Hall; Derby.

Derbyshire & Staffordshire

intricate designs into frames of wet clay & erected over the wells, where they stay damp & fresh for days.

The mining of lead & the prosperity of the farms brought great wealth to the landowning families who were able to employ the finest of architects & craftsmen to design & build their great houses. Haddon Hall is a perfectly preserved 12th century manor house with with terraced gardens of roses & old-fashioned flowers. 17th century Chatsworth, the "Palace of the Peak", houses a splendid collection of paintings, drawings, furniture & books, & stands in gardens with elaborate fountains.

Staffordshire
(Heart of England)

Staffordshire is a contrast of town & county. Miles of moorland & dramatic landscapes lie to the north of the country, & to the south is the Vale of Trent & the greenery of Cannock Chase. But the name of Staffordshire invokes that of the Potteries, the area around Stoke-on-Trent where the world-renowned ceramics are made.

The factories that produce the Royal Doulton, Minton, Spode & Coalport china will arrange tours for visitors, & there is a purpose-built visitor centre at Barlaston displaying the famous Wedgwood tradition.

The Gladstone Pottery Museum is set in a huge Victorian potbank, & the award-winning City museum in Stoke-on-Trent has a remarkable ceramics collection.

There is lovely scenery to be found where the moorlands of Staffordshire meet the crags & valleys of the Peak District National Park. From the wild & windy valleys of The Roaches (from the French 'roche') you can look across the county to Cheshire & Wales. Drivers can take high moorland roads that are marked out as scenic routes.

The valleys of the Dove & Manifold are beautiful limestone dales & ideal for walking or for cycling. Sir Izzak Walton, author of 'The Compleat Angler', drew his inspiration, & his trout, from the waters here.

The valley of the River Churnet is both pretty & peaceful, being largely inaccessible to cars. The Caldon Canal, with its colourful narrowboats, follows the course of the river & there are canalside pubs, picnic areas, boat rides & woodland trails to enjoy. The river runs through the grounds of mock-Gothic Alton Towers, now a leisure park.

The Vale of Trent is largely rural with small market towns, villages, river & canals.

Cannock Chase covers 20 square miles of heath & woodland & is the home of the largest herd of fallow deer in England. Shugborough Hall stands in the Chase. The ancestral home of Lord Lichfeld, it also houses the Staffordshire County Museum & a farm for rare breeds including the famous Tamworth Pig.

Burton-on-Trent is known as the home of the British brewery industry & there are two museums in the town devoted to the history of beer.

Lichfield is a small & picturesque city with a cathedral which dates from the 12th century & has three graceful spires known as the 'Ladies of the Vale'. Dr. Samuel Johnson was born in the city & his house is now a museum dedicated to his life & work.

One of the Vale's villages retains its mediaeval tradition by performing the Abbot's Bromley Horn Dance every September.

Derbyshire & Staffordshire

Derbyshire

Gazeteer

Areas of outstanding natural beauty.
Peak National Park. The Dales.

Houses & Castles

Chatsworth - Bakewell
17th century, built for 1st. Duke of Devonshire. Furniture, paintings & drawings, books, etc. Fine gardens & parklands.
Haddon Hall - Bakewell
Mediaeval manor house - complete. Terraced rose gardens.
Hardwick Hall - Nr. Chesterfield
16th century - said to be more glass than wall. Fine furniture, tapestries & furnishings. Herb garden.
Kedlestone Hall - Derby
18th century - built on site of 12th century Manor house. Work of Robert Adam - has world famous marble hall. Old Master paintings. 11th century church nearby.
Melbourne Hall - Nr. Derby
12th century origins - restored by Sir John Coke. Fine collection of pictures & works of art. Magnificent gardens & famous wrought iron pagoda
Sudbury Hall - Sudbury
Has examples of work of the greatest craftsmen of the period-Grinling Gibbons,Pierce and Laguerre.
Winster Market House   Nr. Matlock
17th century stone built market house.

Cathedrals & Churches

Chesterfield (St. Mary & All Saints)
13th & 14th centuries.
4 chapels, polygonal apse, mediaeval screens, Jacobean pulpit.
Derby (All Saints)
Perpendicular tower - classical style - 17th century plate, 18th century screen.
Melbourne (St. Michael & St. Mary)
Norman with two west towers & crossing tower.
Splendid plate, 18th century screen.
Normbury (St. Mary & St. Barloke)
14th century - perpendicular tower. Wood carving & brasses.
Wirksworth (St. Mary)
13th century, restored & enlarged.

Staffordshire

Gazeteer

Houses & Castles

Ancient High House - Stafford
16th century - largest timber-framed town house in England.
Shugborough - Nr. Stafford
Ancestral home of the Earl of Lichfield. Mansion house, paintings, silver, ceramics, furniture. County Museum. Rare Breeds Farm.
Moseley Old Hall - Nr. Wolverhampton
Elizabethan house formerly half-timbered.
Stafford Castle
Large & well-preserved Norman castle in grounds with castle trail.
Tamworth Castle
Norman motte & bailey castle with later additions. Museum.

Cathedrals & Churches

Croxden Abbey
12th century foundation Cistercian abbey. Ruins of 13th century church.
Ingestre (St. Mary the Virgin)
A rare Wren church built in1676.
Lichfield Cathedral
Unique triple-spired 12th century cathedral.
Tamworth (St. Editha's)
Founded 963, rebuilt 14th century. Unusual double spiral staircase.
Tutbury (St. Mary's)
Norman church with impressive West front.

Museums & Galleries

City Museum & Art Gallery - Stoke-on-Trent
Modern award-winning museum. Ceramics, decorative arts, etc.
Dr. Johnson Birthplace Museum - Lichfield
Gladstone Pottery Museum - Longton
Izaak Walton Cottage & Museum - Shallowfield, Nr. Stafford
National Brewery Museum & the Bass Museum of Brewing-both in Stoke-on-Trent
Stafford Art Gallery & Craft Shop - Stafford
Major gallery for the visual arts & centre for quality craftsmanship.

DERBYSHIRE & STAFFORDSHIRE

Map reference

1	Stevenson	11	Singleton
2	Chambers	12	Heelis
3	Moore	13	Wilkins
4	Tunnicliffe	14	Chapman
5	Moffett	16	Hulme
6	Harry	17	Winterton
6	Mackenzie	18	Whitelegg
7	Ford	19	Egerton-Orme
8	Lewis	19	Ball
9	Marsh	20	Grey
10	Bailey	20	White

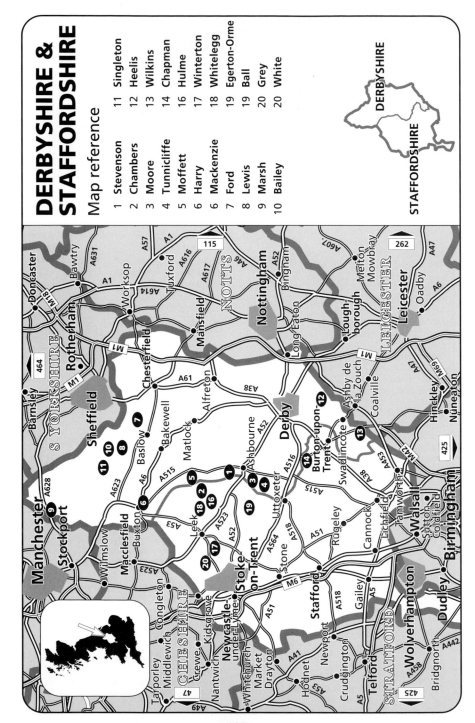

DERBYSHIRE

STAFFORDSHIRE

Derbyshire

	Nearest Road	rate from £ per person	children taken	evening meals	animals taken
Mr & Mrs C. Stevenson **Hinchley Wood** **Mappleton** **Ashbourne** **DE6 2AB** **Tel: (01335) 350219** Fax 01335 300485 **Open: JAN - NOV** **Map Ref No. 01**	Nearest Road: A.515, A.52 Hinchley Wood is situated in the Derbyshire Dales & Peak National Park, & overlooks the Valley of the Dove. The Georgian house is set in extensive grounds & is elegantly furnished & decorated. Ideally situated for visits to Wedgwood, Crown Derby & Royal Doulton in the Potteries or walking in Dovedale. Nearby are many stately homes: Chatsworth, Haddon Hall & Calke Abbey. Ashbourne & Bakewell have excellent antique shops & restaurants. Alton Towers 5 miles. Children over 12. Dinner by arrangement.	£30.00 (no smoking)	Y	Y	N
N. Chambers & N. Lourie **Stanshope Hall** **Stanshope** **Ashbourne DE6 2AD** **Tel: (01335) 310278** Fax 01335 310470 **Open: ALL YEAR** **Map Ref No. 02**	Nearest Road: A.515 Stanshope Hall, with its informal feel but with every comfort, stands in splendid isolation among the dry stone walls of the southern Peak District. Walks from the door lead to verdant Dovedale or the undiscovered seclusion of the Manifold Valley. The en-suite rooms have hand-painted walls & frescos in the bathrooms. Candle-lit dinners are prepared using uncomplicated but imaginative recipes with local & garden produce.	£25.00 CREDIT CARD VISA M'CARD	Y	Y	N
Mrs Cynthia Moore **Rose Cottage** **Snelston** **Ashbourne DE6 2DL** **Tel: (01335) 324230** Fax 01335 324230 **Open: ALL YEAR** **Map Ref No. 03**	Nearest Road: A.515 A mid-Victorian house in 6 acres, Rose Cottage is a family home in quiet, unspoilt, beautiful & peaceful countryside. Bedrooms have panoramic views over Dove Valley towards Weaver Hills (George Eliot's 'Adam Bede' country). Ideal for visiting Dales, walking, country houses (Chatsworth, Haddon Hall etc.), potteries & Alton Towers (9 miles). Comfortable double rooms, private bathrooms, 1 en-suite, T.V., tea-making facilities in rooms. Children over 12.	£22.50 (no smoking)	Y	N	N
Barbara Tunnicliffe **Beeches Farmhouse** **Waldley** **Doveridge** **Ashbourne DE6 5LR** **Tel: (01889) 590288** Fax 01889 590559 **Open: ALL YEAR (Excl. Xmas)** **Map Ref No. 04**	Nearest Road: A.50 A delightful 18th-century farmhouse situated in the Derbyshire Dales. 10 elegant en-suite bedrooms, each well-appointed & furnished to a high standard. Enjoy dining in the award-winning, oak-beamed, licensed restaurant - after exploring the Derbyshire countryside, or the thrills of Alton Towers. Children will love feeding the many animals on this 160-acre working dairy farm. A charming home within easy reach of a wealth of places of interest. E-mail: BEECHESFA@AOL.COM	£26.00 *see PHOTO over* CREDIT CARD VISA M'CARD AMEX	Y	Y	N
Dr & Mrs J.D. Harry **Coningsby** **6 Macclesfield Road** **Buxton SK17 9AH** **Tel/Fax: (01298) 26735** **Open: MAR - NOV** **Map Ref No. 06**	Nearest Road: A.515, A.53 John & Linda look forward to welcoming guests, old & new, to their home & can confidently assure them of a wonderful stay. Coningsby is an elegant Victorian guest house situated in a lovely landscaped garden within walking distance of the town & offers 3 delightful en-suite bedrooms. This is an ideal base from which to explore the beautiful Peak District. No smoking, children or animals please. Car parking.	£25.00 (no smoking)	N	Y	N

Beeches Farmhouse. Waldley.

Derbyshire

	rate from £ per person	children taken	evening meals	animals taken
James Moffett **Biggin Hall** **Biggin-by-Hartington** **Buxton** **SK17 0DH** **Tel: (01298) 84451** **Fax 01298 84681** **Open: ALL YEAR** **Map Ref No. 05**	Nearest Road: A.515 A delightful 17th-century stone house, completely restored & keeping all the character of its origins, with massive oak beams. 15 comfortable rooms, all charmingly furnished, 1 with a 4-poster bed, all with en-suite facilities & modern amenities. Guests have the choice of 2 sitting rooms, 1 with a log fire, 1 with colour T.V. & library, & there is a lovely garden. The house is beautifully furnished, with many antiques. Non-smoking areas. Children over 12. Animals by arrangement. **E-mail: 100610.1573@compuserve.com**	**£25.00** *see PHOTO over* CREDIT CARD VISA M'CARD	Y	Y	Y
Mrs M. A. Mackenzie **Staden Grange Country House** **Staden Lane, Staden** **Buxton SK17 9RZ** **Tel: (01298) 24965** **Fax 01298 72067** **Open: ALL YEAR (Excl. Xmas & New Year)** **Map Ref No. 06**	Nearest Road: A.515 A pleasant, spacious country house set in 25 acres & enjoying splendid uninterrupted views over open farmland. Attractive & comfortable en-suite rooms, 1 with 4-poster, each with colour satellite T.V., radio, 'phone & tea/coffee makers. The 'Foxlow Restaurant' offers excellent cuisine, & menus change daily. Lovely lounge & cocktail bar & large garden. Riding & shooting, sauna, jacuzzi & a golf course nearby. Only 2 miles from Buxton & ideal for touring, walking & riding in this magnificent scenic region.	**£25.00** CREDIT CARD VISA M'CARD AMEX	Y	Y	Y
Mrs Margaret Ford **Horsleygate Hall** **Horsleygate Lane** **Holmesfield** **Chesterfield** **S18 5WD** **Tel: (0114) 2890333** **Open: ALL YEAR** **Map Ref No. 07**	Nearest Road: A.621 This delightful country house, built in 1783, stands in 2 acres of beautiful secluded gardens of particular interest to the plantsman. Assorted chickens, geese & horses enliven the adjacent stableyard while doves cavort along the low stone roofs. This good-looking house incorporates a comfortable mix of country furniture, flagstone floors, old pine fittings & colourful furnishings. Bedrooms are spacious & appealing with homely touches, 1 is en-suite. Set in the Cordwell Valley on the eastern fringe of the Peak Park, minutes from Chatsworth House. Children over 5 years.	**£19.50** 🚭	Y	N	N
David & Meirlys Lewis **Delf View House** **Church Street** **Eyam** **S32 5QH** **Tel: (01433) 631533** **Fax 01433 631972** **Open: ALL YEAR** **Map Ref No. 08**	Nearest Road: A.623 Beautiful & tranquil accommodation in an elegant listed Georgian country house in historic Eyam village in the magnificent Peak National Park. Guests are warmly welcomed in the drawing room, delightfully furnished with antiques, pictures & books. 3 superb bedrooms, 1 en-suite include a Sheraton 4-poster & 18th century French twin beds. Sumptuous breakfasts served in the oak beamed dining room. Restaurants nearby, 1 within 3 mins' walk. Ideal for visiting Chatsworth, Haddon & Eyam Hall. Children over 8. **E-mail: lewis@delfview.demon.co.uk**	**£25.00** 🚭	Y	N	N

When booking your accommodation please mention
The Best Bed & Breakfast

Biggin Hall. Biggin by Hartington.

Derbyshire

	rate from £ per person	children taken	evening meals	animals taken
Peter Marsh **The Wind in the Willows** **Hotel** **Derbyshire Level** **Glossop SK13 9PT** **Tel: (01457) 868001** **Fax 01457 853354** **Open: ALL YEAR** **Map Ref No. 09**	Nearest Road: A.57 An early-Victorian house with 5 acres of land, set amidst the unspoilt views of the Peak District National Park & the Pennine Hills. Providing an escape from the pressures of modern-day life in the atmosphere & surroundings of a bygone era. A wealth of oak-panelled rooms, with traditional furnishings & open fires. All bedrooms are en-suite & very well-equipped with comfort in mind. With an emphasis upon friendliness, relaxation & first-class home-cooking, your hosts will ensure your stay is memorable. Children over 10. CREDIT CARD VISA M'CARD AMEX	£37.50	Y	Y	Y
Mary Bailey **Carr Head Farm** **Church Bank** **Hathersage** **Hope Valley S32 1BR** **Tel: (01433) 650383** **Fax 01433 651441** **Open: ALL YEAR** **Map Ref No. 10**	Nearest Road: A.625 In a most peaceful setting high on the hillside above the village of Hathersage, an unusual farmhouse dating back to 1650, full of character & charm. Surrounded by beautiful mature gardens, all rooms have magnificent unspoilt views. 2 spacious & superbly furnished en-suite bedrooms, 1 with 4-poster. Oak-beamed dining room & an elegant drawing room. Decorated throughout in period style. The village offers a wide choice of eating places & has Charlotte Bronte connections. **E-mail: michael.bailey@tyzack.com**	£24.00	N	N	N
Mr & Mrs Anton Singleton **Underleigh House** **Edale Road, Hope** **Hope Valley S33 6RF** **Tel: (01433) 621372** **Fax 01433 621324** **Open: ALL YEAR** **Map Ref No. 11**	Nearest Road: A.625 A 19th-century farmhouse-style home in a superb, secluded hillside position, with beautiful countryside views, in the heart of the National Park. Each of the 7 en-suite/private rooms are furnished to the highest standard, with many extras, & each has a resident teddy bear! Renowned for hearty breakfasts & gourmet house-party dinners prepared by the owner/chef. Ideally situated for walking or exploring the area by car. CREDIT CARD VISA M'CARD	£28.00	N	Y	N
Mr & Mrs Robert Heelis **Shaw House** **Robinsons Hill** **Melbourne** **DE73 1DJ** **Tel: (01332) 863827** **Open: ALL YEAR** **Map Ref No. 12**	Nearest Road: A.42, M.1 Shaw House is a Grade II listed 18th-century country house set on the edge of Melbourne. 3 spacious & elegantly appointed bedrooms, each with an en-suite bathroom, T.V. & tea/coffee. A delicious breakfast & super evening meals are served in the attractive dining room. Enjoy the friendly, convivial atmosphere in tasteful surroundings. It is conveniently situated for visiting Calke Abbey & several other stately homes. Donington Park & East Midlands Airport 3 miles.	£25.00	N	Y	N
Mrs Clemency Wilkins **The Old Hall, Netherseal** **Swadlincote DE12 8DF** **Tel: (01283) 760258** **Fax 01283 762991** **Open: ALL YEAR (Excl.** **Xmas & New Year)** **Map Ref No. 13**	Nearest Road: A.444, A.42 A Grade II listed manor house situated in 18 acres of private gardens & woodland, overlooking a lake. The house, built originally as a monastery, dates from 1644, & despite all modern conveniences retains its unique character & original features. Many of the rooms are panelled, & all are decorated in a country-house style. 4 attractive, well-equipped bedrooms with en-suite/ private facilities. Traditional English food is served (by arrangement). Children over 14 years.	£22.50	N	Y	N

Staffordshire

	rate from £ per person	children taken	evening meals	animals taken
James & Elizabeth Chapman **The Mill House** **Cornmill Lane, Tutbury** **Burton-on-Trent DE13 9HA** **Tel: (01283) 813634** **Tel: (01283) 813300** **Open: ALL YEAR** **Map Ref No. 14** Nearest Road: A.50, A.38 A corn mill has occupied this site since the Domesday Book. Situated in open countryside, 1/2 mile from the village, the Georgian mill & adjoining red-brick mill house are easy to find. The 3 spacious bedrooms are beautifully furnished & en-suite, with colour T.V. & tea-making facilities. Delicious breakfasts are served in the inglenook breakfast room. Conveniently placed for N.T. properties, Kedleston, Calke & Sudbury. Ideal North/South stop-over.	£23.00	Y	N	N
Mr & Mrs R. Hulme **Porch Farmhouse** **Grindon** **ST13 7TP** **Tel: (01538) 304545** **Fax 01538 304545** **Open: ALL YEAR** **Map Ref No. 16** Nearest Road: A.523 Porch Farmhouse is a peaceful, sympathetically restored 17th-century stone farmhouse, with beautiful views over the hills & dales of the Peak District. All 3 bedrooms, en-suite, offer every luxury. Excellent breakfasts & imaginative candlelit dinners are served, using local produce when available. A perfect base for visiting many historic houses & gardens, or enjoying the beautiful walks & scenery of the National Park. Brochure available. **E-mail: PorchFarmhouse@msn.com**	£25.00 *see PHOTO over* CREDIT CARD VISA M'CARD	N	Y	Y
Mrs Elizabeth Winterton **Brook House Farm** **Brook House Lane** **Cheddleton** **Leek ST13 7DF** **Tel: (01538) 360296** **Open: ALL YEAR** **Map Ref No. 17** Nearest Road: A.520 Brook House is a dairy farm in a picturesque valley 1/2 a mile from the A.520, down a private lane. Many pleasant walks locally; convenient for the Peak District, pottery museums and Alton Towers. Comfortable rooms in the farmhouse, and 2 spacious family rooms with patio doors in a tastefully converted annex. All en-suite & centrally heated, with tea/coffee facilities. Good farmhouse food served in a conservatory with magnificent views. A warm welcome assured.	£17.00	Y	N	N
Miss Nicky Whitelegg **Butterton Moor House** **Parsons Lane** **Butterton** **Leek** **ST13 7PD** **Tel: (01538) 304506** **Open: ALL YEAR** **Map Ref No. 18** Nearest Road: A.523 Butterton Moor House is a lovingly restored 17th-century farmhouse overlooking the Manifold Valley. 4 attractively furnished bedrooms, each with an en-suite bathroom, T.V. & tea/coffee. Guests may choose to relax in the comfortable sitting room, or for the more energetic there is an indoor heated swimming pool & games room. A wide choice of breakfasts is served. Evening meals are available by prior arrangement, & the menu is changed daily. Within easy reach of the Peak District & Alton Towers.	£20.00	Y	Y	N
Mrs Muriel Egerton-Orme **Bank House** **Farley Lane, Oakamoor** **Stoke-on-Trent** **ST10 3BD** **Tel: (01538) 702810** **Fax 01538 702810** **Open: ALL YEAR (Excl. Xmas)** **Map Ref No. 19** Nearest Road: A.52, A.5 A handsome house, overlooking the picturesque Churnet Valley. This elegantly furnished home provides superb en-suite accommodation. All rooms are extremely well-equipped. The aim at Bank House is to create a relaxed & friendly 'house party' ambience for guests, & the facilities are all that one might expect from a friend's country house that has all the comforts of a quality hotel. Excellent 4-course evening meals served. Wonderful centre for touring this region. **E-mail: john.orme@dial.pipex.com**	£26.00 CREDIT CARD VISA M'CARD	Y	Y	Y

Porch Farmhouse. Grindon.

Staffordshire

		rate from £ per person	children taken	evening meals	animals taken
Mrs I. H. Grey **The Old Vicarage** **Leek Road, Endon** **Stoke-on-Trent** **ST9 9BH** **Tel: (01782) 503686** **Open: ALL YEAR** **Map Ref No. 20**	Nearest Road: A.53 A friendly atmosphere is found at this delightful 70-year-old former vicarage. It is situated in a quiet spot in the village of Endon, between the Staffordshire moorlands & Stoke-on-Trent. Accommodation is in 3 rooms, all with modern amenities, T.V. & tea/coffee-making facilities. There is a separate guests' lounge. This makes a good base from which to visit the world-famous potteries, the wonderful countryside & museums.	£17.50	Y	N	N
Mrs Barbara White **Micklea Farm** **Micklea Lane, Longsdon** **Stoke-on-Trent ST9 9QA** **Tel: (01538) 385006** **Fax 01538 382882** **Open: ALL YEAR** **Map Ref No. 20**	Nearest Road: A.53 Micklea Farm is an 18th-century cottage set in a lovely quiet garden. There are 2 double/twin & 2 single rooms, with cots available. There is also a charming sitting room for guests, with an open fire & colour T.V.. Evening meals are available, using home-grown garden produce & home baking. A choice of English or Continental breakfast; also, packed lunches. Conveniently situated for the potteries, Alton Towers & the Peak District.	£17.00	Y	Y	N
Christopher M. Ball **Manor House Farm** **Quixhill Lane** **Prestwood, Denstone** **Uttoxeter ST14 5DD** **Tel: (01889) 590415** **Fax 01335 342198** **Open: ALL YEAR** **Map Ref No. 19**	Nearest Road: A.50 A beautiful Grade II listed farmhouse, set amid rolling hills & rivers. Accommodation is in 3 attractive bedrooms, all with 4-poster beds & an en-suite bathroom. (1 can be used as a twin.) Tastefully furnished with antiques & retaining traditional features including an oak panelled breakfast room. Guests may relax in the extensive gardens with grass tennis court & Victorian summer house. Ideal for visiting Alton Towers, the Peak District or the potteries.	£20.00 *see PHOTO over*	Y	N	N

When booking your accommodation please mention
The Best Bed & Breakfast

Manor House Farm. Prestwood.

Devon

Devon
(West Country)

Here is a county of tremendous variety. Two glorious & contrasting coastlines with miles of sandy beaches, sheltered coves & rugged cliffs. There are friendly resorts & quiet villages of cob & thatch, two historic cities, & a host of country towns & tiny hamlets as well as the wild open spaces of two national parks.

From the grandeur of Hartland Point east to Foreland Point where Exmoor reaches the sea, the north Devon coast is incomparable. At Westward Ho!, Croyde & Woolacombe the rolling surf washes the golden beaches & out to sea stands beautiful Lundy Island, ideal for bird watching, climbing & walking. The tiny village of Clovelly with its cobbled street tumbles down the cliffside to the sea. Ilfracombe is a friendly resort town & the twin towns of Lynton & Lynmouth are joined by a cliff railway.

The south coast is a colourful mixture of soaring red sandstone cliffs dropping to sheltered sandy coves & the palm trees of the English Riviera. This is one of England's great holiday coasts with a string of popular resorts; Seaton, Sidmouth, Budleigh Salterton, Exmouth, Dawlish, Teignmouth & the trio of Torquay, Paignton & Brixham that make up Torbay. To the south, beyond Berry Head are Dartmouth, rich in navy tradition, & Salcombe, a premiere sailing centre in the deep inlet of the Kingsbridge estuary. Plymouth is a happy blend of holiday resort, tourist centre, historic & modern city, & the meeting-point for the wonderful old sailing vessels for the Tall Ships Race.

Inland the magnificent wilderness of Dartmoor National Park offers miles of sweeping moorland, granite tors, clear streams & wooded valleys, ancient stone circles & clapper bridges. The tors, as the Dartmoor peaks, are called are easily climbed & the views from the tops are superb. Widecombe-in-the-Moor, with its imposing church tower, & much photographed Buckland-in-the-Moor are only two of Dartmoor's lovely villages.

The Exmoor National Park straddles the Devon/Somerset border. It is a land of wild heather moorland above deep wooded valleys & sparkling streams, the home of red deer, soaring buzzards & of legendary Lorna Doone from R.D. Blackmore's novel. The south west peninsula coastal path follows the whole of the Exmoor coastline affording dramatic scenery & spectacular views, notably from Countisbury Hill.

The seafaring traditions of Devon are well-known. Sir Walter Raleigh set sail from Plymouth to Carolina in 1584; Sir Francis Drake began his circumnavigation of the world at Plymouth in the "Golden Hind" & fought the Spanish Armada off Plymouth Sound. The Pilgrim Fathers sailed from here & it was to here that Sir Francis Chichester returned having sailed around the world in 1967.

Exeter's maritime tradition is commemorated in an excellent museum located in converted riverside warehouses but the city's chief glory is the magnificent 13th century cathedral of St. Mary & St. Peter, built in an unusual decorated Gothic style, with its west front covered in statues.

The River Dart near Dittisham.

Devon

Devon
Gazeteer

Areas of outstanding natural beauty.
North, South, East Devon.

Houses & Castles

Arlington Court - Barnstaple
Regency house, collection of shell, pewter & model ships.

Bickleigh Castle - Nr. Tiverton
Thatched Jacobean wing. Great Hall & armoury. Early Norman chapel, gardens & moat.

Buckland Abbey - Nr. Plymouth
13th century Cistercian monastery - 16th century alterations. Home of Drake - contains his relics & folk gallery.

Bradley Manor - Newton Abbot
15th century Manor house with perpendicular chapel.

Cadhay - Ottery St. Mary
16th century Elizabethan Manor house.

Castle Drogo - Nr.Chagford
Designed by Lutyens - built of granite, standing over 900 feet above the gorge of the Teign river.

Chambercombe Manor - Illfracombe
14th-15th century Manor house.

Castle Hill - Nr. Barnstaple
18th century Palladian mansion - fine furniture of period, pictures, porcelain & tapestries.

Hayes Barton - Nr. Otterton
16th century plaster & thatch house. Birthplace of Walter Raleigh.

Oldway - Paignton
19th century house having rooms designed to be replicas of rooms at the Palace of Versailles.

Powederham Castle - Nr. Exeter
14th century mediaeval castle much damaged in Civil War. Altered in 18th & 19th centuries. Fine music room by Wyatt.

Saltram House - Plymouth
Some remnants of Tudor house built into George II house, with two rooms by Robert Adam. Excellent plasterwork & woodwork.

Shute Barton - Nr. Axminster
14th century battlemented Manor house with Tudor & Elizabethan additions.

Tiverton Castle - Nr. Tiverton
Fortress of Henry I. Chapel of St. Francis. Gallery of Joan of Arc.

Torre Abbey Mansion - Torquay
Abbey ruins, tithe barn. Mansion house with paintings & furniture.

Cathedrals & Churches

Atherington (St. Mary)
Perpendicular style - mediaeval effigies & glass, original rood loft. Fine screens, 15th century bench ends.

Ashton (St. John the Baptist)
15th century - mediaeval screens, glass & wall paintings. Elizabethan pulpit with canopy, 17th century altar railing.

Bere Ferrers (St. Andrew)
14th century rebuilding - 14th century glass, 16th century benches, Norman font.

Bridford (St. Thomas a Becket)
Perpendicular style - mediaeval glass & woodwork. Excellent rood screen c.1530.

Cullompton (St. Andrew)
15th century perpendicular - Jacobean west gallery - fan tracery in roof, exterior carvings.

Exeter Cathedral
13th century decorated - Norman towers. Interior tierceron ribbed vault (Gothic) carved corbels & bosses, moulded piers & arches. Original pulpitum c.1320. Choir stalls with earliest misericords in England c.1260.

Haccombe (St. Blaize)
13th century effigies, 14th century glass, 17th century brasses, 19th century screen, pulpit & reredos.

Kentisbeare (St. Mary)
Perpendicular style - checkered tower. 16th century rood screen.

Ottery St. Mary (St. Mary)
13th century, 14th century clock, fan vaulted roof, tomb with canopy, minstrel's gallery, gilded wooded eagle. 18th century pulpit.

Parracombe (St. Petrock)
Unrestored Georgian - 16th century benches, mostly perpendicular, early English chancel.

Sutcombe (St. Andrew)
15th century - some part Norman. 16th century bench ends, restored rood screen, mediaeval glass & floor tiles.

Swimbrige (St. James)
14th century tower & spire - mediaeval stone pulpit, 15th century rood screen, font cover of Renaissance period.

Devon

Tawstock (St. Peter)
14th century, Italian plasterwork ceiling, mediaeval glass, Renaissance memorial pew, Bath monument.
Buckfast Abbey
Living Benedictine monastery, built on mediaeval foundation. Famous for works of art in church, modern stained glass, tonic wine & bee-keeping.

Museums & Galleries

Bideford Museum - Bideford
Geology, maps, prints, shipwright's tools, North Devon pottery.
Burton Art Gallery - Bideford
Hubert Coop collection of paintings etc.
Butterwalk Museum - Dartmouth
17th century row of half timbered buildings, nautical museum. 140 model ships.
Newcomen Engine House - Nr.
Butterwalk Museum
Original Newcomen atmospheric/pressure steam engine c.1725.
Royal Albert Memorial Museum Art Gallery - Exeter
Collections of English watercolours, paintings, glass & ceramics, local silver, natural history & anthropology.
Rougemont House Museum - Exeter
Collections of archaeology & local history. Costume & lace collection
Guildhall - Exeter
Mediaeval structure with Tudor frontage - City regalia & silver.
Exeter Maritime Museum - Exeter
Largest collection in the world of working boats, afloat, ashore & under cover.
The Steam & Countryside Museum - Exmouth
Very large working layout - hundreds of exhibits.
Including Victorian farmhouse - farmyard pets for children.
Shebbear - North Devon
Alcott Farm Museum with unique collections of agricultural implements & photographs, etc.
The Elizabethan House - Totnes
Period costumes & furnishings, tools, toys, domestic articles, etc.
The Elizabethan House - Plymouth
16th century house with period furnishings.

City Museum & Art Gallery - Plymouth
Collections of pictures & porcelain, English & Italian drawing. Reynolds' family portraits, early printed books, ship models.
Cookworthy Museum - Kingsbridge
Story of china clay. Local history, shipbuilding tools, rural life.
Honiton & Allhallows Public Museum - Honiton
Collection of Honiton lace, implements etc. Complete Devon Kitchen.
Lyn & Exmoor Museum - Lynton
Life & history of Exmoor.
Torquay & Natural History Society Museum - Torquay
Collection illustrating Kent's Cavern & other caves - natural history & folkculture.

Historic Monuments

Okehampton Castle - Okehampton
11th -14th century chapel, keep & hall.
Totnes Castle - Totnes
13th - 14th century ruins of Castle.
Blackbury Castle - Southleigh
Hill fort - well preserved.
Dartmouth Castle - Dartmouth
15th century castle - coastal defence.
Lydford Castle - Lydford
12th century stone keep built upon site of Saxon fortress town.
Hound Tor - Manaton
Ruins of mediaeval hamlet.

Other things to see & do

The Big Sheep - Abbotsham
Sheep-milking parlour, with gallery, dairy & production rooms. Exhibition & play area.
Dartington Crystal - Torrington
Watch skilled craftworkers make lead crystalware. Glass centre & exhibition.
Dartmoor Wildlife Park - Sparkwell Nr. Plymouth
Over 100 species, including tigers, lions, bears, deer, birds of prey & waterfowl.
The Devon Guild of Craftsmen - Riverside Mill, Bovey Tracey
Series of quality exhibitions throughout the year.
Paignton Zoological & Botanical Gardens - Paignton
Third largest zoo in England. Botanical gardens, tropical house, "The Ark" family activity centre.

DEVON

Map reference

1	Hopewell	24	Chilcott
2	Payne	25	Cumming
3	Jones	26	Williams
4	May	27	Oakey
4	Langton	28	Wiemeyer
5	Tunnicliffe	29	Bell
7	Barnes	30	Gregson
8	Daniel	31	Merchant
9	Johnson-King	32	Pakenham
11	Butt	33	Merritt
13	Turner	38	Turner
13	Green	39	Tagert
14	Capel-Jones	40	Adie
15	Rattenbury	42	Wright
15	Hyde	44	Graeme
17	Sanders	45	Allan
18	Broster	45	Brown
19	Gable	46	Shaw
20	Balkwill	47	Pugsley
20	Lancaster	48	Hill-King
21	Kamp	49	Burnell
21	Bennett	50	Allnutt
21	Sapsford	51	Sexon
22	Pile	52	Worth
23	Kinder	54	Boorman
		55	Flint

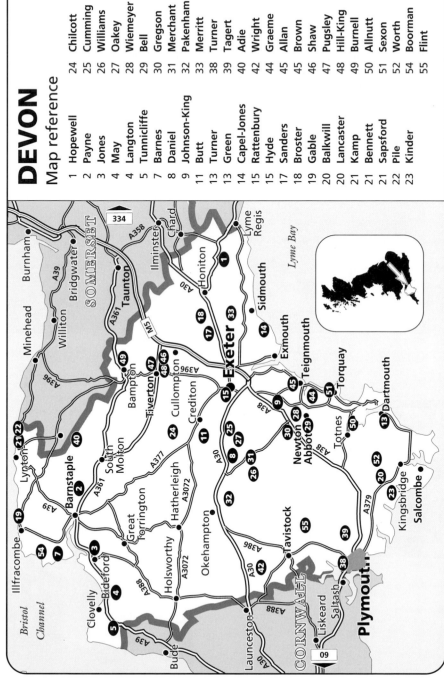

131

Lower Weytown. Horns Cross.

Devon

		rate from £ per person	children taken	evening meals	animals taken
Mrs Helga Hopewell **Lambley Brook** **Springhead Lane** **Kilmington** **Axminster EX13 7SS** **Tel: (01297) 35033** **Open: FEB - DEC** **Map Ref No. 01**	Nearest Road: A.35 A warm & friendly atmosphere is found at this delightful, secluded, 19th-century, converted cottage, standing in its own grounds, & surrounded by open countryside & woodland, on the outskirts of this picturesque village. Offering comfortable & spacious accommodation in 3 pleasant bedrooms, with tea/coffee trays & lovely views. An idyllic retreat for nature lovers. Cosy, elegant lounge, with colour T.V.. Children over 10 years welcome. (Mobile No: 0467 222339.)	£18.00	Y	N	N
Jackie & Antony Payne **Huxtable Farm** **West Buckland** **Barnstaple EX32 0SR** **Tel: (01598) 760254** **Fax 01598 760254** **Open: ALL YEAR (Excl. Xmas)** **Map Ref No. 02**	Nearest Road: A.361 Enjoy a memorable candlelit dinner of farm/local produce with complimentary homemade wine in this wonderful mediaeval longhouse with original oak panelling, beams & bread ovens. This secluded sheep farm with abundant wildlife & panoramic views is ideally situated on the Tarka Trail for exploring Exmoor & N. Devon's coastline. Tennis court, sauna, fitness & games room. Log fires in winter. 5 en-suite bedrooms & 1 with a private bathroom, each with T.V. & tea/coffee.	£23.00	Y	Y	N
Jenny & Barry Jones **The Pines at Eastleigh** **Eastleigh** **Bideford** **EX39 4PA** **Tel: (01271) 860561** **Fax 01271 861248** **Open: ALL YEAR** **Map Ref No. 03**	Nearest Road: A.386 Rediscover peace & relaxation at this Grade II listed Georgian home. Set in 7 acres of gardens & paddocks with views of Bideford, Lundy & Hartland Point. Licensed. Books & maps to borrow & an audio system for guest use. Generous farmhouse-style cooking featuring fresh local produce. Special diets catered for. 7 attractive bedrooms, en-suite or private facilities, T.V., 'phones, tea/coffee, hairdryers. Ground-floor courtyard rooms & king-size beds available. **E-mail: barry@barpines.demon.co.uk**	£26.00 🚭 CREDIT CARD VISA M'CARD	Y	Y	Y
Mrs Caroline May **Lower Waytown** **Horns Cross** **Bideford EX39 5DN** **Tel/Fax: (01237) 451787** **Open: ALL YEAR (Excl. Xmas & New Year)** **Map Ref No. 04**	Nearest Road: A.39 This beautifully converted barn & roundhouse have created a delightful, spacious & comfortable home offering superb accommodation. Extensive grounds with ponds & ornamental waterfowl, & a coastal footpath nearby. The en-suite bedrooms, 2 double (1 ground floor) & 1 twin-bedded, are tastefully furnished, & each has T.V., hairdryers & tea/coffee facilities. The unique, round, beamed sitting room adjoins the spacious dining room, where breakfast is served. Children over 12.	£22.50 🚭 *see PHOTO over*	Y	N	N
Jean & Jack Langton **The Old Rectory** **Rectory Lane** **Parkham** **Bideford EX39 5PL** **Tel: (01237) 451443** **Open: ALL YEAR (Excl. Xmas & New Year)** **Map Ref No. 04**	Nearest Road: A.39 Charming, delightfully furnished country house. Log fires, unique ambience & superb cuisine. 3 en-suite/private-facility bedrooms, very prettily decorated & furnished with every comfort in mind. Dine with your hosts, & enjoy good wine with your excellent evening meal, which, using fresh local produce, is home-cooked by Jean to the highest of standards. Set in an Area of Outstanding Natural Beauty, it is ideally situated for the coast, picturesque Clovelly & Exmoor. Children over 12.	£36.00 🚭 *see PHOTO over*	Y	Y	N

The Old Rectory. Parkham.

Denham Farm & Country House. North Buckland.

Devon

		rate from £ per person	children taken	evening meals	animals taken
Petre Josephine Tunnicliffe **Henaford Manor Farm** **Welcombe** **Bideford** **EX39 6HE** **Tel: (01288) 331252** **Open: ALL YEAR** **Map Ref No. 05**	Nearest Road: A.39 Henaford Manor is a 13th-century farmhouse, set in 226 acres, retaining many traditional features, including beamed ceilings & large fireplaces. 5 tastefully furnished bedrooms, 2 en-suite, all with modern amenities incl. tea/coffee-making facilities, & some with 'phone, radio, T.V.. Guests can relax in the spacious garden or lounge throughout the day. Excellent meals, & guests may bring their own wine. Within 3 miles of Devon's Atlantic coast, where there are several beaches & small coves, including Clovelly & Tintagel.	£18.50	Y	Y	Y
Mrs Jean Barnes **Denham Farm & Country House** **North Buckland** **Braunton EX33 1HY** **Tel/Fax: (01271) 890297** **Open: ALL YEAR (Excl. Xmas)** **Map Ref No. 07**	Nearest Road: A.361 Denham is beautifully situated in the heart of the countryside, with 160 acres of its own farmland. Only a short drive away are superb beaches, breathtaking scenery & lovely coastal walks. Situated only 3 miles from a championship golf course, this delightful house offers 10 en-suite bedrooms, each with colour T.V. & tea/coffee-making facilities. The inglenook fireplace & bread oven are a part of the character of this country home, built in the 1700s.	£25.00 *see PHOTO over* CREDIT CARD VISA M'CARD	Y	Y	N
Tim Daniel **Parford Well** **Sandy Park** **Chagford** **TQ13 8JW** **Tel: (01647) 433353** **Open: ALL YEAR** **Map Ref No. 08**	Nearest Road: A.382 Parford Well is a comfortable & cosy house, surrounded by its own walled garden, set in the tiny hamlet of Sandy Park in the Dartmoor National Park. It is the ideal place to stay if you want to get away from it all, relax & be well-looked-after. Accommodation is in 3 charming & attractively furnished bedrooms, each with an en-suite/private bathroom. There are wonderful walks on the doorstep both in the wooded valley of the River Teign & on the open moor. Children over 10.	£20.00	Y	N	N
Peter & Patricia Johnson-King **Oakfield** **Exeter Road** **Chudleigh TQ13 0DD** **Tel/Fax: (01626) 852194** **Open: Easter - OCT** **Map Ref No. 09**	Nearest Road: A.38 This lovely old family home, beautifully furnished with antiques, & surrounded by 20 acres of delightfully landscaped gardens, orchards & paddocks, with glorious views of the Devon countryside, offers perfect peace & tranquillity. Peter & Patricia treat their guests as friends, & emphasise comfort, relaxation & excellent food. 3 very attractive en-suite bedrooms. Guests may also enjoy the drawing room, billiards room, library & swimming pool.	£30.00 *see PHOTO over*	N	N	N
Richard Turner **Ford House** **44 Victoria Road** **Dartmouth TQ6 9DX** **Tel: (01803) 834047** **Fax 01803 834047** **Open: MAR - OCT** **Map Ref No. 13**	Nearest Road: A.3122 Ford House is an attractive Grade II listed Regency house, centrally situated within walking distance of the many shops, restaurants & pubs. Accommodation is in very comfortable, en-suite, individually decorated bedrooms equipped with either king or queen-size double beds or twin beds. Each room has a fridge, 'phone, hairdryer, T.V. etc. Breakfast is served from 8 a.m. until 12 noon & ranges from traditional full English to scrambled eggs & smoked salmon. Parking.	£25.00 CREDIT CARD VISA M'CARD AMEX	Y	Y	Y

Oakfield. Chudleigh.

Devon

		rate from £ per person	children taken	evening meals	animals taken
Paul & Irene Butt **The New Inn** **Coleford** **Crediton EX17 5BZ** **Tel: 01363 84242** **Fax 01363 85044** **Open: ALL YEAR (Excl.** **Xmas/Boxing Day)** **Map Ref No. 11**	Nearest Road: A.377 The New Inn is a 13th-century thatched inn nestling in a quiet valley by the side of a brook. Accommodation in this attractive property includes 5 en-suite bedrooms with 'phone, T.V. & tea/coffee-making facilities. There is also an extensive menu, using fresh local produce whenever possible. Local amenities include several golf courses, fishing, horse riding & sport & leisure facilities. Easy access to Dartmoor, Exmoor & the north & south Devon coasts. **E-mail: new-inn@mailzynet.co.uk**	£27.00 *see PHOTO over* CREDIT CARD VISA M'CARD AMEX	Y	Y	N
Robert & Brenda Green **Boringdon House** **1 Church Road** **Dartmouth TQ6 9HQ** **Tel: (01803) 832235** **Open: ALL YEAR** **Map Ref No. 13**	Nearest Road: A.3122, A.379 Boringdon is a lovely, welcoming Georgian house in a quiet part of Dartmouth, lying within a large, secluded leafy garden & looking down to the town & river, & sea beyond. Courtyard parking. Only a short, 10-min walk through picturesque lanes down to the historic town. 3 spacious en-suite bedrooms, attractively furnished with Laura Ashley drapes. Comfortable & relaxing, with colour T.V., c/h & tea/coffee facilities.	£22.50	N	N	N
David & Jennie Capel-Jones **Thorn Mill Farm** **Frogmore Road** **East Budleigh EX9 7BB** **Tel: (01395) 444088** **Open: ALL YEAR (Excl. Xmas)** **Map Ref No. 14**	Nearest Road: A.3052 A warm welcome awaits you at this 16th-century family home with beamed lounge & inglenook fireplace in a classic Devon village. The house faces south over the River Otter Valley, with footpaths to coastal paths. Close to Bicton Gardens & N.T. properties, in a designated Area of Outstanding Natural Beauty. 1 double en-suite, 1 twin & 2 singles, all with h&c, colour T.V., radio & hospitality trays. Children over 8 yrs.	£20.00	Y	N	N
Rick & Sue Hyde **Raffles** **11 Blackall Road** **Exeter** **EX4 4HD** **Tel: (01392) 270200** **Fax 01392 270200** **Open: ALL YEAR** **Map Ref No. 15**	Nearest Road: M.4/5 Raffles is a spacious Victorian townhouse situated a few minutes' walk from the heart of one of England's cathedral cities. The family has run an antique business in Devon for 30 years, & the house is furnished throughout with antique furniture. The accommodation is fully en-suite, & emphasis is placed on your comfort & care. A traditional English breakfast is served between 07.30 & 09.30. Dinner can be provided with your preferences discussed & there is a residential table licence. Secure garages are available.	£23.00 CREDIT CARD VISA M'CARD AMEX	Y	Y	Y
Mike & Joanne Sanders **Down House** **Wood Hayes Lane** **Whimple** **Exeter EX5 2QR** **Tel: (01404) 822860** **Open: ALL YEAR** **Map Ref No. 17**	Nearest Road: A.30, M.5 Down House offers peace, quiet & seclusion in an elegantly furnished Edwardian farmhouse set in 6 acres of gardens, orchards & paddocks. The house is in the style of Charles Rennie Mackintosh. Personal service & a family atmosphere are priorities. Double, twin, single & family en-suite rooms of a high standard are available including a twin ground-floor room. A good central base for discovering the richness of the east Devon countryside. Animals by arrangement.	£18.00	Y	N	Y

The New Inn. Coleford.

Devon

	rate from £ per person	children taken	evening meals	animals taken
Michael & Kay Rattenbury **The Edwardian** **30 & 32 Heavitree Road** **Exeter EX1 2LQ** **Tel/Fax: (01392) 276102** **Tel/Fax: (01392) 254699** **Open: ALL YEAR** **Map Ref No. 15**	Nearest Road: M.5, A.30, A.38 Elegant Edwardian townhouses with tasteful, period decor, near Roman walls, cathedral & city centre. Choice of en-suite rooms from singles, twins, doubles (including 3 romantic 4-posters - 1 on the ground floor) & rooms for 3 or 4 persons. Spa bath. English & vegetarian, freshly prepared breakfasts. Local hosts with wide knowledge of the West Country. Large car park opposite. Discounts for stays of 3 nights or more.	**£22.00** *see PHOTO over* CREDIT CARD VISA M'CARD AMEX	Y	N	Y
Gordon Broster **Colestocks Country** **House Hotel** **Payhembury** **Honiton EX14 0JR** **Tel: (01404) 850633** **Fax 01404 850901** **Open: APR - OCT** **Map Ref No. 18**	Nearest Road: A.30 Pink-washed & newly re-thatched, a lovely 16th-century, Grade II listed country house set in 2 acres of gardens. Tranquil rural situation, & well placed for touring the West Country. All rooms have en-suite bath/shower, colour T.V. & tea-making facilities. Many antiques, 1 4-poster, 1 canopied brass bed & 2 half testers. Log fires in the huge inglenook fireplace. Excellent restaurant, all home-cooking. Wines personally chosen & imported by the proprietor. Children over 10 years. Reduced rates for 2 nights or more.	**£27.50** 🚭 CREDIT CARD VISA M'CARD	Y	Y	Y
Roy & Barbara Gable **Varley House** **Chambercombe Park** **Ilfracombe EX34 9QW** **Tel: (01271) 863927** **Fax 01271 863927** **Open: MAR - OCT** **Map Ref No. 19**	Nearest Road: A.399 An attractive, elegant Victorian character house, originally built to revitalise & refresh returning officers from the Boer War. Situated on the outskirts of Ilfracombe. The Gables aim is quality, comfort, courtesy & care with the personal touch. 9 delightful non-smoking rooms, all fully en-suite & with all the little touches to make you feel really pampered. Their home is tastefully furnished & the food served is imaginative & plentiful. Ideal for exploring this lovely area. Children over 5 years.	**£21.50** CREDIT CARD VISA M'CARD AMEX	Y	Y	Y
Mrs Christine Lancaster **Helliers Farm** **Ashford, Aveton Gifford** **Kingsbridge TQ7 4ND** **Tel/Fax: (01548) 550689** **Open: ALL YEAR (Excl. Xmas)** **Map Ref No. 20**	Nearest Road: A.379 Set in the heart of South Hams countryside, this recently modernised farmhouse offers accommodation in 4 pleasant bedrooms with tea/coffee-making facilities. Also, a spacious dining room, where good farmhouse breakfasts are served, a comfortable lounge, with T.V., & a games room. Close to the beaches, moors, golf courses, N.T. walks & the city of Plymouth.	**£17.00** 🚭	Y	N	N

When booking your accommodation please mention
The Best Bed & Breakfast

The Edwardian. Exeter.

	rate from £ per person	children taken	evening meals	animals taken

		rate from £ per person	children taken	evening meals	animals taken
John & Jill Balkwill **Court Barton** **Aveton Gifford** **Kingsbridge TQ7 4LE** **Tel: (01548) 550312** 01548 550312 **Open: ALL YEAR (Excl. Xmas)** **Map Ref No. 20**	Nearest Road: A.379 An absolutely delightful 16th-century, listed manor farmhouse situated on a 40-acre farm. 7 comfortable bedrooms, 6 with en-suite facilities & all with T.V. & tea/coffee-making facilities. A comfortable, well-furnished T.V. lounge with lots of books. Delicious country breakfasts are served in the sunny breakfast room. Full central heating & log fires in cooler weather. Close to moorland & beaches. Ideal for walking, sailing & fishing. **E-mail: jill@devfarms.avel.co.uk**	£20.00 *see PHOTO over* CREDIT CARD VISA M'CARD	Y	N	N
Trebles Cottage Hotel **Kingston** **Kingsbridge** **TQ7 4PT** **Tel: (01548) 810268** **Fax 01548 810268** **Open: ALL YEAR** **Map Ref No. 23**	Nearest Road: A.379, B.3392 Originally a family cottage (built in 1801), & now a small hotel set in secluded grounds on the edge of an attractive, unspoilt village. 5 bedrooms, all en-suite & tastefully & individually furnished, with colour T.V., radio/alarm, tea/coffee makers & hair dryers. A small cocktail bar complements the excellent restaurant. Lovely coastal walks, a picturesque beach & golf nearby. Your hosts offer a warm welcome, personal service & a high standard of comfort & good food. Special Xmas packages available. Children over 12 yrs.	£27.00 CREDIT CARD VISA M'CARD AMEX	Y	Y	Y
June & Adrian Kamp **Southcliffe** **34 Lee Road** **Lynton EX35 6BS** **Tel/Fax: (01598) 753328** **Open: MAR - OCT** **Map Ref No. 21**	Nearest Road: A.39 A charming private hotel of the Victorian era. Modernised throughout, yet retaining many original features, such as the natural pitch-pine staircase & doors. Beautifully appointed bedrooms, all with private bathrooms, colour T.V. & beverage makers. June & Adrian Kamp have been at Southcliffe since 1978, & have a reputation for good food, comfort, cleanliness & value for money. Children over 8. Animals by arrangement.	£19.00 CREDIT CARD VISA M'CARD	Y	Y	Y
Ben & Jane Bennett **Victoria Lodge** **Lee Road** **Lynton** **EX35 6BS** **Tel: (01598) 753203** **Fax 01598 753203** **Open: FEB - NOV** **Map Ref No. 21**	Nearest Road: A.39 An award-winning hotel where a warm & friendly welcome awaits you. Relax in elegant, comfortable surroundings, enjoy the friendly hospitality & food that is a gourmet's delight. (Dinner is available Thurs to Sun.) This gracious house provides charming period features, with modern conveniences. 9 beautifully appointed en-suite bedrooms, all with T.V., radio, hairdryer & tea/coffee. All are decorated to a very high standard, including deluxe bedrooms with 4-poster & Victorian brass beds. Conveniently located to explore Exmoor & the picturesque coastline.	£25.00 CREDIT CARD VISA M'CARD	Y	Y	N
Mrs Bryony Sapsford **Longmead House Hotel** **9 Longmead** **Lynton EX35 6DQ** **Tel/Fax: (01598) 752523** **Open: MAR - OCT** **Map Ref No. 21**	Nearest Road: A.39 A haven for good home-cooking, with that little extra flair which makes many guests return. Bryony & Brian offer a warm welcome to their home, & encourage a relaxed, friendly atmosphere. The 7 bedrooms are all individual, comfortable & attractive; 5 are en-suite. Set in a large garden with ample parking, & close to the Valley of Rocks, Longmead provides an ideal base from which to discover Exmoor.	£17.00 CREDIT CARD VISA M'CARD	Y	Y	Y

Court Barton. Aveton Gifford.

Wigham.   Morchard Bishop.

Devon

rate from £ per person
children taken
evening meals
animals taken

		rate from £ per person	children taken	evening meals	animals taken
Rosemary & Susan Pile **Coombe Farm** **Countisbury** **Lynton EX35 6NF** **Tel: (01598) 741236** **Open: MAR - NOV** **Map Ref No. 22**	Nearest Road: A.39 Coombe is a 365-acre, hill-sheep farm, with an early-17th-century farmhouse set betwixt Lynmouth & the legendary Doone Valley. The coast path runs through the farm at Desolate. All within the spectacular Exmoor National Park. The bedrooms are 2 doubles, en-suite, 1 twin & 2 family. All have hot-drink facilities, shaver points, & bath & hand towels. Central heating. A lounge with woodburner fire & colour T.V..	£18.00	Y	N	N
Stephen & Dawn Chilcott **Wigham** **Morchard Bishop** **EX17 6RJ** **Tel/Fax: (01363) 877350** **Open: ALL YEAR** **Map Ref No. 24**	Nearest Road: A.377 Wigham is a 16th-century Devon longhouse, with a 30-acre farm which provides fresh fruit, vegetables & dairy produce for imaginative meals. Accommodation is in 5 double rooms, including a 4-poster suite. All with colour T.V. & video & full private bathroom. There are 2 sitting rooms in which guests may relax & a snooker lounge & outdoor heated pool for pleasure. Licensed. Stabling - livery by arrangement. *see PHOTO over* CREDIT CARD VISA M'CARD AMEX	£29.00	Y	Y	N
Mrs Mary Cuming **Wooston Farm** **Moretonhampstead** **TQ13 8QA** **Tel: (01647) 440367** **Fax 01647 440367** **Open: ALL YEAR (Excl. Xmas)** **Map Ref No. 25**	Nearest Road: B.3212, A.30 Wooston, once part of the Manor House Estate owned by Lord Hambledon, is situated high above the Teign Valley in the Dartmoor National Park, with views over open moorland, & plenty of walks, golf, fishing & riding nearby. The farmhouse is surrounded by a delightful & well-managed garden of 1/2 an acre. 3 pleasant bedrooms, 2 en-suite, 1 with 4-poster, 1 with private bathroom, with every facility included. Excellent breakfasts are served. Also, a guests' lounge for your relaxation after a day exploring the Devon countryside. Children over 8 years.	£19.00	Y	N	N
John & Sheila Williams **Gate House** **North Bovey** **Moretonhampstead** **TQ13 8RB** **Tel: (01647) 440479** **Fax 01647 440479** **Open: ALL YEAR** **Map Ref No. 26**	Nearest Road: A.30, A.38 North Bovey is an historic village set within the Dartmoor National Park. Gate House, near the village green is a listed 500-year-old thatched mediaeval longhouse with beamed ceilings, old granite fireplaces & bread oven. It is set within an acre of private gardens with a swimming pool. Guest rooms are charmingly furnished, & the bedrooms combine country-style elegance with en-suite/private bathrooms. Lovely walks amidst breath-taking scenery, secluded areas for bird watching & N.T. properties within easy reach. *see PHOTO over*	£25.00	N	Y	Y
Gill & David Oakey **Great Doccombe Farm** **Doccombe** **Moretonhampstead** **TQ13 8SS** **Tel: (01647) 440694** **Open: ALL YEAR** **Map Ref No. 27**	Nearest Road: A.30 Great Doccombe Farm is situated in the pretty hamlet of Doccombe, within the Dartmoor National Park, on the B.3212 from Exeter. An ideal base for walking in the Teign Valley & nearby moors, with golf, riding & fishing nearby. This lovely 16th-century granite farmhouse is surrounded by gardens & fields. The bedrooms (1 ground-floor) are all en-suite, & have shower, T.V. & tea/coffee facilities. Traditional English breakfast served.	£17.00	Y	N	N

Gate House. North Bovey.

Sampsons Farm Restaurant. Newton Abbot

Devon

	rate from £ per person	children taken	evening meals	animals taken
Klaus & Janice Wiemeyer **The Thatched Cottage** **9 Crossley Moor Road** **Kingsteignton** **Newton Abbot TQ12 3LE** **Tel: (01626) 365650** **Open: ALL YEAR** **Map Ref No. 28**	Nearest Road: A.380 A beautiful 400-year-old, Grade II listed, thatched longhouse where old oak beams & a large open fireplace lend a cosy & welcoming atmosphere. There are 3 en-suite bedrooms, all with colour T.V. & tea/coffee-making facilities. A full English breakfast is served. Character bar & restaurant, where table d'hote & a la carte menus are available each evening. A pretty garden for guests' use. An ideal base for touring, with a warm welcome. CREDIT CARD VISA M'CARD AMEX	£20.00	Y	Y	N
Nigel Bell **Sampsons Farm** **Restaurant** **Preston** **Newton Abbot TQ12 3PP** **Tel: (01626) 354913** **Fax 01626 354913** **Open: ALL YEAR** **Map Ref No. 29**	Nearest Road: B.3193, A.38 A super, relaxed, family atmosphere is found at this traditional thatched Devon longhouse. This Grade II listed building, of historical importance, retains much of its original charm & character, with oak beams, panelling & inglenook fireplaces. All rooms have modern amenities, & there are 4-poster & en-suite rooms available. A delicious breakfast is served, & an extensive a la carte & table d'hote menu is offered in the evening. A view of Dartmoor from the windows. A short distance from the coast. Riding, fishing, golf nearby. CREDIT CARD VISA M'CARD AMEX	£17.50 *see PHOTO over*	Y	Y	Y
Mrs Madeleine Gregson **Penpark** **Bickington** **Newton Abbot TQ12 6LH** **Tel: (01626) 821314** **Fax 01626 821101** **Open: ALL YEAR** **Map Ref No. 30**	Nearest Road: A.38 In the Dartmoor National Park, with secluded, beautiful woodland gardens, tennis court & glorious panoramic views, Penpark is an elegant country house, a gem of its period, designed by Clough Williams Ellis of Portmerion fame. 3 charming rooms: a spacious double/twin with balcony; a single next-door & a further double - all with wonderful views; private facilities; tea/coffee & T.V.. The Gregsons offer you a truly relaxed stay in beautiful & friendly surroundings.	£23.00 *see PHOTO over*	Y	N	N
Mrs Trudie Merchant **Great Sloncombe Farm** **Moretonhampstead** **Newton Abbot TQ13 8QF** **Tel: (01647) 440595** **Fax 01647 440595** **Open: ALL YEAR** **Map Ref No. 31**	Nearest Road: A.382 Great Sloncombe Farm is a listed, granite-&-cob-built, 13th-century farmhouse. Set in a peaceful Dartmoor valley, the rambling house has a magical atmosphere, & is furnished with oak & pine, antique china & interesting old photographs. The 3 warm & pleasant bedrooms are all en-suite, with every facility included. Delicious breakfasts, with home-made bread & plentiful Devonshire suppers, are served. Children over 8 yrs.	£20.00	Y	Y	Y
Maureen & John Pakenham **Tor Down House** **Belstone** **Okehampton EX20 1QY** **Tel: (01837) 840731** **Open: ALL YEAR (Excl.** **Xmas & New Year)** **Map Ref No. 32**	Nearest Road: A.30 Imagine a Helen Allingham cottage, honeysuckle around the door, little bedroom windows peeping from under thatch & delightful gardens only 100 paces from the open moor. This is Tor Down House, a 14th-century Dartmoor Longhouse (Grade II) where visitors arrive as guests & leave as friends. Old oak beams, huge granite fireplaces, cats on Persian rugs, 4-poster beds, private shower rooms etc. Sumptuous breakfasts. Dinner by prior arrangement. CREDIT CARD VISA M'CARD	£27.50	N	Y	N

Penpark. Bickington.

Devon

		rate from £ per person	children taken	evening meals	animals taken
S. Merritt & D. Fishman **Venn Ottery Barton Hotel** **Venn Ottery** **Ottery St. Mary** EX11 1RZ **Tel: (01404) 812733** **Fax 01404 814713** **Open: ALL YEAR** **Map Ref No. 33**	Nearest Road: A.3052 Lovely 16th-century listed building, with beams, Bible cupboards & big log fires, set amidst 2 1/2 acres of mature gardens in the heart of the countryside. Just 5 miles from the Devon Heritage Coast at Sidmouth, easy access from the M.5 or A.30; plenty of parking, some ground-floor bedrooms. A charming home. Peaceful, friendly & relaxing, with watercolour & walking holidays for the more active. Dogs welcome.	£30.00 CREDIT CARD VISA M'CARD	Y	Y	Y
John & Daphne Turner **Westways** **706 Budshead Road** **Crownhill** **Plymouth PL6 5DY** **Tel/Fax: (01752) 776617** **Open: ALL YEAR** **Map Ref No. 38**	Nearest Road: A.38 Situated approx. 3 1/2 miles from Plymouth city centre, this attractive detached house offers pleasant accommodation in 3 well-furnished rooms, with tea/coffee facilities. Excellent breakfasts are served in the elegant dining room. Guests may choose to relax & plan their excursions in the comfortable sitting room. Also, a small T.V. room. A homely & friendly base both for visitors wishing to make the most of the many attractions in the area, & for touring Devon. Children over 12.	£20.00 CREDIT CARD VISA M'CARD	N	N	N
Mr & Mrs B. Tagert **The Barn** **Windwhistle Farm** **Hemerdon** **Plymouth PL7 5BU** **Tel: (01752) 347016** **Fax 01752 335670** **Open: ALL YEAR (Excl. Xmas)** **Map Ref No. 39**	Nearest Road: A.38 This beautifully converted old stone barn, on the edge of Dartmoor, yet only 5 miles from Plymouth city centre, offers 3 charming, peaceful en-suite rooms with all comforts. Guests have their own sitting room & the use of the lovely garden in summer. Enjoy a drink in the evening in front of a log fire in the drawing room & an excellent dinner (by arrangement) in the beamed dining 'hall' with fresh vegetables from the garden. Licensed. Children over 14 years welcome.	£28.00	Y	Y	N
John & Penny Adie **Barkham** **Sandyway** **South Molton EX36 3LU** **Tel: (01643) 831370** **Fax 01643 831370** **Open: ALL YEAR** **Map Ref No. 40**	Nearest Road: A.361 Lovely 18th-century farmhouse in 12 acres of woodland, pasture & streams in the middle of Exmoor, & yet only 3 hours from Heathrow. Oak-panelled dining room & guest drawing room with patio leading to the croquet lawn & the superb valley with its unusual tree-house. Excellent English breakfasts & delicious evening meals served. Wonderful riding country, & convenient for North Devon coastline.	£18.00	Y	Y	N
Mrs Jennifer Graeme **Fonthill** **Torquay Road** **Shaldon** **Teignmouth TQ14 0AX** **Tel/Fax: (01626) 872344** **Open: MAR - NOV** **Map Ref No. 44**	Nearest Road: A.381, B.3199 Visitors are warmly welcomed to this lovely Georgian house, for a peaceful holiday in charming & very comfortable accommodation. Fonthill stands in 20 acres of beautiful gardens, woodland & fields on the edge of Shaldon, a pretty village on the South Devon coast. 3 delightful rooms, with en-suite/private bathrooms & every comfort. The lovely garden is for guests' enjoyment, & there is also a tennis court in the grounds. Several sandy beaches nearby, & an 18-hole golf course.	£25.00 *see PHOTO over*	Y	N	N

Fonthill. Shaldon

Thomas Luny House. Teignmouth.

Devon

		rate from £ per person	children taken	evening meals	animals taken
David & Jill Wright **Quither Mill** **Quither** **Tavistock PL19 0PZ** **Tel: (01822) 860160** **Open: ALL YEAR** **Map Ref No. 42**	Nearest Road: A.30, A.386 Quither Mill is situated in a sleepy hamlet & is listed as being of architectural & historical interest. Dating from the 18th century, the mill wheel & workings are intact. Guests enjoy the comfort of beamed en-suite bedrooms & full English breakfast. The hosts are proud of their reputation for fine cooking drawn from 20 years in the hotel world, which makes dinner a memorable experience. Animals by arrangement.	£25.00 (no smoking)	Y	Y	Y
Alison & John Allan **Thomas Luny House** **Teign Street** **Teignmouth** **TQ14 8EG** **Tel: (01626) 772976** **Open: FEB - DEC** **Map Ref No. 45**	Nearest Road: A.381 A Grade II listed Georgian house, built by the marine artist Thomas Luny. Tucked away in the old quarter of Teignmouth, it forms a quiet oasis surrounded by its own high walls. Each superb, en-suite bedroom is individual in style, some with views over the River Teign. Alison & John & their family love to share their home, & they spare no effort in preparing the delicious breakfasts & attending to their guests' general well-being. Licensed. Children over 12 yrs.	£25.00 *see PHOTO over*	Y	N	N
Jenny Richardson Brown **Wytchwood** **West Buckeridge** **Teignmouth** **TQ14 8NF** **Tel: (01626) 773482** **Open: ALL YEAR** **Map Ref No. 45**	Nearest Road: A.381 Ideally placed in this delightful county, close to many beautiful golf courses, award-winning Wytchwood has an outstanding reputation for lavish hospitality & traditional home-cooking. To stay here is to be truly pampered! Pretty en-suite bedrooms with co-ordinating decor & fabrics & lovely views. Homemade bread & rolls, jams, preserves, orchard honey & garden produce. Delicious Devonshire cream teas. Many culinary awards. A warm welcome is assured.	£22.50 (no smoking)	Y	N	N
Mrs Jenny Shaw **Poole Farm** **Ash Thomas** **Tiverton EX16 4NS** **Tel: (01884) 820201** **Open: ALL YEAR** **Map Ref No. 46**	Nearest Road: M.5, A.361 An attractive old farmhouse, recently renovated, with 18 acres & a pretty garden. Set in a peaceful hamlet, Poole Farm has 2 comfortable, en-suite bedrooms, with colour T.V., tea tray & full central heating. There are plenty of good places to eat nearby, but evening meals can usually be provided by prior arrangement. It is an ideal touring base or stop-over en-route.	£20.00 (no smoking)	Y	N	Y
Mrs Barbara Pugsley **Hornhill** **Exeter Hill** **Tiverton** **EX16 4PL** **Tel: (01884) 253352** **Fax 01884 253352** **Open: ALL YEAR** **Map Ref No. 47**	Nearest Road: A.361, M.5 Hornhill, originally a coaching inn, has panoramic views over the beautiful Exe valley. Set in a large garden & surrounded by farmland. The charming hosts offer guests comfort, warmth, delicious home-cooking & a happy atmosphere. The house, furnished with antiques, has 3 attractive bedrooms (1 with a Victorian 4-poster), each with private bathroom, T.V. & tea/coffee facilities. 1 is suitable for the partially disabled. Guests are invited to relax in the elegant drawing room, with plenty of books & a log fire on chilly evenings. A perfect place from which to explore Devon.	£19.50 (no smoking) *see PHOTO over*	N	N	N

Hornhill. Tiverton.

The Old Forge at Totnes.   Totnes.

Devon

	rate from £ per person	children taken	evening meals	animals taken
Mrs Ruth Hill-King **Little Holwell** **Collipriest** **Tiverton EX16 4PT** **Tel: (01884) 257590** **Fax 01884 257590** **Open: ALL YEAR (Excl. Xmas)** **Map Ref No. 48**	Nearest Road: A.361, B.3391 A warm welcome awaits you in this 13th-century home, set amidst rolling hills & woodland in the favoured Exe Valley. Offering 3 very comfortable rooms, 1 en-suite, all with tea/coffee facilities. There is an inglenook fireplace, oak beams, a spiral staircase & relaxing views. Home cooking. An ideal centre for touring the coast & moors, all within easy reach. From the A.361, take the B.3391 to the 4th roundabout, proceed for approx. 2 miles & it is the last house on the right.	£16.00 CREDIT CARD VISA M'CARD	N	Y	N
Mrs Diane Burnell **The Old Mill** **Shillingford** **Tiverton** **EX16 9BW** **Tel: (01398) 331064** **Fax 01398 331598** **Open: ALL YEAR** **Map Ref No. 49**	Nearest Road: B.3227 Set in a pretty riverside 'edge of village' location, The Old Mill, a former water-powered corn mill, offers superb accommodation in self-contained suites. Suite 1 is suitable for 2 - 4 persons, while Suite 2 offers 1/2 family bedrooms. Each has private or en-suite bathrooms, colour T.V. & tea/coffee-making facilities. A beautiful garden & 4 large patios provide ample relaxation areas. Shooting, fishing & horse-riding breaks available. Restaurant licence. Children over 5 yrs. **E-mail: oldmill@deanteam.demon.co.uk**	£25.00 CREDIT CARD VISA M'CARD	Y	Y	N
Brian & Anita Sexon **Kingston House** **75 Avenue Road** **Torquay TQ2 5LL** **Tel: (01803) 212760** **Open: ALL YEAR** **Map Ref No. 51**	Nearest Road: A.3022 Everyone is assured of a warm West Country welcome from Brian & Anita. Kingston House combines Victorian elegance with modern amenities, ensuring a relaxing, enjoyable visit. There are 6 tastefully decorated en-suite bedrooms with complimentary tea/coffee facilities & T.V. Situated only a short level walk from the seafront, harbour & town via the beautiful Torre Abbey & Gardens. A charming home. Children over 8.	£15.00 CREDIT CARD VISA M'CARD	Y	N	N
Mrs Jeannie Allnutt **The Old Forge at Totnes** **Seymour Place** **Totnes** **TQ9 5AY** **Tel: (01803) 862174** **Fax 01803 865385** **Open: ALL YEAR** **Map Ref No. 50**	Nearest Road: A.381, A.384 A delightfully converted, working, 600-year-old smithy. This family-run hotel, located in the centre of Totnes, offers visitors a choice of 10 comfortable, well-equipped bedrooms, 9 en-suite, all with radio, T.V., 'phone & tea/coffee-making facilities. A cottage suite also available for families. There is also a pleasant walled garden for guests' use, where delicious cream teas are served. The Old Forge is ideally located for touring the Torbay coast & Dartmoor. Golf breaks a speciality. Licensed. Leisure lounge with whirlpool spa.	£25.00 *see PHOTO over* CREDIT CARD VISA M'CARD	Y	N	N
Mrs Helen Worth **Orchard House** **Horner** **Halwell** **Totnes TQ9 7LB** **Tel: (01548) 821448** **Open: MAR - NOV** **Map Ref No. 52**	Nearest Road: A.381 Tucked away in a rural hamlet of the South Hams, between Totnes & Kingsbridge, Orchard House nestles within an old cider orchard. It offers superb accommodation: all bedrooms are en-suite with colour T.V., radio, tea/coffee-making facilities & beautiful furnishings. Breakfasts are ample, with cereals, juice, yoghurts & grapefruit, followed by a cooked platter with toast & croissants. Also, guests' own sitting & dining room, with a log fire. Large garden & private parking.	£18.00 *see PHOTO over*	Y	N	N

Orchard House. Horner.

		rate from £ per person	children taken	evening meals	animals taken
Jean & Charles Boorman **Sandunes** **Beach Road** **Woolacombe** **EX34 7BT** **Tel: (01271) 870661** **Open: MAR - OCT** **Map Ref No. 54**	Nearest Road: A.361 'Sandunes' is a very pleasant, most comfortable modern guest house where you are assured of a friendly welcome, a relaxed atmosphere & courteous service. Conveniently located for Woolacombe Sands & the village. The comfortable accommodation is in 7 en-suite bedrooms, many with lovely sea views. The well appointed guest lounge & sun patio have marvellous panoramic views out to sea. This is an ideal base for touring, with sandy beaches, Illfracombe, Lynton, Lynmouth & Exmoor within easy reach.	£17.00	N	Y	N
John & Liz Flint **Burrator House** **Sheepstor** **Yelverton** **PL20 6PF** **Tel: (01822) 855669** **Fax 01822 855669** **Open: ALL YEAR** **Map Ref No. 55**	Nearest Road: A.386 Burrator House, historically connected with the White Rajah of Sarawk, is delightfully situated in a wooded valley within the Dartmoor National Park, adjacent to the picturesque Burrator Reservoir. Fishing licences available. Splendid walking country, stabling & grazing on-site. The Flints offer a warm welcome into their home which has been recently tastefully refurbished. 5 bedrooms, 3 en-suite & 1 with private bathroom, each with colour T.V., radio & 'phone. Guest lounge. Secluded garden with 21 acres.	£20.00 CREDIT CARD VISA M'CARD	Y	N	Y

All the establishments mentioned in this guide are members of
The Worldwide Bed & Breakfast Association

When booking your accommodation please mention
The Best Bed & Breakfast

Dorset

Dorset
(West Country)

The unspoilt nature of this gem of a county is emphasised by the designation of virtually all of the coast & much of the inland country as an Area of Outstanding Natural Beauty. Along the coast from Christchurch to Lyme Regis there are a fascinating variety of sandy beaches, towering cliffs & single banks, whilst inland is a rich mixture of downland, lonely heaths, fertile valleys, historic houses & lovely villages of thatch & mellow stone buildings.

Thomas Hardy was born here & took the Dorset countryside as a background for many of his novels. Few writers can have stamped their identity on a county more than Hardy on Dorset, forever to be known as the "Hardy Country". Fortunately most of the area that he so lovingly described remains unchanged, including Egdon Heath & the county town of Dorchester, famous as Casterbridge.

In the midst of the rolling chalk hills which stretch along the Storr Valley lies picturesque Cerne Abbas, with its late mediaeval houses & cottages & the ruins of a Benedictine Abbey. At Godmanstone is the tiny thatched "Smiths Arms" claiming to be the smallest pub in England.

The north of the county is pastoral with lovely views over broad Blackmoor Vale. Here is the ancient hilltop town of Shaftesbury, with cobbled Gold Hill, one of the most photographed streets in the country.

Coastal Dorset is spectacular. Poole harbour is an enormous, almost circular bay, an exciting mixture of 20th century activity, ships of many nations & beautiful building of the 15th, 18th & early 19th centuries.

Westwards lies the popular resort of Swanage, where the sandy beach & sheltered bay are excellent for swimming. From here to Weymouth is a marvellous stretch of coast with scenic wonders like Lulworth Cove & the arch of Durdle Door.

Chesil Beach is an extraordinary bank of graded pebbles, as perilous to shipping today as it was 1,000 years ago. It is separated from the mainland by a sheltered lagoon known as the Fleet. From here a range of giant cliffs rises to 617 feet at Golden Gap & stretches westwards to Lyme Regis, beloved by Jane Austen who wrote "Persuasion" whilst living here.

Dorset has many interesting archaeological features. Near Dorchester is Maiden Castle, huge earthwork fortifications on a site first inhabited 6,000 years ago. The Badbury rings wind round a wooded hilltop near Wimborne Minster; legend has it that King Arthur's soul, in the form of a raven, inhabited this "dread" wood. The giant of Cerne Abbas is a figure of a man 180 feet high carved into the chalk hillside. Long associated with fertility there is still speculation about the figures' origins, one theory suggesting it is a Romano-British depiction of Hercules. A Roman amphitheatre can be seen at Dorchester, & today's road still follows the Roman route to Weymouth.

Corfe Castle.

Dorset

Dorset
Gazeteer

Areas of outstanding natural beauty.
The Entire County.

Houses & Castles

Athelthampton
Mediaeval house - one of the finest in all England. Formal gardens.

Barneston Manor - Nr. Church Knowle
13th - 16th century stone built manor house.

Forde Abbey - Nr. Chard
12th century Cistercian monastery - noted Mortlake tapestries.

Manor House - Sandford Orcas
Mansion of Tudor period, furnished with period furniture, antiques, silver, china, glass, paintings.

Hardy's Cottage - Higher Bockampton
Birthplace of Thomas Hardy, author (1840-1928).

Milton Abbey - Nr. Blandford
18th century Georgian house built on original site of 15th century abbey.

Purse Caundle Manor - Purse Caundle
Mediaeval Manor - furnished in style of period.

Parnham House - Beaminster
Tudor Manor - some later work by Nash. Leaded windows & heraldic plasterwork. Home of John Makepeace & the International School for Craftsmen in Wood. House, gardens & workshops.

Sherborne Castle - Sherborne
16th century mansion - continuously occupied by Digby family.

No. 3 Trinity Street - Weymouth
Tudor cottages now converted into one house, furnished 17th century.

Smedmore - Kimmeridge
18th century manor.

Wolfeton House - Dorchester
Mediaeval & Elizabethan Manor. Fine stone work, great stair. 17th century furniture - Jacobean ceilings & fireplaces.

Cathedrals & Churches

Bere Regis (St. John the Baptist)
12th century foundation - enlarged in 13th & 15th centuries.
Timber roof & nave, fine arcades.
16th century seating.

Blandford (St. Peter & St. Paul)
18th century - ashlar - Georgian design. Galleries, pulpit, box pews, font & mayoral seat.

Bradford Abbas (St. Mary)
14th century - parapets & pinnacled tower, panelled roof. 15th century bench ends, stone rood screen. 17th century pulpit.

Cerne Abbas (St. Mary)
13th century - rebuilt 15th & 16th centuries, 14th century wall paintings, 15th century tower, stone screen, pulpit possibly 11th century.

Chalbury (dedication unknown)
13th century origin - 14th century east windows, timber bellcote. Plastered walls, box pews, 3-decker pulpit, west gallery.

Christchurch (Christ Church)
Norman nave - ribbed plaster vaulting - perpendicular spire. Tudor renaissance Salisbury chantry - screen with Tree of Jesse: notable misericord seats.

Milton Abbey (Sts. Mary, Michael, Sampson & Branwaleder)
14th century pulpitum & sedilla, 15th century reredos & canopy, 16th century monument, Milton effigies 1775.

Sherborne (St. Mary)
Largely Norman but some Saxon remains - excellent fan vaulting, of nave & choir. 12th & 13th century effigies - 15th century painted glass.

Studland (St. Nicholas)
12th century - best Norman church in the country. 12th century font, 13th century east windows.

Whitchurch Canonicorum (St. Candida & Holy Cross)
12th & 13th century. 12th century font, relics of patroness in 13th century shrine, 15th century painted glass, 15th century tower.

Wimbourne Minster (St. Cuthberga)
12th century central tower & arcade, otherwise 13th-15th century. Former collegiate church. Georgian glass, some Jacobean stalls & screen. Monuments & famed clock of 14th century.

Yetminster (St. Andrew)
13th century chancel - 15th century rebuilt with embattled parapets. 16th century brasses & seating.

Dorset

Museums & Galleries

Abbey Ruins - Shaftesbury
Relics excavated from Benedictine
Nunnery founded by Alfred the Great.
Russell-Cotes Art Gallery & Museum -
Bournemouth
17th-20th century oil paintings,
watercolours, sculptures, ceramics,
miniatures, etc.
Rothesay Museum - Bournemouth
English porcelain, 17th century furniture,
collection of early Italian paintings, arms &
armour, ethnography, etc.
**Bournemouth Natural Science
Society's Museum**
Archaeology & local natural history.
Brewery Farm Museum - Milton Abbas
Brewing & village bygones from Dorset.
Dorset County Museum - Dorchester
Geology, natural history, pre-history.
Thomas Hardy memorabilia
Philpot Museum - Lyme Regis
Old documents & prints, fossils, lace & old
fire engine.
Guildhall Museum - Poole
Social & civic life of Poole during 18th &
19th centuries displayed in two-storey
Georgian market house.
Scapolen's Court - Poole
14th century house of local merchant

exhibiting local & archaeological history of
town, also industrial archaeology.
Sherborne Museum - Sherborne
Local history & geology - abbey of AD
705, Sherborne missal AD 1400, 18th
century local silk industry.
Gallery 24 - Shaftesbury
Art exhibitions - paintings, pottery, etc.
Red House Museum & Art Gallery -
Christchurch
Natural history & antiques of the region.
Georgian house with herb garden.
Priest's House Museum - Wimbourne
Minster
Tudor building in garden exhibiting local
archaeology & history.

Other things to see & do

Abbotsbury Swannery - Abbotsbury
Unique colony of Swans established by
monks in the 14th century. 16th century
duck decoy, reed walk, information centre.
Dorset Rare Breeds Centre - Park Farm,
Gillingham
Poole Potteries - the Quay, Poole
Sea Life Centre - Weymouth
Variety of displays, including Ocean
Tunnel, sharks, living "touch" pools.

West Bay.

DORSET
Map reference

1	O'Rouke	14	C. Smith
2	Thompson	15	Griffin
3	Edwards	16	T. Norman
3	W. Smith	16	Lake
3	Du Faur	17	Bryceson
4	Walker	18	Bradley-Watson
5	Davies	19	W. Norman
6	Diment	20	Ingleton
7	Vear	21	Eley
8	Swann	22	Partridge
9	Millorit	23	Hookham-Bassett
10	McCarthy	24	Newson-Smith
10	Buncall	25	Kerridge
11	Hipwell	26	Pow
12	Tomblin	27	Gregory
13	Haggert	28	Turnbull
		29	Spender

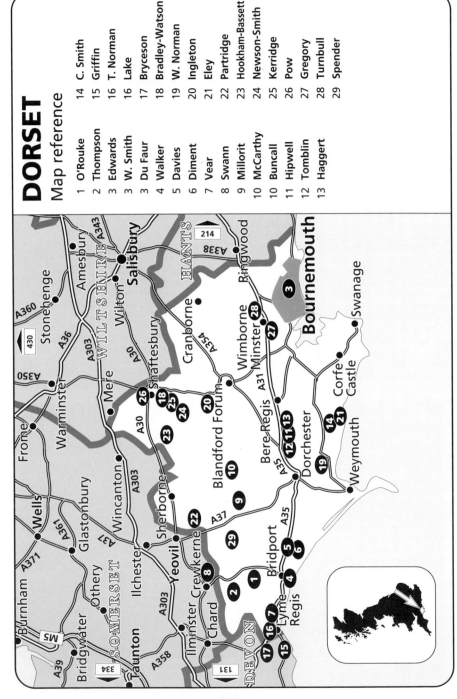

Dorset

		rate from £ per person	children taken	evening meals	animals taken
Michael J. O'Rourke **The Lodge Country House** **Beaminster** **DT8 3BL** **Tel: (01308) 863468** **Open: ALL YEAR** **Map Ref No. 01**	Nearest Road: A.3066 The Lodge is a fine Grade II listed Georgian house on the edge of the charming town of Beaminster. The interior is particularly interesting, retaining all the original features. There are 5 very attractive en-suite/private bedrooms. The kitchen provides good English home-cooking, most of the ingredients coming from the kitchen garden. There are 2 all-weather tennis courts & a swimming pool for your enjoyment. A friendly welcome awaits you from your host. Children over 12.	£25.00 *see PHOTO over* CREDIT CARD VISA M'CARD	Y	N	Y
Judy Thompson **Higher Langdon** **Beaminster** **DT8 3NN** **Tel: (01308) 862537** **Fax 01308 862537** **Open: ALL YEAR** **Map Ref No. 02**	Nearest Road: A.356 Imagine a haven of tranquillity where in summer skylarks soar & in the autumn the landscape is a riot of reds, russets & ochre hues. Higher Langdon is a spacious & homely working farm, set in acres of rolling countryside. Offering a relaxed, informal atmosphere, combined with traditional farmhouse cooking & charming accommodation (2 guest rooms with en-suite/private facilities). Easy access to Beaminster, Bridport, Dorchester & Weymouth. Evening meals by arrangement.	£20.00	Y	Y	N
Alan & Jackie Edwards **Gervis Court Hotel** **38 Gervis Road** **East Cliff** **Bournemouth BH1 3DH** **Tel: (01202) 556871** **Fax 01202 556871** **Open: ALL YEAR** **Map Ref No. 03**	Nearest Road: A.338 Gervis Court is a family-run, licensed hotel, set among the pines on the fashionable East Cliff, 2 mins from the cliff top, cliff lift & sea. Each bedroom is en-suite, tastefully furnished with comfort in mind, & has modern amenities, including T.V. & tea/coffee-making facilities. Many are situated on the ground floor. An ideal place to visit the beautiful Dorset countryside, yet only a short walk to the theatres, cinemas, pier & gardens - & the town centre, with its fashionable shops. Activity breaks available.	£18.00 CREDIT CARD VISA M'CARD	Y	N	N
Jo & Bill Smith **Silver Trees** **57 Wimborne Road** **Bournemouth BH3 7AL** **Tel: (01202) 556040** **Fax 01202 556040** **Open: ALL YEAR** **Map Ref No. 03**	Nearest Road: A.347 A charming Victorian house standing in its own wooded grounds, with sweeping lawns, colourful flowers & shrubs. Offering comfortable accommodation in 5 en-suite bedrooms with colour T.V.. Breakfast is cooked to order in the elegant dining room overlooking the garden. Early morning tea & refreshments are available on request & served in your room, or in the lounge. Ideally located for visiting the New Forest & Dorset. **E-mail: billsmith@zetnet.co.uk**	£21.00 CREDIT CARD VISA M'CARD AMEX	N	N	N
Jean & Colin Du Faur **Sandhurst Private Hotel** **16 Southern Road** **Southbourne** **Bournemouth BH6 3SR** **Tel: (01202) 423748** **Open: MAR - OCT** **Map Ref No. 03**	Nearest Road: A.35 Guests' comfort is a priority at this friendly, welcoming hotel. There's a choice of 8 comfortable rooms. 5 of these large rooms (incl. a ground-floor one) have private facilities. All have colour T.V. & tea/coffee makers. Good home-cooked breakfasts, & evening meals available. Situated 2 mins from the beach in a quiet suburb of Bournemouth. An ideal centre for touring, with Christchurch, Beaulieu, the New Forest, Salisbury & Dorchester a short drive. Private parking.	£17.00	Y	Y	N

The Lodge. Beaminster.

Dorset

		rate from £ per person	children taken	evening meals	animals taken
Ann & Dan Walker MHCIMA **Britmead House** **West Bay Road** **Bridport** **DT6 4EG** **Tel: (01308) 422941** **Fax 01308 422516** **Open: ALL YEAR** **Map Ref No. 04**	Nearest Road: A.35 A friendly welcome in a relaxed & comfortable atmosphere. Renowned for good food, a high standard of facilities, personal service & attention to detail. Situated between Bridport, the fishing harbour of West Bay, Chesil Beach & the Dorset Coastal Path. 7 individually decorated en-suite bedrooms, 1 ground floor, all with T.V., tea facilities & hairdryer. South-facing lounge & dining room overlook the garden & open countryside beyond. Optional dinner, incorporating local fish & produce. Licensed. Parking. Children over 5.	£20.00 CREDIT CARD VISA M'CARD AMEX	Y	Y	Y
Sydney & Jayne Davies **Innsacre Farmhouse** **Shipton Gorge** **Bridport** **DT6 4LJ** **Tel: (01308) 456137** **Fax 01308 456137** **Open: ALL YEAR (Excl. Xmas)** **Map Ref No. 05**	Nearest Road: A.35 Innsacre is a 17th-century farmhouse plus barns, hidden midway between Lyme Regis & Dorchester, 3 miles from the sea & N.T. coastal path. A magical & peaceful setting, south-facing, with 10 acres of spinneys, steep hillsides, orchards & lawns. All rooms are en-suite, with antique French. (Each room has a T.V. & tea tray.) Large sitting-room with inglenook fireplace - log fires, beams & delicious breakfasts. An easy atmosphere. Evening meals unavailable on Saturdays from Easter to Oct. Children over 9.	£29.00 CREDIT CARD VISA M'CARD	Y	Y	Y
Mrs Sue Diment **Rudge Farm** **Chilcombe** **Bridport DT6 4NF** **Tel: (01308) 482630** **Fax 01308 482635** **Open: MAR - OCT** **Map Ref No. 06**	Nearest Road: A.35 Rudge Farm is peacefully situated on a gentle south-facing slope overlooking the beautiful Bride Valley, just over 2 miles from the sea. After a day spent exploring the lovely West Dorset countryside, relax in this comfortable Victorian farmhouse before trying one of the excellent pubs or restaurants. The large attractively furnished rooms are all en-suite, with T.V., tea tray & far-reaching views. Children over 10 years. E-mail: rudge@wdi.co.uk	£22.00	Y	N	N
Anne & Vernon Vear **Newlands House** **Stonebarrow Lane** **Charmouth DT6 6RA** **Tel: (01297) 560212** **Open: MAR - OCT** **Map Ref No. 07**	Nearest Road: A.35 A house of character set in about 2 acres of garden & orchard on the eastern fringe of Charmouth village. Offering good food & wines, comfort & an ambience of quiet relaxation. There is no smoking, except in the bar lounge. Ample car parking. Newlands House is surrounded by an Area of Outstanding Natural Beauty, & is perfect either for walking & or as a centre for touring. Children over 6 yrs.	£23.75	Y	Y	N
Gillian & Robert Swann **Broadview Gardens** **East Crewkerne** **Crewkerne TA18 7AG** **Tel: (01460) 73424** **Fax 01460 73424** **Open: ALL YEAR** **Map Ref No. 08**	Nearest Road: A.30 Unusual Colonial bungalow built in an era of quality. Achieving top-quality awards for comfort, cooking & friendliness. Carefully furnished in the Edwardian style. En-suite rooms overlooking an acre of beautiful gardens. All bedrooms with T.V., tea facilities, hairdryer, easy chairs & fans. Traditional English home-cooking. Perfect touring base for country & garden lovers, N.T. houses, antique enthusiasts, moors & quaint old villages. Dorset coast 20 mins. List of 50 places provided.	£25.00 *see PHOTO over* CREDIT CARD VISA M'CARD	Y	Y	Y

Broadview. Crewkerne.

Dorset

		rate from £ per person	children taken	evening meals	animals taken
Anita & Andre Millorit **Brambles, Woolcombe** **Melbury Bubb** **Dorchester DT2 0NJ** **Tel: (01935) 83672** **Fax 01935 83003** **Open: ALL YEAR (Excl. Xmas)** **Map Ref No. 09**	Nearest Road: A.37 Set in beautiful, tranquil countryside, Brambles is a pretty thatched cottage offering every comfort, superb views & a friendly welcome. There is a choice of of en-suite twin, double or single rooms, all having colour T.V. & tea/coffee-making facilities. Pretty garden available for relaxing. Full English or Continental breakfast served. There are many interesting places to visit & wonderful walks for enthusiasts. Children over 1 year welcome.	£20.00 *see PHOTO over*	Y	N	N
Rupert & Annette McCarthy **Rew Cottage** **Buckland Newton** **Dorchester** **DT2 7DN** **Tel: (01300) 345467** **Open: JAN - Mid DEC** **Map Ref No. 10**	Nearest Road: A.352 A warm welcome awaits you in a peaceful cottage in the heart of Hardy's Dorset. Surrounded by green farmland with lovely views on all sides. An ideal centre for walking or touring & within easy reach of Sherborne, Dorchester & the sea. Bedrooms are comfortably furnished; double, twin & single rooms (with tea/coffee facilities & T.V.). 2 private bathrooms adjacent. Attractive pubs within easy reach for evening meals. Children & animals by arrangement.	£19.00	Y	N	Y
Mrs Tia Bunkall **Holyleas House** **Buckland Newton** **Dorchester** **DT2 7DP** **Tel: (01300) 345214** **Open: ALL YEAR** **Map Ref No. 10**	Nearest Road: A.37 Holyleas House is an attractive home set in a pretty garden. It is tastefully decorated throughout in a country-house style & is elegantly furnished to the highest standard. Accommodation is in 3 delightful bedrooms which are light & airy & comfortable & have tea/coffee-making facilities. (2 with private bathroom.) A delicious breakfast & good evening meals are served in the attractive dining room. Wood fires in winter. A charming home, ideally placed for exploring Devon. Evening meals by arrangement.	£20.00 🚭	Y	N	Y
Anthea & Michael Hipwell **The Old Vicarage** **Affpuddle** **Dorchester DT2 7HH** **Tel/Fax: (01305) 848315** **Open: ALL YEAR (Excl. Xmas & New Year)** **Map Ref No. 11**	Nearest Road: A.35, B.3390 The Old Vicarage is a traditional country house standing in a large mature garden in the charming Piddle Valley, at the heart of the Dorset countryside. Accommodation is in 3 comfortable & attractively furnished rooms, each with private bathroom; all facilities are at hand, at your request. Your hosts will be pleased to help with advice on the numerous places of interest & places to dine. (Evening meals are offered during the winter & only by arrangement.) Children over 10 years.	£22.50	Y	Y	N
Marian Tomblin **Lower Lewell Farmhouse** **West Stafford** **Dorchester** **DT2 8AP** **Tel: (01305) 267169** **Open: ALL YEAR** **Map Ref No. 12**	Nearest Road: A.35, A.352 Lower Lewell Farmhouse dates from the 17th century, & is situated in the delightful Frome Valley in the midst of Thomas Hardy country. Indeed, the house is reputed to be the Talbothays Dairy portrayed in Hardy's novel 'Tess of the D'Urbervilles'. 3 bedrooms are available, equipped with tea/coffee-making facilities, & a full English breakfast is served. There is a sitting room with colour T.V.. A delightful touring centre.	£18.00	Y	N	N

Brambles. Woolcombe.

Dorset

		rate from £ per person	children taken	evening meals	animals taken
Mrs D. M. Haggett **Vartrees House** **Moreton** **Dorchester** **DT2 8BE** **Tel: (01305) 852704** **Open: ALL YEAR** **Map Ref No. 13**	Nearest Road: B.3390 off A.35 Peaceful & secluded character country house set in 3 acres of picturesque woodland gardens. Built by Hermann Lea, friend of Thomas Hardy. Accommodation throughout is spacious & comfortable. Tea/coffee makers in all 3 rooms, 1 en-suite. T.V. lounge. Situated near the pretty village of Moreton, with its renowned church & burial place of Lawrence of Arabia. Coast 4 miles. Station 1/4 of mile. Excellent local pubs. Children over 10 years welcome.	£18.00	Y	N	Y
Charles & Jennie Smith **Manor House** **Winfrith Newburgh** **Dorchester** **DT2 8JR** **Tel: (01305) 852988** **Fax 01305 854988** **Open: ALL YEAR** **Map Ref No. 14**	Nearest Road: A.352 This much-loved manor house with large walled garden is near Lulworth Cove, a spectacular coast path & Hardy Country. A Jacobean staircase ascends to the Green Room with a large double bed, 18th-century panelling & an en-suite bathroom with roll-top bath. The Victorian Room has twin brass beds with a private shower room adjacent. Both have T.V., tea-making facilities & antique furniture. A self-contained wing also available. 2 nearby pubs serve excellent evening meals. Min. stay 2 nights.	£21.00 (no smoking)	Y	N	N
Geoffrey & Elizabeth Griffin **Willow Cottage** **Ware Lane** **Lyme Regis** **DT7 3EL** **Tel: (01297) 443199** **Open: ALL YEAR (Excl. Xmas)** **Map Ref No. 15**	Nearest Road: A.3052 Willow Cottage enjoys tranquillity & unrivalled views over N.T. pastureland & coastline. Within 200 yards is the south-west coast path, & a short cliff-top walk brings you to the Cobb, Lyme's ancient harbour. The double-bedded en-suite room has colour T.V. & tea-making facilities. For a third member of a party, there is an adjacent single room. Both rooms command splendid sea views & the main room opens onto a sun balcony. Children over 8 years.	£21.00	Y	N	N
Tony & Vicky Norman **The Red House** **Sidmouth Road** **Lyme Regis DT7 3ES** **Tel: (01297) 442055** **Fax 01297 442055** **Open: MAR - NOV** **Map Ref No. 16**	Nearest Road: A.3052 This distinguished house, set in mature grounds, enjoys spectacular coastal views, & yet is only a short walk to the centre of Lyme Regis. The 3 en-suite bedrooms (1 for family use; 2 are especially spacious) are furnished with every comfort, including tea/coffee, T.V., clock-radio, desk, armchairs, a drink refrigerator, central heating & electric heaters. Fresh flowers & magazines are among the little extras. Breakfast can be taken on the garden balcony. Parking. Children over 8.	£20.00 (no smoking) CREDIT CARD VISA	Y	N	N
Mrs Diana Lake **Rashwood Lodge** **Clappentail Lane** **Lyme Regis DT7 3LZ** **Tel: (01297) 445700** **Open: FEB - NOV** **Map Ref No. 16**	Nearest Road: A.3052, A.35 Rashwood Lodge is an unusual octagonal house, located on the western hillside with views over Lyme Bay. Just a short walk away is the coastal footpath & Ware Cliff, famed for its part in 'The French Lieutenant's Woman'. The bedrooms have their own facilities & benefit from their south-facing aspect overlooking a large & colourful garden set in peaceful surroundings. Golf course 1 mile. A charming home. Children over 4 years.	£20.00 (no smoking)	Y	N	N

Dorset

	rate from £ per person	children taken	evening meals	animals taken
Andrew & Katie Bryceson **Amherst Lodge Farm** **Uplyme** **Lyme Regis DT7 3XH** **Tel: (01297) 442773** Fax 01297 442625 Open: ALL YEAR (Excl. Xmas) Map Ref No. 17 Nearest Road: A.35 Originally a Devon long house, converted in the 20's in 'the grand manner', Amherst Lodge Farm lies in a wooded valley with trout lakes, Jacob sheep & an abundance of wildlife. The River Lyme runs through the old established & informal garden extending to 2 acres of maples, rhododendrons & orchard. There are 3 bedrooms, all with en-suite bathrooms, colour T.V. & tea/coffee-making facilities. Children over 13 yrs. **E-mail: 100530.77@compuserve.com**	£22.00	N	N	N
Joyce & Bill Norman **Dingle Dell** **Church Lane** **Osmington DT3 6EW** **Tel: (01305) 832378** Fax 01305 832378 Open: MAR - OCT Map Ref No. 19 Nearest Road: A.353 Dingle Dell is situated on the edge of the village of Osmington, in its own charming garden, with roses covering the mellow stone walls. 2 spacious & comfortable bedrooms (1 en-suite), furnished to the highest of standards, & with each overlooking the garden & countryside. Both rooms have T.V. & tea/coffee. A generous English breakfast is served. Dingle Dell provides a truly peaceful spot to rest & relax, & is a convenient base for exploring the many attractions of Dorset.	£19.50 (no smoking)	N	N	N
Richard & Tavy Bradley-Watson **Melbury Mill** **Melbury Abbas** **Shaftesbury** **SP7 0DB** **Tel: (01747) 852163** Open: ALL YEAR Map Ref No. 18 Nearest Road: A.350, A.30 Mr & Mrs Bradley-Watson offer a warm welcome at this old working mill, set in 9 acres of meadows & overlooking a mill pond abounding with waterfowl. All bedrooms are large & centrally heated, & have en-suite facilities. Located just south of Shaftesbury, famous for its Gold Hill, it is in picturesque Thomas Hardy countryside. Ideal for walkers, with N.T. downland & the properties of Stourhead & Kingston Lacy close by. 3-course dinners are provided using fresh local produce. An ideal base for a short-break holiday.	£22.50 *see PHOTO over*	Y	Y	N
Tim & Lucy Kerridge **The Old Forge** **Compton Abbas** **Shaftesbury SP7 0NQ** **Tel: (01747) 811881** Fax 01747 811881 Open: ALL YEAR Map Ref No. 25 Nearest Road: A.350 The Old Forge, dating back to the 1700s, is a building full of local history. The blacksmith's forge has been restored as a museum of a traditonal Dorset rural blacksmith. Set in an Area of Outstanding Natural Beauty, it is ideally placed for exploring Hardy's Wessex & many N.T. properties including Stourhead, Corfe Castle & Brownsea Island are all within easy distance. There are 3 elegantly furnished & well-appointed bedrooms, 2 with an en-suite/private bathroom.	£20.00 (no smoking)	Y	N	N
Mr & Mrs D. J. Pow **Cliff House** **Breach Lane** **Shaftesbury SP7 8LF** **Tel: (01747) 852548** Fax 01747 852548 Open: ALL YEAR Map Ref No. 26 Nearest Road: A.30 A fine example of a spacious Grade II listed period property with quiet rooms. Within walking distance of the ancient Saxon hilltop town which is one of the oldest & highest in southern England, having magnificent views & the famous Gold Hill. An ideal central position for visiting the surrounding countryside of Wessex which abounds with historic country houses, cathedrals & abbeys. Many good pubs & restaurants locally. 2 bedrooms, with private/en-suite bathrooms. Children over 5.	£21.00 (no smoking)	Y	N	N

Melbury Mill. Melbury Abbas.

Manor Farmhouse. Yetminster.

Dorset

	rate from £ per person	children taken	evening meals	animals taken

Mrs Ann Partridge **Manor Farmhouse** **High Street** **Yetminster** **Sherborne DT9 6LF** **Tel: (01935) 872247** **Open: ALL YEAR** **Map Ref No. 22**	Nearest Road: A.37 This 17th-century farmhouse, with oak panelling, beams & inglenook fireplaces, offers every comfort to the discerning visitor. 4 bedrooms, all with private facilities & modern amenities, including T.V. & tea/coffee. Delicious meals served, made from traditional recipes & using fresh local produce. The village is described as the best 17th-century stone-built village in the south of England. An excellent centre for visiting Sherborne, Glastonbury, New Forest & Hardy's Dorset.	£25.00 *see PHOTO over* CREDIT CARD VISA M'CARD	N	Y	N
Jill & Ken Hookham-Bassett **Stourcastle Lodge** **Gough's Close** **Sturminster Newton** **DT10 1BU** **Tel: (01258) 472320** **Fax 01258 473381** **Open: ALL YEAR** **Map Ref No. 23**	Nearest Road: A.357 Stourcastle Lodge is a family-run business, offering a very high standard of accommodation, with personal service & excellent cuisine. A superb breakfast is served in the attractive dining room. Each of the elegant bedrooms are south-facing & overlook the delightful garden, which is stocked full of herbaceous & perennial borders. Stourcastle Lodge is a beautiful home, & an ideal base for exploring Dorset & its many attractions.	£26.50 *see PHOTO over* CREDIT CARD VISA M'CARD	Y	Y	N
Mary-Ann Newson-Smith **Lovells Court, Marnhull** **Sturminster Newton** **DT10 1JJ** **Tel: (01258) 820652** **Fax 01258 820487** **Open: ALL YEAR** **Map Ref No. 24**	Nearest Road: A.30, A.303 Lovells Court is a rambling old house of character, set in the delightful countryside of Thomas Hardy, & with fine views across the Blackmore Vale. The market town of Sturminster Newton & the Abbeys of Sherborne & Milton Abbas are nearby. An excellent base for enjoying rural Dorset & its many N.T. properties. There are 2 en-suite rooms & 1 with private bathroom, all with T.V., radio & tea-making facilities. 2 excellent village inns for food all year round. Children over 12 years.	£23.00	Y	N	N
J. Ingleton **Fiddleford Millhouse** **Fiddleford** **Sturminster Newton** **DT10 2BX** **Tel: (01258) 472786** **Open: ALL YEAR** **Map Ref No. 20**	Nearest Road: A.357 An idyllically situated, Grade I listed 16th-century farm/manor house of great architectural interest overlooking the River Stour in peacefully secluded countryside. A beautifully furnished & decorated family home. 3 large, comfortable bedrooms, 1 with a 16th-century moulded plaster ceiling & en-suite bathroom, the other 2 sharing a bathroom. All have tea facilities & T.V.. A beautiful garden with a sitting area. 2 pubs within easy walking distance. Country pursuits available locally.	£17.50	N	N	N
Tony & Mary Eley **Gatton House** **West Lulworth** **Wareham BH20 5RU** **Tel: (01929) 400252** **Fax 01929 400252** **Open: MAR - SEPT** **Map Ref No. 21**	Nearest Road: A.352 Spectacularly positioned, quiet & comfortable, this small hotel is set amongst the Purbeck Hills, yet only a strolling distance from famous Lulworth Cove. There are lovely lounge areas, a breakfast room & attractive bedrooms. Outside, the terrace provides a perfect venue for morning coffee or afternoon tea. Gatton House is an ideal location for walking or touring Dorset's beauty spots, & it is within easy reach of Bournemouth, Poole, Swanage, Dorchester & Weymouth.	£22.50 CREDIT CARD VISA M'CARD	Y	N	Y

Stourcastle Lodge. Sturminster Newton.

Dorset

		rate from £ per person	children taken	evening meals	animals taken
Mrs Margaret Gregory **Ashton Lodge** **10 Oakley Hill** **Wimborne BH21 1QH** **Tel: (01202) 883423** **Fax 01202 886180** **Open: ALL YEAR** **Map Ref No. 27**	Nearest Road: A.31 A detached family residence with a relaxed family atmosphere. The dining room overlooks an attractively-laid-out garden. Full English breakfast is a speciality. 2 of the 4 bedrooms have en-suite facilities, & all have colour T.V., tea/coffee-making facilities & hairdryers. Ironing facilities are available on request, & packed lunches can be arranged with prior notice. Ashton Lodge is conveniently placed for the coast, New Forest & cross channel ferries.	£20.00 CREDIT CARD VISA M'CARD	Y	N	N
Sara & John Turnbull **Thornhill** **Holt** **Wimborne** **BH21 7DJ** **Tel: (01202) 889434** **Open: ALL YEAR** **Map Ref No. 28**	Nearest Road: A.31 Visitors are warmly welcomed to this large, thatched family house located in rural surroundings 3 1/2 miles from Wimborne. Large garden. Hard tennis court available. Double, twin & single rooms. 1 private bathroom, & another which may be shared. Sitting room with colour T.V. & coffee/tea-making & laundry facilities. Plenty of good local pubs. Well situated for exploring the coast, New Forest & Salisbury area.	£20.00	N	N	N
Mr & Mrs Peter Spender **Halstock Mill** **Halstock** **Yeovil BA22 9SJ** **Tel: (01935) 891278** **Fax 01935 891278** **Open: ALL YEAR (Excl. Xmas)** **Map Ref No. 29**	Nearest Road: A.37 At the end of a 1/2-mile private lane is 17th-century Halstock Mill. The 400 acres of pastureland surrounding it ensure a peaceful, relaxing stay. Accommodation is in 4 spacious en-suite bedrooms with colour T.V. & tea/coffee makers. The beamed drawing room has an inglenook log fire. Jane offers a superb 4-course dinner (by arrangement), prepared with home/local produce. An ideal base for touring Dorset, Somerset & Devon. Children over 5 years.	£24.00 *see PHOTO over* CREDIT CARD VISA M'CARD AMEX	Y	Y	Y

When booking your accommodation please mention
The Best Bed & Breakfast

Halstock Mill. Halstock.

Essex

Essex
(East Anglia)

Essex is a county of commerce, busy roads & busier towns, container ports & motorways, yet it is also a landscape of mudflats & marshes, of meadows & leafy lanes, villages & duckponds. Half timbered buildings & thatched & clapboard cottages stand among rolling hills topped by orange brick windmills.

The coast on the east, now the haunt of wildfowl, sea-birds, sailors & fishermen has seen the arrival of Saxons, Romans, Danes, Vikings & Normans. The names of their settlements remain - Wivenhoe, Layer-de-la-Haye, Colchester & Saffron Walden - the original Saxon name was Walden, but the Saffron was added when the crocus used for dyes & flavouring was grown here in the 15th century.

The seaside resorts of Southend & Clacton are bright & cheery, much-loved by families for safe beaches. Harbours here are great favourites with anglers & yachtsmen.

Inland lie the watermeadows & windmills, willows & cool green water which shaped the life & work of John Constable, one of the greatest landscape painters. Scenes are instantly recognisable today as you walk to Dedham along the banks of the swiftly flowing River Stour.

Colchester is England's oldest recorded town, once the Roman capital of Britain trading in corn & cattle, slaves & pearls. Roman remains are still to be seen & their original street plan is the basis of much of modern Colchester. A great feast is held here annually to celebrate the famous oyster - the "Colchester native".

South Essex, though sliced through by the M.25 motorway is still a place of woodland & little rivers. The ancient trees of Epping Forest, hunting ground for generations of monarchs, spread 6,000 acres of leafy glades & heathland into the London suburbs.

Audley End. Saffron Walden.

Essex

Essex
Gazeteer
Areas of outstanding natural beauty.
Dedham Vale (part), Epping Forest.

Houses & Castles
Audley End House - Saffron Walden
1603 - Jacobean mansion on site of
Benedictine Abbey. State rooms & Hall.
Castle House - Dedham
Home of the late Sir A. Munnings.
President R.A. Paintings & other works.
Hedingham Castle - Castle Hedingham
Norman keep & Tudor bridge.
Layer Marney Tower - Nr. Colchester
1520 Tudor brick house. 8 storey gate
tower. Formal yew hedges & lawns.
Payecock's - Coggeshall
1500 - richly ornamented - merchant's
house - National Trust.
St. Osyth's Priory - St. Osyth
Was Augustinian Abbey for 400 years until
dissolution in 1537, 13th-18th century
buildings. 13th century chapel. Wonderful
gatehouse containing works of art
including ceramics & Chinese Jade.
Spains Hall - Finchingfield
Elizabethan Manor incorporating parts of
earlier timber structure. Paintings,
furniture & tapestries.

Cathedrals & Churches
Brightlingsea (All Saints)
15th century tower - some mediaeval
painting fragments. Brasses.
Castle Hedingham (St. Nicholas)
12th century doorways, 14th century rood
screen, 15th century stalls, 16th century
hammer beams, altar tomb.
Copford (St. Michael & All Angels)
12th century wall paints. Continuous
vaulted nave & chancel
.**Finchingfield** (St. John the Baptist)
Norman workmanship. 16th century tomb
-18th centuary tower & cupola.
Layer Marney (St. Mary)
Tudor brickwork, Renaissance
monuments, mediaeval screens, wall
paintings.
Little Maplestead (St. John the Baptist)
14th century, one of the five round

churches in England, having hexagonal
nave, circular aisle, 14th century arcade.
Newport (St. Mary the Virgin)
13th century. Interesting 13th century
altar (portable) with top which becomes
reredos when opened. 15th century
chancel screen. Pre-Reformation Lectern.
Some old glass.

Museums & Galleries
Dutch Cottage Museum - Canvey Island
17th century thatched cottage of octagonal
Dutch design. Exhibition of models of
shipping used on the Thames through the
ages.
Ingatestone Hall - Ingatestone
Documents & pictures of Essex.
The Castle - Colchester
Norman Keep now exhibiting
archeological material from Essex &
especially Roman Colchester.
Southchurch Hall - Southend-on-Sea
14th century moated & timber framed
manor house - Tudor wing, furnished as
meiaeval manor.
Thurrock - Grays
Prehistoric, Romano-British & pagan
Saxon archaeology.

Other things to see & do
Colchester Oyster Fishery - Colchester
Tour showing cultivating, harvesting,
grading & packing of oysters. Talk, tour
& sample.

Burnham on Crouch.

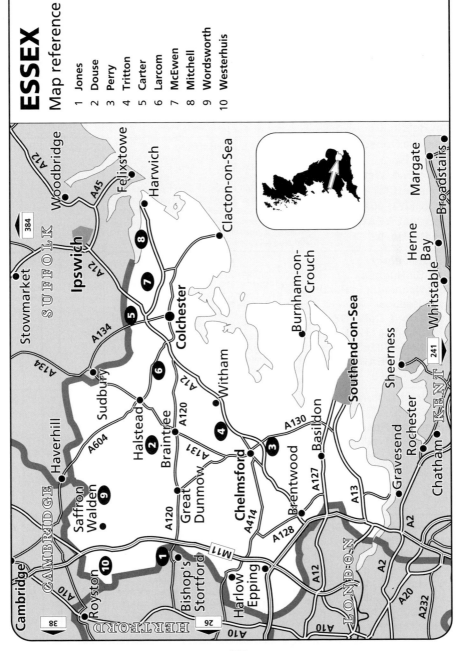

ESSEX

Map reference

1 Jones
2 Douse
3 Perry
4 Tritton
5 Carter
6 Larcom
7 McEwen
8 Mitchell
9 Wordsworth
10 Westerhuis

179

Essex

		rate from £ per person	children taken	evening meals	animals taken
Peter & Rosemary Jones **The Cottage** **71 Birchanger Lane** **Birchanger** **Bishops Stortford** **CM23 3QA** **Tel/Fax: (01279) 812349** **Open: ALL YEAR (Excl. Xmas)** **Map Ref No. 01**	Nearest Road: A.120, M.11 Situated within a quiet village, this charming 17th-century listed house offers 15 comfortable en-suite bedrooms, all with colour T.V. & tea/coffee makers. Oak-panelled reception rooms with log burners, & a conservatory/dining room looking onto mature gardens. A convenient base for trips to Cambridge, London & East Anglia, & within easy reach of Stansted Airport & Bishops Stortford. Private parking available. A delightful home, ideal for a relaxing short break. CREDIT CARD VISA M'CARD	£25.00	Y	N	N
Mrs Delia Douse **Spicers Farm** **Rotten End, Wethersfield** **Braintree CM7 4AL** **Tel: (01371) 851021** **Open: ALL YEAR** **Map Ref No. 02**	Nearest Road: A.120 Rotten End is a quiet, secluded hamlet in an area designated of special landscape value. The attractive farmhouse is well-situated & offers 3 charming & comfortable en-suite bedrooms with colour T.V., tea/coffee-making facilities, clock/radio & lovely views. Enjoy a delicious breakfast in the sunny conservatory overlooking the large garden. Conveniently situated for Harwich, Stansted & Cambridge.	£16.00	Y	N	N
Mrs Glen Perry **Little Sir Hughes** **West Hanningfield Road** **Great Baddow** **Chelmsford CM2 7SZ** **Tel: (01245) 471701** **Fax 01245 473763** **Open: ALL YEAR** **Map Ref No. 03**	Nearest Road: A.1114, A.12 Little Sir Hughes is a 300 year old Grade II listed country house set in a 2 1/2 acre formal garden. Set in a very peaceful location, yet only 5 mins from A.12, 10 mins from Chelmsford & 35 mins by rail from London. All rooms are beautifully furnished & decorated. 3 double bedrooms, all en-suite & each with hairdryer, T.V., radio & tea/coffee-making facilities. Delightful guests' drawing room with colour T.V. & log fire. Superb breakfasts with homemade preserves a speciality. Evening meals on request. Parking. Children over 10.	£24.00	Y	Y	N
Mrs Linda Tritton **The Wick** **Terling Hall Road** **Hatfield Peverel** **Chelmsford CM3 2EZ** **Tel: (01245) 380705** **Open: ALL YEAR** **Map Ref No. 04**	Nearest Road: A.12 Grade II listed, 16th-century farmhouse offering a friendly, warm atmosphere in a peaceful rural setting. Large garden with ornamental herb garden, beautiful terrace & paddock with duck pond & stream. 2 comfortable twin-bedded rooms with tea-making facilities, 1 with wash basin & T.V. sharing a large bathroom. Cosy drawing room with log fire, T.V. & video. The house is delightfully decorated. Extensive breakfast menu - delicious evening meals on request. Parking.	£20.00	Y	Y	N
Col. & Mrs Jeremy Carter **Round Hill House** **Church Road** **Boxted** **Colchester CO4 5ST** **Tel/Fax: (01206) 272392** **Open: ALL YEAR** **Map Ref No. 05**	Nearest Road: A.134 Round Hill House is an attractive, comfortable house with beautiful views & a delightful garden set in Constable country overlooking the Dedham Vale. Tennis & coarse fishing available on the premises & sailing nearby. Rural East Anglia is on the doorstep with its mediaeval villages, churches & antique shops, music festivals, art galleries, great houses & gardens. Walking, racing at Newmarket, golf, riding, trout fishing & beaches within easy distance. Dinner by arrangement.	£20.00	Y	Y	Y

Essex

		rate from £ per person	children taken	evening meals	animals taken
Lady Larcom **Elm House** **14 Upper Holt Street** **Earls Colne** **Colchester CO6 2PG** **Tel: (01787) 222197** **Open:** ALL YEAR (Excl. Xmas) **Map Ref No. 06**	Nearest Road: A.604 A comfortable & welcoming 18th-century family home in a village of great architectural interest, & with a delightful, secluded garden. Imaginative cuisine using local produce. There are 3 charming bedrooms, 2 with en-suite/private bathroom. Within easy reach of Colchester (Roman walls, Norman castle), Dedham Vale (immortalised by Constable's paintings), Cambridge, Long Melford & Beth Chatto's gardens.	£19.00	Y	Y	Y
Mr & Mrs C. McEwen **Aldhams** **Bromley Road** **Lawford** **Manningtree CO11 2NE** **Tel/Fax: (01206) 393210** **Open:** ALL YEAR (Excl. Xmas) **Map Ref No. 07**	Nearest Road: A.120, A.12 Set in 3 acres of grounds, Aldhams is a fine example of a converted Queen Anne farmhouse. The charming hosts offer 3 elegantly furnished & very comfortable bedrooms, each with radio, tea/coffee-making facilities & colour T.V., 2 with en-suite bathroom. A delicious full English or Continental breakfast is served. Vegetarians catered for. Within easy reach of Colchester (Britain's oldest recorded town), Norwich, London & the beautiful Constable country.	£22.50	Y	N	N
Mrs H. P. Mitchell **New Farm House** **Spinnel's Lane** **Wix** **Manningtree CO11 2UJ** **Tel: (01255) 870365** **Fax 01255 870837** **Open: ALL YEAR** **Map Ref No. 08**	Nearest Road: A.120 Modern farmhouse set in a picturesque garden welcomes visitors with its friendly atmosphere. The location offers proximity to Constable Country, Colchester & Ipswich, & is within 10 min's drive of Harwich Port. 12 modern bedrooms, all with T.V., radio, tea/coffee & the option of en-suite facilities. 2 guests' lounges, including snack-making facilities. Breakfast menu with choice of farmhouse, Continental, etc. All diets catered for. Children welcome: cots, etc., & play area with equipment & space for activities. Licensed.	£21.00 CREDIT CARD VISA M'CARD AMEX	Y	Y	Y
Antony & Anne Wordsworth **Little Brockholds Farm** **Radwinter** **Saffron Walden** **CB10 2TF** **Tel: (01799) 599458** **Fax(01799) 599458** **Open: ALL YEAR** **Map Ref No. 09**	Nearest Road: B.1053 An Elizabethan farmhouse, surrounded by fields & gardens, with ponds, shrubs, old-fashioned roses & marvellous wildlife. A secluded rural setting with excellent walks & safe bicycling. Antony & Anne are keen gardeners. It is well-situated to explore East Anglia, being close to the mediaeval towns of Saffron Walden & Thaxted. Cambridge, Newmarket, Duxford & Stansted Airport are all within 30 mins drive. Anne is an experienced cook & produces delicious dinners, using her own fresh herbs & vegetables.	£30.00	Y	Y	N
Mrs Tineke Westerhuis **Rockells Farm** **Duddenhoe End** **Saffron Walden CB11 4UY** **Tel: (01763) 838053** **Fax 01763 837001** **Open:** ALL YEAR (Excl. Xmas) **Map Ref No. 10**	Nearest Road: A.11.M, B.1039 Rockells is an arable farm in a beautiful corner of Essex. The Georgian house has a large garden with a 3-acre lake for course fishing. All 3 rooms have private facilities. 1 room is on the ground floor. On the farm are several footpaths. Beautiful villages in the area. Within easy reach are Audley End House, Duxford Air Museum & Cambridge. London is approx. 1 hour by car or train. Stansted Airport 30 mins by car.	£18.00	Y	N	N

Gloucestershire

Gloucestershire
(Heart of England)

The landscape is so varied the people speak not of one Gloucestershire but of three - Cotswold, Vale & Forest. The rounded hills of the Cotswolds sweep & fold in graceful compositions to form a soft & beautiful landscape in which nestle many pretty villages. To the east there are wonderful views of the Vale of Berkeley & Severn, & across to the dark wooded slopes of the Forest of Dean on the Welsh borders.

Hill Forts, ancient trackways & long barrows of neolithic peoples can be explored, & remains of many villas from late Roman times can be seen. A local saying "Scratch Gloucester & find Rome" reveals the lasting influence of the Roman presence. Three major roads mark the path of invasion & settlement. Akeman street leads to London, Ermine street & the Fosse Way to the north east. A stretch of Roman road with its original surface can be seen at Blackpool Bridge in the Forest of Dean, & Cirencester's museum reflects its status as the second most important Roman city in the country.

Offa's Dyke, 80 miles of bank & ditch on the Welsh border was the work of the Anglo-Saxons of Mercia who invaded in the wake of the Romans. Cotswold means "hills of the sheepcotes" in the Anglo-Saxon tongue, & much of the heritage of the area has its roots in the wealth created by the wool industry here.

Fine Norman churches such as those at Tewkesbury & Bishops Cleeve were overshadowed by the development of the perpendicular style of building made possible by the growing prosperity. Handsome 15th century church towers crown many wool towns & villages as at Northleach, Chipping Camden & Cirencester, & Gloucester has a splendid 14th century cathedral. Detailing on church buildings gives recognition to the source of the wealth-cloth-workers shears are depicted on the north west buttresses of Grantham church tower & couchant rams decorate church buttresses at Compton Bedale.

Wool & cloth weaving dominated life here in the 14th & 15th centuries with most families dependent on the industry. The cottage craft of weaving was gradually overtaken by larger looms & water power. A water mill can be seen in the beautiful village of Lower Slaughter & the cottages of Arlington Row in Bibury were a weaving factory.

The Cotswold weaving industry gave way to the growing force of the Lancashire mills but a few centres survive. At Witney you can still buy the locally made blankets for which the town is famous.

From the 16th century the wealthy gentry built parks & mansions. Amongst the most notable are the Jacobean Manor house at Stanway & the contrasting Palladian style mansion at Barnsley Park. Elizabethan timber frame buildings can be seen at Didbrook, Dymock & Deerhurst but houses in the local mellow golden limestone are more common, with Chipping Camden providing excellent examples.

Cheltenham was only a village when, in 1716 a local farmer noticed a flock of pigeons pecking at grains of salt around a saline spring in his fields. He began to bottle & sell the water & in 1784 his son-in-law, Henry Skillicorne, built a pump room & the place received the name of Cheltenham Spa. Physicians published treatises on the healing qualities of the waters, visitors began to flock there & Cheltenham grew in style & elegance.

Gloucestershire

Gloucestershire Gazeteer

Areas of outstanding natural beauty
The Cotswolds, Malvern Hills & the Wye Valley.

Houses & Castles

Ashleworth Court - Ashleworth
15th century limestone Manor house.
Badminton House - Badminton
Built in the reign of Charles II. Stone newel staircase.
Berkeley Castle - Berkeley
12th century castle - still occupied by the Berkeley family. Magnificent collections of furniture, paintings, tapestries & carved timber work. Lovely terraced gardens & deer park.
Chavenage - Tetbury
Elizabethan Cotswold Manor house, Cromwellian associations.
Clearwell Castle - Nr. Coleford
A Georgian neo-Gothic house said to be oldest in Britain, recently restored.
Court House - Painswick
Cotswold Manor house - has original court room & bedchamber of Charles I. Splendid panelling & antique furniture.
Dodington House - Chipping Sodbury
Perfect 18th century house with superb staircase. Landscape by Capability Brown.
Horton Court - Horton
Cotswold manor house altered & restored in 19th century.
Kelmscott Manor - Nr. Lechlade
16th century country house - 17th century additions. Examples of work of William Morris, Rosetti & Burne-Jones.
Owlpen Manor - Nr. Dursley
Historic group of traditional Cotswold stone buildings. Tudor Manor house with church, barn, court house & a grist mill. Holds a rare set of 17th century painted cloth wall hangings.
Snowshill Manor - Broadway
Tudor house with 17th century facade. Unique collection of musical instruments & clocks, toys, etc. Formal garden.
Sudeley Castle - Winchcombe
12th century - home of Katherine Parr, is rich in historical associations, contains art treasures & relics of bygone days.

Cathedrals & Churches

Bishops Cleeve (St. Michael & All Saints)
12th century with 17th century gallery. Magnificent Norman west front & south porch. Decorated chancel.   Fine window.
Bledington (St.Leonards)
15th century glass in this perpendicular church, Norman bellcote. Early English east window.
Buckland (St. Michael)
13th century nave arcades. 17th century oak panelling, 15th century glass.
Cirencester (St. John the Baptist)
A magnificent church - remarkable exterior, 3 storey porch, 2 storey oriel windows, traceries & pinnacles. Wine-glass pulpit c.1450. 15th century glass in east window, monuments in Lady chapel.
Gloucester Cathedral
Birthplace of Perpendicular style in 14th century. Fan vaulting, east windows commemorate Battle of Crecy - Norman Chapter House.
Hailes Abbey - Winchcombe
14th century wall paintings, 15th century tiles, glass & screen, 17th century pulpit. Elizabethan benches.
Iron Acton (St. James the Less)
Perpendicular - 15th century memorial cross. 19th century mosaic floors, Laudian alter rails, Jacobean pulpit, effigies.
Newland (All Saints)
13th century, restored 18th century. Pinnacled west tower, effigies.
Prinknash Abbey - Gloucester
14th & 16th century - Benedictine Abbey.
Tewkesbury Abbey - Tewkesbury
Dates back to Norman times, contains Romanesque & Gothic styles. 14th century monuments.
Yate (St. Mary)
Splendid perpendicular tower.

Museums & Galleries

Bishop Hooper's Lodgings - Gloucester
3 Tudor timber frame buildings - museum of domestic life & agriculture in Gloucester since 1500.
Bourton Motor Museum - Bourton-on-the-Water
Collection of cars & motor cycles.
Cheltenham Art Gallery - Cheltenham.

Gloucestershire

Lower Slaughter.

Gallery of Dutch paintings, collection of oils, watercolours, pottery, porcelain, English & Chinese; furniture.
City Wall & Bastion - Gloucester
Roman & mediaeval city defences in an underground exhibition room.
Stroud Museum - Cirencester
Depicts earlier settlements in the area & has a very fine collection of Roman antiquities.

Historic Monuments

Chedworth Roman Villa - Yanworth
Remains of Romano-British villa.
Belas Knap Long Barrow - Charlton Abbots
Neolithic burial ground - three burial chambers with external entrances.
Hailes Abbey - Stanway
Ruins of beautiful mediaeval abbey built by son of King John, 1246.
Witcombe Roman Villa - Nr. Birdlip

Large Roman villa - Hypocaust & mosaic pavements preserved.
Ashleworth Tithe Barn - Ashleworth
15th century tithe barn - 120 feet long - stone built, interesting roof timbering.
Odda's Chapel - Deerhurst
Rare Saxon chapel dating back to 1056.
Hetty Pegler's Tump - UleLong Barrow- fairly complete, chamber is 120 feet long.

Other things to see & do

Cheltenham International Festival of Music & Literature - Annual event.
Cotswolds Farm Park - dozens of rare breeds of farm animals.
The Three Choirs Festival - music festival staged in alternating years at Gloucester, Hereford & Worcester Cathedrals.
Slimbridge - Peter Scott's Wildfowl Trust.

GLOUCESTERSHIRE
Map reference

1	Boxall	15	Cassidy
1	Bolton	16	Langton
1	Wright	17	Keyser
1	Adams	18	Parsons
2	Thornely	19	Fletcher
3	Moodie	20	Beddows
4	Paz	21	Reid
5	Beauvoisin	22	Helm
6	Gamez	23	Sayers
6	Berg	24	Dean
6	Stone	25	Anderson
7	Enstone	26	Thompson
8	Ellis	27	Gisby
8	Minchin	28	Marshall
9	Burrough	29	Peacock
10	Whent	30	Veen
11	Loving	31	Bonniwell
12	Wilson	33	Brunsdon
13	Brown	34	Tremellen
14	Carey-Wilson	35	Eyre

Dial House Hotel. Bourton.

Gloucestershire

		rate from £ per person	children taken	evening meals	animals taken
Mr & Mrs Boxall **Dial House Hotel** **The Chestnuts** **Bourton-on-the-Water** **GL54 2AN** **Tel: (01451) 822244** **Open: ALL YEAR** **Map Ref No. 01**	Nearest Road: A.436 Built in 1698 from Cotswold stone, Dial House Hotel has the feel of an English country house & enjoys views of the River Windrush & has a quite unexpected & beautiful 1 1/2 acre walled garden. All of the 10 bedrooms have either an en-suite or private bathroom & are individually furnished, some with antique 4-posters. Dine by candle light in the inglenook, beamed restaurant. Log fires in winter. A warm welcome all year. Parking. (Hosts can be contacted by fax on 01451 810126.) *see PHOTO over* CREDIT CARD VISA M'CARD AMEX	£25.00	N	Y	N
Mrs Karin Bolton **Clapton Manor** **Clapton-on-the-Hill** **Bourton-on-the-Water** **GL54 2LG** **Tel: (01451) 810202** **Fax 01451 821804** **Open: ALL YEAR (Excl. Xmas)** **Map Ref No. 01**	Nearest Road: A.40, A.429 Clapton Manor is a 17th-century manor house at the top of a secluded village with stunning views across the Windrush Valley. The house affords either complete privacy, the guests having their own log-fired sitting-room, or more integration with the family as preferred. With its beams & huge inglenook fireplaces, it is both informal & comfortable. Karin cooks delicious meals using local produce when possible. The garden has many unusual plants & James is a designer & historian & can advise on gardens to visit. *see PHOTO over* CREDIT CARD VISA M'CARD	£28.00	Y	Y	N
Mrs Julia Wright **Farncombe** **Clapton-on-the-Hill** **Bourton-on-the-Water** **GL54 2LG** **Tel/Fax: (01451) 820120** **Open: ALL YEAR** **Map Ref No. 01**	Nearest Road: A.429, A.40 Come & share the peace, tranquillity & superb views of Farncombe, & eat, drink & sleep - smoke-free - 700ft above sea level & only 2 miles from Bourton-on-the-Water. 2 attractive doubles, with showers, & 1 twin en-suite. A spacious dining room, with tea/coffee-making facilities, & a comfortable T.V. lounge. Tourist information, maps & books & current menus for your choice when eating out. Numerous walks & drives, with easy access to all attractions & places of interest.	£18.50	N	N	N
Mrs Helen Adams **Upper Farm** **Clapton-on-the-Hill** **Bourton-on-the-Water** **GL54 2LG** **Tel: (01451) 820453** **Fax 01451 810185** **Open: MAR - NOV** **Map Ref No. 01**	Nearest Road: A.40, A.429 If peace & tranquillity is what you require, then this charming undiscovered village 2 miles from Bourton is certainly the spot. Clapton enjoys one of the finest Cotswold views from its hill position. Here, you will find Upper Farm, with its 17th-century stone farmhouse lovingly restored & yet retaining a wealth of original charm. Delightful accommodation, commanding views & personal attention are complemented with fresh farmhouse fayre. Children over 6 years welcome.	£17.00	Y	N	N
Mr & Mrs David Moodie **The Elms, Olveston** **Bristol BS12 3DR** **Tel: (01454) 614559** **Fax 01454 618607** **Open: ALL YEAR** **Map Ref No. 03**	Nearest Road: A.38 A Grade II listed Georgian village house with stables adjoining, & recently converted into extra accommodation & a self-contained wing. No toxic materials were used in the conversion, & the establishment is very allergy-conscious; whenever possible food is organic. The Grooms' Room (which comprises a double bedroom, bathroom & sitting room) has its own access. Ideally located for M.4/M.5 & Bristol. Bath, Cheltenham.	£25.00	N	N	Y

Clapton Manor. Clapton on the Hill.

The Old Rectory. Willersey.

Milton House Hotel. Cheltenham.

Gloucestershire

		rate from £ per person	children taken	evening meals	animals taken
Mrs Ann Thornely **Eastcote Cottage** **Knapp Road East** **Thornbury** **Bristol BS12 2HJ** **Tel: (01454) 413106** **Open:** ALL YEAR (Excl. Xmas) **Map Ref No. 02**	Nearest Road: M.4, M.5, A.38 Eastcote is a charming 200-year-old stone house located in a lovely rural setting, with splendid views across open countryside. Guests have a choice of 4 comfortable bedrooms with modern amenities. A colour-T.V. lounge is available for guests' use. Conveniently situated for the M.4/M.5 interchange for the Cotswolds, with Bristol, Bath, Cheltenham & the Wye Valley easily accessible. Private parking available. (Hosts can be contacted by fax on 01454 281812.)	£22.00	Y	N	N
John & Daphne Paz **Dornden Guest House** **15 Church Lane** **Old Sodbury** **Bristol BS17 6NB** **Tel: (01454) 313325** **Open: ALL YEAR (Excl. Xmas & New Year)** **Map Ref No. 04**	Nearest Road: A.432 Dornden, built of local Cotswold stone, stands in a beautiful garden enjoying the peace of the countryside & magnificent views to the west. 9 attractive rooms, 5 en-suite, overlooking the garden and the open country beyond. Delicious meals are prepared, using home-grown produce (where possible) and free-range eggs. There is also a grass tennis court available to guests. A delightful home, with a warm, friendly atmosphere, ideal for exploring the beautiful West Country. (Hosts can be contacted by fax on 01454 312263.)	£25.00	Y	Y	Y
Mrs Elizabeth Beauvoisin **The Old Rectory** **Church Street, Willersey** **Broadway WR12 7PN** **Tel: (01386) 853729** **Fax 01386 858061** **Open:** ALL YEAR (Excl. Xmas) **Map Ref No. 05**	Nearest Road: B.4632 Hidden at the end of a lane, opposite the 11th-century church, this old Georgian rectory, built of Cotswold stone, is very quiet & comfortable. Superb en-suite, spacious rooms, 4-posters. In winter, a roaring log fire greets you at breakfast, in the elegant dining room, & in summer the walled garden, with its 300-year-old Mulberry tree, offers tranquillity. Only 300 yards to the excellent 13th-century Bell Inn. Children over 8. **E-mail: beauvoisin@btinternet.com**	£30.00 *see PHOTO over* CREDIT CARD VISA M'CARD	Y	N	N
Penny & Alex Gamez **Milton House Hotel** **12 Royal Parade** **Bayshill Road** **Cheltenham GL50 3AY** **Tel: (01242) 582601** **Fax 01242 222326** **Open: ALL YEAR** **Map Ref No. 06**	Nearest Road: A.40, M.5 Milton House stands in a quiet tree-lined avenue of elegant Regency homes. Situated just a 4-min stroll from the imposing promenade, restaurants & the Imperial Gardens. 8 en-suite, individually styled & decorated bedrooms, all with colour T.V., 'phone & tea/coffee makers. A choice of healthy & generously proportioned breakfasts is available, together with the morning papers. There is also a pretty sun lounge with bar & T.V.. An ideal base from which to explore the Cotswolds.	£26.00 *see PHOTO over* CREDIT CARD VISA M'CARD AMEX	Y	N	Y
John & Marian Enstone **Cleeve Hill Hotel** **Cleeve Hill** **Cheltenham** **GL52 3PR** **Tel: (01242) 672052** **Open: ALL YEAR** **Map Ref No. 07**	Nearest Road: A.46 Situated in an Area of Outstanding Natural Beauty, Cleeve Hill has the friendly, relaxed atmosphere of a family home. All bedrooms have superb views, some to the Malvern Hills, & all are en-suite & equipped to the highest standards with 'phone, T.V., radio/alarm & beverage facilities. The excellent breakfasts are generous, & provide the perfect start to the day. Located in the heart of the Cotswolds, it is ideally placed for visiting Bath, Oxford, Stratford, Warwick. Children over 8.	£30.00 *see PHOTO over* CREDIT CARD VISA M'CARD AMEX	Y	N	N

Cleeve Hill Hotel. Cleeve Hill.

Charlton House. Charlton Kings.

Gloucestershire

		rate from £ per person	children taken	evening meals	animals taken
Jurgen & Annette Berg **Hollington House Hotel** **115 Hales Road** **Cheltenham GL52 6ST** **Tel: (01242) 256652** **Fax 01242 570280** **Open: ALL YEAR** **Map Ref No. 06**	Nearest Road: A.40, A.435 An elegant Victorian house, easy to find off the London Road/A.40, with a large garden, croquet lawn & ample parking. Spacious bedrooms, with en-suite facilities, tea/coffee trays & colour T.V.. Good food for breakfast & dinner, with a choice of menu. A pleasant, relaxed atmosphere, with proprietors' personal attention, & a comfortable lounge with a bar. The perfect location, within easy driving distance of Oxford, Bath, Stratford-upon-Avon & the Cotswolds. Children over 3. CREDIT CARD VISA M'CARD AMEX	£25.00	Y	Y	N
Mera & Bev Stone **Charlton House** **18 Greenhills Road** **Charlton Kings** **Cheltenham GL53 9EB** **Tel/Fax: (01242) 238997** **Open: ALL YEAR** **Map Ref No. 06**	Nearest Road: A.435 Charlton House is a friendly, family-run guest house located in a good residential area of Cheltenham with views of the Cotswold Hills. This comfortable home is fully double-glazed & centrally heated, with good-quality fitments & furnishings throughout. Excellent home-cooking. Your special dietary requirements provided for by a trained nutritionist. Reductions for extended stays. Ample off-road parking. Charlton House is completely non-smoking. Children over 8 years. *see PHOTO over*	£20.00	Y	Y	N
Graham & Diana Ellis **Coombe House** **Rissington Road** **Bourton-on-the-Water** **Cheltenham GL54 2DT** **Tel: (01451) 821966** **Fax 01451 810477** **Open: ALL YEAR** **Map Ref No. 08**	Nearest Road: A.429, A.424 This quiet Cotswold home offers gentle elegance, a garden with unusual plants, & an easy riverside walk to the renowned village centre. The 7 pretty, thoughtfully equipped bedrooms have en-suite facilities. A delightful small drawing room. Heaps of assistance. Ample parking. Begin the day with a delicious English/Continental breakfast, then meander through the beautiful Cotswolds. Within easy reach of Hidcote, Barnsley, Oxford, Blenheim, Stratford & Warwick. *see PHOTO over* CREDIT CARD VISA M'CARD AMEX	£28.50	Y	N	N
Michael & Pamela Minchin **The Ridge** **Whiteshoots Hill** **Bourton-on-the-Water** **Cheltenham GL54 2LE** **Tel: (01451) 820660** **Open: ALL YEAR (Excl. Dec 25)** **Map Ref No. 08**	Nearest Road: A.429 The Ridge stands in 2 acres of beautiful secluded grounds just 1 mile from the centre of Bourton-on-the-Water. A large country house with 4 individually decorated, centrally heated bedrooms, most with en-suite facilities. 1 is on the ground floor. This house provides an extremely pleasant & comfortable base for touring the Cotswolds. A delicious full English breakfast is served. Good restaurants & pubs nearby serve excellent evening meals. Children over 6 years welcome.	£19.50	Y	N	N
Jenny & David Burrough **Windrush Farm** **Bourton-on-the-Water** **Cheltenham GL54 3BY** **Tel: (01451) 820419** **Fax 01451 820419** **Open: MAR - NOV** **Map Ref No. 09**	Nearest Road: A.436 This 150-acre farm is situated in the heart of the glorious Cotswolds, renowned for its beauty & interest. The traditional, stone-mullioned farmhouse has a lovely garden & commands superb views, & yet is only 2 miles from Bourton. The guest rooms are tastefully furnished, & comprise 1 twin-bedded & 1 double room, with en-suite bathrooms & beverage-making facilities. A delicious English breakfast is served. Jenny & David enjoy helping to plan your day.	£20.00	N	N	N

Coombe House.   Bourton-on-the-Water.

Halewell Close. Withington.

Westward. Sudeley.

		rate from £ per person	children taken	evening meals	animals taken
Elaine & Graham Whent **Cotteswold House** Market Place, Northleach Cheltenham GL54 3EG Tel/Fax: (01451) 860493 Open: ALL YEAR (Excl. Xmas & New Year) Map Ref No. 10	Nearest Road: A.40, A.429 Relax in this 350 year old Cotswold stone wool merchant's home with beamed ceilings, 13th-century panelling & Tudor archway. Offering a choice of a double suite or 2 double bedrooms, each with their own bathroom - all spacious, elegant & well-equipped. Enjoy traditional English food & a friendly welcome. Cotteswold House is located in the centre of this ancient market town of Northleach in the heart of the beautiful Cotswolds. An ideal touring base.	£22.50 🚭 CREDIT CARD VISA M'CARD	N	Y	N
Mrs Pauline Loving **Northfield B & B** Cirencester Rd, Northleach Cheltenham GL54 3JL Tel: (01451) 860427 Open: ALL YEAR (Excl. Xmas & New Year) Map Ref No. 11	Nearest Road: A.429, A.40 Detached family house in country, with large gardens, & own garden produce to complement home-cooking. Close to all local services in the small market town of Northleach. Accommodation is in 3 comfortable & attractively furnished en-suite bedrooms. It is an excellent centre for visiting many lovely Cotswold villages. Also easily reached by car are Cheltenham, Oxford, Cirencester & Stratford.	£20.00 🚭	Y	Y	N
Mrs Elizabeth J. Carey-Wilson, Halewell Close Withington Cheltenham GL54 4BN Tel: (01242) 890238 Fax 01242 890332 Open: ALL YEAR Map Ref No. 14	Nearest Road: A.40 Halewell is a Cotswold stone house dating back in parts to the early 15th century. Situated on the edge of the very quiet & pretty village of Withington in a glorious setting in the hills. There are 6 superb, large well-equipped double & twin-bedded en-suite rooms of individual character. 1 twin is located at ground level. An outstanding country home with easy access to the delights of the Cotswolds & surrounding area. Children, evening meals & animals by arrangement.	£41.50 *see PHOTO over* CREDIT CARD VISA M'CARD AMEX	Y	Y	Y
Mrs Susie Wilson **Westward, Sudeley** Winchcombe Cheltenham GL54 5JB Tel/Fax: (01242) 604372 Open: ALL YEAR Map Ref No. 12	Nearest Road: A.40 The Wilson families share this beautiful Georgian house on the scarp of the Cotswolds above Sudeley Castle, sitting within its own 600-acre estate with spectacular views to the Malverns. The heart of the Cotswolds is very close, with Broadway, Oxford & Stratford within easy reach. The Wilsons combine good food - Susie trained at Prue Leith's - with elegance & comfort in a relaxed family home. 2 delightful en-suite rooms available.	£32.50 *see PHOTO over* CREDIT CARD VISA M'CARD	N	Y	Y
Nick, Jean & Julian Brown **The Malt House** Broad Campden Chipping Campden GL55 6UU Tel: (01386) 840295 Fax 01386 841334 Open: ALL YEAR (Excl. Xmas) Map Ref No. 13	Nearest Road: A.44, A.429 Nick & Jean Brown have achieved a blend of relaxed & yet professional service, welcoming guests as part of an extended house party. This 17th-century former malting house is set in extensive gardens, with an orchard & croquet lawn. Public rooms are furnished with antiques. Bedrooms are en-suite & individually decorated, with T.V., tea/coffee & hairdryers, & overlook the gardens. The Windrush Suite has an 18th-century 4-poster bed, & family & private garden suites are available. Excellent table d'hote evening meals.	£39.50 *see PHOTO over* CREDIT CARD VISA M'CARD AMEX	Y	Y	Y

The Malt House. Broad Campden.

Lady Lamb Farm. Meysey Hampton.

Winstone Glebe. Winstone.

Gloucestershire

		rate from £ per person	children taken	evening meals	animals taken
Stephen & Anna Langton **The Little House** **6 Coxwell Street** **Cirencester** **GL7 2BH** **Tel: (01285) 653164** **Open: ALL YEAR (Excl. Xmas)** **Map Ref No. 16**	Nearest Road: A.417, A.419 The Little House is a 3-storey town house originally built as a wool merchant's house in around 1680, with 18th century additions. Situated in a very old narrow street of great historical interest, just 2 mins' walk from the Parish Church (very fine) & all the shops & facilities. 3,000 acre Cirencester Park is 5 mins' walk away. The house has been renovated & decorated to a high standard & provides 1 twin-bedded en-suite room & 1 twin & 1 single sharing a bathroom. Children over 4.	£23.50	Y	N	N
Mrs Jeanie Keyser **Lady Lamb Farm** **Meysey Hampton** **Cirencester** **GL7 5LH** **Tel: (01285) 712206** **Fax 01285 712206** **Open: ALL YEAR (Excl. Xmas)** **Map Ref No. 17**	Nearest Road: A.417 Lady Lamb Farm is a Cotswold stone farmhouse, surrounded by countryside & situated less than a mile from the small market town of Fairford. 3 attractively furnished guest rooms, each with T.V. & tea/coffee facilities. (1 is en-suite.) A swimming pool & tennis court are available. Set on the edge of the Cotswolds, Bath, Oxford & many Cotswold towns & wonderful gardens are within easy reach. Cotswold Water Park offers a wide range of watersports & golf, riding & fishing are available nearby. Animals by arrangement.	£25.00 *see PHOTO over* CREDIT CARD VISA M'CARD	Y	N	Y
Shaun & Susanna Parsons **Winstone Glebe** **Winstone** **Cirencester** **GL7 7JL** **Tel: (01285) 821451** **Fax 01285 821451** **Open: ALL YEAR** **Map Ref No. 18**	Nearest Road: A.417 A small Georgian rectory overlooking a Saxon church in a Domesday-listed village, & enjoying spectacular rural views. Ideally situated for exploring Cotswold market towns, with their mediaeval churches, antique shops & rich local history. 3 delightful rooms, each with private/en-suite bathroom. Being an Area of Outstanding Natural Beauty, there are well-signposted walks. The more energetic can borrow a bicycle & explore, or just enjoy warm hospitality & good food cooked by Susanna, who was a professional cook.	£25.00 *see PHOTO over* CREDIT CARD VISA M'CARD	Y	Y	Y
Deborah & Richard Fletcher **Tudor Farmhouse Hotel** **& Restaurant** **High Street, Clearwell** **Coleford GL16 8JS** **Tel: (01594) 833046** **Fax 01594 837093** **Open: ALL YEAR (Excl. Xmas)** **Map Ref No. 19**	Nearest Road: A.466 Situated in a charming village between the Forest of Dean & the beautiful Wye Valley, this 13th-century farmhouse features a wealth of oak beams, original panelling & an historic spiral staircase. Exquisitely furnished bedrooms are located in the main house & in charmingly converted stone cider makers' cottages. All are well-appointed. Imaginative cuisine is prepared by the chef & served in the stylish dining room. The charming hosts will ensure that your stay is very special.	£28.50 *see PHOTO over* CREDIT CARD VISA M'CARD AMEX	Y	Y	Y
Mrs E. M. Beddows **New House Farm** **Barrel Lane** **Longhope GL17 0LS** **Tel/Fax: (01452) 830484** **Open: ALL YEAR** **Map Ref No. 20**	Nearest Road: A.40 Clive & Betty Beddows give you a warm welcome to their Georgian farmhouse, set in 80 acres of farmland, with many lovely walks. All bedrooms have private or en-suite bathrooms, radio/alarms, satellite T.V., electric blankets & tea/coffee facilities. Full English breakfast & hearty evening meals are all home-cooked, with a selection of wines from the small but well-stocked bar.	£20.00	Y	Y	Y

Tudor Farmhouse. Clearwell.

Hunters Lodge. Minchinhampton.

Gloucestershire

	rate from £ per person	children taken	evening meals	animals taken
Ian & Mary Cassidy **Waterton Garden Cottage** **Ampney Crucis** **Cirencester** **GL7 5RX** **Tel: (01285) 851303** **Open: ALL YEAR** **Map Ref No. 15** Nearest Road: A.417 Situated in the heart of the Cotswolds, Waterton Garden Cottage, part of a late-Victorian stable block, has been sympathetically converted, & retains many original features. A high standard of comfort, & an ambience which would match many small country houses, are both to be found. All bedrooms are en-suite & one can expect fine cuisine, comfort & attention to detail without unnecessary formality. Every effort is made to ensure that your stay is memorable & enjoyable. Children over 9 years. (no smoking)	£22.50	Y	Y	N
Mrs Marie-Teresa Sayers **The Old Rectory** **Didmarton** **GL9 1DS** **Tel: (01454) 238233** **Open: ALL YEAR (Excl. Xmas)** **Map Ref No. 23** Nearest Road: A.433 The Old Rectory (Grade II listed) is a charming home, where a happy & relaxed atmosphere prevails. The friendly hosts offer very comfortable accommodation in 3 attractive bedrooms, each with an en-suite/private bathroom & T.V.. Also, a cosy lounge with T.V. & a pretty garden in which guests may choose to relax. A delicious breakfast is served. An ideal base from which to explore this beautiful region. Children over 12.	£19.00	Y	N	N
Sheila & James Reid **Edale House** **Folly Road, Parkend** **Lydney GL15 4JF** **Tel: (01594) 562835** **Fax 01594 564488** **Open: FEB - DEC** **Map Ref No. 21** Nearest Road: A.48 Edale House is a fine Georgian residence facing the cricket green in the village of Parkend in the heart of the Royal Forest of Dean. Once the home of local G.P. Bill Tandy, author of 'A Doctor in the Forest', the house has been tastefully restored to provide comfortable en-suite accommodation with every facility for guests. Enjoy delicious dinners prepared by your hosts, previously chef/proprietors of a well-known local restaurant. Animals by arrangement. CREDIT CARD VISA M'CARD	£20.00	N	Y	Y
Margaret Helm **Hunters Lodge** **Dr Brown's Road** **Minchinhampton GL6 9BT** **Tel: (01453) 883588** **Fax 01453 731449** **Open: ALL YEAR (Excl. Xmas)** **Map Ref No. 22** Nearest Road: A.419, A.46 A friendly and helpful welcome is assured for guests at this beautifully furnished Cotswold stone country house situated adjoining 600 acres of N.T. common land and golf course. Central heating throughout. All bedrooms have T.V., tea/coffee facilities & en-suite/private bathrooms. A visitors' lounge, with colour T.V., adjoins a delightful conservatory overlooking a large garden. An ideal centre for Bath, Cheltenham, Cirencester & the Cotswolds. Peter is a registered tourist guide. (no smoking) *see PHOTO over*	£20.00	Y	N	N
David & Caroline Anderson **Gunn Mill House** **Lower Spout Lane** **Mitcheldean** **GL17 0EA** **Tel: (01594) 827577** **Fax 01594 827577** **Open: ALL YEAR** **Map Ref No. 25** Nearest Road: A.4136, A.48 Bounded by its mill stream & the Forest of Dean, the Andersons' Georgian country home stands in 5 acres of gardens & meadows. Refurbished to a high standard, the galleried sitting room & large en-suite bedrooms (5: doubles, twins, family suites) are filled with antiques & collectables from around the world. Share your hosts' love of good food, including some ethnic fare, homemade breads & jams. Vegetarians catered for. Liquor licence. Overseas visitors especially welcomed. **E-mail: alexs@star.co.uk** (no smoking) *see PHOTO over*	£20.00	Y	Y	Y

Gunn Mill House. Mitcheldean.

Orchard House. Kilcot.

Gloucestershire

		rate from £ per person	children taken	evening meals	animals taken

Mrs Elizabeth M. Dean **Treetops** **London Road** **Moreton-in-Marsh** GL56 0HE **Tel/Fax: (01608) 651036** **Open: ALL YEAR** **Map Ref No. 24**	Nearest Road: A.44 A beautiful family home offering traditional Bed & Breakfast. 6 attractive bedrooms, all with a bathroom en-suite, & 2 of which are on the ground floor and thus suitable for disabled persons or wheelchair users. All rooms have T.V., radio and tea/coffee facilities. Cots and high chairs available. Delightful secluded gardens to relax in. Ideally situated for exploring the Cotswolds. A warm and homely atmosphere awaits you here.	£21.00 CREDIT CARD VISA M'CARD	Y	N	Y
Sybil Gisby **College House** **Chapel Street, Broadwell** **Moreton-in-Marsh** GL56 0TW **Tel: (01451) 832351** **Open: ALL YEAR (Excl.** **Xmas & New Year)** **Map Ref No. 27**	Nearest Road: A.429 Hidden in an enchanting & unspoilt Cotswold village, College House offers the most luxurious accommodation in lovely bedrooms with en-suite facilities. Exposed beams & ancient flagstone floors, & mullioned windows with hand-painted shutters. A tranquil sitting room, with a massive stone fireplace. Every comfort is provided, & Mrs Gisby enjoys spending time with her guests. This is the ideal base for a relaxing break.	£23.00	N	Y	N
Mrs Anne Thompson **Orchard House** **Aston Ingham Road** **Kilcot** **Newent GL18 1NP** **Tel: (01989) 720417** **Fax 01989 720770** **Open: ALL YEAR** **Map Ref No. 26**	Nearest Road: M.50, B.4222 This beautiful, Tudor-style country house is completely surrounded by 5 acres of well-tended lawns, paddocks & woodland trails. A relaxed & friendly atmosphere with every modern comfort & delicious food - traditional & vegetarian. The elegant & finely furnished rooms include 4 attractive double bedrooms overlooking the gardens, an original beamed T.V. lounge, with log fires in winter, & a spacious dining room. A residential licence. Well located for visiting the Wye Valley, the Cotswolds & the Malverns.	£24.50 *see PHOTO over* CREDIT CARD VISA M'CARD	N	Y	N
Mrs Linda Marshall **Damsells Cross** **Painswick GL6 6SR** **Tel: (01452) 814385** **Tel: (01452) 814384** **Fax 01452 814408** **Open: ALL YEAR** **Map Ref No. 28**	Nearest Road: A.46 Set in the ancient deer park to King Henry VIII's hunting lodge, Damsells Cross is a fine Cotswold house offering outstanding views, heated swimming pool, tennis court, croquet lawn & extensive grounds overlooking the beautiful Painswick Valley on the Cotswold Way. Choose a comfortable bedroom or charming apartment, all decorated in true English fine country-house style. Log fires, comfortable library & a beautiful drawing room. A charming home.	£30.00 CREDIT CARD VISA M'CARD	N	N	N
Gillie Peacock **Cinderhill House** **St. Briavels** **GL15 6RH** **Tel: (01594) 530393** **Fax 01594 530098** **Open: ALL YEAR** **Map Ref No. 29**	Nearest Road: A.466 A pretty, 14th-century house tucked into the hill below the castle in St. Briavels, with magnificent views across the Wye Valley to the Brecon Beacons & Black Mountains. A lovingly restored & tastefully furnished house with 5 beautiful bedrooms (& 2 4-posters), each with a private or en-suite bathroom. Gillie is a professional cook, & takes delight in ensuring that all meals are well cooked using local produce. 3 self-catering cottages, 1 for the disabled. Licensed.	£27.00 *see PHOTO over*	Y	Y	N

Cinderhill House. St. Briavels.

The Dial Cottage. Amberley.

Gloucestershire

		rate from £ per person	children taken	evening meals	animals taken
David & Pamela Veen **The Dial Cottage** **Amberley** **Minchinhampton Common** **Stroud GL5 5AL** **Tel: (01453) 872563** **Fax 01453 873057** **Open: MAR - NOV** **Map Ref No. 30**	Nearest Road: M.5, M.4 The Dial Cottage is a 17th-century Cotswold stone cottage, situated between Cirencester & Stroud on 800 acres of N.T. land. Within the 'Royal Triangle' explore the historic Cotswolds, Cheltenham, Gloucester, Bath & Wales. A warm & friendly atmosphere is assured with attractive country comforts, antique beds, en-suite facilities & all amenities. London (by rail) 1 1/2 hrs. Good walking, golf, gliding & horse riding nearby. Children over 10 years.	£25.00 *see PHOTO over*	Y	N	N
Mrs Frances Bonniwell **Wishanger Manor** **Miserden** **Stroud GL6 7HX** **Tel: (01285) 821212** **Fax 01285 821674** **Open: APR - OCT** **Map Ref No. 31**	Nearest Road: A.417 Wishanger is a 16th-century, Grade II listed manor house steeped in history & tucked away in its own peaceful valley. The house has been recently restored & refurbished & now provides a comfortable home of character with antiques & traditonal furnishings. Behind the house is a model Victorian farmyard built of Cotswold stone, around a central courtyard. An ideal position from which to explore the Cotswolds, with Cheltenham Spa only a short drive away.	£20.00	Y	N	N
Sheila & Garth Brunsdon **Hope Cottage Guest** **House, Box** **Stroud GL6 9HD** **Tel: (01453) 832076** **Open: JAN - NOV** **Map Ref No. 33**	Nearest Road: A.46, A.419 For peace & tranquillity, this charming, undiscovered village 10 miles from Cirencester is unrivalled. Box is in an Area of Outstanding Natural Beauty enjoying glorious Cotswold views. Here, you can savour the charm of this delightful country house, set in 3 acres of landscaped gardens & with a heated pool. Comfortable en-suite rooms, all with colour T.V. & hospitality tray. Sumptuous traditional English breakfasts.	£20.00 *see PHOTO over*	Y	N	N
Janet & Tim Tremellen **Tavern House** **Willesley** **Tetbury** **GL8 8QU** **Tel: (01666) 880444** **Fax 01666 880254** **Open: ALL YEAR** **Map Ref No. 34**	Nearest Road: A.433 A Grade II listed, part-17th-century, former staging post that has been sympathetically refurbished to provide an exceptionally high standard of accommodation. All rooms have bath/shower en-suite, direct-dial telephones, T.V., etc. Delightful, secluded, walled gardens in which to relax. Ideally situated for Westonbirt Arboretum, & convenient for Bath, Cheltenham & Gloucester. A genuine country-house atmosphere, & an excellent base from which to explore the Cotswolds. Charming inns offering dinner close-by. Children over 10.	£28.50 *see PHOTO over* CREDIT CARD VISA M'CARD	Y	N	N
Major & Mrs J. V. Eyre **Boyts Farm, Tytherington** **Wotton-under-Edge** **GL12 8UG** **Tel/Fax: (01454) 412220** **Open: ALL YEAR (Excl.** **Xmas & New Year)** **Map Ref No. 35**	Nearest Road: A.38 A 16th-century stone farmhouse with beams & open fires set in 2 acres of landscaped gardens including a minature canal, a walled garden potager & rose & lavender gardens. 2 delightful guest rooms, each with an en-suite bathroom. Convenient for M.4/M.5, Severn Bridge, Bristol, Bath, Tetbury & the Cotswolds. Nearby is Berkeley Castle, Wildfowl & Wetlands Trust Slimbridge, Westonbirt Arboretum. Theatres at Bath & Bristol & racing at Cheltenham, Chepstow & Bath.	£25.00	N	N	Y

Hope Cottage Guest House. Box.

Tavern House. Willesley.

Hampshire & Isle of Wight

Hampshire
(Southern)

Hampshire is located in the centre of the south coast of England & is blessed with much beautiful & unspoilt countryside. Wide open vistas of rich downland contrast with deep woodlands. Rivers & sparkling streams run through tranquil valleys passing nestling villages. There is a splendid coastline with seaside resorts & harbours, the cathedral city of Winchester & the "jewel" of Hampshire, the Isle of Wight.

The north of the county is known as the Hampshire Borders. Part of this countryside was immortalised by Richard Adams & the rabbits of 'Watership Down'. Beacon Hill is a notable hill-top landmark. From its slopes some of the earliest aeroplane flights were made by De Haviland in 1909. Pleasure trips & tow-path walks can be taken along the restored Basingstoke Canal.

The New Forest is probably the area most frequented by visitors. It is a landscape of great character with thatched cottages, glades & streams & a romantic beauty. There are herds of deer & the New Forest ponies wander at will. To the N.W. of Beaulieu are some of the most idyllic parts of the old forest, with fewer villages & many little streams that flow into the Avon. Lyndhurst, the "capital" of the New Forest offers a range of shops & has a contentious 19th century church constructed in scarlet brickwork banded with yellow, unusual ornamental decoration, & stained glass windows by William Morris.

The Roman city of Winchester became the capital city of Saxon Wessex & is today the capital of Hampshire. It is famous for its beautiful mediaeval cathedral, built during the reign of William the Conquerer & his notorious son Rufus. It contains the great Winchester Bible.

William completed the famous Domesday Book in the city, & Richard Coeur de Lion was crowned in the cathedral in 1194.

Portsmouth & Southampton are major ports & historic maritime cities with a wealth of castles, forts & Naval attractions from battleships to museums.

The channel of the Solent guarded by Martello towers, holds not only Southampton but numerous yachting centres, such as Hamble, Lymington & Bucklers Hard where the ships for Admiral Lord Nelson's fleet were built.

The River Test.

The Isle of Wight

The Isle of Wight lies across the sheltered waters of the Solent, & is easily reached by car or passenger ferry. The chalk stacks of the Needles & the multi-coloured sand at Alum Bay are among the best known of the island's natural attractions & there are many excellent beaches & other bays to enjoy. Cowes is a famous international sailing centre with a large number of yachting events throughout the summer. Ventnor, the most southerly resort is known as the "Madeira of England" & has an exotic botanic garden. Inland is an excellent network of footpaths & trails & many castles, manors & stately homes.

Hampshire & Isle of Wight

Hampshire

Gazeteer

Areas of outstanding natural beauty.
East & South Hampshire, North Wessex
Downs & Chichester Harbour.

Houses & Castles

Avington Park - Winchester
16th century red brick house, enlarged in
17th century by the addition of two wings
& a classical portico. Stateroom, ballroom
with wonderful ceiling. Red drawing room,
library, etc.

Beaulieu Abbey & Palace House -
Beaulieu
12th century Cistercian abbey - the
original gatehouse of abbey converted to
palace house 1538. Houses historic car
museum.

Breamore House - Breamore
16th century Elizabethan Manor House,
tapestries, furniture, paintings. Also
museum.

Jane Austen's Home - Chawston
Personal effects of the famous writer.

Broadlands - Romsey
16th century - park & garden created by
Capability Brown. Home of the Earl
Mountbatten of Burma.

Mottisfont Abbey - Nr. Romsey
12th century Augustinian Priory until
Dissolution. Painting by Rex Whistler
trompe l'oeil in Gothic manner.

Stratfield Saye House - Reading
17th century house presented to the Duke
of Wellington 1817. Now contains his
possessions - also wild fowl sanctuary.

Sandham Memorial Chapel - Sandham,
Nr. Newbury
Paintings by Stanley Spencer cover the
walls.

The Vyne - Sherbourne St. John
16th century red brick chapel with
Renaissance glass & rare linenfold
panelling. Alterations made in 1654 -
classical portico. Palladian staircase
dates form 1760.

West Green House - Hartley Wintney
18th century red brick house set in a
walled garden.

Appuldurcombe House - Wroxall, Isle of
Wight
The only house in the 'Grand Manner' on
the island. Beautiful English baroque east
facade. House now an empty shell
standing in fine park.

Osbourne House - East Cowes, Isle of
Wight
Queen Victoria's seaside residence.

Carisbrooke Castle - Isle of Wight
Oldest parts 12th century, but there was a
wooden castle on the mound before that.
Museum in castle.

Cathedrals & Churches

Winchester Cathedral
Largest Gothic church in Europe. Norman
& perpendicular styles, three sets of
mediaeval paintings, marble font c.1180.
Stalls c.1320 with 60 misericords.
Extensive mediaeval tiled floor.

Breamore (St. Mary) - Breamore
10th century Saxon. Double splayed
windows, stone rood.

East Meon (All Saints)
15th century rebuilding of Norman fabric.
Tournai marble front.

Idsworth (St. Hubert)
16th century chapel - 18th century bell
turret. 14th century paintings in chancel.

Pamber (dedication unknown)
Early English - Norman central tower, 15th
central pews, wooden effigy of knight
c.1270.

Romsey (St. Mary & St. Ethelfleda)
Norman - 13th century effigy of a lady -
Saxon rood & carving of crucifixion, 16th
century painted reredos.

Silchester (St. Mary)
Norman, perpendicular, 14th century effigy
of a lady, 15th century screen, Early
English chancel with painted patterns on
south window splays, Jacobean pulpit with
domed canopy.

Winchester (St. Cross)
12th century. Original chapel to Hospital.
Style changing from Norman at east to
decorated at west. Tiles, glass,
wall painting.

HAMPSHIRE
Map reference

1 Humphryes		16 Barnfield	
2 Mason		17 Cutmore	
3 Mallam		17 Gallagher	
4 Biddolph		17 Thompson	
5 Whitaker		17 Messenger	
6 Buckley		18 Ames	
7 Rowbotham		19 Matthews	
8 Tose		20 Baigent	
9 Cadman		21 Skelton	
10 Duckworth		22 Taylor	
11 Dawson		23 Nixon	
11 Yates		24 Ford	
12 Ratcliffe		25 Hughes	
13 Allison		26 Chivers	
14 Watling		27 Talbot	
15 Poulter		28 Parker	

Upavon · Hungerford · Newbury · Wokingham · Woking · Guildford
WILTSHIRE · BERKS · SURREY · SUSSEX
Camberley · Farnborough · Aldershot · Farnham · Milford · Guildford
397 · 404 · A272
Basingstoke · Alton · Hindhead · Haslemere · Midhurst · Petworth · Pulborough · Arundel
Andover · New Alresford · Petersfield · Chichester · Bognor Regis
Winchester · A272 · Havant · Fareham · Portsmouth · Selsey
Salisbury · Romsey · Eastleigh · Southampton · Gosport
Amesbury · Stonehenge · Lymington · Cowes · Ryde · Sandown · Shanklin
Cranborne · Ringwood · Lyndhurst · Newport · Isle of Wight · Niton
Bournemouth · Freshwater · The Solent
DORSET · English Channel

159 · 450 · 26

Malt Cottage. Upper Clatford.

Hampshire

		rate from £ per person	children taken	evening meals	animals taken
Adam & Laraine Humphryes **Belmont House** **Gilbert Street, Ropley** **Alresford SO24 0BY** **Tel: (01962) 772344** **Open: ALL YEAR (Excl. Xmas & Easter)** **Map Ref No. 01**	Nearest Road: A.31 An attractive Georgian house dating back to the 18th century, set in a pretty acre of garden with rural views. Offering 1 comfortably furnished twin-bedded room with tea/coffee-making facilities & use of study with colour T.V.. A short walk to the village, ancient church, shop, 2 pubs & the famous Watercress Steam Railway. Within easy reach of Winchester, Salisbury & 1 hour (approx.) from London airports.	£18.00	N	N	N
Mrs Patricia Mason **Malt Cottage** **Upper Clatford** **Andover SP11 7QL** **Tel: (01264) 323469** **Fax 01264 334100** **Open: ALL YEAR** **Map Ref No. 02**	Nearest Road: A.303 Walk around the beautiful 6-acre garden with chalk stream & lakes, or sit by the fire in the beamed sitting room. Malt Cottage, an ideal stop en-route from London/Heathrow to the West Country, is situated in a picturesque village with many thatched cottages. 3 attractive bedrooms with en-suite/private facilities. There are many places to visit locally, including Stonehenge, Salisbury & Winchester. A delightful home.	£20.00 *see PHOTO over*	Y	N	N
Mrs Carolyn Mallam **Broadwater** **Amport** **Andover SP11 8AY** **Tel/Fax: (01264) 772240** **Open: ALL YEAR** **Map Ref No. 03**	Nearest Road: A.303 Broadwater is a 17th-century, listed, thatched cottage situated in a peaceful unspoilt village just off the A.303. It is an ideal base for sightseeing in Hampshire, with easy access to the West Country & London. The cottage offers 2 delightful, double/twin-bedded rooms, both with en-suite facilities. A private & very comfortable sitting room, with an inglenook & a private dining room, together with home cooking, are all available. Colour T.V..	£22.50	Y	N	N
Tom & Fiona Biddolph **May Cottage** **Thruxton** **Andover SP11 8LZ** **Tel: (01264) 771241** **Fax 01264 771770** **Open: ALL YEAR (Excl. Xmas & New Year)** **Map Ref No. 04**	Nearest Road: A.303 May Cottage dates back to 1740 & is situated in the heart of this picturesque tranquil village with Post Office & old inn. A most comfortable home with 1 single & 3 twin rooms with en-suite/private bathrooms, 1 on the ground floor. All with colour T.V. & tea trays. Guests' own sitting/dining room with T.V.. An ideal base for visiting ancient cities, stately homes & gardens, yet within easy reach of ports & airports. Excellent home-cooking & dinner by prior arrangement. Parking. Children over 12. (Hosts can be contacted on mobile 0468 242166.)	£20.00	Y	Y	N
Jeremy & Philippa Whitaker **Land of Nod** **Headley** **Bordon** **GU35 8SJ** **Tel: (01428) 713609** **Fax 01428 717698** **Open:** ALL YEAR (Excl. Xmas) **Map Ref No. 05**	Nearest Road: A.3 A large neo-Georgian house set in 7 acres of garden in the centre of 100 acres of a private woodland estate. This attractive home affords 2 twin-bedded rooms with private or en-suite bathroom, T.V. & tea/coffee-making facilities. Situated just 1 hour from London, Heathrow, Gatwick & Portsmouth, & within easy reach of some of the finest gardens & historic houses in the south of England, the Land of Nod is the perfect spot for a relaxing break. A car, though, is essential for maximum enjoyment.	£25.00 *see PHOTO over*	N	Y	N

Land of Nod. Headley.

Hampshire

		rate from £ per person	children taken	evening meals	animals taken

Details	Description	rate from £ per person	children taken	evening meals	animals taken
Mrs Wendy Buckley **Tothill House** **Black Lane, Forest Road** **Burley, New Forest** **Christchurch BH23 8DZ** Tel: (01425) 674414 Fax 01425 672235 Open: JAN - NOV Map Ref No. 06	Nearest Road: A.35 An Edwardian country house set in 12 acres of woodland. An Area of Outstanding Natural Beauty noted for its flora & fauna. 5 mins from Burley village, a popular New Forest tourist attraction. Offering good food & 3 attractive en-suite rooms, individually decorated, with T.V. & tea-making facilities. Very secluded, with peace & tranquillity. Local sporting & recreational activities, & a variety of places to visit. Children over 16. The perfect spot for a relaxing break.	£25.00 🚭	Y	N	N
Michael Rowbotham **Merry Hall Hotel** **73 Horndean Road** **Emsworth PO10 7PU** Tel: (01243) 431377 Fax 01243 431411 Open: ALL YEAR Map Ref No. 07	Nearest Road: A.27 Merry Hall is situated in a delightful fishing village, set midway between Chichester & Portsmouth. Although a modern hotel, there are log fires & a very cosy, relaxed atmosphere. The 9 attractive bedrooms are well-equipped & have T.V. & tea/coffee facilities; 6 are en-suite. Some bedrooms & the conservatory overlook the pretty garden, which has an abundance of birdlife. Emsworth is well placed for exploring Hampshire & has a number of good local restaurants & pubs.	£20.00 CREDIT CARD VISA M'CARD	Y	N	Y
Nigel & Sandra Tose **Rudge House** **Itchel Lane, Crondall** **Farnham GU10 5PR** Tel: (01252) 850450 Fax 01252 850829 Open: ALL YEAR Map Ref No. 08	Nearest Road: A.287 Elegant, spacious family home, dating from the 1850s, featuring a 4-acre garden with tennis court & croquet lawn. Edging an historic village, the house is quiet & secluded, bordering farmland, yet within 45 mins of Heathrow, Gatwick & London. Windsor, Ascot, Winchester & Oxford highly accessible. Extremely comfortable accommodation, offering en-suite/private facilities & pump showers, plus T.V. lounge & tea/coffee. Evening meal & packed lunches by arrangement.	£27.50 🚭 *see PHOTO over*	N	Y	N
Mrs G. Cadman **Cottage Crest** **Castle Hill, Woodgreen** **Fordingbridge SP6 2AX** Tel: (01725) 512009 Open: ALL YEAR Map Ref No. 09	Nearest Road: A.338 Woodgreen is a typical New Forest village, with cottages surrounded by thick hedges to keep out the cattle & ponies. Cottage Crest is a Victorian drover's cottage set high in its own 4 acres, & enjoying superb views of the River Avon & valley below. Bedrooms are spacious & decorated to a very high standard. All have an en-suite bathroom/shower & w.c.. Children over 8 yrs welcome.	£20.00	Y	N	N
Brig. & Mrs G. Duckworth **Weir Cottage** **Bickton** **Fordingbridge** **SP6 2HA** Tel: (01425) 655813 Open: ALL YEAR Map Ref No. 10	Nearest Road: A.338 Bickton is a tiny hamlet on the River Avon half a mile from the New Forest & 30 mins from Salisbury, Bournemouth & Southampton. 200-year-old Weir Cottage offers 2 comfortable bedrooms: 1 double en-suite & 1 twin-bedded room with a private bathroom. Enjoy attractive views as you breakfast in the splendid, upstairs, beamed living room overlooking the river as it flows under the mill. The Garden Room, with colour T.V., leads out into the secluded terraced garden. 2 pianos available on request. Children over 6 yrs.	£20.00 🚭	Y	Y	N

Rudge House. Crondall.

Hampshire

		rate from £ per person	children taken	evening meals	animals taken
Bruce & Janet Dawson **Hucklesbrook Cottage** **South Gorley** **Fordingbridge** SP6 2PN Tel: **(01425) 653048** Open: **ALL YEAR** Map Ref No. 11	Nearest Road: A.338 Hucklesbrook Cottage is an attractive cottage furnished with antiques, on the western edge of the New Forest. Offering 2 comfortable en-suite bedrooms, both with tea/coffee-making facilities. Spacious guests' sitting room with open fire & T.V.. Interesting evening meals prepared with prior notice. Forest ponies & donkeys wander past the cottage & lucky walkers may see deer. Salisbury, Winchester & Dorset coast within easy reach. Children over 12 years.	£20.00	Y	Y	N
Mrs Pat Ratcliffe **Hendley House** **Rockbourne** **Fordingbridge SP6 3NA** Tel: **(01725) 518303** Fax 01725 518546 Open: **FEB - NOV** Map Ref No. 12	Nearest Road: A.338, A.354 Beautiful, south-facing, 16th-century Grade II listed house with oak beams & later additions, overlooking water meadows & farmland. Elegantly decorated, log fires in winter & heated swimming pool in spacious garden in summer. You will be assured of a warm welcome as Nick & Pat love entertaining (Nick is a wine merchant). 2 charming bedrooms with en-suite shower or private bathroom. Ideal base for exploring New Forest, Wessex & the South Coast. Children over 10.	£24.00	Y	N	N
Mrs Joanne Allison **Northwood Farmhouse** **Northwood Lane** **Hayling Island PO11 0LR** Tel: **(01705) 469262** Mobile 0850 860921 Open: **ALL YEAR** Map Ref No. 13	Nearest Road: A.27, M.27 An elegant 1820s Georgian farmhouse furnished throughout with antiques. This peaceful setting makes an ideal base for sight-seeing in the south. 1 1/2 hours from London. Your hostess welcomes you with friendly service offering fine home-cooked international cuisine. Conservatory & outdoor summer dining available. The beautiful interior-designed rooms combine luxury & comfort, & a French bridal suite is offered complete with en-suite jacuzzi bathroom. Dinner by arrangement.	£24.00	Y	Y	Y
Mrs Geraldine Watling **The Grange** **Alverstone** **Sandown** **Isle of Wight PO36 0EZ** Tel/Fax: **(01983) 403729** Open: **FEB - NOV** Map Ref No. 14	Nearest Road: A.3056, A.3055 Enjoy a peaceful stay at The Grange. Set in a large garden beneath the Downs, it is ideally situated for all aspects of the island. A nature trail passes through the village, & there are sandy beaches just 2 miles away. 7 tastefully furnished bedrooms with en-suite facilities. The house is centrally heated & there is a comfortable lounge with a log fire. Traditional English breakfast is served to start the day, & there is an excellent, varied menu for evening meals.	£19.00	Y	Y	N
Mr & Mrs N. Poulter **Quinces** **Cranmore Avenue** **Yarmouth** **Isle of Wight PO41 OXS** Tel: **(01983) 760080** Open: **ALL YEAR** Map Ref No. 15	Nearest Road: A.3054 An attractive cedar house, centrally heated throughout, peacefully set between a vineyard & a dairy farm on a private road 2 miles from Yarmouth. 2 delightful bedrooms, with tea/coffee-making facilities. Also available to guests is a comfortable living room with colour T.V. & log fires in season. The Poulters offer an ideal base for exploring the lovely & varied countryside & coastline of the West Wight, as well as the option of wildlife holidays tailored to your interests.	£18.00	Y	N	Y

The Nurse's Cottage. Sway.

	rate from £ per person	children taken	evening meals	animals taken

Mr R.A. Barnfield
The Nurse's Cottage
Station Road
Sway
Lymington SO41 6BA
Tel: (01590) 683402
Fax 01590 683402
Open: XMAS - Mid NOV
Map Ref No. 16

Nearest Road: A.337
"Wining & dining can be one of the great pleasures in life", says Tony Barnfield, who has transformed the former District Nurse's cottage in this New Forest village into an award-winning licensed guest house. Guests are welcomed with afternoon tea, & the overnight rate includes a 3-course dinner from an extensive menu incl. over 70 wines from around the world. 3 en-suite, ground-floor bedrooms with many comforts, fresh fruit & flowers, bottled water & Beaulieu Chocolates, T.V., etc. Reductions for 2-7 night stays. Children over 10.

£45.00 — Y Y Y

see PHOTO over

CREDIT CARD
VISA
M'CARD
AMEX

Jennifer & Peter Cutmore
Wheatsheaf House
Gosport Street
Lymington SO41 9BG
Tel: (01590) 679208
Fax 01590 672720
Open: ALL YEAR
Map Ref No. 17

Nearest Road: A.337
A beautifully appointed early-17th-century former tavern, Wheatsheaf House is close to the centre of this charming Georgian market town, & only 3 mins' walk from the historic town quay. Tea/coffee is available on request in a choice of 3 large comfortable rooms with either en-suite or private facilities. Ideally placed for sailing, the New Forest & for touring the whole region. You are assured of a warm welcome. Self-catering accommodation also available.

£23.00 — Y N Y

Wendy M. Gallagher
Albany House
3 Highfield
Lymington
SO41 9GB
Tel: (01590) 671900
Open: ALL YEAR (Excl. Xmas)
Map Ref No. 17

Nearest Road: A.337
This fine Regency house, built in 1842, provides a warm welcoming atmosphere in a traditionally furnished home. There are views over the town of Solent & the Isle of Wight. 3 very comfortably furnished bedrooms, each with en-suite facilities, colour T.V. & tea/coffee makers. Delicious meals are served in the elegant dining room using freshly prepared ingredients. In season, shellfish & New Forest game will be provided. (Evening meals, children & animals by arrangement.)

£26.00 — Y Y Y

Mrs P. A. Thomson
St. Mary's Lodge
Captains Row
Lymington
SO41 9RR
Tel: (01590) 678576
Fax 01590 678576
Open: ALL YEAR
Map Ref No. 17

Nearest Road: A.37
A superbly furnished, gracious Georgian house, Grade II listed, in a splendid position with lovely views over the Lymington River, Solent & Isle of Wight beyond. Close to the Old Town quay & marinas. Excellent restaurants & pubs, & Lymington town with its famous Saturday market & good shops. 4 delightful bedrooms, each with an en-suite/private bathroom. The New Forest, walks, cycling, golf, riding, a ferry to I.o.W., within 5 mins' walk. Enviable comfort for a memorable stay. Children over 5 years.

£23.00 — Y N Y

Mrs Jan Messenger
Mulberries
6 West Hayes
Lyminton SO41 3RL
Tel: (01590) 679549
Open: ALL YEAR
Map Ref No. 17

Nearest Road: A.337, M.27
An elegant detached house situated in a quiet cul-de-sac only 5 mins walk from the high street, quay & marinas. Secluded south-facing walled garden, full of choice plants. Heated outdoor pool for guests' use in the summer. 2 large double en-suite bedrooms & 1 single en-suite, all with tea/coffee facilities. Comfortable drawing room with T.V.. Ideal base for exploring the New Forest, I.O.W. & surrounding area. Children over 12.

£25.00 — Y N N

Cockle Warren Cottage Hotel. Hayling Island.

Hampshire

	rate from £ per person	children taken	evening meals	animals taken

Paul T. Ames
Ormonde House
Southampton Road
Lyndhurst SO43 7BT
Tel: (01703) 282806
Fax 01703 282004
Open: ALL YEAR (Excl. Xmas)
Map Ref No. 18

Nearest Road: A.35
Ormonde House is set back from the main forest road & is directly opposite the open forest; easy for an early morning walk. The village of Lyndhurst is a convenient 5 min walk away. The public rooms are adorned with comfortable settees & armchairs which lead into the flower-filled hotel gardens. 17 en-suite bedrooms, some with bath & shower, plus T.V., 'phone & tea facilities. The licensed restaurant offers dinner 7 nights a week April - October & on request through the winter.

£24.00 — Y Y Y
CREDIT CARD
VISA
M'CARD

Mrs Daphne Matthews
Yew Tree Farm
Bashley Common Road
Bashley
New Milton BH25 5SH
Tel/Fax: (01425) 611041
Open: ALL YEAR
Map Ref No. 19

Nearest Road: A.35
Yew Tree Farm offers 2 lovely, spacious bed-sitting rooms, marvellously comfortable, with double or twin beds & both with their own bathrooms, in a traditional, cosy thatched farmhouse on the edge of the New Forest. Extensive breakfasts (taken in bedroom) & home-made dinners (if ordered in advance), using top-quality produce. Private entrance & ample parking. Very easily located about 1 mile off the A.35 road on the B.3058 road.

£27.50 — N Y N

Mrs G. W. Baigent
Trotton Farm
Trotton
Petersfield GU31 5EN
Tel: (01730) 813618
Fax 01730 816093
Open: ALL YEAR
Map Ref No. 20

Nearest Road: A.272
This charming home, set in 200 acres of farmland, offers comfortable accommodation in 2 twin-bedded rooms & 1 double-bedded room each with en-suite shower & modern amenities, including tea/coffee-making facilities. Residents' lounge is available throughout the day. Games room & pretty garden for guests' relaxation. Ideally situated for visiting many local, historical & sporting attractions, & 1 hour from Gatwick & Heathrow. Single supplement.

£17.50 — Y N Y

David & Diane Skelton
Cockle Warren Cottage
36 Seafront, Hayling Island
Portsmouth PO11 9HL
Tel: (01705) 464961
Tel/Fax: (01705) 464838
Open: ALL YEAR
Map Ref No. 21

Nearest Road: A. 27, M.27
A delightful seaside cottage hotel with large gardens & heated swimming pool. All the lovely rooms are en-suite with colour T.V. etc.; some have 4-poster beds & overlook the sea. French & English country cooking, homemade bread & French wine can be enjoyed in the pretty conservatory. In winter, relax by the open log fire in the lounge with its antiques & memorabilia, to the sound of the sea just a few yards away. National Award Winners. Children over 12.

£29.00 — Y Y Y
see PHOTO over
CREDIT CARD
VISA
M'CARD
AMEX

Dr. & Mrs A. Taylor
11 Clarence Parade
Southsea
Portsmouth
PO5 3NU
Tel: (01705) 736510
Fax 01705 874844
Open: ALL YEAR (Excl. Xmas)
Map Ref No. 22

Nearest Road: M.27, A.3
This elegant, Georgian-style house overlooks Southsea Common, with magnificent views across the Solent & the Isle of Wight. Convenient for the Continental Ferry Port, I.O. W. ferries & ancient ships. Parking in front of house. 3 large, beautifully decorated & comfortable bedrooms, 2 en-suite & 1 with private bathroom, all with T.V., coffee/tea facilities, etc. The seafront, tennis courts, shops & restaurants are all within 2 mins' walk. A warm welcome awaits you. German is spoken. Children over 10. (Mobile 0402 986145.)

£20.00 — Y N N

Hampshire

		rate from £ per person	children taken	evening meals	animals taken
Mrs Yvonne Nixon **The Nest** **10 Middle Lane,** **Off School Lane** **Ringwood** **BH24 1LE** **Tel/Fax: (01425) 476724** **Mobile 0589 854505** **Open: ALL YEAR** **Map Ref No. 23**	Nearest Road: A.31, B.3347 A charming Victorian house situated in a quiet residential lane 5 mins' walk to Ringwood centre, a New Forest market town with many restaurants & inns. A former schoolmaster's residence, 'The Nest' offers excellent-value, character accommodation in pretty, well-equipped 'Laura Ashley'-style bedrooms. Convenient location with ample off-road parking. Close to Bournemouth, Poole, Portsmouth, Salisbury & Southampton. Breakfast is served in the delightful, sunny 'Garden Room' surrounded by an unusual collection of old potties! Reductions for longer stays.	£17.00	Y	N	N
Jane Yates **Plantation Cottage** **Mockbeggar** **Ringwood BH24 3NL** **Tel: (01425) 477443** **Open: ALL YEAR** **Map Ref No. 11**	Nearest Road: A.338 Charming 200 year old Grade II listed cottage set in 3 acres where wild ponies graze by the roadside. Ideal for exploring the beautiful New Forest. Riding stables, cycle hire, excellent pubs & restaurants close by. All bedrooms are en-suite, tastefully decorated & have colour T.V., hairdryer, radio & tea/coffee facilities. Guests' lounge & garden available all day. Also, holiday cottage to let.	£25.00 CREDIT CARD VISA M'CARD	N	N	N
Robin & Mary Ford **Holmans** **Bisterne Close** **Burley** **Ringwood BH24 4AZ** **Tel/Fax: (01425) 402307** **Open: ALL YEAR** **Map Ref No. 24**	Nearest Road: A.35, A.31 Holmans is a charming country house in the heart of the New Forest, set in 4 acres with stabling available for guests' own horses. Superb walking, horse riding & carriage driving, with a golf course nearby. A warm, friendly welcome is assured. All bedrooms are tastefully furnished & en-suite with tea/coffee-making facilities, radio & hairdryers. Colour T.V. in guests' lounge with adjoining orangery & log fires in winter.	£20.00	Y	N	Y
Anthea Hughes **Spursholt House** **Salisbury Rd** **Romsey SO51 6DJ** **Tel: (01794) 512229** **Fax 01794 523142** **Open: ALL YEAR** **Map Ref No. 25**	Nearest Road: A.27 Spursholt House dates from the 17th century, with Victorian extensions for Lord Palmerston. The gardens extend to 2 acres, with paved terraces, a topiary, a parterre & roses. Rooms are furnished with antiques, & the 3 bedrooms are spacious & panelled, with large beds. The sitting room, available at all times, is super, with knole sofas, T.V. & telephone at hand. Coffee/tea facilities. Excellent touring area, equidistant from Winchester, Salisbury & New Forest.	£22.00	Y	N	Y
Mrs Y. Chivers **Montrose** **Solomons Lane** **Shirrell Heath** **Wickham SO32 2HU** **Tel/Fax: (01329) 833345** **Open: ALL YEAR** **Map Ref No. 26**	Nearest Road: A.32 Montrose offers accommodation of a high standard in tasteful surroundings. 3 delightful bedrooms, 1 en-suite. Comfort & personal attention has helped to build a superb reputation. Situated in the Meon Valley between the historical villages of Wickham & Bishops Waltham, & yet close to the M.27, M.3 & continental ferry ports, thus providing an ideal base for exploring the towns of Winchester, Portsmouth & Southampton, & the lovely Hampshire countryside & coastline.	£23.00 CREDIT CARD VISA M'CARD	N	N	N

Hampshire

		rate from £ per person	children taken	evening meals	animals taken
James & Jean Talbot **Church Farm** **Barton Stacey** **Winchester SO21 3RR** **Tel: (01962) 760268** **Fax 01962 760268** **Open: ALL YEAR** **Map Ref No. 27**	Nearest Road: A.303, A.30 Church Farm is a 15th-century tithe barn with Georgian & modern additions. It features an adjacent coach house & groom's cottage, recently converted, where guests may be totally self-contained, or be welcomed to the log-fired family drawing room & dine on locally produced fresh food. There are 7 beautiful bedrooms for guests, most with en-suite, T.V., tea/coffee-making facilities. Horses are kept. Swimming pool & croquet. Tennis court adjacent.	£22.00 CREDIT CARD VISA M'CARD AMEX	Y	Y	Y
John & Judy Parker **East View** **16 Clifton Hill** **Winchester SO22 5BL** **Tel: (01962) 862986** **Open: ALL YEAR** **Map Ref No. 28**	Nearest Road: A.272, A.34 This Victorian townhouse is set in its own secluded, landscaped garden, & yet is only 5 mins from the city centre. East View has splendid views over the city & cathedral to the South Downs beyond. 3 attractive bedrooms, each with en-suite/private facilities, T.V., radio, tea/coffee trays. Elegant sitting room & dining room furnished with antiques. In summer, breakfast is served in the conservatory. Private car park.	£22.50 CREDIT CARD VISA M'CARD	N	N	N

All the establishments mentioned in this guide are members of
The Worldwide Bed & Breakfast Association

When booking your accommodation please mention
The Best Bed & Breakfast

Hereford & Worcester

Hereford & Worcester
(Heart of England)

Hereford is a beautiful ancient city standing on the banks of the River Wye, almost a crossing point between England & Wales. It is a market centre for the Marches, the border area which has a very particular history of its own.

Hereford Cathedral has a massive sandstone tower & is a fitting venue for the Three Choirs festival which dates from 1727, taking place yearly in one or the other of the three great cathedrals of Hereford, Worcester & Gloucester.

The county is fortunate in having many well preserved historic buildings. Charming "black & white" villages abound here, romantically set in a soft green landscape.

The Royal Forest of Dean spreads its oak & beech trees over 22,000 acres. When people first made their homes in the woodlands it was vaster still. There are rich deposits of coal & iron mined for centuries by the foresters, & the trees have always been felled for charcoal. Ancient courts still exist where forest dwellers can & do claim their rights to use the forest's resources.

The landscape alters dramatically as the land rises to merge with the great Black Mountain range at heights of over 2,600 feet. It is not possible to take cars everywhere but a narrow mountain road, Gospel Pass, takes traffic from Hay-on-Wye to Llanthony with superb views of the upper Wye Valley.

The Pre-Cambrian Malvern Hills form a natural boundary between Herefordshire & Worcestershire & from the highest view points you can see over 14 counties. At their feet nestle pretty little villages such as Eastonor with its 19th century castle in revived Norman style that looks quite mediaeval amongst the parklands & gardens.

There are, in fact, five Malverns. The largest predictably known as Great Malvern was a fashionable 19th century spa & is noted for the purity of the water which is bottled & sold countrywide.

The Priory at Malvern is rich in 15th century stained glass & has a fine collection of mediaeval tiles made locally. William Langland, the 14th century author of "Piers Ploughman", was educated at the Priory & is said to have been sleeping on the Malvern Hills when he had the visionary experience which led to the creation of the poem. Sir Edward Elgar was born, lived & worked here & his "Dream of Gerontius" had its first performance in Hereford Cathedral in 1902.

In Worcestershire another glorious cathedral, with what remains of its monastic buildings, founded in the 11th century, stands beside the River Severn. College Close in Worcester is a lovely group of buildings carefully preserved & very English in character.

The Severn appears to be a very lazy waterway but flood waters can reach astonshing heights, & the "Severn Bore" is a famous phenomenon.

A cruise along the river is a pleasant way to spend a day seeing villages & churches from a different perspective, possibly visiting a riverside inn. To the south of the county lie the undulating Vales of Evesham & Broadway - described as the show village of England.

The Malvern Hills.

Hereford & Worcester

Hereford & Worcester Gazeteer

Areas of outstanding natural beauty.
The Malvern Hills, The Cotswolds, The Wye Valley.

Historic Houses & Castles

Berrington Hall - Leominster
18th century - painted & plastered ceilings. Landscape by Capability Brown.

Brilley - Cwmmau Farmhouse - Whitney-on-Wye
17th century timber-framed & stone tiled farmhouse.

Burton Court - Eardisland
14th century great hall. Exhibition of European & Oriental costume & curios. Model fairground.

Croft Castle - Nr. Leominster
Castle on the Welsh border - inhabited by Croft family for 900 years.

Dinmore Manor - Nr. Hereford
14th century chapel & cloister.

Eastnor Castle - Nr. Ledbury
19th century - Castellated, containing pictures & armour. Arboretum.

Eye Manor - Leominster
17th century Carolean Manor house - excellent plasterwork, paintings, costumes, books, secret passage. Collection of dolls.

Hanbury Hall - Nr. Droitwich
18th century red brick house - only two rooms & painted ceilings on exhibition.

Harvington Hall - Kidderminster
Tudor Manor house with moat, priest's hiding places.

The Greyfriars - Worcester
15th century timber-framed building adjoins Franciscan Priory.

Hellen's - Much Marcle
13th century manorial house of brick & stone. Contains the Great hall with stone table - bedroom of Queen Mary. Much of the original furnishings remain.

Kentchurch Court - Hereford
14th century fortified border Manor house. Paintings & Carvings by Grinling Gibbons.

Moccas Court - Moccas
18th century - designed by Adam - Parklands by Capability Brown - under restoration.

Pembridge Castle - Welsh Newton
17th century moated castle.

Sutton Court - Mordiford
Palladian mansion by Wyatt, watercolours, embroideries, china.

Cathedrals & Churches

Amestry (St. John the Baptist & St.Alkmund)
16th century rood screen.

Abbey Dore (St. Mary & Holy Trinity)
17th century glass & great oak screen - early English architecture.

Brinsop (St. George)
14th century, screen & glass, alabaster reredos, windows in memory of Wordsworth, carved Norman tympanum.

Bredon (St. Giles)
12th century - central tower & spire. Mediaeval heraldic tiles, tombs & early glass.

Brockhampton (St. Eadburgh)
1902. Central tower & thatched roof.

Castle Frome (St. Michael & All Angles)
12th century carved font, 17th century effigies in alabaster.

Chaddesley Corbett (St. Cassian)
14th century monuments, 12th century font.

Elmley (St. Mary)
12th century & 15th century font, tower, gargoyles, mediaeval.

Great Witley (St. Michael)
Baroque - Plasterwork, painted ceiling, painted glass, very fine example.

Hereford (All Saints)
13th-14th centuries, spire, splendid choir stalls, chained library.

Hereford Cathedral
Small cathedral.
Fine central tower c.1325, splendid porch, brasses, early English Lady Chapel with lancet windows. Red sandstone.

Kilpeck (St. Mary & St. David)
Romanesque style - mediaeval windows - fine carvings.

Leominster (St. Peter & St. Paul)
12th century doorway, fine Norman arches, decorated windows.

Much Marcle (St. Bartholomew)
13th century. 14th & 17th century monuments.

HEREFORD & WORCESTER

Map reference

1 Ailesbury
2 Bengry
3 Lee
4 Batson
5 Watson
6 Young
7 Conolly
8 Fothergill
9 Allen
10 G. Williams
11 Foreman
12 Meekings
13 Kemp
16 Rowan
17 J. Williams
19 Lloyd

Herefordshire

		rate from £ per person	children taken	evening meals	animals taken
Caroline Ailesbury **The Old Rectory** **Garway** **HR2 8RH** **Tel: (01600) 750363** Fax 01600 750364 **Open: MAR - NOV** **Map Ref No. 01**	Nearest Road: A.466 This home is Victorian, with a wonderfully welcoming atmosphere. Much of the furniture has been in the family for generations. Log fires & Aga cooking combine to make you feel at home. The Blue Room has a double 4-poster & the Pink Room has twin beds. Although they share a bathroom, each has a handbasin. The acre of mature garden is peaceful & has beautiful views overlooking the Monnow Valley to the Brecon Beacons & the Black Mountains. Children over 8. Dinner by prior arrangement. Single supplement.	£18.00 CREDIT CARD VISA M'CARD	Y	Y	N
Mr & Mrs J. Bengry **The Vauld Farm** **Marden** **Hereford** **HR1 3HA** **Tel: (01568) 797898** **Open: ALL YEAR** **Map Ref No. 02**	Nearest Road: A.49 The Vauld Farm is a delightful 16th-century black-&-white former farmhouse, set in a beautiful garden. It retains many period features throughout & affords attractive accommodation. 3 charming & elegantly furnished bedrooms, each with an en-suite bathroom, T.V. & tea/coffee-making facilities. (1 with 4-poster.) Hearty breakfasts & delicious evening meals are served in the tastefully decorated dining room. A beautiful home & the perfect location for a relaxing break.	£22.50	N	Y	N
Mrs G. Lee **Cwm Craig Farm** **Little Dewchurch** **Hereford HR2 6PS** **Tel: (01432) 840250** **Open: ALL YEAR** **Map Ref No. 03**	Nearest Road: A.49 Spacious Georgian farmhouse, surrounded by superb unspoilt countryside. Situated between the cathedral city of Hereford & Ross-on-Wye, & just a few mins' drive from the Wye Valley. Ideal base for touring the Forest of Dean. All 3 bedrooms have modern amenities, shaver points & tea/coffee facilities. 2 are en-suite. There is a lounge & separated dining room, both with colour T.V.. A full English breakfast is served.	£15.00	Y	N	N
Anthony J. Batson **Bredwardine Hall** **Bredwardine** **Hereford** **HR3 6DB** **Tel: (01981) 500596** **Open: ALL YEAR** **Map Ref No. 04**	Nearest Road: A.438 A charming 19th-century manor house with immense character and literary interest, standing in secluded, wooded gardens & providing elegant and well-appointed accommodation. 5 delightful bedrooms; spacious en-suite/private bathrooms; full central heating; tea/coffee facilities; T.V.s; ample parking. Excellent food and wine; a relaxed, friendly atmosphere; personal service. Set in the tranquil Wye Valley, near Hay-on-Wye and its world-famous bookshops. Children over 8.	£24.00	Y	Y	Y
Grace Watson **Hall's Mill House** **Huntington** **Kington** **HR5 3QA** **Tel: (01497) 831409** **Open: ALL YEAR (Excl. Xmas)** **Map Ref No. 05**	Nearest Road: A.438, A.44 Hall's Mill House has recently been restored & is situated in peaceful, idyllic countryside overlooking the River Arrow. Offering 3 attractively furnished rooms with en-suite/private bathrooms available. A comfortable lounge in which guests may choose to relax. An excellent base from which to explore the area. Easy access to Offa's Dyke, the Black Mountains, Hay-on-Wye, black-&-white villages, Welsh border country, churches & castles. Many excellent pubs & restaurants locally.	£18.00	Y	N	N

The Hills Farm. Leystors.

Herefordshire

		rate from £ per person	children taken	evening meals	animals taken
Roger & Judy Young **Priors Court** **Aylton** **Ledbury** **HR8 2QE** **Tel: (01531) 670748** **Fax 01531 670860** **Open: ALL YEAR** **Map Ref No. 06**	Nearest Road: A.438 You will be warmly welcomed at Priors Court, a Tudor farmhouse whose origins date back to the Domesday Book. Set in the rolling Herefordshire countryside, in its own peaceful farmland, it also has 2 acres of delightful gardens with a stream & a lake. Each comfortable beamed bedroom has a colour T.V., radio, tea/coffee facilities & a private bathroom. Traditional English breakfasts include home-made bread, marmalade & jams. Ideal for walks in the Malverns, Cotswolds or Welsh Hills. Cheltenham, Stratford & Bath within easy reach.	£20.00	Y	N	N
Peter & Jane Conolly **The Hills Farm** **Leysters** **Leominster HR6 0HP** **Tel: (01568) 750205** **Fax 01568 750205** **Open: MAR - NOV** **Map Ref No. 07**	Nearest Road: A.4112 Magnificent views & a splendid welcome await you at this 15th-century farmhouse on the edge of the village of Leysters betwixt Ludlow & Leominster. Delightful en-suite bedrooms have T.V.s & beverage facilities. 3 are in charming barn conversions offering complete seclusion. Scrumptious dinners, traditional or vegetarian, are available in the individually tabled dining room - the dairy in days gone by - which is unlicensed, so bring your own wine. A wonderful escape. *see PHOTO over* CREDIT CARD VISA M'CARD	£23.00	N	Y	Y
Catherine & Marguerite **Fothergill** **Highfield** **Ivington Road, Newtown** **Leominster HR6 8QD** **Tel: (01568) 613216** **Open: ALL YEAR** **Map Ref No. 08**	Nearest Road: A.44, A.49 Twins Catherine & Marguerite are eager to make you feel welcome & at home in their elegant Edwardian house, set in a rural tranquil location. You will be very comfortable in any of the 3 attractive bedrooms, all with a bathroom (1 being en-suite) & tea/coffee-making facilities. There is a large garden & a T.V. lounge with a crackling fire in which guests may relax, & the home-made food is absolutely delicious. Residential licence.	£17.50	N	Y	N
Mike & Anne Allen **Broxwood Court** **Broxwood** **Leominster** **HR6 9JJ** **Tel: (01544) 340245** **Fax 01544 340573** **Open: ALL YEAR (Excl. Feb)** **Map Ref No. 09**	Nearest Road: A.44 Broxwood Court occupies a commanding position, with superb views of the Black Mountains & surrounding countryside. The garden, with its sweeping lawns, magnificent trees & lake, offers a unique atmosphere of peace & tranquillity. Pure white & coloured peacocks roam the grounds. The delightful bedrooms have either en-suite or private bathrooms. Anne is an excellent Cordon Bleu cook, & meals include produce from the extensive organic kitchen garden. Ideal for exploring this beautiful area. Children over 10. *see PHOTO over* CREDIT CARD VISA M'CARD	£35.00	Y	Y	Y
Geoff & Peggy Williams **Sunnymount Hotel** **Ryefield Road** **Ross-on-Wye** **HR9 5LU** **Tel: (01989) 563880** **Open: ALL YEAR (Excl. Xmas)** **Map Ref No. 10**	Nearest Road: M.50, A.40 Quietly situated on the edge of the town, this attractive Edwardian house is warm & inviting. Offering 6 well-appointed bedrooms, with en-suite bathrooms & tea/coffee-making facilities. The sitting rooms (1 with colour T.V.) & dining room overlook the pretty garden. A wide choice of breakfasts using home & local produce freshly prepared for each meal. English/French cooking. Licensed. Ample private parking. An ideal base from which to explore this fascinating area. CREDIT CARD VISA M'CARD AMEX	£24.50	Y	Y	N

Broxwood Court. Broxwood.

Cowley House. Broadway.

Herefordshire & Worcestershire

		rate from £ per person	children taken	evening meals	animals taken
Malcolm & Diane Foreman **Bollitree Lawns** **Weston-under-Penyard** **Ross-on-Wye** **HR9 7PF** **Tel: (01989) 786129** **Open: MAR - NOV** **Map Ref No. 11**	Nearest Road: M.50, A.40 Relax in this elegant Victorian country home, set in 19 acres of peaceful garden & pastureland with fine views. Malcolm & Di pay close attention to detail to ensure their guests' complete enjoyment. The recently restored house is furnished in comfort & style, & both bedrooms, a double & a twin, have excellent en-suite bathrooms. Food lovers & keen gardeners, the owners are restoring the Victorian/Edwardian garden. Children over 12.	£25.00	Y	Y	N

Worcestershire

		rate from £ per person	children taken	evening meals	animals taken
Mary Kemp **Cowley House** **Church Street** **Broadway** **WR12 7AE** **Tel: (01386) 853262** **Open: ALL YEAR** **Map Ref No. 13**	Nearest Road: A.44 Cowley House is a delightful 17th-century Cotswold stone house set in 3/4 acre garden, situated just off Broadways village green in a central but secluded position. It has beautiful antiques, and a wealth of charm & character with exposed stone walls, stone flagged floors & ceiling beams. Bedrooms have private facilities & hairdryers. Complementary beverages are available. Ample car parking. Children over 5.	£25.00 *see PHOTO over*	Y	N	N
Mrs Barbara Ann Meekings **Leasow House** **Laverton Meadow** **Broadway** **WR12 7NA** **Tel: (01386) 584526** **Fax 01386 584596** **Open: ALL YEAR** **Map Ref No. 12**	Nearest Road: A.44 Leasow is a charming 17th-century Cotswold stone farmhouse. Recently renovated, it offers 7 delightful spacious bedrooms, with shower/bath en-suite, T.V. & tea/coffee-making facilities. Set in the peaceful tranquillity of the open countryside, it is only 2 1/2 miles from Broadway village. The house has wonderful panoramic views of the Cotswold escarpment. Ideally situated for touring the Cotswolds & the Vale of Evesham. A warm welcome from the friendly hosts is assured. E-mail: BMEEKINGS@CIX.COMPULINK.CO.UK	£27.00 *see PHOTO over* CREDIT CARD VISA M'CARD AMEX	Y	N	N
Barbara & Richard Rowan **The Red Gate** **32 Avenue Road** **Malvern** **WR14 3BJ** **Tel: (01684) 565013** **Fax 01684 565013** **Open: ALL YEAR** **Map Ref No. 16**	Nearest Road: A.449 Situated in a tree-lined avenue within walking distance of the town centre & hills. This late Victorian house has retained much of its traditional charm, which is matched by the courtesy & hospitality you would expect from a friendly family-run hotel. Each of the 6 bedrooms is quite different, some high & spacious, some cottagey with stripped pine furniture. All are non-smoking, have en-suite bathrooms, colour T.V., tea/coffee & the small comforts one would like to find when away from home. The Red Gate is a very special place. Children over 8 years.	£24.00 CREDIT CARD VISA M'CARD	Y	N	N

Leasow House. Broadway.

Worcestershire

		rate from £ per person	children taken	evening meals	animals taken
Judith & Jon Williams **Wyche Keep** **22 Wyche Road** **Malvern** **WR14 4EG** **Tel: (01684) 567018** **Fax 01684 892304** **Open: ALL YEAR** **Map Ref No. 17**	Nearest Road: B.4218, A.449 Wyche Keep is a unique arts-&-crafts castle-style house, perched high on the Malvern Hills, built by the family of Sir Stanley Baldwin, Prime Minister, to enjoy the spectacular 60-mile views, & having a long history of elegant entertaining. 3 large double suites, including a 4-poster. Traditional English cooking is a speciality & guests can savour memorable 4-course candle-lit dinners, served in a 'house party' atmosphere in front of a log fire. A magical setting with private parking. Home of Brother John Mediaeval Britain Tours, & acclaimed in USA for scholarship & inspiration.	£25.00 🚭 *see PHOTO over*	N	Y	N
Mrs Val Lloyd **40 Britannia Square** **Worcester** **WR1 3DN** **Tel: (01905) 611920** **Fax 01905 27152** **Open: ALL YEAR** **Map Ref No. 19**	Nearest Road: A.449, A.38 A lovely Regency house in a quiet conservation square near the city centre. Spacious, comfortable bedrooms with en-suite bathrooms, tea/coffee facilities & colour T.V.. Decorated with period furnishings to a very high standard & featured in design magazines. A gourmet English breakfast is served in the elegant dining room. Easy walking distance to the cathedral, Royal Worcester Porcelain, racecourse, county cricket gound, theatre & shopping. A pretty garden where guests may relax. An ideal base for touring.	£25.00 CREDIT CARD VISA M'CARD AMEX	Y	N	N

All the establishments mentioned in this guide are members of
The Worldwide Bed & Breakfast Association

When booking your accommodation please mention
The Best Bed & Breakfast

Wyche Keep. Malvern.

Kent

Kent
(South East)

Kent is best known as "the garden of England". At its heart is a tranquil landscape of apple & cherry orchards, hop-fields & oast-houses, but there are also empty downs, chalk sea-cliffs, rich marshlands, sea ports, castles & the glory of Canterbury Cathedral.

The dramatic chalk ridgeway of the North Downs links the White Cliffs of Dover with the north of the county which extends into the edge of London. It was a trade route in ancient times following the high downs above the Weald, dense forest in those days. It can be followed today & it offers broad views of the now agricultural Weald.

The pilgrims who flocked to Canterbury in the 12th-15th centuries, (colourfully portrayed in Chaucer's Canterbury Tales), probably used the path of the Roman Watling Street rather than the high ridgeway.

Canterbury was the cradle of Christianity in southern England & is by tradition the seat of the Primate of All England. This site, on the River Stour, has been settled since the earliest times & became a Saxon stonghold under King Ethelbert of Kent. He established a church here, but it was in Norman times that the first great building work was carried out, to be continued in stages until the 15th century. The result is a blending of styles with early Norman work, a later Norman choir, a vaulted nave in Gothic style & a great tower of Tudor design. Thomas Becket was murdered on the steps of the Cathedral in 1170. The town retains much of its mediaeval character with half-timbered weavers' cottages, old churches & the twin towers of the west gate.

Two main styles of building give the villages of Kent their special character. The Kentish yeoman's house was the home of the wealthier farmers & is found throughout the county. It is a timber-frame building with white lath & plaster walls & a hipped roof of red tiles. Rather more modest in style is a small weatherboard house, usually painted white or cream. Rolvenden & Groombridge have the typical charm of a Kentish village whilst Tunbridge Wells is an attractive town, with a paved parade known as the Pantiles & excellent antique shops.

There are grand houses & castles throughout the county. Leeds Castle stands in a lake & dates back to the 9th century. It has beautifully landscaped parkland. Knowle House is an impressive Jacobean & Tudor Manor House with rough ragstone walls, & acres of deer-park & woodland.

Kent is easily accessible from the Channel Ports, Gatwick Airport & London.

Leeds Castle.

Kent

Kent
Gazeteer

Areas of outstanding natural beauty.
Kent Downs.

Historic Houses & Castles

Aylesford, The Friars - Nr. Maidstone
13th century Friary & shrine of Our Lady,
(much restored), 14th century cloisters -
original.

Allington Castle -Nr. Maidstone
13th century. One time home of Tudor
poet Thomas Wyatt. Restored early 20th
century. Icons & Renaissance paintings.

Black Charles - Nr. Sevenoaks
14th century Hall house - Tudor fireplaces,
beautiful panelling.

Boughton Monchelsea Place - Nr.
Maidstone
Elizabethan Manor House - grey stone
battlements - 18th century landscaped
park, wonderful views of Weald of Kent.

Chartwell - Westerham
Home of Sir Winston Churchill.
Chiddingstone Castle - Nr. Edenbridge
18th century Gothic revival building
encasing old remains of original Manor
House - Royal Stuart & Jacobite
collection.
Ancient Egyptian collection - Japanese
netsuke, etc.

Eyehorne Manor - Hollingbourne
15th century Manor house with 17th
century additions.

Cobham Hall - Cobham
16th century house - Gothic &
Renaissance - Wyatt interior. Now school
for girls.

Fairfield - Eastry, Sandwich
13th-14th centuries - moated castle. Was
home of Anne Boleyn. Beautiful gardens
with unique collection of classical statuary.

Knole - Sevenoaks
15th century - splendid Jacobean interior -
17th & 18th century furniture. One of the
largest private houses in England.

Leeds Castle- Nr. Maidstone
Built in middle of the lake, it was the home
of the mediaeval Queens of England.

Lullingstone Castle - Eynsford
14th century mansion house - frequented
by Henry VIII & Queen Anne.
Still occupied by descendants of the
original owners

Long Barn - Sevenoaks
14th century house - said to be home of
William Caxton. Restored by Edwin
Lutyens; 16th century barn added to
enlarge house. Galleried hall - fine
beaming & fireplaces. Lovely gardens
created by Sir Harold Nicholson & his wife
Vita Sackville-West.

Owletts - Cobham
Carolean house of red brick with
plasterwork ceiling & fine staircase.

Owl House - Lamberhurst
16th century cottage, tile hung; said to be
home of wool smuggler. Charming
gardens.

Penshurst Place - Tonbridge
14th century house with mediaeval Great
Hall perfectly preserved.English Gothic.
Birthplace of Elizabethan poet, Sir Philip
Sidney
Fine staterooms, splendid picture gallery,
famous toy museum. Tudor gardens &
orchards.

Saltwood Castle - Nr. Hythe
Mediaeval - very fine castle & is privately
occupied. Was lived in by Sir Ralph de
Broc, murderer of Thomas a Becket.

Squerreys Court - Westerham
Manor house of William & Mary period,
with furniture, paintings & tapestries of
time. Connections with General Wolfe.

Stoneacre - Otham
15th century yeoman's half-timbered
house.

Cathedrals & Churches

Brook (St. Mary)
11th century paintings in this unaltered
early Norman church.

Brookland (St. Augustine)
13th century & some later part. Crown-
post roofs, detached wooden belfry with
conical cap. 12th century lead font.

Canterbury Cathedral
12th century wall paintings, 12th & 13th
century stained glass. Very fine Norman
crypt. Early perpendicular nave &
cloisters which have heraldic bosses.
Wonderful central tower.

Charing (St. Peter & St. Paul)
13th & 15th century interior with 15th
century tower. 17th century restoration.

Kent

Cobham (St. Mary)
16th century carved & painted tombs - unequalled collection of brasses in county.
Elham (St. Mary the Virgin)
Norman wall with 13th century arcades, perpendicular clerestory. Restored by Eden.
Lullingstone (St. Botolph)
14th century mainly - 16th century wood screen. Painted glass monuments.
Newington-on-the-Street (St. Mary the Virgin)
13th & 14th century - fine tower. 13th century tomb. Wall paintings.
Rochester Cathedral
Norman facade & nave, otherwise early English.
12th century west door. 14th century doorway to Chapter room.
Stone (St. Mary)
13th century - decorated - paintings, 15th century brass, 16th century tomb.
Woodchurch (All Saints)
13th century, having late Norman font & priest's brass of 1320. Arcades alternating octagonal & rounded columns. Triple lancets with banded marble shafting at east end.

Museums & Galleries

Royal Museums - Canterbury
Archaeological, geological, mineralogical exhibits, natural history, pottery & porcelain. Engravings, prints & pictures.
Westgate - Canterbury
Museum of armour, etc. in 14th century gatehouse of city.
Dartford District Museum - Dartford
Roman, Saxon & natural history.
Deal Museum - Deal
Prehistoric & historic antiquities.
Dicken's House Museum - Broadstairs
Personalia of Dickens; prints, costume & Victoriana.
Down House - Downe
The home of Charles Darwin for 40 years, now his memorial & museum.
Dover Museum - Dover
Roman pottery, ceramics, coins, zoology, geology, local history, etc.
Faversham Heritage Society - Faversham
1000 years of history & heritage.
Folkestone Museum & Art Gallery - Folkestone
Archeology, local history & sciences.

Herne Bay Museum - Herne Bay
Stone, Bronze & Early Iron Age specimens. Roman material from Reculver excavations. Items of local & Kentish interest.
Museum & Art Gallery - Maidstone
16th century manor house exhibiting natural history & archaeolgical collections. Costume Gallery, bygones, ceramics, 17th century works by Dutch & Italian painters. Regimental museum

Historic Monuments

Eynsford Castle - Eynsford
12th century castle remains.
Rochester Castle - Rochester
Storied keep - 1126-39
Roman Fort & Anglo-Saxon Church - Reculver
Excavated remains of 3rd century fort & Saxon church.
Little Kit's Coty House - Aylesford
Ruins of burial chambers from 2 long barrows.
Lullingstone Roman Villa - Lullingstone
Roman farmstead excavations.
Roman Fort & Town - Richborough
Roman 'Rutupiae' & fort
Tonbridge Castle - Tonbridge
12th century curtain walls, shell of keep & 14th century gatehouse.
Dover Castle - Dover
Keep built by Henry II in 1180. Outer curtain built 13th century.

Gardens

Chilham Castle Gardens - Nr. Canterbury
25 acre gardens of Jacobean house, laid out by Tradescant.
Lake garden, fine trees & birds of prey. Jousting & mediaeval banquets.
Great Comp Gardens - Nr. Borough Green
Outstanding 7 acre garden with old brick walls.
Owl House Gardens - Lamberhurst
16th century smugglers cottage with beautiful gardens of roses, daffodils & rhododendrons.
Sissinghurst Castle Gardens - Sissinghurst
Famous gardens created by Vita Sackville-West around the remains of an Elizabethan mansion.

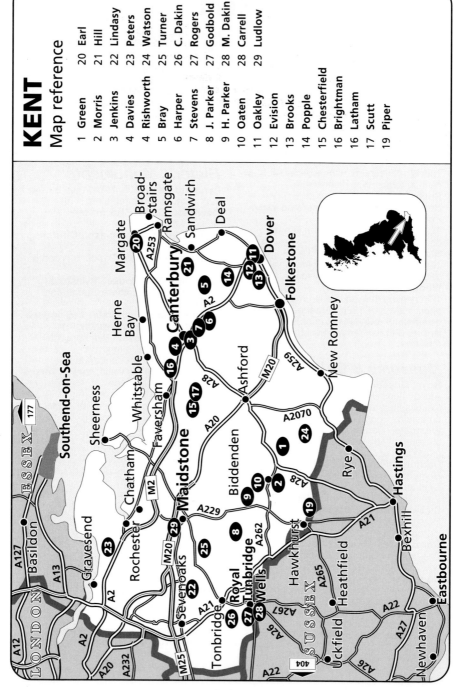

KENT
Map reference

1 Green	20 Earl
2 Morris	21 Hill
3 Jenkins	22 Lindasy
4 Davies	23 Peters
4 Rishworth	24 Watson
5 Bray	25 Turner
6 Harper	26 C. Dakin
7 Stevens	27 Rogers
8 J. Parker	27 Godbold
9 H. Parker	28 M. Dakin
10 Oaten	28 Carrell
11 Oakley	29 Ludlow
12 Evision	
13 Brooks	
14 Popple	
15 Chesterfield	
16 Brightman	
16 Latham	
17 Scutt	
19 Piper	

Hales Place. High Halden.

Kent

		rate from £ per person	children taken	evening meals	animals taken
Roger & Ellen Green **Hales Place** **High Halden** **Ashford TN26 3JQ** **Tel: (01233) 850219** Fax 01233 850716 **Open: ALL YEAR** **Map Ref No. 01**	Nearest Road: A.28, M.20 Off the beaten track & set in 11 acres, award-winning Hales Place dates from the 14th century & is the ideal touring base for Kent. A prolific kitchen garden provides organic fruit & vegetables for candlelit dinners & homemade preserves & chutneys. 3 delightful bedrooms with en-suite/private facilities. The private cinema in the grounds is a firm favourite with guests. Special cinema weekends can be arranged. 🚭 *see PHOTO over* CREDIT CARD VISA M'CARD	£25.00	Y	Y	N
Mrs Susan Morris **Tudor Cottage** **25 High Street** **Biddenden** **Ashford TN27 8AL** **Tel: (01580) 291913** **Open: ALL YEAR** **Map Ref No. 02**	Nearest Road: A.262 Tudor Cottage is a beautiful 15th-century house in the centre of the charming & historic village of Biddenden, with 2 good restaurants nearby. Accommodation is in 3 delightful double bedrooms, 2 en-suite, 1 with private facilities, each well-equipped with colour T.V. & tea/coffee-making facilities. Children over 10 welcome. Tudor Cottage is an ideal location from which to explore beautiful Kent & East Sussex.	£19.50	Y	N	N
Jill & David Jenkins **Thanington Hotel** **140 Wincheap** **Canterbury** **CT1 3RY** **Tel: (01227) 453227** Fax 01227 453225 **Open: ALL YEAR** **Map Ref No. 03**	Nearest Road: A.28 Spacious Georgian hotel, ideally situated 10 mins stroll from the city centre. 15 en-suite bedrooms, beautifully decorated & furnished, all in immaculate condition with modern-day extras. King-size 4-poster beds, antique bedsteads & 2 large family rooms. Walled garden with patio, indoor heated swimming pool, bar, guest lounge & snooker/games room. Delicious breakfast served in the elegant dining room. Car park. An oasis in a busy tourist city, convenient for channel ports, tunnel & historic houses of Kent. Gatwick 60 mins. E-mail: Thanington_Hotel@Compuserve.Com *see PHOTO over* CREDIT CARD VISA M'CARD AMEX	£30.00	Y	N	Y
Ann & John Davies **Magnolia House** **36 St Dunstan's Terrace** **Canterbury CT2 8AX** **Tel/Fax: (01227) 765121** **Mobile 0585 595970** **Open: ALL YEAR** **Map Ref No. 04**	Nearest Road: A.2, M.2 Magnolia House is a charming, detached late-Georgian house situated in a quiet, residential street a 10-min walk from the city centre. The 7 bedrooms are individually coordinated to a high standard, & have every facility for an enjoyable stay. A varied breakfast menu is served in the dining room overlooking the attractive walled garden, where you are welcome to relax after a busy day's sightseeing. Evening meals available Nov-Feb. Children over 12. 🚭 *see PHOTO over* CREDIT CARD VISA M'CARD AMEX	£30.00	Y	Y	N
Keith & Anthea Rishworth **Oriel Lodge** **3 Queens Avenue** **Canterbury CT2 8AY** **Tel/Fax: (01227) 462845** **Open: ALL YEAR** **Map Ref No. 04**	Nearest Road: A.2, M.2 In a tree-lined residential road, 5 mins' walk from the city centre & restaurants, Oriel Lodge is an attractive Edwardian detached house retaining a warm & restful period character. There are 6 well-furnished rooms with up-to-date facilities, a comfortable lounge with log fire & attractive gardens. Smoking in lounge area only. Private parking. Children over 6 years. CREDIT CARD VISA M'CARD	£19.00	Y	N	N

Thanington Hotel. Canterbury.

Magnolia House. Canterbury.

Kent

			rate from £ per person	children taken	evening meals	animals taken
Mrs Rosemary Bray **Ratling House** Ratling, Aylesham Canterbury CT3 3HL Tel: (01304) 842200 Open: ALL YEAR Map Ref No. 05	Nearest Road: A.2 A comfortable 18th-century country house in a quiet rural setting near the A.2. Off the B.2046 approx. 1 mile east of Adisham, & 1 mile north of Aylesham. Centrally heated & attractively furnished double bedrooms, 1 with en-suite facilities, T.V., etc., 2 with an adjacent bathroom. Large gardens of 2 acres. Ample private parking. Convenient for Channel ports & Tunnel. Dover & Canterbury 9 miles.	£20.00	Y	N	N
Hilary Harper **East Bridge Country Hotel** Bridge Hill, Bridge Canterbury CT4 5AS Tel: (01227) 830808 Fax 01227 832181 Open: ALL YEAR Map Ref No. 06	Nearest Road: A.2 A friendly, elegant & comfortable Georgian house in a pretty village. 15 mins from the sea ports of Dover & Folkestone. Overlooking open countryside of outstanding beauty, the house offers accommodation in 8 comfortable rooms, 4 en-suite, all with modern amenities, T.V. & tea/coffee-making facilities. Ideal for walking, riding, fishing. Close to Kent's historic castles. Tasty English breakfasts. A licensed restaurant available to residents & non-residents.	£20.00 CREDIT CARD VISA M'CARD	Y	Y	N
Colin & Rosemary Stevens **Iffin Farmhouse** Iffin Lane Canterbury CT4 7BE Tel: (01227) 462776 Fax 01227 462776 Open: ALL YEAR Map Ref No. 07	Nearest Road: A.2 A warm welcome awaits you in this old 18th-century farmhouse, renovated to a very high standard. 3 large double bedrooms, each with views to the garden & orchards, T.V., tea/coffee-making facilities & an en-suite/private bathroom. Enjoy a full English breakfast, served in a lovely dining room. Set in 10 acres of gardens, paddocks & orchards, Iffin Farmhouse (only 6 mins' drive from historic Canterbury) is a delightful spot for touring Kent. Children over 5 years.	£20.00 *see PHOTO over*	Y	N	N
Jeremy & Annie Parker **West Winchet** Winchet Hill, Goudhurst Cranbrook TN17 1JX Tel: (01580) 212024 Fax 01580 212250 Open: ALL YEAR (Excl. Xmas & New Year) Map Ref No. 08	Nearest Road: A.262 West Winchet is the west wing of a substantial Victorian mansion surrounded by parkland in a secluded & peaceful setting. 2 beautifully decorated rooms, 1 double with private bathroom & 1 twin with en-suite shower. Each with T.V., radio & tea/coffee facilities. Both rooms are on the ground floor, & the twin bedded room has French windows onto the terrace & into the garden. A magnificent drawing room for guests' use. An ideal touring centre for Kent & East Sussex. 2 1/2 miles mainline station (London 55 mins).	£22.50	Y	N	Y
Heather & Kenneth Parker **Maplehurst Mill** Mill Lane, Frittenden Cranbrook TN17 2DT Tel: (01580) 852203 Fax 01580 852203 Open: ALL YEAR Map Ref No. 09	Nearest Road: A.229 Maplehurst Mill is a beautiful water mill, attached to a mediaeval mill house & standing in 11 acres of landscaped gardens. Offering 3 attractively furnished guest rooms (incl. 1 4-poster), with en-suite/private bathroom, T.V., etc. Each has views over the water & the surrounding countryside. A breakfast & candlelit dinner are served in the mediaeval miller's house, in a beautiful beamed dining room with inglenook, antiques & silver. A delightful home, where a warm welcome awaits you. Children over 12.	£29.00 CREDIT CARD VISA M'CARD	Y	Y	N

Iffin Farmhouse. Canterbury.

Kent

	Nearest Road	rate from £ per person	children taken	evening meals	animals taken
Bridget & Robin Oaten **Hancocks Farmhouse** **Tilsden Lane** **Cranbrook TN17 3PH** **Tel: (01580) 714645** **Fax 01580 714645** **Open: ALL YEAR** **Map Ref No. 10**	Nearest Road: A.229, A.262 Extended in the late 16th century, Hancocks Farmhouse is now a lovely Grade II listed building, surrounded by farmland on the edge of the Wealden town of Cranbrook. Comfortably furnished with antiques. 3 beautifully decorated bedrooms, 1 with a 4-poster, each with an en-suite/private bathroom, T.V., radio & tea/coffee facilities. Dinner here is delicious, & all the bread rolls, cakes & jams are home-made. Guests may relax in the pretty garden. Children over 12.	£30.00	Y	Y	Y
Chris & Lea Oakley **Wallett's Court, West Cliffe** **St. Margarets-at-Cliffe** **Dover CT15 6EW** **Tel: (01304) 852424** **Fax 01304 853430** **Open: ALL YEAR (Excl. Xmas.)** **Map Ref No. 11**	Nearest Road: A.258, A.2 A wonderful 17th-century manor house, home of William Pitt the Younger, situated in countryside above the White Cliffs of Dover. Accommodation is in 10 delightful & very comfortable bedrooms, all en-suite. Oak beams & inglenook fireplaces. A true 17th-century atmosphere. Home-made produce for breakfast, & Saturday is 'Gourmet Evening' in the award-winning restaurant. Kingsdown Golf Course close by. A very warm welcome awaits all visitors to this lovely house.	£32.50 CREDIT CARD VISA M'CARD AMEX	Y	Y	N
Mrs Judy Evison **The Old Vicarage** **Chilverton Elms** **Hougham** **Dover CT15 7AS** **Tel: (01304) 210668** **Fax 01304 225118** **Open: ALL YEAR** **Map Ref No. 12**	Nearest Road: A.2, A.20, M.20 Many guests are totally surprised by the peaceful atmosphere & commanding position of this house, given its closeness to Dover. This is a beautiful country house built around 1870 & totally restored as their home by the present owners, retaining many original features. It is elegantly furnished with antiques & provides everything for your stay to the very highest standards, 2 en-suite bedrooms & 1 with private bathroom. Excellent base for touring east Kent. 2 miles ferry ports/9 miles Channel Tunnel. Parking. Dinner by arrangement.	£27.50 CREDIT CARD VISA M'CARD	Y	Y	N
Diana Brooks **Rose Hill Farm, Mill Lane** **West Hougham** **Dover CT15 7BD** **Tel: (01304) 240609** **Open: ALL YEAR** **Map Ref No. 13**	Nearest Road: A.20, M.20 Following a successful feature in the guide at Lucy's, Hythe, the Brookses are now at a delightful 17th-century listed farmhouse with antique furniture, beams, log fires & charming en-suite bedrooms; 2 lovely cottages. A 1 1/2 acre garden with heated swimming pool, croquet lawn & lovely garden views - Dover Castle in the distance. Less than 10 mins' drive to Dover Port & the Channel Tunnel. A quiet & idyllic setting.	£21.00	Y	N	N
Barry & Lyn Popple **Sunshine Cottage** **The Green, Mill Lane** **Shepherdswell** **Dover CT15 7LQ** **Tel: (01304) 831359** **Tel: (01304) 831218** **Open: ALL YEAR** **Map Ref No. 14**	Nearest Road: A.2 A 17th-century, Grade II listed cottage, overlooking Shepherdswell village green, with a wealth of beams, an inglenook fireplace & 2 lounges. Tastefully furnished, & with a homely atmosphere. 6 attractive bedrooms. A pretty garden & courtyard available to guests. Good home-cooking & home-made preserves. Good food also available at a nearby pub. Shepherdswell is situated halfway between Canterbury & Dover, 25 mins from the Channel Tunnel. BR station 5 mins' walk away.	£20.00	Y	Y	N

Kent

		rate from £ per person	children taken	evening meals	animals taken
Mr & Mrs M. Chesterfield **Frith Farm House** **Otterden** **Faversham ME13 0DD** **Tel: (01795) 890701** **Fax 01795 890009** **Open: ALL YEAR** **Map Ref No. 15**	Nearest Road: A.20 A warm welcome awaits guests at this restored Georgian farmhouse, surrounded by lovely cherry trees. It stands in an Area of Outstanding Natural Beauty. Accommodation is in a choice of 3 comfortable en-suite rooms with radio, T.V. & tea/coffee-making facilities. This makes a pleasant base from which to tour the whole of Kent. Leeds Castle, Rochester, Chilam & Canterbury are nearby. A delightful home.	£23.50 *see PHOTO over* CREDIT CARD VISA M'CARD	N	Y	N
Mrs Annette Brightman **The Granary** **Plumford Lane,** **Brogdale Road** **Faversham ME13 0DS** **Tel: (01795) 538416** **Fax 01795 538416** **Open: ALL YEAR** **Map Ref No. 16**	Nearest Road: A.2 Set deep in apple-orchard country, The Granary - recently part of a working farm - has been tastefully & beautifully converted to provide an interesting & spacious home. All rooms are delightfully furnished to a very high standard, whilst retaining a rustic charm. 3 charming bedrooms with en-suite/private bathrooms. The guests' lounge, with balcony, overlooks the surrounding countryside. Good local pubs offering excellent food. Ideal for touring historic Kent. **E-mail: thegranary@compuserve.com**	£22.00 CREDIT CARD VISA M'CARD	Y	N	N
Mrs Corrine Scutt **Leaveland Court** **Leaveland** **Faversham** **ME13 0NP** **Tel: (01233) 740596** **Open: FEB - NOV** **Map Ref No. 17**	Nearest Road: A.251 Guests are warmly welcomed to this enchanting 15th-century timbered farmhouse, & its delightful gardens with heated swimming pool. Situated in a quiet rural setting, between 13th-century Leaveland church & woodlands, & surrounded by a 300-acre downland farm. All of the attractive bedrooms have en-suite facilities, colour T.V. & tea/coffee tray. Conveniently placed only 5 mins from M.2 & Faversham, 20 mins Canterbury & 30 mins Channel ports. A charming home.	£20.00 CREDIT CARD VISA M'CARD	Y	N	N
Prudence Latham **Tenterden House** **209 The Street** **Boughton** **Faversham ME13 9BL** **Tel: (01227) 751593** **Open: ALL YEAR** **Map Ref No. 16**	Nearest Road: A.2, M.2 Tenterden House is a listed Tudor building in the village of Boughton, which is 6 miles from Canterbury & 1 mile from the M.2. The old gardener's cottage has been renovated to provide a bathroom & 2 bedrooms (1 double & 1 twin), h&c, T.V. & tea/coffee facilities. Full English breakfast is served in the main house. Restaurants & pubs within walking distance, as is Boughton Golf Course. An ideal centre for walking, touring, bird-watching & reaching all Channel Ports.	£19.00	Y	N	N
Mrs Rosemary Piper **Conghurst Farm** **Conghurst Lane** **Hawkhurst TN18 4RW** **Tel: (01580) 753331** **Fax 01580 754579** **Open: FEB - NOV** **Map Ref No. 19**	Nearest Road: A.268 Set in peaceful, totally unspoilt countryside, Conghurst Farm offers a perfect spot for a restful holiday. Within easy reach of all the marvellous houses & gardens that this part of the country has to offer. Accommodation is in 3 very comfortable bedrooms, all with en-suite/private bathrooms. There is a drawing room, a separate T.V. room &, in the summer, a delightful garden for guests to enjoy. An ideal base from which to explore Kent.	£24.00	N	Y	N

Frith Farm House. Otterden.

Jordans. Plaxtol.

Kent

	rate from £ per person	children taken	evening meals	animals taken
Mrs Ann Earl **The Greswolde Hotel** **20 Surrey Road** **Cliftonville** **Margate CT9 2LA** **Tel: (01843) 223956** **Open: ALL YEAR** **Map Ref No. 20**	Nearest Road: M.2, A.299 The Greswolde is a 6-bedroomed Victorian hotel retaining much of its original character & charm. All rooms have en-suite facilities, with colour T.V. & tea makers. There is a quiet, relaxing lounge/ reading room. Located 100 yds from the promenade, & close to championship indoor & outdoor bowling greens. Many golf courses also within easy reach. Pubs & eating places are nearby. Ideal for touring, with Channel ports close by. Children over 8 years welcome.	£18.50 CREDIT CARD VISA M'CARD	Y	N	Y
Mary Hill **Ringlemere Oast** **Ringlemere Farm** **Woodnesborough** **Sandwich CT13 0PS** **Tel/Fax: (01304) 812646** **Open: APR - SEPT** **Map Ref No. 21**	Nearest Road: A.257 A substantial twin kilned oast house with large gardens in the quiet of the east Kent countryside, offering 3 double bedrooms with en-suite facilities, elegant dining room & comfortable lounge leading to secluded patio. Centrally situated for the Channel Tunnel & the ferry terminals, with Canterbury, the Cinque Ports & resort towns easily reached. Golf & watersports mingle with country pubs & relaxing moments.	£25.00 *see PHOTO over* CREDIT CARD VISA M'CARD	N	N	N
Mrs Jo Lindsay N.D.D.,A.T.D. **Jordans** **Sheet Hill** **Plaxtol** **Sevenoaks** **TN15 0PU** **Tel: (01732) 810379** **Open: Mid JAN-Mid DEC** **Map Ref No. 22**	Nearest Road: A.25, A.227 Beautiful, picture-postcard, 15th-century Tudor house, (awarded a 'Historic Building of Kent' plaque) in the picturesque village of Plaxtol, among orchards & parkland. It is beautifully furnished, & has leaded windows, inglenook fireplaces, massive oak beams & an enchanting old English garden with roses & espalier trees. Within easy reach are Ightham Mote, Leeds & Hever Castle, Penshurst, Chartwell & Knole. 3 lovely rooms, with en-suite/private facilities. London 35 mins by train, & easy access to airports. Children over 12.	£26.00 🚭 *see PHOTO over*	Y	N	N
Mrs V. A. Peters **Gardeners Cottage** **Puckle Hill** **Shorne Ridgeway** **DA12 3LB** **Tel/Fax: (01474) 823269** **Open: ALL YEAR** **Map Ref No. 23**	Nearest Road: A.2 Gardeners Cottage is an attractive house set in 5 acres of gardens with a bluebell wood, a magnificent ancient lime tree, croquet lawn & rhododendron-lined driveway. 3 attractively furnished bedrooms, each with an en-suite/private bathroom, tea/coffee facilities & T.V.. It retains many original features including oak beams, inglenooks & wood-burning stoves. Close to the A.2/M.2 & M.25, it is ideally situated for touring Kent - historic Rochester 4 miles - & for visiting London. Ashford International Station 35 mins.	£25.00 🚭	Y	Y	N
Mr & Mrs Ian Watson **Wittersham Court** **Wittersham** **Tenterden TN30 7EA** **Tel/Fax: (01797) 270425** **Open: ALL YEAR (Excl. Xmas & New Year)** **Map Ref No. 24**	Nearest Road: A.28 Wittersham Court is a Grade II listed period house, tastefully furnished & set in an acre of peaceful garden on the famous Isle of Oxney, midway between Tenterden & Rye. 3 attractive bedrooms, each with an en-suite/private bathroom. Excellent evening meals available. There are many beautiful gardens & castles in the area to visit, as well as Romney Marsh with its lovely churches. Only 45 mins from Dover & Folkestone. Single supplement.	£30.00 🚭 CREDIT CARD VISA M'CARD	N	Y	N

Ringlemere Oast. Woodnesborough.

Swale Cottage. Penshurst.

Kent

		rate from £ per person	children taken	evening meals	animals taken
Mrs Anne G. Turner **Leavers Oast** **Stanford Lane** **Hadlow** **Tonbridge TN11 0JN** **Tel/Fax: (01732) 850924** **Open: ALL YEAR** **Map Ref No. 25**	Nearest Road: A.26 A warm, friendly welcome & imaginative cooking is to be found in this beautiful 19th-century oast. An en-suite bedroom in the barn & 2 roundel bedrooms provide comfortable accommodation. The house is furnished with interesting antiques, & the lovely garden overlooks open country. Excellent communications make it an ideal base for visiting many historic houses & gardens. London 40 mins by rail. Children over 12 years. Evening meals by arrangement.	£26.00	Y	N	N
Mrs Cynthia Dakin **Swale Cottage** **Poundsbridge Lane** **Penshurst** **Tonbridge** **TN11 8AH** **Tel: (01892) 870738** **Open: ALL YEAR** **Map Ref No. 26**	Nearest Road: A.26, B.2176 Swale Cottage is a beautifully converted Kentish barn, formerly part of a 13th-century Yeoman farm. Now a spacious home offering 3 well-appointed en-suite bedrooms with T.V. (4-poster, double & a twin) & an elegant breakfast room, all furnished in English country cottage style. The rooms are adorned with watercolours & pastels painted by your hostess. The setting is idyllic, with glorious views of gardens & countryside. Prestigious awards. Close to Penshurst Place, Hever & Chartwell. Gatwick 40 mins.	£28.00 *see PHOTO over*	Y	N	N
Richard & Sue Rogers **Ash Tree Cottage** **7 Eden Road** **Tunbridge Wells TN1 1TS** **Tel/Fax: (01892) 541317** **Open: ALL YEAR (Excl. Xmas & New Year)** **Map Ref No. 27**	Nearest Road: A.21 Ashtree Cottage is situated in a quiet private road just above the famous Pantiles, & within a few minutes' walk of the high street & station. There are 2 charming & attractively furnished bedrooms with en-suite bathrooms, radio, T.V., tea/coffee-making facilities & plenty of tourist information. There is an excellent choice of restaurants & country pubs nearby, & many places of interest are within easy reach. Children over 8.	£21.00	Y	N	N
Mary & Tony Dakin **The Old Parsonage** **Church Lane, Frant** **Tunbridge Wells** **TN3 9DX** **Tel: (01892) 750773** **Fax 01892 750773** **Open: ALL YEAR** **Map Ref No. 28**	Nearest Road: A.267 This award-winning country house is peacefully situated by the church in pretty Frant village with its 2 character pubs & restaurant nearby. Overlooking Lord Abergavenny's deer park on one side & the church on the other, this Georgian house provides superb accommodation including luxurious en-suite bedrooms, antique-furnished reception rooms & a flower-filled conservatory where guests may relax in comfort. Short drive to 15 historic houses & gardens. Gatwick 40 mins. Heathrow 70 mins. London 45 mins by train.	£30.00 *see PHOTO over* CREDIT CARD VISA M'CARD	Y	N	Y
Mrs Carolyn Carrell **Rowden House Farm** **Frant** **Tunbridge Wells** **TN3 9HS** **Tel: (01892) 750259** **Open: APR - OCT** **Map Ref No. 28**	Nearest Road: A.267 A delightful Elizabethan house, listed as of architectural interest, standing in 20 acres, with sheep, horses, dogs & chickens. Surrounded by the beautiful, rolling, wooded countryside of Sussex, it is perfectly placed for visiting the stately homes & towns of Kent & Sussex. 1 twin-bedded room, with private bathroom, & 2 singles with wash basins. All have tea/coffee-making facilities. An attractive drawing room, with T.V.. Gatwick 1 hour, London 1 1/4 hours. Children over 10.	£21.50	Y	N	N

The Old Parsonage. Frant.

Kent

	rate from £ per person	children taken	evening meals	animals taken
Angela & Michael Godbold **Danehurst House Hotel** **41 Lower Green Road** **Rusthall** **Tunbridge Wells TN4 8TW** **Tel: (01892) 527739** **Fax 01892 514804** **Open: ALL YEAR** **Map Ref No. 27**	Nearest Road: A.264 Danehurst is a charming gabled house in a village setting in the heart of Kent. The tastefully furnished bedrooms afford excellent accommodation, & a delicious breakfast is served in the Victorian conservatory. Guests may also enjoy a candle-lit dinner in the elegant dining room between Oct. & May. Angela & Michael are delighted to welcome you to their home & will ensure that your stay is relaxing & enjoyable. Private parking available. Children over 8 years. (Please note Danehurst is closed the last week in August.)	£25.00 🚭 *see PHOTO over* CREDIT CARD VISA M'CARD AMEX	Y	Y	N
Judy Ludlow **Woodgate** **Birling Road** **Leybourne** **West Malling ME19 5HT** **Tel: (01732) 843201** **Open: JAN - NOV** **Map Ref No. 29**	Nearest Road: A.228 This is a very pretty 17th-century cottage, situated in a rural location & yet within easy reach of the M.20. Set in 4 acres of woodland garden, with tropical bird aviaries. Unusual chickens wander freely during daylight hours. Rooms are tastefully & distinctively decorated, with antiques collected during the years spent living overseas. Meals (available with prior notice) are a speciality, & are unusual & interesting. **E-mail: ludlow@easynet.co.uk**	£20.00 🚭	Y	Y	Y

All the establishments mentioned in this guide are members of
The Worldwide Bed & Breakfast Association

When booking your accommodation please mention
The Best Bed & Breakfast

Danehurst House Hotel. Rustall.

Leicestershire, Nottinghamshire & Rutland

Leicestershire (East Midlands)

Rural Leicestershire is rich in grazing land, a peaceful, undramatic landscape broken up by the waterways that flow through in the south of the county.

The River Avon passes on its way to Stratford, running by 17th century Stanford Hall & its motorcycle museum. The Leicester section of the Grand Union Canal was once very important for the transportation of goods from the factories of the Midlands to London Docks. It passes through a fascinating series of multiple locks at Foxton. The decorative barges, the 'narrow boats' are pleasure craft these days rather than the lifeblood of the closed community of boat people who lived & worked out their lives on the canals.

Rutland was formerly England's smallest county, but was absorbed into East Leicestershire in the 1970's. Recently, once again, it has become a county in its' own right. Rutland Water, is one of Europe's largest reservoirs & an attractive setting for sailing, fishing or enjoying a trip on the pleasure cruiser. There is also the Rutland Theatre at Tolethorpe Hall, where a summer season of Shakespeare's plays is presented in the open air.

Melton Mowbray is famous for its pork pies & it is also the centre of Stilton cheese country. The "King of Cheeses" is made mainly in the Vale of Belvoir where Leicestershire meets Nottinghamshire, & the battlements & turrets of Belvoir Castle overlook the scene from its hill-top.

To the north-west the Charnwood Forest area is pleasantly wooded & the deer park at Bradgate surrounding the ruined home of Lady Jane Grey, England's nine-day queen, is a popular attraction.

Nottinghamshire (East Midlands)

Nottinghamshire has a diversity of landscape from forest to farmland, from coal mines to industrial areas.

The north of the county is dominated by the expanse of Sherwood Forest, smaller now than in the time of legendary Robin Hood & his Merry Men, but still a lovely old woodland of Oak & Birch.

The Dukeries are so called because of the numerous ducal houses built in the area & there is beautiful parkland on these great estates that can be visited. Clumber Park, for instance has a huge lake & a double avenue of Limes.

Newstead Abbey was a mediaeval priory converted into the Byron family home in the 16th century. It houses the poet Byron's manuscripts & possessions & is set in wonderful gardens.

More modest is the terraced house in Eastwood, where D.H. Lawrence was born into the mining community on which his novels are based.

Nottingham was recorded in the Domesday Book as a thriving community & that tradition continues. It was here that Arkwright perfected his cotton-spinning machinery & went on to develop steam as a power source for industry.

Textiles, shoes, bicycles & tobacco are all famous Nottingham products, & the story of Nottingham Lace can be discovered at the Lace Hall, housed in a former church.

Nottingham Castle, high on Castle Rock, was built & destroyed & rebuilt many times during its history. It now houses the city's Art Gallery & Museum. The Castle towers over the ancient 'Trip to Jerusalem' Inn, said to be so named because crusaders stopped there for a drink on their way to fight in the Holy Land.

Leicestershire, Nottinghamshire & Rutland

Leicestershire Gazeteer

Areas of outstanding natural beauty.
Charnwood Forest, Rutland Water.

Historic Houses & Castles

Belvoir Castle - Nr. Grantham
Overlooking the Vale of Belvoir, castle rebuilt in 1816, with many special events including jousting tournaments. Home of the Duke of Rutland since Henry VIII. Paintings, furniture, historic armoury, military museums, magnificent stateroom.

Belvoir Castle

Belgrave Hall - Leicester
18th century Queen Anne house - furnishing of 18th & 19th centuries.
Langton Hall - Nr. Market Harborough
Privately occupied - perfect English country house from mediaeval times - drawing rooms have 18th century Venetian lace.

Oakham Castle - Oakham
Norman banqueting hall of late 12th C.
Stanford Hall - Nr Lutterworth
17th century William & Mary house - collection of Stuart relics & pictures, antiques & costumes of family from Elizabeth I onward. Motor cycle museum.
Stapleford Park - Nr. Melton Mowbray
Old wing dated 1500, restored 1663. Extended to mansion in 1670. Collection of pictures, tapestries, furniture & Balston's Staffordshire portrait figures of Victorian age.

Cathedrals & Churches

Breedon-on-the-Hill (St. Mary & St. Hardulph)
Norman & 13th century. Jacobean canopied pew, 18th century carvings.
Empingham (St. Peter)
14th century west tower, front & crocketed spire. Early English interior - double piscina, triple sedilla.
Lyddington (St. Andrew)
Perpendicular in the main - mediaeval wall paintings & brasses.
Staunton Harol (Holy Trinity)
17th century - quite unique Cromwellian church - painted ceilings.

Museums & Galleries

Bosworth Battlefield Visitor Centre - Nr Market Bosworth
Exhibitions, models, battlefield trails at site of 1485 Battle of Bosworth where Richard III lost his life & crown to Henry.
Leicestershire Museum of Technology - Leicester
Beam engines, steam shovel, knitting machinery & other aspects of the county's industrial past.
Leicester Museum & Art Gallery - Leicester
Painting collection.
18th & 19th century, watercolours & drawings, 20th century French paintings, Old Master & modern prints.
English silver & ceramics, special exhibitions.
Jewry Wall Museum & Site - Leicester
Roman wall & baths site adjoining museum of archaeology.

Leicestershire, Nottinghamshire & Rutland

Melton Carnegie Museum-Melton Mowbray
Displays of Stilton cheese, pork pies & other aspects of the past & present life of the area.

Rutland County Museum - Oakham
Domestic & agricultural life of Rutland, England's smallest county.

Donnington Collection of Single-Seater Racing Cars - Castle Donington
Large collection of grand prix racing cars & racing motorcycles, adjoining Donington Park racing circuit..

Wygson's House Museum of Costume - Leicestershire
Costume, accessories & shop settings in late mediaeval buildings.

The Bellfoundry Museum - Loughborough
Moulding, casting, tuning & fitting of bells, with conducted tours of bellfoundry.

Historic Monuments

The Castle - Ashby-de-la-Zouch
14th century with tower added in 15th century.

Kirby Muxloe Castle - Kirby Muxloe
15th century fortified manor house with moat ruins.

Other things to see & do

Rutland Farm Park - Oakham
Rare & commercial breeds of livestock in 18 acres of park & woodland, with early 19th century farm buildings.

Stoughton Farm Park - Nr. Leicester
Shire horses, rare breeds, small animals & modern 140 dairy herd. Milking demonstrations, farm museum, woodland walks. Adventure playground.

Twycross Zoo - Nr. Atherstone
Gorillas, orang-utans, chimpanzees, gibbons, elephants, giraffes, lions & many other animals.

The Battlefield Line Nr. Market Bosworth
Steam railway & collection of railway relics, adjoining Bosworth Battlefield.

Great Central Railway - Loughborough
Steam railway over 5-mile route in Charnwood Forest area, with steam & diesel museum.

Rutland Railway Museum - Nr. Oakham
Industrial steam & diesel locomotives.

Nottinghamshire Gazeteer

Historic Houses & Castles

Holme Pierrepont Hall - Nr. Nottingham
Outstanding red brick Tudor manor, in continuous family ownership, with 19th century courtyard garden.

Newark Castle - Newark
Dramatic castle ruins on riverside site, once one of the most important castles of the north.

Newstead Abbey - Nr. Mansfield
Priory converted to country mansion, home of poet Lord Byron with many of his possessions & manuscripts on display. Beautiful parkland, lakes & gardens.

Nottingham Castle - Nottingham
17th century residence on site of mediaeval castle.
Fine collections of ceramics, silver, Nottingham alabaster carvings, local historical displays. Art gallery. Special exhibitions & events.

Wollaton Hall - Nottingham
Elizabethan mansion now housing natural history exhibits. Stands in deer park, with Industrial Museum in former stables, illustrating the city's bicycle, hosiery, lace, pharmaceutical & other industries.

Cathedrals & Churches

Egmanton (St. Mary)
Magnificent interior by Comper. Norman doorway & font. Canopied rood screen, 17th century altar.

Newark (St. Mary Magdalene)
15th century. 2 painted panels of "Dance of Death". Reredos by Comper.

Southwell Cathedral
Norman nave, unvaulted, fine early English choir. Decorated pulpitum, 6 canopied stalls, fine misericords. Octagonal chapter house..

Terseval (St. Catherine)
12th century - interior 17th century unrestored.

Museums & Galleries

Castlegate Museum - Nottingham
Row of Georgian terraced houses showing costume & textile collection.
Lace making equipment & lace collection.

Leicestershire, Nottinghamshire & Rutland

Nottingham Castle Museum - Nottingham
Collections of ceramics, glass & silver. Alabaster carvings.

D.H. Lawrence Birthplace - Eastwood
Home of the novelist & poet, as it would have been at time of his birth, 1885.

Millgate Museum of Social & Folk Life - Newark
Local social & folk life, with craft workshops.

Brewhouse Yard Museum - Nottingham
Daily life in Nottingham, displayed in 17th century cottages & rock-cut cellars.

The Lace Hall - Nottingham
The story of Nottingham Lace audio-visual display & exhibition with lace shops, in fine converted church.

Museum of Costume & Textiles - Nottingham
Costumes, lace & textiles on display in fine Georgian buildings.

Bassetlaw Museum - Retford
Local history of north Nottinghamshire.

Canal Museum - Nottinghamshire
History of the River Trent & canal history, in former canal warehouse.

Ruddington Framework Knitters' Museum - Ruddington
Unique complex of early 19th-century framework knitters' buildings with over 20 hand frames in restored workshop.

Other things to see & do

The Tales of Robin Hood - Nottingham
A 'flight to adventure' from mediaeval Nottingham to Sherwood Forest through the tales of the world's most famous outlaw.

Clumber Park - Nr. Worksop
Landscaped parkland, with double avenue of limes, lake, chapel. One of the Dukeries' estates, though the house no longer remains.

Rufford - Nr. Ollerton
Parkland, lake & gallery with fine crafts, around ruin of Cistercian abbey.

Sherwood Forest Visitor Centre - Nr. Edwinstowe
Robin Hood exhibition.
450 acres of ancient oak woodland associated with the outlaw & his merry men.

Sherwood Forest Farm Park - Nr. Edwinstowe
Rare breeds of cattle, sheep, pigs & goats. Lake with wildfowl.

White Post Farm Centre - Farnsfield, Nr Newark
Working modern farm with crops & many animals, including cows, sheep, pigs, hens, geese, ducks, llamas, horses. Indoor displays & exhibits.

Newark Castle.

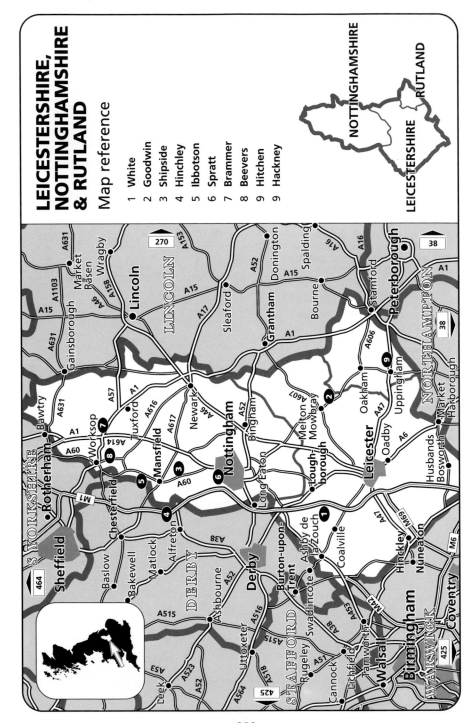

LEICESTERSHIRE, NOTTINGHAMSHIRE & RUTLAND

Map reference

1 White
2 Goodwin
3 Shipside
4 Hinchley
5 Ibbotson
6 Spratt
7 Brammer
8 Beevers
9 Hitchen
9 Hackney

NOTTINGHAMSHIRE
RUTLAND
LEICESTERSHIRE

Leicestershire & Nottinghamshire

		rate from £ per person	children taken	evening meals	animals taken
Audrey, Bill & Carolyn White **Abbots Oak Country House** **Warren Hills Road,** **Greenhill** **Coalville LE67 4UY** **Tel/Fax: (01530) 832328** **Open: ALL YEAR** **Map Ref No. 01**	Nearest Road: A.50, M.1 A Grade II listed building with a wealth of oak panelling, & including the staircase reputedly from Nell Gwynn's town house. Set in mature gardens & woodland, with natural granite outcrops. 4 delightful rooms, all with en-suite/private bathroom. Open fires create a warm & welcoming atmosphere, & Carolyn's superb dinners are served in the candlelit dining room. Stratford, Belvoir Castle & Rutland Water can all be reached within the hour. Tennis court, billiard room.	£32.50	N	Y	Y
Mrs Sue Goodwin **Hillside House** **27 Melton Rd, Burton Lazars** **Melton Mowbray LE14 2UR** **Tel: (01664) 566312** **Fax 01664 501819** **Open: ALL YEAR (Excl. Xmas)** **Map Ref No. 02**	Nearest Road: A.606 A charmingly converted farmhouse with superb views over open countryside, in the small village of Burton Lazars. Comfortable accommodation is offered in 3 double bedrooms, each with an en-suite/private bathroom. All have tea/coffee-making facilities & a colour T.V.. A pleasant garden, on sunny days. Close to Melton Mowbray, famous for its pork pies & Stilton cheese, & with Burghley House, Belvoir Castle & Rutland Water within easy reach. Children over 10. Mobile 0585 068956.	£16.50	Y	N	N

Nottinghamshire

		rate from £ per person	children taken	evening meals	animals taken
Mrs Ann Shipside **Holly Lodge, Ricket Lane,** **Ravenshead,** **Blidworth NG2 10NQ** **Tel: (01623) 793853** **Fax 01623 490977** **Open: ALL YEAR** **Map Ref No. 03**	Nearest Road: A.60 Holly Lodge is situated just off the A.60, 9 miles north of Nottingham. This attractive former hunting lodge stands in 15 acres of grounds. The 4 comfortable & attractive, en-suite guest rooms are housed within the converted stables. There are panoramic countryside views on all sides, with woodland walks, tennis, golf & riding nearby. Ideally situated for a peaceful, rural holiday base with a relaxed & friendly atmosphere. *see PHOTO over* CREDIT CARD VISA M'CARD AMEX	£21.00	Y	N	N
Mrs Betty Hinchley **Titchfield House** **300/302 Chesterfield Road** **North, Pleasley,** **Mansfield NG19 7QU** **Tel/Fax: (01623) 810356** **Tel: (01623) 810921** **Open: ALL YEAR** **Map Ref No. 04**	Nearest Road: A.617 This is 2 houses converted into 1 family-run guest house, offering 8 comfortable rooms, a lounge with T.V., a kitchen for guests' use, a bathroom & showers. It also has an adjoining garage. Near to Mansfield, which is a busy market town. Sherwood Forest & the Peak District are both easily accessible. Titchfield House is a very handy location for touring this lovely area, & for onward travel. A warm & friendly welcome is assured at this charming home. CREDIT CARD VISA M'CARD AMEX	£17.00	Y	N	Y
June M. Ibbotson **Blue Barn Farm** **Langwith,** **Mansfield NG20 9JD** **Tel/Fax: (01623) 742248** **Open: ALL YEAR (Excl. Xmas Day & New Year)** **Map Ref No. 05**	Nearest Road: A.616, A.1, M.1 An enjoyable visit is guaranteed at this family-run, 250-acre farm, set in tranquil countryside on the edge of Sherwood Forest (Robin Hood country). 3 guest bedrooms, each with modern amenities including h&c, tea/coffee-making facilities & a guest bathroom with shower. 1 bedroom is en-suite. A colour-T.V. lounge & garden are also available. Guests are very welcome to walk around the farm. Many interesting places, catering for all tastes, only a short journey away.	£17.00	Y	N	N

Holly Lodge. Blidworth.

Nottinghamshire & Rutland

		rate from £ per person	children taken	evening meals	animals taken
Sheila & Michael Spratt **Greenwood Lodge** **Third Avenue** **Sherwood Rise** **Nottingham NG7 6JH** **Tel/Fax: (0115) 9621206** **Open: ALL YEAR** **Map Ref No. 06**	Nearest Road: A.60 A warm, welcoming Victorian house situated in a quiet cul-de-sac, 1 mile from the city centre. The home of Sheila & Michael Spratt, The Lodge is furnished mainly with antiques, & boasts a fine 4-poster bed. All rooms are en-suite & individually decorated & furnished to a high standard, with T.V., hairdryer, trouser press & hospitality tray. Evening meals are by prior arrangement. An ideal base from which to explore Nottingham & its many places of interest. CREDIT CARD VISA M'CARD	£28.00	Y	Y	Y
Rosalie Brammer **The Barns Country** **Guesthouse** **Morton Farm, Babworth** **Retford DN22 8HA** **Tel: (01777) 706336** **Fax 01777 709773** **Open: ALL YEAR** **Map Ref No. 07**	Nearest Road: A.1, B.6420 A delightfully warm welcome & a pleasant, relaxed atmosphere await you at 'The Barns'. This beautifully converted 18th-century barn boasts open fires & many oak beams, & offers guests a choice of 6 comfortable & attractively furnished rooms, all with en-suite facilities, T.V. & tea/coffee makers. A charming home & an interesting base for touring this lovely area. It is located at Babworth - home of the Pilgrim Fathers - only 2 miles from Robin Hood country. CREDIT CARD VISA M'CARD AMEX	£21.00	Y	N	N
Beverley Beevers **Duncan Wood Lodge** **Carburton** **Worksop** **S80 3BP** **Tel: (01909) 483614** **Open: ALL YEAR** **Map Ref No. 08**	Nearest Road: A.1, A.60 Built in 1850, Duncan Wood Lodge is a beautiful stone lodge which has been tastefully refurbished. Accommodation is in 7 very comfortable bedrooms, 3 with en-suite facilities. Each bedroom has T.V., hospitality tray & hairdryer, & in addition, most have satellite T.V. & a trouser press. A comfortable guest lounge with views of the garden. A varied range of good evening meals are served together with a selection of wines in the attractive dining room. A charming home. CREDIT CARD VISA M'CARD	£18.00	Y	Y	Y

Rutland

		rate from £ per person	children taken	evening meals	animals taken
Jenny Hitchen **Rutland House** **61 High Street** **Uppingham LE15 9PY** **Tel/Fax: (01572) 822497** **Open: ALL YEAR** **Map Ref No. 09**	Nearest Road: A.47 Rutland House offers excellent accommodation in 5 delightful guest rooms. All rooms are en-suite, with central heating, colour T.V., radio/alarms & tea/coffee facilities. Being a small establishment, the rooms are quiet & homely. Full English or Continental breakfast served. Close to Rutland Water & Burghley House. Children over 5 yrs. A lovely home well-placed for touring. CREDIT CARD VISA M'CARD	£20.00	Y	N	Y
Ian & Christine Hackney **The Garden Hotel** **High Street West** **Uppingham LE15 9QD** **Tel: (01572) 822352** **Fax 01572 821156** **Open: ALL YEAR** **Map Ref No. 09**	Nearest Road: A.47 Regarded as Uppingham's best kept secret, this historic hotel has a reputation for friendly, homely service. All rooms en-suite, with T.V., 'phone & tea/coffee . Comfortable lounge & separate bar, together with large, well-tended garden, provide country-home comforts. The restaurant is renowned for traditional British home cooking. Good wine list. Candlelit French Bistro available Mon-Sat. Summer tea in the garden. Car park. CREDIT CARD VISA M'CARD AMEX	£32.50	Y	Y	Y

Lincolnshire

Lincolnshire
(East Midlands)

Lincolnshire is an intriguing mixture of coast & country, of flat fens & gently rising wolds.

There are the popular resorts of Skegness & Mablethorpe as well as quieter coastal regions where flocks of wild birds take food & shelter in the dunes. Gibraltar Point & Saltfleetby are large nature reserves.

Fresh vegetables for much of Britain are produced in the rich soil of the Lincolnshire fens, & windmills punctuate the skyline. There is a unique 8-sailed windmill at Heckington. In spring the fields are ablaze with the red & yellow of tulips. The bulb industry flourishes around Spalding & Holbeach, & in early May tulip flowers in abundance decorate the huge floats of the Spalding Flower Parade.

The city of Lincoln has cobbled streets & ancient buildings & a very beautiful triple-towered Cathedral which shares its hill-top site with the Castle, both dating from the 11th century. There is a 17th century library by Wren in the Cathedral, which has amongst its treasures one of the four original copies of Magna Carta.

Boston has a huge parish church with a distincive octagonal tower which can be seen for miles across the surrounding fenland, & is commonly known as the 'Boston Stump'. The Guildhall Museum displays many aspects of the town's history, including the cells where the early Pilgrim Fathers were imprisioned after their attempt to flee to the Netherlands to find religious freedom. They eventually made the journey & hence to America.

One of England's most outstanding towns is Stamford. It has lovely churches, ancient inns & other fine buildings in a mellow stone.

Sir Isaac Newton was born at Woolsthorpe Manor & educated at nearby Grantham where there is a museum which illustrates his life & work.

The poet Tennyson was born in the village of Somersby, where his father was Rector.

Lincoln Cathedral.

Lincolnshire

Lincolnshire Gazeteer

Areas of outstanding natural beauty.
Lincolnshire Wolds.

Historic Houses & Castles

Auborn House - Nr. Lincoln
16th century house with imposing carved staircase & panelled rooms.
Belton House - Grantham
House built 1684-88 - said to be by Christopher Wren - work by Grinling Gibbons & Wyatt also. Paintings, furniture, porcelain, tapestries, Duke of Windsor mementoes. A great English house with formal gardens & extensive grounds with orangery.
Doddington Hall - Doddington, Nr. Lincoln
16th century Elizabethan mansion with elegant Georgian rooms & gabled Tudor gatehouse. Fine furniture, paintings, porcelain, etc. Formal walled knot gardens, roses & wild gardens.
Burghley House - Stamford
Elizabethan - England's largest & grandest house of the era. Famous for its beautiful painted ceilings, silver fireplaces & art treasures.
Gumby Hall - Burgh-le-Marsh
17th century manor house. Ancient gardens.
Harrington Hall - Spilsby
Mentioned in the Domesday Book - has mediaeval stone base - Carolinean manor house in red brick. Some alterations in 1678 to mullioned windows. Panelling, furnishings of 17th & 18th century.
Marston Hall - Grantham
16th century manor house. Ancient gardens.
The Old Hall - Gainsborough
Fine mediaeval manor house built in 1480's with original kitchen, rebuilt after original hall destroyed during Wars of the Roses. Tower & wings, Great Hall. It was the first meeting place of the "Dissenters", later known as the Pilgrim Fathers.
Woolsthorpe Manor - Grantham
17th century house. Birthplace of Sir Isaac Newton.
Fydell House - Boston
18th century house, now Pilgrim College.

Lincoln Castle - Lincoln
William the Conqueror castle, with complete curtain wall & Norman shell keep. Towers & wall walk. Unique prisoners' chapel.
Tattershall Castle - Tattershall
100 foot high brick keep of 15th century moated castle, with fine views over surrounding country.

Cathedrals & Churches

Addlethorpe (St. Nicholas)
15th century - mediaeval stained glass - original woodwork.
Boston (St. Botolph)
14th century decorated - very large parish church. Beautiful south porch, carved stalls.
Brant Broughton (St. Helens)
13th century arcades - decorated tower & spire - perpendicular clerestory. Exterior decoration.
Ewerby (St. Andrew)
Decorated - splendid example of period - very fine spire. 14th century effigy.
Fleet (St. Mary Magdalene)
14th century - early English arcades - perpendicular windows - detached tower & spire.
Folkingham (St. Andrew)
14th century arcades - 15th century windows - perpendicular tower - early English chancel.
Gedney (St. Mary Magdalene)
Perpendicular spire (unfinished). Early English tower. 13th-14th century monuments, 14th-15th century stained glass.
Grantham (St. Wulfram)
14th century tower & spire - Norman pillars - perpendicular chantry - 14th century vaulted crypt.
Lincoln Cathedral - Lincoln
Magnificent triple-towered Gothic building on fine hill-top site.
Norman west front,
13th century - some 14th century additions. Norman work from 1072. Angel choir - carved & decorated pulpitum - 13th century chapter house - 17th century library by Wren (containing one of the four original copies of Magna Carta).

Lincolnshire

St. Botolph's Church - Boston
Fine parish church, one of the largest in
the country, with 272 foot octagonal tower
dominating the surrounding fens.
Long Sutton (St. Mary)
15th century south porch, mediaeval brass
lectern, very fine early English spire.
Louth (St. James)
Early 16th century - mediaeval Gothic -
wonderful spire.
Scotter (St. Peter)
Saxon to perpendicular - early English
nave - 15th century rood screen.
Stow (St. Mary)
Norman - very fine example, particularly
west door. Wall painting.
Silk Willoughby (St. Denis)
14th century - tower with spire & flying
buttresses. 15th-17th century pulpit.
Stainfield (St. Andrew)
Queen Anne - mediaeval armour & early
needlework.
Theddlethorpe (All Saints)
14th century - 15th century & reredos of
15th century, 16th century parcloses, 15th
century brasses - some mediaeval glass.
Wrangle (St. Mary the Virgin & St.
Nicholas)
Early English - decorated - perpendicular -
Elizabethan pulpit. 14th century east
window & glass.

Museums & Galleries

Alford Manor House - Alford
Tudor manor house - thatched - folk
museum. Nearby windmill.
Boston Guildhall Museum - Boston
15th century building with mayor's parlour,
court room & cells where Pilgrim Fathers
were imprisoned in 1607. Local exhibits.
Lincoln Cathedral Library - Lincoln
Built by Wren housing early printed books
& mediaeval manuscripts.
Lincoln Cathedral Treasury - Lincoln
Diocesan gold & silver plate.
Lincoln City & Country Museum -
Lincoln
Prehistoric, Roman & mediaeval
antiquities with local associations. Armour
& local history.
Museum of Lincolnshire Life - Lincoln
Domestic, agricultural, industrial & social
history of the county. Edwardian room
settings, shop settings, agricultural machinery.

Usher Gallery - Lincoln
Paintings, watches, miniatures, porcelain,
silver, coins & medals. Temporary
exhibitions. Tennyson collection. Works
of English watercolourist Peter de Wint.
Grantham Museum - Grantham
Archeology, prehistoric, Saxon & Roman.
Local history with special display about
Sir Isaac Newton, born nearby & educated
in Grantham.
Church Farm Museum - Skegness
Farmhouse & buildings with local
agricultural collections & temporary
exhibitions & special events.
Stamford Museum - Stamford
Local history museum, with temporary
special exhibitions.
Battle of Britain Memorial Flight -
Coningsby
Lancaster bomber, five Spitfires & two
Hurricanes with other Battle of Britain
memorabilia.
National Cycle Museum - Lincoln
Development of the cycle.
Stamford Steam Brewery Museum -
Stamford
Complete Victorian steam brewery with
19th century equipment.

Other things to see & do

Springfield - Spalding
Show gardens of the British bulb industry,
& home of the Spalding Flower Parade
each May. Summer bedding plants &
roses.
Butlins Funcoast World - Skegness
Funsplash Water World with amusements
& entertainments
Castle Leisure Park - Tattershall
Windsurfing, water-skiing, sailing, fishing &
other sports & leisure facilities.
Long Sutton Butterfly Park - Long
Sutton
Walk-through tropical butterfly house with
outdoor wildflower meadows & pets
corner.
Skegness Natureland Marine Zoo -
Skegness
Seal sanctuary with aquaria, tropical
house, pets corner & butterfly house.
Windmills - at Lincoln (Ellis Mill - 4 sails),
Boston (Maud Foster - 5 sails), Burgh-le-
Marsh (5 sails), Alford (5 sails), Sibsey (6
sails), Heckington (8 sails).

LINCOLNSHIRE
Map reference

1 Armstrong
2 Robinson
3 Honnor
4 Pritchard
4 Brown
5 Acton

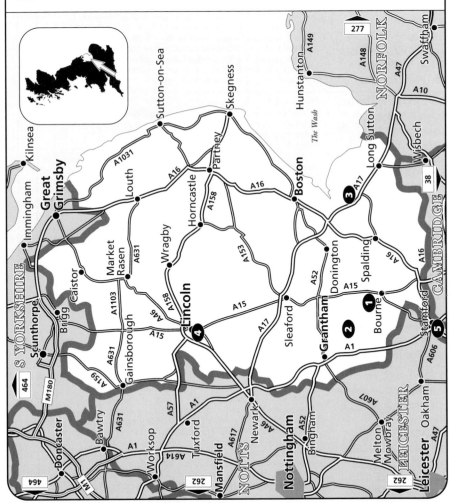

Lincolnshire

		rate from £ per person	children taken	evening meals	animals taken
Mrs Chantal Armstrong **Cawthorpe Hall** **Cawthorpe** **Bourne PE10 0AB** **Tel: (01778) 423830** **Fax 01778 426620** **Open: ALL YEAR** **Map Ref No. 01**	Nearest Road: A.15 This fine, old listed house is surrounded by a large pretty garden & fields of roses supplying the rose distillery with fragrant blooms. The rooms are bright, spacious & comfortably furnished & have a bathroom en-suite. A full English breakfast will be served in a family country kitchen. Country lovers can enjoy beautiful woodland walks. Horse riding or golf, Grimsthorpe Castle & Park are all within easy reach. A charming home.	£20.00	Y	Y	Y
Mrs Sue Robinson **Sycamore Farm** **Bassingthorpe** **Grantham NG33 4ED** **Tel: (01476) 585274** **Open: MAR - NOV** **Map Ref No. 02**	Nearest Road: A.1, B.6403 Set in peaceful unspoilt countryside, Sycamore Farm offers the perfect place to relax & unwind. Spacious, pretty bedrooms with en-suite bathrooms (1 private), elegant guest lounge, fresh flowers, log fires, fine views, books & board games. Ideally placed for A.1 (4 miles), Stamford, Lincoln, historic Belton & Burghley & Geoff Hamilton's 'Barnsdale'. Children over 12 years.	£20.00	Y	N	N
Mrs Lesley Honnor **Pipwell Manor** **Washway Road** **Saracens Head** **Holbeach** **PE12 8AL** **Tel: (01406) 423119** **Open: ALL YEAR (Excl. Xmas)** **Map Ref No. 03**	Nearest Road: A.17 Pipwell Manor is a Grade II listed Georgian manor house, built in around 1740, set in paddocks & gardens in a small quiet village in the Lincolnshire Fens, just off the A.17. Beautifully restored & decorated in English-country style, but retaining many original features, Pipwell Manor is a delightful place to stay. 4 comfortably furnished & attractive bedrooms, each with an en-suite/private bathroom & tea/coffee-making facilities. Guests are welcomed with tea & home-made cake. Parking.	£20.00	Y	N	N
Gillian & John Pritchard **Carline Guest House** **1-3 Carline Road** **Lincoln** **LN1 1HL** **Tel: (01522) 530422** **Open: ALL YEAR (Excl. Xmas & New Year)** **Map Ref No. 04**	Nearest Road: A.57, A.46, A.15 Gill & John Pritchard extend a warm welcome. Excellent accommodation, in 12 attractively furnished bedrooms, 10 with en-suite facilities. Each room has T.V., radio, beverage facilities, hair dryers & trouser press. The Carline is a short, pleasant stroll from the Lawns Tourism & Conference Centre, & from the historic Uphill area of Lincoln. There are several restaurants & public houses nearby for your lunch or evening meal. Ask for recommendations. Children over 2 yrs.	£20.00	Y	N	N
Mr Raymond H. Brown **Minster Lodge Hotel** **3 Church Lane** **Lincoln** **LN2 1QJ** **Tel: (01522) 513220** **Fax 01522 513220** **Open: ALL YEAR** **Map Ref No. 04**	Nearest Road: A.15, A.46 Minster Lodge is a delightful small hotel refurbished to a high standard. Offering 6 attractive en-suite bedrooms with radio, colour T.V. & beverage facilities. Ideally situated within 50 yards of Newport Arch - the only remaining Roman Arch still in use - & 5 mins' walk from Lincoln's major tourist attractions of Lincoln Cathedral & Castle, as well as a colourful mixture of antique shops, gift shops & boutiques, which are situated in the mediaeval area surrounding the cathedral & castle.	£26.00 CREDIT CARD VISA M'CARD	Y	N	N

Lincolnshire

		rate from £ per person	children taken	evening meals	animals taken
John & Moya Acton **The Priory** **Church Road** **Ketton** **Stamford** **PE9 3RD** **Tel: (01780) 720215** **Fax 01780 721881** **Open: ALL YEAR (Excl. Xmas)** **Map Ref No. 05**	Nearest Road: A.1, A.6121 Historic listed country house in quiet village setting near Stamford - England's finest stone town. Award-winning bed & breakfast with spacious en-suite bedrooms offering every comfort & many thoughtful extras. Bedrooms are individually designed with oversize handmade beds, high ceilings, luxurious fabrics, original panelling & splendid views over the gardens. Resident chef prepares a choice of dishes every day from fresh local produce complemented by an extensive wine list. Eat in the large conservatory & relax in the guests' lounge. Private parking. Close to Rutland Water. **E-mail: Priory.a0504924@infotrade.co.uk**	£35.00 *see PHOTO over* CREDIT CARD VISA M'CARD	Y	Y	N

All the establishments mentioned in this guide are members of
The Worldwide Bed & Breakfast Association

When booking your accommodation please mention
The Best Bed & Breakfast

The Priory. Ketton.

Norfolk

Norfolk
(East Anglia)

One of the largest of the old counties, Norfolk is divided by rivers from neighbouring counties & pushes out into the sea on the north & east sides. This is old East Anglia.

Inland there is great concentration on agriculture where fields are hedged with hawthorn which blossoms like snow in summer. A great deal of land drainage is required & the area is crisscrossed by dykes & ditches - some of them dating back to Roman times.

Holkham Hall.

The Norfolk Broads were formed by the flooding of mediaeval peat diggings to form miles & miles of inland waterways, navigable & safe. On a bright summer's day, on a peaceful backwater bounded by reed & sedge, the Broads seem like paradise. Here are hidden treasures like the Bittern, that shyest of birds, the Swallowtail butterfly & the rare Marsh orchid.

Contrasting with the still inland waters is a lively coastline which takes in a host of towns & villages as it arcs around The Wash. Here are the joys of the seaside at its best, miles of safe & sandy golden beaches to delight children, dunes & salt marshes where birdlife flourishes, & busy ports & fishing villages with pink-washed cottages.

Cromer is a little seaside town with a pier & a prom, cream teas & candy floss, where red, white & blue fishing boats are drawn up on the beach.

Hunstanton is more decorous, with a broad green sweeping down to the cliffs. Great Yarmouth is a boisterous resort. It has a beach that runs for miles, with pony rides & almost every amusement imaginable.

It is possible to take a boat into the heart of Norwich, past warehouses, factories & new penthouses, & under stone & iron bridges. Walking along the riverbank you reach Pulls Ferry where a perfectly proportioned grey flint gateway arcs over what was once a canal dug to transport stone to the cathedral site. Norwich Cathedral is magnificent, with a sharply soaring spire, beautiful cloisters & fine 15th century carving preserved in the choir stalls. Cathedral Close is perfectly preserved, as is Elm Hill, a cobbled street from mediaeval times. There are many little shops & narrow alleys going down to the river.

Norfolk is a county much loved by the Royal family & the Queen has a home at Sandringham. It is no castle, but a solid, comfortable family home with red brick turrets & French windows opening onto the terrace.

Norfolk

Norfolk Gazeteer

Areas of outstanding beauty.
Norfolk coast (part)

Historic Houses & Castles

Anna Sewell House - Great Yarmouth
17th century Tudor frontage. Birthplace of writer Anna Sewell.

Blicking Hall - Aylsham
Great Jacobean house. Fine Russian tapestry, long gallery with exceptional ceiling. Formal garden.

Felbrigg Hall - Nr. Cromer
17th century, good Georgian interior. Set in wooded parklands.

Holkham Hall - Wells
Fine Palladian mansion of 1734. Paintings, statuary, tapestries, furnishings & formal garden by Berry.

Houghton Hall - Wells
18th century mansion. Pictures, china & staterooms.

Oxburgh Hall - Swafftham
Late 15th century moated house. Fine gatehouse tower. Needlework by Mary Queen of Scots.

Wolterton Hall - Nr. Norwich
Built in 1741 contains tapestries, porcelain, furniture.

Trinity Hospital - Castle Rising
17th century, nine brick & tile almshouses, court chapel & treasury.

Cathedrals & Churches

Attleborough (St. Mary)
Norman with late 14th century. Fine rood screen & frescoes.

Barton Turf (St. Michael & All Angles)
Magnificent screen with painting of the Nine Orders of Angles.

Beeston-next-Mileham (St. Mary)
14th century. Perpendicular clerestory tower & spire. Hammer Beam roof, parclose screens, benches, front cover. Tracery in nave & chancel windows.

Cawston (St. Agnes)
Tower faced with freestone. Painted screens, wall paintings, tower, screen & gallery. 15th century angel roof.

East Harding (St. Peter & St. Paul)
14th century, some 15th century alterations. Monuments of 15th-17th century. Splendid mediaeval glass.

Erpingham (St. Mary)
14th century military brass to John de Erpingham, 16th century Rhenish glass. Fine tower.

Gunton (St. Andrew)
18th century. Robert Adam - classical interior in dark wood - gilded.

King's Lynn (St. Margaret)
Norman foundation. Two fine 14th century Flemish brasses, 14th century screens, reredos by Bodley, interesting Georgian pulpit with sounding board.

Norwich Cathedral
Romanesque & late Gothic with 15th century spire. Perpendicular lierne vaults in nave, transeptsand presbytery.

Ranworth (St. Helens)
15th century screen, very fine example. Sarum Antiphoner, 14th century illuminated manuscript - East Anglian work.

Salle (St. Peter & St. Paul)
15th century. Highly decorated west tower & porches. Mediaeval glass, pulpit with 15th century panels & Jacobean tester. Stalls, misericords, brasses & monuments, sacrament font.

Terrington (St. Clement)
Detached perpendicular tower. Western front has fire-light window & canopied niches. Georgian panelling west of nave. 17th century painted font cover. Jacobean commandment boards.

Trunch (St. Botolph)
15th century screen with painted panels, mediaeval glass, famous font canopy with fine carving & painting, ringer's gallery, Elizabethan monument.

Wiggenhall (St. Germans)
17th century pulpit, table, clerk's desk & chair, bench ends 15th century.

Wymondham (St. Mary & St. Thomas of Canterbury)
Norman origins including arcades & triforium windows, 13th century font fragments, complete 15th century font. 15th century clerestory & roof. Comper reredos, famous Corporas Case, rare example of 13th century Opus Anglicanum.

Museums & Galleries

Norwich Castle Museum
Art collection, local & natural history,

Norfolk

Strangers Hall - Norwich
Mediaeval mansion furnished as museum of urban domestic life in 16th-19th centuries.

St. Peter Hungate Church Museum - Norwich
15th century church for the exhibition of ecclesiastical art & East Anglican antiquities.

Sainsbury Centre for Visual Arts - University, Norwich
Collection of modern art, ancient, classical & mediaeval art, Art Nouveau, 20th century constructivist art.

Bridewell Museum of Local Industries - Norwich
Crafts, industries & aspects of city life.

Museum of Social History - King's Lynn
Exhibition of domestic life & dress, etc., noted glass collection.

Bishop Bonner's Cottages
Restored cottages with coloured East Anglia pargetting, c. 1502, museum of archaeological discoveries, exhibition of rural crafts.

The Guildhall - Thetford
Duleep Singh Collection of Norfolk & Suffolk portraits.

Shirehall Museum - Walsingham
18th century court room having original fittings, illustrating Walsingham life.

Historic Monuments

Binham Priory & Cross - Binham
12th century ruins of Benedictine foundation.

Caister Castle - Great Yarmouth
15th century moated castle - ruins. Now motor museum.

The Castle - Burgh Castle
3rd century Saxon fort - walls - ruin.

Mannington Hall - Saxthorpe
Saxon church ruin in gardens of 15th century moated house.

Castle Rising - Castle Rising
Splendid Norman keep & earthworks.

Castle Acre Priory & Castle Gate - Swaffham

Other things to see & do

African Violet Centre - Terrington St. Clements.
60 varieties of African Violets. Talks & Tours.

Norfolk Lavender Centre - Heacham
Open to the public in July & August. Demonstrations of harvesting & distilling the oil.

Thetford Forest
Forest walks, rides & picnic places amongst conifers, oak, beech & birch.

The Broads.

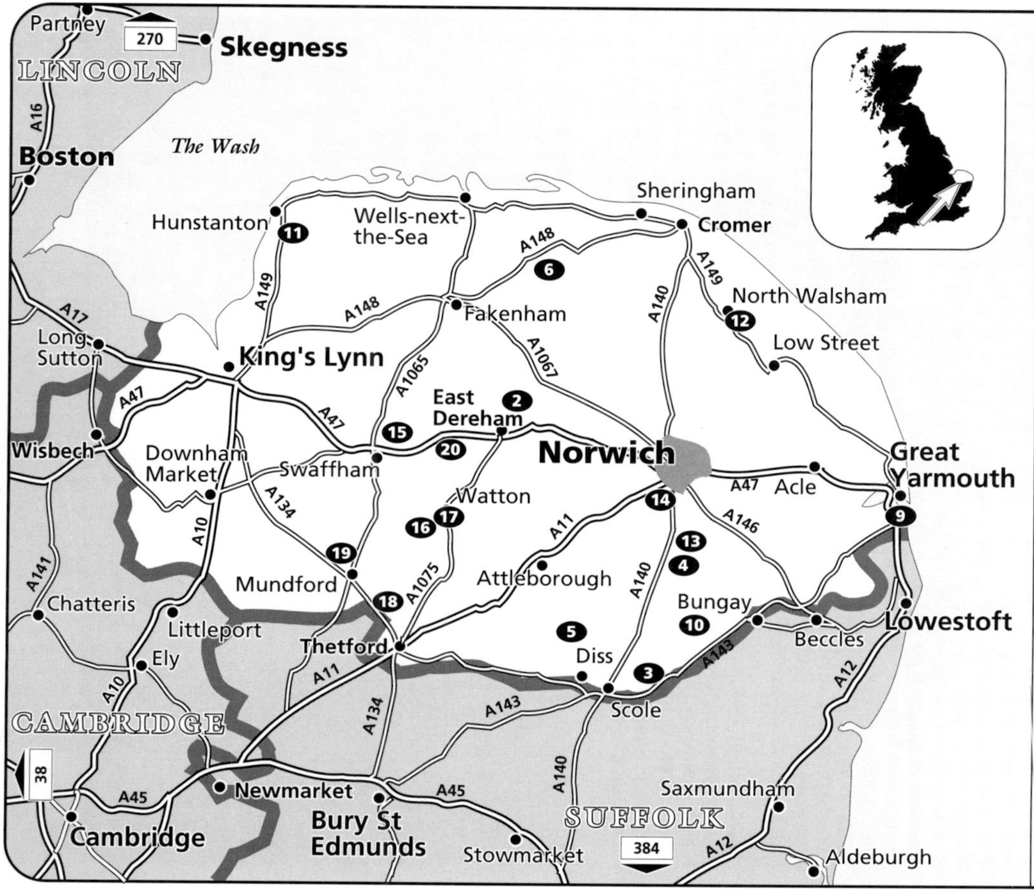

NORFOLK

Map reference

2 Bartlett
3 Morrish
4 Croft
5 Webb
6 Greenhalgh
9 Wells
10 Baxter
11 Tweedy Smith
11 Morison
12 Tofts
13 Douglas
14 Lovatt
15 Hickey
16 Garnier
17 Carr
18 Collins
19 Ford
20 Lock

Skegness
Partney
LINCOLN
270
A16
Boston
A17
The Wash
Long Sutton
Wisbech
A47
A141
Chatteris
Littleport
Ely
A10
CAMBRIDGE
Cambridge
A45
Newmarket
Bury St Edmunds
Stowmarket
A14
38
SUFFOLK
Saxmundham
Aldeburgh
A12
384
Lowestoft
Beccles
A146
Bungay
A143
Thetford
A11
Mundford
A134
Swaffham
A47
King's Lynn
Downham Market
A10
A149
Hunstanton
Wells-next-the-Sea
A148
Fakenham
A1067
A1065
East Dereham
Watton
Attleborough
A11
Diss
Scole
A140
A143
Norwich
A140
A149
Cromer
Sheringham
North Walsham
Low Street
Acle
A47
Great Yarmouth

Norfolk

		rate from £ per person	children taken	evening meals	animals taken
David & Annie Bartlett **Bartles Lodge** **Church Street, Elsing** **Dereham NR20 3EA** **Tel: (01362) 637177** **Open: ALL YEAR** **Map Ref No. 02**	Nearest Road: A.47, A.1067 Bartles Lodge is in the peaceful, unspoilt village of Elsing, set in 12 acres of landscaped meadows inhabited by plenty of wildlife. The rooms, centred around the patio, pond & fountain, are beautifully furnished in country style, & most overlook the Bartletts' own lakes. All rooms are en-suite with colour T.V.'s, etc. Although Bartles Lodge is licensed, the local village inn is nearby.	£20.00 CREDIT CARD VISA M'CARD	Y	N	Y
Mrs Angela Morrish **Grove Thorpe** **Grove Road** **Brockdish** **Diss IP21 4JE** **Tel: (01379) 668305** **Fax 01379 668305** **Open: ALL YEAR** **Map Ref No. 03**	Nearest Road: A.143 Grove Thorpe is a Grade II listed 17th-century farmhouse which has been beautifully renovated to a very high standard, with inglenook fireplaces & beamed rooms. Set in mature, secluded gardens & grounds of 6 acres with livery facilities available for horses. All guest bedrooms are en-suite & have beverage facilities. Laze around log fires in winter or sit in the gardens through the summer. Excellent evening meals. Conveniently situated for Norfolk, Suffolk, Bressingham, Norwich, Norfolk Broads & the Otter Trust. Children over 12.	£22.00	Y	Y	Y
Martin & Jean Croft **The Old Bakery** **Church Walk** **Pulham Market** **Diss IP21 4SJ** **Tel/Fax: (01379) 676492** **Open: ALL YEAR (Excl. Xmas & New Year)** **Map Ref No. 04**	Nearest Road: A.140 The Old Bakery is a 16th-century oak-framed house on a private road in the centre of an award-winning conservation village among thatched period houses. All 3 double rooms are fully en-suite, have colour T.V., clock/radio & hospitality tray. The Old Bakery is licensed, & offers excellent traditional meals prepared by Martin, a Master Chef. These are served in the beamed & log-fired dining room, which glows with warmth & history. Situated near Bressingham, Norwich, the Broads & the Heritage Coast.	£20.00 *see PHOTO over*	Y	Y	N
Ken & Brenda Webb **Strenneth** **Airfield Road** **Fersfield** **Diss IP22 2BP** **Tel: (01379) 688182** **Fax 01379 688260** **Open: ALL YEAR** **Map Ref No. 05**	Nearest Road: A.1066 Strenneth is situated in unspoilt countryside a short drive from Bressingham Gardens & the picturesque market town of Diss. The original 17th-century building has been carefully renovated to a high standard with a wealth of oak beams & a newer single-storey courtyard wing. Parking & plenty of walks nearby. All 7 bedrooms, including a 4-poster & an executive, are tastefully arranged with period furniture & distinctive beds, each having T.V., hospitality tray & en-suite facilities. **E-mail: ken@mainline.co.uk**	£20.00 CREDIT CARD VISA M'CARD AMEX	Y	N	Y
Pam & Alan Greenhalgh **The Old Brick Kilns** **Little Barney Lane, Barney** **Fakenham NR21 0NL** **Tel: (01328) 878305** **Fax 01328 878948** **Open: ALL YEAR** **Map Ref No. 06**	Nearest Road: A.148 3 cottages converted into a house of fine character, set in a private 7-acre park which achieved an award for conservation in 1996. Cetnrally located for all the attractions & activities of north Norfolk. All meals are prepared from fresh produce, dietary requirements catered for with prior notice. Accommodation is in 3 very attractive en-suite bedrooms. A friendly, warm welcome awaits you at this quiet, quality home-from-home.	£20.00 CREDIT CARD VISA M'CARD	Y	Y	N

The Old Bakery. Pulham Market.

Norfolk

	rate from £ per person	children taken	evening meals	animals taken
Mrs Barbara Wells **Spindrift Private Hotel** 36 Wellesley Road Great Yarmouth NR30 1EU Tel/Fax: (01493) 858674 Open: ALL YEAR (Excl. Xmas) Map Ref No. 09	Nearest Road: A.47 Good food & comfortable accommodation are the by-words at 'Spindrift'. Attractively situated adjacent to the sea front, the Golden Mile, bowling greens, tennis courts & the water ways. Easy-going atmosphere, with keys provided for access at all times. 8 bedrooms, some with excellent sea views, & 5 bedrooms with en-suite facilities. All with modern amenities, colour T.V. & tea/coffee-making facilities. Good on road parking; public car park at rear, if space allows. Children over 3.	£15.00 CREDIT CARD VISA M'CARD AMEX	Y	N	N
Mrs Christina Baxter **Starston Hall** Starston Harleston IP20 9PU Tel: (01379) 854252 Fax 01379 852966 Open: ALL YEAR Map Ref No. 10	Nearest Road: A.143 Starston Hall, a house of Elizabethan origin, is Grade II listed & stands in 4 acres of gardens, including the original moat, & is surrounded by a large estate. It has recently been extensively renovated, many of the original features have been sympathetically restored & it is furnished comprehensively with antique furniture. Your host offers by prior arrangement varied dinner menus, including vegetarian, & is fluent in French, German & Italian. Children over 12 years. **E-mail: w.w.w.starstonhall.co.uk**	£30.00 🚭 *see PHOTO over*	Y	Y	N
Sheila Tweedy Smith **Fieldsend House** Homefields Road Hunstanton PE36 5HL Tel: (01485) 532593 Open: ALL YEAR Map Ref No. 11	Nearest Road: A.149 Fieldsend is a large Carrstone house, built at the turn of the century & enjoying lovely sea views. There are canopied beds, plus 1 en-suite bedroom with 4-poster. Colour T.V., tea/coffee makers & an oak-panelled sitting room. Guests will enjoy a leisurely stay at this country-house-style home, which is only 4 mins from the centre of town. Delicious breakfasts served by a Cordon Bleu cook. Parking available.	£20.00	Y	N	N
Mrs Susan Morison **Pinewood House** 26 Northgate Hunstanton PE36 6AP Tel: (01485) 533068 Open: MAR - OCT Map Ref No. 11	Nearest Road: A.149 Enjoy comfort & hospitality in this charming Victorian house with a natural pine look, interesting pictures & antiques. Offering 8 delightfully decorated bedrooms, 1 with a Victorian bedstead & Laura Ashley decor & some with sea views. 4 are en-suite & all have T.V. & tea/coffee-making facilities. Ideal family accommodation. A licensed bar. Log fires in winter. A choice of breakfast, freshly brewed coffee & homemade marmalade. A perfect base for Sandringham (7 miles), Lavender Fields or the wonderful coastline.	£18.50 CREDIT CARD VISA M'CARD AMEX	Y	N	Y
Annette Tofts **The Toll Barn** Norwich Road North Walsham NR28 0JB Tel: (01692) 403063 Fax 01692 406582 Open: ALL YEAR Map Ref No. 12	Nearest Road: A.149 Nominated for prestigious B & B awards, Toll Barn offers outstanding comfort & privacy in a relaxed, informal atmosphere. Delightful, spacious guest lodges are situated within pretty courtyard gardens, each decorated in classic English country-house style. All en-suite with T.V., fridge & tea/coffee. Enjoy farmhouse breakfasts in the exposed brick & beamed dining room, or choose room service. Ideal for exploring north Norfolk, Broads, coast & Norwich. Children over 12.	£22.00 🚭	N	N	N

Starston Hall.   Starston.

Norfolk

		rate from £ per person	children taken	evening meals	animals taken
Joanna Douglas **Greenacres Farmhouse** **Woodgreen** **Long Stratton** **Norwich NR15 2RR** Tel: (01508) 530261 Open: ALL YEAR Map Ref No. 13	Nearest Road: A.140 A period 17th-century farmhouse on a 30 acre common with ponds & wildlife, only 10 miles from Norwich. All en-suite bedrooms (2 double/1 twin) are tastefully furnished to complement the oak beams & period furniture, with tea/coffee facilities & T.V.. The beamed sitting room with inglenook fireplace invites you to relax. A sunny dining room encourages you to enjoy a leisurely breakfast. Snooker table & all-weather tennis court. Enjoy the peace & tranquillity of this charming home.	£18.00	Y	Y	Y
Eddie & Margaret Lovatt **Edmar Lodge** **64 Earlham Road** **Norwich** **NR2 3DF** Tel: (01603) 615599 Open: ALL YEAR Map Ref No. 14	Nearest Road: A.11 A welcoming smile, friendly service & every comfort are all provided at Edmar Lodge, situated only 10 mins' walk from the city centre & with 2 car parks. Ideal for exploring Norwich & the Norfolk countryside. Advice is readily given on walks in the city with its attractions from modern shops to fascinating museums, together with tour planning in & around the county. 4 bedrooms with every amenity, including tea/coffee & T.V. (44 channels). (2 en-suite & 2 standard rooms with vanity units sharing a bathroom - ideal for a family.)	£18.00	Y	N	N
Linda & Martin Hickey **Corfield House** **Sporle** **Swaffham PE32 2EA** Tel: (01760) 723636 Open: MAR - DEC Map Ref No. 15	Nearest Road: A.47 Corfield House is an attractive brick-built house standing in 1/2 an acre of lawned gardens in the peaceful village of Sporle near Swaffham, an ideal base for touring Norfolk. Some of the 4 comfortable & attractive en-suite bedrooms (1 ground-floor) have fine views across open fields, & all have T.V., clock/radio & a fact-file on places to visit. Good home-cooked food using excellent local produce. Licensed.	£21.50 (no smoking) CREDIT CARD VISA M'CARD	Y	Y	N
Lavender Garnier **College Farm** **Thompson** **Thetford** **IP24 1QG** Tel: (01953) 483318 Open: ALL YEAR Map Ref No. 16	Nearest Road: A.1075 Built 600 years ago as a College of Priests, & became a manor house when Henry VIII dissolved the monasteries. College Farm has been modernised to provide 3 charming rooms, 2 en-suite & all with T.V. & superb views over farmland & mature trees. Delicious breakfasts served in the panelled dining room. An excellent thatched pub in the village offers tasty meals. Norfolk coast, Norwich, Cambridge & Sandringham within easy reach by car. Children over 7 years.	£18.00	Y	N	N
Mrs Shirley Carr **White Hall** **Carbrooke** **Watton** **Thetford IP25 6SG** Tel/Fax: (01953) 885950 Open: ALL YEAR Map Ref No. 17	Nearest Road: A.1075 Elegant Georgian country house in delightful grounds of 3 acres, with large natural pond. 3 attractive, comfortable bedrooms (1 en-suite) & spacious, sunny drawing room with colour T.V.. Traditional breakfast served in fine dining room. Early morning tea, evening drinks, full central heating, log fires, etc., ensure that your stay is enjoyable and relaxing. Ideal touring centre, lots of local interest. Good food, golf, swimming nearby. Animals by arrangement.	£19.00	Y	N	Y

	rate from £ per person	children taken	evening meals	animals taken
Mrs Christine Collins **Cedar Lodge** **West Tofts** **Thetford** **IP26 5DB** **Tel: (01842) 878281** **Open: ALL YEAR** **Map Ref No. 18**	Nearest Road: A.134 Guests receive a true country welcome at this cedar colt house. Standing in a well-kept garden, it is located in the heart of Thetford Forest. Traditionally furnished & offering comfortable guest rooms, 2 with private bathroom, & all with tea/coffee-making facilities. Christine is Cordon Bleu trained, loves entertaining her guests & is pleased to provide packed lunches. The North Norfolk coast, Cambridge, Norwich & Newmarket are within 45 mins' drive. Children over 12 yrs. Animals by arrangement.	£17.50	Y	Y	Y
Mrs Marion Ford **Old Bottle House** **Cranwich, Mundford** **Thetford IP26 5JL** **Tel: (01842) 878012** **Open: ALL YEAR** **Map Ref No. 19**	Nearest Road: A.134 Old Bottle House is a 275-year-old former coaching inn, on the edge of Thetford Forest. Guests have a choice of 3 spacious, colour-co-ordinated bedrooms with tea/coffee-making facilities & colour T.V.. Delicious meals are served in the dining room, which has an inglenook fireplace. A charming house with every comfort, and a warm, friendly welcome. Children over 5 please.	£17.00	Y	Y	N
Jennie & Alex Lock **Greenbanks Country** **Hotel** **Swaffham Road** **Wendling NR19 2AB** **Tel: (01362) 687742** **Open: ALL YEAR** **Map Ref No. 20**	Nearest Road: A.47 Charming, small, 18th-century hotel, with delightful country restaurant, situated in 9 acres of meadows & lakes. Spectacular gardens. Elegant & attractive en-suite rooms, offering peace & comfort. Superb cuisine, with excellent choice from varied menu: special diets catered for. Greenbanks is 15 mins from the fine city of Norwich, & within easy reach of the coast, the Broads & many stately homes. Walking, fishing & golfing breaks available.	£32.00 CREDIT CARD VISA M'CARD	Y	Y	Y

When booking your accommodation please mention
The Best Bed & Breakfast

Northumbria

Northumbria

Mountains & moors, hills & fells, coast & country are all to be found in this Northern region which embraces four counties - Northumberland, Durham, Cleveland & Tyne & Wear.

Saxons, Celts, Vikings, Romans & Scots all fought to control what was then a great wasteland between the Humber & Scotland.

Northumberland

Northumberland is England's Border country, a land of history, heritage & breathtaking countryside. Hadrian's Wall, stretching across the county from the mouth of the Tyne in the west to the Solway Firth, was built as the Northern frontier of the Roman Empire in 122 AD. Excavations along the Wall have brought many archaeological treasures to light. To walk along the wall is to discover the genius of Roman building & engineering skill. They left a network of roads, used to transport men & equipment in their attempts to maintain discipline among the wild tribes.

Through the following centuries the Border wars with the Scots led to famous battles such as Otterburn in 1388 & Flodden in 1513, & the construction of great castles including Bamburgh & Lindisfarne. Berwick-on-Tweed, the most northerly town, changed hands between England & Scotland 13 times.

Northumberland's superb countryside includes the Cheviot Hills in the Northumberland National Park, the unforgettable heather moorlands of the Northern Pennines to the west, Kielder Water (Western Europe's largest man-made lake), & 40 miles of glorious coastline.

Holy Island, or Lindisfarne, is reached by a narrow causeway that is covered at every incoming tide. Here St. Aidan of Iona founded a monastery in the 7th century, & with St. Cuthbert set out to Christianise the pagan tribes. The site was destroyed by the Danes, but Lindisfarne Priory was built by the monks of Durham in the 11th century to house a Benedictine community. The ruins are hauntingly beautiful.

Durham

County Durham is the land of the Prince Bishops, who with their armies, nobility, courts & coinage controlled the area for centuries. They ruled as a virtually independent State, holding the first line of defence against the Scots.

In Durham City, the impressive Norman Castle standing proudly over the narrow mediaeval streets was the home of the Prince Bishops for 800 years.

Durham Cathedral, on a wooded peninsula high above the River Wear, was built in the early 12th century & is undoubtably one of the world's finest buildings, long a place of Christian pilgrimage.

The region's turbulent history led to the building of forts & castles. Some like Bowes & Barnard Castle are picturesque ruins whilst others, including Raby, Durham & Lumley still stand complete.

The Durham Dales of Weardale, Teesdale & the Derwent Valley cover about one third of the county & are endowed with some of the highest & wildest scenery. Here are High Force, England's highest waterfall, & the Upper Teesdale National Nature Reserve.

The Bowes Museum at Barnard Castle is a magnificent French-style chateau & houses an important art collection.

In contrast is the award-winning museum at Beamish which imaginatively recreates Northern life at the turn of the century.

Northumbria

Cleveland

Cleveland, the smallest 'shire' in England, has long been famous for its steel, chemical & shipbuilding industries but it is also an area of great beauty. The North Yorkshire National Park lies in the south, & includes the cone-shaped summit of Roseberry Topping, "Cleveland's Matterhorn".

Cleveland means 'land of cliffs', & in places along the magnificent coastline, cliffs tower more than 600 feet above the sea, providing important habitat for wild plants & sea-birds.

Pretty villages such as Hart, Elwick & Staithes are full of steep, narrow alleys. Marton was the birthplace of Captain James Cook & the museum there traces the explorer's early life & forms the start of the 'Cook Heritage Trail'.

The Tees estuary is a paradise for birdwatchers, whilst walkers can follow the Cleveland Way or the 38 miles of the Langbaurgh Loop. There is surfing, windsurfing & sailing at Saltburn, & for the less energetic, the scenic Esk Valley Railway runs from Middlesbrough to Whitby.

Tyne & Wear

Tyne & Wear takes its name from the two rivers running through the area, & includes the large & lively city of Newcastle-on-Tyne.

Weardale lies in a beautiful valley surrounded by wild & bleak fells. Peaceful now, it was the setting for a thriving industry mining coal & silver, zinc & lead. Nature trails & recreation areas have been created among the old village & market towns.

The county was the birthplace of George Stephenson, railway engineer, who pioneered the world's first passenger railway on the Stockton to Darlington Line in 1825.

Durham Cathedral.

Northumbria

Northumbria Gazeeter

Areas of Outstanding Natural Beauty
The Heritage Coast, the Cheviot Hills, the North Pennine chain.

Historic Houses & Castles

Alnwick Castle - Alnwick
A superb mediaeval castle of the 12th century.
Bamburgh Castle-Bamburgh
A restored 12th century castle with Norman keep.
Callaly Castle - Whittingham
A 13th century Pele tower with 17th century mansion. Georgian additions.
Durham Castle - Durham
Part of the University of Durham - a Norman castle.
Lindisfarne Castle - Holy Island
An interesting 14th century castle.
Ormesby Hall - Nr. Middlesbrough
A mid 18th century house.
Raby Castle - Staindrop, Darlington
14th century with some later alteration . Fine art & furniture. Large gardens.
Wallington Hall -Combo
A 17th century house with much alteration & addition.
Washington Old Hall-Washington
Jacobean manor house, parts of which date back to 12th century.

Cathedrals & Churches

Brancepeth (St. Brandon)
12th century with superb 17th century woodwork. Part of 2 mediaeval screens. Flemish carved chest.
Durham Cathedral
A superb Norman cathedral. A unique Galilee chapel & early 12th century vaults.
Escombe
An interesting Saxon Church with sundial.
Hartlepool (St. Hilda)
Early English with fine tower & buttresses.
Hexham (St. Andrews)
Remains of a 17th century church with Roman dressing. A unique night staircase & very early stool. Painted screens.
Jarrow (St. Pauls)
Bede worshipped here. Strange in that it was originally 2 churches until 11th century. Mediaeval chair.

Newcastle (St. Nicholas)
14th century with an interesting lantern tower.
Heraldic font. Roundel of 14th century glass.
Morpeth (St. Mary the Virgin)
Fine mediaeval glass in east window - 14th century.
Pittington (St. Lawrence)
Late Norman nave with wall paintings. Carved tombstone - 13th century.
Skelton (St. Giles)
Early 13th century with notable font, gable crosses, bell-cote & buttresses.
Staindrop (St. Mary)
A fine Saxon window.
Priests dwelling.
Neville tombs & effigies.

Museums & Galleries

Aribea Roman Fort Museum - South Shields
Interesting objects found on site.
Berwick-on-Tweed Museum - Berwick
Special exhibition of interesting local finds.
Bowes Museum - Bernard Castle
European art from mediaeval to 19th century.
Captain Cook Birthplace Museum - Middlesbrough
Cook's life & natural history relating to his travels.
Clayton Collection - Chollerford
A collection of Roman sculpture, weapons & tools from forts.
Corbridge Roman Station - Corbridge
Roman pottery & sculpture.
Dormitory Musuem - Durham Cathedral
Relics of St. Cuthbert.
Mediaeval seats & manuscripts.
Gray Art Gallery - Hartlepool
19th-20th century art & oriental antiquities.
Gulbenkian Museum of Oriental Art - University of Durham
Chinese pottery & porcelain, Chinese jade & stone carvings, Chinese ivories, Chinese textiles, Japenese & Tibetan art. Egyptian & Mesopotamian antiquities.
Jarrow Hall - Jarrow
Excavation finds of Saxon & mediaeval monastery.
Fascinating information room dealing with early Christian sites in England.

Northumbria

Keep Museum - Newcastle-upon-Tyne
Mediaeval collection.
Laing Art Gallery - Newcastle-upon-Tyne
17th-19th century British arts, porcelain,
glass & silver.
National Music Hall Museum -
Sunderland
19th-20th century costume & artefacts
associated with the halls.
Preston Hall Museum - Stockton-on-Tees
Armour & arms, toys, ivory period room
University - New Castle -Upon -Tyne
The Hatton Gallery - housing a fine
collection of Italian paintings.
Museum of Antiquities
Prehistoric, Roman & Saxon collection
with an interesting reconstruction of a
temple.
**Beamish North of England Open Air
Museum** - European Museum of the Year
Chantry Bagpipe Museum - Morpeth
Darlington Museum & Railway Centre.

Historic Monuments

Ariiea Roman Fort - South Shields
Remains which include the gateways &
headquarters.
Barnard Castle - Barnard Castle
17th century ruin with interesting keep.
Bowes Castle - Bowes
Roman Fort with Norman keep.
The Castle & Town Walls - Berwick-on-
Tweed
12th century remains, reconstructed later.
Dunstanburgh Castle - Alnwick
14th century remains.
Egglestone Abbey - Barnard Castle
Remains of a Poor House.
Finchdale Priory - Durham
13 th century church with much
remaining.
Hadrian's Wall - Housesteads
Several miles of the wall including castles
& site museum.
Mithramic Temple - Carrawbrough
Mithraic temple dating back to the 3rd
century.
Norham Castle - Norham
The partial remains of a 12th century
castle.
Prudhoe Castle - Prudhoe
Dating from the 12th century with
additions. Bailey & gatehouse well
preserved.

The Roman Fort - Chesters
Extensive remains of a Roman bath
house.
Tynemouth Priory & Castle - Tynemouth
11th century priory - ruin - with 16th
century towers & keep.
Vindolanda - Barton Mill
Roman fort dating from 3rd century.
Warkworth Castle - Warkworth
Dating from the 11th century with
additions.
A great keep & gatehouse.
Warkworth Hermitage - Warkworth
An interesting 14th century Hermitage.
Lindisfarne Priory - Holy Island
(Lindisfarne)
11th century monastery. Island accessible
only at low tide.

Other things to see & do

Botanical Gardens - Durham University
Bird & Seal Colonies - Farne Islands
Conducted tours by boat
Marine Life Centre & Fishing Museum -
Seahouses
Museum of sealife, & boat trips to the
Farne Islands.
Tower Knowe Visitor Centre - Keilder
Water

Saltburn Victorian Festival.

NORTHUMBERLAND, DURHAM & TYNE & WEAR

Map reference

1	Inkster	14	Peel
2	Jackson	15	Close
4	Laverack	16	Todd
5	Weightman	19	Whitley
7	Graham-Tomlinson	20	Reed
7	Elliott	21	Delin
8	Carr		
9	Lee		
11	Courage		
12	Minchin		
13	Gay		

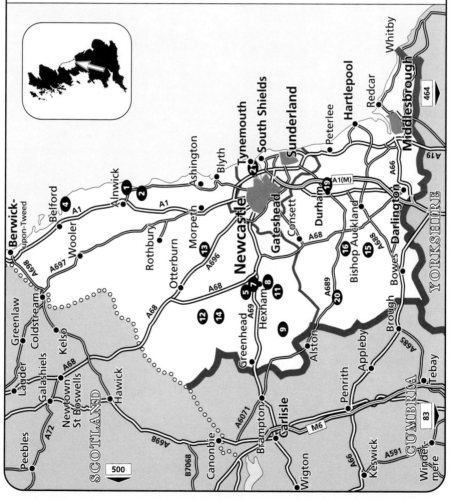

291

Marine House. Alnmouth.

Northumberland

		rate from £ per person	children taken	evening meals	animals taken
Gordon & Sheila Inkster **Marine House Private Hotel** **1 Marine Road** **Alnmouth NE66 2RW** **Tel: (01665) 830349** **Open: FEB - DEC** **Map Ref No. 01**	Nearest Road: A.1 A 200-year-old listed building of considerable charm, situated on the edge of the village golf links with magnificent views of the sea. 10 individually appointed bedrooms, some with tester & crown drapes. All en-suite, with T.V. & tea/coffee. Delicious, imaginative home cooking by a dedicated & creative resident chef, with menus changing daily. The prevailing atmosphere of comfort is enhanced by open log fires. Children over 7. (Min. 2-night stay, & rate incl. dinner).	£36.00 *see PHOTO over* CREDIT CARD VISA M'CARD	Y	Y	Y
Mrs Dorothy Jackson **Bilton Barns Farmhouse** **Bilton Barns** **Alnmouth** **Alnwick NE66 2TB** **Tel: (01665) 830427** **Fax 01665 830063** **Open: MAR - Mid OCT** **Map Ref No. 02**	Nearest Road: A.1 This spacious & well furnished farmhouse has beautiful, panoramic views over Alnmouth & Warkworth Bay, only 1 1/2 miles away. Set in lovely countryside, & excellently situated for the many magnificent beaches, castles, walks & recreational activities. All rooms are centrally heated, & large bedrooms have their own washbasin, T.V. & tea/coffee facilities, 3 with private bathroom. Dorothy makes many dishes with a distinctly local flavour. Brian is pleased to show any interested visitors around the farm.	£19.00	Y	Y	N
Anita & Peter Laverack **Waren House Hotel** **Waren Mill** **Belford NE70 7EE** **Tel: (01668) 214581** **Fax 01668 214484** **Open: ALL YEAR** **Map Ref No. 04**	Nearest Road: A.1 Lovingly restored traditional country house set in 6 acres of wooded grounds on the edge of Budle Bay, overlooking the Holy Island of Lindisfarne. Beautiful bedrooms, some with 4-poster, all with both spacious bathrooms & all the facilities you would expect from one of Northumbria's premier award-winning hostelries. Magnificent dining room offering excellent food. 200-plus bin wine list. No smoking except in library. Bamburgh Castle 2 miles. Children over 14. (Rate includes dinner.)	£55.00 CREDIT CARD VISA M'CARD AMEX	N	Y	Y
Margaret & Bill Weightman **The Courtyard** **Mount Pleasant, Sandhoe** **Corbridge NE46 4LX** **Tel: (01434) 606850** **Fax 01434 606632** **Open: ALL YEAR** **Map Ref No. 05**	Nearest Road: A.69, A.68 A warm family welcome greets visitors to this lovingly restored & beautifully furnished country house, dating from 1730. Surrounded by open countryside, with wonderful panoramic views over Corbridge & Corstopitum Roman Fort, both 1 1/2 miles away, & the Tyne Valley. All rooms have exposed oak beams, en-suite bath/shower rooms, T.V. & tea/coffee; 1 has an antique 4-poster bed. Dinner available with prior notice. Licensed. E-mail: courtyard@northumbria.co.uk	£25.00 🚭 *see PHOTO over*	N	N	N
Patricia Graham-Tomlinson **West Close House** **Hextol Terrace** **Hexham** **NE46 2AD** **Tel: (01434) 603307** **Open: ALL YEAR** **Map Ref No. 07**	Nearest Road: A.69, B.6305 Surrounded by lovely, secluded, prize-winning gardens, this charming & immaculately maintained detached 1920s Villa is situated in a peaceful, leafy cul-de-sac with private parking. 4 delightful bedrooms (1 a superb double en-suite) offer wash basins, radio/alarms, hairdryers & beverage trays. There is an elegant sitting room & a cosy dining/T.V. room. Wholefood Continental or Full English breakfasts are varied, generous & wholesome. A warm, friendly & relaxing ambience ensure a memorable stay. Children over 10.	£18.00 🚭	Y	N	N

The Courtyard. Sandhoe.

Northumberland

	rate from £ per person	children taken	evening meals	animals taken
Mrs Eileen Elliott **Middlemarch** **Hencotes** **Hexham NE46 2EB** **Tel: (01434) 605003** **Fax 01434 605003** **Open: ALL YEAR** **Map Ref No. 07**	Nearest Road: A.68, A.69 A beautifully restored, award-winning, listed Georgian presbytery perfectly placed in the mediaeval market town. A good stop for exploring Northumberland & the Roman Wall, or for going to & from Scotland. The well-appointed, spacious bedrooms comprise 1 4-poster en-suite, 1 family, 1 double & 1 twin. 2 are en-suite, & all have w.b., tea/coffee facilities, r/c colour T.V., radio/alarms & hairdryers. Private parking. Children over 12 yrs. Animals by arrangement.	£22.00	Y	N	Y
Mrs Susan Carr **East Peterel Field Farm** **Hexham** **NE46 2JT** **Tel: (01434) 607209** **Fax 01434 601753** **Open: ALL YEAR** **Map Ref No. 08**	Nearest Road: A.69 An attractive, listed farmhouse offering super accommodation in 4 well-proportioned guest rooms. Each is well equipped with modern-day comforts, including colour T.V., radio & tea/ coffee-making facilities. 2 have en-suite bathrooms. Hearty breakfasts & delicious evening meals are served, & special diets can be catered for. Riding holidays are easily arranged, & 2 golf courses are within easy reach. Children very welcome. Ample parking. An ideal centre for touring & within easy reach of Hadrian's Wall. **E-mail: bookings@petfield.demon.co.uk**	£23.00	Y	Y	N
David & Isobel Lee **Planetrees** **Keenley** **Allendale** **Hexham** **NE47 9NT** **Tel: (01434) 345236** **Open: ALL YEAR (Excl. Xmas)** **Map Ref No. 09**	Nearest Road: A.686 If you want to feel on top of the world, Planetrees is for you. A panoramic setting high in the Northern Pennines, with views to Hadrians Wall & the Cheviot Hills. Comfortable accommodation for relaxing in after exploring this Area of Outstanding Natural Beauty. Residents lounge with log fire, T.V. & video. Centrally heated bedrooms with hairdryer, electric blankets, radios & tea-making facilities. Convenient for English lakes, Beamish, Newcastle Ferry (1 hour drive) & overnight stop for Scotland. Local inns nearby.	£17.00	Y	N	Y
Elizabeth Courage **Rye Hill Farm** **Slaley** **Hexham NE47 OAH** **Tel: (01434) 673259** **Fax 01434 673608** **Open: ALL YEAR** **Map Ref No. 11**	Nearest Road: A.68, A.69 Rye Hill Farm dates back some 300 years & is a traditional livestock unit in beautiful countryside just 5 miles south of Hexham. Recently, some of the stone barns adjoining the farmhouse have been converted into superb modern guest accommodation. There are 6 bedrooms, all with private facilities, & all have radio, T.V. & tea/ coffee-making facilities. Delicious home-cooked meals. Perfect for a get-away-from-it-all holiday. **E-mail: enquiries@courage.u-net.com**	£20.00	Y	Y	Y
David & June Minchin **Westfield House** **Bellingham** **Hexham NE48 2DP** **Tel/Fax: (01434) 220340** **Open: ALL YEAR** **Map Ref No. 12**	Nearest Road: A.68 Westfield is a truly hospitable home. Built as an elegant, but cosy Victorian gentleman's residence, with nearly an acre of gardens. The 5 bedrooms, including 3 en-suite & a 4-poster, are all totally comfortable, with more than a touch of luxury. Breakfast & dinner are superb, with traditional cooking at its best. Wonderful countryside - ideal touring spot - Roman Wall, castles & N.T. properties, so come & bide-awhile & be spoilt.	£19.00 *see PHOTO over* CREDIT CARD VISA M'CARD	Y	Y	Y

Westfield. Bellingham.

Northumberland & Durham

		rate from £ per person	children taken	evening meals	animals taken
David & Sally Peel **Low Stead** **Wark** **Hexham** **NE48 3DP** **Tel: (01434) 230352** **Open: APR - OCT** **Map Ref No. 14**	Nearest Road: A.69 The unspoilt countryside of Northumberland's National Park surrounds Low Stead. A 16th-century 'bastle house' built to repel border reivers, its present tranquillity & solitude provide a haven for walkers, wildlife enthusiasts & country lovers. 2 delightful en-suite bedrooms. Imaginatively presented meals using local produce are served in the log-fired oak-beamed dining room. Peace, history & total comfort combine to make Low Stead's unique atmosphere. Children over 9.	£24.50 (no smoking) *see PHOTO over*	Y	Y	N
Stephen & Celia Gay **Shieldhall** **Wallington** **Morpeth** **NE61 4AQ** **Tel: (01830) 540387** **Fax 01830 540387** **Open: MAR - NOV** **Map Ref No. 13**	Nearest Road: A.696 Within acres of well-kept gardens, offering unimpeded views & overlooking the National Trust's Wallington estate, this meticulously restored 18th-century farmhouse is built around a pretty courtyard. All of the 5 bedrooms are beautifully furnished & have en-suite facilities. There are very comfortable lounges & an extremely charming inglenooked dining room where home produce is often used for delicious meals which are especially prepared when booked in advance.	£19.50 (no smoking) CREDIT CARD VISA M'CARD	Y	Y	N

Durham

		rate from £ per person	children taken	evening meals	animals taken
Anthony & Marguerite Todd **Coves House Farm** **Wolsingham** **Bishop Auckland** **DL13 3BG** **Tel: (01388) 527375** **Fax 01388 526157** **Open: ALL YEAR** **Map Ref No. 16**	Nearest Road: A.689 Historically important, listed early-17th-century farmhouse, lovingly restored by the present owners. Secluded setting in 400 acres of hill farmland. Extremely comfortable twin-bedded room with private bathroom & sitting room in own wing. Extra twin-bedded room available if required for a family or group of friends. Full central heating. Home-cooked food using local produce, by owner with professional catering qualifications. Children over 12 years. Animals by arrangement.	£26.00	Y	Y	Y
Helene & Russell Close **Grove House** **Hamsterley Forest** **Bishop Auckland** **DL13 3NL** **Tel: (01388) 488203** **Fax 01207 520366** **Open: ALL YEAR** **Map Ref No. 15**	Nearest Road: A.68 Grove House, once an aristocrat's shooting lodge, is tastefully furnished throughout, & is situated in an idyllic setting in the middle of Hamsterley Forest. A spacious lounge with log fire gives a warm & comfortable country-house atmosphere. The grandeur & fineness of the dining room reminds one of an age gone by. (Take note of the door handles!) There are 3 bedrooms, all en-suite or with private bathrooms, which are well-appointed. Helene does all the cooking herself to ensure freshness & quality to her evening meals. A delightful home & wonderful base from which to explore this little-known region. Children over 8.	£20.00 (no smoking)	Y	Y	N

Low Stead. Wark.

Durham & Tyne & Wear

		rate from £ per person	children taken	evening meals	animals taken
Alan & Rhona Whitley **The Bracken** **Bank Foot** **Shincliffe** **Durham DH1 2PD** **Tel: (0191) 3862966** **Fax 0191 3845423** **Open: ALL YEAR** **Map Ref No. 19**	Nearest Road: A.177 The Bracken Guest House is situated on the outskirts of Durham City in the nearby village of Shincliffe. The property stands in 2 acres of wood grounds, with safe parking in front of the house. Just 2 mins' drive from the city centre on the A.177 which links up with the A.1/M. All of the attractive bedrooms are en-suite, & 1 is situated on the ground floor & has wheelchair access. There is a residents' lounge/bar in which to relax. An ideal centre from which to explore this lovely region & its many attractions. Animals by arrangement. CREDIT CARD VISA M'CARD	£25.00	Y	Y	Y
Mrs B. Reed **Lands Farm** **Westgate-in-Weardale** **DL13 1SN** **Tel: (01388) 517210** **Open: MAR - OCT** **Map Ref No. 20**	Nearest Road: A.689 You will be warmly welcomed to Lands Farm, an old stone-built farmhouse within walking distance of Westgate village. A walled garden with stream meandering by. Accommodation is in centrally heated double & family rooms with luxury en-suite facilities, T.V., tea/coffee making. Full English breakfast or Continental alternative served in an attractive dining room. This is an ideal base for touring (Durham, Hadrian's Wall, Beamish Museum, etc.) & for walking.	£20.00	Y	N	N

Tyne & Wear

		rate from £ per person	children taken	evening meals	animals taken
Anna & Pascal Delin **Hope House** **47 Percy Gardens** **Tynemouth** **NE30 4HH** **Tel: (0191) 2571989** **Fax 0191 2571989** **Open: ALL YEAR** **Map Ref No. 21**	Nearest Road: A.1058 Hope House is a beautifully refurbished Victorian house occupying an unrivalled position overlooking the Long Sands on the seafront of Tynemouth. Offering 3 spacious & comfortable double bedrooms with magnificent sea views, tasteful en-suite facilities, T.V. & hospitality tray. In the beautiful dining room, you will be entranced by the unique ambience which is complemented by works of art & fine antiques, & where French & English cuisine is served using only the finest ingredients. Tynemouth village, only a few mins stroll away, features a 900-year-old castle & priory, tea shops & restaurants. A wonderful location. CREDIT CARD VISA M'CARD AMEX	£37.50	Y	Y	N

When booking your accommodation please mention
The Best Bed & Breakfast

Oxfordshire

Oxfordshire
(Thames & Chilterns)

Oxfordshire is a county rich in history & delightful countryside. It has prehistoric sites, early Norman churches, 15th century coaching inns, Regency residences, distinctive cottages of black & white chalk flints & lovely Oxford, the city of dreaming spires.

The countryside ranges from lush meadows with willow-edged river banks scattered with small villages of thatched cottages, to the hills of the Oxfordshire Cotswolds in the west, the wooded Chilterns in the east & the distinctive ridge of the Berkshire Downs in the south. "Old Father Thames" meanders gently across the county to Henley, home of the famous regatta.

The ancient track known as the Great Ridgeway runs across the shire, & a walk along its length reveals barrows, hill forts & stone circles. The 2,000 year old Uffington Horse cut into the chalk of the hillside below an ancient hill fort site, is some 360 feet in length & 160 feet high.

The Romans built villas in the county & the remains of one, including a magnificent mosaic can be seen at North Leigh. In later centuries lovely houses were built. Minster Lovell stands beside the Windrush; Rousham house with its William Kent gardens is situated near Steeple Aston & beside the Thames lies Elizabethan Mapledurham House with its working watermill.

At Woodstock is Blenheim Palace, the largest private house in Britain & birthplace of Sir Winston Churchill. King Alfred's statue stands at Wantage, commemorating his birth there, & Banbury has its cross, made famous in the old nursery rhyme.

Oxford is a town of immense atmosphere with fine college buildings around quiet cloisters, & narrow cobbled lanes. It was during the 12th century that Oxford became a meeting place for scholars & grew into the first established centre of learning, outside the monasteries, in England.

The earliest colleges to be founded were University College, Balliol & Merton. Further colleges were added during the reign of the Tudors, as Oxford became a power in the kingdom. There are now 35 university colleges & many other outstanding historic buildings in the city . Christ Church Chapel is now the Cathedral of Oxford, a magnificent building with a deservedly famous choir.

St. Mary's Church.

Oxfordshire

Oxfordshire Gazeteer

Areas of Oustanding Natural Beauty
The North Wessex Downs. The Chiltern Hills. The Cotswolds.

Historic Houses & Castles

Ashdown House - Nr. Lambourn
17th century, built for Elizabeth of Bohemia, now contains portraits associated with her. Mansard roof has cupola with golden ball.

Blenheim Palace - Woodstock
Sir John Vanbrugh's classical masterpiece. Garden designed by Vanbrugh & Henry Wise. Further work done by Capability Brown who created the lake. Collection of pictures & tapestries.

Broughton Castle- Banbury.
14th century mansion with moat - interesting plaster work fine panelling & fire places

Chasleton House-Morton in Marsh
17th century,fine examples of plaster work & panelling.Still has original furniture & tapestries. topiary garden from1700.

Grey Court - Henly-on-Thames
16th century house containing 18th century plasterwork & furniture. Mediaeval ruins. Tudor donkey-wheel for raising water from well.

Mapledurham House - Mapledurham
16th century Elizabethan house. Oak staircase, private chapel, paintings, original moulded ceilings. Watermill nearby.

Milton Manor House - Nr. Abingdon
17th century house designed by Inigo Jones - Georgian wings, walled garden, pleasure grounds.

Rousham House - Steeple Ashton
17th century - contains portraits & miniatures.

University of Oxford Colleges

University college ------------------1249
Balliol----------------------------------1263
Merton---------------------------------1264
Hertford-------------------------------1284
Oriel------------------------------------1326
New-------------------------------------1379
All Souls-------------------------------1438
Brasenose-----------------------------1509
Christ Church----------------------1546
St. John's---------------------------1555
Pembroke--------------------------1624
Worcester-------------------------1714
Nuffield ----------------------------1937
St. Edmund Hall-------------------1270
Exeter-------------------------------1314
The Queen's-----------------------1340
Lincoln------------------------------1427
Magdalen --------------------------1458
Corpus Christi ---------------------1516
Trinity-------------------------------1554
Jesus--------------------------------1571
Wadham----------------------------1610
Keble--------------------------------1868

Cathedrals & Churches

Abingdon (St. Helen)
14th-16th century perpendicular. Painted roof. Georgian stained & enamelled glass.

Burford (St. John the Baptist)
15th century. Sculptured table tombs in churchyard.

Chislehampton (St. Katherine)
18th century. Unspoilt interior of Georgian period. Bellcote.

Dorchester (St. Peter & St. Paul)
13th century knight in stone effigy. Jesse window.

East Hagbourne (St. Andrew)
14th -15th century. Early glass, wooden roofs, 18th century tombs.

North Moreton (All Saints)
13th century with splendid 14th century chantry chapel - tracery.

Oxford Cathedral
Smallest of our English cathedrals. Stone spire form 1230. Norman arcade has double arches, choir vault.

Ryecote (St. Michael & All Angels)
14th century benches & screen base. 17th century altar-piece & communion rails, old clear glass, good ceiling.

Stanton Harcourt (St. Michael)
Early English - old stone & marble floor. Early screen with painting, monuments of 17th -19th century.

Yarnton (St. Bartholomew)
13th century - late perpendicular additions. Jacobean screen. 15th century alabaster reredos.

Oxfordshire

Museums & Galleries

The Ashmolean Museum of Art & Archaeology - Oxford
British ,European ,Mediterranean, Egyptian & Near Eastern archaeology. Oil paintings of Italian, Dutch, Flemish, French & English schools. Old Master watercolours, prints, drawings, ceramics, silver, bronzes & sculptures. Chinese & Japanese porcelain, lacquer & painting, Tibetan, Islamic & Indian art.
Christ Church Picture Gallery - Oxford
Old Master drawings & paintings.
Museum of Modern Art - Oxford
Exhibitiors of contemporary art.
Museum of Oxford
Many exhibits depicting the history of Oxford & its University.
The Rotunda - Oxford
Privately owned collection of dolls' houses 1700-1900, with contents such as furniture, china, silver, dolls, etc.
Oxford University Museum
Entomological, zoological, geological & mineralogical collections.
Pendon Museum of Miniature Landscape & Transport - Abingdon.
Showing in miniature the countryside & its means of transport in the thirties, with trains & thatched village. Railway relics.

Town Museum - Abingdon
17th century building exhibiting fossil, archaeological items & collection of charters & documents.
Tolsey Museum - Burford
Seals, maces, charters & bygones - replica of Regency room with period furnishings & clothing.

Historic Monuments

Uffington Castle & White Horse - Uffington
White horse cut into the chalk - iron age hill fort.
Rollright Stones - Nr. Chipping Norton
77 stones placed in circle - an isolated King's stone & nearby an ancient burial chamber.
Minster Lovell House - Minster Lovell
15th century mediaeval house - ruins.
Deddington Castle - Deddington

Other things to see & do

Didcot railway centre -a large collection of locomotives etc., from Brunel's Great Western Railway.
Filkins -a working wool mill where rugs & garments are woven in traditional way.

Blenheim Palace. Woodstock.

OXFORDSHIRE

Map reference

0	Lloyd	17	Welham
1	Welfare	17	Price
2	Canning	17	Tompkins
4	Wills	17	Trafford
5	Grove-White	17	Anderson
6	Allday	17	Morris
7	Pasrons	17	Edwards
8	Jones	20	Aitken
9	Scavuzzo	21	Cole
9	Weir	22	Hill
10	Wadsworth	23	Simpson
11	Talfourd-Cook	26	Crofts
12	Fulford-Dobson		
15	Krasker		

Fallowfields.   Abingdon.

Oxfordshire

		rate from £ per person	children taken	evening meals	animals taken
Anthony & Peta Lloyd **Fallowfields Country** **Hotel, Faringdon Road** **Southmoor** **Abingdon OX13 5BH** **Tel: (01865) 820416** **Fax 01865 821275** **Open: ALL YEAR** **Map Ref No. 00**	Nearest Road: A.420 Fallowfields, the former home of Begum Aga Khan, is an absolutely delightful 300-year-old Gothic-style manor house. Beautifully furnished, with the emphasis on gracious elegance. The 2 lounges are spacious & comfortable. The pleasant bedrooms have pretty linens, tea/coffee-making facilities, hairdryer, radio, 'phone & valet press. The elegant dining room befits the super cuisine served. Guests are also encouraged to use the tennis court, croquet lawn & the outdoor swimming pool. Children over 10 years.	£42.50 🚭 *see PHOTO over* CREDIT CARD VISA M'CARD AMEX	Y	Y	Y
Mrs Deborah Welfare **Rooks Orchard** **Little Wittenham** **Abingdon OX14 4QY** **Tel: (01865) 407765** **Open: ALL YEAR** **Map Ref No. 01**	Nearest Road: A.4130 In a tranquil hamlet on the Rover Thames, this listed 17th-century family house with inglenook fireplaces, beams & period furniture is set in large gardens surrounded by orchards & a nature reserve with public access. Little Wittenham is a designated Area of Outstanding Natural Beauty within easy reach of Oxford, Wallingford, Abingdon & Didcot. Delightful accommodation. Local villages offer good pubs & restaurants.	£24.00	Y	N	Y
P. Ritter & M. Canning **La Madonette Country** **Guest House** **North Newington** **Banbury OX15 6AA** **Tel: (01295) 730212** **Fax 01295 730363** **Open: ALL YEAR** **Map Ref No. 02**	Nearest Road: A.422, M.40 A peacefully situated 17th-century millhouse set in rural surroundings, where Patti & Michael offer a warm welcome to their guests. The 5 spacious double en-suite bedrooms are comfortably furnished with full facilities & are attractively decorated. Well located for the Cotswolds, Stratford-upon-Avon, Oxford & Blenheim. Good local pubs & restaurants offering evening meals nearby. An attractive lounge, gardens & swimming pool for guests' use. Licensed.	£25.50 CREDIT CARD VISA M'CARD	Y	N	N
Stephen & Mary Pen Wills **Fulford House** **The Green, Culworth** **Banbury OX17 2BB** **Tel: (01295) 760355** **Fax 01295 768304** **Open: ALL YEAR** **Map Ref No. 04**	Nearest Road: B.4525 Peace, quiet & comfort is assured in this charming 17th-century home. Whether wandering in the old tranquil gardens, watching horses training or chatting with other guests & hosts, there is a great ambience. 3 delightfully furnished bedrooms with en-suite/private facilities & T.V.. A drawing room is for guests' use. 1 hour from Heathrow, Fulford House is in rolling Northamptonshire countryside, near Warwick, Stratford & Oxford. A central stop-over for travellers. Licensed. Children over 5.	£24.00 *see PHOTO over*	Y	N	Y
Col. & Mrs Grove-White **Home Farmhouse** **Charlton** **Banbury** **OX17 3DR** **Tel/Fax: (01295) 811683** **Open: ALL YEAR** **Map Ref No. 05**	Nearest Road: M.40, A.43 This charming, listed stone house dating from 1637, with its attractive, colourful, paved courtyard, provides an excellent base for visiting Oxford, Blenheim, Stratford-upon-Avon, Warwick & the beautiful Cotswold villages. Mrs Grove-White has used her expertise as a professional interior designer to ensure that the 3 double/twin bedded rooms, with en-suite bathroom & colour T.V., are comfortable & elegantly furnished. Evening meals by arrangement only. Children over 12 yrs.	£24.00 🚭 *see PHOTO over* CREDIT CARD VISA M'CARD	N	Y	N

Fulford House.   Banbury.

Home Farmhouse. Charlton.

Oxfordshire

	rate from £ per person	children taken	evening meals	animals taken
Stephen & Sara Allday **College Farmhouse** **Kings Sutton** **Banbury OX17 3PS** **Tel: (01295) 811473** **Fax 01295 812505** **Open: ALL YEAR** **Map Ref No. 06** Nearest Road: A.43, M.40 Fine period farmhouse, with lovely views, set in its own secluded grounds, which include a lake, tennis court & organic vegetable garden. Ideally located for visits to Oxford, Warwick, Stratford-upon-Avon & the Cotswolds. Excellent home-produced food - special diets catered for. Stephen & Sara have considerable local knowledge. They enjoy gardening, bridge & racing. You will be sure of a very comfortable & peaceful stay. Evening meals & animals by arrangement.	£25.00 *see PHOTO over*	Y	Y	Y
Glen & Caroline Parsons **Home Farm House** **Middle Aston** **Bicester OX6 3PX** **Tel: (01869) 340666** **Fax (01869) 340666** **Open: ALL YEAR** **Map Ref No. 07** Nearest Road: A.4260 Home Farm House is an attractive 17th-century house with a wonderful garden & stunning views. The attractive bedrooms, 1 double & 1 twin, are delightfully furnished & have either en-suite or private bathroom. Home Farm House is excellently placed for visiting Woodstock & Blenheim Palace, Oxford & the Cotswolds. Evening meals by arrangement. Glen & Caroline look forward to welcoming you to their home.	£20.00	Y	N	N
Mrs Wendy Jones **Hillborough House &** **Willows Restaurant** **The Green, Shipton Rd** **Milton-under-Wychwood** **Chipping Norton OX7 6JH** **Tel: (01993) 830501** **Fax 01993 832005** **Open: FEB - DEC** **Map Ref No. 08** Nearest Road: A.424 An elegant Victorian house with conservatory restaurant, facing the village green in this delightful Cotswold village. All of the attractive rooms are en-suite, spacious, warm & cheerful, & some of cottage character are annexed across the courtyard from the main house. Cosy lounge & secluded lawned gardens. Dinner served 5 nights a week (Tues-Sat) in separately run Willows Restaurant. Excellent walking area, & touring of Cotswolds, Stratford & the university city of Oxford. Animals by arrangement.	£26.00 CREDIT CARD VISA M'CARD AMEX	Y	Y	Y
Mrs Audrey Scavuzzo **The Forge House** **Churchill** **Chipping Norton** **OX7 6NJ** **Tel: (01608) 658173** **Open: ALL YEAR** **Map Ref No. 09** Nearest Road: A.361 The Forge House is a 150-year-old, traditional Cotswold stone cottage, with inglenook log fires & exposed beams, combining the charm of tradition with the comfort of contemporary living. 4 tastefully furnished en-suite rooms, 2 with 4-poster beds & 1 with jacuzzi. All have radio, T.V. & tea/coffee facilities. A lounge & garden available for guests' use. Personal service & advice on touring the surrounding area. Convenient for Oxford, Stratford-upon-Avon, Warwick Castle, Blenheim Palace & the Cotswolds.	£25.00 *see PHOTO over*	Y	N	N

When booking your accommodation please mention
The Best Bed & Breakfast

College Farmhouse. King Sutton.

The Forge House. Chipping Norton.

The Craven.   Uffington.

Oxfordshire

	Nearest Road	rate from £ per person	children taken	evening meals	animals taken
Janet Weir **Cotswold Cottage** **Chapel Street** **Bledington** **Chipping Norton OX7 6XA** Te/FaxI: **(01608) 658996** **Open: ALL YEAR** **Map Ref No. 09**	Nearest Road: B.4450 A period cottage with lots of character, flagstone floors & beams, in an unspoilt Cotswold village only 4 miles from Stow-on-the-Wold. Ideally situated for relaxing or for exploring villages of Bourton-on-the-Water, the Slaughters, Chipping Campden & Broadway. A very warm welcome is assured. Beautiful, en-suite rooms, 1 with 4-poster, 1 with jacuzzi, all have colour T.V., hairdryer, clock/radio & tea-making facilities. 15th-century inn on village green only 3 mins' walk.	£25.00	N	N	N
Mrs Carol Wadsworth **The Craven** **Fernham Rd, Uffington** **Faringdon SN7 7RD** Tel: **(01367) 820449** **Open: ALL YEAR** **Map Ref No. 10**	Nearest Road: A.420 An extremely attractive 17th-century thatched farmhouse with exposed beams & open log-burning fire. Accommodation is very comfortable, & comprises 5 bedrooms, 1 with 4-poster bed & private bathroom. Good home cooking with fresh local produce. The Craven offers a friendly, relaxed atmosphere. The perfect base for touring this fascinating area.	£20.00 *see PHOTO over* CREDIT CARD VISA M'CARD	Y	Y	N
Mr & Mrs Talfourd-Cook **Holmwood, Shiplake Row** **Binfield Heath** **Henley-on-Thames** **RG9 4DP** Tel: **(0118) 9478747** Fax 0118 9478637 **Open: ALL YEAR** **Map Ref No. 11**	Nearest Road: A.4155 Holmwood is a large elegant Georgian country house, Grade II listed, furnished with antique, period furniture. There is a galleried hall, coved mahogany doors & marble fireplaces (wood fires in winter). All bedrooms are spacious & have en-suite facilities. The beautiful gardens extend to 3 1/2 acres & have extensive views over the Thames Valley. A good base for London & the South East. Heathrow Airport 30 mins, Reading 4 miles, Henley 2 1/2 miles. Children over 10 years.	£25.00	N	N	N
Mrs Susan Fulford-Dobson **Shepherds** **Shepherds Green** **Rotherfield Greys** **Henley-on-Thames** **RG9 4QL** Tel/Fax: **(01491) 628413** **Open:** ALL YEAR (Excl. Xmas) **Map Ref No. 12**	Nearest Road: A.4130 A warm & welcoming country home (part 18th-century), covered in roses, wisteria, clematis & jasmine. Shepherds stands on a peaceful village green on its own 8-acre grounds. The 4 pretty bedrooms all have en-suite or private facilities, T.V. & tea/coffee trays. Delightful drawing room for guests with antiques & wood fire. An ideal centre from which to explore the Thames Valley, Chilterns, Windsor & Oxford. Heathrow 35 mins, Gatwick 1 1/4 hrs. Children over 12 welcome. Many pubs & restaurants within easy reach.	£21.00 *see PHOTO over*	Y	N	N
Judy Krasker **Conygree Gate Hotel** **Church Street** **Kingham OX7 6YA** Tel: **(01608) 658389** Fax 01608 659467 **Open: ALL YEAR** **Map Ref No. 15**	Nearest Road: A.436, A.361 A 17th-century converted Cotswold stone farmhouse in a quiet & peaceful village, surrounded by glorious Cotswold countryside. Leaded windows, oak beams & window seats in many of the rooms & inglenook fireplaces in the 2 lounges. Secluded walled garden. 9 bedrooms, mostly en-suite, all with colour T.V. & tea/coffee facilities. Excellent food from the chef in the restaurant. A very friendly & informal atmosphere.	£27.50 CREDIT CARD VISA M'CARD	Y	Y	Y

Shepherds. Rotherfield Greys.

Oxfordshire

		rate from £ per person	children taken	evening meals	animals taken
Mr & Mrs P. Welham **Norham Guest House** **16 Norham Road** **Oxford OX2 6SF** **Tel: (01865) 515352** **Fax 01865 793162** **Open: ALL YEAR** **Map Ref No. 17**	Nearest Road: A.423, A.4165 A delightful Victorian house situated in a conservation area yet convenient for the many attractions of Oxford. 7 tastefully furnished en-suite guest rooms & 1 family room with modern amenities. All rooms have T.V. & tea/coffee facilities. Delicious breakfasts are served. Vegetarian diets by arrangement. Convenient for the city centre. Ideal for visiting the Cotswolds & Stratford-upon-Avon. Children over 5 years.	£27.00	Y	N	N
Mrs L. G. Price **Arden Lodge** **34 Sunderland Avenue** **Off Woodstock Road** **Oxford OX2 8DX** **Tel: (01865) 552076** **Open: ALL YEAR** **Map Ref No. 17**	Nearest Road: A.40 A modern detached house, set in a tree-lined avenue, in one of Oxford's most select areas. Offering 3 attractively furnished bedrooms, with private facilities, colour T.V. & beverage tray. An excellent base for touring: within easy reach of London, the Cotswolds, Stratford & Warwick. Convenient for the city centre, parks, river, meadows, golf course & country inns, including the world famous 'Trout Inn'. Children over 3. (Hosts can be contacted on Mobile 0402 068697.)	£21.00	Y	N	N
Sally & Tony Tompkins **Gables Guest House** **6 Cumnor Hill** **Oxford OX2 9HA** **Tel: (01865) 862153** **Fax 01865 864054** **Open: ALL YEAR** **Map Ref No. 17**	Nearest Road: A.420 Gables is an attractive detached house with a conservatory lounge overlooking the beautiful garden. Ideally situated close to the city centre, bus & railway stations. Easy access to A.34 & equally for the Cotswolds & London. A large private car park. The 6 high-quality rooms are fully equipped with satellite T.V., direct-dial 'phones, hairdryer, tea/coffee facilities & clock/radio. Full range of English, Continental & vegetarian breakfasts available.	£21.00 CREDIT CARD VISA M'CARD	Y	N	N
Mr & Mrs E. Trafford **Tilbury Lodge Hotel** **5 Tilbury Lane** **Eynsham Rd, Botley** **Oxford OX2 9NB** **Tel: (01865) 862138** **Fax 01865 863700** **Open: ALL YEAR** **Map Ref No. 17**	Nearest Road: A.34, B.4044 Tilbury Lodge is a pleasant, family-run private hotel situated in a quiet residential area. Offering Accommodation is in 9 en-suite rooms with radio, T.V., 'phone, hairdryer & tea/coffee-making facilities. 1 four-poster & 2 ground-floor rooms. A pleasant jacuzzi bath is also available. Ample parking. Residents' lounge & garden in which guests may choose to relax. Located 2 miles west of the city centre, with good pubs & restaurants a few minutes' walk away. Good bus service.	£28.00 CREDIT CARD VISA M'CARD	Y	N	N
Dr. B. & Mrs A. Anderson **Sandfield Guest House** **19 London Road** **Headington** **Oxford OX3 7RE** **Tel: (01865) 762406** **Fax (01865) 762406** **Open: ALL YEAR (Excl. Xmas)** **Map Ref No. 17**	Nearest Road: A.40 A family-run guest house offering a high standard of comfort to guests preferring personal service & attention. Quiet & attractive accommodation which is tastefully decorated. The well-proportioned rooms are all en-suite or have a private bathroom, colour T.V., hospitality tray & hairdryer. Guest lounge & gardens. Convenient for city centre buses. Easy walking distance to Redcliffe Hospital Complex & Oxford Brookes University. On direct coach routes to London & Heathrow & Gatwick Airports. Ample on-site parking. Children over 6.	£22.50 CREDIT CARD VISA M'CARD AMEX	Y	N	N

Shipton Grange House. Shipton–under–Wychwood.

Oxfordshire

		rate from £ per person	children taken	evening meals	animals taken
Mr & Mrs P. D. Morris **Pine Castle Hotel** **290-292 Iffley Road** **Oxford** **OX4 4AE** **Tel: (01865) 241497** **Fax 01865 727230** **Open: ALL YEAR (Excl. Xmas)** **Map Ref No. 17**	Nearest Road: A.4158 A warm welcome awaits you at this Edwardian guest house which still retains many of its period features. It is conveniently situated on a main bus route into the city centre. An alternative route is a short walk along the tow path beside the Thames which is both convenient & picturesque. Cots are provided, T.V. & tea/coffee-making facilities in each of the 8 en-suite rooms. Breakfasts vary from the healthy to the positively indulgent. Evening meals with prior notice. **E-mail: pinebeds.oxfhotel@pop3hiway.co.uk**	£28.00 CREDIT CARD VISA M'CARD	Y	Y	N
Doreen & Bertram Edwards **Highfield House** **91 Rose Hill** **Oxford OX4 4HT** **Tel/Fax: (01865) 774083** **Open: ALL YEAR** **Map Ref No. 17**	Nearest Road: A.4158 A pleasing & friendly house, with good access to the city centre & ring road. Accommodation is in 7 spacious bedrooms, all attractively furnished & with matching decor. 5 with en-suite bathroom. All have colour T.V. & tea/coffee-making facilities. A short walk brings you to the old attractive village of Iffley. An excellent base for exploring the historic delights of Oxford.	£19.00 CREDIT CARD VISA M'CARD	Y	N	N
Mrs Veronica Hill **Shipton Grange House** **Shipton-under-** **Wychwood OX7 6DG** **Tel: (01993) 831298** **Fax 01993 832082** **Open: ALL YEAR (Excl. Xmas & New Year)** **Map Ref No. 22**	Nearest Road: A.361 A unique conversion of a Georgian coach house & stabling situated in the former grounds of Shipton Court. Secluded in its own walled garden, & approached by a gated archway. There are 3 elegantly furnished guest rooms, each with an en-suite/private bathroom, colour T.V. & beverage facilities. Delicious breakfasts served in the attractive dining room. The friendly hosts are animal lovers & have a number of pet dogs. Shipton Grange is a delightful house, & ideal for visiting Oxford, Blenheim, etc. Children over 12.	£25.00 *see PHOTO over*	Y	N	N
Peter Cole **The Dairy B & B** **Moreton** **Thame OX9 2HX** **Tel: (01844) 214075** **Fax (01844) 214075** **Open: ALL YEAR** **Map Ref No. 21**	Nearest Road: A.329 This former milking parlour, set in over 4 acres, provides a beautiful, peaceful & comfortable stay. All bedrooms are large, bright & airy & include hairdryers, writing tables, fresh flowers, biscuits & comfortable sofas & chairs. There is a large open-plan lounge with views of the Chilterns. The property is very convenient for London either by train, coach or car, all less than an hour's journey. Oxford is 25 mins by car.	£30.00	N	N	N
Euan & Marjorie Aitken **Upper Green Farm** **Manor Road, Towersey** **Thame OX9 3QR** **Tel: (01844) 212496** **Fax 01844 260399** **Open: ALL YEAR (Excl. Xmas & New Year)** **Map Ref No. 20**	Nearest Road: A.4129 A long immaculate drive leads to this 15th-century thatched farmhouse & 18th-century barn, surrounding a lawned farmyard with flower tubs & borders in profusion. Guests may choose to stay in the farmhouse or Paradise Barn where breakfast is served in the old stables. All bedrooms have private/en-suite facilities & lovely views, & are furnished with country antiques, lace & patchwork. Also, there are 2 rooms suitable for the disabled. A charming base from which to explore this region.	£22.50 *see PHOTO over*	N	N	N

Upper Green Farm. Towersey.

Oxfordshire

		rate from £ per person	children taken	evening meals	animals taken
Liz & John Simpson **Field View** **Wood Green** **Witney OX8 6DE** **Tel: (01993) 705485** **Mobile 0468 614347** **Open: ALL YEAR (Excl. Xmas)** **Map Ref No. 23**	Nearest Road: A.40, A.4095 An attractive Cotswold stone house set in 2 acres, situated on picturesque Wood Green, midway between Oxford University & the Cotswolds. It is an ideal centre for touring, yet only 8 minutes' walk from the centre of this lively Oxfordshire market town. A peaceful setting & a warm, friendly atmosphere await you. Accommodation is in 3 comfortable en-suite rooms with modern amenities & tea/coffee-making facilities.	£21.00	N	N	N
Jean A. Crofts **Crofters Guest House** **29 Oxford Hill** **Witney OX8 6JU** **Tel/Fax: (01993) 778165** **Open: ALL YEAR** **Map Ref No. 26**	Nearest Road: A.40 Situated in a lively market town, 10 miles from Oxford, on the edge of the Cotswolds, Blenheim Palace & Burford, & within easy reach of Stratford. Guests are accommodated in comfortable family, double & twin rooms, all with excellent facilities. En-suite & ground-floor available. Your hosts Jean & Peter will make your stay a memorable experience. Arrive as a guest, leave as a friend.	£20.00	Y	N	N

All the establishments mentioned in this guide are members of
The Worldwide Bed & Breakfast Association

When booking your accommodation please mention
The Best Bed & Breakfast

Shropshire

Shropshire
(Heart of England)

Shropshire is a borderland with a very turbulent history. Physically it straddles highlands & lowlands with border mountains to the west, glacial plains, upland, moorlands & fertile valleys & the River Severn cutting through. It has been quarrelled & fought over by rulers & kings from earliest times. The English, the Romans & the Welsh all wanted to hold Shropshire because of its unique situation. The ruined castles & fortifications dotted across the county are all reminders of its troubled life. The most impressive of these defences is Offa's Dyke, an enormous undertaking intended to be a permanent frontier between England & Wales.

Shropshire has great natural beauty, countryside where little has changed with the years. Wenlock Edge & Clun Forest, Carding Mill Valley, the Long Mynd, Caer Caradoc, Stiperstones & the trail along Offa's Dyke itself, are lovely walking areas with magnificent scenery.

Shrewsbury was & is a virtual island, almost completely encircled by the Severn River. The castle was built at the only gap, sealing off the town. In this way all comings & goings were strictly controlled. In the 18th century two bridges, the English bridge & the Welsh bridge, were built to carry the increasing traffic to the town but Shrewsbury still remains England's finest Tudor city.

Massive Ludlow Castle was a Royal residence, home of Kings & Queens through the ages, whilst the town is also noted for its Georgian houses.

As order came out of chaos, the county settled to improving itself & became the cradle of the Industrial Revolution. Here Abraham Darby discovered how to use coke (from the locally mined coal) to smelt iron. There was more iron produced here in the 18th century than in any other county. A variety of great industries sprang up as the county's wealth & ingenuity increased. In 1781 the world's first iron bridge opened to traffic.

There are many fine gardens in the county. At Hodnet Hall near Market Drayton, the grounds cover 60 acres & the landscaping includes lakes & pools, trees, shrubs & flowers in profusion. Weston Park has 1,000 acres of parkland, woodland gardens & lakes landscaped by Capability Brown.

The house is Restoration period & has a splendid collection of pictures, furniture, china & tapestries.

Shrewsbury hosts an annual poetry festival & one of England's best flower shows whilst a Festival of Art, Music & Drama is held each year in Ludlow with Shakespeare performed against the castle ruins.

Coalbrookedale Museum.

Shropshire

Shropshire Gazeteer

Areas of Outstanding Natural Beauty
The Shropshire Hills.

Historic Houses & Castles

Stokesay Castle - Craven Arms
13th century fortified manor house. Still occupied - wonderful setting - extremely well preserved. Fine timbered gatehouse.
Weston Park - Nr. Shifnal
17th century - fine example of Restoration period - landscaping by Capability Brown. Superb collection of pictures.
Shrewsbury Castle - Shrewsbury
Built in Norman era - interior decorations - painted boudoir.
Benthall Hall - Much Wenlock
16th century. Stone House - mullioned windows. Fine wooden staircase - splendid plaster ceilings.
Shipton Hall - Much Wenlock
Elizabethan. Manor House - walled garden - mediaeval dovecote.
Upton Cressett Hall - Bridgnorth
Elizabethan. Manor House & Gatehouse. Excellent plaster work. . 14th century great hall.

Cathedrals & Churches

Ludlow (St. Lawrence)
14th century nave & transepts. 15th century pinnacled tower. Restored extensively in 19th century. Carved choir stalls, perpendicular chancel - original glass. Monuments.
Shrewsbury (St. Mary)
14th, 15th, 16th century glass. Norman origins.
Stottesdon (St. Mary)
12th century carvings.Norman font. Fine decorations with columns & tracery.
Lydbury North (St. Michael)
14th century transept, 15th century nave roof, 17th century box pews and altar rails. Norman font.
Longor (St. Mary the Virgin)
13th century having an outer staircase to West gallery.
Cheswardine (St. Swithun)
13th century chapel - largely early English. 19th century glass and old brasses. Fine sculpture.

Tong (St. Mary the Virgin with St. Bartholomew)
15th century. Golden chapel of 1515, stencilled walls, remains of paintings on screens, gilt fan vaulted ceiling. Effigies, fine monuments

Museums & Galleries

Clive House - Shrewsbury
Fine Georgian House - collection of Shropshire ceramics. Regimental museum of 1st Queen's Dragoon Guards.
Rowley's House Museum - Shrewsbury
Roman material from Viroconium and prehistoric collection.
Coleham Pumping Station - Old Coleham
Preserved beam engines
Acton Scott Working Farm Museum - Nr. Church Stretton
Site showing agricultural practice before the advent of mechanization.
Ironbridge Gorge Museum - Telford
Series of industrial sites in the Severn Gorge.
CoalBrookdale Museum & Furnace Site
Showing Abraham Darby's blast furnace history. Ironbridge information centre is next to the world's first iron bridge.
Mortimer Forest Museum - Nr. Ludlow
Forest industries of today and yesterday. Ecology of the forest.
Whitehouse Museum of Buildings & Country life - Aston Munslow
4 houses together in one, drawing from every century 13th to 18th, together with utensils and implements of the time.
The Buttercross Museum - Ludlow
Geology, natural & local history of area.
Reader`s House-Ludlow
Splendid example of a 16th century town house. 3 storied porch.
Much Wenlock Museum.-Much Wenlock
Geology, natural & local history.
Clun Town Museum - Clun
Pre-history earthworks, rights of way, commons & photographs.

Historic Monuments

Acton Burnell Castle - Shrewsbury
13th century fortified manor house - ruins only.

Shropshire

Boscobel House - Shifnal
17th century house.
Bear Steps - Shrewsbury
Half timbered buildings. Mediaeval.
Abbot's House - Shrewsbury
15th century half-timbered.
Buildwas Abbey - Nr. Telford
12th century - Savignac Abbey - ruins.
The church is nearly complete with 14
Norman arches.
Haughmond Abbey - Shrewsbury
12th century - remains of house of
Augustinian canons.
Wenlock Priory - Much Wenlock
13th century abbey - ruins.
Roman Town - Wroxeter
2nd century - remains of town of
Viroconium including public baths and
colonnade.
Moreton Corbet Castle - Moreton Corbet
13th century keep, Elizabethan features -
gatehouse altered 1519.
Lilleshall Abbey
12th century - completed 13th century,
West front has notable doorway.
Bridgnorth Castle - Bridgnorth
Ruins of Norman castle whose angle of
incline is greater than Pisa.
Whiteladies Priory - Boscobel
12th century cruciform church - ruins.
Old Oswestry - Oswestry
Iron age hill fort covering 68 acres; five
ramparts and having an elaborate western
portal.

Other things to see & do

Ludlow Festival of Art and Drama -
annual event
Shrewsbury Flower Show - every August
Severn Valley Railway - the longest full
guage steam railway in the country

Kings Head Inn. Shrewsbury.

SHROPSHIRE

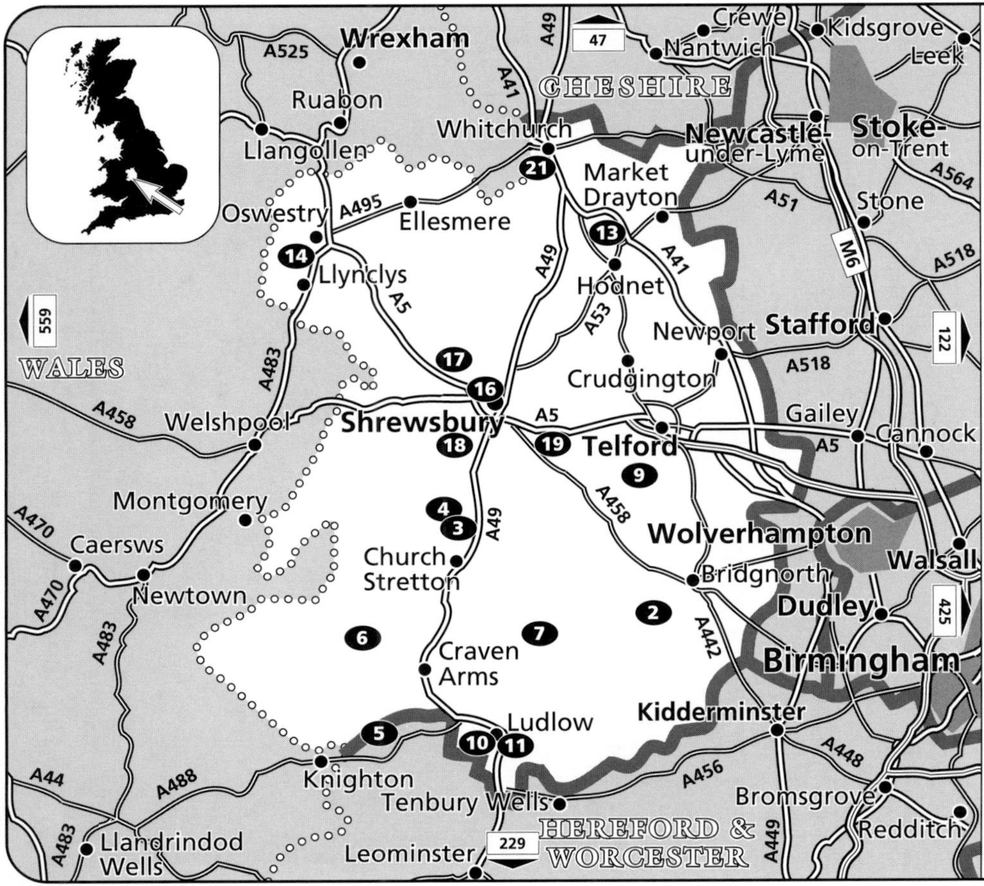

Map reference

2 Rowlands
3 Tory
4 Davies
5 Lloyd
6 Villar
7 Wrigley
9 Hanningan
10 Ross
11 Sanders
13 Williamson
14 Hunter
16 Harris
17 Bovill
18 Mitchell
19 Yates-Roberts
21 Bebbington

Rectory Farm. Woolstaston.

Shropshire

		rate from £ per person	children taken	evening meals	animals taken
Mary Rowlands **Middleton Lodge** **Middleton Priors** **Bridgnorth WV16 6UR** **Tel: (01746) 712228** **Fax 01746 712675** **Open: ALL YEAR (Excl. Xmas)** **Map Ref No. 02**	Nearest Road: B.4268 Middleton Lodge is set in 20 acres of beautiful rural Shropshire countryside overlooking Brown Clee Hill. Accommodation is in 3 extremely attractive en-suite bedrooms, 1 with a 4-poster. There are many places of interest within easy reach of Middleton: the scenic Severn Valley Railway, Ironbridge, Stokesay Castle, the breathtaking beauty of the Long Mynd & the picturesque Carding Mill Valley.	£30.00 🚭	N	N	N
Mrs Jan & Miss Kate Tory **Jinlye Guest House** **Castle Hill** **All Stretton** **Church Stretton SY6 6JP** **Tel/Fax: (01694) 723243** **Open: ALL YEAR** **Map Ref No. 03**	Nearest Road: A.49 A 16th-century country guest house nestling in the Shropshire highlands - a completely unspoilt part of England. At a height of 1400 feet, adjacent to 6000 acres of N.T. land, each room has its own breathtaking scenery. Delightfully furnished in period decor. A wealth of old beams & open log fires. Delicious home cooking served in the Jacobean style dining hall. Colour brochure available. Children over 12 years.	£23.00	Y	Y	N
Mrs Jeanette Davies **Rectory Farm** **Woolstaston** **Church Stretton** **SY6 6NN** **Tel: (01694) 751306** **Open: FEB - DEC** **Map Ref No. 04**	Nearest Road: A.49 An extremely attractive half-timbered farmhouse dating back to 1620, offering 3 charming & tastefully furnished rooms, all with bath en-suite & T.V. & tea/coffee-making facilities. Situated on the edge of the N.T. Long Mynd Hills, it has marvellous views & superb walking right from the door. There is much for the sportsman here: golf, riding, fishing & gliding. Many historic houses & wonderful beauty spots are a short drive away. Children over 12 years. Restricted smoking. Best Bed & Breakfast Award Winner.	£22.00 *see PHOTO over*	Y	N	N
Hayden & Yvonne Lloyd **Upper Buckton** **Leintwardine** **Craven Arms** **SY7 0JU** **Tel: (01547) 540634** **Open: ALL YEAR** **Map Ref No. 05**	Nearest Road: A.4113, A.4110 Set amidst the beautiful unspoilt Teme Valley, a delightful riverside farm situated in the secluded hamlet of Buckton. The Georgian house is surrounded by an attractive garden, millstream & a 12th century motte. The well-appointed rooms with many antiques & paintings make this a lovely home. Log fires. There are 3 elegant bedrooms with private bathrooms & tea/coffee trays. Superb Cordon Bleu Dinners. Guests' own wine welcome. In the centre of the Welsh Marches with much of scenic & historic interest. Ludlow, Offa's Dyke, N.T. properties & gardens.	£25.00 🚭 *see PHOTO over*	Y	Y	N

When booking your accommodation please mention
The Best Bed & Breakfast

Upper Buckton Farm. Leintwardine.

Old Rectory. Hopesay.

Shropshire

		rate from £ per person	children taken	evening meals	animals taken
Michael & Roma Villar **The Old Rectory** **Hopesay** **Craven Arms SY7 8HD** **Tel: (01588) 660245** Fax 01588 660502 Open: ALL YEAR (Excl. Xmas) Map Ref No. 06	Nearest Road: A.49 The Old Rectory, dating from the 17th century, is set in beautiful grounds of almost 2 acres. All bedrooms are en-suite, 2 with large double beds & 1 twin bedded room. All have T.V. & tea/coffee. A drawing room, with a log fire & French windows to a garden, & a splendid dining room with an attractive Gothic window. Furnished with antiques & period pieces. Superb cooking using fresh garden/local produce. Licensed. Ideal for the Welsh Marches, Ludlow, Shrewsbury & Ironbridge.	£32.00 (no smoking) *see PHOTO over*	N	Y	N
Patrick & Lucinda Wrigley **Delbury Hall** **Diddlebury** **Craven Arms** **SY7 9DH** **Tel: (01584) 841267** Fax 01584 841441 Open: ALL YEAR (Excl. Xmas) Map Ref No. 07	Nearest Road: A.49 A beautiful Georgian house (1753), in a stately & tranquil setting in the Corvedale, near Ludlow. Flower-filled gardens, an ornamental lake, trout fishing & a hard tennis court. Home-produced vegetables, milk, eggs, hand-churned Jersey butter, smoked salmon & prosciutto. Beautifully furnished, spacious bedrooms, 1 4-poster, 1 half-tester, with T.V., 'phone, coffee & tea. A guests' sitting room, dining room and, by arrangement, delicious food prepared by your host. E-mail: wrigley@delbury.demon.co.uk	£40.00 *see PHOTO over* CREDIT CARD VISA M'CARD	Y	Y	N
Jim & Pauline Hannigan **The Severn Trow** **Church Road** **Jackfield** **Ironbridge TF8 7ND** **Tel: (01952) 883551** Open: JAN - OCT Map Ref No. 09	Nearest Road: A.442 The Severn Trow is a wonderful place which has seen a hand of hospitality extended by successive occupants for many centuries. It stands on the riverbank where originally travellers would berth their trows before retiring to recuperate. It has been renovated, & yet it has retained many original features which enhance its character, such as an inglenook & a Jackfield mosaic tile floor. Rooms are delightful: each is en-suite (1 ground floor) & well-appointed. A choice of eating houses nearby.	£20.00 (no smoking)	N	N	N
Patricia & Philip Ross **Number Twenty Eight** **28 Lower Broad Street** **Ludlow** **SY8 1PQ** **Tel: (01584) 876996** Fax 01584 876996 Open: ALL YEAR Map Ref No. 10	Nearest Road: A.49, B.4361 A warm welcome awaits you in this guest house which now comprises 3 period houses, in this historic street. Snug sitting rooms, book-lined walls, pictures, prints, plates & open fires make for a relaxing atmosphere. Every bedroom is en-suite & each is individually furnished. Tea/coffee & T.V.. Ludlow has a wealth of excellent eating houses, all within walking distance. Riverside & hill walks, castles & lots of book & antique shops to explore in this most lovely of Tudor & Georgian market towns, near the Welsh border.	£25.00 (no smoking) CREDIT CARD VISA M'CARD AMEX	Y	N	Y
Mrs Judith Sanders **Middleton Court** **Middleton** **Ludlow** **SY8 2DZ** **Tel: (01584) 872842** Open: MAR - NOV Map Ref No. 11	Nearest Road: A.49 Middleton Court is a fine country house on a working farm, situated 2 1/2 miles from Ludlow. 1 master en-suite bedroom, with a double & single bed, & 1 double & 1 twin-bedded room each with a private bathroom. All are comfortably furnished with antiques, & have beautiful views over the terraced gardens & woods beyond. Sitting room, with T.V. & log fires. Super full English breakfasts & traditional 4-course evening meals. Ideal for exploring Shropshire & the Welsh border country.	£20.00 (no smoking)	N	Y	N

Delbury Hall. Diddlebury.

Pen–Y–Dyffryn Hall. Rhydycroesau.

Shropshire

		rate from £ per person	children taken	evening meals	animals taken
Mrs Pauline Williamson **Mickley House** **Faulsgreen** **Tern Hill** **Market Drayton** **TF9 3QW** **Tel: (01630) 638505** **Open:** ALL YEAR (Excl. Xmas) **Map Ref No. 13**	Nearest Road: A.41, A.53 When visiting Ironbridge, Shrewsbury, Chester or Wedgewood, experience peace, quiet & comfort in this Victorian farmhouse. Oak doors, beams, leaded windows. The tranquillity of the house spills out into landscaped gardens. Relax or meander through rose-scented pergolas to pools & a trickling waterfall. The restful drawing room beckons after sight-seeing. Excellent restaurants/ pubs nearby. En-suite bedrooms of different style & decor, with all facilities. Master bedroom with Louis XIV king-size bed. Ground floor if preferred.	£20.00	Y	N	N
Miles & Audrey Hunter **Pen-Y-Dyffryn Country** **Hotel** **Rhydycroesau** **Oswestry SY10 7JD** **Tel/Fax: (01691) 653700** **Open: ALL YEAR** **Map Ref No. 14**	Nearest Road: A.5 Peace, comfort & a warm welcome await you in this former Georgian rectory, splendidly situated in the Shropshire/Welsh hills just 3 miles west of Oswestry. An ideal base for exploring Chester, Shrewsbury & North Wales. Delicious home-cooked evening meals using English & Welsh local produce. Fully licensed. Log fires in the lounge & restaurant. All bedrooms beautifully furnished, en-suite, colour T.V.. 5 acres of grounds. 1 ground-floor bedroom available.	£30.00 *see PHOTO over* CREDIT CARD VISA M'CARD AMEX	Y	Y	Y
Mrs Mair Harris **Tudor House** **2 Fish Street** **Shrewsbury SY1 1UR** **Tel: (01743) 351735** **Open: ALL YEAR** **Map Ref No. 16**	Nearest Road: A.5 This Grade II listed building is centrally situated in a quiet mediaeval street in picturesque & historic Shrewsbury (Brother Cadfael country). Dating from 1460, it has a wealth of oak beams, & has been tastefully redecorated & refurbished. Some rooms have en-suite facilities; all have washbasins, colour T.V. & central heating. Special diets available in non-smoking dining room. Drinks are served in residents' licensed lounge.	£20.00	N	N	N
John & Hermione Bovill **Mytton Hall** **Montford Bridge** **Shrewsbury** **SY4 1EU** **Tel: (01743) 850264** **Open: ALL YEAR** **Map Ref No. 17**	Nearest Road: A.5 An elegant, white, listed Georgian house built in 1790, & with spectacular views. There are 3 attractive & tastefully furnished bedrooms, all en-suite, & a sitting room with T.V. & log fire. Full central heating. Lovely gardens adjoining the River Perry. Private fishing. A tennis court. The welcoming atmosphere of a fine old English country house, located 6 miles from Shrewsbury & within easy reach of Ironbridge & many other attractions. Children over 12 yrs.	£24.00 *see PHOTO over*	N	N	N
Mrs Christine Yates-Roberts **Upper Brompton Farm** **Cross Houses** **Shrewsbury** **SY5 6LE** **Tel: (01743) 761629** **Open: MAR - OCT** **Map Ref No. 19**	Nearest Road: A.458 This delightful Georgian farmhouse with extensive lawns & gardens is a haven of peace, comfort & elegance. 5 mins from Shrewsbury - England's finest Tudor town - & 15 mins from Ironbridge, the birthplace of industry. It is ideally situated for exploring Housman's Shropshire. The 3 en-suite bedrooms are beautifully furnished with many welcoming touches. The 2 double rooms have 4-poster beds & wonderful views to the Shropshire hills. Breakfast in the sun-filled dining room. Relax in front of an open fire. Children over 6.	£24.00	Y	N	N

Mytton Hall. Montford Bridge.

Shropshire

		rate from £ per person	children taken	evening meals	animals taken
Mike & Gill Mitchell **The White House** **Hanwood** **Shrewsbury** **SY5 8LP** **Tel: (01743) 860414** **Fax 01743 860414** **Open: ALL YEAR** **Map Ref No. 18**	Nearest Road: A.488, A.5 A lovely, 16th-century, black-and-white, half-timbered guest house with nearly 2 acres of gardens and river, 3 miles south-west of mediaeval Shrewsbury. Ironbridge, Mid-Wales and the Long Mynd within a half-hour drive. 6 guest rooms, some en-suite, each with full central heating & tea/coffee facilities. 2 sitting rooms, 1 with T.V.. Car parking. The dining room offers a fresh, varied menu supplemented by vegetables and herbs from the garden, and the house hens provide your breakfast eggs!	£22.50 🚭 *see PHOTO over*	N	Y	N
Charles & Jane Bebbington **Dearnford Hall** **Whitchurch** **SY13 3JJ** **Tel: (01948) 662319** **Fax 01948 666670** **Open: ALL YEAR (Excl. Xmas)** **Map Ref No. 21**	Nearest Road: A.41, A.49 Relax & unwind in this beautiful 17th-century country house on the picturesque borders of Shropshire, Cheshire & the Welsh Marches, in the heart of cheese-making country. Log fires, a comfortable drawing room & lovely en-suite bedrooms overlooking sweeping lawns & a clematis-clad entrance. Simply stroll in the gardens, play golf, or enjoy some outstanding fly-fishing at the hosts' own spring-fed trout pool; wander by the cornfields, watch the plovers, skylarks & swallows overhead & the partridges by the hedgerows. Superb restaurants & pubs nearby. Business visitors welcome. Parking.	£25.00 🚭 CREDIT CARD VISA M'CARD	N	N	N

All the establishments mentioned in this guide are members of
The Worldwide Bed & Breakfast Association

When booking your accommodation please mention
The Best Bed & Breakfast

The White House. Hanwood.

Somerset, Bath & Bristol

Somerset
(West Country)

Fabulous legends, ancient customs, charming villages, beautiful churches, breathtaking scenery & a glorious cathedral, Somerset has them all, along with a distinctively rich local dialect. The essence of Somerset lies in its history & myth & particularly in the unfolding of the Arthurian tale.

Legend grows from the bringing of the Holy Grail to Glastonbury by Joseph of Arimathea, to King Arthur's castle at Camelot, held by many to be sited at Cadbury, to the image of the dead King's barge moving silently through the mists over the lake to the Isle of Avalon. Archaeological fact lends support to the conjecture that Glastonbury, with its famous Tor, was an island in an ancient lake. Another island story surrounds King Alfred, reputedly sheltering from the Danes on the Isle of Athelney & there burning his cakes.

Historically, Somerset saw the last battle fought on English soil, at Sedgemoor in 1685. The defeat of the Monmouth rebellion resulted in the wrath of James II falling on the West Country in the form of Judge Jeffreys & his "Bloody Assize".

To the west of the county lies part of the Exmoor National Park, with high moorland where deer roam & buzzards soar & a wonderful stretch of cliffs from Minehead to Devon. Dunster is a popular village with its octagonal Yarn market, & its old world cottages, dominated at one end by the castle & at the other by the tower on Conygar Hill.

To the east the woods & moors of the Quantocks are protected as an area of outstanding natural beauty. The Vale of Taunton is famous for its apple orchards & for the golden cider produced from them.

The south of the county is a land of rolling countryside & charming little towns, Chard, Crewkerne, Ilchester & Ilminster amongst others.

To the north the limestone hills of Mendip are honeycombed with spectacular caves & gorges, some with neolithic remains, as at Wookey Hole & Cheddar Gorge.

Wells is nearby, so named because of the multitude of natural springs. Hardly a city, Wells boasts a magnificent cathedral set amongst spacious lawns & trees. The west front is one of the glories of English architecture with its sculptured figures & soaring arches. A spectacular feature is the astronomical clock, the work of 14th century monk Peter Lightfoot. The intricate face tells the hours, minutes, days & phases of the moon. On the hour, four mounted knights charge forth & knock one another from their horses.

Wells Cathedral Choir.

Somerset, Bath & Bristol

Bath is one of the most loved historic cities in England. It owes its existence to the hot springs which bubble up five hundred thousand gallons of water a day at a temperature of some 120' F. According to legend, King Bladud appreciated the healing qualities of the waters & established his capital here, calling it Aquae Sulis. He built an elaborate healing & entertainment centre around the springs including reservoirs, baths & hypercaust rooms.

The Roman Baths, not uncovered until modern times, are on the lowest of three levels. Above them came the mediaeval city & on the top layer at modern street level is the elegant Georgian Pump Room.

Edward was crowned the first King of all England in 973, in the Saxon Abbey which stood on the site of the present fifteenth century abbey. This building, in the graceful perpendicular style with elegant fan vaulting, is sometimes called the "lantern of the West", on account of its vast clerestories & large areas of glass.

During the Middle Ages the town prospered through Royal patronage & the development of the wool industry. Bath became a city of weavers, the leading industrial town in the West of England.

The 18th century gave us the superb Georgian architecture which is the city's glory. John Wood, an ambitious young architect laid out Queen Anne's Square in the grand Palladian style, & went on to produce his masterpiece, the Royal Crescent. His scheme for the city was continued by his son & a number of other fine architects, using the beautiful Bath stone. Bath was a centre of fashion, with Beau Nash the leader of a glittering society.

In 1497 John & Sebastian Cabot sailed from the Bristol quayside to the land they called Ameryke, in honour of the King's agent in Bristol, Richard Ameryke. Bristol's involvement in the colonisation of the New World & the trade in sugar, tobacco & slaves that followed, made her the second city in the kingdom in the 18th century. John Cabot is commemorated by the Cabot Tower on grassy Brandon Hill - a fine vantage point from which to view the city. On the old docks below are the Bristol Industrial Museum & the SS Great Britain, Brunel's famous iron ship. Another achievement of this master engineer, the Clifton Suspension Bridge, spans Bristol's renowned beauty spot, the Clifton Gorge. For a glimpse of Bristol's elegant past, stroll through Clifton with its stately terraces & spacious Downs.

A short walk from the busy city centre & modern shopping area, the visitor in search of history will find cobbled King Street with its merchant seamen's almshouses & The Theatre Royal, the oldest theatre in continuous use in England, & also Llandoger Trow, an ancient inn associated with Treasure Island & Robinson Crusoe.

Bath Abbey.

Somerset, Bath & Bristol

Somerset, Bath & Bristol Gazeteer

Areas of Outstanding Natural Beauty
Mendip Hills. Quantock Hills. National Park - Exmoor. The Cotswolds.

Historic Houses & Castles

Abbot's Fish House - Meare
14th century house.
Barrington Court - Illminster
16th century house & gardens.
Blaise Castle House - Henbury Nr. Bristol
18th century house - now folk museum, extensive woodlands.
Brympton D'Evercy - Nr. Yeovil
Mansion with 17th century front & Tudor west front. Adjacent is 13th century priest's house & church. Formal gardens & vineyard.
Claverton Manor - Nr. Bath
Greek revival house - furnished with 17th, 18th, 19th century American originals.
Clevedon Court - Clevedon
14th century manor house, 13th century hall, 12th century tower. Lovely garden with rare trees & shrubs. This is where Thackerey wrote much of 'Vanity Fair'.
Dyrham Park - Between Bristol & Bath
17th century house - fine panelled rooms, Dutch paintings, furniture.
Dunster Castle - Dunster
13th century castle with fine 17th century staircase & ceilings.
East Lambrook Manor - South Petherton
15th century house with good panelling.
Gaulden Manor - Tolland
12th century manor. Great Hall having unique plaster ceiling & oak screen. Antique furniture.
Halsway Manor - Crowcombe
14th century house with fine panelling.
Hatch Court - Hatch Beauchamp
Georgian house in the Palladian style with China room.
King John's Hunting Lodge - Axbridge
Early Tudor merchant's house.
Lytes Carry - Somerton
14th & 15th century manor house with a chapel & formal garden.
Montacute House - Yeovil
Elizabethan house with fine examples of Heraldic Glass, tapestries, panelling & furniture. Portrait gallery of Elizabethan & Jacobean paintings.
Tintinhull House - Yeovil
17th century house with beautiful gardens.
Priory Park College - Bath
18th century Georgian mansion, now Roman Catholic school.
No. 1 Royal Crescent - Bath
An unaltered Georgian house built 1767.
Red Lodge - Bristol
16th century house - period furniture & panelling.
St. Vincent's Priory - Bristol
Gothic revival house, built over caves which were sanctuary for Christians.
St Catherine's Court - Nr. Bath
Small Tudor house - associations with Henry VIII & Elizabeth I.

Cathedrals & Churches

Axbridge (St. John)
1636 plaster ceiling & panelled roofs.
Backwell (St. Andrew)
12th to 17th century, 15th century tower, repaired 17th century. 15th century tomb & chancel, 16th century screen, 18th century brass chandelier.
Bath Abbey
Perpendicular - monastic church, 15th century foundation. Nave finished 17th century, restorations in 1674.
Bishop's Lydeard (St. Mary)
15th century. Notable tower, rood screen & glass.
Bristol Cathedral
Mediaeval. Eastern halfnave Victorian. Chapterhouse richly ornamented. Iron screen, 3 fonts, "fairest parish church in all England".
Bristol (St. Mary Radcliffe)
Bristol (St. Stephens')
Perpendicular - monuments, magnificent tower.
Bruton (St. Mary)
Fine 2 towered 15th century church. Georgian chancel, tie beam roof, Georgian reredos. Jacobean screen. 15th century embroidery.
Chewton Mendip (St. Mary Magdalene)
12th century with later additions. 12th century doorway, 15th century bench ends, magnificent 16th century tower & 17th century lecturn.

Somerset, Bath & Bristol

Crewkerne (St. Bartholomew)
Magnificent west front & roofs, 15th & 16th century. South doorway dating from 13th century, wonderful 15th century painted glass & 18th century chandeliers.
East Brent (St. Mary)
Mainly 15th century. Plaster ceiling, painted glass & carved bench ends.
Glastonbury (St. John)
One of the finest examples of perpendicular towers. Tie beam roof, late mediaeval painted glass, mediaeval vestment & early 16th century altar tomb.
High Ham (St. Andrew)
Sumptuous roofs & vaulted rood screen. Carved bench ends. Jacobean lectern, mediaeval painted glass. Norman font.
Kingsbury Episcopi (St. Martin)
14th-15th century. Good tower with fan vaulting. Late mediaeval painted glass.
Long Sutton (Holy Trinity)
15th century with noble tower & magnificent tie beam roof. 15th century pulpit & rood screen, tower vaulting.
Martock (All Saints)
13th century chancel. Nave with tie beam roof, outstanding of its kind. 17th century paintings of Apostles.
North Cadbury (St. Michael)
painted glass.
Pilton (St. John)
12th century with arcades. 15th century roofs.
Taunton (St. Mary Magdalene)
Highest towers in the county. Five nave roof, fragments of mediaeval painted glass.
Trull (All Saints)
15th century with many mediaeval art treasures & 15th century glass.
Wells Cathedral-Wells
Magnificent west front with carved figures. Splendid tower. Early English arcade of nave & transepts. 60 fine misericords c.1330. Lady chapel with glass & star vault. Chapter House & Bishop's Palace.
Weston Zoyland (St. Mary)
15th century bench ends. 16th century heraldic glass. Jacobean pulpit.
Wrington (All Souls)
15th century aisles & nave; font, stone pulpit, notable screens.

Museums & Galleries

Admiral Blake Museum - Bridgewater
Exhibits relating to Battle of Sedgemoor, archaeology.
American Museum in Britain - Claverton Nr. Bath
American decorative arts 17th to 19th century displayed in series of furnished rooms & galleries of special exhibits. Paintings, furniture, glass wood & metal work, textiles, folk sculpture, etc.
Borough Museum - Hendford Manor Hall, Yeovil
Archaeology, firearms collections & Bailward Costume Collection.
Bristol Industrial Museum - Bristol
Collections of transport items of land, sea & air. Many unique items.
Burdon Manor - Washford
14th century manor house with Saxon fireplace & cockpit.
City of Bristol Art Gallery - Bristol
Permanent & loan collections of paintings, English & Oriental ceramics.
Glastonbury Lake Village Museum - Glastonbury
Late prehistoric antiquities.
Gough's Cave Museum - Cheddar
Upper Paleolithic remains, skeleton, flints, amber & engraved stones.
Holburne of Menstrie Museum - Bath
Old Master paintings, silver, glass, porcelain, furniture & miniatures in 18th century building. Work of 20th century craftworkers.
Hinton Priory - Hinton Charterhouse
13th century - ruins of Carthusian priory.
Kings Weston Roman Villa - Lawrence Weston
3rd & 4th centuries - mosaics of villa - some walls.
Museum of Costume - Bath
Collection of fashion from 17th century to present day.
Roman Baths - Bath
Roman Museum - Bath
Material from remains of extensive Roman baths & other Roman sites.
Stoney Littleton Barrow - Nr. Bath
Neolithic burial chamber - restoration work 1858.
St. Nicholas Church & City Museum - Bristol
Mediaeval antiquities relating to local

Somerset, Bath & Bristol

history, Church plate & vestments.
Altarpiece by Hogarth.
Temple Church - Bristol
14th & 15th century ruins.
Victoria Art Gallery - Bath
Paintings, prints, drawings, glass,
ceramics, watches, coins, etc. Bygones -
permanent & temporary exhibitions.
Geology collections.
Wookey Hole Cave Museum - Wookey
Hole
Remains from Pliocene period. Relics of
Celtic & Roman civilization. Exhibition of
handmade paper-making.

Historic Monuments

Cleeve Abbey - Cleeve
Ruined 13th century house, with timber
roof & wall paintings.
Farleigh Castle - Farleigh Hungerford
14th century remains - museums in
chapel.
Glastonbury Abbey - Glastonbury
12th & 13th century ruins of St. Joseph's

chapel & Abbot's kitchen.
Muchelney Abbey - Muchelney
15th century ruins of Benedictine abbey.

Other things to see & do

Black Rock Nature Reserve - Cheddar
Circular walk through plantation woodland,
downland grazing.
Cheddar Caves
Show caves at the foot of beautiful
Cheddar Gorge.
Clifton Zoological Gardens - Bristol
Flourishing zoo with many exhibits -
beautiful gardens.
Clifton Suspension Bridge - Bristol
Designed by Isambard Kingdom Brunel,
opened in 1864. Viewpoint & picnic spot
Camera Obscura.
Cricket St. Thomas Wildlife Park - Nr.
Chard
Wildlife park, heavy horse centre,
countryside museum, etc.
The Pump Room - Bath
18th century neo-classical interior. Spa.

Clifton Suspension Bridge. Bristol.

SOMERSET, BATH & BRISTOL

Map reference

1	Dodd	7	Laidler
1	Besley	8	Dyer
1	Webber	9	Healey
1	Warwick-Smith	10	Shellard
1	Beckett	11	Tasker
1	Addison	12	Newman-Coburn
1	Napier	13	Smith
1	Kitching	14	Gregory
1	Cox	15	Forshaw
1	Stabbins	15	Bradshaw
1	Ashman-Marr	16	Collins
1	James	17	Vicary
1	Humphrey	18	Redmond
1	Gaunt	21	Brewer
1	Wroe-Parker	23	Middle
1	Taylor	24	Copeland
1	King	25	Clark
1	Burton	26	Mitchem
1	Hall	27	Willcox
1	Bryan	28	Ritchie
1	Williams	29	Eyre
1	Selby	30	Muers-Raby
1	Keeling	31	Hughes
1	Youngs	32	White
2	Westlake	33	Thompson
3	Davies	34	Frost
4	Whitwam	35	Nowell
4	Graham	36	Clover
4	Walker	37	Durbin
5	Holder	38	Criddle
6	Bowles	39	Somerville

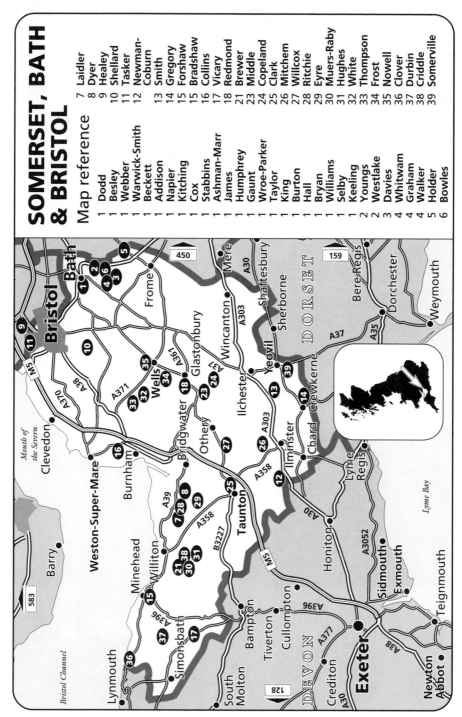

Gainsborough Hotel. Bath.

Somerset
Bath & Bristol

		rate from £ per person	children taken	evening meals	animals taken
Marion Dodd **Brocks** **32 Brock Street** **Bath BA1 2LN** **Tel: (01225) 338374** **Fax (01225) 334245** **Open: ALL YEAR** **Map Ref No. 01**	Nearest Road: A.4 Brocks is a beautiful Georgian town house situated between the Circus and Royal Crescent. Very close to the Roman Baths, Assembly Rooms, etc. This really is a wonderful part of Bath. This historic house has all modern conveniences & all of the comfortable bedrooms have private facilities. The aim here is to offer guests the highest standards, and personal attention. A delightful base from which to explore beautiful Bath.	£27.00 CREDIT CARD VISA M'CARD	Y	N	N
Mrs Chrissie Besley **The Old Red House** **37 Newbridge Road** **Bath BA1 3HE** **Tel: (01225) 330464** **Fax 01225 331661** **Open: ALL YEAR** **Map Ref No. 01**	Nearest Road: A.4 This charming Victorian Gingerbread House is colourful, comfortable & warm; full of unexpected touches & intriguing little curiosities. Its leaded & stained glass windows are now double-glazed to ensure a peaceful stay. The extensive breakfast menu, a delight in itself, is served in a sunny conservatory. Parking. Special rates for 3 or more nights. Dinner available at a local riverside pub. A brochure on request. Children over 4 yrs.	£22.00 *see PHOTO over* CREDIT CARD VISA M'CARD AMEX	Y	N	Y
Arthur & Christine Webber **Cranleigh** **159 Newbridge Hill** **Bath** **BA1 3PX** **Tel: (01225) 310197** **Fax 01225 423143** **Open: ALL YEAR** **Map Ref No. 01**	Nearest Road: A.431 Situated in a quiet residential area, this comfortable Victorian house has great character, with exceptionally spacious, stylishly decorated en-suite bedrooms. Most have lovely views across the Avon Valley. Breakfast includes such choices as fresh-fruit salad & scrambled eggs with smoked salmon. Easy access to the heart of Bath. Parking. Around their home, the Webbers have many interesting items from their own travels, & they keep a wealth of information to help you make the most of your stay. Children over 4. **E-mail: Cranleigh@btinternet.com**	£29.00 *see PHOTO over* CREDIT CARD VISA M'CARD	Y	N	N
Mrs R. M. Warwick-Smith **Gainsborough Hotel** **Weston Lane** **Bath BA1 4AB** **Tel: (01225) 311380** **Fax 01225 447411** **Open: ALL YEAR** **Map Ref No. 01**	Nearest Road: A.4 The Gainsborough is a large country-house hotel, comfortably furnished & set in its own grounds near the Botanical Gardens & Victoria Park. Offering 17 attractive en-suite bedrooms, each with colour T.V., direct-dial telephone, tea/coffee-making facilities & hairdryer. The dining room & small cocktail bar overlook the lawns, where guests often relax during the summer on the sun terrace. Private parking available.	£26.00 *see PHOTO over* CREDIT CARD VISA M'CARD AMEX	Y	N	N
Derek & Maria Beckett **Cedar Lodge** **13 Lambridge** **London Rd** **Bath BA1 6BJ** **Tel: (01225) 423468** **Open: ALL YEAR** **Map Ref No. 01**	Nearest Road: A.4, A.46 Within easy level walk to the historic city centre, this beautiful, detached Georgian house offers period elegance with modern amenities. 3 lovely bedrooms (1 with 4-poster, 1 half-tester, 1 twin), all with en-suite/private bathrooms. Delightful gardens & comfortable drawing room, with fire, to relax in. Ideally situated for excursions to Avebury, Stonehenge, Salisbury, Longleat, Wells, Cotswolds, Wales & many other attractions. Secure private parking. Children over 12.	£25.00	Y	N	N

The Old Red House. Bath.

Cranleigh. Bath.

Bailbrook Lodge. Bath.

		rate from £ per person	children taken	evening meals	animals taken
Mr & Mrs K. M. Addison **Bailbrook Lodge Hotel** **35-37 London Road West** **Bath BA1 7HZ** **Tel/Fax: (01225) 859090** **Fax 01225 852299** **Open:** ALL YEAR (Excl. Xmas) **Map Ref No. 01**	Nearest Road: A.4, A.46 Bailbrook Lodge is an imposing Georgian house located 1 mile east of Bath. There is a choice of 12 elegantly furnished en-suite bedrooms (some 4-posters), all with T.V. & hospitality tray. Evening meals with traditional English cuisine are provided. The lounge bar & dining room overlook the garden. Bailbrook Lodge is an ideal base for exploring Bath & touring the beautiful surrounding countryside. Ample car-parking.	£26.00 *see PHOTO over* CREDIT CARD VISA M'CARD AMEX	Y	Y	N
John & Rosamund Napier **Eagle House** **Church Street** **Bathford** **Bath BA1 7RS** **Tel/Fax: (01225) 859946** **Open: ALL YEAR** **Map Ref No. 01**	Nearest Road: A.363, A.4 Eagle House is a fine Georgian Grade II listed house set in 2 acres of garden in the heart of picturesque Bathford. There are 8 comfortable, en-suite bedrooms with 'phone, T.V. & tea/coffee-making facilities, plus spacious public rooms - the drawing room has a 16-ft ceiling, as well as views over the garden down the valley. The house is elegant, yet the atmosphere is informal, & all are welcome. There is also a lovely cottage for 4.	£29.50 *see PHOTO over* CREDIT CARD VISA M'CARD	Y	N	Y
Geoff & Avril Kitching **Wentworth House Hotel** **106 Bloomfield Road** **Bath BA2 2AP** **Tel: (01225) 339193** **Fax 01225 310460** **Open:** ALL YEAR (Excl. Xmas) **Map Ref No. 01**	Nearest Road: A.367 Stay 3 nights & receive a 10% discount at this imposing Victorian Bath stone mansion (1887) standing in secluded grounds with stunning views of the valley. Situated in a quiet part of the city with a large car park in the grounds. Within walking distance of the city, Abbey & Roman Baths. All 18 rooms, with private facilities, are individual with a high standard of comfort. A licensed bar lounge. An outdoor swimming pool, golf & walks close by. Lots of information on Bath, the area & Somerset.	£25.00 CREDIT CARD VISA M'CARD AMEX	Y	N	N
Bridget & Malcolm Cox **Bloomfield House** **146 Bloomfield Rd** **Bath BA2 2AS** **Tel: (01225) 420105** **Fax 01225 481958** **Open: ALL YEAR** **Map Ref No. 01**	Nearest Road: A.367 An elegant Georgian country house in a sylvan setting with stunning views over the city. Antique furniture, French crystal chandeliers, silver-service breakfast & open fires. All rooms have an en-suite bath/shower, direct-dial telephone, T.V. & canopied or 4-poster beds. Also, the lavish principal bedroom of the Mayor & Mayoress of Bath (1902/3). Bloomfield House offers the finest, the friendliest, the best. Car park. 2-bed, self-contained family flat also available.	£30.00 (non-smoking) *see PHOTO over* CREDIT CARD VISA M'CARD	N	N	N
Mrs Nicky Stabbins **The Hollies** **Hatfield Rd, Wellsway** **Bath BA2 2BD** **Tel/Fax: (01225) 313366** **Open: ALL YEAR (Excl. Xmas & New Year)** **Map Ref No. 01**	Nearest Road: A. 367 The Hollies is a lovely old Victorian, Grade II listed house situated within walking distance of the city. With just 3 pretty guest rooms, personal attention and hospitality are assured. Each room has en-suite or private facilities, colour T.V., beverage-making facilities, hairdryer & radio/alarm clock. A wide breakfast menu is served. Private parking is available. Rooms overlook the secluded garden of apple trees, herbs & roses. The Hollies is a charming home, ideal for exploring Bath.	£20.00 (non-smoking) CREDIT CARD VISA M'CARD	Y	N	N

Eagle House. Bathford.

Bloomfield House. Bath.

Haydon House. Bath.

Highways House.   Bath.

Somerset
Bath & Bristol

		rate from £ per person	children taken	evening meals	animals taken

Mrs M. Ashman-Marr
Haydon House
9 Bloomfield Park
Bath
BA2 2BY
Tel/Fax: (01225) 444919
Tel/Fax: (01225) 427351
Open: ALL YEAR
Map Ref No. 01

Nearest Road: A.367
A true oasis of tranquillity, this secluded, elegantly furnished Edwardian townhouse is situated in a quiet residential area with easy parking, not far from the city centre. Every conceivable comfort is offered in the 5 tastefully decorated en-suite bedrooms, including hospitality tray. Guests can enjoy a welcoming cup of tea in the beautifully appointed antique-filled sitting room, with sunshine filtering through the vine-clad pergola, & innovative breakfasts are stylishly served to a background of gentle classical music. Children by arrangement.

£28.50 | Y | N | N

(no smoking symbol)

see PHOTO over

CREDIT CARD
VISA
M'CARD
AMEX

David & Davina James
Highways House
143 Wells Road
Bath BA2 3AL
Tel: (01225) 421238
Fax 01225 481169
Open: ALL YEAR (Excl. Xmas)
Map Ref No. 01

Nearest Road: A.367
An elegant, Victorian, family-run home offering superior accommodation in 7 rooms (including 1 twin room on the ground floor) with en-suite or private facilities, colour T.V. & tea/coffee makers. A tastefully decorated home, with a lovely guest lounge. A full English breakfast is served. Located only 10 mins from the city centre. A perfect base from which to tour the Cotswolds, Stonehenge, Salisbury & Wells. Children over 5 years. Parking.

£26.00 | Y | N | N

see PHOTO over

CREDIT CARD
VISA
M'CARD

Berkeley & Moira Gaunt
Oldfields Guest House
102 Wells Road
Bath BA2 3AL
Tel: (01225) 317984
Fax 01225 444471
Open: ALL YEAR (Excl. Xmas)
Map Ref No. 01

Nearest Road: A.367
Elegant & traditional bed & breakfast at this beautiful bath stone Victorian house, 10 mins from the city centre. 14 rooms with colour T.V., direct-dial 'phone, hairdryer & tea/coffee-making facilities. All rooms are equipped with a private bath or shower. Experience the true ambience of the 19th-century; beautiful antique furniture, rich fabrics & warm decor. A full English breakfast is served, or select from the extensive buffet.

£27.50 | Y | N | N

(no smoking symbol)

see PHOTO over

CREDIT CARD
VISA
M'CARD

Mrs Wroe-Parker & Mr Chiles
Cheriton House
9 Upper Oldfield Park
Bath BA2 3JX
Tel: (01225) 429862
Fax 01225 428403
Open: ALL YEAR
Map Ref No. 01

Nearest Road: A.367
Situated on the southern slope of Bath with splendid views of the city, Cheriton House has been carefully restored & redecorated, & the rooms are attractively furnished. All of the bedrooms have private bathrooms (en-suite), colour T.V. & hot-drink-making facilities. There is a choice of delicious breakfasts including traditional English & Continental. Guests are welcome to enjoy the beautiful, peaceful garden.

£25.00 | Y | N | N

CREDIT CARD
VISA
M'CARD
AMEX

When booking your accommodation please mention
The Best Bed & Breakfast

Oldfields. Bath.

Dorian House. Bath.

Somerset
Bath & Bristol

		rate from £ per person	children taken	evening meals	animals taken

	Nearest Road: A.367	£32.00	Y	N	N
Jane & Brian Taylor **Dorian House** **1 Upper Oldfield Park** **Bath BA2 3JX** **Tel: (01225) 426336** **Fax 01225 444699** **Open: ALL YEAR** **Map Ref No. 01**	A warm welcome and an aura of nostalgic luxury await every guest at this gracious Victorian house. Accommodation is in 8 charming bedrooms, all en-suite, fully appointed, with tea/coffee trays, hairdryers, telephones and colour T.V.. There is a lounge & a small licensed bar, and a full English breakfast menu is served. Parking available, and only a 10-minute stroll to the city centre. Dorian House is ideal for a relaxing break.	*see PHOTO over* CREDIT CARD VISA M'CARD AMEX			

	Nearest Road: A.367	£26.00	N	N	N
David & Jenny King **Oakleigh House** **19 Upper Oldfield Park** **Bath BA2 3JX** **Tel: (01225) 315698** **Fax 01225 448223** **Open: ALL YEAR** **Map Ref No. 01**	Your comfort is assured at Oakleigh House, quietly situated only 10 mins from the city centre. Oakleigh combines Victorian elegance with today's comforts to make your stay that extra bit special. All of the 4 bedrooms are attractively furnished & have an en-suite bath/shower & w.c., hair-dryers, colour T.V., clock radios & tea/coffee-making facilities. A private car park. Oakleigh is an ideal base for beautiful Bath and beyond.	CREDIT CARD VISA M'CARD AMEX			

	Nearest Road: A.367	£26.00	Y	N	N
John & Sue Burton **Badminton Villa** **10 Upper Oldfield Park** **Bath BA2 3JZ** **Tel: (01225) 426347** **Fax 01225 420393** **Open: ALL YEAR (Excl. Xmas)** **Map Ref No. 01**	John & Sue welcome you to the friendly & relaxed atmosphere of Badminton Villa, with its magnificent views of Bath. Conveniently situated in a quiet road just a 10-min walk from the city centre. The attractive bedrooms are all en-suite & have colour T.V. & tea/coffee facilities. Badminton Villa, with a private car park, is the perfect location for visitors to Bath or for exploring the beautiful West Country. Children over 5 yrs.	CREDIT CARD VISA M'CARD			

	Nearest Road: A.367	£38.00	Y	N	N
Mr George H. Hall **Holly Lodge** **8 Upper Oldfield Park** **Bath** **BA2 3JZ** **Tel: (01225) 424042** **Fax 01225 481138** **Open: ALL YEAR** **Map Ref No. 01**	Holly Lodge is a fine Victorian townhouse set in its own grounds in an elevated position, with superb views over the city & only 10 mins' walk from the city centre. It boasts 7 individually designed rooms, which are beautifully decorated. All have luxury bathrooms & a host of extras including satellite T.V. & tea/coffee-making facilities. (Some have 4-poster or queen-size beds.) Imaginative breakfasts are served in the delightful conservatory breakfast room. Holly Lodge is the ideal haven for relaxation & is perfect for exploring Bath.	*see PHOTO over* CREDIT CARD VISA M'CARD AMEX			

	Nearest Road: A.36	£27.50	N	N	N
Patrick & Hilary Bryan **Ravenscroft** **North Road, Bathwick** **Bath BA2 6HZ** **Tel: (01225) 461919** **Fax 01225 461919** **Open: ALL YEAR** **Map Ref No. 01**	Built in 1876, Ravenscroft is an elegant Victorian residence with a wealth of period features. Its elevated position provides spectacular views over the city of Bath & countryside beyond. Only a few minutes from the city centre, it is surrounded by an acre of secluded, mature gardens which offer guests peace & tranquillity. There are 2 lovely bedrooms with colour T.V., tea/coffee & hair-drying facilities. Private parking.	*see PHOTO over*			

Holly Lodge. Bath.

Ravenscroft. Bathwick.

Villa Magdela. Bath.

Brompton House. Bath.

Somerset
Bath & Bristol

		rate from £ per person	children taken	evening meals	animals taken
Mrs Alison Williams **Villa Magdala Hotel** **Henrietta Road** **Bath BA2 6LX** **Tel: (01225) 466329** **Fax 01225 483207** **Open: ALL YEAR** **Map Ref No. 01**	Nearest Road: A.36 Ideally situated, this charming Victorian town house hotel enjoys a peaceful location overlooking Henrietta Park, only 5 mins level walk to the city centre & the famous Roman Baths. All of the 17 spacious rooms have private bathroom, T.V., direct-dial 'phone, refreshment trays & pleasant views. Private parking is available for guests in the hotel grounds. **E-mail: villa@btinternet.com**	£30.00 *see PHOTO over* CREDIT CARD VISA M'CARD AMEX	Y	N	N
David & Sue Selby **Brompton House** **St. Johns Road** **Bath BA2 6PT** **Tel: (01225) 420972** **Fax 01225 420505** **Open: ALL YEAR (Excl. Xmas & New Year)** **Map Ref No. 01**	Nearest Road: A.4, A.36 Built as a rectory in 1777, Brompton House is an elegant Georgian residence with a car park & beautiful mature gardens. Only 5 mins walk from many of Bath's historic sights, it is run by the Selbys who offer every comfort & service to their guests. The attractive sitting room is furnished with antiques & the tastefully decorated en-suite bedrooms offer T.V., radio/alarm, 'phone & tea/coffee. Breakfast is a delicious choice of full English, Continental or wholefood. Children over7. **E-mail: BROMPTON_HOUSE@compuserve.com**	£27.50 *see PHOTO over* CREDIT CARD VISA M'CARD AMEX	Y	N	N
David & Susan Keeling **Bath Tasburgh Hotel** **Warminster Road** **Bath BA2 6SH** **Tel: (01225) 425096** **Fax 01225 463842** **Open: ALL YEAR** **Map Ref No. 01**	Nearest Road: A.36 Built in 1890, this lovely Victorian residence provides ideal country comfort in a city setting. The hotel sits in over an acre of beautiful gardens overlooking the Avon Valley, with the adjacent canal towpath proving an idyllic walk into Bath. 12 tastefully furnished en-suite bedrooms (including 4-posters) providing all the comforts & amenities. Elegant drawing room, dining room & stunning conservatory/terrace. Parking. Licensed. Every effort is made to ensure a memorable stay.	£32.50 *see PHOTO over* CREDIT CARD VISA M'CARD AMEX	Y	Y	N
Mrs Joan Youngs **Lindisfarne** **41a Warminster Road** **Bathampton** **Bath BA2 6XJ** **Tel: (01225) 466342** **Open: DEC - OCT** **Map Ref No. 02**	Nearest Road: A.36 Situated just 1 1/2 miles from the city centre. Lindisfarne is a lovely home offering comfortable en-suite accommodation with colour T.V. & refreshment facilities. Many good eating venues within walking distance. A large private car park & a frequent bus service to Bath centre. The perfect place from which to explore this beautiful city. A warm welcome & personal attention guaranteed by the resident owners.	£20.00	Y	N	Y
Mr & Mrs M. Westlake **Monkshill** **Shaft Road** **Monkton Combe** **Bath BA2 7HL** **Tel: (01225) 833028** **Fax 01225 833028** **Open: ALL YEAR** **Map Ref No. 02**	Nearest Road: A.3062 This distinguished Edwardian house is set in its own beautiful gardens, on an English-country hilltop commanding spectacular countryside views, & yet lies only 5 mins from the centre of Bath. Stroll through the small mediaeval village of Monkton Combe, at the valley's base, & return to tea amid the elegant antiques, fireplace & grand piano that complement the drawing room. The bedrooms are elegant, with colourful flowing drapes, charming brass beds, bath/shower & fine views over the gardens & valley below.	£27.50 *see PHOTO over* CREDIT CARD VISA M'CARD	Y	N	N

The Tasburgh Bath. Bath.

Monkshill. Monkton Combe.

Green Lane House. Hinton.

Somerset
Bath & Bristol

		rate from £ per person	children taken	evening meals	animals taken

Christopher & Juliet Davies
Green Lane House
Hinton Charterhouse
Bath BA3 6BL
Tel: (01225) 723631
Fax 01225 723773
Open: ALL YEAR
Map Ref No. 03

Nearest Road: A.36, B.3110
Five miles south of Bath in undulating countryside on the borders of Somerset & Wiltshire lies the conservation village of Hinton Charterhouse. Green Lane House, originally 3 terraced 18th-century stone cottages, has been tastefully renovated & attractively furnished. Traditional features such as exposed beams & open log fireplaces combine with modern comforts introduced throughout the distinctively decorated bedrooms, residents' lounge & breakfast room.

£20.00 | Y | N | N

see PHOTO over

CREDIT CARD
VISA
M'CARD
AMEX

Jon & Janet Whitwam
The Plaine
Norton St. Philip
Bath BA3 6LE
Tel: (01373) 834723
Fax 01373 834101
Open: ALL YEAR
Map Ref No. 04

Nearest Road: A.36
The Plaine is a delightful listed building, dating from the 16th century & situated in the heart of an historic conservation village. There are 3 beautiful en-suite rooms, all with 4-poster beds. Opposite is the famous George Inn - one of the oldest hostelries in England. Delicious breakfasts are prepared with local produce and free-range eggs. A convenient location for Bath, Wells, Longleat and the Cotswolds. Parking. Children over 3.

£24.00 | Y | N | N

see PHOTO over

CREDIT CARD
VISA
M'CARD
AMEX

Leslie & Traudle Graham
Monmouth Lodge
Norton St. Philip
Bath
BA3 6LH
Tel: (01373) 834367
Open: ALL YEAR
Map Ref No. 04

Nearest Road: A.36, A.366
Set in an acre of attractive garden, looking on to the Somerset Hills surrounding this historic village. 3 attractively furnished ground floor en-suite bedrooms, with colour T.V., tea/coffee facilities, king-size beds & own patio doors, which offer space & comfort. In the charming sitting room & stylish dining room, there is the same attention to detail & quality, where a good choice of excellent breakfast is served. Ideally situated for Bath, Wells, Stonehenge etc. Private parking. Famous 13th century pub nearby.

£27.00 | Y | N | N

CREDIT CARD
VISA
M'CARD

Graham & Nicola Walker
Bath Lodge Hotel
Warminster Road
Norton St. Philip
Bath BA3 6NH
Tel: (01225) 723040
Fax 01225 723737
Open: ALL YEAR
Map Ref No. 04

Nearest Road: A.36
Bath Lodge is a superbly converted, Heritage Grade II listed, former gatehouse to Farleigh Castle, with both the alterations & landscaping having been completed within the last few years. All of the rooms are beautifully located & have many castellated features within them. Private balconies from 3 of the rooms overlook the natural gardens & adjacent deer forest. Bath Lodge is situated just 7 miles south of Bath on the A.36. Children over 10 years welcome.

£27.50 | Y | N | Y

see PHOTO over

CREDIT CARD
VISA
M'CARD
AMEX

Mrs Clare Lewis
Church Farm
Woolverton
Bath BA3 6QT
Tel: (01373) 831003
Fax 01373 831005
Open: ALL YEAR
Map Ref No. 06

Nearest Road: A.36
Church Farm is a 17th-century country house, conveniently placed 10 mins south of Bath & close to many places of interest. It is no longer a working farm, but is situated in its own grounds with lakes, paddocks & stabling. You will receive a warm welcome & private, comfortable en-suite accommodation with T.V. & tea/coffee. A delightful home, tastefully furnished throughout. Well placed for visiting Bath, Bristol, Cheddar Gorge, Longleat, Stourhead & Wells. (Reductions for children.)

£25.00 | Y | N | N

CREDIT CARD
VISA

The Plaine. Norton St. Philip.

Bath Lodge. Norton St. Philip.

Irondale House. Rode.

Somerset
Bath & Bristol

		rate from £ per person	children taken	evening meals	animals taken
Jayne Holder **Irondale House** **67 High Street** **Rode** **Bath BA3 6PB** Tel: (01373) 830730 Fax 01373 830730 Open: ALL YEAR Map Ref No. 05	Nearest Road: A.36 A warm welcome is extended by Jane & Oliver to their late-18th-century home, set in a quiet rural village within a lovely walled garden, 10 miles south of Bath. The bedrooms are decorated to the highest standard, with super king-size beds, colour T.V. & hairdryers, 1 en-suite & 1 with private facilities. An excellent breakfast is served in the attractive dining room, & guests can relax in the comfortable drawing room. Ideal for touring the West Country, including Bath, Wells, Salisbury, Stourhead & Longleat. Children over 12. *see PHOTO over* CREDIT CARD VISA M'CARD	£25.00	Y	N	N
Mrs Pam Laidler **Quantock House** **Holford** **Bridgwater TA5 1RY** Tel: (01278) 741439 Open: ALL YEAR Map Ref No. 07	Nearest Road: A.39 Quantock House is in the small picturesque village of Holford, historically connected with Wordsworth and Coleridge. Relax in this 400-year-old thatched home with cottage garden. The spacious rooms have en-suite bathrooms, T.V. & tea/coffee-making facilities. Sample the home cooking on offer, or enjoy nearby homely hostelries. Set near hills & the sea, Quantock House is a perfect centre for exploring by car or on foot. *see PHOTO over*	£20.00	Y	Y	Y
Mrs Ann Dyer **Blackmore Farm** **Blackmore Lane** **Cannington** **Bridgwater TA5 2NE** Tel: (01278) 653442 Fax 01278 653442 Open: ALL YEAR Map Ref No. 08	Nearest Road: A.39 Blackmore Farm is a Grade I listed, 14th-century manor house, set in pleasant rural surroundings with views to the Quantock Hills. The house retains many of its period features, including stone archways, garderobes & oak beams. Accommodation includes a 4-poster bedroom & 'The Gallery', with a private sitting room. Breakfast is taken in the Great Hall around the 16ft carved oak table. There are a range of excellent local restaurant facilities. Within easy reach of the Quantock Hills, west Somerset coast & Exmoor.	£19.00	Y	N	N
Christine Healey **The Old Bakery** **The Street, Olveston** **Bristol BS12 3DR** Tel: (01454) 616437 Open: ALL YEAR Map Ref No. 09	Nearest Road: A.38 The Old Bakery is situated in the centre of the village of Olveston, just 12 miles north of Bristol. This lovely 200 year-old cottage provides comfortable accommodation in 2 attractive twin-bedded rooms. A lounge with colour T.V./video is provided exclusively for guests which overlooks a pretty walled garden. Easy access to Bath, Forest of Dean, South Cotswolds & M.4/M.5. Children over 4 years welcome.	£22.00	Y	N	Y
Ruth Shellard **Overbrook, Stowey Bottom** **Bishop Sutton** **Bristol BS18 4TN** Tel: (01275) 332648 Fax 01179 352052 Open: ALL YEAR (Excl. Xmas) Map Ref No. 10	Nearest Road: A.368 Overbrook is a charming wisteria-clad house, tastefully furnished, with a lovely garden by a brook. Situated in rural seclusion in a quiet & peaceful lane, with a little ford by the front gate. There are 2 beautifully furnished bedrooms, each with an en-suite/private facilities. Overbrook is only 1/2 mile from the village & close to the beautiful Chew Valley Lake. Cheddar Gorge, Bath, Wells & Bristol are within easy reach.	£18.00	Y	N	N

Quantock House. Holford.

Dollons House. Dunster.

	rate from £ per person	children taken	evening meals	animals taken
Mrs Philippa Tasker **Downs Edge, Saville Rd** **Stoke Bishop** **Bristol BS9 1JD** **Tel/Fax: (0117) 9683264** **Mobile: 0585 866463** **Open: ALL YEAR** **Map Ref No. 11**	Nearest Road: A.4018 Downs Edge is situated in a superb position on the very edge of Bristol's famous Downs - an open park of some 450 acres. Furnished with fine period furniture, the house is set in magnificent gardens close to the spectacular Avon Gorge & its breathtaking views. This uniquely peaceful location is ideally situated for the city centre, Clifton & the university. Downs Edge is served by an excellent public transport system with easy access to the motorway network. **CREDIT CARD** VISA M'CARD	£28.00	Y	Y	N
Mr & Mrs R. Newman-Coburn **Hawthorne House** **Bishopswood** **Chard** **TA20 3RS** **Tel: (01460) 234482** **Open: ALL YEAR** **Map Ref No. 12**	Nearest Road: A.303 Hawthorne House is a cosy 19th-century stone house set in the Blackdown Hills, an Area of Outstanding Natural Beauty. It is ideally situated for an overnight stay en-route to Cornwall, & for visiting N.T. properties & the many other attractions in Somerset & Devon. Each of the 3 comfortable bedrooms has an en-suite/private bathroom & tea/coffee-making facilities. The attractive dining room has panoramic views over the extensive gardens & surrounding hills. Children over 12.	£17.50	Y	Y	Y
Guy & Charmian Smith **Chinnock House** **Middle Chinnock** **Crewkerne TA18 7PN** **Tel: (01935) 881229** **Fax 01935 881229** **Open: ALL YEAR** **Map Ref No. 13**	Nearest Road: A.30, A.303 A beautiful Ham stone Georgian house set in a walled garden with glorious views in a quiet Somerset hamlet. Offering 2 twin-bedded rooms, each with a private/en-suite bathroom, & 1 en-suite double. An ideal centre for visiting Bath, Stonehenge, Wells, Glastonbury, Sherborne, Dorchester & Hardy Country. Evening meals by prior arrangement, with fresh salmon, home-grown vegetables & raspberries & cream a speciality. Swimming pool & laundry service.	£27.50	Y	Y	N
John & Sally Gregory **Dryclose** **Newbery Lane, Misterton** **Crewkerne TA18 8NE** **Tel: (01460) 73161** **Open: ALL YEAR (Excl.** **Xmas & New Year)** **Map Ref No. 14**	Nearest Road: A.30, A.303 Dryclose is an attractive, 16th-century, listed, beamed & panelled former farmhouse, set in 2 acres of lovely garden, with an outdoor swimming pool. There are 3 charming bedrooms, 1 twin, 1 single & 1 twin en-suite. All have hot-drinks facilities. There are 2 sitting rooms, each with T.V., for guests. The area abounds with beautiful gardens & historic houses, & the coast is only 15 miles away. An ideal spot for a relaxing break & for exploring Somerset. Children over 8.	£18.50	Y	Y	N
Major & Mrs H.E. Bradshaw **Dollons House** **10 Church Street** **Dunster TA24 6SH** **Tel: (01643) 821880** **Fax 01643 822016** **Open: ALL YEAR (Excl.** **Xmas/Boxing Days)** **Map Ref No. 15**	Nearest Road: A.39 17th-century Dollons House nestles beneath the castle in this delightful mediaeval village in the Exmoor National Park. Dunster is ideal for touring Exmoor & the North Devon Coast. Accommodation is in 3 attractive & very comfortable en-suite rooms, each with its own character & special decor. 100 years ago, the local pharmacist had his shop in Dollons, & in the back he made marmalade for the Houses of Parliament. A delightful home. **see PHOTO over** **CREDIT CARD** VISA M'CARD	£25.00	N	N	N

Somerset
Bath & Bristol

	Nearest Road / Description	rate from £ per person	children taken	evening meals	animals taken
Jane Forshaw **The Old Priory** **Dunster** **TA24 6RY** **Tel: (01643) 821540** **Open: ALL YEAR** **Map Ref No. 15**	Nearest Road: A.39 The Old Priory is a small mediaeval house, located in old-fashioned, walled gardens in a peaceful setting opposite a dovecote. 3 tastefully furnished bedrooms, including 1 4-poster. Each has an en-suite or private bathroom & tea/coffee-making facilities. Super wholefood/farmhouse breakfasts served. An interesting home, combining high standards with an informal atmosphere. The Old Priory is an ideal base for exploring Somerset.	£22.50	N	N	N
Jaqui Collins **Knoll Lodge** **Church Road** **East Brent** **TA9 4HZ** **Tel: (01278) 760294** **Open: ALL YEAR** **Map Ref No. 16**	Nearest Road: A.38, A.370 Knoll Lodge is a 19th-century, listed Somerset house in an acre of orchard, where you are offered comfortable accommodation & quality food in friendly & peaceful rural surroundings. 3 spacious bedrooms - 2 double en-suite, 1 twin with private bathroom. Centrally heated, & attractively decorated with antique pine furniture & hand-made American patchwork quilts. Colour T.V.s & tea/coffee facilities. Dinner by arrangement. Children over 12.	£21.00 (no smoking)	Y	Y	N
Trevor & Pat Redmond **Number Three** **3 Magdalene Street** **Glastonbury** **BA6 9EW** **Tel: (01458) 832129** **Open: Easter - NOV** **Map Ref No. 18**	Nearest Road: M.5 Ex. 23, A.39 An attractive Grade II listed Georgian house adjoining the ruin of the once-powerful Abbey. The tomb of King Arthur & Guinevere is claimed to have been discovered here in the 13th-century. There are 4 very attractive rooms, each with private facilities, telephone, radio, T.V. & tea/coffee makers. Sports massage therapy & aromatherapy by a highly trained & licensed practitioner available. An excellent base for touring: Cheddar Gorge, Wookey Hole, Wells Cathedral & Bath are within easy reach.	£32.50 (no smoking) CREDIT CARD VISA M'CARD	Y	N	N
Mrs V. A. Vicary **Larcombe Foot** **Winsford** **Minehead** **TA24 7HS** **Tel: (01643) 851306** **Open: APR - DEC** **Map Ref No. 17**	Nearest Road: A.396 Larcombe Foot, a comfortable old country house set in the beautiful & tranquil Upper Exe Valley, is an ideal base for walking, riding, fishing & touring Exmoor. Guests' comfort is paramount. Accommodation is in 3 bedrooms, 2 with private bathroom, & tea/coffee makers in all rooms. A comfortable sitting room with log fire & T.V., plus a pretty garden to relax in. Evening meals by prior arrangement. Winsford is considered one of the prettiest villages on the moor.	£18.00	Y	Y	Y

When booking your accommodation please mention
The Best Bed & Breakfast

The Lynch Country House Hotel. Somerton.

Somerset
Bath & Bristol

		rate from £ per person	children taken	evening meals	animals taken
Mrs Diana Brewer **Wood Advent Farm** **Roadwater** **TA23 0RR** **Tel: (01984) 640920** **Fax 01984 640920** **Open: ALL YEAR** **Map Ref No. 21**	Nearest Road: A.39 Set in the Exmoor National Park, Wood Advent Farm is a 340-acre, working sheep farm, with beautiful views & breathtaking parks. 5 relaxing en-suite bedrooms, with tea/coffee facilities. A chintz lounge, with log fire, is available, & an inglenook woodburner heats the dining room, where country dishes are served, most of the produce being home-produced on the farm or locally. A grass tennis court & outdoor, heated pool. A wonderful base for the West Country.	£18.50 CREDIT CARD VISA	N	Y	N
Mr & Mrs B. H. Middle **Church Farm Guest House** **Compton Dundon** **Somerton TA11 6PE** **Tel: (01458) 272927** **Open: ALL YEAR (Excl. Xmas)** **Map Ref No. 23**	Nearest Road: B.3151 A superb thatched cottage, over 400 years old. 5 delightful rooms, all with en-suite facilities, T.V.& tea/coffee. Most rooms in a converted barn. Imaginative home cooking from fresh produce (24 hrs' notice please); licensed, with a choice of wines. Nestling below St. Andrew's Church in a lovely village, with marvellous views, in the heart of the Vale of Avalon. Walking & wildlife on the doorstep. Ideal for coast & countryside, historic houses & towns. Car park. Children over 5.	£19.50	Y	Y	N
Roy Copeland **The Lynch Country House** **4 Behind Berry** **Somerton TA11 7PD** **Tel: (01458) 272316** **Fax 01458 272590** **Open: ALL YEAR (Excl. Xmas)** **Map Ref No. 24**	Nearest Road: A.303 The Lynch is a charming small hotel, standing in acres of carefully tended, wonderfully mature grounds. Beautifully refurbished & decorated to retain all its Georgian style & elegance, it now offers 5 attractively presented rooms, some with 4-posters, others with Victorian bedsteads, all with thoughtful extras including bathrobes & magazines. Each room has en-suite facilities, 'phone, radio, T.V. & tea/coffee. The elegant dining room overlooks the lawns & lake. Single occupancy supplement. Children over 10.	£24.50 *see PHOTO over* CREDIT CARD VISA M'CARD AMEX	Y	N	N
Mrs C. Clark **Meryan House Hotel** **Bishops Hull** **Taunton TA1 5EG** **Tel: (01823) 337445** **Fax 01823 322355** **Open: ALL YEAR** **Map Ref No. 25**	Nearest Road: A.38 A charming, 17th-century, listed building of architectural & historical interest. It is set in its own grounds, yet only 1 1/4 miles from Taunton. All bedrooms are elegantly furnished with antiques, & have en-suite, colour T.V. (satellite & video channels) & tea/coffee-making facilities. A delightful house, with a wealth of beams & inglenook fireplaces. Excellent cuisine prepared from home-grown produce.	£29.00 CREDIT CARD VISA M'CARD	Y	Y	Y
Peter & Fiona Willcox **Langford Manor** **Fivehead** **Taunton TA3 6PH** **Tel: (01460) 281674** **Fax 01460 281585** **Open: ALL YEAR** **Map Ref No. 27**	Nearest Road: A.378 This beautiful Grade II manor house set in 9 acres on the edge of the Somerset Levels offers peace, tranquillity & seclusion. The house, dating from the 13th century, affords every comfort whilst retaining the original character. All rooms are en-suite & the panelled drawing room & dining room are available for guests. Relax in the garden, play croquet or tennis followed by an excellent dinner; soak up the country house atmosphere. Children over 14 years welcome.	£35.00 *see PHOTO over*	Y	Y	N

Langford Manor. Fivehead.

Higher House. West Bagborough.

Higher Vexford House. Lydeard St. Lawrence.

Somerset
Bath & Bristol

		rate from £ per person	children taken	evening meals	animals taken
Mrs Claire Mitchem **Whittles Farm** **Beercrocombe** **Taunton TA3 6AH** **Tel: (01823) 480301** **Fax 01823 480301** **Open: MAR - OCT** **Map Ref No. 26**	Nearest Road: A.358 Guests at Whittles Farm can be sure of a high standard of accommodation & service. A superior 16th-century farmhouse set in 200 acres of pastureland, it is luxuriously carpeted & furnished in traditional style. Inglenook fireplaces & log-burners. 3 en-suite bedrooms, individually furnished, T.V. & tea/coffee. Super farmhouse food, using own meat, eggs & vegetables, & local Cheddar cheese & butter. Evening meals by arrangement. Table licence. Children over 12.	£23.00	Y	Y	N
Charles & Jane Ritchie **Bashfords Farmhouse** **West Bagborough** **Taunton** **TA4 3EF** **Tel: (01823) 432015** **Fax 01823 432520** **Open: ALL YEAR** **Map Ref No. 28**	Nearest Road: A.358 Bashfords Is a beautIfully restored stone-bullt farmhouse offering a superb level of comfort in a glorious rural area. For those who enjoy wildlife & walking, the Quantocks are unsurpassed. For those whose interests are less energetic, there are many historic properties & gardens within easy reach. Bashfords is the perfect centre for a peaceful & relaxing stay in an Area of Outstanding Natural Beauty. Children over 10. Evening meals by prior arrangement. **E-mail: critchie@abling.co.uk**	£19.50	N	Y	N
Mr & Mrs Martin Eyre **Higher House** **West Bagborough** **Taunton TA4 3EF** **Tel: (01823) 432996** **Fax 01823 433568** **Open: ALL YEAR** **Map Ref No. 29**	Nearest Road: A.358 Higher House is set 650 feet up on the southern slopes of the Quantock Hills. The views from the house & gardens are exceptional. The principal part of the house is 17th-century, built around 2 courtyards, 1 with a heated pool. Each bedroom has its own bathroom, 'phone, colour T.V., tea/coffee facilities, books, magazines. There is a beautifully presented drawing room. An all-weather tennis court is also available.	£22.50 *see PHOTO over*	Y	Y	N
Phillida J. Hughes **Redlands House** **Trebles Holford** **Combe Florey** **Taunton TA4 3HA** **(01823) 433159** **Open: ALL YEAR** **Map Ref No. 31**	Nearest Road: A.358 Originally a barn, Redlands is now a lovely family home, which offers a very warm & friendly welcome. It nestles in the sheltered, peaceful hamlet of Trebles Holford with views to the surrounding Quantock Hills. The area is renowned for its beautiful walks, picturesque villages & wild life. This is an excellent base for exploring the region, Exmoor, Dartmoor & the beaches of North & South Devon. There are 3 attractive guest rooms, each with en-suite/private facilities.	£22.00 *see PHOTO over*	Y	Y	Y
Nigel & Finny Muers-Raby **Higher Vexford House** **Higher Vexford** **Lydeard St. Lawrence** **Taunton TA4 3QF** **Tel: (01984) 656267** **Fax 01984 656707** **Open: ALL YEAR** **Map Ref No. 30**	Nearest Road: A.358 This beautiful large Quantock stone country house is located in stunning countryside between The Quantocks, Brendons & Exmoor. A spacious sitting room & dining room all furnished with antiques, log fires & flagstone floors. Lovely bedrooms decorated in traditional country-house style. Books, magazines, tea/coffee facilities. A pretty walled garden with views down this hidden valley. A friendly welcome awaits you. A great place to come & relax & unwind. **E-mail: 101752.1124@compuserve.com**	£28.00 *see PHOTO over*	Y	N	Y

Redlands House.   Combe Florey.

Curdon Mill. Williton.

Somerset
Bath & Bristol

	rate from £ per person	children taken	evening meals	animals taken
Richard & Daphne Criddle **Curdon Mill** **Vellow** **Williton** **Taunton TA4 4LS** **Tel: (01984) 656522** **Fax 01984 656197** **Open: ALL YEAR** **Map Ref No. 38** Nearest Road: A.358 Curdon Mill is a lovely working water mill situated on farmland at the foot of the beautiful Quantock Hills. 6 pretty, en-suite bedrooms with T.V. & tea/coffee-making facilities. A lounge is available for guests' use. Meals are delicious & are available Mon-Sat. Real country cuisine using local or home-produced meat & fish, with fresh fruit, vegetables & herbs from the garden. A lovely base for touring the region. A heated outdoor pool in a spacious relaxing garden. Licensed for civil marriages. Stabling for horses also available.	£25.00 *see PHOTO over* CREDIT CARD VISA M'CARD AMEX	N	Y	Y
Carolyn White **Box Tree House** **Westbury-sub-Mendip** **Wells** **BA5 1HA** **Tel: (01749) 870777** **Open: ALL YEAR** **Map Ref No. 32** Nearest Road: A.371 A warm welcome is assured at this delightful, converted, 17th-century farmhouse located in the heart of the village with an excellent local inn for evening meals. 3 comfortable en-suite bedrooms with tea/coffee-making facilities. A charming T.V. lounge is also available. Box Tree House is renowned for its English breakfasts with local preserves, croissants & home-made muffins. Also, workshops for stained glass & picture framing, with many unique items for sale.	£19.00	Y	N	N
Mrs Wendy Thompson **Stoneleigh House** **Westbury-sub-Mendip** **Wells BA5 1HF** **Tel: (01749) 870668** **Fax 01749 870668** **Open: ALL YEAR (Excl. Xmas)** **Map Ref No. 33** Nearest Road: A.371 This 18th-century farmhouse is set in beautiful countryside with wonderful views, & surrounded by its own gardens. Stoneleigh House has long enjoyed a reputation for its comfort & congenial atmosphere. It has been carefully modernised so that the wealth of historical features complement the present-day comforts. En-suite rooms available, with T.V. & beverage facilities. Delicious breakfasts are prepared including home made preserves & free-range eggs. Children over 10.	£20.00 *see PHOTO over*	Y	N	N
Anita & Chris Frost **Southway Farm** **Polsham** **Wells BA5 1RW** **Tel: (01749) 673396** **Fax 01749 670373** **Open: FEB - NOV** **Map Ref No. 34** Nearest Road: A.39 Southway Farm is a Grade II listed Georgian farmhouse situated halfway between Glastonbury & Wells. Accommodation is in 3 comfortable & attractively furnished bedrooms, 1 en-suite & 2 with a private bathroom. A delicious full English breakfast is served, although vegetarians are also catered for. Guests may relax in the cosy lounge, with colour T.V., or in the pretty, tranquil garden. An ideal location for a restful holiday, or for touring the glorious West Country.	£20.00	Y	N	N
Eddie & Holly Nowell **Beryl** **Off Hawkers Lane** **Wells BA5 3JP** **Tel: (01749) 678738** **Fax 01749 670508** **Open: ALL YEAR (Excl. Xmas)** **Map Ref No. 35** Nearest Road: A.371 Beryl is a precious gem in a perfect setting, situated 1 mile from the cathedral city of Wells. This striking 19th-century Gothic mansion has beautifully furnished en-suite bedrooms, interesting views & all the accoutrements of luxury living. Dinner is available by arrangement & is served in the exquisite dining room. Eddie & Holly are charming hosts, & your stay at their home is sure to be memorable.	£32.50 CREDIT CARD VISA M'CARD	Y	Y	Y

Stoneleigh House. Westbury- sub- Mendip.

Cutthorne. Luckwell Bridge.

Somerset
Bath & Bristol

		rate from £ per person	children taken	evening meals	animals taken
Stephen Blue & Peter Clover **Bales Mead** **West Porlock** **TA24 8NX** **Tel: (01643) 862565** **Open: ALL YEAR** **Map Ref No. 36**	Nearest Road: A.39 A stylish, elegant Edwardian country house offering superb accommodation & noted for its lavish, memorable breakfasts. An outstanding & peaceful setting situated midway between the pretty village of Porlock & the picturesque harbour at Porlock Weir. Set in lovely gardens with panoramic views towards the sea & spectacular unspoilt countryside of Exmoor. 3 exquisitely furnished double bedrooms with every comfort & private bathrooms. An excellent base for walking/touring Exmoor & the North Devon Coast.	£26.00	N	N	N
Ann & Philip Durbin **Cutthorne** **Luckwell Bridge** **Wheddon Cross** **TA24 7EW** **Tel/Fax: (01643) 831255** **Open: FEB - DEC** **Map Ref No. 37**	Nearest Road: A.396 Tucked away in the heart of Exmoor National Park, Cutthorne offers a quiet & relaxing haven for country lovers. Situated in an Area of Outstanding Natural Beauty, walking & riding are unrivalled, whether by the coast or on the moors. Nearby are Lynton & Lynmouth, Tarr Steps & Dunster. The pretty bedrooms all have bathrooms & 1 a 4-poster bed. The cuisine is traditional or vegetarian, using the finest local meat & organic vegetables. *see PHOTO over*	£22.00	N	Y	Y
Jackie Somerville **Holywell House** **Holywell** **East Coker** **Yeovil BA22 9NQ** **Tel: (01935) 862612** **Fax 01935 863035** **Open: ALL YEAR (Excl. Xmas)** **Map Ref No. 39**	Nearest Road: A.30 Lovingly restored, tastefully decorated & furnished with many fine antiques. Guests' every need seems to have been anticipated, even down to the hot water bottle for chilly nights! Jackie enjoys cosseting her guests, which is why she wins top awards. There are 3 delightful en-suite bedrooms. Standing in 3 acres of glorious grounds, with tennis court & croquet lawn, Holywell House has literary connections with Thomas Hardy & T. S. Eliot. Evening meals by prior arrangement. *see PHOTO over*	£30.00	Y	Y	N

When booking your accommodation please mention
The Best Bed & Breakfast

Holywell House. Holywell.

Suffolk

Suffolk
(East Anglia)

In July, the lower reaches of the River Orwell hold the essence of Suffolk. Broad fields of green and gold with wooded horizons sweep down to the quiet water. Orwell Bridge spans the wide river where yachts and tan-sailed barges share the water with ocean-going container ships out of Ipswich. Downstream the saltmarshes echo to the cry of the Curlew. The small towns and villages of Suffolk are typical of an area with long seafairing traditions. This is the county of men of vision; like Constable and Gainsborough, Admiral Lord Nelson and Benjamin Britten.

The land is green and fertile and highly productive. The hedgerows shelter some of our prettiest wild flowers, & the narrow country lanes are a pure delight. Most memorable is the ever-changing sky, appearing higher and wider here than elsewhere in England. There is a great deal of heathland, probably the best known being Newmarket where horses have been trained and raced for some hundreds of years. Gorse-covered heath meets sandy cliffs on Suffolks Heritage Coast. Here are bird reserves and the remains of the great mediaeval city of Dunwich, sliding into the sea.

West Suffolk was famous for its wool trade in the Middle Ages, & the merchants gave thanks for their good fortune by building magnificent "Wool Churches". Much-photographed Lavenham has the most perfect black & white timbered houses in Britain, built by the merchants of Tudor times. Ipswich was granted the first charter by King John in 1200, but had long been a trading community of seafarers. Its history can be read from the names of the streets - Buttermarket, Friars Street, Cornhill, Dial Lane & Tavern Street. The latter holds the Great White Horse Hotel mentioned by Charles Dickens in Pickwick Papers. Sadly not many ancient buildings remain, but the mediaeval street pattern and the churches make an interesting trail to follow. The Market town of Bury St. Edmunds is charming, with much of its architectural heritage still surviving, from the Norman Cornhill to a fine Queen Anne House. The great Abbey, now in ruins, was the meeting place of the Barons of England for the creation of the Magna Carta, enshrining the principals of individual freedom, parliamentary democracy and the supremacy of the law. Suffolk has some very fine churches, notably at Mildenhall, Lakenheath, Framlingham, Lavenham & Stoke-by-Nayland, & also a large number of wonderful houses & great halls, evidence of the county's prosperity.

Lavenham.

Suffolk

Suffolk Gazeteer

Areas of Outstanding Natural Beauty
Suffolk Coast. Heathlands. Dedham Vale.

Historic Houses & Castles

Euston Hall - Thetford
18th century house with fine collection of pictures. Gardens & 17th century Parish Church nearby.

Christchurch Mansion - Ipswich
16th century mansion built on site of 12th century Augustinian Priory. Gables & dormers added in 17th century & other alteration & additions made in 17th & 18th centuries.

Gainsborough's House - Sudbury
Birthplace of Gainsborough, well furnished, collection of paintings.

The Guildhall - Hadleigh
15th century.

Glemham Hall - Nr Woodbridge
Elizabethan house of red brick - 18th century alterations. Fine stair, panelled rooms with Queen Anne furniture.

Haughley Park - Nr. Stowmarket
Jacobean manor house.

Heveningham Hall - Nr. Halesworth
Georgian mansion - English Palladian - Interior in Neo-Classical style. Garden by Capability Brown.

Ickworth - Nr. Bury St. Edmunds
Mixed architectural styles - late Regency & 18th century. French furniture, pictures & superb silver. Gardens with orangery.

Kentwell Hall - Long Melford
Elizabethan mansion in red brick, built in E plan, surrounded by moat.

Little Hall - Lavenham
15th century hall house, collection of furniture, pictures, china, etc.

Melford Hall - Nr. Sudbury
16th century - fine pictures, Chinese porcelain, furniture. Garden with gazebo.

Somerleyton Hall - Nr. Lowestoft
Dating from 16th century - additional work in 19th century. Carving by Grinling Gibbons. Tapestries, library, pictures.

Cathedrals & Churches

Bury St. Edmunds (St. Mary)
15th century. Hammer Beam roof in nave, wagon roof in chancel. Boret monument 1467.

Bramfield (St. Andrew)
Early circular tower. Fine screen & vaulting. Renaissance effigy.

Bacton (St. Mary)
15th century timbered roof. East Anglian stone & flintwork.

Dennington (St. Mary)
15th century alabaster monuments & bench ends. Aisle & Parclose screens with lofts & parapets.

Earl Stonhay (St. Mary)
14th century - rebuilt with fine hammer roof & 17th century pulpit with four hour-glasses.

Euston (St. Genevieve)
17th century. Fine panelling, reredos may be Grinling Gibbons.

Framlingham (St. Michael)
15th century nave & west tower, hammer beam roof in false vaulting. Chancel was rebuilt in 16th century for the tombs of the Howard family, monumental art treasures. Thamar organ. 1674.

Fressingfield (St. Peter & St. Paul)
15th century woodwork - very fine.

Lavenham (St. Peter & St. Paul)
15th century. Perpendicular. Fine towers. 14th century chancel screen. 17th century monument in alabaster.

Long Melford (Holy Trinity)
15th century Lady Chapel, splendid brasses. 15th century glass of note. Chantry chapel with fine roof. Like cathedral in proportions.

Stoke-by-Nayland (St. Mary)
16th-17th century library, great tower. Fine nave & arcades. Good brasses & monuments.

Ufford (St. Mary)
Mediaeval font cover - glorious.

Museums & Galleries

Christchurch Mansion - Ipswich
Country house, collection of furniture, pictures, bygones, ceramics of 18th century. Paintings by Gainsborough, Constable & modern artists.

Ipswich Museum - Ipswich
Natural History; prehistory, geology & archaeology to mediaeval period.

Suffolk

Moyse's Hall Musuem - Bury St. Edmunds
12th century dwelling house with local antiquities & natural history.
Abbot's Hall Museum of Rural Life - Stowmarket
Collections describing agriculture, crafts & domestic utensils.
Gershom-Parkington Collection - Bury St. Edmunds
Queen Anne House containing collection of watches & clocks.
Dunwich Musuem - Dunwich
Flora & fauna; local history.

Historic Monuments

The Abbey - Bury St. Edmunds
Only west end now standing.

Framlingham Castle
12th & 13th centuries - Tudor almshouses.
Bungay Castle - Bungay
12th century. Restored 13th century drawbridge & gatehouse.
Burgh Castle Roman Fort - Burgh
Coastal defences - 3rd century.
Herringfleet Priory - Herringfleet
13th century - remains of small Augustinian priory.
Leiston Abbey - Leiston
14th century - remains of cloisters, choir & trancepts.
Orford Castle - Orford
12th century - 18-sided keep - three towers.

The House in the Clouds. Thorpeness.

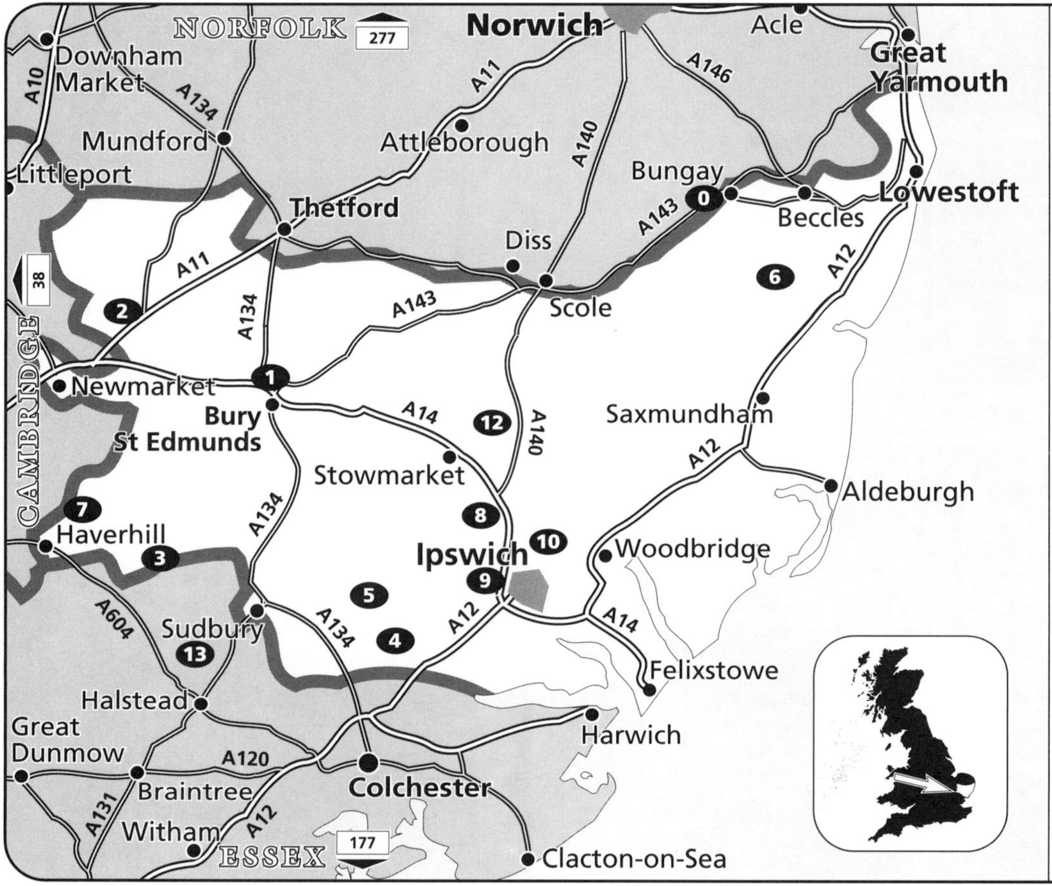

SUFFOLK
Map reference

0 Watchorn
1 Skellett
2 Jakobson
3 Tuffill
4 Watkins
5 Rolfe
6 Middleton-Stewart
7 Sheppard
8 Hackett-Jones
9 Debenham
10 Hilton
12 Ridsdale
13 Morse

NORFOLK 277

CAMBRIDGE 38

ESSEX 177

Great Yarmouth
Acle
A146
A10
Downham Market
Littleport
Mundford
A134
Attleborough
A11
Norwich
Thetford
A143
A11
Newmarket
Bury St Edmunds
A134
Haverhill
A604
Halstead
Great Dunmow
A131
Braintree
A120
Witham
A12
Colchester
Sudbury
A134
Stowmarket
A14
Diss
Scole
A140
Bungay
A143
Beccles
A12
Lowestoft
Saxmundham
A12
Aldeburgh
Woodbridge
A14
Felixstowe
Harwich
Clacton-on-Sea
Ipswich
A14
A140
A12

0
6
10
12
8
9
5
4
1
2
7
3
13

387

Fornham Hall. Fornham All Saints.

Suffolk

		rate from £ per person	children taken	evening meals	animals taken
Mrs Bobbie Watchorn **Earsham Park Farm** **Harleston Road** **Earsham** **Bungay NR35 2AQ** **Tel/Fax: (01986) 892180** **Open: ALL YEAR** **Map Ref No. 00**	Nearest Road: A.143 A Victorian farmhouse set on a hill overlooking the Waveney Valley, with superb views. Park Farm offers 3 really delightful guest rooms, all furnished to a high standard. Each is en-suite, & well-equipped with T.V., radio/alarm & tea/coffee facilities. 1 4-poster. Breakfast is served in the lovely dining room. Within easy reach of Norwich, Lowestoft & Southwold. A wonderful home, where comfort & a relaxed atmosphere prevail.	£19.00	Y	Y	N
Susan Skellett **Fornham Hall** **Fornham All Saints** **Bury St. Edmunds** **IP28 6JJ** **Tel: (01284) 725266** **Fax 01284 703424** **Open: ALL YEAR** **Map Ref No. 01**	Nearest Road: A.14 Listed Georgian country home with Tudor origins in quiet & peaceful partly walled gardens, 2 miles from Bury St. Edmunds & major roads & set on the edge of a pretty village. A traditionally furnished home with superior en-suite accommodation, white linens, bone china tea services, fresh flowers & many extras. Enjoy afternoon tea on the lawn & a game of croquet, or just relax by the pond & feed the resident ducks. An informal, warm, friendly atmosphere prevails. Children over 10 years are welcome.	£25.00 *see PHOTO over* CREDIT CARD VISA M'CARD	Y	N	Y
Mrs Genny Jakobson **Brambles** **Mildenhall Rd, Worlington** **Bury St. Edmunds** **IP28 8RY** **Tel/Fax: (01638) 713121** **Open: ALL YEAR (Excl. Xmas)** **Map Ref No. 02**	Nearest Road: A.11 Set in 3 acres of lovely gardens, close to the A.11, an ideal base for visits to Cambridge, Bury St. Edmunds, Ely & Newmarket (8 miles). Brambles is a peaceful house, with a relaxing atmosphere, where a warm welcome & comfortably furnished rooms combine with Genny's imaginative & creative cooking for a stay to remember. Try their Newmarket racing tours - morning gallops, stables, studs. Brochure available, Children over 8.	£27.50 *see PHOTO over*	Y	Y	N
Alastair & Jean Tuffill **Cobwebs** **26 Nethergate Street** **Clare CO10 8NP** **Tel: (01787) 277539** **Fax 01787 278252** **Open: ALL YEAR** **Map Ref No. 03**	Nearest Road: A.1092 Cobwebs is a delightful listed, beamed 14th century house in one of the loveliest ancient parts of East Anglia. Within the house there is 1 single & 1 twin-bedded room. Set within the charming walled garden is a separate & secluded twin-bedded en-suite cottage with its own access. Parking is no problem. Cobwebs is within easy walking distance of excellent pubs & restaurants. Children over 6.	£20.00	Y	N	Y
Nowell & Penny Watkins **The Bauble** **Higham** **Colchester CO7 6LA** **Tel: (01206) 337254** **Fax 01206 337263** **Open: ALL YEAR** **Map Ref No. 04**	Nearest Road: A.12 The Bauble is a delightful house offering accommodation in 3 attractively furnished bedrooms, with modern amenities including T.V. & tea/coffee-making facilities. A full English breakfast is served. Lounge, garden, heated pool & tennis court available for guests' use. Higham lies in the heart of Constable country & is within easy reach of many wool villages, with their churches, antiques shops & National Trust properties. Children over 12 years welcome.	£20.00	Y	N	N

Brambles. Worlington.

Edgehill Hotel. Hadleigh.

Suffolk

	rate from £ per person	children taken	evening meals	animals taken
Mrs Angela Rolfe **Edgehill** **2 High Street** **Hadleigh IP7 5AP** **Tel: (01473) 822458** **Open:** ALL YEAR (Excl. Xmas) **Map Ref No. 05** Nearest Road: A.12, A.14 Edgehill is a family-run Georgian house in central Hadleigh. Beautifully restored & tastefully modernised, the hotel offers the ultimate in accommodation. Particular attention is paid to friendly service & traditional home cooking with organic vegetables. Situated in the most picturesque part of Suffolk, it is a good base from which to visit the surrounding towns & pretty villages of East Anglia.	£25.00 see PHOTO over	Y	Y	Y
Judith Middleton-Stewart **St. Peter's House** **Spexhall** **Halesworth** **IP19 0RQ** **Tel: (01986) 873329/874567** **Fax 01986 875275** **Open: ALL YEAR** **Map Ref No. 06** Nearest Road: A.12, A.144 This converted 17th-century tithe barn is set in a peaceful garden with duck ponds & visiting ducks. The unique accommodation, in rolling Suffolk farmland, provides 2 attractive double bedrooms (ground floor) & 1 twin room, all with en-suite/ private facilities, & abundantly equipped. Robust breakfasts, including Suffolk fish & local fare. Dinner only to order. Well placed for Southwold, Aldeburgh & the Heritage Coast & memorable mediaeval monuments. A charming home. **E-mail: jms.leo@lineone.net**	£22.00 see PHOTO over	N	Y	Y
Mrs Jane Sheppard **The Old Vicarage** **Great Thurlow** **Haverhill** **CB9 7LE** **Tel: (01440) 783209** **Open: ALL YEAR** **Map Ref No. 07** Nearest Road: A.1307 Set in mature grounds & woodlands, this delightful old vicarage has a friendly family atmosphere. Complete peace & comfort are assured. Wonderful views of the Suffolk countryside. Open log fires welcome you in winter. Perfectly situated for Newmarket, Cambridge, Long Melford & Constable country, the attractively furnished bedrooms have en-suite or private facilities, & tea & coffee trays. (No smoking in bedrooms.) Evening meals are available at prior notice. Children over 7 welcome, & pets by arrangement.	£22.00 see PHOTO over	Y	Y	Y
Penny Debenham **Mulberry Hall** **Burstall** **Ipswich IP8 3DP** **Tel: (01473) 652348** **Open:** ALL YEAR (Excl. Xmas) **Map Ref No. 09** Nearest Road: A.1071 A lovely 16th-century timber-framed farmhouse, once owned by Cardinal Wolsey, standing in 1 1/2 acres of garden. A choice of 3 bedrooms with modern amenities, hair dryer & ironing facilities are available. The house is comfortably & prettily furnished, & guests may use the lounge, with log-burning, inglenook fireplace. Plenty of games & reading matter, plus information on local events. Tennis, badminton & croquet available.	£18.00	Y	Y	N
Lise & Michael Hilton **Bowerfield House** **Helmingham Road** **Otley** **Ipswich IP6 9NR** **Tel: (01473) 890742** **Fax 01473 890059** **Open: MAR - OCT** **Map Ref No. 10** Nearest Road: A.12, A.140 A large, handsome, 17th-century, listed stable & barn conversion, set in mature grounds with terraces & a croquet lawn. Beautifully furnished en-suite rooms, with antiques, T.V., radio & tea/ coffee facilities. Also, a billiard room & a drawing room with log fires & grand piano for guests' use. Full English or Scandinavian breakfast served. Evening meals by arrangement mid-week only. Lise is the winner of several B & B awards. Within easy reach of Woodbridge, Ipswich, Aldeburgh, Minsemere, Snape Concert Hall, Constable Country & golf courses. Children over 12.	£23.00 🚭	Y	Y	N

St. Peters House. Spexhall.

The Old Vicarage. Great Thurlow.

	rate from £ per person	children taken	evening meals	animals taken
Raewyn Hackett-Jones **Pipps Ford** **Norwich Road** **Needham Market** **Ipswich IP6 8LJ** **Tel: (01449) 760208** **Fax 01449 760561** **Open: Mid JAN - Mid DEC** **Map Ref No. 08**	Nearest Road: A.14, A.140 A beautiful, Tudor, beamed guest house in a pretty, old-fashioned garden by the Gipping river. 7 very attractive bedrooms, with private bathrooms & tea/coffee-making facilities. A very extensive breakfast menu & delicious 4-course evening meals, served in the delightful conservatory. Licensed. Colour T.V., tennis court & swimming pool. Winner of The Best Bed & Breakfast award for East Anglia. A good central position for touring all of East Anglia. Children over 5 years welcome. Animals by arrangement.	£27.50 *see PHOTO over*	Y	Y	Y
Martin & Diana Ridsdale **Cherry Tree Farm** **Mendlesham Green** **Stowmarket IP14 5RQ** **Tel: (01449) 766376** **Open: ALL YEAR (Excl. Xmas & New Year)** **Map Ref No. 12**	Nearest Road: A.140 Traditional timber-framed farmhouse, standing in three quarters of an acre of garden, with orchard & duck ponds, in a peaceful Suffolk village. 3 bedrooms, each with en-suite facilities. A spacious & comfortable lounge, inglenook fireplaces with log fire. Hearty English breakfast served in the oak-beamed dining room. Home-baked bread, own preserves & honey. Imaginative evening meals, with garden & local produce, good cheeses & fine English wines.	£22.00	N	Y	N
Catherine & David Morse **St. Mary Hall** **Belchamp Walter** **Sudbury CO10 7BB** **Tel: (01787) 237202** **Fax 01787 238302** **Open: ALL YEAR** **Map Ref No. 13**	Nearest Road: A.604, A.134 Fine example of a mediaeval Suffolk manor house in lovely 4-acre garden, 1 mile south of the village of Belchamp Walter (guests advised to obtain directions in advance). On arrival, you will be warmly welcomed. Two twin/double and one single room, each with private bathroom. Book-lined library with T.V.. Pretty dining room. Large outdoor pool, tennis court, croquet. Catherine, a keen cook, will provide dinner at 24 hr's notice.	£25.00 CREDIT CARD VISA M'CARD	Y	Y	Y

When booking your accommodation please mention
The Best Bed & Breakfast

Pipps Ford.   Needham Market.

Surrey

Surrey
(South East)

One of the Home Counties, Surrey includes a large area of London, south of the Thames. Communications are good in all directions so it is easy to stay in Surrey & travel either into central London or out to enjoy the lovely countryside which, despite urban development, survives thanks to the 'Green Belt' policy. The county is also very accessible from Gatwick Airport.

The land geographically, is chalk sandwiched in clay, & probably the lack of handy building material was responsible for the area remaining largely uninhabited for centuries. The North Downs were a considerable barrier to cross, but gradually settlements grew along the rivers which were the main

Polesden Lacey.

routes through. The Romans used the gap created by the River Mole to build Stane Street between London & Chichester, this encouraged the development of small towns. The gap cut by the passage of the River Wey allows the Pilgrims Way to cross the foot of the Downs. Dorking, Reigate & Farnham are small towns along this route, all with attracitve main streets & interesting shops & buildings.

Surrey has very little mention in the Domesday Book, &, although the patronage of the church & of wealthy families established manors which developed over the years, little happened to disturb the rural tranquility of the region. As a county it made little history but rather reflected passing times, although Magna Carta was signed at Egham in 1215.

The heathlands of Surrey were a Royal playground for centuries. The Norman Kings hunted here & horses became part of the landscape & life of the people, as they are today on Epsom Downs.

Nearness to London & Royal patronage began to influence the area, & the buildings of the Tudor period reflect this. Royal palaces were built at Hampton Court & Richmond, & great houses such as Loseley near Guildford often using stone from the monasteries emptied during the Reformation. Huge deer parks were enclosed & stocked. Richmond, described as the "finest village in the British Dominions", is now beset by 20th century traffic but still has a wonderful park with deer, lakes & woodland that was enclosed by Charles I. The terraces & gardens of such buildings as Trumpeters House & Asgill House on the slopes of Richmond overlooking the Thames, have an air of spaciousness & elegance & there are lovely & interesting riverside walks at Richmond.

Surrey

Surrey Gazeteer

Historic Houses & Castles

Albury Park - Albury, Nr. Guildford
A delightful country mansion designed by Pugin.

Clandon Park - Guildford
A fine house in the Palladian style by Leoni. A good collection of furniture & pictures. The house boasts some fine plasterwork.

Claremont - Esher
A superb Palladian house with interesting interior.

Detillens - Limpsfield
A fine 15th century house with inglenook fireplaces & mediaeval furniture. A large, pleasant garden.

Greathed Manor- Lingfield
An imposing Victorian manor house.

Hatchlands - East Clandon
A National Trust property of the 18th century with a fine Adam interior

Loseley House - Guildford
A very fine Elizabethan mansion with superb panelling, furniture & paintings.

Polesden Lacy - Dorking
A Regency villa housing the Grevill collection of tapestries, pictures & furnishings. Extensive gardens.

Cathedrals & Churches

Compton (St. Nicholas)
The only surviving 2-storey sanctuary in the country. A fine 17th century pulpit.

Esher (St. George)
A fine altar-piece & marble monument.

Hascombe (St. Peter)
A rich interior with much gilding & painted reredos & roofs.

Lingfield (St. Peter & St. Paul)
15th century. Holding a chained bible.

Ockham (St. Mary & All Saints)
Early church with 13th century east window.

Stoke D'Abernon (St. Mary)
Dating back to Pre-conquest time with additions from the 12th-15th centuries. A fine 13th century painting. Early brasses.

Museums & Galleries

Charterhouse School Museum - Godalming
Peruvian pottery, Greek pottery, archaeology & natural history.

Chertsey Museum - Chertsey
18th-19th century costume & furnishing displayed & local history.

Guildford House - Guildford
The house is 17th century & of architectural interest housing monthly exhibitions.

Guildford Museum - Guildford
A fine needlework collection & plenty on local history.

Old Kiln Agricultural - Tilford
A very interesting collection of old farm implements.

Watermill Museum - Haxted
A restored 17th century mill with working water wheels & machinery.

Weybridge Museum - Weybridge
Good archaeological exhibition plus costume & local history.

The Gardens. Wisley

398

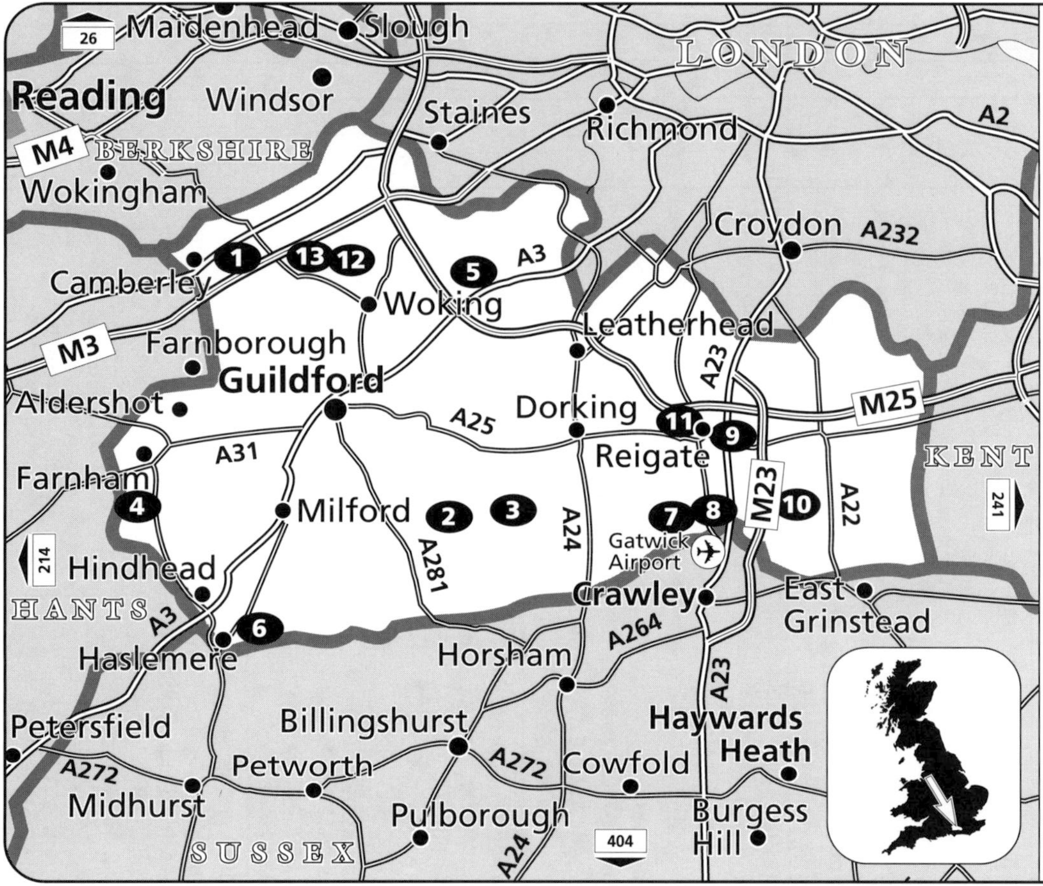

SURREY
Map reference

1 McCarthy
2 Franklin-Adams
3 Hill
4 Conrad-Pickles
5 Leggett
6 Carmichael
7 Lees
7 Blok
8 Grinsted
9 Warren
10 Wolf
11 Bussandri
12 Leeper
13 Rowse

LONDON

KENT

A2

241

M25

A232 Croydon

A22

East Grinstead

M23

10

Leatherhead

A23

9

8

Hayways Heath

Burgess Hill

A3

Woking

Dorking

Reigate

11

7

Gatwick Airport

Crawley

A23

Cowfold

A272

404

5

A25

A24

Horsham

Billingshurst

Pulborough

Richmond

Staines

A24

3

Petworth

A281

Milford

2

Guildford

Farnborough

13 12

Camberley

1

Aldershot

A31

Farnham

4

Hindhead

6

Haslemere

Petersfield

Midhurst

A272

SUSSEX

HANTS

A3

214

M3

M4

26

Reading

Windsor

Wokingham

Slough

Maidenhead

BERKSHIRE

A264

399

Surrey

	rate from £ per person	children taken	evening meals	animals taken

Tommy & Ann McCarthy
Pineleigh
10 Castle Road (off
Waverley Drive)
Camberley GU15 2DS
Tel/Fax: (01276) 64787
Open: ALL YEAR
Map Ref No. 01

Nearest Road: M.3, A.325
Pineleigh is a spacious Edwardian house, built in 1906 & set in half an acre of mature garden in a very quiet area. Accommodation is in 4 comfortable guest rooms, all en-suite with telephone, T.V. & hospitality tray. Attractively furnished in Victorian style with many old prints & pictures. A full English breakfast is served, evening meals by arrangement. Conveniently located for Heathrow Airport & London.

£25.00 — N — N — N

CREDIT CARD
VISA
M'CARD
AMEX

Mrs Carol Franklin-Adams
High Edser
Shere Road, Ewhurst
Cranleigh GU6 7PQ
Tel: (01483) 278214
Fax 01483 278200
Open: ALL YEAR
Map Ref No. 02

Nearest Road: A.25
A large, handsome Grade II listed home, the earliest part built in the 16th century, situated in an Area of Outstanding Natural Beauty. There are three rooms available: two doubles and one twin with private facilities. Residents' lounge and T.V.. Tennis court in grounds, and golf nearby. 35 minutes to Gatwick and London Airports. Approximately an hour's drive to London. A delightful home, ideal for a relaxing break.

£20.00 — Y — N — Y

Mrs Gill Hill
Bulmer Farm
Holmbury St. Mary
Dorking
RH5 6LG
Tel: (01306) 730210
Open: ALL YEAR
Map Ref No. 03

Nearest Road: A.25, B.2126
Enjoy a warm welcome at this delightful 17th-century farmhouse, complete with many beams & an inglenook fireplace. Offering 3 charming rooms, all with h/c & tea/coffee-making facilities. Adjoining the house around a courtyard are 5 attractive barn-conversion en-suite bedrooms for non-smokers. Farm produce & home-made preserves are provided. Situated in a picturesque village, it is convenient for London airports. Children over 12 years.

£19.00 — N — N — Y

Mrs Pam Conrad-Pickles
Liscombe
Hamlash Lane
Frensham
GU10 3AT
Tel: (01252) 794409
Fax 01252 795313
Open: ALL YEAR (Excl. Xmas)
Map Ref No. 04

Nearest Road: A.287
A delightful family country house set in 4 acres of beautiful grounds. A heated swimming pool, & tennis court, close to Frensham Ponds. 3 attractively decorated bedrooms, 1 double, 1 twin & 1 single, all with en-suite facilities. Dinner by prior arrangement. An excellent touring base for Windsor, Hampton Court, Portsmouth & H.M.S. Victory, Petworth Park & Chawton, home of Jane Austen. Approx 50 mins to London, Heathrow & Gatwick. Children over 10 years.

£25.00 — Y — Y — N

Mrs Lynn Legget
Foxholm
Redhill Road, Cobham
Guildford KT11 1EF
Tel: (01932) 867961
Fax 01932 866310
Open: ALL YEAR
Map Ref No. 05

Nearest Road: A.3, A.245
Grade II listed Victorian Gothic detached country house furnished with antiques. Set in 14 acres of woodland, planted with azaeleas, camelias & rhododendrons. Bordered on 2 sides by Silvermere Golf Course. Within 2 miles of M.25 Jt. 10 with the A.3 giving easy access to London by road or rail. Close to Royal Horticultural Society Gardens at Wisley, Painshill Park, Hampton Court, Windsor & both Heathrow & Gatwick.

£23.00 — N — N — N

Surrey

		rate from £ per person	children taken	evening meals	animals taken
Mrs Elizabeth Carmichael **Deerfell** **Blackdown Park** **Fernden Lane** **Haslemere GU27 3LA** **Tel: (01428) 653409** Fax 01428 656106 **Open:** Mid JAN - Mid DEC **Map Ref No. 06**	Nearest Road: A.286 A warm welcome at a spacious & comfortable stone-built home set in downland countryside, with breathtaking views to the hills & valleys of Surrey/Sussex. Accommodation is in 2 pretty en-suite rooms which are very comfortable & have tea/coffee facilities & T.V.. Wonderful walks on doorstep. Light suppers available. Close by - Haslemere station (4 miles), London (45 mins), Guildford/Chichester (20 miles), Heathrow/Gatwick Airports 1 hour.	£20.00	Y	N	N
Mrs Jean Lees **Latchetts Cottage** **Ricketts Wood Road** **Norwood Hill** **Horley RH6 0ET** **Tel: (01293) 862831** **Open: ALL YEAR** **Map Ref No. 07**	Nearest Road: A.217, A.23 Latchetts Cottage is situated in the small hamlet of Norwood Hill, yet is less than 10 mins from Gatwick Airport & the station. This cosy cottage has comfortable accommodation, with a warm welcome & a homely atmosphere. All bedrooms have fine views over uninterrupted countryside. The village pub offers a varied menu, & is within walking distance. N.T. properties & walks nearby. Parking & courtesy transport available.	£18.50	Y	N	N
Mrs G. Blok **Crutchfield Farm** **Crutchfield Lane** **Hookwood** **Horley RH6 0HT** **Tel: (01293) 863110** Fax 01293 863233 **Open: ALL YEAR** **Map Ref No. 07**	Nearest Road: A.217 Crutchfield Farm is a listed 15th-century timber framed farmhouse overlooking its own swan lake, only 3 miles from Gatwick & set in 10 acres of landscaped gardens with swimming pool & tennis court. There are many massive exposed oak beams & an inglenook fireplace. The beautiful bedrooms are tastefully furnished with colour T.V. & tea/coffee-making facilities. London & the south coast 30 mins. Rate includes airport transfer if required. Parking available. A delightful home & an ideal touring base.	£20.00	Y	N	Y
Carole & Adrian Grinsted **The Lawn Guest House** **30 Massetts Road** **Horley RH6 7DE** **Tel: (01293) 775751** Fax 01293 821803 **Open: ALL YEAR** **Map Ref No. 08**	Nearest Road: A.23 A well-appointed Victorian house 4 minutes from Gatwick & 25 miles to London or Brighton. Very useful as a base for travelling, it is close to the rail station & town centre. There are 7 bedrooms, all with en-suite facilities & very comfortable & well decorated, with colour T.V. & tea/coffee-making facilities. Also, a pleasant breakfast room & a garden for guests' use. There is a supplement payable for single use of rooms. Parking. CREDIT CARD VISA M'CARD AMEX	£22.50	Y	N	Y
Mr & Mrs Warren **Ashleigh House Hotel** **39 Redstone Hill** **Redhill RH1 4BG** **Tel: (01737) 764763** Fax 01737 780308 **Open:** ALL YEAR (Excl. Xmas) **Map Ref No. 09**	Nearest Road: A.25 An Edwardian merchant's house situated within 600 yards of Redhill centre with rail links to Gatwick (15 mins.) & London (30 mins.) & 4 miles from M.25 motorway with many historic houses within easy reach. The house is comfortably furnished & offers 8 bedrooms, 6 en-suite. The breakfast room overlooks an English garden. Jill & Michael extend a very hospitable welcome to all their guests from around the world. Parking. CREDIT CARD VISA M'CARD	£24.00	Y	N	N

Surrey

		rate from £ per person	children taken	evening meals	animals taken
Mr & Mrs Philip Wolf **The Old Farmhouse** **Wasp Green Lane** **Outwood** **Redhill RH1 5QE** **Tel: (01342) 842313** **Fax 01342 844744** **Open:** ALL YEAR (Excl. Xmas) **Map Ref No. 10**	Nearest Road: A.25 An early-15th-century mediaeval 4-bay hall house, which is little altered & retains many original features, including the diamond mullions for the hall window & fine panelling. It also has one of the longest unsupported crossing beams in Surrey. 2 of the attractively furnished bedrooms have brass bedsteads, & 1 has an original oak 4-poster bed. A delightful home. The Old Farmhouse is perfect for exploring the south east of England & many places of historic interest. Children over 10.	£25.00	Y	Y	N
Mr & Mrs G. Bussandri **The Cranleigh Hotel** **41 West Street** **Reigate RH2 9BL** **Tel: (01737) 223417** **Fax 01737 223734** **Open: ALL YEAR** **Map Ref No. 11**	Nearest Road: A.25, M.25 The Cranleigh Hotel has a reputation for comfort, cleanliness & hospitality. Its modern facilities include hairdryers, T.V. & a pleasant bar & lounge, etc. Comfortable accommodation in 9 guest rooms. 45 mins from London, & a few minutes from Gatwick Airport, the hotel stands in lovely gardens, which provide flowers & fresh food for the table. Very convenient for travellers to the South-West. Ideal for first or last night of travel.	£35.00 CREDIT CARD VISA M'CARD AMEX	Y	Y	N
Teresa & Kevin Leeper **Knaphill Manor** **Carthouse Lane** **Woking** **GU21 4XT** **Tel: (01276) 857962** **Fax 01276 855503** **Open: ALL YEAR** **Map Ref No. 12**	Nearest Road: M.25 Jt. 11 A delightful, large family home, dating back to the 1700's, set in 6 acres of grounds, with a tennis court & croquet lawn. Located in a farming area, the house is quiet & secluded, yet Heathrow & Gatwick are only a 35-min. drive away. Accommodation is very comfortable, with en-suite or private facilities plus T.V. & tea/coffee makers. A guests' colour-T.V. lounge is also available. Early morning arrivals are welcome. London 25 mins. Ascot, Windsor & Oxford are also easily reached. Children over 8 yrs.	£32.50 *see PHOTO over* CREDIT CARD VISA M'CARD	Y	N	N
Tony & Susie Rowse **Pankhurst** **Bagshot Road** **West End** **Woking GU24 9QR** **Tel/Fax: (01276) 858149** **Open:** ALL YEAR (Excl. Xmas) **Map Ref No. 13**	Nearest Road: A.319 Pankhurst is an attractive & historic Grade II listed country house, set in a walled garden amid 8 acres of gardens & woods. Situated close to the picturesque village of Chobham, it has 3 beautiful guest rooms, each equipped with T.V., radio & tea/coffee, etc. There is also a tennis court & heated outdoor swimming pool. Close to Heathrow & Gatwick Airports, Ascot, Windsor, Sunningdale & Wentworth. 3 miles M.3. 7 miles M.25.	£30.00	Y	N	N

When booking your accommodation please mention
The Best Bed & Breakfast

Knaphill Manor.   Knaphill.

Sussex

Sussex
(South East)

The South Downs of Sussex stretch along the coast, reflecting the expanse of the North Downs of Kent, over the vast stretches of the Weald.

The South Downs extend from dramatic Beachy Head along the coast to Chichester & like the North Downs, they are crossed by an ancient trackway. There is much evidence of prehistoric settlement on the Downs. Mount Caburn, near Lewes, is crowned by an iron age fort, & Cissbury Ring is one of the most important archaeological sites in England. This large earthwork covers 80 acres & must have held a strategic defensive position. Hollingbury Fort carved into the hillside above Brighton, & the Trundle (meaning circle) date from 300-250 B.C., & were constructed on an existing neolithic settlement. The Long Man of Wilmington stands 226 feet high & is believed to be Nordic, possibly representing Woden, the God of War.

Only two towns are located on the Downs but both are of considerable interest. Lewes retains much of its mediaeval past & there is a folk museum in Ann of Cleves' house, which itself is partly 16th century. Arundel has a fascinating mixture of architectural styles, a castle & a superb park with a lake, magnificent beech trees & an unrivalled view of the Arun valley.

The landscape of the inland Weald ranges from bracken-covered heathlands where deer roam, to the deep woodland stretches of the Ashdown Forest, eventually giving way to soft undulating hills & valleys, patterned with hop-fields, meadows, oast houses, windmills & fruit orchards. Originally the whole Weald was dense with forest. Villages like Midhurst & Wadhurst hold the Saxon suffix "hurst" which means wood. As the forests were cleared for agriculture the names of the villages changed & we find Bosham & Stedham whose suffix "ham" means homestead or farm.

Battle, above Hastings, is the site of the famous Norman victory & 16th century Bodiam Castle, built as defence against the French in later times, has a beautiful setting encircled by a lily-covered moat.

Sussex has an extensive coastline, with cliffs near Eastbourne at Beachy Head, & at Hastings. Further east, the great flat Romney Marshes stretch out to sea, & there is considerable variety in the coastal towns.

Chichester has a magnificent cathedral & a harbour reaching deep into the coastal plain that is rich in archaeological remains. The creeks & mudflats make it an excellent place for bird watching.

Brighton is the most famous of the Sussex resorts with its Pier, the Promenade above the beaches, the oriental folly of George IV's Royal Pavilion & its Regency architecture. "The Lanes" are a maze of alleys & small squares full of fascinating shops, a thriving antique trade, & many good pubs & eating places. Hastings to the east preserves its "Old Town" where timbered houses nestle beneath the cliffs & the fishing boats are drawn up on the shingle whilst the nets are hung up to dry in curious tall, thin net stores. Winchelsea stands on a hill where it was rebuilt in the 13th century by Edward I when the original town was engulfed by the sea. It is a beautiful town with a fine Norman church, an excellent museum in the Town Hall, & many pretty houses. Across the Romney Marshes on the next hill stands Rye, its profile dominated by its church. It is a fascinating town with timbered houses & cobbled streets.

Sussex

Areas of Outstanding Natural Beauty
The Sussex Downs. Chichester Harbour.

Historic Houses & Castles

Arundel Castle - Arundel
18th century rebuilding of ancient castle, fine portraits, 15th century furniture.
Cuckfield Park - Cuckfield
Elizabethan manor house, gatehouse. Very fine panelling & ceilings.
Danny - Hurstpierpoint
16th century - Elizabethan .
Goodwood House - Chichester
18th century - Jacobean house - Fine Sussex flintwork, paintings by Van Dyck, Canaletto & Stubbs, English & French furniture, tapestries & porcelain.
Newtimber Place - Newtimber
Moated house - Etruscan style wall paintings.
Purham - Pulborough
Elizabethan house containing important collection of Elizabethan, Jacobean & Georgian portraits, also fine furniture.
Petworth House - Petworth
17th century - landscaped by Capability Brown - important paintings - 14th century chapel.
St. Mary's - Bramber
15th century timber framed house - rare panelling.
Tanyard - Sharpthorne
Mediaeval tannery - 16th & 17th century additions.
The Thatched Cottage - Lindfield
Close-studded weald house - reputedly Henry VII hunting lodge.
Uppark - Petersfield
17th century - 18th century interior decorations remain unaltered.
Alfriston Clergy House - Nr. Seaford
14th century parish priest's house - pre-reformation.
Battle Abbey - Battle
Founded by William the Conqueror.
Charleston Manor - Westdean
Norman, Tudor & Georgian architectural styles - Romanesque window in the Norman wing.
Bull House - Lewes
15th century half-timbered house - was home of Tom Paine.

Bateman's - Burwash
17th century - watermill - home of Rudyard Kipling.
Bodiam Castle - Nr. Hawkshurst
14th century - noted example of mediaeval moated military architecture.
Great Dixter - Northiam
15th century half-timbered manor house - great hall - Lutyens gardens
Glynde Place - Nr. Lewes
16th century flint & brick - built around courtyard-collection of paintings by Rubens, Hoppner, Kneller, Lely, Zoffany.
Michelham Priory - Upper Dicker, Nr. Hailsham
13th century Augustinian Priory - became Tudor farmhouse - working watermill, ancient stained glass, etc., enclosed by moat.
Royal Pavilion - Brighton
Built for Prince Regent by Nash upon classical villa by Holland. Exotic Building - has superb original works of art lent by H.M. The Queen. Collections of Regency furniture also Art Nouveau & Art Deco in the Art Gallery & Museum.
Sheffield Park - Nr. Uckfield
Beautiful Tudor House - 18th century alterations - splendid staircase.

Cathedrals & Churches

Alfriston (St. Andrew)
14th century - transition from decorated style to perpendicular, Easter sepulchre.
Boxgrove (St. Mary & St. Blaise)
13th century choir with 16th century painted decoration on vaulting. Relic of Benedictine priory. 16th century chantry. Much decoration.
Chichester Cathedral
Norman & earliest Gothic. Large Romanesque relief sculptures in south choir aisle.
Etchingham (St. Mary & St. Nicholas)
14th century. Old glass, brasses, screen, carved stalls.
Hardham (St. Botolph)
11th century - 12th century wall paintings.
Rotherfield (St. Denys)
16th century font cover, 17th century canopied pulpit, glass by Burne-Jones, wall paintings, Georgian Royal Arms.

Sussex

Sompting (St. Mary)
11th century Saxon tower - Rhenish Helm Spire - quite unique.
Worth (St. Nicholas)
10th century - chancel arch is the largest Saxon arch in England. German carved pulpit c.1500 together with altar rails.
Winchelsea (St. Thomas the Apostle)
14th century - choir & aisles only.
Canopied sedilia & piscina.

Museums & Galleries

Barbican House Museum - Lewes
Collection relating to pre-historic, Romano-British & , mediaeval antiquities of the area. Prints & water colours of the area.
Battle Museum-Battle
Remains from archeological sites in area. Diorama of Battle of Hastings.
Bignor Roman Villa Collection - Bignor
4th century mosaics, Samian pottery, hypocaust, etc.
Brighton Museum & Art Gallery - Brighton
Old Master Paintings, watercolours, ceramics, furniture. Surrealist paintings, Art Nouveau & Art Deco applied art, musical instruments & many other exhibits.

Marlipins Museum - Shoreham
12th century building housing collections of ship models, photographs, old maps, geological specimens, etc.
Royal National Lifeboat Institution Museum - Eastbourne
Lifeboats of all types used from earliest times to present.
Tower 73 - Eastbourne
Martello tower restored to display the history of these forts. Exhibition of equipment, uniforms & weapons of the times.
The Toy Museum - Rottingdean, Brighton
Toys & playthings from many countries - children's delight.

Other things to see & do

Bewl Water - Nr. Wadhurst
Boat trips, walks, adventure playground
Chichester Festival Theatre - Chichester
Summer season of plays from May to September.
Goodwood Racecourse

The Royal Pavilion. Brighton.

SUSSEX

Map reference

3	Fuente	21	Fowler
4	Field	22	Thomas
4	Waller	23	P. Cooper
4	Trotman	25	Cox
5	Buxton	26	Skinner
5	P. Collins	27	Hook
5	Hansell	28	Pontifex
6	Gregory	29	Mulcare
7	Grocott	30	Field
8	Bruford	31	Francis
10	Blencowe	32	Steel
11	Dridge	33	Apperly
12	Richardson	33	Brinkhurst
13	Wilson	33	Hadfield
14	Scull	34	Woodhams
15	D. Collins	35	Jempson
18	C. Cooper	36	Carver
19	Kent	37	Salmon
20	Birchell	38	Warton

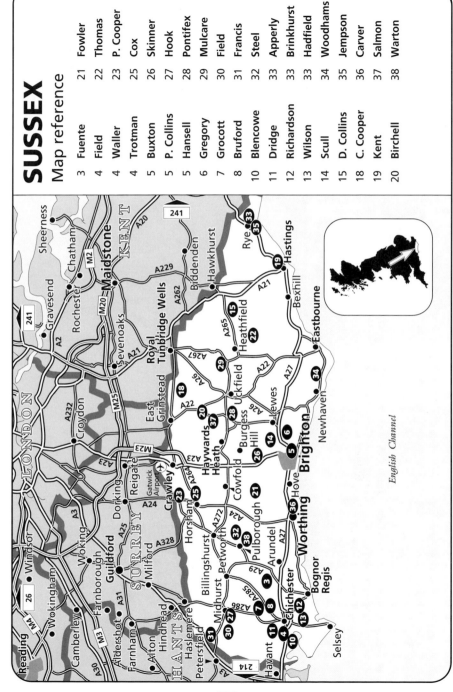

English Channel

407

Critchfield House. Bosham.

Sussex

		rate from £ per person	children taken	evening meals	animals taken
Peter & Sarah Fuente **Mill Lane House** **Slindon** **Arundel** **BN18 0RP** **Tel: (01243) 814440** **Open: ALL YEAR** **Map Ref No. 03**	Nearest Road: A.27, A.29 Magnificent views to the coast. Situated in a beautiful downland village with many miles of footpaths. Superb bird-watching locally. 7 en-suite rooms, each with T.V.. Within easy reach are Pagham & Chichester Harbour, Arundel Castle, Fishbourne Roman Palace, Goodwood, Chichester, the cathedral & the Festival Theatre. Beaches 6 miles. Excellent pubs within walking distance. Evening meals available on request.	£19.25	Y	Y	Y
Mrs Janetta Field **Critchfield House** **Bosham Lane** **Old Bosham** **Bosham PO18 8HG** **Tel/Fax: (01243) 572370** **Open: MAR - OCT** **Map Ref No. 04**	Nearest Road: A.259 Critchfield is an 18th-century village house with a rich welcoming atmosphere. The lovely double & twin-bedded rooms have private or en-suite bathrooms, T.V., hot drink facilities with biscuits & fruit. The excellent breakfast is served in the oak beamed dining room with freshly squeezed juices, homemade marmalade etc. The picturesque harbour of Bosham renowned by sailors & artists is a few mins away. There is a hotel-restaurant & 2 pubs nearby. Children over 8 years.	£22.50 *see PHOTO over*	Y	N	Y
Ruth & Clive Buxton **Adelaide Hotel** **51 Regency Square** **Brighton** **BN1 2FF** **Tel: (01273) 205286** **Fax 01273 220904** **Open: ALL YEAR** **Map Ref No. 05**	Nearest Road: A.259 A warm welcome, friendly service, comfort & delicious food are the hallmarks of this elegant Grade II listed Regency town-house hotel, modernised but retaining the charm of yesteryear. Centrally situated in Brighton's premier sea-front square with NCP parking beneath. There are 12 peaceful en-suite bedrooms, tastefully furnished & equipped with 'phone, colour T.V., etc. A beautiful 4-poster bedroom available. Easy access to A.23, 30 mins Gatwick. **E-mail: adelaide@pavilion.co.uk**	£32.50 CREDIT CARD VISA M'CARD AMEX	Y	N	N
Paul & Pauline Collins **Topps Hotel** **17 Regency Square** **Brighton BN1 2FG** **Tel: (01273) 729334** **Fax 01273 203679** **Open: ALL YEAR** **Map Ref No. 05**	Nearest Road: A.23 Quietly situated in a regency square at the heart of Brighton, the Topps Hotel is only 2 mins walk from the sea & the Metropole Conference Centre with the Lanes & Royal Pavilion nearby. With its friendly welcome & efficient service, Topps Hotel is certainly deserving of its name. The spacious bedrooms are all elegantly appointed, & every need of the discerning visitor has been considered. A charming base for a relaxing break.	£39.50 CREDIT CARD VISA M'CARD AMEX	Y	N	N
John & Daphne Hansell **Trouville Hotel** **11 New Steine** **Brighton** **BN2 1PB** **Tel: (01273) 697384** **Open: FEB - DEC** **Map Ref No. 05**	Nearest Road: A.23, A.259 The Trouville is a Regency, Grade II listed townhouse, tastefully restored & furnished. Accommodation is in 9 attractive rooms, each with colour T.V. & tea/coffee-making facilities. En-suite & 4-poster rooms available. Situated in a charming sea-front square, the Trouville is convenient for shopping, the Pavilion, the Lanes, Marina & Conference Centre & the many restaurants which are all within walking distance.	£19.00 CREDIT CARD VISA M'CARD AMEX	Y	N	N

Hatpins. Old Bosham.

Sussex

		rate from £ per person	children taken	evening meals	animals taken
Mr C. B. Gregory **Braemar Guest House** **Steyning Road** **Rottingdean** **Brighton BN2 7GA** **Tel: (01273) 304263** **Open: ALL YEAR** **Map Ref No. 06**	Nearest Road: A.259 A charming house, family-run, offering 15 pleasant, comfortable rooms with modern facilities. The proprietors really go out of their way to make their guests' stay a memorable one. From here, Rudyard Kipling's house is only 2 mins' walk. The town is a famous smuggling place, with many ancient buildings & a Saxon church. There is a multitude of places to discover in the area, making this an ideal place for touring.	£15.00	Y	N	Y
Mr Allan Bruford **The Bruford's** **66 The Street** **Boxgrove** **Chichester** **PO18 0EE** **Tel: (01243) 774085** **Open: ALL YEAR** **Map Ref No. 08**	Nearest Road: A.27 Opposite Boxgrove Priory (c. 1105 A.D.) & 1 mile from Goodwood. This turn-of-the-century village house, with rear annex accommodation, offers en-suite twin & 4-poster bedrooms, both with r/c colour T.V., radio/alarm & tea/coffee-making facilities. Trouser press in 4-poster bedroom. Approached through the quiet garden, & with its own private breakfast room, this accommodation is renowned for its sumptuous English breakfasts, & features beamed & flint walls.	£20.00	N	N	N
Mr R. Grocott **The Old Store Guest House** **Stane Street, Halnaker** **Chichester PO18 0QL** **Tel/Fax: (01243) 531977** **Open: ALL YEAR** **Map Ref No. 07**	Nearest Road: A.27, A.285 An impressive 18th-century Grade II listed house, adjoining the Goodwood Estate. All 7 rooms at The Old Store have en-suite shower rooms, tea/coffee-making facilities, colour T.V.s, hairdryer & trouser press. A full English breakfast is served in a most charming breakfast room. Car park. Excellent pub/restaurant within walking distance. Ideally situated for Chichester, Bosham, Portsmouth, Petworth, Arundel & Brighton.	£27.50 CREDIT CARD VISA M'CARD	Y	N	N
Mrs Mary Waller **Hatpins, Bosham Lane** **Old Bosham** **Chichester PO18 8HG** **Tel/Fax: (01243) 572644** **Tel: (01243) 575816** **Open: ALL YEAR** **Map Ref No. 04**	Nearest Road: A.259 Situated in the charming, picturesque harbour village of Old Bosham, 3 miles west of Chichester, & near to Goodwood House, H.M.S. Victory & the Mary Rose, this elegant property offers luxurious & inviting interior-designed decor & antiques, including a half-tester & Victorian brass beds, & a sauna. Suitable, & welcoming, for honeymoon couples. All rooms have private/en-suite bathrooms. A charming home.	£25.00 *see PHOTO over*	Y	N	N
Peter & Anna Blencowe **The Old Rectory** **Cot Lane** **Chidham** **Chichester PO18 8TA** **Tel/Fax: (01243) 572088** **Open: ALL YEAR** **Map Ref No. 10**	Nearest Road: A.259 The Old Rectory is a large, comfortable period house, set in a country lane in the quiet village of Chidham. 5 charming bedrooms, 3 with private facilities, a colour T.V., tea-making facilities, a radio & electric underblankets. There is a delightful lounge, with a colour T.V. & grand piano, & a large garden with a swimming pool. Opposite the Saxon church, & close to the village pub serving excellent meals. Chichester Harbour is nearby.	£21.00	Y	N	Y

White Barn. Bosham.

Sussex

		rate from £ per person	children taken	evening meals	animals taken
Susan & Antony Trotman **White Barn** **Crede Lane** **Old Bosham** **Chichester PO18 8NX** **Tel/Fax: (01243) 573113** **Open: ALL YEAR** **Map Ref No. 04**	Nearest Road: A.259 An outstanding unique, open-plan single-storey house with heavily timbered interior. Located in the attractive Saxon harbour village of Old Bosham. Accommodation is in 3 delightful en-suite bedrooms with comfortable beds, colour T.V., radio & tea/coffee-making facilities. Relax in the charming sitting room, with log fire on chilly evenings. Memorable dinners & breakfasts served overlooking the pretty, colourful garden. A very warm welcome. Children over 10.	£28.00 *see PHOTO over* CREDIT CARD VISA M'CARD	Y	Y	N
Mrs Jeannette Dridge **Chichester Lodge** **Oakwood School Drive** **Oakwood** **Chichester PO18 9AL** **Tel: (01243) 786560** **Open: ALL YEAR** **Map Ref No. 11**	Nearest Road: B.2178 A picturesque, Grade II listed 1840s Gothic Lodge set in very quiet country surroundings, yet only 4 mins' drive from the city centre and the Festival Theatre. Accommodation is in 3 tastefully furnished bedrooms with 4-poster beds & en-suite bathrooms. An adjoining garden room has tea-making facilities & a cosy log-burning fire. You are assured of a warm and friendly welcome at this charming home.	£20.00	N	N	N
Lesley Wilson **Crouchers Bottom** **Country Hotel** **Birdham Road, Apuldram** **Chichester PO20 7EH** **Tel: (01243) 784995** **Fax 01243 539797** **Open: ALL YEAR** **Map Ref No. 13**	Nearest Road: A.27 A delightful country hotel set in its own grounds. Offering 9 en-suite bedrooms, 7 on the ground floor, with good wheelchair access. All the rooms have 'phone, tea/coffee facilities, hairdryer, colour T.V. & radio/alarm clocks. Each room has been beautifully refurbished. The restaurant offers excellent Cordon Bleu cuisine. Crouchers Bottom is set in lovely countryside with views of Chichester cathedral. Close to Chichester harbour & the yacht basin. You can be sure of a warm friendly welcome at Crouchers Bottom.	£42.00 CREDIT CARD VISA M'CARD AMEX	Y	Y	Y
Robert & Helen Scull **Longcroft House** **Beacon Road** **Ditchling BN6 8UZ** **Tel/Fax: (01273) 842740** **Open: ALL YEAR** **Map Ref No. 14**	Nearest Road: A.273, A.27 Longcroft House is situated in 2 1/2 acres of garden & meadow, near the foot of the Ditchling Beacon, & within easy walking distance of the ancient village centre. Offering 3 prettily furnished bedrooms (including 1 with 4-poster). Each has a colour T.V. & tea/coffee. (Complementary morning tea in bed.) Helen specialises in fireside dining, & meals are delicious. Homemade bread, preserves & afternoon tea available.	£22.50	Y	Y	N
Mrs D. Collins **Glydwish Place** **Fontridge Lane** **Burwash** **Etchingham TN19 7DG** **Tel: (01435) 882869** **Fax 01435 882749** **Open: ALL YEAR** **Map Ref No. 15**	Nearest Road: A.21, A.265 Glydwish Place is a charming home. A wing of this split-level house, on a lovely wooded site with far reaching views, has been created for your comfort & relaxation. 4 attractively furnished rooms, a double (which can be self-contained) & lounge/dining room & 3 further rooms, 1 incl. an executive 7ft sq. bed. The surrounding countryside is a delight with many interesting places to visit. Lovely walks & good pubs in surrounding villages. Use of games room, sauna, solarium & gymnasium. (Babies & children over 10 welcome.)	£20.00	Y	N	N

Bolebroke Watermill.   Hartfield.

Sussex

			rate from £ per person	children taken	evening meals	animals taken

Mrs Christine Cooper **Bolebroke Watermill** **Edenbridge Road** **Hartfield** **TN7 4JP** **Tel: (01892) 770425** **Fax 01892 770425** **Open:** ALL YEAR (Excl. Xmas) **Map Ref No. 18**	Nearest Road: A.264 A magical watermill, first recorded in 1086 A.D., & an Elizabethan miller's barn offer 5 en-suite rooms of genuine, unspoilt rustic charm, set amid woodland, water & pasture, & used as the idyllic setting for the film 'Carrington'. The mill is complete with machinery, trap doors & very steep stairs. The barn has low doors & beamed ceilings, & includes the enchanting honeymooners' hayloft with a 4-poster bed. Light supper trays are available, & award-winning breakfasts are served in the adjoining mill-house. Children over 7.	£28.50 *see PHOTO over* CREDIT CARD VISA M'CARD AMEX	Y	N	N
Mr Brian W. Kent **Parkside House** **59 Lower Park Road** **Hastings TN34 2LD** **Tel: (01424) 433096** **Fax 01424 421431** **Open: ALL YEAR** **Map Ref No. 19**	Nearest Road: A.21, A.259 Located in a quiet residential conservation area, & set in an elevated position opposite a beautiful park. This elegant Victorian house retains all its original features, but with every modern facility. High standards of hospitality, comfort & good home-cooking are provided, creating an informal, friendly & welcoming atmosphere. Bedrooms are en-suite, & offer every luxury. The 'Apricot' room has an antique French bed. A quiet location only 15 mins' walk from the town centre & sea front.	£23.00 CREDIT CARD VISA M'CARD	Y	N	N
Mrs D. A. Birchell **Holly House** **Beaconsfield Road** **Chelwood Gate** **Haywards Heath** RH17 7LF **Tel: (01825) 740484** **Open: ALL YEAR** **Map Ref No. 20**	Nearest Road: A.275 Holly House, an early-Victorian forest farmhouse with character, offers a warm, friendly welcome to visitors. A 1-acre garden with long views. Situated in an Ashdown Forest village & ideal for touring Sussex, with many N.T. properties nearby. A comfortable lounge is available, & breakfast is taken in the conservatory overlooking the garden. The 5 pleasant rooms, 3 en-suite, have tea-making facilities & T.V.. A small swimming pool heated during the summer. Animals welcome.	£20.00	Y	Y	Y
Richard & Ruth Thomas **Great Crouch's** **Rushlake Green** **Heathfield** **TN21 9QD** **Tel: (01435) 830145** **Open: ALL YEAR** **Map Ref No. 22**	Nearest Road: A.265, A.267 This Grade II country house is set in the conservation village of Rushlake Green, an Area of Outstanding Natural Beauty, in the heart of rural East Sussex. Oak beams, original doors & antiques furnish the house, whilst the bedrooms, both with en-suite or private bathroom, have T.V., books, magazines & tea/coffee-making facilities. 15 acres of garden & pasture, an indoor heated swimming pool, plus a warm & friendly welcome, make this a great place to relax & unwind.	£25.00	N	N	N

When booking your accommodation please mention
The Best Bed & Breakfast

Sussex

		rate from £ per person	children taken	evening meals	animals taken
Mrs Sylvia Fowler **Frylands** **Frylands Lane, Wineham** **Henfield BN5 9BP** **Tel: (01403) 710214** **Fax 01403 711449** **Open: ALL YEAR (Excl. Xmas & New Year)** **Map Ref No. 21**	Nearest Road: A.272, A.23 Frylands is a timber-framed Tudor farmhouse in a quiet setting of farmland, woods & river. There are 3 lovely bedrooms, 1 with private facilities, & all with colour T.V., radio & tea/coffee tray with home-made biscuits. A traditional breakfast, cooked to order, is served with a selection of home-made preserves & local honey. Large garden with heated swimming pool. Good pubs & food nearby. 20 mins Gatwick & Brighton. **E-mail: fowler@pavilion.co.uk**	£18.00	Y	N	N
Mrs Elizabeth Cox **Glebe End** **Church Street** **Warnham** **Horsham** **RH12 3QW** **Tel: (01403) 261711** **Fax 01403 257572** **Open: ALL YEAR** **Map Ref No. 25**	Nearest Road: A.24 Glebe End is a fascinating mediaeval house, with a secluded, sunny, walled garden, set in the heart of Warnham village. It retains many original features, including heavy flagstones, curving ships' timbers & an inglenook fireplace. 4 single, twin or king-sized en-suite rooms, charmingly furnished with antiques & each with T.V. & hot-drink trays. Mrs Cox is an excellent cook, & meals (by arrangement) are delicious & include home-grown produce. Tennis & golf nearby. 20 mins to Gatwick Airport. Animals by arrangement.	£18.00	Y	Y	Y
Peggy Cooper **Blackfriars** **Friday Street** **Rusper** **Horsham RH12 4QA** **Tel/Fax: (01293) 871263** **Open: ALL YEAR (Excl. Xmas & New Year)** **Map Ref No. 23**	Nearest Road: A.24 Blackfriars is a charming country house set in its own 4 acres. Although reputedly dating back to Jacobean days, Blackfriars offers every modern amenity including a swimming pool & tennis court which guests may use. The accommodation in the adjacent guest cottage offers comfortable bedrooms, a sitting room & a fridge. Convenient for Gatwick & central London. A warm welcome from Peggy & John awaits all guests. Children over 2 years welcome.	£24.50	Y 🚭	N	N
Mike & Susie Skinner **Clayton Wickham** **Farmhouse** **Belmont Lane** **Hurstpierpoint BN6 9EP** **Tel: (01273) 845698** **Fax 01273 846546** **Open: ALL YEAR** **Map Ref No. 26**	Nearest Road: A.23 A delightful, secluded 16th-century farmhouse with lovely views, set amidst the beautiful Sussex countryside. The friendly hosts have refurbished their home to a high standard, yet have retained many original features, hence there are a wealth of beams & a huge inglenook fireplace in the drawing room. There are also a variety of tastefully furnished & well-appointed bedrooms, including a super 4-poster en-suite. Excellent 4-course candlelit dinner by arrangement, & lovely 3-acre grounds with tennis court. Ample parking.	£21.00	Y	Y	Y

When booking your accommodation please mention
The Best Bed & Breakfast

Huggetts Furnace Farm. Five Ashes.

Sussex

		rate from £ per person	children taken	evening meals	animals taken

Carol Pontifex **Fairseat House** **Newick** **Lewes** **BN8 4PJ** **Tel: (01825) 722263** **Open: ALL YEAR** **Map Ref No. 28**	Nearest Road: A.272 Comfortable, elegant Edwardian house with 4 acres of garden & pasture, heated covered swimming pool, period furniture & interesting historical & family artifacts. 3 spacious, prettily decorated rooms with en-suite bathroom, including the Edwardian 4-poster bedroom. Warm, relaxed atmosphere. Excellent food with choice of kippers, fresh fruit salad or traditional English breakfasts, & delicious home-cooked dinners & light suppers. Convenient Gatwick & Glyndbourne. **E-mail: bnbuk@pavilion.co.uk**	£20.00 (non-smoking) CREDIT CARD VISA M'CARD AMEX	Y	Y	Y
Gillian & John Mulcare **Huggetts Furnace Farm** **Stonehurst Lane** **Five Ashes** **Mayfield TN20 6LL** **Tel: (01825) 830220** **Fax 01825 830722** **Open: ALL YEAR** **Map Ref No. 29**	Nearest Road: A.272 A beautiful mediaeval farmhouse (Grade II listed) set well off the beaten track in tranquil countryside. 3 attractive bedrooms, all with en-suite/private facilities, radio & tea/coffee. The oak-beamed guests' room has an inglenook fireplace (log fires on chilly evenings) & a T.V.. Super dinners & breakfasts use the best home-grown & local produce. Heated outdoor swimming pool, & 120 acres of grounds. Self-catering cottage (non-smokers). Gatwick 45 mins. 30 mins coast. Nearby, many N.T. properties. Children over 8.	£25.00 *see PHOTO over*	Y	Y	N
Sue & Mike Hook **The Old Cottage** **Didling** **Midhurst** **GU29 0LQ** **Tel: (01730) 813680** **Open: ALL YEAR** **Map Ref No. 27**	Nearest Road: A.272 The Old Cottage is a peaceful 16th-century shepherds cottage, newly restored & extended with a large garden, wildlife pond & panoramic views. Accommodation is in 2 centrally heated twin-bedded rooms with washbasins, clock/radios & tea/coffee-making facilities. Excellent evening meals are available from the local country pubs. On-site parking. For keen gardeners', special garden design holidays are available. A warm welcome is assured at this lovely home.	£20.00 (non-smoking) CREDIT CARD VISA M'CARD	N	N	N
John & Lois Field **Mill Farm** **Trotton** **Petersfield GU31 5EL** **Tel: (01730) 813080** **Fax 01730 815080** **Open: ALL YEAR** **Map Ref No. 30**	Nearest Road: A.272 A Sussex country house set in 15 acres of pasture. A large garden, with a grass tennis court. Delightful accommodation in 4 pleasant rooms, 1 en-suite, each with superb views over the South Downs. Colour T.V.s & tea-making facilities. Log fires in the hall & drawing room. Lovely walks & excellent pubs. Chichester, Goodwood & Petworth Houses, Arundel Castle, Heathrow, Gatwick & the coast within easy reach. Ideal as a holiday base.	£17.50 (non-smoking)	Y	N	Y
Mr & Mrs J. C. Francis **Mizzards Farm, Rogate** **Petersfield GU31 5HS** **Tel: (01730) 821656** **Fax 01730 821655** **Open: ALL YEAR (Excl. Xmas)** **Map Ref No. 31**	Nearest Road: A.3, A.272 This beautifully modernised farmhouse is set in gardens & farmland by the River Rother. All of the bedrooms have en-suite facilities & colour T.V.. There is an elegant drawing room, & breakfast is served in a magnificent vaulted hall dating from the 16th century. There is a covered swimming pool, for guests' use, & beautiful gardens. Situated close to the South Downs, the coast & several National Trust houses.	£26.00 *see PHOTO over*	N	N	N

Mizzards Farm. Rogate.

Sussex

		rate from £ per person	children taken	evening meals	animals taken
Alma Steele **New House Farm** **Broadford Bridge Road** **West Chiltington** **Pulborough RH20 2LA** **Tel: (01798) 812215** **Fax 01798 813209** **Open: ALL YEAR** **Map Ref No. 32**	Nearest Road: A.29 A lovely 15th-century house with oak beams & inglenook fireplaces. Situated in a village with a 12th-century church. 3 delightful rooms, 2 with en-suite facilities. T.V. & tea/coffee makers. A pleasant lounge with T.V. & a lovely garden. Gatwick Airport is easily reached. Parham Gardens, W. Sussex golf course, Amberley Wild Brooks, Arundel Castle, Petworth House. Polo at Cowdray Park. Children over 12 years accepted. Good evening meals available at local inns nearby. W. Chiltington golf course nearby.	£22.00	Y	N	N
Mrs Fiona Warton **No. 1 Lime Chase** **Fryern Road (Off)** **Storrington** **Pulborough** **RH20 4LX** **Tel: (01903) 740437** **Fax 01903 740437** **Open: ALL YEAR** **Map Ref No. 38**	Nearest Road: A.283 Quiet, secluded village location in the South Downs an Area of Outstanding Natural Beauty, with woodland/hilltop walks. Elegant twin, double & family rooms with antiques, T.V., beverage facilities & superior bathrooms including en-suite. Enjoy afternoon tea in the ambience of the conservatory or by the log fire. Traditional English breakfast with homemade bread. Romantic breaks a speciality. Excellent restaurants/pubs within walking distance. Good touring location: Arundel, Goodwood, Chichester, Brighton. Gatwick 35 mins. Heathrow 75 mins. Children over 12 years.	£22.50 🚭	Y	N	N
Jane Apperly **Cadborough Farm** **Udimore Road** **Rye TN31 6AA** **Tel: (01797) 225426** **Fax 01797 224097** **Open: FEB - NOV** **Map Ref No. 33**	Nearest Road: A.259 Cadborough is a lovely country house set in 24 acres with outstanding views towards the sea overlooking Camber Castle & the ancient towns of Rye & Winchelsea. Spacious sunny bedrooms with en-suite facilities & sea views & a self-contained suite with inner hall, bedroom, sitting room & bathroom. Drawing room with log fire. Superb English & Continental breakfast. Short walk from town centre. Children over 8.	£20.00 CREDIT CARD VISA M'CARD	Y	N	Y
Francis & Jenny Hadfield **Jeake's House** **Mermaid Street** **Rye** **TN31 7ET** **Tel: (01797) 222828** **Fax 01797 222623** **Open: ALL YEAR** **Map Ref No. 33**	Nearest Road: A.259, A.268 Jeakes House is an outstanding 17th-century listed building. Retaining original features, including oak beams & wood panelling, & decorated throughout with antiques. 12 comfortable rooms overlook the peaceful gardens, with either en-suite or private facilities, T.V. & tea/coffee-making facilities. 4-poster available. Dine in the galleried former Baptist chapel, where a choice of full English, wholefood vegetarian or Continental breakfast is served. Located in one of Britain's most picturesque mediaeval streets. **E-mail: jeakeshouse@btinternet**	£24.50 *see PHOTO over* CREDIT CARD VISA M'CARD	Y	N	Y

When booking your accommodation please mention
The Best Bed & Breakfast

Jeake's House. Rye.

The Old Parsonage. West Dean.

		rate from £ per person	children taken	evening meals	animals taken
Sara Brinkhurst **Little Orchard House** **West Street** **Rye** **TN31 7ES** **Tel: (01797) 223831** **Fax 01797 223831** **Open: ALL YEAR** **Map Ref No. 33**	Nearest Road: A.259, A.268 This charming Georgian townhouse, with traditional walled garden & Smuggler's Watchtower, is at the heart of ancient Rye. Whilst a perfect touring base, it retains many original features. Open fires, antique furnishings & books ensure a peaceful, relaxed atmosphere. Generous country breakfasts feature organic & free-range local products. 3 lovely en-suite bedrooms - 1 with 4-poster - have T.V. & hot drinks tray. A romantic suite with kitchen facilities in the detached Tower offers seclusion. Children over 12.	£30.00 CREDIT CARD VISA M'CARD	Y	N	N
Mr & Mrs R. Woodhams **The Old Parsonage** **West Dean, Alfriston** **Seaford BN25 4AL** **Tel: (01323) 870432** **Open: ALL YEAR (Excl.** **Xmas & New Year)** **Map Ref No. 34**	Nearest Road: A.259 The Old Parsonage, built in 1280 & reputed to be the oldest continually inhabited small house in England, is situated in a hamlet in the Friston Forest, 1 mile from the Seven Sisters coastline. With chalk & flint walls 2 1/2 feet thick, massive oak beams, stone spiral staircases, log fires & extensive gardens, the house beautifully combines an antique setting with modern comforts. Eastbourne, Brighton & Glyndebourne nearby. Children over 12 yrs.	£27.50 *see PHOTO over*	Y	N	N
Jean & David Salmon **Sliders Farm** **Sliders Lane** **Furners Green, Danehill** **Uckfield TN22 3RT** **Tel: (01825) 790258** **Fax 01825 790125** **Open: ALL YEAR (Excl. Xmas)** **Map Ref No. 37**	Nearest Road: A.275 A listed 16th-century farmhouse, with a wealth of oak beams & inglenook fireplaces, in a secluded setting on the Sussex Weald. All rooms are en-suite, with T.V. & tea/coffee. Home-grown produce & home-cooking. Dining room & lounge with inglenooks & billiard table. An outdoor pool, tennis court & own private trout fishing. Convenient for Ardingly Showground, Sheffield Park Gardens, the Bluebell Railway & N.T. properties & gardens. Coast & Gatwick 30 mins (car). London 45 mins (train). Dinner available for parties of 4 or more.	£19.00 *see PHOTO over*	Y	N	N
Mrs Sarah Jempson **Cleveland House** **Rookery Lane** **Winchelsea TN36 4EE** **Tel: (01797) 226256** **Fax 01797 226256** **Open: ALL YEAR** **Map Ref No. 35**	Nearest Road: A.259 A beautiful listed 18th-century house in the centre of historic Winchelsea, completely quiet & peaceful & with wonderful sea views. Magnificent 1 1/2 acre walled garden with heated swimming pool featured on T.V. & in magazines. 1 double room with sea view & private bathroom, 1 twin room overlooking the rose garden with en-suite shower room. Both rooms have colour T.V. & tea/coffee-making facilities. 2 miles from Rye. 3 mins' walk from 2 inns serving lunchtime & evening meals.	£27.50 CREDIT CARD VISA M'CARD	Y	N	Y
John & Doreen Carver **Bonchurch House** **1 Winchester Road** **Worthing BN11 4DJ** **Tel: (01903) 202492** **Open: ALL YEAR** **Map Ref No. 36**	Nearest Road: A.259 Bonchurch is a home-from-home guest house where a warm welcome is extended to all guests by John & Doreen Carver, resident proprietors for 26 years. bedrooms, all well-equipped with shaver points & an en-suite/private shower/bathroom, colour T.V., easy chairs & tea/coffee facilities. Home cooking is a speciality. Ideally situated in a picturesque setting, yet close to the sea front, shops & entertainment. Children over 3.	£19.00 CREDIT CARD VISA M'CARD	Y	Y	N

Sliders Farm. Furners Green.

Warwickshire

Warwickshire
(Heart of England)

Warwickshire contains much that is thought of as traditional rural England, but it is a county of contradictions. Rural tranquillity surrounds industrial towns, working canals run along with meandering rivers, the mediaeval splendour of Warwick Castle vies with the handsome Regency grace of Leamington Spa.

Of course, Warwickshire is Shakespeare's county, with his birthplace, Stratford-upon-Avon standing at the northern edge of the Cotswolds. You can visit any of half a dozen houses with Shakespearian associations, see his tomb in the lovely Parish church or enjoy a performance by the world famous Royal Shakespeare Company in their theatre on the banks of the River Avon.

Warwickshire was created as the Kingdom of Mercia after the departure of the Romans. King Offa of Mercia left us his own particular mark - a coin which bore the imprint of his likeness known as his "pen" & this became our penny. Lady Godiva was the wife of an Earl of Mercia who pleaded with her husband to lessen the taxation burden on his people. He challenged her to ride naked through the streets of Coventry as the price of her request. She did this knowing that her long hair would cover her nakedness, & the people, who loved her, stayed indoors out of respect. Only Peeping Tom found the temptation irresistible.

The 15th, 16th, & 17th centuries were the heyday of fine building in the county, when many gracious homes were built. Exceptional Compton Wynyates has rosy pink bricks, twisted chimney stacks, battlements & moats & presents an unforgettably romantic picture of a perfect Tudor House.

Coventry has long enjoyed the reputation of a thriving city, noted for its weaving of silks and ribbons, learned from the refugee Huguenots. When progress brought industry, watches, bicycles & cars became the mainstay of the city. Coventry suffered grievously from aerial bombardment in the war & innumerable ancient & treasured buildings were lost.

A magnificent new Cathedral stands besides the shell of the old. Mystery plays enacting the life of Christ are performed in the haunting ruin.

Warwick Castle.

Warwickshire

Warwickshire
Gazeteer

Areas of Outstanding Natural Beauty
The Edge Hills

Historic Houses & Castles

Arbury Hall - Nuneaton
18th century Gothic mansion - made famous by George Elliot as Cheverel Manor - paintings, period furnishings, etc.

Compton Wynyates
15th century - famous Tudor house - pink brick, twisted chimneys, battlemented walls. Interior almost untouched - period furnishing.

Coughton Court - Alcester
15th century - Elizabethan half-timbered wings. Holds Jacobite relics.

Harvard House - Stratford-upon-Avon
16th century - home of mother of John Harvard, University founder.

Homington Hall - Shipston-on-Stour
17th century with fine 18th century plasterwork.

Packwood House - Hockley Heath
Tudor timber framed house - with 17th century additions. Famous yew garden.

Ragley Hall - Alcester
17th century Palladian - magnificent house with fine collection of porcelain, paintings, furniture, etc. & a valuable library.

Shakespeare's Birthplace Trust Properties - Stratford-upon-Avon
Anne Hathaway's Cottage - Shottery
The thatched cottage home of Anne Hathaway.

Hall's Croft - Old Town
Tudor house where Shakespeare's daughter Susanna lived.

Mary Arden's House - Wilmcote
Tudor farmhouse with dovecote. Home of Shakespeare's mother.

New Place - Chapel Street
Shakespeare's last home - the foundations of his house are preserved in Elizabethan garden.

Birthplace of Shakespeare - Henley Street
Many rare Shakespeare relics exhibited in this half-timbered house.

Lord Leycester Hospital - Warwick
16th century timber framed group around courtyard - hospital for poor persons in the mediaeval guilds.

Upton House - Edge Hill
Dating from James II reign - contains Brussels tapestries, Sevres porcelain, Chelsea figurines, 18th century furniture & other works of art, including Old Masters.

Warwick Castle - Warwick
Splendid mediaeval castle - site was originally fortified more than a thousand years ago. Present castle 14th century. Armoury.

Cathedrals & Churches

Astley (St. Mary the Virgin)
17th century - has remains of 14th century collegiate church. 15th century painted stalls.

Beaudesert (St. Nicholas)
Norman with fine arches in chancel.

Brailes (St. George)
15th century - decorated nave & aisles - 14th century carved oak chest.

Crompton Wynyates
Church of Restoration period having painted ceiling.

Lapworth (St. Mary)
13th & 14th century - steeple & north aisle connected by passage.

Preston-on-Stour (The Blessed Virgin Mary)
18th century. Gilded ceiling, 17th century glass

Tredington (St. Gregory)
Saxon walls in nave - largely14th century, 17th century pulpit. Fine spire.

Warwick (St. Mary)
15th century Beauchamp Chapel, vaulted choir, some 17th century Gothic.

Wooten Wawen (St. Peter)
Saxon, with remnants of mediaeval wall painting, 15th century screens & pulpit: small 17th century chained library.

Museums & Galleries

The Royal Shakespeare Theatre Picture Gallery - Stratford-upon-Avon
Original designs & paintings, portraits of famous actors, etc.

Motor Museum - Stratford-upon-Avon
Collection of cars, racing, vintage, exotic, replica of 1930 garage. Fashions, etc. of 1920's era.

WARWICKSHIRE
Map reference

1 Wilson	13 Machin
2 Mahon	13 Wootton
3 Lawson	13 Everitt
3 Powell	13 Andrews
6 Lea	13 P. Evens
7 Walliker	13 Walters
8 Hutsby	13 Spencer
9 Mills	13 Tozer
10 Smith	13 Mander
10 Vernon Miller	14 Crook
11 Mawle	15 Lyon
12 Lowe	16 Draisey
13 S. Evans	17 Stanton
13 Pettitt	18 Howard
13 Workman	19 Trought
13 Castelli	20 Kitchen
13 M. Evans	21 Waterworth

STAFFORDSHIRE
Telford
Galley
Bridgnorth
Wolverhampton
Cannock
Lichfield
Coalville
Ashby de la Zouch
Tamworth
Walsall
Dudley
Birmingham
Sutton Coldfield
Nuneaton
Hinckley
Leicester
LEICESTER
Oadby
Husbands Bosworth
Kidderminster
Bromsgrove
Redditch
Alcester
Coventry
Rugby
Royal Leamington Spa
Warwick
Daventry
NORTHAMPTON
Towcester
Brackley
Buckingham
Stratford
Banbury
OXFORD
Chipping Norton
Worcester
Great Malvern
Evesham
Stow-on-the-Wold
GLOUCESTER

262
115
319
229
182
300
38

M1 M6 M69 M40 M42 M5
A47 A5 A45 A423 A422 A423 A34 A429 A422 A439 A34 A44 A435 A22 A44 A449 A448 A456 A442 A103 A38 A442

8 Clarendon Crescent. Leamington Spa.

Warwickshire

		rate from £ per person	children taken	evening meals	animals taken
Mrs Joan Wilson **Ferndale Guest House** **45 Priory Road** **Kenilworth CV8 1LL** **Tel: (01926) 853214** **Fax 01926 858336** **Open: ALL YEAR** **Map Ref No. 01**	Nearest Road: A.46 You are assured of a warm welcome in this family-run, spacious Victorian house situated in a quiet tree-lined avenue only 5 mins' walk from the town centre. All 7 bedrooms are en-suite & tastefully decorated & include colour T.V. & coffee/tea-making facilities. A guests' T.V. lounge is available throughout the day. Ideally located for Warwick, Coventry, Leamington Spa, the N.E.C., Stoneleigh Agricultural Centre & Warwick University.	£18.00	Y	N	Y
Mrs Kim Mahon **Marston House** **Byfield Road** **Priors Marston** **Leamington Spa CV23 8RP** **Tel: (01327) 260297** **Fax 01327 262846** **Open: ALL YEAR** **Map Ref No. 02**	Nearest Road: A.361 Situated in a conservation village of great charm, Marston House is a stylish turn-of-the-century house. It offers beautifully furnished accommodation in 1 double & 1 twin-bedded room, each with a private bathroom. Guests may choose to relax in the charming lounge or wander around the attractive garden. Evening meals are available on request. Conveniently situated within easy reach of Stratford, Warwick, Leamington & other haunts of interest. Children over 6 years.	£23.00	Y	Y	Y
Christine & David Lawson **8 Clarendon Crescent** **Leamington Spa** **CV32 5NR** **Tel: (01926) 429840** **Open: ALL YEAR** **Map Ref No. 03**	Nearest Road: A.452 A Grade II listed Regency house overlooking a private dell. Situated in a quiet backwater of Leamington. Elegantly furnished with antiques, & offering accommodation in 6 tastefully furnished bedrooms, 5 en-suite. A delicious full English breakfast is served. Only 5 minutes' walk from the town centre. Very convenient for Warwick, Stratford, Stoneleigh Agricultural Centre, Warwick University & the N.E.C.. Children over 3 yrs.	£25.00 *see PHOTO over*	Y	N	N
Bill & Barbara Powell **Flowerdale House** **58 Warwick New Road** **Leamington Spa CV32 6AA** **Tel: (01926) 426002** **Fax 01926 883699** **Open: ALL YEAR** **Map Ref No. 03**	Nearest Road: A.452 Flowerdale House, a Victorian building, stands back from the main road midway between Leamington & Warwick. Offering a warm welcome, the 6 bedrooms all have en-suite facilities, T.V. & tea/coffee trays. A residential licence, with several lounging areas creating an informal atmosphere. The dining room can spill over into a plant-filled conservatory with a very inviting garden beyond. Ideally located for Warwick Castle, Stratford-upon-Avon, Warwick University, the N.A.C. & N.E.C.	£19.00 CREDIT CARD VISA M'CARD	Y	N	N
Deborah Lea **Crandon House** **Avon Dassett** **Leamington Spa** **CV33 0AA** **Tel: (01295) 770652** **Fax (01295) 770652** **Open: ALL YEAR (Excl. Xmas)** **Map Ref No. 06**	Nearest Road: B.4100, M.40 Crandon House offers an especially warm welcome & exceptionally high standard of accommodation & comfort. Set in 20 acres of beautiful countryside. 5 pretty bedrooms (1 ground floor) with en-suite/private bathroom, T.V. & tea/coffee. Log fire. Extensive breakfast menu. A tranquil rural retreat, yet within easy reach of Stratford, Warwick, Oxford & the Cotswolds. Located between the M.40 Jts 11 & 12 (4 miles). Animals by arrangement. Children over 12 yrs. Special winter breaks.	£20.00 CREDIT CARD VISA M'CARD	Y	N	Y

Ambion Court Hotel.   Dadlington.

Warwickshire

		rate from £ per person	children taken	evening meals	animals taken
John & Wendy Walliker **Ambion Court Hotel** **The Green** **Dadlington** **Nuneaton CV13 6JB** **Tel: (01455) 212292** Fax 01455 213141 **Open: ALL YEAR** **Map Ref No. 07**	Nearest Road: A.5, M.69. A charming, modernised Victorian farmhouse, overlooking Dadlington's village green, set in rolling countryside 2 miles north of Hinckley. Rustic character abounds, & each room is well-appointed with en-suite bathroom, T.V., radio, 'phone & hospitality tray. The Pine Room is particularly imposing. A lounge, cocktail bar & excellent restaurant. Comfort, hospitality & exceptional tranquillity for those seeking complete relaxation. No smoking in restaurant/bedrooms. **E-mail: ambion@aol.com**	£25.00 *see PHOTO over* CREDIT CARD VISA M'CARD	Y	Y	Y
Sue Hutsby **Nolands Farm** **Oxhill** **CV35 0RJ** **Tel: (01926) 640309** Fax 01926 641662 **Open: JAN - NOV** **Map Ref No. 08**	Nearest Road: A.422 Nolands Farm is situated in a tranquil valley surrounded by fields, woods & a lake for fishing. The 9 en-suite bedrooms are annexed to the house in converted stables, with some ground-floor bedrooms, some with a romantic 4-poster. Tea/coffee makers & T.V. Dinner must be reserved in advance, & is available in the licensed granary-style restaurant, serving the freshest produce & fine cuisine. Everything for the discerning country lover. Clay-pigeon shooting, bicycles for hire & riding nearby. Children over 7.	£18.00 *see PHOTO over* CREDIT CARD VISA M'CARD	Y	Y	N
Alison Mills **Tibbit Farm** **Nethercote** **Rugby** **CV23 8AS** **Tel: (01788) 890239** **Open: ALL YEAR** **Map Ref No. 09**	Nearest Road: A.425, A.45 Retreat along the pretty country lanes on the border of Warwickshire & Northamptonshire to the haven of this totally secluded 17th-century house, beautifully furnished with antiques, where superb accommodation is offered. The spacious & pretty bedrooms have books, tea/coffee facilities, T.V. & en-suite bathroom. Idyllically situated within acres of rolling countryside, providing an ideal base for exploring an area rich in places of historical, scenic & cultural interest.	£22.50	Y	N	Y
Ken & Jackie Smith **Lower Farm** **Darlingscott** **Shipston-on-Stour** **CV36 4PN** **Tel/Fax: (01608) 682750** **Open: ALL YEAR** **Map Ref No. 10**	Nearest Road: A.429 On the edge of the Cotswolds, just off the Fosse Way in the pretty, unspoilt hamlet of Darlingscott stands this fine, 18th-century, listed farmhouse. The guest accommodation comprises 3 attractive double rooms, each with en-suite bathroom, colour T.V. & tea-making facilities. This is the perfect location from which to visit Chipping Campden. The magnificent gardens of Hidcote & Kiftsgate are just 5 miles away, & Stratford-upon-Avon only 9 miles. Children over 8 yrs.	£20.00	Y	N	N
Rebecca Mawle **Lower Farm Barn** **Great Wolford** **Shipston-on-Stour** **CV36 5NQ** **Tel: (01608) 674435** **Open: ALL YEAR** **Map Ref No. 11**	Nearest Road: A.3400 This lovely, 100-year-old, converted barn stands in the small, peaceful Warwickshire village of Great Wolford. The property retains much of its original form, including exposed beams & ancient stone work. Now tastefully modernised, it makes a very comfortable home. 2 beautifully furnished double rooms with en-suite facilities. A delightful base from which to explore this fascinating area, & within easy reach of Stratford-upon-Avon.	£17.00	Y	N	N

Nolands Farm & Country Restaurant.   Oxhill.

Blackwell Grange, Shipston-on-Stour.

Warwickshire

		Nearest Road	rate from £ per person	children taken	evening meals	animals taken
Mr & Mrs S. Lowe **Folly Farm Cottage** **Back Street, Ilmington** **Shipston-on-Stour** **Stratford-upon-Avon** **CV36 4LJ** **Tel/Fax: (01608) 682425** **Open: ALL YEAR** **Map Ref No. 12**	Nearest Road: A.3400 Large country cottage in delightful undiscovered quiet Cotswold village with country pubs & pretty cottages within easy reach of Stratford-upon-Avon or Warwick. Offering outstanding accommodation for that special occasion. Romantic en-suite double or 4-poster rooms with T.V. & hospitality tray. As an added luxury breakfast may be served in your room overlooking large cottage gardens. Honeymoon apartment suite with whirlpool bath. **E-mail: slowe@mcmail.com**	£22.00	N	N	N
Mrs Liz Vernon Miller **Blackwell Grange Farm** **Blackwell** **Shipston-on-Stour** **Stratford-upon-Avon** **CV36 4PF** **Tel/Fax: (01608) 682357** **Open: MAR-DEC** **Map Ref No. 10**	Nearest Road: A.3400, A.429 A Grade II listed farmhouse, part of which dates from 1603. Set on the edge of a peaceful village, with fine views of the Ilmington Hills & countryside. Good food, log fires & comfortable rooms makes this a great place for relaxation. Accommodation incl. 2 ground-floor en-suite bedrooms, suitable for the disabled, in converted stables. Ideal for touring the Cotswolds, Shakespeare Country & N.T. properties & gardens. Stratford-upon-Avon 7 miles, Moreton-in-Marsh 8 miles. Children over 7 years. Evening meals by arrangement.	£25.00 *see PHOTO over* CREDIT CARD VISA M'CARD AMEX	Y	Y	N
Susan Evans **Oxstalls Farm** **Warwick Road** **Stratford-upon-Avon** **CV37 0NS** **Tel: (01789) 205277** **Open: ALL YEAR** **Map Ref No. 13**	Nearest Road: A.439 This charming, thoroughbred stud farm overlooks the beautiful Welcombe Hill & golf course. It provides excellent accommodation for touring or relaxing in peaceful surroundings. 24 tastefully furnished bedrooms, many with en-suite facilities, T.V. & tea/coffee makers & some with 4-poster. For the keen fisherman there is also a well-stocked trout pond. A guided tour of the farm to see the animals is available. 1 mile from Stratford town centre & the Royal Shakespeare Theatre.	£17.50	Y	N	N
Mrs Eileen Crook **Burton Farm, Bishopton** **Stratford-upon-Avon** **CV37 0RW** **Tel: (01789) 293338** **Fax 01789 262877** **Open: ALL YEAR** **Map Ref No. 14**	Nearest Road: A.46 Burton Farm is a 140 acre working farm only 1 1/2 miles from Stratford-upon-Avon. The farmhouse & barns date from Tudor times & are steeped in the character for which the area is world famous. The accommodation, all of which has en-suite facilities, is quietly situated & enjoys an environment of colourful gardens & pools which support wildlife & a collection of rare birds & plants. The friendly atmosphere & quiet retreat will ensure a pleasant stay. A charming home.	£22.50 *see PHOTO over*	Y	N	N
Roger & Joanna Pettitt **Parkfield Guest House** **3 Broad Walk** **Stratford-upon-Avon** **CV37 6HS** **Tel/Fax: (01789) 293313** **Open: ALL YEAR** **Map Ref No. 13**	Nearest Road: A.439 A delightful Victorian house, in a quiet location in Old Town just 5 minutes' walk to the town centre & the Royal Shakespeare Theatre. Ideally situated for touring the Cotswolds, Warwick Castle, etc.. 7 spacious & comfortable rooms, 5 en-suite, all with colour T.V. & tea/coffee-making facilities. Excellent breakfasts. Private parking. Lots of tourist information available. Guests can be collected from the station. Children over 7 yrs.	£18.00 CREDIT CARD VISA M'CARD	Y	N	N

Burton Farm. Bishopston.

Kawartha House. Stratford-upon-Avon.

Warwickshire

	rate from £ per person	children taken	evening meals	animals taken
Mr R.W. Workman **Ravenhurst** **2 Broad Walk** **Stratford-upon-Avon** **CV37 6HS** **Tel/Fax: (01789) 292515** **Open: ALL YEAR** **Map Ref No. 13** Nearest Road: A.4390 A Victorian town house with a warm & friendly atmosphere. Ideally situated on the edge of the old town & only a few minutes' walk from the Shakespeare Theatre, town centre & places of historical interest. Enjoy the comfort & quiet of this family-run guest house, where all bedrooms have colour T.V. & tea/coffee-making facilities. Special double en-suite rooms available with 4-poster beds. The Workmans are Stratfordians, therefore local knowledge is a speciality.	£20.00 (non-smoking) CREDIT CARD VISA M'CARD AMEX	N	N	N
Mr & Mrs I. Castelli **Minola Guest House** **25 Evesham Place** **Stratford-upon-Avon** **CV37 6HT** **Tel: (01789) 293573** **Open: ALL YEAR** **Map Ref No. 13** Nearest Road: A.439 A comfortable house with a relaxed atmosphere, offering good accommodation in 5 rooms, 1 with private shower, 3 en-suite; all have T.V. & tea/coffee makers. Stratford offers a myriad of delights for the visitor, including the Royal Shakespeare Theatre. Set by the River Avon, this makes a lovely place for a picnic lunch or early evening meal before the performance. Cots are provided. Italian & French spoken. (Smoking restricted.)	£20.00	Y	N	N
Mrs Mavis Evans **Kawartha House** **39 Grove Road** **Stratford-upon-Avon** **CV37 6PB** **Tel: (01789) 204469** **Fax 01789 292837** **Open: ALL YEAR** **Map Ref No. 13** Nearest Road: A.439 Kawartha House is a well-appointed town house with a friendly atmosphere, overlooking the 'old town' park. It is located just a few minutes' walk from the town centre & is ideal for visiting the places of historic interest. Private parking is available. With pretty en-suite bedrooms & quality food, these are the ingredients for a memorable stay. This is a delightful base from which to explore Warwickshire & is within easy reach of the Cotswolds with its many attractive villages.	£15.00 (non-smoking) *see PHOTO over* CREDIT CARD VISA M'CARD	Y	N	Y
Michael & Yvonne Machin **Stretton House** **38 Grove Road** **Stratford-upon-Avon** **CV37 6PB** **Tel/Fax: (01789) 268647** **Open: ALL YEAR (Excl. Xmas)** **Map Ref No. 13** Nearest Road: A.439 Stretton House is a 'home from home' where a warm & friendly welcome awaits you. Very comfortable accommodation at reasonable prices. Pretty, full en-suite bedrooms & standard rooms, all having T.V. & tea/coffee facilities. Excellent full English breakfast, vegetarians catered for. Limited car parking. Situated opposite lovely Fir Park, within touch of the country, yet only 3 mins' walk from the town centre. Children over 8 years.	£15.00 (non-smoking) *see PHOTO over*	Y	N	N
Drenagh & Simon Wootton **Hardwick House** **1 Avenue Road** **Stratford-upon-Avon** **CV37 6UY** **Tel: (01789) 204307** **Fax 01789 296760** **Open: ALL YEAR (Excl. Xmas)** **Map Ref No. 13** Nearest Road: A.439 Hardwick House is situated in a quiet, residential area of Stratford-upon-Avon, away from main roads yet only a 5 min walk into the town. All 14 bedrooms are non-smoking, clean & comfortable, with tea/coffee-making facilities & T.V.. Resident proprietors ensure a warm welcome & attention to detail. There is an on-site car park. Directions from M.40: on the A.439, take the first right turn past the 30 mph sign into St. Gregory's Road, & Hardwick House is 200 yards on the right.	£21.00 (non-smoking) *see PHOTO over* CREDIT CARD VISA M'CARD AMEX	Y	N	N

Stretton House. Stratford-upon-Avon.

Hardwick House. Stratford-upon-Avon.

Melita Hotel. Stratford-upon-Avon.

Warwickshire

	rate from £ per person	children taken	evening meals	animals taken

Mrs Margaret Everitt **Eastnor House Hotel** **33 Shipston Road** **Stratford-upon-Avon** **CV37 7LN** **Tel: (01789) 268115** **Fax 01789 266516** **Open: ALL YEAR** **Map Ref No. 13**	Nearest Road: A.3400 By the River Avon, 125 metres from Clopton Bridge, with private parking & just a stroll from theatres & birthplace. This large Victorian townhouse, built for a wealthy draper, offers excellent accommodation, with oak panelling, central open staircase, a pleasant breakfast room & an elegant lounge. 9 spacious, tastefully furnished bedrooms with private bathrooms, T.V. & welcome tray. Breakfast is individually prepared, completing a comfortable & restful stay.	£25.00 🚭 CREDIT CARD VISA M'CARD AMEX	Y	N	N
Patricia Anne Andrews **Melita Private Hotel** **37 Shipston Road** **Stratford-upon-Avon** **CV37 7LN** **Tel: (01789) 292432** **Open: ALL YEAR (Excl. Xmas)** **Map Ref No. 13**	Nearest Road: A.3400 An extremely friendly family-run hotel. Offering pleasant service, good food & accommodation in 12 excellent bedrooms, with private facilities, T.V., tea/coffee & 'phones. A comfortable lounge/ bar & pretty, award-winning garden for guests' use. Parking. A pleasant 5-minute walk to Shakespearian properties/theatres, shopping centre & riverside gardens. Superbly situated for Warwick Castle, Coventry & the Cotswolds. Hosts can be contacted by fax on 01789 204867.	£24.50 🚭 *see PHOTO over* CREDIT CARD VISA M'CARD AMEX	Y	N	Y
Philip & Jean Evans **Sequoia House Hotel** **51-53 Shipston Road** **Stratford-upon-Avon** **CV37 7LN** **Tel: (01789) 268852** **Fax 01789 414559** **Open: ALL YEAR** **Map Ref No. 13**	Nearest Road: A.3400 A beautifully appointed private hotel situated across the River Avon from the Royal Shakespeare Theatre. 26 bedrooms (mostly en-suite), a cocktail bar, a cottage annex & a garden restaurant. The hotel is comfortably furnished, & decorated in a warm & restful style, with many extra thoughtful touches. The garden overlooks the town cricket ground & the old tramway. Pleasant walks along the banks of the River Avon opposite the Theatre & Holy Trinity Church. Children over 5. **E-mail: sequoiahotel@msn.com**	£25.00 🚭 *see PHOTO over* CREDIT CARD VISA M'CARD AMEX	Y	N	N
Mrs Marian J. Walters **Church Farm, Dorsington** **Stratford-upon-Avon** **CV37 8AX** **Tel: (01789) 720471** **Fax 01789 720830** **Open: ALL YEAR** **Map Ref No. 13**	Nearest Road: B.439 A warm welcome awaits you at this mixed working farm with lakes, equestrian course & woodlands to explore. Situated on the edge of a quiet, pretty village, yet close to Stratford, Warwick, the Cotswolds & the N.E.C.. Accommodation is in 7 delightful rooms, some en-suite. Stabling & fishing available. An excellent base from which to explore the region. Mrs Walters can also be contacted by mobile on 0831 504194.	£16.50	Y	N	Y
Mrs G. Lyon **Winton House, The Green** **Upper Quinton** **Stratford-upon-Avon** **CV37 8SX** **Tel: (01789) 720500** **Mobile 0831 485483** **Open: ALL YEAR** **Map Ref No. 15**	Nearest Road: B.4632 Built in 1856, this Victorian farmhouse is situated in a peaceful hamlet in an Area of Outstanding Natural Beauty. The bedrooms, 2 en-suite & 1 with private bathroom, are furnished with antique wrought iron 4-posters, a pine cupboard bed, old lace & handmade quilts. Award-winning breakfasts with homemade jam & a 'Winton house special' that changes daily. Log fires. 2 village pubs. Ideally situated for touring, walking (Heart of England way) & cycling. **E-mail: lyong@ibm.net**	£23.00 🚭	Y	N	N

Sequoia House. Stratford-upon-Avon.

Moonraker House. Stratford-upon-Avon.

Victoria Spa Lodge. Stratford-upon-Avon.

		rate from £ per person	children taken	evening meals	animals taken
Mr & Mrs M. Spencer **Moonraker House** **40 Alcester Road** **Stratford-upon-Avon** **CV37 9DB** **Tel: (01789) 299346/267115** **Fax 01789 295504** **Open: ALL YEAR (Excl. Xmas)** **Map Ref No. 13**	Nearest Road: A.422 Pretty hanging baskets adorn Moonraker, which is situated on the north-west side of town - an easy 5-10 mins stroll from the city centre. Moonraker is 2 separate buildings offering 19 beautifully decorated en-suite rooms with T.V. & tea/coffee-making facilities. The charming 4-poster rooms also have a garden terrace. Moonraker II has the advantage of a spacious sun lounge. An excellent location from which to explore Stratford & its many attractions. Children over 10. **E-mail: moonraker.spencer@virgin.net**	£23.50 *see PHOTO over* CREDIT CARD VISA M'CARD	Y	N	Y
Paul & Dreen Tozer **Victoria Spa Lodge** **Bishopton Lane, Bishopton** **Stratford-upon-Avon** **CV37 9QY** **Tel: (01789) 267985** **Fax 01789 204728** **Open: ALL YEAR** **Map Ref No. 13**	Nearest Road: A.46, A.3400 Large 19th-century house in country setting, overlooking Stratford canal, with ample parking. A royal coat of arms was built into the gables (with the permission of Queen Victoria) of this Grade II listed building. There are 7 very attractive & comfortable en-suite bedrooms, each having a hostess tray, colour T.V., radio/alarm & hairdryer. 1 1/2 miles from the centre of town. Victoria Spa Lodge is an excellent base for the Cotswolds & Shakespearian properties. Pleasant walks along the tow path to Stratford & Wilmcote.	£22.50 (no smoking) *see PHOTO over* CREDIT CARD VISA M'CARD	Y	N	N
Mrs Margaret Mander **Pear Tree Cottage** **7 Church Road, Wilmcote** **Stratford-upon-Avon** **CV37 9UX** **Tel: (01789) 205889** **Fax 01789 262862** **Open: ALL YEAR (Excl. Xmas)** **Map Ref No. 13**	Nearest Road: A.3400, M.40 A delightful half-timbered 16th-century house located in the Shakespeare village of Wilmcote. It retains all its original charm & character, with oak beams, flagstone floors, inglenook fireplaces, thick stone walls with deep-set windows, & antiques. Offering 7 very comfortable en-suite rooms, all with tea/coffee-making facilities & colour T.V.. A delicious breakfast is served each morning in the dining room. A comfortable lounge is also provided. Children over 3 yrs. A lovely base from which to tour the whole region.	£22.50 (no smoking) *see PHOTO over*	Y	N	N
Mrs Elizabeth Draisey **Forth House** **44 High Street** **Warwick CV34 4AX** **Tel: (01926) 401512** **Fax 01926 490809** **Open: ALL YEAR** **Map Ref No. 16**	Nearest Road: M.40, A.429 This rambling Georgian family home in the centre of Warwick provides 2 peaceful guest suites hidden away at the back. 1 family-sized ground-floor suite with private bathroom, sitting room (with T.V.), fridge & drink facilities opens onto the garden, whilst the other room, also en-suite, overlooks the garden. Ideally situated for holidays or business. Junction 15 (M.40), 2 miles away, brings Oxford, Birmingham (Airport & N.E.C.), Stratford & the Cotswolds within easy reach.	£23.00 (no smoking)	Y	N	Y
Mrs Judith Stanton **Redlands Farm** **Banbury Rd, Lighthorne** **Warwick CV35 0AH** **Tel: (01926) 651241** **Open: APR - OCT** **Map Ref No. 17**	Nearest Road: M.40, B.4100 A lovely 16th-century farmhouse in 2 acres of garden, with a swimming pool. A quiet location, with delightful views over open countryside. Large, beamed bedrooms are tastefully decorated, 1 en-suite with Victorian brass bed. All centrally heated, with tea/coffee facilities. There is a comfortable guests' lounge with T.V., log fires & homely atmosphere. Ideal for Warwick, Stratford, Cotswolds & Motor Heritage Museum. Parking.	£18.00	Y	N	N

Pear Tree Cottage. Wilmcote.

The Old Rectory. Sherbourne.

Warwickshire

		rate from £ per person	children taken	evening meals	animals taken
Carolyn Howard **Docker's Barn Farm** **Oxhill Bridle Road** **Pillerton Hersey** **Warwick CV35 0RL** **Tel: (01926) 640475** **Fax 01926 641747** **Open:** ALL YEAR (Excl. Xmas) **Map Ref No. 18**	Nearest Road: A.422 Docker's Barn is an idyllically situated barn conversion surrounded by its own land, handy for Stratford, Warwick, N.A.C., N.E.C., the Cotswolds & the Heritage Motor Centre. (Jt. 12 M.40 - 6 miles.) The 3 attractive, beamed en-suite bedrooms have tea/coffee trays & T.V. & the 4-poster suite has its own entrance. Wildlife abounds & lovely walks lead from the barn. Hens & livestock are kept. Service is friendly & attentive & French & Spanish are spoken. Children over 8.	£18.50	Y	N	Y
Mrs Topsy Trought **Brookland** **Peacock Lane** **Tysoe** **Warwick CV35 0SG** **Tel: (01295) 680202** **Open: ALL YEAR (Excl. Xmas & New Year)** **Map Ref No. 19**	Nearest Road: A.422 Dating from 1634, Brookland is beautifully situated in the pretty village of Tysoe, resting in the Vale of the Red Horse. 3 prettily furnished bedrooms. A comfortable lounge with an open fire & T.V.. Topsy provides excellent cuisine, using fresh home-grown produce, served in a 17th-century dining room that includes an inglenook fireplace & wooden beams. Tysoe, a conservation area, is well placed for visiting Shakespeare's country, the Cotswolds & the South Midlands. Only 20 mins from Stratford-upon-Avon.	£17.50	Y	Y	N
Ian & Dawn Kitchen **The Old Rectory** **Vicarage Lane** **Sherbourne** **Warwick CV35 8AB** **Tel: (01926) 624562** **Fax 01926 624995** **Open: ALL YEAR** **Map Ref No. 20**	Nearest Road: A.46 A licensed Georgian country house rich in beams, flagstones & inglenooks. Situated in a gem of an English village, 1/3 mile from M.40, junction 15. Accommodation is in 14 elegantly appointed en-suite bedrooms which thoughtfully provide all possible comforts, many antique brass beds & some wonderful, Victorian-style bathrooms. Hearty breakfasts served amid antique oak. A delightful home & an ideal base from which to tour the area & its many attractions.	£23.00 *see PHOTO over* CREDIT CARD VISA M'CARD AMEX	Y	Y	Y
Mrs H Waterworth **Sandbarn Farm** **Hampton Lucy** **Warwick** **CV35 8AU** **Tel: (01789) 842280** **Open:** ALL YEAR (Excl. Xmas) **Map Ref No. 21**	Nearest Road: A.439 17th-century farmhouse in charming village, offering luxury bed and breakfast accommodation. Tranquil setting with lovely views, only 3 miles from Stratford-upon-Avon. Warwick and Kenilworth Castles are nearby; also, many National Trust houses and parks. Of the 5 guest bedrooms, 4 are en-suite and 1 private. Single availability. Residents' lounge and T.V.. Children over 5 please. Easy access to N.E.C. & N.A.C..	£25.00 *see PHOTO over*	Y	N	N

When booking your accommodation please mention
The Best Bed & Breakfast

Sandbarn Farm. Hampton Lucy.

Wiltshire

Wiltshire
(West Country)

Wiltshire is a county of rolling chalk downs, small towns, delightful villages, fine churches & great country houses. The expanse of Salisbury Plain is divided by the beautiful valleys of Nadder, Wylye, Ebble & Avon. In a county of open landscapes, Savernake Forest, with its stately avenues of trees strikes a note of contrast. In the north west the Cotswolds spill over into Wiltshire from neighbouring Gloucestershire.

No other county is so rich in archaeological sites. Long barrows and ancient hill forts stand on the skylines as evidence of the early habitation of the chalk uplands. Many of these prehistoric sites are at once magnificent and mysterious. The massive stone arches and monoliths of Stonehenge were built over a period of 500 years with stones transported over great distances. At Avebury the small village is completely encircled by standing stones and a massive bank and ditch earthwork. Silbury Hill is a huge, enigmatic man-made mound. England's largest chambered tomb is West Kennet Long Barrow and at Bush Barrow, finds have included fine bronze and gold daggers and a stone sceptre-head similar to one found at Mycenae in Greece.

Some of England's greatest historic houses are in Wiltshire. Longleat is an Elizabethan mansion with priceless collections of paintings, books & furniture. The surrounding park was landscaped by Capability Brown and its great fame in recent years has been its Safari Park, particularly the lions which roam freely around the visiting cars. Stourhead has celebrated 18th century landscaped gardens which are exceptional in spring when rhododendrons bloom.

Two delightful villages are Castle Combe, nestling in a Cotswold valley, & Lacock where the twisting streets hold examples of buildings ranging from mediaeval half-timbered, to Tudor & Georgian. 13th century Lacock Abbey, converted to a house in the 16th century, was the home of Fox Talbot, pioneer of photography.

There are many notable churches in Wiltshire. In Bradford-on-Avon, a fascinating old town, is the church of St. Lawrence, a rare example of an almost perfect Saxon church from around 900. Farley has an unusual brick church thought to have been designed by Sir Christopher Wren, & there is stained glass by William Morris in the church at Rodbourne.

Devizes Castle

Salisbury stands where three rivers join, on a plain of luxuriant water-meadows, where the focal point of the landscape is the soaring spire of the Cathedral; at 404 feet, it is the tallest in England. The 13th century cathedral has a marvellous & rare visual unity. The body of the building was completed in just 38 years, although the spire was added in the next century. Salisbury, or "New Sarum" was founded in 1220 when the Bishop abandoned the original cathedral at Old Sarum, to start the present edifice two miles to the south. At Old Sarum you can see the foundation of the old city including the outline of the first cathedral.

Wiltshire

Wiltshire Gazeteer

Area of Outstanding Natural Beauty
The Costwolds & the North Wessex Downs.

Historic Houses & Castles

Corsham Court - Chippenham
16th & 17th centuries from Elizabethan & Georgian periods. 18th century furniture, British, Flemish & Italian Old Masters. Gardens by Capability Brown.

Great Chalfield Manor - Melksham
15th century manor house - moated.

Church House - Salisbury
15th century house.

Chalcot House - Westbury
17th century small house in Palladian manner.

Lacock Abbey - Nr. Chippenham
13th century abbey. In 1540 converted into house - 18th century alterations. Mediaeval cloisters & brewery.

Longleat House - Warminster
16th century - early Renaissance, alterations in early 1800's. Italian Renaissance decorations. Splendid state rooms, pictures, books, furniture. Victorian kitchens. Game reserve.

Littlecote - Nr. Hungerford
15th century Tudor manor. Panelled rooms, moulded plaster ceilings.

Luckington Court - Luckington
Queen Anne for the most part - fine ancient buildings.

Malmesbury House - Salisbury
Queen Anne house - part 14th century. Rococo plasterwork.

Newhouse - Redlynch
17th century brick Jacobean trinity house - two Georgian wings,

Philips House - Dinton
1816 Classical house.

Sheldon Manor - Chippenham
13th century porch & 15th century chapel in this Plantagenet manor.

Stourhead - Stourton
18th century Palladian house with framed landscape gardens.

Westwood Manor - Bradford-on-Avon
15th century manor house - alterations in 16th & 17th centuries.

Wardour Castle - Tisbury
18th century house in Palladian manner.

Wilton House - Salisbury
17th century - work of Inigo Jones & later of James Wyatt in 1810. Paintings, Kent & Chippendale furniture.

Avebury Manor - Nr Malborough
Elizabethan manor house - beautiful plasterwork, panelling & furniture. Gardens with topiary.

Bowood - Calne
18th century - work of several famous architects. Gardens by Capability Brown - famous beechwoods.

Mompesson House - Salisbury
Queen Anne town house - Georgian plasterwork.

Cathedrals & Churches

Salisbury Cathedral
13th century - decorated tower with stone spire. Part of original stone pulpitum is preserved. Beautiful large decorated cloister. Exterior mostly early English.

Salisbury (St. Thomas of Canterbury)
15th century rebuilding - 12th century font, 14th & 15th century glass, 17th century monuments. 'Doom' painting over chancel & murals in south chapel

Amesbury (St. Mary & St. Melor)
13th century - refashioned 15th & restored in 19th century. Splendid timber roofs, stone vaulting over chapel of north transept, mediaeval painted glass, 15th century screen, Norman font.

Bishops Cannings (St. Mary the Virgin)
13th-15th centuries. Fine arcading in transept - fine porch doorway. 17th century almsbox, Jacobean Holy table.

Bradford-on-Avon (St. Lawrence)
Best known of all Saxon churches in England.

Cricklade (St. Sampson)
12th -16th century. Tudor central tower vault, 15th century chapel.

Inglesham (St. John the Baptist)
Mediaeval wall paintings, high pews, clear glass, remains of painted screens.

Malmesbury (St. Mary)
Norman - 12th century arcades, refashioning in 14th century with clerestory, 15th century stone pulpitum added. Fine sculpture.

Wiltshire

Tisbury (St. John the Baptist)
14th-15th centuries. 15th-17th century
roofing to nave & aisles. Two storeyed
porch & chancel.
Potterne (St. Mary)
13th,14th,15th centuries. Inscribed
Norman tub font. Wooden pulpit.

Museums & Galleries

Salisbury & South Wiltshire Museum -
Salisbury
Collections showing history of the area in
all periods. Models of Stonehenge & Old
Sarum - archaeologically important
collection.
Devizes Museum - Devizes
Unique archaeological & geological
collections, including Sir Richard Colt-
Hoare's Stourhead collection of prehistoric
material.
Alexander Keiller Museum - Avebury
Collection of items from the Neolithic &
Bronze ages & from excavations in
district.
Athelstan Museum - Malmesbury
Collection of articles referring to the town -
household, coin, etc.
Bedwyn Stone Museum - Great Bedwyn
Open-air museum showing where
Stonehenge was carved.
Lydiard Park - Lydiard Tregoze
Parish church of St. Mary & a splendid
Georgian mansion standing in park & also
permanent & travelling exhibitions.

**Borough of Thamesdown Museum &
Art Gallery** - Swindon
Natural History & Geology of Wiltshire,
Bygones, coins, etc. 20th century British
art & ceramic collection.
Great Western Railway Museum -
Swindon
Historic locomotives.

Historic Monuments

Stonehenge - Nr. Amesbury
Prehistoric monument - encircling bank &
ditch & Augrey holes are Neolithic. Stone
circles possibly early Bronze age.
Avebury
Relics of enormous circular gathering
place B.C. 2700-1700.
Old Sarum - Nr. Salisbury
Possibly first Iron Age camp, later Roman
area, then Norman castle.
Silbury Hill - Nr. Avebury
Mound - conical in shape - probably a
memorial c.3000-2000 B.C.
Windmill Hill - Nr. Avebury
Causewayed camp c.3000-2300 B.C.
Bratton Camp & White Horse - Bratton
Hill fort standing above White Horse.
West Kennet Long Barrow
Burial place c.4000-2500 B.C.
Ludgershall Castle - Lugershall
Motte & bailey of Norman castle,
earthworks, also flint walling from
later castle.

Castle Combe.

452

WILTSHIRE
Map reference

1	Venables	22	Tucker
2	Roberts	22	Fairbrother
3	Denning	22	Rodwell
4	Sexton	23	Thwaites
6	Steed	24	Sykes
7	Addison	25	Gifford-Mead
8	Stafford	26	Robertson
10	Daniel	27	Lanham
11	O'Flynn	28	Hunt
13	Eavis	29	Threlfall
14	Edwards	32	Humphreys
15	Roe	33	Corp
16	Davies	34	Singer
21	Ross	35	Wilson

Burghope Manor. Bradford-upon-Avon.

Wiltshire

David & Helga Venables **The Coach House** **Upper Farm** **Upper Wraxall** **Bath SN14 7AG** **Tel/Fax: (01225) 891026** **Open: ALL YEAR** **Map Ref No. 01**	Nearest Road: A.420 A tranquil & attractive Cotswold stone barn conversion with a spacious, elegant interior creating a comfortable, relaxed atmosphere. Set in a large landscaped garden with tennis court & croquet lawn as well as an informal parkland. 3 pretty bedrooms have their own private bathroom, T.V. & tea/coffee makers. (8 miles north-east of Bath, near Jt. 17 or 18 of the M.4.) Close to many delightful Cotswold villages. Children over 6. **E-mail: venables@compuserve.com**	£20.00	Y	Y	N
Priscilla & Peter Roberts **Bradford Old Windmill** **4 Masons Lane** **Bradford-on-Avon** BA15 1QN **Tel: (01225) 866842** **Fax 01225 866648** **Open: ALL YEAR** **Map Ref No. 02**	Nearest Road: A.363 A cosy, relaxed atmosphere greets you at this converted windmill high on the hill above the town. The old stone tower overflows with character, & with the many finds picked up by Peter & Priscilla on their backpacking trips around the world. Most of the unusually shaped bedrooms have their own distinctive en-suite bathrooms. Imaginative breakfasts are served beneath the massive grain weighing scales. 5 minutes' walk from the town centre. Children over 6 years.	£22.50 🚭 CREDIT CARD VISA M'CARD AMEX	Y	Y	N
Elizabeth & John Denning **Burghope Manor, Winsley** **Bradford-on-Avon** **BA15 2LA** **Tel: (01225) 723557** **Fax 01225 723113** **Open: ALL YEAR (Excl.** **Xmas & New Year)** **Map Ref No. 03**	Nearest Road: A.36 This historic 13th-century family home is set in beautiful countryside on the edge of the village of Winsley - overlooking the Avon Valley - 5 miles from the centre of Bath & 1 1/2 miles from Bradford-on-Avon. Although steeped in history, Burghope Manor is first & foremost a living family home, which has been carefully modernised so that the wealth of historical features may complement the present-day comforts, which include en-suite bathrooms. A village pub & restaurant within short walking distance. Evening meals for groups only. Children over 10. Single supplement.	£35.00 *see PHOTO over* CREDIT CARD VISA M'CARD AMEX	Y	Y	N
Mrs Elaine Sexton **Elm Farmhouse** **The Green** **Biddestone** **Chippenham SN14 7DG** **Tel/Fax: (01249) 713354** **Open: ALL YEAR** **Map Ref No. 04**	Nearest Road: A.4, A.420 Elm Farmhouse is located in the centre of beautiful Biddestone & is a fine Grade II listed building retaining many original features. 3 attractive bedrooms are offered (1 double, 1 twin & 1 family room), each with private facilities, tea/coffee & T.V.. Built in 1778, the house is situated opposite the pond & is close to 2 village pubs. The charming rooms have views overlooking the pond & walled garden. Biddestone is between Lacock & Castle Combe & is only 9 miles from Bath.	£20.00 🚭	Y	N	Y
Richard & Gloria Steed **The Cottage** **Westbrook** **Bromham** **Chippenham SN15 2EE** **Tel: (01380) 850255** **Open: ALL YEAR** **Map Ref No. 06**	Nearest Road: A.342, A.3102 This delightful cottage is reputed to have been a coaching inn, & dates back to 1450. There are 3 charming bedrooms, all with private shower, T.V. & tea/coffee makers, in a beautifully converted barn. Also, many exposed beams that were once ships' timbers. Breakfast is served in the old beamed dining room. A lovely garden & paddock for guests' use. An ideal centre for visiting Bath, Bristol, Devizes, Marlborough, Avebury, Stonehenge, Longleat, Castle Combe & Lacock.	£20.00	Y	N	N

Wiltshire

		rate from £ per person	children taken	evening meals	animals taken
Mrs Margaret Addison **The Old Rectory** **Cantax Hill, Lacock** **Chippenham SN15 2JZ** **Tel: (01249) 730335** **Fax 01249 730166** **Open: ALL YEAR** **Map Ref No. 07**	Nearest Road: A.350 Situated in the mediaeval village of Lacock, the Old Rectory, built in 1866, is a fine example of Victorian Gothic architecture, with creeper-clad walls & mullioned windows. It stands in 12 acres of its own carefully tended grounds, which include a tennis court & croquet lawn. The Old Rectory offers 3 very attractive bedrooms, all with en-suite facilities. An excellent base from which to explore the glorious West Country.	£22.50 *see PHOTO over*	Y	N	N
Mrs Gill Stafford **Pickwick Lodge Farm** **Guyers Lane** **Corsham SN13 0PS** **Tel: (01249) 712207** **Fax 01249 701904** **Open: ALL YEAR (Excl. Xmas & New Year)** **Map Ref No. 08**	Nearest Road: A.4 A delightful 17th-century Cotswold stone farmhouse, set in peaceful surroundings. Accommodation is in 2 well-appointed, comfortable & tastefully furnished bedrooms, each with an en-suite/private bathroom, radio, T.V. & tea/coffee-making facilities. Hearty & delicious breakfasts are served. Ideally situated for visiting many sites of historical interest, such as the Wiltshire White Horses, Avebury & Stonehenge; many stately homes & National Trust properties within easy reach. Ample car parking.	£18.00	Y	N	N
Peter & Jenny Daniel **Heatherly Cottage** **Ladbrook Lane** **Gastard** **Corsham SN13 9PE** **Tel: (01249) 701402** **Fax 01249 701412** **Open: ALL YEAR** **Map Ref No. 10**	Nearest Road: A.4, A.350 Heatherly Cottage was built in the 17th-century & has a large garden with plenty of parking space & beautiful views towards the Westbury White Horse. Each of the 3 attractive bedrooms is well-equipped & has a T.V. & tea/coffee-making facilities & an en-suite or private bathroom. In nearby Lacock & Gastard there are traditional English pubs which serve excellent lunches & evening meals. The hosts aim to ensure that you enjoy your stay & are happy to advise of local attractions, walks etc. Children over 10 years.	£18.00	Y	N	N
Mrs Jeannie O'Flynn **Wyneshore House** **West Lavington** **Devizes SN10 4LW** **Tel/Fax: (01380) 818180** **Open: ALL YEAR (Excl. Xmas & New Year)** **Map Ref No. 11**	Nearest Road: A.360 Wyneshore House is set in 3 acres of garden on the edge of the village, with views to Salisbury Plain. It offers spacious & elegantly furnished accommodation with a galleried hall. The 2 twin-bedrooms have a private bathroom/shower room & tea/coffee-making facilities. There is a comfortable guest sitting room with a colour T.V.. West Lavington has 3 pubs offering good evening meals & is well-situated for visiting Bath, Salisbury & historic houses & gardens. Children over 12.	£19.00	Y	N	N
Mrs Ross Eavis **Manor Farm** **Corston** **Malmesbury SN16 0HF** **Tel: (01666) 822148** **Fax 01666 822148** **Open: ALL YEAR (Excl. Xmas)** **Map Ref No. 13**	Nearest Road: A.429 Relax & unwind in this charming, award-winning, 17th-century listed farmhouse on a working dairy/arable farm. 6 spacious tastefully furnished bedrooms, 4 en-suite, all with tea/coffee-making facilities, radio & T.V.. A beautiful lounge with inglenook fireplace as well as a secluded garden for guests' use. Meals available in the local pub within walking distance. An ideal base for exploring the Cotswolds, Bath, Stonehenge & many stately homes. Children over 8.	£20.00 CREDIT CARD VISA M'CARD	Y	N	N

Old Rectory. Lacock.

Wiltshire

			rate from £ per person	children taken	evening meals	animals taken

Mrs Edna Edwards
Stonehill Farm
Charlton
Malmesbury SN16 9DY
Tel: (01666) 823310
Fax 01666 823310
Open: ALL YEAR
Map Ref No. 14

Nearest Road: B.4040, M.4
Stonehill Farm is a 15th-century Cotswold stone farmhouse situated on a working dairy farm in the lush & rolling countryside on the Wiltshire-Gloucestershire border. 1 of the bedrooms has its own shower room en-suite, & all rooms have tea/coffee-making facilities. A full English breakfast is served in the guests' sitting/dining room. Ideal for 1 night or several days. Oxford, Bath, Stratford, Stonehenge & the delightful Cotswold Hills & villages are all within easy reach by car.

£17.50 | Y | N | Y

Mrs Judy Davies
Marridge Hill
Ramsbury
Marlborough
SN8 2HG
Tel: (01672) 520237
Fax 01672 520053
Open: APR - DEC
Map Ref No. 16

Nearest Road: M.4, B.4192
A mainly Victorian family home set in glorious countryside, yet only 1 hour's drive from Heathrow Airport. You will be warmly welcomed into a relaxed, informal atmosphere. 3 comfortable & attractive rooms (1 with spacious en-suite facilities) & both bathrooms have power showers. Pleasant lounge & dining room, with books galore, & an acre of well-kept garden. An ideal base for touring this historic area, including Neolithic Avebury, Salisbury, Bath, Oxford & the Cotswolds. Good pubs & restaurants nearby. Children over 5.
E-mail: dando@impedaci.demon.co.uk

£18.00 | Y | N | Y

CREDIT CARD
VISA
M'CARD

Clarissa Roe
Clench Farmhouse
Clench
Marlborough SN8 4NT
Tel: (01672) 810264
Mobile 0374 784601
Open: ALL YEAR
Map Ref No. 15

Nearest Road: A.345, A.346
A warm & friendly atmosphere awaits guests when they arrive at this attractive 18th century farmhouse, which is set in its own grounds & surrounded by lovely countryside. There are 2 double bedrooms & 1 twin bedroom, each with either an en-suite or private bathroom. All well decorated & furnished. Delicious dinners are also served. There is a tennis court & outdoor heated swimming pool. Well situated for Bath, Stonehenge & Salisbury. Ample parking.

£22.00 | Y | Y | Y

Colin & Susan Ross
Chetcombe House Hotel
Chetcombe Road
Mere BA12 6AZ
Tel: (01747) 860219
Fax 01747 860111
Open: ALL YEAR
Map Ref No. 21

Nearest Road: A.303
Chetcombe is a country-house hotel set in an acre of lovely garden in the picturesque little town of Mere. Accommodation is in 5 attractively furnished rooms with en-suite facilities & modern amenities, including T.V. & tea/coffee makers. Delicious meals are served. Guests may relax in the comfortable lounge or enjoy the pretty garden. Ideal as a stop-over en-route to the West Country, or as a base for exploring the delights of Wiltshire.

£25.00 | Y | Y | Y

CREDIT CARD
VISA
M'CARD
AMEX

Mrs Mary Tucker
1 Riverside Close
Laverstock
Salisbury SP1 1QW
Tel: (01722) 320287
Fax 01722 320287
Open: ALL YEAR
Map Ref No. 22

Nearest Road: A.30
An executive's home in a quiet area 1 1/2 miles from Salisbury Cathedral. A tastefully furnished ground-floor suite, with a private shower room, & a double & single room with a patio door opening onto a beautiful flower arranger's garden. A double en-suite bedroom is also available. Guests have their own T.V. & tea/coffee-making facilities. An excellent base for visiting this historic city. Guests will receive every consideration here.

£22.50 | Y | N | N

Wiltshire

		rate from £ per person	children taken	evening meals	animals taken
Patrick Fairbrother & Felicity Watts **Glen Lyn House** **6 Bellamy Lane** **Milford Hill** **Salisbury SP1 2SP** **Tel/Fax: (01722) 327880** **Open: ALL YEAR** **Map Ref No. 22**	Nearest Road: A.36 Situated in a quiet tree-lined lane, 5 mins' walk from the city centre, Glen Lyn is an elegant Victorian house offering 6 individually appointed bedrooms, 4 en-suite & all with colour T.V.. Enjoy a great English breakfast & superb home-produced dinner, then relax in the lounge or listen to birdsong in the beautiful garden. The ideal tranquil base for visiting the cathedral & Stonehenge, & for exploring the New Forest. Ample parking. Children over 12. Evening meals by prior arrangement.	£26.00	N	Y	Y
Mrs G. Rodwell **Farthings** **9 Swaynes Close** **Salisbury SP1 3AE** **Tel: (01722) 330749** **Open: ALL YEAR** **Map Ref No. 22**	Nearest Road: A.30 Farthings is a comfortable old house in a very quiet tree-lined street conveniently close to Salisbury's market square & its many excellent restaurants. There are 4 bedrooms, 2 single & 2 double/twin en-suite, each with tea/coffee makers. Residents' lounge with colour T.V., & an interesting collection of old photos. A delicious choice of breakfast is available.	£18.00	N	N	N
R. R. & L. D. Thwaites **The Old Mill Hotel** **Town Path** **West Harnham** **Salisbury SP2 8EU** **Tel: (01722) 327517** **Fax 01722 333367** **Open: ALL YEAR** **Map Ref No. 23**	Nearest Road: A.3094 Beautifully situated on the River Nadder, this historic Grade I listed mill dates back to 1135. In 1550, the river was diverted through the building to drive 3 water wheels, & the water continues to cascade through the restaurant to this day. A cosy beamed bar serves inexpensive Wiltshire dishes & local real ale. The restaurant offers a full a la carte menu & specialises in seafood. All bedrooms are en-suite & have beautiful river views. Salisbury city is a 10 min walk over the delightful town path.	£35.00 *see PHOTO over* CREDIT CARD VISA M'CARD AMEX	Y	Y	N
Christine Sykes **Elm Tree Cottage** **Chain Hill** **Stapleford** **Salisbury SP3 4LH** **Tel: (01722) 790507** **Open: MAR - OCT** **Map Ref No. 24**	Nearest Road: A.36 Elm Tree Cottage is a 17th-century character cottage with inglenook & beams & a lower garden to relax in. The bedrooms, each with an en-suite/ private bathroom, are light & airy, are attractively decorated & have T.V. & tea/coffee facilities. The atmosphere is relaxed & warm, & breakfast is served as required. Situated in a picturesque village, there are views across various valleys & it is a good centre for Salisbury, Wilton, Longleat, Stonehenge, Avebury, etc.	£23.00	Y	N	N

When booking your accommodation please mention
The Best Bed & Breakfast

Old Mill Hotel. West Harnham.

Wiltshire

		rate from £ per person	children taken	evening meals	animals taken

Diana Gifford Mead **The Mill House** **Berwick St. James** **Salisbury SP3 4TS** **Tel: (01722) 790331** **Open: ALL YEAR** **Map Ref No. 25**	Nearest Road: A.36, A.303 Stonehenge - a lovely walk - is 3 1/2 miles from Mill House built by the Miller in 1785 & set in a Nature Reserve surrounded by water, abounding in old-fashioned roses, wild flowers & birds. Diana & Michael welcome you to share the idyllic peace, the wonderful walks, English pubs, antiquities, historic houses, fishing & healthy eating. Golf & riding available. Help with your itinerary. Children over 5 years welcome.	£20.00	Y *see PHOTO over*	N	N
Mr & Mrs I. Robertson **Wyndham Cottage** **St. Mary's Road** **Dinton** **Salisbury** **SP3 5HH** **Tel: (01722) 716343** **Open: ALL YEAR** **Map Ref No. 26**	Nearest Road: A.30 Stonehenge lies 2 beautiful valleys north, an evening's drive of 15 mins from this idyllic thatched 300-year-old cottage, an English dream set in a N.T. area. Most sensitively renovated for extreme comfort. The views & walks are exceptional, as are the bluebells, lambs & calves in the spring. Ian, a horticulturalist, has created a delightful cottage garden. Excellent pubs nearby. Close to Salisbury, Wilton House, Longleat, Stourhead & Bath. 2 delightful bedrooms with private bathroom, tea/coffee & T.V.. Children over 12.	£20.00	Y	N	N
Suzi Lanham **Newton Farmhouse** **Southampton Road** **Whiteparish** **Salisbury** **SP5 2QL** **Tel: (01794) 884416** **Open: ALL YEAR** **Map Ref No. 27**	Nearest Road: A.36 This historic listed 16th-century farmhouse, on the borders of the New Forest, was formerly part of the Trafalgar Estate & is situated 8 miles south of Salisbury, convenient for Stonehenge, Romsey, Winchester, Portsmouth & Bournemouth. All rooms are en-suite & are delightfully decorated, 3 with 4-poster beds. The beamed dining room houses a collection of Nelson memorabilia & antiques & has flagstone floors & an inglenook fireplace. The superb English breakfast includes homemade breads & preserves & free-range eggs. (Dinner by arrangement.) Swimming pool.	£17.50	Y	Y	N
Mrs Norma Hunt **Bridge Farm** **Lower Road, Britford** **Salisbury SP5 4DY** **Tel: (01722) 332376** **Open: ALL YEAR** **Map Ref No. 28**	Nearest Road: A.338 A warm welcome & a hearty English breakfast are assured at this charming 18th-century farmhouse on a 120-hectare farm on the southern edge of Salisbury. It is within easy walking distance of the cathedral, & has famous views of the spire along the River Avon that flows alongside the beautiful gardens. Centrally situated for touring the area, with many attractions including Stonehenge, Wilton House & the New Forest.	£20.00	Y	N	N
Mrs Valerie Threlfall **1 Cove House** **Ashton Keynes** **Swindon SN6 6NS** **Tel: (01285) 861226** **Fax 01793 814990** **Open: ALL YEAR** **Map Ref No. 29**	Nearest Road: A.419 Southern half of a beautiful 17th-century manor house in a pretty Cotswold village. There are 2 doubles & 1 twin-bedded room, all elegantly decorated, 2 with en-suite/private facilities. The guests' sitting room is located in the beamed attic, whose interior reflects the hosts' joint hobbies of vintage-car & costume collection. A walled garden/garden room is reached via a recently renovated ballroom. 3 local hostelries offering meals within easy walking distance.	£25.00	Y	N	Y

The Mill House. Berwick St. James

Wiltshire

	rate from £ per person	children taken	evening meals	animals taken
Diane & Barry Humphreys **The Old Manor Hotel** **Trowle** **Trowbridge** **BA14 9BL** **Tel: (01225) 777393** **Fax 01225 765443** **Open: ALL YEAR** **Map Ref No. 32**	Nearest Road: A.363 An attractive, Grade II listed, 500-year-old farmhouse, peacefully situated in 4 1/2 acres. Converted barns form a charming ground-floor courtyard complex (traditional lounges in the main house). Many rooms feature antiques, pine & romantic 4-posters. Tastefully furnished, & yet retaining many period features, all have beverage facilities, an en-suite bathroom & satellite T.V.. Parking. A good base for touring the Cotswolds, Stonehenge, Glastonbury & the West Country. **E-mail: queen.anne.house@dial.pipex.com**	£35.00 CREDIT CARD VISA M'CARD AMEX	Y	Y	N
Mrs Lynn Corp **Sturford Mead Farm** **Corsley** **Warminster BA12 7QU** **Tel: (01373) 832213** **Fax 01373 832213** **Open: ALL YEAR** **Map Ref No. 33**	Nearest Road: A.362 Sturford Mead is conveniently located between Frome & Warminster, opposite Longleat with its Safari Park, lake & grounds. Offering comfortable accommodation in a choice of 3 attractive & tastefully furnished rooms, 1 with private facilities, 2 en-suite, all with radio, tea/coffee makers & T.V.. There is also a T.V. lounge & garden for guests' use. This is an ideal base for visiting the ancient cities of Wells & Bath. Cheddar Gorge & Wookey Hole are close by. Single supplement.	£20.00	Y	N	N
Rachel & Colin Singer **Springfield House** **Crockerton** **Warminster** **BA12 8AU** **Tel: (01985) 213696** **Open: ALL YEAR** **Map Ref No. 34**	Nearest Road: A.350 Situated in the beautiful Wylye Valley, on the edge of the famous Longleat Estate, Springfield House is a charming village house dating from the 17th-century. Rachel & Colin welcome you to their home, with its beams, open fires, fresh flowers & sunny en-suite rooms, overlooking the garden & grass tennis court. Dinner by candlelight in the inglenook dining room (by prior arrangement) is much recommended, & is a wonderful way to end the day. Marvellous base for touring, walking or relaxing. Bath, Salisbury, Wells, Stonehenge, Stourhead all easily reached. Single supplement.	£24.00	Y	Y	N
Bernard & Diane Wilson **Home Farm** **Farleigh Road** **Wingfield BA14 9LG** **Tel: (01225) 764492** **Open: ALL YEAR** **Map Ref No. 35**	Nearest Road: A.366 Home Farm is set in a garden of almost 2 acres with an abundance of private parking. Pretty, comfortable bedrooms which contain all you need for a relaxed & happy stay are available on the ground floor, with a double/twin/family room upstairs. Ideal for visiting Bradford-on-Avon, Bath, Longleat, Avebury & many more places of historic interest. A warm welcome awaits you. Evening meals by arrangement.	£22.50 CREDIT CARD VISA M'CARD	Y	N	N

When booking your accommodation please mention
The Best Bed & Breakfast

Yorkshire

Yorkshire & Humberside

England's largest county is a region of beautiful landscapes, of hills, peaks, fells, dales & forests with many square miles of National Park. It is a vast area taking in big industrial cities, interesting towns & delightful villages. Yorkshire's broad rivers sweep through the countryside & are an angler's paradise. Cascading waterfalls pour down from hillside & moorland.

The North sea coast can be thrilling, with wild seas & cliff-top walks, or just fun, as at the many resorts where the waves break on long beaches & trickle into green rock-pools. Staithes & Robin Hoods Bay are fascinating old fishing villages. Whitby is an attractive port where, Abbey, the small town tumbles in red-roofed tiers down to the busy harbour from which Captain Cook sailed.

The Yorkshire Dales form one of the finest landscapes in England. From windswept moors to wide green valleys the scenery is incomparable. James Herriot tells of of the effect that the broad vista of Swaledale had on him. "I was captivated", he wrote, "completely spell-bound....". A network of dry stone walls covers the land; some are as old as the stone-built villages but those which climb the valley sides to the high moors are the product of the 18th century enclosures, when a good wall builder would cover seven meters a day.

Each of the Dales has a distinctive character; from the remote upper reaches of Swaledale & Wensleydale, where the air sings with the sound of wind, sheep, & curlew, over to Airedale & the spectacular limestone gorges of Malham Cove & Gordale Scar, & down to the soft meadows & woods of Wharfedale where the ruins of Bolton Priory stand beside the river.

To the east towards Hull with its mighty River Humber crossed by the worlds largest single-span suspension bridge, lie the Yorkshire Wolds. This is lovely countryside where villages have unusual names like Fridaythorpe & Wetwang. Beverley is a picture-postcard town with a fine 13th century Minster.

The North Yorks National Park, where the moors are ablaze with purple fire of heather in the late summer, is exhilarating country. There is moorland to the east also, on the Pennine chain; famous Ilkley Moor with its stone circle known as the twelve apostles, & the Haworth Moors around the plain Yorkshire village where the Bronte sisters lived; "the distant dreamy, dim blue chain of mountains circling every side", which Emily Bronte describes in Wuthering Heights.

The Yorkshire Pennines industrial heritage is being celebrated in fascinating museums, often based in the original Woolen Mills & warehouses, which also provide workshop space for skilled craftspeople.

Yorkshires Monastic past is revealed in the ruins of its once great Abbeys. Rievaulx, Jervaux & Fountains, retain their tranquil beauty in their pastoral settings. The wealth of the county is displayed in many historic houses with glorious gardens, from stately 18th Century Castle Howard of 'Brideshead Revisited' fame to Tudor Shibden Hall, portrayed in Wuthering Heights.

York is the finest mediaeval city in England. It is encircled by its limestone city walls with four Great Gates. Within the walls are the jumbled roof line, dog-leg streets & sudden courtyards of a mediaeval town. Half timbered buildings with over-sailing upper storeys jostle with Georgian brick houses along the network of narrow streets around The Shambles & King Edward Square.

Yorkshire

Yorkshire Gazeteer

Areas of Outstanding Natural Beauty.
The North Yorkshire Moors & The Yorkshire Dales.

Historic Houses & Castles.

Carlton Towers
17th century, remodelled in later centuries. paintings, silver, furniture, pictures. Carved woodwork, painted decorations, examples of Victorian craftmanship.

Castle Howard - Nr. York
18th century - celebrated architect, Sir John Vanbrugh - paintings, costumes, furniture by Chippendale, Sheraton, Adam. Not to be missed.

East Riddlesden Hall - Keighley
17th century manor house with fishponds & historic barns, one of which is regarded as very fine example of mediaeval tithe barn.

Newby Hall - Ripon
17th century Wren style extended by Robert Adam. Gobelins tapestry, Chippendale furniture, sculpture galleries with Roman rotunda, statuary. Award-winning gardens.

Nostell Priory - Wakefield
18th century, Georgian mansion, Chippendale furniture, paintings.

Burton Constable Hall - Hull
16th century, Elizabethan, remodelled in Georgian period. Stained glass, Hepplewhite furniture, gardens by Capability Brown.

Ripley Castle - Harrogate
14th century, parts dating during 16th & 18th centuries. Priest hole, armour & weapons, beautiful ceilings.

The Treasurer's House - York
17th & 18th centuries, splendid interiors, furniture, pictures.

Harewood House - Leeds
18th century - Robert Adam design, Chippendale furniture, Italian & English paintings. Sevres & Chinese porcelain.

Benningbrough Hall - York
18th century. Highly decorative woodwork, oak staircase, friezes etc. Splendid hall.

Markenfield Hall - Ripon
14th to 16th century - fine Manor house surrounded by moat.

Heath Hall - Wakefield

18th century, palladian. Fine woodwork & plasterwork, rococo ceilings, excellent furniture, paintings & porcelain

Bishops House - Sheffield
16th century. Only complete timber framed yeoman farmhouse surviving. Vernacular architecture. Superb

Skipton Castle- Skipton
One of the most complete & well preserved mediaeval castles in England.

Cathedral & Churches

York Minster
13th century. Greatest Gothic Cathedral north of the Alps. Imposing grandeur - superb Chapter house, contains half of the mediaeval stained glass of England. Outstandingly beautiful.

York (All Saints, North Street)
15th century roofing in parts - 18th century pulpit wonderful mediaeval glass.

Ripon Cathedral
12th century - though in some parts Saxon in origin. Decorated choir stalls - gables buttresses. Church of 672 preserved in crypt, , Caxton Book, ecclesiastic treasures.

Bolton Percy (All Saints)
15th century.
Maintains original glass in east window. Jacobean font cover. Georgian pulpit. Interesting monuments.

Rievaulx Abbey
12th century, masterpiece of Early English architecture.
One of three great Cistercian Abbeys built in Yorkshire.
Impressive ruins.

Campsall (St. Mary Magdalene)
Fine Norman tower - 15th century rood screen, carved & painted stone altar.

Fountains Abbey - Ripon
Ruins of England's greatest mediaeval abbey - surrounded by wonderful landscaped gardens. Enormous tower, vaulted cellar 300 feet long.

Whitby (St. Mary)
12th century tower & doorway, 18th century remodelling - box pews much interior woodwork painted - galleries. High pulpit. Table tombs.

Yorkshire

Whitby Abbey - Whitby (St. Hilda)
7th century superb ruin - venue of Synod of 664. Destroyed by Vikings, restored 1078 - magnificent north transept.
Halifax (St. John the Baptist)
12th century origins, showing work from each succeeding century - heraldic ceilings. Cromwell glass.
Beverley Minster - Beverley
14th century. Fine Gothic Minster - remarkable mediaeval effigies of musicians playing instruments. Founded as monastery in 700.
Bolton Priory - Nr. Skipton
Nave of Augustinian Priory, now Bolton's Parish Church, amidst ruins of choir & transepts, in beautiful riverside setting.
Selby Abbey - Selby
11th century Benedictine abbey of which the huge church remains. Roof & furnishings are modern after a fire of 1906, but the stonework is intact.

Museums & Galleries

Aldborough Roman Museum - Boroughbridge
Remnants of Roman period of the town - coins, glass, pottery, etc.
Great Ayton
Home of Captain Cook, explorer & seaman. Exhibits of maps, etc.
Art Gallery - City of York
Modern paintings, Old Masters, watercolours, prints, ceramics.
Lotherton Hall - Nr. Leeds
Museum with furniture, paintings, silver, works of art from the Leeds collection & oriental art gallery.
National Railway Museum - York
Devoted to railway engineering & its development.
York Castle Museum
The Kirk Collection of bygones including cobbled streets, shops, costumes, toys, household & farm equipment - fascinating collection.
Cannon Hall Art Gallery - Barnsley
18th century house with fine furniture & glass, etc. Flemish & Dutch paintings. Also houses museum of the 13/18 Royal Hussars.
Mappin Art Gallery - Sheffield
Works from 18th,19th & 20th century.

Graves Art gallery-Sheffield.
British portraiture. European works, & examples of Asian & African art. Loan exhibitions are held there.
Royal Pump Room Museum - Harrogate
Original sulphur well used in the Victorian Spa. Local history costume & pottery.
Bolling Hall - Bradford
A period house with mixture of styles - collections of 17th century oak furniture, domestic utensils, toys & bygones.
Georgian Theatre - Richmond
Oldest theatre in the country - interesting theatrical memorabilia.
Jorvik Viking Centre - York
Recently excavated site in the centre of York showing hundreds of artifacts dating from the Viking period. One of the most important archaeological discoveries this century.
Abbey House Museum - Kirkstall, Leeds
Illustrated past 300 years of Yorkshire life. Shows 3 full streets from 19th century with houses, shops & workplaces.
Piece Hall - Halifax
Remarkable building - constructed around huge quadrangle - now Textile Industrial Museum, Art Gallery & has craft & antique shops.
National Museum of Photography, Film & Television - Bradford
Displays look at art & science of photography, film & T.V. Britain's only IMAX arena.
The Colour Museum - Bradford
Award-winning interactive museum,which allows visitors to explore the world of colour & discover the story of dyeing & textile printing.
Calderdale Industrial Museum - Halifax
Social & industrial Museum of the year 1987
Shibden Hall & Folk Museum of Halifax
Half-timbered house with folk museum, farmland, miniature train & boating lake.
Leeds City Art Gallery & Henry Moore Sculpture Gallery
Yorkshire Sculpture Park - Wakefield
Yorkshire Museum of Farming - Murton
Award-winning museum of farming & the countryside.

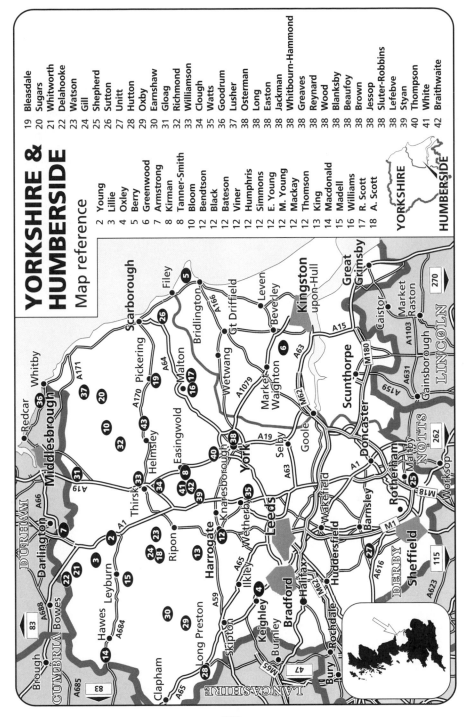

YORKSHIRE & HUMBERSIDE

Map reference

#	Name		#	Name
2	Young		19	Bleasdale
3	Lillie		20	Sugars
4	Oxley		21	Whitworth
5	Berry		22	Delahooke
6	Greenwood		23	Watson
7	Armstrong		24	Gill
8	Kirman		25	Shepherd
8	Tanner-Smith		26	Sutton
10	Bloom		27	Unitt
12	Bendtson		28	Hutton
12	Black		29	Oxby
12	Bateson		30	Earnshaw
12	Viner		31	Gloag
12	Humphris		32	Richmond
12	Simmons		33	Williamson
12	E. Young		34	Clough
12	M. Young		35	Watts
12	Mackay		36	Goodrum
12	Thomson		37	Lusher
13	King		38	Osterman
14	Macdonald		38	Long
15	Madell		38	Easton
16	Williams		38	Jackman
17	R. Scott		38	Whitbourn-Hammond
18	A. Scott		38	Greaves
			38	Reynard
			38	Wood
			38	Blanksby
			38	Beaufoy
			38	Brown
			38	Jessop
			38	Sluter-Robbins
			38	Lefebve
			39	Styan
			40	Thompson
			41	White
			42	Braithwaite

YORKSHIRE

HUMBERSIDE

Elmfield Country House. Arrathorne.

Yorkshire

		rate from £ per person	children taken	evening meals	animals taken
Jane & Peter Young **The Old Vicarage** **Crakehall** **Bedale** **DL8 1HE** **Tel: (01677) 422967** **Open: ALL YEAR** **Map Ref No. 02**	Nearest Road: A.684 The Old Vicarage is a charming Georgian house set in a lovely garden of 1 acre, with many unusual plants. Cosy afternoon teas, & evening drinks served in front of a log fire. Hearty breakfasts, including home-cooked ham, fruits from the garden & home-made preserves. 5 spacious bedrooms - some en-suite - with tea/coffee-making facilities, colour T.V. & radio. An ideal base for exploring the Dales & Moors. Local golf club & riding nearby. Children over 5.	£20.00 (no smoking)	Y	N	N
James & Edith Lillie **Elmfield House** **Arrathorne** **Bedale DL8 1NE** **Tel: (01677) 450558** **Fax 01677 450557** **Open: ALL YEAR** **Map Ref No. 03**	Nearest Road: A.1, A.684 Located in its own grounds in the country. Enjoy a relaxed, friendly atmosphere in spacious surroundings, with a high standard of furnishings. 9 en-suite bedrooms comprising twin bedded, double & family rooms. 2 rooms have been adapted for disabled guests, & another has a 4-poster bed. All rooms have satellite colour T.V., 'phone, radio/alarm & tea/coffee makers. A games room & solarium are also available. Excellent farmhouse cooking. Residential licence. A delightful home.	£21.00 *see PHOTO over* CREDIT CARD VISA M'CARD	Y	Y	N
Mrs Patricia Oxley **Five Rise Locks Hotel** **Beck Lane** **Bingley BD16 4DD** **Tel: (01274) 565296** **Fax 01274 568828** **Open: ALL YEAR (Excl.** **Xmas & New Year)** **Map Ref No. 04**	Nearest Road: A.650 Standing in mature terraced gardens overlooking the Aire Valley, minutes' walk from Bingley & the Five Rise Locks. Each of the attractive & well-appointed en-suite bedrooms has been individually designed & tastefully furnished. Enjoy delicious home-cooking prepared with intelligence & imagination - wines from a well-chosen list, in elegant yet comfortable surroundings. Experience Haworth - the Brontes, Esholt, steam trains, museums & tranquil, vast open spaces. An excellent spot for a relaxing break.	£20.00 CREDIT CARD VISA M'CARD	Y	Y	Y
Lesley Berry **The Manor House** **Flamborough** **Bridlington YO15 1PD** **Tel: (01262) 850943** **Fax 01262 850943** **Open: ALL YEAR (Excl. Xmas)** **Map Ref No. 05**	Nearest Road: A.165, A.166 A manor of Flamborough is recorded in the Domesday Book. The current Georgian house is a handsomely proportioned family home offering spacious & comfortable accommodation in well-appointed rooms. Historic Flamborough Head is designated a Heritage Coast, with many interesting walks & a nearby bird reserve. Ideally placed for exploration of North & East Yorkshire. Dinner, by prior arrangement, features local seafood when available. Children over 8 yrs.	£30.00 CREDIT CARD VISA M'CARD AMEX	Y	Y	N
Mrs P. B. Greenwood **Rudstone Walk Farm** **South Cave** **Brough HU15 2AH** **Tel: (01430) 422230** **Fax 01430 424552** **Open: ALL YEAR** **Map Ref No. 06**	Nearest Road: A.1034 Rudstone Walk is renowned for its hospitality & good food. Accommodation is in the very tastefully converted farm buildings, adjacent to the main farmhouse where meals are served. Each of the attractive bedrooms has excellent en-suite facilities, colour T.V., 'phone, hairdryer & much more. Rudstone provides a peaceful retreat after a tiring day. It is ideal for a relaxing break, & is within easy reach of York & many other attractions.	£25.50 CREDIT CARD VISA M'CARD AMEX	Y	Y	N

Clow-beck House. Croft-on-Tees.

Yorkshire

			rate from £ per person	children taken	evening meals	animals taken
Heather & David Armstrong **Clow Beck House** **Monk End Farm** **Croft-on-Tees** **Darlington DL2 2SW** **Tel: (01325) 721075** **Fax 01325 720419** **Open: ALL YEAR** **Map Ref No. 07**	Nearest Road: A.1, A.167 Clow Beck House is decorated with some flamboyance - chandeliers, antiques & Adam-style panels. This award-winning country house exudes warmth, friendliness & relaxation with a tinge of luxury. 11 beautiful, individually styled en-suite rooms with many extras. Excellent for Herriot country, York & the Dales - route planning is your hosts' speciality. Facilities are available for families & those with impaired mobility. Be pampered with old-fashioned hospitality & service, coupled with delicious food in an oasis of calm.	*see PHOTO over* CREDIT CARD VISA M'CARD	£25.00	Y	N	N
Christine & John Kirman **The Old Vicarage** **Market Place** **Easingwold YO6 3AL** **Tel: (01347) 821015** **Fax 01347 823465** **Open: FEB - NOV** **Map Ref No. 08**	Nearest Road: A.19 A listed property of immense character built in the 18th century & thoughtfully brought up to modern standards, & yet still retaining many delightful features. Now offering 5 en-suite rooms with T.V. & tea/coffee makers. Standing in extensive lawned gardens, overlooking the market square, & with a croquet lawn & a walled rose garden, it is an ideal touring centre for York, the Dales, the Yorkshire Moors & 'Herriot' countryside. Parking.	*see PHOTO over*	£22.50	Y	N	N
Mrs D. Tanner-Smith **Alderside** **Thirsk Road** **Easingwold** **YO6 3HJ** **Tel: (01347) 822132** **Open: ALL YEAR** **Map Ref No. 08**	Nearest Road: A.19 Alderside is a comfortable Edwardian former school house set in large private gardens. 2 comfortable double bedrooms, with en-suite/ private bathroom, & 1 twin room with basin for a relative/friend, each with T.V., radio & tea/coffee facilities. A full English breakfast is served using local produce & home-made preserves. A pleasant walk to Easingwold market place, with its variety of shops, pubs, etc. Easy access to York & surrounding countryside. Children over 12. **E-mail: john.tsmith@btinternet.com**		£19.00	Y	N	N
Dr & Mrs M.S. Bloom **Manor House Farm** **Ingleby Greenhow** **Great Ayton** **TS9 6RB** **Tel: (01642) 722384** **Open: ALL YEAR (Excl. Xmas)** **Map Ref No. 10**	Nearest Road: A.172 A charming old farm in idyllic surroundings at the foot of the Cleveland Hills in the North York Moors National Park. Set in park & woodland, this lovely house, with beams & open fires, has 3 delightful rooms with en-suite/private facilities, a pretty lounge, with T.V. for guests, & a garden. Very friendly, personal service. The hosts are proud of their reputation for fine cooking. Wine & dine by candlelight. Horse riding & golf locally, plus stabling if you can bring your own mount. Children over 12 welcome. Animals by arrangement.	CREDIT CARD VISA M'CARD	£27.50	Y	Y	Y
John & Roberta Black **Alexa House Hotel** **26 Ripon Road** **Harrogate HG1 2JJ** **Tel: (01423) 501988** **Fax 01423 504086** **Open: ALL YEAR** **Map Ref No. 12**	Nearest Road: A.61 Built in 1830 for Baron de Ferrier, Alexa House & Stable Cottages is now an elegant & welcoming small hotel. It is conveniently situated within 5 mins' walk of the town centre where the many restaurants are a gourmet's delight. With its tasteful decoration, warm hospitality & a breakfast that's second to none, it offers 13 en-suite bedrooms, a licensed bar, large car park & a chance to unwind at one of the north's finest health & fitness spas.	CREDIT CARD VISA M'CARD AMEX	£27.00	Y	Y	N

The Old Vicarage. Easingwold.

Yorkshire

		rate from £ per person	children taken	evening meals	animals taken
Gill & Kristian Bendtson **Ashwood House** **7 Spring Grove** **Harrogate HG1 2HS** **Tel: (01423) 560081** **Fax 01423 527928** **Open: ALL YEAR (Excl. Xmas & New Year)** **Map Ref No. 12**	Nearest Road: A.61 A charming 9 bedroomed Edwardian house retaining many of its original features quietly situated in a residential cul-de-sac mins from the town centre. The attractive en-suite bedrooms are spacious, some with 4-poster beds, all with hospitality tray, T.V., hairdryer & complimentary toiletries. A delicious breakfast is served from lovely Royal Copenhagen china in the elegant dining room. A high standard of service & a warm welcome is assured. Scandinavian languages spoken. Children over 7 years.	£23.00	Y	N	N
Peter & Dee Bateson **Acacia Lodge** **21 Ripon Road** **Harrogate** **HG1 2JL** **Tel: (01423) 560752** **Fax 01423 503725** **Open: ALL YEAR** **Map Ref No. 12**	Nearest Road: A.61 Acacia Lodge is a warm, lovingly restored & charming small family-run hotel with pretty gardens in a select central conservation area just a short stroll from Harrogate's fashionable shops, many restaurants & attractions. It retains all its original character with fine furnishings, antiques & old paintings. Bedrooms are en-suite & well-furnished with every comfort. Award-winning breakfasts served in the oak furnished dining room & guests can relax in the lounge with open fire & library of books. Private floodlit car park. Children over 7.	£25.00	Y	N	N
Rupert & Marian Viner **Delaine Hotel, 17 Ripon Rd** **Harrogate HG1 2JL** **Tel: (01423) 567974** **Fax 01423 561723** **Open: ALL YEAR (Excl. Xmas)** **Map Ref No. 12**	Nearest Road: A.61 The Delaine is a Victorian, family-run hotel set in beautiful award-winning gardens. Offering guests a warm welcome & the personal attention of owners Rupert & Marian Viner. All of the delightful bedrooms have en-suite facilities, are very comfortable & have co-ordinated furnishings, & all the usual amenities & more. Excellent home-cooked meals are available. This is the perfect base for touring the Yorkshire Dales.	£27.50 CREDIT CARD VISA M'CARD AMEX	Y	Y	N
Mrs Julia Humphris **Crescent Lodge** **20 Swan Road** **Harrogate** **HG1 2SA** **Tel: (01423) 503688** **Fax 01423 503688** **Open: ALL YEAR (Excl. Xmas)** **Map Ref No. 12**	Nearest Road: A.61, A.1 This charming, period, Grade II listed family home, overlooking crescent gardens & only a short walk from the Valley Gardens & Pump Rooms, offers 4 well-appointed rooms, 2 en-suite, each with tea/coffee makers & complimentary toiletries. A hairdryer & laundry facilities available. An elegant guests' drawing room with colour T.V.. Ideally placed for the conference centre, exhibition halls, shops & theatre, as well as Yorkshire's finest Dales scenery. French, German & Spanish spoken.	£23.00	N	N	N
Mrs Elizabeth Young **Daryl House Hotel** **42 Dragon Parade** **Harrogate HG1 5DA** **Tel: (01423) 502775** **Open: ALL YEAR** **Map Ref No. 12**	Nearest Road: A.59 A small, friendly, family-run house offering excellent accommodation in 6 most pleasant rooms with every modern comfort. Tea/coffee makers & T.V. in all rooms. An attractive lounge with colour T.V. & garden for guests' enjoyment. Home-cooked food & personal attention are the hallmarks of Daryl House. Close to the town centre with its conference facilities. A very warm welcome awaits all visitors.	£16.00	Y	Y	Y

High Winsley Cottage. Burnt Yates.

Yorkshire

		rate from £ per person	children taken	evening meals	animals taken
John & Maria Simmons **The Ruskin Hotel** **1 Swan Road** **Harrogate** **HG1 2SS** **Tel: (01423) 502045** **Fax 01423 506131** **Open: ALL YEAR** **Map Ref No. 12**	Nearest Road: A.61, A.1 A truly outstanding small Victorian hotel, set in lovely lawned grounds (with a car park). In a quiet conservation area only mins' stroll from the town, theatres & magnificent gardens. Beautiful, spacious en-suite bedrooms, antique furnished & offering every facility. Superior beds including 4-poster. Charming drawing room with open fire, antique furniture & books create a relaxed atmosphere. Renowned for superb breakfasts & English/French cuisine served in the Victorian style restaurant. A warm welcome awaits you.	£35.00 CREDIT CARD VISA M'CARD	Y	Y	N
Mike & Tricia Young **Shannon Court Hotel** **65 Dragon Avenue** **Harrogate HG1 5DS** **Tel: (01423) 509858** **Fax 01423 530606** **Open: ALL YEAR (Excl. Xmas & New Year)** **Map Ref No. 12**	Nearest Road: A.59 Charming Victorian house hotel overlooking the 'stray' in High Harrogate. Enjoy real home cooking in this family-run hotel. Accommodation is in 8 delightful bedrooms, all of which are en-suite & have every modern comfort including radio, colour T.V. & tea/coffee-making facilities. Licensed for residents & their guests. Close to town centre, railway station & conference centre, with easy parking, & direct to main routes for moors & dales. Shannon Court Hotel is an excellent touring base.	£23.00	Y	Y	N
Mrs Jennifer Mackay **Franklin View** **19 Grove Road** **Harrogate HG1 5EW** **Tel: (01423) 541388** **Open: ALL YEAR** **Map Ref No. 12**	Nearest Road: A.59, A.61 A warm & friendly welcome awaits guests in this fine Edwardian house standing in attractive rockery gardens. The accommodation has been carefully refurbished to a high standard & the bedrooms have private facilities, colour T.V. & tea/coffee makers. A short walk takes you into the famous spa town centre with superb shopping & restaurant facilities. Ideal touring base for historical interests & the wonderful scenery of the Yorkshire Dales.	£20.00	Y	N	N
Peter & Marion Thomson **Knox Mill House** **Knox Mill Lane** **Killinghall** **Harrogate HG3 2AE** **Tel/Fax: (01423) 560650** **Open: ALL YEAR (Excl. Xmas & New Year)** **Map Ref No. 12**	Nearest Road: A.61 Built in 1785, this lovely old millhouse stands on the banks of a stream in a quiet rural setting, & yet is only 1 1/2 miles from the centre of Harrogate. Beautifully renovated, it still retains all its original features: oak beams, an inglenook fireplace & stone arches. There are 3 delightful rooms, attractively & comfortably furnished. 2 are en-suite, & all have tea/coffee makers & views over the stream & fields. A delightful lounge with colour T.V., & a garden for guests' enjoyment.	£20.00	N	N	N
Clive & Gill King **High Winsley Cottage** **Burnt Yates** **Harrogate HG3 3EP** **Tel: (01423) 770662** **Open: MAR - DEC** **Map Ref No. 13**	Nearest Road: A.61 Traditional Dales cottage in Nidderdale, situated well off the road in peaceful countryside, with lovely views all around, & ideally placed for both town & country. 3 twin & 2 double rooms, well-appointed & all with en-suite facilities. 2 large sitting rooms, with guide books, games, T.V., etc. Imaginative home cooking using produce from the extensive kitchen garden, complemented by wines from an interesting list. Children over 11.	£23.50 *see PHOTO over*	Y	Y	N

Waterford House. Middleham.

Yorkshire

		rate from £ per person	children taken	evening meals	animals taken

Gail Ainley & Ann Macdonald **Brandymires Guest House** **Muker Road** **Hawes DL8 3PR** **Tel: (01969) 667482** **Open: APR - NOV** **Map Ref No. 14**	Nearest Road: A.684 A warm welcome awaits you in this comfortable mid-19th-century stone house in a tranquil rural setting. Every room has a splendid view over the fells. 4 spacious & attractive double bedrooms, 2 with 4-poster beds, full central heating. Good home cooking, including homemade bread, is an important feature, & dinner is available with prior notice, except on Thursdays. Brandymires is an ideal centre for exploring both the glorious countryside of the Yorkshire Dales & the historic surrounding towns. No T.V.. Ample parking.	£18.00 🚭	N	Y	Y
Everyl & Brian Madell **Waterford House** **Kirkgate** **Middleham** **Leyburn DL8 4PG** **Tel: (01969) 622090** **Fax 01969 624020** **Open: ALL YEAR** **Map Ref No. 15**	Nearest Road: A.1 A beautiful, traditional stone-built Georgian residence overlooking the market square of Middleham. Once the centre of government in mediaeval England & featuring the ruins of Richard III's castle. There are 5 spacious en-suite bedrooms, some beamed, including a 4-poster & exquisitely decorated in keeping with the period atmosphere. The restaurant has an a la carte menu that changes daily & over 700 wines, many of them from the 50's, 60's & 70's. Ideal base for the Dales & Herriot country.	£32.50 *see PHOTO over* CREDIT CARD VISA M'CARD	Y	Y	Y
Paul & Pat Williams **Newstead Grange** **Beverley Road, Norton** **Malton YO17 9PJ** **Tel: (01653) 692502** **Fax 01653 696951** **Open: MAR - Mid NOV** **Map Ref No. 16**	Nearest Road: A.64, B.1248 An elegant Georgian country house set in 2 1/2 acres of gardens & grounds with delightful views of the North Yorkshire moors & wolds. The style of the house is tastefully enhanced by antique furniture, open log fires burn in cooler weather & the bedrooms are individually furnished. The proprietors personally prepare the meals to a very high standard from vegetables & fruit in the organic kitchen garden & fresh local produce. Totally non-smoking. Children over 9.	£30.00 🚭 *see PHOTO over* CREDIT CARD VISA M'CARD	Y	Y	N
Richard & Stella Scott **Red House** **Wharram-le-Street** **Malton** **YO17 9TL** **Tel: (01944) 768455** **Open: ALL YEAR (Excl. Xmas)** **Map Ref No. 17**	Nearest Road: A.64, B.1248 Stella & Richard warmly welcome everyone to their elegant 19th-century home. Standing in an acre of garden in the heart of the Yorkshire Wolds, it offers 3 very comfortable bedrooms, with en-suite facilities, T.V. & tea/coffee makers, & a guests' lounge with lovely log fires. Good home cooking, using their own produce. Special diets catered for. Licensed dining rooms. Nearby are Castle Howard, Sledmere House & Nunnington Hall. York 23 miles. Grass tennis facility.	£22.50 🚭	Y	Y	Y
Avril Scott **Pasture House** **Healey** **Masham HG4 4LJ** **Tel: (01765) 689149** **Fax 01765 689990** **Open: ALL YEAR** **Map Ref No. 18**	Nearest Road: A.6108 Pasture House is a large, comfortable house providing guests with pleasant accommodation in the quiet of the lovely Yorkshire Dales. A perfect centre for walkers & horse-racing enthusiasts, with several courses & Middleham training gallops nearby. 4 comfortable rooms with T.V. & tea/coffee makers, a residents' lounge & large garden are also available. Pony trekking, golf & fishing locally. Children & pets welcome. Facilities for babies. A lovely home.	£16.00	Y	Y	Y

Newstead Grange. Norton.

Yorkshire

		rate from £ per person	children taken	evening meals	animals taken

Mrs E. Bleasdale **The Old Manse Guest** **House, Middleton Road** **Pickering YO18 8AL** **Tel: (01751) 476484** Fax 01751 477124 **Open:** ALL YEAR (Excl. Xmas) **Map Ref No. 19**	Nearest Road: A.170 The Old Manse, a former home of Methodist ministers, is a fine Edwardian house in its own grounds in the picturesque market town of Pickering. There are 8 en-suite rooms, a large secluded garden, orchard & private car park. Pickering - gateway to the N. Yorkshire Moors & 'Heartbeat' country, is the start of 18 miles of the scenic N.Y.M. Steam Railway & an ideal location for touring & walking. Children over 10.	£19.00	Y	N	N
Linda Sugars **Sevenford House** **Thorgill** **Rosedale Abbey** **Pickering YO18 8SE** **Tel: (01751) 417283** Fax 01751 417505 **Open: ALL YEAR** **Map Ref No. 20**	Nearest Road: A.170 Originally a vicarage, & built from the stones of Rosedale Abbey, 'Sevenford House' stands in 4 acres of lovely gardens in the heart of the beautiful Yorkshire Moors National Park. 3 tastefully furnished, en-suite bedrooms, with T.V., radio, & tea/coffee, offer wonderful views overlooking valley & moorland. A relaxing guests' lounge/ library with an open fire. An excellent base for exploring the region. Riding & golf locally. Also, ruined abbeys, Roman roads, steam railways, the beautiful coastline & pretty fishing towns.	£19.50 🚭 *see PHOTO over*	Y	N	N
Ian & Angela Whitworth **The White House** **Arkle Town** **Arkengarthdale** **Richmond DL11 6RB** **Tel: (01748) 884203** **Open: MAR - NOV** **Map Ref No. 21**	Nearest Road: A.66, A.1 An 18th-century former farmhouse, modernised, tastefully decorated and furnished to a high standard. 3 rooms offer modern amenities (2 en-suite). Cosy visitors' lounge with open fire. Only the best ingredients used, in tasty, home-cooked meals. In the heart of Herriot country, and set above the road with superb uninterrupted views, the ideal centre for exploring the Yorkshire Dales. Reduced rates for 2 or more nights inc. dinner. Hosts can be contacted by fax on 01748 884088.	£18.50 🚭 CREDIT CARD VISA M'CARD	N	Y	N
Mrs A. Delahooke **The Coach House** **The Old Rectory** **Barningham** **Richmond DL11 7DW** **Tel: (01833) 621251** Fax 01833 621421 **Open: APR - OCT** **Map Ref No. 22**	Nearest Road: A.66 Old stone steps on the outside of this charming 18th-century coach house lead to an attractive, beamed double bedroom & bathroom, with all amenities including T.V. & tea/coffee-making facilities. Set in a beautiful old yard, adjacent to the Old Rectory, in the middle of the unspoilt hamlet of Barningham. A perfect half-way house for travellers to & from Scotland. Situated 2 miles from the A.66 main Pennine route with spectacular views, yet delightfully secluded.	£25.00 🚭	N	N	Y
Mrs Elaine M. Watson **Sleningford Grange** **North Stainley** **Ripon HG4 3HX** **Tel: (01765) 635252** Fax 01765 635252 **Open: ALL YEAR** **Map Ref No. 23**	Nearest Road: A.1 A delightful listed manor house dating from the 15th century, Sleningford Grange stands in lovely & extensive gardens on the verge of the Yorkshire Dales. The interior is elegant, & furnished with antiques. There are 4 most comfortable & spacious bedrooms with en-suite facilities & views across rolling countryside. An ideal base for exploring the Dales/Moors & the wealth of historic towns & abbeys - or for an overnight break midway between London & Edinburgh.	£35.00 🚭	Y	N	N

Sevenford House. Rosedale Abbey.

Yorkshire

		rate from £ per person	children taken	evening meals	animals taken

Phillip Gill & Anton Van Der Horst **Bank Villa** **The Avenue, Masham** **Ripon HG4 4DB** **Tel: (01765) 689605** **Open: APR - OCT** **Map Ref No. 24**	Nearest Road: A.6108, A.1 A fine Georgian house overlooking the River Ure in large terraced gardens, offering delightful accommodation in 7 comfortable double rooms, some with private showers. It is a super base for visiting the Druids Temple, Jervaulx Abbey, Middleham Castle, Fountains Abbey & the wonderful 'James Herriot Country'. Dutch is spoken. Meals are excellent value. Children over 5 years welcome.	£18.50	Y	Y	Y
Mr & Mrs M. A. Shepherd **Stonecroft Residential Hotel, Main Street** **Bramley** **Rotherham S66 2SF** **Tel: (01709) 540922** **Open: ALL YEAR** **Map Ref No. 25**	Nearest Road: M.18 Ex. 1 Stonecroft is a Grade II listed building with a homely atmosphere. The main building is 300 years old, with a profusion of oak beams & open fireplaces. Accommodation is in 8 tastefully furnished rooms, 7 with en-suite bathroom, all with modern amenities including colour T.V., radio & tea/coffee-making facilities. A residents' lounge & delightful garden also available for guests to relax in. Ideally situated for visiting the many attractions in Yorkshire & Derbyshire. CREDIT CARD VISA M'CARD	£21.75	Y	N	Y
Mrs Virginia Sutton **Willerby Wold Farm** **Staxton** **Scarborough YO12 4TF** **Tel: (01944) 710747** **Fax 01944 710747** **Open: ALL YEAR (Excl. Xmas)** **Map Ref No. 26**	Nearest Road: A.64 Peacefully situated on an 800-acre farm on the edge of the Yorkshire Wolds, this elegant country house is ideally located for exploring the east coast, the North York Moors & York. The 3 attractive bedrooms have private bathrooms, tea & coffee facilities & colour T.V.. Guests are welcome to use the garden & all-weather tennis court. Stabling available. Evening meals by arrangement. A delightful family home.	£18.00	Y	Y	N
Phil & Ann Unitt **Aldermans Head Manor** **Hartcliffe Hill Road** **Langsett, Stocksbridge** **Sheffield S36 4SY** **Tel: (01226) 766209** **Fax 01226 766209** **Open: ALL YEAR** **Map Ref No. 27**	Nearest Road: A.616 An historic, licensed, country manor house set in dramatic countryside with panoramic views across the Derbyshire Peak District. 3 spacious en-suite bedrooms with excellent views, T.V., radio/alarm, tea/coffee, 1 with 4-poster & spa bath. Residents' lounge with log fire. Traditional English breakfast served in the oak-beamed dining room or the conservatory. Extensive mature gardens lead into 50 acres of woodland & pasture. Ideal for local walking or exploring Yorkshire & Derbyshire, providing a very peaceful & special experience. *see PHOTO over* CREDIT CARD VISA M'CARD	£22.50	N	Y	Y
Mrs D. E. Hutton **The Country House Hotel** **Long Preston** **Skipton BD23 4NJ** **Tel: (01729) 840246** **Fax 01729 840246** **Open: FEB - Mid DEC** **Map Ref No. 28**	Nearest Road: A.65 An elegant Victorian country house, situated in its own grounds in the Yorkshire Dales. 7 bedrooms with en-suite/private bathroom, colour T.V. & tea/ coffee facilities. Drawing room with log fire & extensive library. Fine food, but please bring your own wine. A sauna & spa bath are also provided for relaxation. Delightful house, offering a personal service in homely, informal & restful surroundings. Children over 4 years.	£27.00	Y	Y	N

Aldermans Head Manor. Langsett.

Yorkshire

		rate from £ per person	children taken	evening meals	animals taken
Julia Oxby **Greenways House** **Wharfeside Ave** **Threshfield** **Skipton BD23 5BS** Tel: (01756) 752598 Open: ALL YEAR Map Ref No. 29	Nearest Road: A.65 Greenways is situated 1/2 mile from Grassington in a tranquil position on the banks of the River Wharfe, set in a large garden with private access to the river. Greenways is a comfortable Edwardian villa, all bedrooms are attractively furnished & are en-suite. This is an ideal centre for exploring the beautiful Yorkshire Dales, Bronte country, Fountains Abbey, historic York, Grassington, Malham & Bolton Abbey.	£20.00 🚭	Y	N	N
Tim Earnshaw & Robin **Martin** **High Fold** **Kettlewell** **Skipton** **BD23 5RJ** Tel: (01756) 760390 Open: FEB - DEC Map Ref No. 30	Nearest Road: A.59, B.6160 High Fold is a dales barn, recently converted to a high standard of accommodation, offering elegant yet relaxing surroundings in a quiet & picturesque location. Enhanced by beamed ceilings, stone features & antiques. 4 beautifully furnished & well-equipped en-suite bedrooms. 2 are situated on the ground floor & have been carefully designed for disabled/elderly guests. A large drawing room with log fire, books, etc. Imaginative cuisine using quality produce. An ideal base for the Dales, Skipton, Grassington, Malham & Bolton Abbey.	£27.00	Y	Y	Y
Mrs Anne Gloag **Busby House** **Stokesley** **TS9 5LB** Tel: (01642) 710425 Fax 01642 713838 Open: FEB - NOV Map Ref No. 31	Nearest Road: A.1, A.19, A.172 This is a lovely old farmhouse, with cobbled courtyard to the rear, situated 2 1/2 miles south of Stokesley. Delightfully furnished, the principal rooms look south over the large gardens & fields to the hills beyond. 2 pretty twin bedrooms with private bathrooms. The atmosphere is peaceful & relaxed & exudes warmth & friendliness. Renowned for comfort, & delicious dinners on request. Ideal for exploring the Moors, Dales & coast, York, Durham & many places of historic interest. (A.1. only 25 mins.) Children over 12.	£30.00 🚭	Y	Y	N
Mrs Carol Richmond **Red Hall** **Ingleby Road** **Great Broughton** **Stokesley TS9 7ET** Tel/Fax: (01642) 712300 Open: ALL YEAR Map Ref No. 32	Nearest Road: A.172 Warmly welcoming, Red Hall is an elegant Grade II listed early-Georgian country house set in its own grounds at the foot of the rugged North Yorkshire Moors National Park & surrounded by tranquil meadows & woodland. Red Hall has been carefully (painstakingly) modernised, preserving its classic internal features, & has nicely appointed, spacious bedrooms. Meals are served in the guests' private dining room opening onto the secluded south-facing garden.	£27.50 🚭 *see PHOTO over*	Y	Y	N
Mrs Tess Williamson **Thornborough House** **Farm** **South Kilvington** **Thirsk YO7 2NP** Tel/Fax: (01845) 522103 Open: ALL YEAR Map Ref No. 33	Nearest Road: A.19 A warm welcome awaits you at this 200-year-old farmhouse, set in lovely countryside. Only one & a half miles north of Thirsk, this working farm is situated in the town made famous by James Herriot. 3 comfortable rooms, each with en-suite/private shower room, all with tea/coffee-making facilities. Guests have their own sitting/dining room with colour T.V. & open fire. Good home cooking a speciality. Conveniently located for York, Ripon, the Pennine Dales & the East Coast.	£15.00 CREDIT CARD VISA M'CARD	Y	Y	Y

Red Hall.   Great Broughton.

Yorkshire

		rate from £ per person	children taken	evening meals	animals taken
Ann & Robin Clough **Spital Hill** **York Road** **Thirsk** **YO7 3AE** Tel: (01845) 522273 Fax 01845 524970 Open: ALL YEAR Map Ref No. 34	Nearest Road: A.19 Quiet, peaceful & relaxing, Spital Hill is set in 1 1/2 acres of secluded garden surrounded by parkland, yet only 10 mins from A.1. Originally a Georgian farmhouse, it was extended in 1884, & is now a comfortable home from which to explore York, Harrogate, the Moors, the Dales & Herriot Country. Dinner is en-famille, & the whole meal, incl. a range of breads, is home-prepared drawing from the kitchen garden. Licensed. The bedrooms are delightfully furnished & the bathrooms are well-provisioned. Children over 12 years. CREDIT CARD VISA M'CARD AMEX	£29.50	Y	Y	N
David & Margaret Watts **Four Gables** **Oaks Lane, Boston Spa** **Wetherby LS23 6DS** Tel/Fax: (01937) 845592 Open: ALL YEAR Map Ref No. 35	Nearest Road: A.1 Visitors will love this most unusual 'Lutyens" style house with its wealth of character - wooden floors, original fireplaces & beautiful ceilings throughout. Enjoy its peaceful setting, down a private lane, yet only 5 mins walk from the bustling village of Boston Spa with all its facilities & riverside walks. There are 3 attractive en-suite bedrooms. David & Maggie are welcoming hosts & Maggie (a trained chef) adores preparing interesting food. CREDIT CARD M'CARD	£23.00	Y	Y	Y
Mrs Ashley Goodrum **Cliffemount Hotel** **Bank Top Lane** **Runswick Bay** **Whitby TS13 5HU** Tel: (01947) 840103 Fax 01947 841025 Open: ALL YEAR (Excl. Xmas) Map Ref No. 36	Nearest Road: A.174 As the name implies, this privately-run hotel is situated on a clifftop with panoramic views over Runswick Bay. Built in the 1920s with later additions, the hotel is tastefully decorated throughout. All of the 11 bedrooms are comfortably furnished & have en-suite facilities, & the majority have spectacular sea views. Cliffemount, with its warm & friendly atmosphere, also enjoys a good reputation for its high standard of food. Fully licensed. Log fires in winter. CREDIT CARD VISA M'CARD	£24.00	Y	Y	Y
John & Pauline Lusher **Whitfield House Hotel** **Darnholm** **Goathland** **Whitby YO22 5LA** Tel: (01947) 896215 Open: ALL YEAR Map Ref No. 37	Nearest Road: A.169 Once a 17th-century farmhouse, Whitfield House has been carefully modernised to provide every comfort whilst retaining its old-world charm. 9 cottage-style en-suite bedrooms (no smoking), with T.V., tea maker, telephone, hairdryer & clock/radio alarm. Quietly situated in the heart of the North Moors National Park. Superb country cooking using fresh produce. Residential licence. The perfect base for touring or just relaxing. Children over 5 years. CREDIT CARD VISA M'CARD	£26.00	Y	Y	Y
Mr & Mrs S. Long **Grasmead House Hotel** **1 Scarcroft Hill** **York YO2 1DF** Tel: (01904) 629996 Fax 01904 629996 Open: ALL YEAR Map Ref No. 38	Nearest Road: A.64 An attractive, small, family-run hotel, situated within easy walking distance of the city centre. The charming bedrooms feature antique furniture, 4-poster beds (1 dating back to 1730) & excellent en-suite bathrooms. Plus, of course, tea/coffee-making facilities & T.V.. There is also a comfortable lounge with a small bar where you can relax after spending the day exploring historic York. Delicious breakfasts served in the attractive dining room. Ideal centre for visiting the Dales, Moors & coast. *see PHOTO over* CREDIT CARD VISA M'CARD AMEX	£27.50	Y	N	N

Grasmead House Hotel. York.

Yorkshire

	rate from £ per person	children taken	evening meals	animals taken

		rate from £ per person	children taken	evening meals	animals taken
Elsie & Leonard Osterman **Barbican Hotel** **20 Barbican Road** **York YO1 5AA** **Tel: (01904) 627617** **Fax 01904 647140** **Open: ALL YEAR** **Map Ref No. 38**	Nearest Road: A.19 Small in size but large in character. Barbican Hotel overlooks the mediaeval city walls. Leave your car in the floodlit car park & walk to all the city-centre attractions. All bedrooms are en-suite & attractively furnished with colour T.V., 'phone, coffee/tea, hairdryer, etc. Traditional or vegetarian breakfasts served in the dining room with a lovely original kitchen range in superb condition. A friendly Northern welcome always assured. **E-mail: barbican@thenet.co.uk**	£20.00 CREDIT CARD VISA M'CARD AMEX	Y	N	N
L. M. Keir & M. D. Easton **Easton's** **90 Bishopthorpe Road** **York** **YO2 1JS** **Tel: (01904) 626646** **Open: ALL YEAR** **Map Ref No. 38**	Nearest Road: A.64, A.19 A sympathetically & beautifully restored Victorian wine-merchant's residence, centrally situated just 300 yds from the mediaeval city walls. The period furniture, William Morris decor, open fires & fully equipped bedrooms are in accord with the character of the building, & with the standard of excellence that the owners strive for. The Victorian sideboard breakfast menu follows the same theme of quality, & includes a selection of traditional & vegetarian dishes. Children over 5 yrs.	£22.00 *see PHOTO over* CREDIT CARD VISA M'CARD	Y	N	N
Keith Jackman **Dairy Guest House** **3 Scarcroft Road** **York** **YO2 1ND** **Tel: (01904) 639367** **Open: FEB - DEC** **Map Ref No. 38**	Nearest Road: A.64 The Dairy is a tastefully renovated Victorian house within walking distance of the city centre & just 200 yards from the mediaeval city walls. Decorated & furnished in the styles of Habitat, Sanderson's & Laura Ashley, with the emphasis on pine & plants. 5 bedrooms, some en-suite (& 4-poster available), each with modern amenities, T.V., hot-drink facilities & information on York & Yorkshire. A lovely enclosed courtyard. Breakfast choices are from English to wholefood vegetarian.	£17.50	Y	N	N
Russell & Cherry **Whitbourn-Hammond** **Nunmill House** **85 Bishopthorpe Road** **York YO2 1NX** **Tel: (01904) 634047** **Fax 01904 655879** **Open: FEB - NOV** **Map Ref No. 38**	Nearest Road: A.64, A.59 A warm friendly welcome awaits you at Nunmill House, a delightful late-Victorian house, tastefully restored throughout with Laura Ashley furnishings to enhance the original architectural features. Offering a choice of 8 delightful bedrooms, each with en-suite or private facilities. Ideally situated just outside the mediaeval walls, & a 10-minute walk to all the historic attractions of the city. Complimentary tea & coffee are available, & special diets can be catered for by arrangement.	£22.00	Y	N	N
Malcolm & Liz Greaves **Carlton House Hotel** **134 The Mount** **York YO2 2AS** **Tel: (01904) 622265** **Fax 01904 637157** **Open: ALL YEAR (Excl. Xmas & New Year)** **Map Ref No. 38**	Nearest Road: A.64 Each & every guest will receive a warm & friendly welcome from proprietors Liz & Malcolm Greaves. This pleasant, family-run hotel offers guests a choice of 13 attractive en-suite rooms, all with colour T.V., radio & tea/coffee makers. The spacious lounges are comfortable & pleasantly furnished. A traditional English breakfast is cooked to order. Light refreshments are available at most times throughout the day. Nearby are York race course & the Minster. **E-mail: carltonuk@aol.com**	£25.00	Y	N	N

Easton's. York.

Arndale Hotel. York.

Yorkshire

David & Gillian Reynard **Arndale Hotel** **290 Tadcaster Road** **York** **YO2 2ET** **Tel: (01904) 702424** **Open: ALL YEAR (Excl.** **Xmas & New Year)** **Map Ref No. 38**	Nearest Road: A.64, A.1036 A delightful Victorian house, directly overlooking York's famous race course, with beautiful enclosed walled gardens giving a country-house atmosphere within the city. There is a spacious, elegant lounge, complete with antiques, fresh flowers, paintings & a small bar. The 10 outstanding & thoughtfully equipped bedrooms are all en-suite. Many bathrooms are Victorian in style, with modern whirlpool baths. Antique half-tester/4-poster beds. Delicious quality breakfasts. Friendly, attentive service. Large enclosed gated car park. Children over 7 years.	£24.50 *see PHOTO over* CREDIT CARD VISA M'CARD	Y	N	N
Richard & Wendy Wood **Curzon Lodge & Stable** **Cottages** **23 Tadcaster Road** **Dringhouses** **York YO2 2QG** **Tel: (01904) 703157** **Open: ALL YEAR** **Map Ref No. 38**	Nearest Road: A.64, A.1036 A charming 17th-century Grade II listed house & oak-beamed stables within city conservation area overlooking the racecourse. Once a home of renowned York chocolate makers, guests are now invited to share the unique atmosphere in 10 delightful & fully-equipped en-suite rooms. Some 4-poster & brass beds. Country antiques, old prints, books, maps, fresh flowers & sherry in the cosy sitting room lend traditional ambience. Warm & informal. Delicious English breakfasts. Parking in grounds. Restaurants within 1 min. walk.	£24.50 *see PHOTO over* CREDIT CARD VISA M'CARD	Y	N	N
Bill Pitts & Rosie Blanksby **Holmwood House Hotel** **114 Holgate Road** **York YO2 4BB** **Tel: (01904) 626183** **Fax 01904 670899** **Open: ALL YEAR** **Map Ref No. 38**	Nearest Road: A.59 The conversion of 2 listed, early-Victorian town houses has created an elegant hotel that offers guests a feeling of home with a touch of luxury. All rooms - which, of course, have en-suite facilities - are different both in size & decoration, & there are now 3 honeymoon rooms (2 with 4-poster beds), a suite, on the ground floor, with spa bathroom & a guest sitting room with an open fire. Children over 8 years. **E-mail: holmwoodhouse@dial.pipex.com**	£25.00 🚭 *see PHOTO over* CREDIT CARD VISA M'CARD AMEX	Y	N	N
Mike & Ann Beaufoy **18 St. Paul's Square** **York** **YO2 4BD** **Tel: (01904) 629884** **Open: ALL YEAR** **Map Ref No. 38**	Nearest Road: A.59 A delightful Victorian house located in a pleasant Victorian garden square in the centre of York. Skilfully restored & furnished with period antiques, it now offers 3 very comfortable en-suite/private bedrooms, a guests' colour T.V. lounge & a garden. Mike & Ann enjoy sharing their home & knowledge of York with their guests, & are happy to give advice on where to go & what to see locally.	£35.00 🚭	Y	N	N

When booking your accommodation please mention
The Best Bed & Breakfast

Curzon Lodge. York.

Holmwood House Hotel.   York.

Bloomsbury Hotel. York.

Yorkshire

		rate from £ per person	children taken	evening meals	animals taken
Mrs Jaqueline Jessop **Bloomsbury Hotel** **127 Clifton** **York** **YO3 6BL** **Tel: (01904) 634031** **Open: ALL YEAR** **Map Ref No. 38**	Nearest Road: A.1237 The Bloomsbury is a beautiful large Victorian town house with adequate car parking. Situated in a conservation area only a 12-minute walk from York Minster in the historic centre of York. Each of the 9 guest rooms in this delightful family-run establishment has been individually designed by the owners for your comfort. The proprietors will gladly give assistance & advice to ensure your stay is enjoyable & successful. Children over 7. *see PHOTO over* CREDIT CARD VISA M'CARD	£24.00	Y	N	N
Mrs Ann & Miss Kim **Sluter-Robbins** **Arnot House** **17 Grosvenor Terrace** **York** **YO3 7AG** **Tel/Fax: (01904) 641966** **Open: ALL YEAR** **Map Ref No. 38**	Nearest Road: A.19 Overlooking Bootham Park, only 5 mins' walk from the York Minster & city centre. Arnot House is a Victorian town-house built for a wealthy merchant in 1865. The house is beautifully decorated & there are fine antiques & paintings. Many of its original features have been retained including marble fireplaces & ornate coving. The 4 attractive bedrooms have either Victorian brass or wooden beds & every facility. An excellent location. Children over 10 years. *see PHOTO over* CREDIT CARD VISA	£22.50	Y	N	N
Will & Penny Lefebve **The Bentley** **25 Grosvenor Terrace** **York** **YO3 7AG** **Tel: (01904) 644313** **Fax 01904 644313** **Open: FEB - DEC (Excl. Xmas)** **Map Ref No. 38**	Nearest Road: A.19 Relax in an elegant Victorian town house, furnished with quality, care & comfort in mind for the really discerning guest. Enjoy the spacious en-suite rooms (with T.V., tea/coffee, etc.), most of which have a fine view across parkland to the beautiful York Minster. The Bentley is just a few minutes' stroll from the city centre & its many historical treats, yet in a quiet one-way street, with parking. York is also a unique shopping experience. Children over 10 years. *see PHOTO over*	£21.00	N	N	N
Tony & Tricia Styan **Primrose Cottage** **Lime Bar Lane, Grafton** **York YO5 9QJ** **Tel: (01423) 322835/322711** **Fax 01423 323985** **Open: ALL YEAR** **Map Ref No. 39**	Nearest Road: A.1 M., A.168 A warm friendly welcome awaits you at Primrose Cottage, in a quiet picturesque village 1 mile east of the A.1. Comfortable bedrooms with washbasins & tea/coffee facilities. 2 bath/shower rooms. Spacious T.V. lounge, & sheltered patio garden with barbecue for guests' use. 2 local inns serving excellent food. Ideally situated 15 mins north of York. Ripon, Harrogate & Yorkshire Dales within easy distance.	£18.00	Y	N	Y
Mrs Yvonne Thompson **Brentwood Cottage** **Main Street** **Shipton-by-Beningbrough** **York YO6 1AB** **Tel: (01904) 470111** **Open: ALL YEAR** **Map Ref No. 40**	Nearest Road: A.19 A warm & friendly welcome awaits all guests at Brentwood Cottage. Located 5 miles outside the historic city of York, it offers guests a choice of 5 very pleasant bedrooms, 2 with en-suite/private facilities & amenities, & each with tea/coffee makers. There is also a comfortable residents' lounge & garden available. Brentwood Cottage makes a good base for touring York & the surrounding countryside. A large car park. CREDIT CARD VISA M'CARD	£17.00	Y	N	N

Arnot House. York.

The Bentley. York.

Laurel Farm. Brafferton.

Yorkshire

		rate from £ per person	children taken	evening meals	animals taken
John & Sue White **Brafferton Hall** **Hall Lane** **Brafferton, Helperby** **York YO6 2NZ** **Tel/Fax: (01423) 360352** **Open: ALL YEAR** **Map Ref No. 41**	Nearest Road: A.1 Brafferton Hall is a comfortable family home set in a quiet village near the River Swale in the heart of North Yorkshire, yet only 4 miles from the A.1. Offering 4 comfortable & attractively furnished bedrooms, each with en-suite or private facilities, T.V., radio & tea/coffee-making facilities. Ideally placed for exploring York, the National Parks & Herriot country all within an easy 30-minute drive. Informality, accompanied by excellent fare, is to be enjoyed at Brafferton Hall. CREDIT CARD VISA M'CARD AMEX	£30.00	Y	Y	Y
Ann & Sam Key **Laurel Manor Farm** **Brafferton Helperby** **York YO6 2NZ** **Tel: (01423) 360436** **Fax 01423 360436** **Open: ALL YEAR** **Map Ref No. 42**	Nearest Road: A.1.M. Hidden up a lane, beside the village church is Laurel Manor Farm, its 28 acres running down to the River Swale. The recently refurbished bedrooms have en-suite/private bathrooms & are furnished with antiques, a 4-poster, family portraits, beams & open fireplaces. Dine with your hosts or walk 2 mins to one of 4 inns. The Keys have a tennis court, croquet lawn, river walks & are licensed. Situated only 4 miles from the A.1m. 12 miles York/Harrogate.	£25.00 *see PHOTO over*	Y	Y	Y
Chris & Sarah Braithwaite **Plumpton Court Guest** **House, High Street** **Nawton, Helmsley** **York YO6 5TT** **Tel: (01439) 771223** **Open: ALL YEAR** **Map Ref No. 43**	Nearest Road: A.170 Plumpton Court is a family-run 17th-century guest house set in the foothills of the North Yorkshire Moors & is ideally situated for York & exploring the east coast. Offering 7 comfortable & well-appointed bedrooms (5 en-suite), all with clock/radio & tea/coffee-making facilities. There is a comfortable lounge in which guests may relax, with real fire, small bar & T.V.. Delicious evening meals served using fresh local produce. Secure, gated car park & garden. A charming home.	£20.50	Y	Y	N
Mrs Julie Brown **Four Seasons Hotel** **7 St. Peters Grove** **Bootham** **York YO3 6AQ** **Tel: (01904) 622621** **Fax 01904 620976** **Open: MAR - DEC** **Map Ref No. 38**	Nearest Road: A.19 An elegant Victorian residence. Ideally situated in a peaceful cul-de-sac only 7 mins' stroll from the Minster & York's many other historic attractions. Accommodation is in 6 beautifully appointed & tastefully furnished en-suite bedrooms, all fully equipped. Four-course English breakfast, residential licence & private car parking. The Four Seasons Hotel is an ideal base to explore York & is within easy reach of Harrogate & the beautiful Yorkshire Dales.	£26.00 *see PHOTO over* CREDIT CARD VISA M'CARD	Y	N	Y

When booking your accommodation please mention
The Best Bed & Breakfast

Four Seasons Hotel. York.

Scotland

Scotland

Scotland's culture & traditions, history & literature, languages & accents, its landscape & architecture, even its wildlife set it apart from the rest of Britain. Much of Scotland's history is concerned with the struggle to retain independence from England.

The Romans never conquered the Scottish tribes, but preferred to keep them at bay with Hadrian's Wall, stretching across the Border country from Tynemouth to the Solway Firth.

Time lends glamour to events, but from the massacre of Glencoe to the Highland Clearances, much of Scotland's fate has been a harsh one. Robert the Bruce did rout the English enemy at Bannockburn after scaling the heights of Edinburgh Castle to take the city, but in later years Mary, Queen of Scots was to spend much of her life imprisoned by her sister Elizabeth I of England. Bonnie Prince Charlie (Charles Edward Stuart) led the Jacobite rebellion which ended in defeat at Culloden.

These events are recorded in the folklore & songs of Scotland. The Border & Highland Gatherings & the Common Ridings are more than a chance to wear the Tartan, they are reminders of national pride.

Highland Games are held throughout the country where local & national champions compete in events like tossing the caber & in piping contests. There are sword dances & Highland flings, the speciality of young men & boys wearing the full dress tartan of their clan.

Scotland's landscape is rich in variety from the lush green lowlands to the handsome splendour of the mountainous Highlands, from the rounded hills of the Borders to the far-flung islands of the Hebrides, Orkney & Shetland where the sea is ever-present.

There are glens & beautiful lochs deep in the mountains, a spectacular coastline of high cliffs & white sandy beaches, expanses of purple heather moorland where the sparkling water in the burns runs brown with peat, & huge skies bright with cloud & gorgeous sunsets.

Argyll & The Islands

This area has ocean & sea lochs, forests & mountains, 3000 miles of coastline, about 30 inhabited islands, the warming influence of the Gulf Stream & the tallest tree in Britain (in Strone Gardens, near Loch Fyne).

Sites both historic & prehistoric are to be found in plenty. There is a hilltop fort at Dunadd, near Crinan with curious cup-&-ring carvings, & numerous ancient sites surround Kilmartin, from burial cairns to grave slabs.

Kilchurn Castle is a magnificent ruin in contrast to the opulence of Inveraray. Both are associated with the once-powerful Clan Campbell. There are remains of fortresses built by the Lords of the Isles, the proud chieftains who ruled the west after driving out the Norse invaders in the 12th century.

Oban is a small harbour town accessible by road & rail & the point of departure for many of the islands including Mull.

Tobermory. Isle of Mull.

Scotland

Mull is a peaceful island with rugged seascapes, lovely walks & villages, a miniature railway & the famous Mull Little Theatre. It is a short hop from here to the tiny island of Iona & St. Columba's Abbey, cradle of Christianity in Scotland.

Coll & Tiree have lovely beaches & fields of waving barley. The grain grown here was once supplied to the Lords of the Isles but today most goes to Islay & into the whisky. Tiree has superb windsurfing.

Jura is a wilder island famous for its red deer. The Isles of Colonsay & Oronsay are joined at low water.

Gigha, 'God's Isle', is a fertile area of gardens with rare & semitropical plants. The Island of Staffa has Fingal's Cave.

The Borders, Dumfries & Galloway

The borderland with England is a landscape of subtle colours & contours from the round foothills of the Cheviots, purple with heather, to the dark green valley of the Tweed.

The Lammermuir Hills sweep eastwards to a coastline of small harbours & the spectacular cliffs at St. Abbs Head where colonies of seabirds thrive.

The Border towns, set in fine countryside, have distinctive personalities. Hawick, Galashiels, Selkirk & Melrose all played their parts in the various Border skirmishes of this historically turbulent region & then prospered with a textile industry which survives today. They celebrate their traditions in the Common Riding ceremonies.

The years of destructive border warfare have left towers & castles throughout the country. Roxburgh was once a Royal castle & James II was killed here during a siege. Now there are only the shattered remains of the massive stone walls. Hermitage Castle is set amid wild scenery near Hawick & impressive Floors Castle stands above Kelso.

At Jedburgh the Augustine abbey is remarkably complete, & a visitors centre here tells the story of the four great Border Abbeys; Jedburgh itself, Kelso, Dryburgh & Melrose.

The lovely estate of Abbotsford where Sir Walter Scott lived & worked is near Melrose. A prolific poet & novelist, his most famous works are the Waverley novels written around 1800. His house holds many of his possessions, including a collection of armour. Scott's View is one of the best vantage points in the borderlands with a prospect of the silvery Tweed & the three distinctive summits of the Eildon Hills.

Eildon Hills.

There are many gracious stately homes. Manderston is a classical house of great luxury, & Mellerstain is the work of the Adam family. Traquair was originally a Royal hunting lodge. Its main gates were locked in 1745 after a visit from Bonnie Prince Charlie, never to be opened until a Stuart King takes the throne.

Dumfries & Galloway to the southwest is an area of rolling hills with a fine coastline.

Plants flourish in the mild air here & there are palm trees at Ardwell House & the Logan Botanic Garden.

Scotland

The gardens at Castle Kennedy have rhododendrons, azaleas & magnolias & Threave Gardens near Castle Douglas are the National Trust for Scotland's School of gardening.

The Galloway Forest Park covers a vast area of lochs & hills & has views across to offshore Ailsa Craig. At Caerlaveroch Castle, an early Renaissance building near the coast of Dumfries, there is a national nature reserve.

The first church in Scotland was built by St. Ninian at Whithorn in 400 on a site now occupied by the 13th century priory. The spread of Christianity is marked by early memorial stones like the Latinus stone at Whithorn, & the abbeys of Dundrennan, Crossraguel, Glenluce & Sweetheart, named after its founder who carried her husband's heart in a casket & is buried with it in the abbey.

At Dumfries is the poet Burns' house, his mausoleum & the Burns Heritage Centre overlooking the River Nith.

In Upper Nithsdale the Mennock Pass leads to Wanlockhead & Leadhills, once centres of the lead-mining industry. There is a fascinating museum here & the opportunity of an underground trip.

Lowland

The Frith of Clyde & Glascow in the west, & the Firth of Forth with Edinburgh in the east are both areas of rich history, tradition & culture.

Edinburgh is the capital of Scotland & amongst the most visually exciting cities in the world. The New Town is a treasure trove of inspired neo-classical architecture, & below Edinburgh Castle high on the Rock, is the Old Town, a network of courts, closes, wynds & gaunt tenements around the Royal Mile.

The Palace of Holyrood House, home of Mary, Queen of Scots for several years overlooks Holyrood Park & nearby Arthur's Seat, is a popular landmark.

The City's varied art galleries include The Royal Scottish Academy, The National Gallery, Portrait Gallery, Gallery of Modern Art & many other civic & private collections.

The Royal Museum of Scotland displays superb historical & scientific material. The Royal Botanic Gardens are world famous.

Cultural life in Edinburgh peaks at Festival time in August. The official Festival, the Fringe, the Book Festival, Jazz Festival & Film Festival bring together artistes of international reputation.

The gentle hills around the city offer many opportunities for walking. The Pentland Hills are easily reached,

Inverary Castle.

with the Lammermuir Hills a little further south. There are fine beaches at Gullane, Yellowcraigs, North Berwick & at Dunbar.

Tantallon Castle, a 14th century stronghold, stands on the rocky Firth of Forth, & 17th century Hopetoun House, on the outskirts of the city is only one of a number of great houses in the area.

North of Edinburgh across the Firth of Forth lies the ancient Kingdom of Fife. Here is St. Andrews, a pleasant town on the seafront, an old university

Scotland

town & Scotland's ecclesiastical capital, but famous primarily for golf.

Glasgow is the industrial & business capital of Scotland. John Betjeman called it the 'finest Victorian city in Britain' & many buildings are remarkable examples of Victorian splendour, notably the City Chambers.

Many buildings are associated with the architect Charles Rennie MacKintosh; the Glasgow School of Art is one of them. Glasgow Cathedral is a perfect example of pre-Reformation Gothic architecture.

Glasgow is Scotland's largest city with the greatest number of parks & fine Botanic Garden. It is home to both the Scottish Opera & the Scottish Ballet, & has a strong & diverse cultural tradition from theatre to jazz. Its museums include the matchless Burrell Collection, & the Kelvingrove Museum & Art Gallery, which houses one of the best civic collections of paintings in Britain, as well as reflecting the city's engineering & shipbuilding heritage.

The coastal waters of the Clyde are world famous for cruising & sailing, with many harbours & marinas. The long coastline offers many opportunities for sea-angling from Largs to Troon & Prestwick, & right around to Luce Bay on the Solway.

There are many places for birdwatching on the Estuary, whilst the Clyde Valley is famous for its garden centres & nurseries.

Paisley has a mediaeval abbey, an observatory & a museum with a fine display of the famous 'Paisley' pattern shawls.

Further south, Ayr is a large seaside resort with sandy beach, safe bathing & a racecourse. In the Ayrshire valleys there is traditional weaving & lace & bonnet making, & Sorn, in the rolling countryside boasts its 'Best Kept Village' award.

Culzean Castle is one of the finest Adam houses in Scotland & stands in spacious grounds on the Ayrshire cliffs.

Robert Burns is Scotland's best loved poet, & 'Burns night' is widely celebrated. The region of Strathclyde shares with Dumfries & Galloway the title of 'Burns Country' . The son of a peasant farmer, Burns lived in poverty for much of his life. The simple house where he was born is in the village of Alloway. In the town of Ayr is the Auld Kirk where he was baptised & the footbridge of 'The Brigs of Ayr' is still in use. The Tam O'Shanter Inn is now a Burns museum & retains its thatched roof & simple fittings. The Burns Trail leads on to Mauchline where Possie Nansie's Inn remains. At Tarbolton the National Trust now care for the old house where Burns founded the 'Batchelors Club' debating society.

Perthshire, Loch Lomond & The Trossachs

By a happy accident of geology, the Highland Boundary fault which separates the Highlands from the Lowlands runs through Loch Lomond, close to the Trossachs & on through Perthshire, giving rise to marvellous scenery.

In former times Highlanders & Lowlanders raided & fought here. Great castles like Stirling, Huntingtower & Doune were built to protect the routes between the two different cultures.

Stirling was once the seat of Scotland's monarchs & the great Royal castle is set high on a basalt rock. The Guildhall & the Kirk of the Holy Rude are also interesting buildings in the town, with Cambuskenneth Abbey & the Bannockburn Heritage Centre close by.

Perth 'fair city' on the River Tay,

Scotland

has excellent shops & its own repertory theatre. Close by are the Black Watch Museum at Balhousie Castle, & the Branklyn Gardens, which are superb in May & June.

Scone Palace, to the north of Perth was home to the Stone or Scone of Destiny for nearly 500 years until its removal to Westminster. 40 kings of Scotland were crowned here.

Pitlochry sits amid beautiful Highland scenery with forest & hill walks, two nearby distilleries, the famous Festival theatre, Loch Faskally & the Dam Visitor Centre & Fish Ladder.

In the Pass of Killiecrankie, a short drive away, a simple stone marks the spot where the Highlanders charged barefoot to overwhelm the redcoat soldiers of General MacKay.

Queens View.

Famous Queen's View overlooks Loch Tummel beyond Pitlochry with the graceful peak of Schiehallion completing a perfect picture.

Other lochs are picturesque too; Loch Earn, Loch Katrine & bonnie Loch Lomond itself, & they can be enjoyed from a boat on the water. Ospreys nest at the Loch of the Lowes near Dunkeld.

Mountain trails lead through Ben Lawers & the 'Arrocher Alps' beyond Loch Lomond. The Ochils & the Campsie Fells have grassy slopes for walking. Near Callander are the Bracklinn Falls, the Callander Crags & the Falls of Leny.

Wooded areas include the Queen Elizabeth Forest Park & the Black Wood of Rannoch which is a fragment of an ancient Caledonian forest. There are some very tall old trees around Killiecrankie, & the world's tallest beech hedge - 26 metres high - grows at Meikleour near Blairgowrie.

Creiff & Blairgowrie have excellent golf courses set in magnificent scenery.

The Grampians, Highlands & Islands

This is spacious countryside with glacier-scarred mountains & deep glens cut through by tumbling rivers. The Grampian Highlands make for fine mountaineering & walking.

There is excellent skiing at Glenshee, & a centre at the Lecht for the less experienced, whilst the broad tops of the giant mountains are ideal for cross-country skiing. The chair-lift at Glenshee is worth a visit at any season.

The Dee, The Spey & The Don flow down to the coastal plain from the heights. Some of the world's finest trout & salmon beats are on these rivers.

Speyside is dotted with famous distilleries from Grantown-on-Spey to Aberdeen, & the unique Malt Whisky Trail can be followed.

Royal Deeside & Donside hold a number of notable castles. Balmoral is the present Royal family's holiday home, & Kildrummy is a romantic ruin in a lovely garden. Fyvie Castle has five dramatic towers & stands in peaceful parkland. Nearby Haddo House, by contrast, is an elegant Georgian home.

There is a 17th century castle at Braemar, but more famous here is the Royal Highland Gathering. There are wonderful walks in the vicinity -

Scotland

Morrone Hill, Glen Quoich & the Linn O'Dee are just a few.

The city of Aberdeen is famed for its sparkling granite buildings, its university, its harbour & fish market & for North Sea Oil. It also has long sandy beaches & lovely year-round flower displays, of roses in particular.

Around the coast are fishing towns & villages. Crovie & Pennan sit below impressive cliffs. Buckie is a typical small port along the picturesque coastline of the Moray Firth.

The Auld Kirk at Cullen has fine architectural features & elegant Elgin has beautiful cathedral ruins. Pluscarden Abbey, Spynie Palace & Duffus Castle are all nearby.

Dunnottar Castle.

Nairn has a long stretch of sandy beach & a golf course with an international reputation. Inland are Cawdor Castle & Culloden Battlefield.

The Northern Highlands are divided from the rest of Scotland by the dramatic valley of the Great Glen. From Fort William to Inverness, sea lochs, canals & the depths of Loch Ness form a chain of waterways linking both coasts.

Here are some of the wildest & most beautiful landscapes in Britain. Far Western Knoydart, the Glens of Cannich & Affric, the mysterious lochs, including Loch Morar, deeper than the North Sea, & the marvellous coastline; all are exceptional.

The glens were once the home of crofting communities, & of the clansmen who supported the Jacobite cause. The wild scenery of Glencoe is a favourite with walkers & climbers, but it has a tragic history. Its name means 'the glen of weeping' & refers to the massacre of the MacDonald clan in 1692, when the Royal troops who had been received as guests treacherously attacked their hosts at dawn.

The valleys are empty today largely as a result of the infamous Highland Clearances in the 19th century when the landowners turned the tenant crofters off the land in order to introduce the more profitable Cheviot sheep. The emigration of many Scots to the U.S.A. & the British Colonies resulted from these events.

South of Inverness lie the majestic Cairngorms. The Aviemore centre provides both summer & winter sports facilities here.

To the north of Loch Ness are the remains of the ancient Caledonian forest where red deer & stags are a common sight on the hills. Rarer are sightings of the Peregrine Falcon, the osprey, the Golden Eagle & the Scottish wildcat. Kincraig has excellent wildlife parks.

Inverness is the last large town in the north, & a natural gateway to the Highlands & to Moray, the Black Isle & the north-east.

The east coast is characterised by the Firths of Moray, Cromarty & Dornoch & by its changing scenery from gentle pastureland, wooded hillsides to sweeping coastal cliffs.

On the Black Isle, which is not a true island but has a causeway & bridge links with the mainland, Fortrose & Rosemarkie in particular have lovely beaches, caves & coastal walks. There is golf on the headland at Rosemarkie & a 13th century cathedral of rosy pink sandstone stands in Fortrose.

Scotland

Scotland Gazeteer

Areas of outstanding natural beauty

It would be invidious, not to say almost impossible, to choose any particular area of Scotland as having a more beautiful aspect than another - the entire country is a joy to the traveller. The rugged Highlands, the great glens, tumbling waters, tranquil lochs - the deep countryside or the wild coastline - simply come & choose your own piece of paradise.

Historic Houses & Castles

Bowhill - Nr. Selkirk
18th-19th century - home of the Duke of Bucceleugh & Queensberry. Has an outstanding collection of pictures by Canaletto, Claude, Gainsborough, Reynolds & Leonardo da Vinci. Superb silver, porcelain & furniture.16th & 17th century miniatures.

Traquair House - Innerleithen
A unique & ancient house being the oldest inhabited home in Scotland. It is rich in associations with every form of political history & after Bonnie Prince Charlie passed through its main gates in 1745 no other visitor has been allowed to use them. There are treasures in the house dating from 12th century, & it has an 18th century library & a priest's room with secret stairs.

Linlithgow Palace - Linlithgow
The birthplace of Mary, Queen of Scots.

Stirling Castle - Stirling
Royal Castle.

Drumlanrigg Castle - Nr. Thornhill
17th century castle of pale pink stone - romantic & historic - wonderful art treasures including a magnificent Rembrandt & a huge silver chandelier. Beautiful garden setting.

Braemar Castle - Braemar
17th century castle of great historic interest. Has round central tower with spiral staircase giving it a fairy-tale appearance.

Drum Castle - Nr. Aberdeen
Dating in part from 13th century, it has a great square tower.

Cawdor Castle - Nairn
14th century fortress - like castle - has always been the home of the Thanes of Cawdor - background to Shakespeare's Macbeth.

Dunvegan Castle - Isle of Skye
13th century - has always been the home of the Chiefs of McLeod.

Hopetoun House - South Queensferry
Very fine example of Adam architecture & has a fine collection of pictures & furniture. Splendid landscaped grounds.

Inverary Castle - Argyll
Home of the Dukes of Argyll. 18th century - Headquarters of Clan Campbell.

Burn's Cottage - Alloway
Birthplace of Robert Burns - 1659 - thatched cottage - museum of Burns' relics.

Bachelors' Club - Tarbolton
17th century house - thatched - where Burns & friends formed their club - 1780.

Blair Castle - Blair Atholl
Home of the Duke of Atholl, 13th century Baronial mansion - collection of Jacobite relics, armour, paintings, china & many other items.

Glamis Castle - Angus
17th century remodelling in Chateau style - home of the Earl of Strathmore & Kinghorne. Very attractive castle - lovely grounds by Capability Brown.

Scone Palace - Perth
has always been associated with seat of Government of Scotland from earliest times. The Stone of Destiny was removed from the Palace in 1296 & taken to Westminster Abbey. Present palace rebuilt in early 1800's still incorporating parts of the old. Lovely gardens.

Edinburgh Castle
Fortress standing high over the town - famous for military tattoo.

Culzean Castle & Country Park - Maybole
Fine Adam house & spacious gardens perched on Ayrshire cliff.

Dunrobin Castle - Golspie
Ancient seat of the Earls & Dukes of Sutherland.

Eilean Donan Castle - Wester Ross
13th century castle, Jacobite relics.

Manderston - Duns
Great classical house with only silver staircase in the world. Stables, marble dairy, formal gardens.

Scotland

Cathedrals & Churches

Dunfermline Abbey - Dunfermline
Norman remains of beautiful church.
Modern east end & tower.

Edinburgh (Church of the Holy Rood)
15th century - was divided into two in 17th
century & re-united 1938. Here Mary,
Queen of Scots was crowned.

Glasgow (St. Mungo)
12th-15th century cathedral - 19th century
interior. Central tower with spire.

Kirkwall (St. Magnus)
12th century cathedral with very fine nave.

Falkirk Old Parish Church - Falkirk
The spotted appearance (faw) of the
church (kirk) gave the town its name. The
site of the church has been used since 7th
century, with succesive churches built
upon it. The present church was much
rebuilt in 19th century. Interesting
historically.

St Columba's Abbey - Iona

Museums & Galleries

Agnus Folk Museum - Glamis
17th century cottages with stone slab
roofs, restored by the National Trust for
Scotland & houses a fine folk collection.

Mary, Queen of Scots' House - Jedburgh
Life & times of the Queen along with
paintings, etc.

Andrew Carnegie Birthplace -
Dunfermline
The cottage where he was born is now
part of a museum showing his life's work.

Aberdeen Art Gallery & Museum -
Aberdeen
Sculpture, paintings, watercolours, prints
& drawings. Applied arts. Maritime
museum exhibits.

Provost Skene's House - Aberdeen
17th century house now exhibiting local
domestic life, etc.

Highland Folk Museum - Kingussie
Examples of craft work & tools - furnished
cottage with mill.

West Highland Museum - Fort William
Natural & local hsitory. Relics of Jacobites
& exhibition of the '45 Rising.

Clan Macpherson House - Newtonmore
Relics of the Clan.

Glasgow Art Gallery & Museum -
Glasgow
Archaeology, technology, local & natural
history. Old Masters, tapestries, porcelain,
glass & silver, etc. Sculpture.

Scottish National Gallery - Edinburgh
20th century collection - paintings &
sculpture - Arp, Leger, Giacometti,
Matisse, Picasso. Modern Scottish
painting.

**National Museum of Antiquities in
Scotland** - Edinburgh
Collection from Stone Age to modern
times - Relics of Celtic Church, Stuart
relics, Highland weapons, etc.

Gladstone Court - Biggar
Small indoor street of shops, a bank,
schoolroom, library, etc.

Burns' Cottage & Museum - Alloway
Relics of Robert Burns - National Poet.

Inverness Museum & Art Gallery -
Inverness
Social history, archaeology & cultural life
of the Highlands. Display of the Life of the
Clans - good Highland silver - crafts, etc.

Kirkintilloch - Nr. Glasgow
Auld Kirk Museum. Local history,
including archaeological specimens from
the Antonine Wall (Roman). Local
industries, exhibitions, etc

Pollock House & Park - Glasgow
18th century house with collection of
paintings, etc. The park is the home of the
award-winning Burrell Collection
The foregoing are but a few of the many
museums & galleries in Scotland - further
information is always freely available from
the Tourist Information.

Historic Monuments

Aberdour Castle - Aberdour
14th century fortification - part still roofed.

Balvenie Castle - Duffton
15th century castle ruins.

Cambuskenneth Abbey - Nr. Stirling
12th century abbey - seat of Bruce's
Parliament in 1326. Ruins.

Dryburgh Abbey - Dryburgh
Remains of monastery.

Loch Leven Castle - Port Glasgow
15th century ruined stronghold - once lived
in by Mary, Queen of Scots.

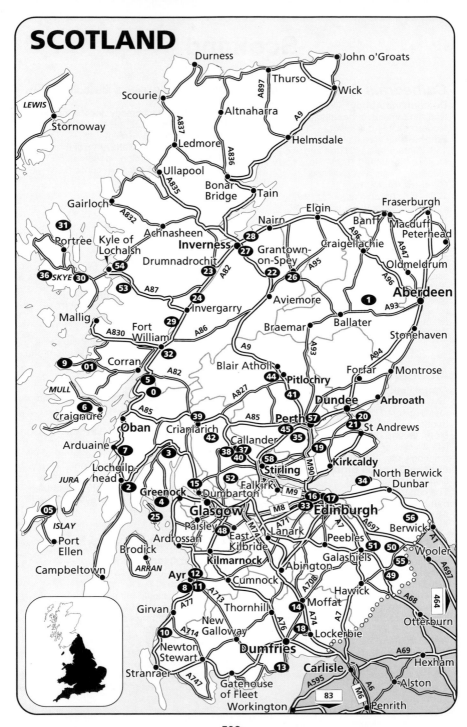

SCOTLAND

LEWIS

Durness   John o'Groats
                 Thurso
Scourie   A897   Wick
Stornoway   Altnaharra
                 A9
          Ledmore   Helmsdale
          A837 A836
LEWIS
          Ullapool
          A835
          Bonar
          Bridge   Tain
Gairloch   A832   Elgin   Fraserburgh
31   Nairn   Banff Macduff
Portree Kyle of Achnasheen 28   Peterhead
         Lochalsh   27   Grantown- Craigellachie
36 SKYE 30 54   Drumnadrochit on-Spey A96   Oldmeldrum
         53 A87   23   A82   22   26   A96
                    24   A95   Aberdeen
         Invergarry   Aviemore   1   A93
Mallig   29   A86   Braemar   Ballater
         Fort   A9   Stonehaven
9 01 William 32   A93 A94
         Corran A82   Blair Atholl   Forfar Montrose
         5   A827 44 Pitlochry   A93
MULL   0   41 Dundee Arbroath
6   A85   Perth 57   20
Craignure   39   A85   45 35 21 St Andrews
         Oban A85 Crianlarich 42   Callander 19 Kirkcaldy
Arduaine   3   38 37
         7   40 58 North Berwick
Lochgilp-   52 Stirling 34 Dunbar
head   15   Falkirk
JURA 2 Greenock Dumbarton M9
      4   Glasgow M8 33 Edinburgh
05   25 Paisley 48 M74 16 17 56
ISLAY   Ardrossan East Lanark A67 Berwick
Port   Kilbride   Peebles 51 50 A1
Ellen Brodick Kilmarnock Galashiels 55 Wooler
Campbeltown ARRAN Ayr 12 Abington 49 A68
         8 11 A713 Cumnock A708 Hawick 464
Girvan A77   Thornhill 14 Moffat A7 Otterburn
      10 A714 New A76 18 A74
Newton Galloway Lockerbie A68
Stewart   Dumfries Hexham
Stranraer A747 13 Carlisle Alston
         Gatehouse A595 83 M6
         of Fleet Workington Penrith

SCOTLAND

Map references

Map of Scotland with regions labelled: OUTER HEBRIDES, LEWIS, WESTERN ISLES, SKYE, INNER HEBRIDES, HIGHLANDS, MORAY, ABERDEENSHIRE, ABERDEEN, MULL, JURA, ISLAY, ARRAN, PERTHSHIRE & KINROSS, ANGUS, DUNDEE, ARGYLL & BUTE, STIRLING, FIFE, EAST LOTHIAN, NORTH AYRSHIRE, SOUTH LANARKSHIRE, EAST AYRSHIRE, BORDERS, SOUTH AYRSHIRE, DUMFRIES & GALLOWAY

1 INVERCLYDE
2 DUNBARTON & CLYDEBANK
3 RENFREWSHIRE
4 EAST RENFREWSHIRE
5 GLASGOW
6 EAST DUNBARTONSHIRE
7 NORTH LANARKSHIRE
8 FALKIRK
9 CLACKMANNAN
10 WEST LOTHIAN
11 EDINBURGH
12 MID LOTHAIN

Scotland
Aberdeenshire & Argyll

		rate from £ per person	children taken	evening meals	animals taken
Anne & Eddie Strachan **Hazlehurst Lodge** **Ballater Road** **Aboyne** **AB34 5HY** **Tel: (013398) 86921** **Fax 013398 86660** **Open: FEB - DEC** **Map Ref No. 1**	Nearest Road: A.93 Charming Victorian coachman's lodge on the way to Aboyne Castle, set in wooded garden. Reflecting the owners' artistic background are 5 beautifully designed bedrooms, all with en-suite facilities. Anne Strachan is a fine chef, with a growing reputation for imaginative cooking using the best of Scottish produce. Her superb meals are served with friendly informality in the small licensed restaurant. Aboyne is an ideal centre for a truly relaxing stay on Royal Deeside, an Area of Outstanding Natural Beauty. **E-mail: scotlanddeluxe@zet.net.co.uk** CREDIT CARD VISA M'CARD AMEX	£27.00	Y	Y	Y
David & Meg White **Lys-Na-Greyne** **Rhu-Na-Haven Road** **Aboyne** **AB34 5JD** **Tel: (013398) 87397** **Fax 013398 86441** **Open: ALL YEAR** **Map Ref No. 1**	Nearest Road: A.93 Lys-Na-Greyne is a beautiful Edwardian mansion situated in idyllic surroundings on the banks of the River Dee on the outskirts of Aboyne in Royal Deeside, standing in grounds of around 3 acres. This is a perfect place for exploring the surrounding countryside where there are many castles & places of historic interest. Golf, riding, gliding, fishing, hill-walking, tennis all available locally. Shooting, stalking available by arrangement with hosts. All rooms with en-suite/private bathroom & breathtaking views over the garden or river. CREDIT CARD VISA M'CARD AMEX	£25.00	Y	N	Y

Argyll

		rate from £ per person	children taken	evening meals	animals taken
Peter & Helen Stockdale **Feorag House** **Glenborrodale** **Acharacle PH36 4JP** **Tel: (01972) 500248** **Fax 01972 500285** **Open: ALL YEAR** **Map Ref No. 01**	Nearest Road: A.861 Set amongst 13 acres of grounds, with its own private shoreline, Feorag House is a haven of comfort, peace, warmth, good food & good friends; surrounded by wild mountainous beauty & the timeless lap of the waves of Loch Sunart. Each bedroom is tastefully furnished & enjoys a sea view & a bathroom en-suite. The home-baking & varied menus make a stay at Feorag House a sheer delight. Children over 10 years welcome. Animals by arrangement. CREDIT CARD VISA M'CARD	£29.50	N	Y	Y
Earle & Stella Broadbent **Lochside Cottage** **Fasnacloich** **Appin PA38 4BJ** **Tel: (01631) 730216** **Open: ALL YEAR** **Map Ref No. 0**	Nearest Road: A.828 Total peace on the shore of Loch Baile Mhic Chailen, in an idyllic glen of outstanding beauty. There are many walks from the cottage garden; or, visit Fort William, Glencoe & Oban, from where you can board a steamer to explore the Western Isles. At the end of the day, a warm welcome awaits you: delicious home-cooked dinner, a log fire & the certainty of a perfect night's sleep in one of 3 en-suite bedrooms.	£20.00	Y	Y	Y

Abbot's Brae. Dunoon.

Scotland
Argyll

		rate from £ per person	children taken	evening meals	animals taken
Margaret & Harvey McKay **'Allt-na-Craig'** **Tarbert Road** **Ardrishaig PA30 8EP** **Tel: (01546) 603245** **Open: ALL YEAR (Excl. Xmas & New Year)** **Map Ref No. 02**	Nearest Road: A.83 The McKays warmly welcome all their guests to 'Allt-na-Craig', a lovely old Victorian mansion set in picturesque grounds overlooking Loch Fyne. Accommodation in 6 comfortable en-suite bedrooms with tea/coffee makers. A guests' lounge with open fire & dining room is also available. This is a perfect base for outdoor activities, like hill-walking, fishing, golf, riding & windsurfing, or for visiting the islands. Delicious evening meals by arrangement.	£30.00	Y	Y	Y
Helen & Gavin Dick **Abbot's Brae Hotel** **West Bay** **Dunoon PA23 7QJ** **Tel: (01369) 705021** **Fax 01369 705021** **Open: ALL YEAR** **Map Ref No. 04**	Nearest Road: A.815 Friendly, family-run Victorian country house hotel in secluded 2-acre woodland glen, with breathtaking views of the sea & hills. 7 tastefully furnished, spacious bedrooms, all en-suite with colour T.V., radio, 'phone & tea/coffee facilities. Unwind with a drink by the fire in the comfortable lounge, dine in the cosy dining room with delicious a la carte menu & select wine list. The ideal base for exploring Argyll & the Western Highlands. Only 1 hour from Glasgow Airport. Licensed.	£24.50 *see PHOTO over* CREDIT CARD VISA M'CARD	Y	Y	Y
Flavia MacArthur **Ardsheal Home Farm** **Kentallen** **Duror in Appin** **PA38 4BZ** **Tel/Fax: (01631) 740229** **Open: APR - OCT (& New Year)** **Map Ref No. 5**	Nearest Road: A.828 A charming Scottish hill farm of 1,000 acres, surrounded by breathtaking scenery on the shores of Loch Linnhe, overlooking the Morvern Hills. A warm welcome is assured from the friendly hosts. 3 attractive bedrooms, comfortable & well-furnished, with tea/coffee-making facilities, electric blankets, etc. Delicious evening meals (no vegetarian) served by arrangement. Convenient for touring, sailing to the inner Isles. An idyllic holiday retreat, there is even 1 mile of private beach. Riding & tennis nearby. Single supplement.	£17.00 🚭	Y	Y	N
Mrs Margaret Rozga **Kilmeny Farmhouse** **Ballygrant** **Isle of Islay PA45 7QW** **Tel: (01496) 840668** **Fax 01496 840668** **Open: ALL YEAR** **Map Ref No. 05**	Nearest Road: A.746 Islay is well-known for its abundant & wonderful wildlife & its many malt-whisky distilleries. Kilmeny Farmhouse, in the heart of a 300-acre beef farm, commands magnificent views of the surrounding hills & glen. This family-run business places emphasis on quality & personal service. The exquisite en-suite bedrooms, with country views, are elegantly furnished. The public rooms are charming, with a country-house influence. A 4-course dinner menu is available. Children over 8.	£30.00 🚭	Y	Y	Y
John & Eleanor Wagstaff **Red Bay Cottage** **Deargphort** **Fionnphort** **Isle of Mull PA66 6BP** **Tel: (01681) 700396** **Open: ALL YEAR** **Map Ref No. 06**	Nearest Road: A.849 A really warm welcome awaits the visitor to this charming modern house, offering 3 very comfortable rooms with modern facilities. Situated only 20 metres from the sea, & overlooking Iona Sound & the white sandy beaches on the Isle of Iona, this surely must be the ideal base for a relaxing & peaceful holiday. Mr Wagstaff offers superb food. Eleanor is a qualified, practising silversmith, so why not enjoy a winter break on their residential silversmithing course?	£16.00	Y	Y	Y

Ardsheal House. Kentallen of Appin.

Scotland
Argyll

		rate from £ per person	children taken	evening meals	animals taken
Neil & Philippa Sutherland **Ardsheal House** **Kentallen of Appin** **PA38 4BX** Tel: (01631) 740227 Fax 01631 740342 Open: MAR - NOV Map Ref No. 5	Nearest Road: A.82 Ardsheal House is spectacularly situated on the shores of Loch Linnhe, in 800 acres of woodlands, fields & gardens. It is a wonderful place for a relaxing holiday. This historic mansion is elegantly furnished throughout with family antiques & pictures, & offers 5 en-suite bedrooms which are attractive & well-appointed. The food at Ardsheal is excellent, it delights the eye & pleases the palate, & includes local fresh produce & homemade bread & preserves. A delightful home.	£35.00 *see PHOTO over* CREDIT CARD VISA M'CARD AMEX	Y	Y	Y
Dr & Mrs D. Bannister **Tigh an Lodan Ford** **Lochgilphead (By)** **PA31 8RH** Tel: (01546) 810287 Fax 01546 810287 Open: MAY - OCT Map Ref No. 07	Nearest Road: A.816 In scenic seclusion at the southern end of Loch Awe, Ford is well situated for enjoying the under-appreciated attractions of mid-Argyll, as well as for fishing & walking. The hosts offer an interesting cuisine in a relaxing environment. Tigh an Lodan has all the comforts you expect, coupled with pampering touches such as an open fire & plentiful books in the elegant sitting room. There is comfortable accommodation for 6 in 3 bedrooms, all en-suite. Children over 13 years welcome.	£19.00 🚭 CREDIT CARD VISA M'CARD	Y	Y	Y
Mrs Sandra Cameron **Thistle House** **St. Catherines** **PA25 8AZ** Tel: (01499) 302209 Fax 01499 302531 Open: APR - OCT Map Ref No. 03	Nearest Road: A.815 Superbly situated Victorian country house retaining many original features. Surrounded by 2 acres of mature garden, commanding spectacular views of Loch Fyne & sitting directly across the Loch from Inverary & its famous castle. 4 en-suite bedrooms with tea/coffee-making facilities & colour T.V.. Lounge with open fire. Good eating place in village & other restaurants nearby for evening meals. The Cowal Peninsula is well located for exploring Argyll & the Loch Lomond area. 1 hour's drive from Glasgow Airport.	£21.00 CREDIT CARD VISA M'CARD	Y	N	N
William Mercer **Arnish Cottage,** **Christian Guest House** **Poll Bay** **St. Catherines PA25 8BA** Tel/Fax: (01499) 302405 Open: ALL YEAR Map Ref No. 03	Nearest Road: A.815 Situated across the Loch from Inveraray, a truly idyllic setting on a private road 20 feet from the Lochside, & approx. 1 hr's drive from Glasgow Airport. A T.V. lounge & viewing conservatory are provided. All of the attractive & comfortable bedrooms are en-suite. Non-smoking throughout. Loch fishing, hill & forest walks, pony trekking, etc., are readily organised. A charming home, ideal for a relaxing break.	£25.00 🚭	N	N	N
Roy & Janet Smith **'Meall Mo Chridhe'** **Country House** **Kilchoan** **West Ardnamurchan** **PH36 4LH** Tel/Fax: (01972) 510238 Open: APR - OCT Map Ref No. 09	Nearest Road: A.861 Meall Mo Chridhe (Little Hill of my Heart) is a Grade II listed former manse (c.1790) situated on the most westerly point of the U.K. mainland. Peace & tranquillity, log fires, elegant furnishings & imaginative cooking using local game & seafoods, incl. venison, quail, king scallops, salmon, & langoustines. Janet makes her own bread, jam preserves & fruit sorbets. Spectacular coastal scenery, walking & wildlife. Car ferry to Tobermory, the ideal location from which to visit Mull, Iona, Coll & Tiree. Children over 12.	£33.00 🚭	Y	Y	Y

Brenalder Lodge.   Doonfoot.

Scotland
Ayrshire

		rate from £ per person	children taken	evening meals	animals taken
Mrs Caroline McDonald **The Crescent** **26 Bellevue Crescent** **Ayr KA7 2DR** **Tel: (01292) 287329** **Open: JAN - NOV** **Map Ref No. 12**	Nearest Road: A.70 Elegant Victorian terraced house set in the heart of Ayr. All rooms are comfortable & individually styled including 1 with 4-poster bed. Each has a private bathroom. Within 5 minutes walk, guests can enjoy a leisurely stroll along the promenade or a relaxing drink in one of Ayr's cosy pubs. Ideal location for golf, Burns Heritage, Culzean Castle & the Galloway Forest. Hosts can also be contacted by fax on 01292 286779. CREDIT CARD VISA M'CARD	£23.00	Y	N	N
Brenda Taylor **Brenalder Lodge** **39 Dunure Road** **Doonfoot** **Ayr** **KA7 4HR** **Tel: (01292) 443939** **Open: ALL YEAR** **Map Ref No. 11**	Nearest Road: A.77 Brenda & Bert Taylor welcome you to Brenalder Lodge. There are panoramic views of the Carrick Hills & the Firth of Clyde. Easy access to Prestwick airport & the world-famous Turnberry & Royal Troon golf courses. An ideal base for touring the Burns country. All rooms have en-suite facilities, T.V. & tea/coffee makers. A delicious 4-course Scottish breakfast is served in the new conservatory-style dining room. All-day access to the Lodge, & parking. A 4-course dinner is served at 6 p.m. with 24 hrs' notice. Children over 7. *see PHOTO over*	£25.00	Y	Y	Y
Mrs Agnes Gemmell **Dunduff Farm** **Dunure** **Ayr KA7 4LH** **Tel: (01292) 500225** **Fax 01292 500222** **Open: FEB - NOV** **Map Ref No. 08**	Nearest Road: A.719 A warm friendly welcome awaits you at Dunduff Farm. Situated just south of Ayr at the coastal village of Dunure, this family run beef & sheep unit of some 600 acres, is only 15 mins from the shore. Excellent accommodation yet homely & comfortable. Bedrooms have panoramic coastal views over Arran, the Holy Isle, Mull of Kintyre & Ailsa Craig. Each is well-equipped & has beverage facilities, T.V. & an en-suite or private bathroom. Good location for exploring south west Scotland. CREDIT CARD VISA M'CARD	£20.00	Y	N	N
Susan & Robin Crosthwaite **Cosses Country House** **Ballantrae** **KA26 0LR** **Tel: (01465) 831363** **Fax 01465 831598** **Open: ALL YEAR (Excl.** **Xmas & New Year)** **Map Ref No. 10**	Nearest Road: A.77 A former shooting lodge (1800's) & home farm (1900's), set in a secluded valley of garden & woodland. Superb accommodation, en-suite facilities, T.V., a hospitality tray & a roaring log fire on chilly evenings. A good base for exploring this delightful part of Scotland. The kitchen & herb garden supplement local produce for you to enjoy the taste of Scotland dinners. Castles (incl. Culzean), gardens, Burns's birthplace, golf courses, fishing, walks & cycling within easy reach. Irish ferry terminals 30 mins' drive. **E-mail: 100636.1047@compuserve.com** *see PHOTO over* CREDIT CARD VISA M'CARD	£33.00	Y	Y	Y
Mrs Janet Beale **Balkissock Lodge** **Ballantrae** **Girvan KA26 0LP** **Tel: (01465) 831537** **Fax 01465 831537** **Open: ALL YEAR** **Map Ref No. 10**	Nearest Road: A.77 Janet & Adrian offer southern Scottish hospitality in their delightful Georgian country home. Guests are accommodated in attractive en-suite rooms. Peace, quiet, sea air & splendid scenery are the perfect combination for a short break. Ideally situated for touring & for the Irish ferries. The imaginative, professionally cooked menus are dedicated to the best of Scottish food, including vegetarian. Guests may bring their own wines. **E-mail: 1006223125@compuserve.com** CREDIT CARD VISA M'CARD	£22.50	Y	Y	N

Cosses. Ballantrae.

Scotland
Ayrshire

		rate from £ per person	children taken	evening meals	animals taken
Mrs Isobel Kyle **Hawkhill Farm** **Old Dailly** **Girvan** **KA26 9RD** **Tel: (01465) 871232** **Open: APR - OCT** **Map Ref No. 10**	Nearest Road: A.77 Superior farmhouse hospitality in spacious 17th-century former coaching inn, where the emphasis is on comfort & good food. 2 delightfully furnished bedrooms with private facilities, central heating, log fires on a chillier day in the Adam-inspired lounge. Hawkhill Farm is in a peaceful setting, & is perfect for exploring south-west Scotland, Culzean Castle, Robert Burns Centre, golf, pony-trekking, walking, cycling (hire one here) & gardens. Brochure available. A charming home.	£21.00	Y	N	N

Berwickshire

		rate from £ per person	children taken	evening meals	animals taken
Michael & Caroline Thomson **Kirkside House** **Bonkyl** **Duns TD11 3RJ** **Tel: (01361) 882825** **Fax 01361 882157** **Open: MAY - OCT** **Map Ref No. 56**	Nearest Road: A.1, A.6112 Kirkside House is an early-Victorian, former manse set in a peaceful, rural location. Charming en-suite/private bedrooms have lovely views to the hills & are thoughtfully equipped. Super breakfasts served using free-range produce. Guests may choose to relax in the delightful walled garden with clematis, honeysuckle & roses. An acclaimed restaurant nearby. An ideal base for local country pursuits, Edinburgh, Berwick & Dunbar. 'Phone for directions. Children over 12 years.	£20.00	Y	N	N

Clackmannanshire

		rate from £ per person	children taken	evening meals	animals taken
Jane & Adrian O'Dell **Westbourne B & B** **10 Dollar Road** **Tillicoultry FK13 6PA** **Tel: (01259) 750314** **Fax 01259 750642** **Open: ALL YEAR** **Map Ref No. 58**	Nearest Road: A.91 A Victorian mill-owner's mansion set in wooded grounds beneath Ochil Hills, in excellent walking country with numerous golf courses. Warm, friendly atmosphere, delicious home-cooking including vegetarian dishes. Log fires, croquet lawn, T.V., radio & tea/coffee-making facilities in all rooms (en-suite is on the ground floor). Centrally situated for Edinburgh, Glasgow, Perth & Stirling, home of 'Braveheart'. Secure off-street parking. **E-mail: odellwestbourne@compuserve.com**	£20.00	Y	N	Y

Dumfriesshire

		rate from £ per person	children taken	evening meals	animals taken
Mr & Mrs F. D. Jeffries **Cavens House** **Kirkbean-by-Dumfries** **DG2 8AA** **Tel: (01387) 880234** **Fax 01387 880234** **Open: ALL YEAR** **Map Ref No. 13**	Nearest Road: A.710 Formerly an old mansion with a strong American historical connection, this charming guest house offers 6 really comfortable rooms with modern facilities, including a private bath or shower. Tea-making facilities & colour T.V. in each room. Standing in 11 acres of mature gardens & woodland, it makes a perfect base for those wishing to explore the joys of the Solway Coast, with its beautiful scenery & excellent beaches. Sailing, fishing, walking, golfing & riding all local. An excellent cuisine here. A friendly atmosphere.	£25.00 *see PHOTO over* CREDIT CARD VISA M'CARD	Y	Y	Y

Cavens House.   Kirkbean-by-Dumfries.

Scotland
Dumfriesshire

		rate from £ per person	children taken	evening meals	animals taken
Frank & Jane Pearson **Applegarth House** **Lockerbie** **DG11 1SX** **Tel: (01387) 810270** Fax 01387 811701 **Open: ALL YEAR** **Map Ref No. 18**	Nearest Road: M.74 Applegarth House is a delightful former manse in a peaceful situation overlooking the River Annan, yet only 3 miles from Lockerbie & Jt.17 on the M.74. It is the perfect centre from which to explore the beautiful Border country, or an ideal overnight stop. Shooting, stalking, fishing & wildfowling can be arranged locally. Jane is an excellent cook & you are assured a warm welcome in their relaxed family home with its comfortable, sunny & spacious rooms. Children over 10. 'Phone for directions. CREDIT CARD VISA M'CARD	£30.00	Y	Y	N
Margaret White **Hartfell House** **Hartfell Crescent** **Moffat DG10 9AL** **Tel: (01683) 220153** **Open: MAR - NOV** **Map Ref No. 14**	Nearest Road: A.74, M.74 Hartfell House is a splendid Victorian manor house located in a rural setting overlooking the hills, yet only a few mins' walk from the town. A listed building known locally for its fine interior woodwork. Offering 8 spacious bedrooms, 5 with en-suite facilities. Standing in landscaped gardens of approximately 2 acres of lawns & trees, & providing an atmosphere of peaceful relaxation.	£18.00	Y	Y	Y

Dunbartonshire

		rate from £ per person	children taken	evening meals	animals taken
Mr & Mrs S. MacDonald **Kirkton House** **Darleith Road** **Cardross** **G82 5EZ** **Tel: (01389) 841951** **Fax (01389) 841868** **Open: ALL YEAR (Excl. Xmas & New Year)** **Map Ref No. 15**	Nearest Road: A.814 Experience a blend of olde worlde charm, modern amenities & superb views at this converted 18/19th-century farmhouse, set in a tranquil location & yet handy for Glasgow Airport (20/25 mins), Loch Lomond, The Trossachs & most West Highland routes. All the spacious bedrooms have full en-suite facilities. The cosy lounge has a roaring fire on chilly evenings. Enjoy home-cooked food & savour a glass of wine at dinner by oil lamplight. Like the lounge, the convivial dining room has the original stone walls & a rustic fireplace, with the old swee from which the cooking pots were hung. **E-mail: KIRKTONHOUSE@COMPUSERVE.COM** CREDIT CARD VISA M'CARD AMEX	£28.50 *see PHOTO over*	Y	Y	Y

Edinburgh

		rate from £ per person	children taken	evening meals	animals taken
Mrs Helen Baird **Arisaig** **64 Glasgow Road** **Corstorphine EH12 8LN** **Tel: (0131) 3342610** **Open: APR - OCT** **Map Ref No. 16**	Nearest Road: M.8, M.9, A.720 A warm Scottish welcome awaits you here at this very pleasant & comfortable detached bungalow, situated only 3 miles from the city centre. There are 2 lovely bedrooms, all with modern amenities, & all kept to a very high standard. Tea/coffee-making & en-suite facilities available. Parking. Excellent bus service. An ideal base from which to explore Edinburgh. Children over 12.	£20.00	N	N	N

Kirkton House. Cardross.

Scotland
Edinburgh

		rate from £ per person	children taken	evening meals	animals taken

Adrian & Jackie Hayes **The Avenue Hotel** **4 Murrayfield Avenue** **Edinburgh EH12 6AX** **Tel: (0131) 3467270** **Fax 0131 3379733** **Open: ALL YEAR** **Map Ref No. 16**	Nearest Road: A.8 An Edwardian terraced villa situated in a quiet tree lined avenue, west of & only mins from the city centre. Ideal for both the business traveller & tourist with easy access to the airport, city by-pass & motorway links to the north & west of Scotland. Adrian & Jackie Hayes look forward to welcoming you. All 9 individually designed rooms have private facilities, T.V. & hospitality tray. Ample free parking available.	£20.00 CREDIT CARD VISA M'CARD	Y	N	Y
Willaim & Eleanor Clark **Tudorbank Lodge** **18 St. John's Road** **Corstorphine** **Edinburgh EH12 6NY** **Tel: (0131) 3347845** **Fax 0131 3345386** **Open: ALL YEAR** **Map Ref No. 16**	Nearest Road: A.8 An enchanting Tudor (C.1900) house set in private gardens with parking, which has been interestingly furnished. Come & enjoy the warmth of Scottish hospitality. Superb breakfasts, freshly cooked to order, with an ample choice for Vegetarians. Colour T.V., hospitality tray, washbasins in all rooms, some en-suite. Ideal for touring, business, golf & especially for the Festival, Fringe & Tatoo. Easy access to city centre, Zoo, Murrayfield, Airport, Ingliston Showground & Forth Bridges.	£25.00	Y	N	Y
Mrs Jan Cairns **Cairn Lodge Guest House** **2 Downie Terrace** **Corstophine** **Edinburgh EH12 7AU** **Tel: (0131) 5392117** **Fax 0131 5398117** **Open: ALL YEAR** **Map Ref No. 16**	Nearest Road: M.8, M.9 Cairn Lodge is an elegant Victorian house, conveniently situated for Murrayfield, the airport, motorways & the city. A warm, friendly Scottish welcome awaits you in this charming house, which has been lovingly restored. Excellent bedrooms with marble fireplaces & original cornices, en-suite facilities, colour T.V. & hospitality trays in all rooms. Superb breakfasts. Private parking & an excellent bus service. An ideal base from which to explore Edinburgh.	£20.00 🚭	Y	N	Y
Susan Turner **Camus House** **4 Seaview Terrace** **Edinburgh EH15 2HD** **Tel/Fax: (0131) 6572003** **Open: ALL YEAR** **Map Ref No. 16**	Nearest Road: A.199 A Victorian, terraced villa overlooking the Firth of Forth, Camus House enjoys the peace of the seaside, along with an excellent bus service to the city centre, with its cultural, historical and leisure interests. The 4 guest rooms are comfortably furnished, and have wash basins, colour T.V., radio alarms & tea/coffee facilities, 2 are en-suite. A genuine and friendly welcome is assured.	£17.00 CREDIT CARD VISA M'CARD	Y	N	Y
Brenda & William Wright **The Salisbury** **45 Salisbury Road** **Edinburgh** **EH16 5AA** **Tel: (0131) 6671264** **Fax 0131 6671264** **Open: ALL YEAR** **Map Ref No. 16**	Nearest Road: A.7 Enjoy real Scottish hospitality in the comfort of this Georgian house. The Wright family offer you tastefully decorated, comfortable bedrooms, all with private facilities, colour T.V. & tea/coffee makers. Their home has been carefully refurbished during their 20-year ownership. Central heating throughout. Secluded garden to the rear. 10 mins by bus to the city centre, railway station & tourist attractions. Private car park. Children over 5 years welcome. **E-mail: brenda.wright@btinternet.com**	£24.00 🚭 CREDIT CARD VISA M'CARD	Y	N	N

Kildonan Lodge Hotel. Edinburgh.

Scotland
Edinburgh

Mrs Dorothy Vidler **Kenvie Guest House** **16 Kilmaurs Road** **Edinburgh EH16 5DA** **Tel: (0131) 6681964** **Fax 0131 6681964** **Open: ALL YEAR** **Map Ref No. 16**	Nearest Road: A.7, A.68, A.1 Kenvie Guest House is charming, comfortable, warm, friendly & inviting. This small Victorian town house is situated in a quiet residential street, 1 small block from the main road, leading to the city centre (an excellent bus service) & the bypass to all routes. Offering, for your comfort, lots of caring touches, including complimentary tea/coffee, colour T.V. & no-smoking rooms. Private facilities available. You are guaranteed a warm welcome from Richard & Dorothy.	£19.00 CREDIT CARD VISA M'CARD	Y	N	N
Maggie Urquhart **Kildonan Lodge Hotel** **27 Craigmillar Park** **Newington** **Edinburgh EH16 5PE** **Tel: (0131) 6672793** **Fax 0131 6679777** **Open: ALL YEAR** **Map Ref No. 16**	Nearest Road: A.701 Ideally situated in central Edinburgh, Kildonan Lodge is an outstanding example of Victorian elegance proving the perfect setting for your visit to Scotland's capital. Relax & enjoy a 'dram' at the Honesty bar. Each of the well-appointed non-smoking en-suite bedrooms have colour T.V., telephone, radio/alarm & welcome tea/coffee trays. Delicious wholesome Scottish breakfasts are served. A warm friendly welcome awaits you.	£28.00 *see PHOTO over* CREDIT CARD VISA M'CARD AMEX	Y	N	N
Wilma, Bill & Sandy Hogg **Kingsley Guest House** **30 Craigmillar Park** **Newington** **Edinburgh EH16 5PS** **Tel/Fax: (0131) 6678439** **Open: ALL YEAR** **Map Ref No. 16**	Nearest Road: A.701 You are assured of a warm welcome & personal attention at this family-run guest house. The pleasant Victorian terraced villa offers 6 comfortable rooms, 4 en-suite. All rooms are well-equipped, with colour T.V., tea/coffee-making facilities & central heating. Conveniently situated on the south side of the city centre, in the residential university area. A really good base for everyone, with an excellent bus service from the door & a private car park. Children over 5.	£17.00 CREDIT CARD VISA M'CARD	Y	N	N
Norah Alexander **Tiree Guest House** **26 Craigmillar Park** **Edinburgh EH16 5PS** **Tel: (0131) 667 7477** **Fax 0131 662 1608** **Open: ALL YEAR** **Map Ref No. 16**	Nearest Road: A.701 Situated on the south side of Edinburgh, about 1 1/2 miles from the city centre. Offering accommodation in 8 comfortable rooms, 5 with en-suite facilities. All rooms have colour T.V. & tea/coffee makers. Conveniently located for Edinburgh University, Holyrood Palace & the shopping centre. Children are very welcome here, & are given reduced rates. A full Scottish breakfast is served.	£17.00	Y	N	N
Annie Deacon **53 Eskside West** **Musselburgh** **Edinburgh** **EH21 6RB** **Tel: (0131) 6652875** **Open: ALL YEAR** **Map Ref No. 16**	Nearest Road: A.1, A.199 A warm & helpful hostess awaits you at this stone-built terraced cottage on the bank of the River Esk. Charmingly decorated to a high standard. Double room en-suite & a twin bedded & single room sharing a luxurious bathroom. Fresh flowers, T.V., radio & tea/coffee-making facilities in all rooms. A professional cook, Annie provides excellent breakfasts & dinners. A super base, 15 mins' from Holyrood & 20 mins' from the centre of Edinburgh. Children over 6.	£16.00	Y	Y	N

Twenty London Street. Edinburgh.

	Nearest Road	rate from £ per person	children taken	evening meals	animals taken
Judith & Harper Cuthbert **Delta House** **16 Carberry Road** **Inveresk, Musselburgh** **Edinburgh EH21 7TN** **Tel: (0131) 6652107** **Open: APR - OCT** **Map Ref No. 17**	Nearest Road: A.720 Delta House is a Victorian detached house built in 1880. This beautiful home has very spacious rooms & is tastefully furnished throughout. First-class accommodation is offered & there are 3 attractive & well-appointed bedrooms, each with an en-suite/private bathroom, T.V., tea/coffee-making facilities & easy chairs. A delicious breakfast is served. Delta House is ideally placed for a relaxing break & is within easy reach of Edinburgh. A delightful home.	£20.00	Y	N	N
Mrs Mairi Dewar **Glenesk, 6 Delta Place** **Smeaton Grove** **Inveresk, Musselburgh** **Edinburgh EH21 7TP** **Tel: (0131) 6653217** **Open: ALL YEAR** **Map Ref No. 17**	Nearest Road: A.1 Quietly situated in the picturesque village of Inveresk, 'Glenesk' is a spacious, detached villa. It is convenient for all the scenic beauties, beaches & sporting activities of the east coast, while only 7 miles from the centre of Edinburgh & 1 mile from the busy shopping centre of Musselburgh. All 3 bedrooms have en-suite shower rooms or bathrooms, colour T.V. & tea/coffee-making facilities. A comfortable lounge. Parking space. No signs displayed: conservation area.	£19.00	Y	N	N
Gloria Stuart **Gloria's Place** **20 London Street** **Edinburgh** **EH3 6NA** **Tel: (0131) 557 0216** **Fax 0131 556 6445** **Open: ALL YEAR** **Map Ref No. 16**	Nearest Road: A.1 Gloria welcomes you to her luxurious Georgian home, minutes on foot from the city centre. An atmosphere of elegance & warmth will be your first impression: a hall vibrant with colour, a magnificent drawing room - yours to enjoy - where breakfast is served. All 3 bedrooms sleep 2 people, & have en-suite (private) bath/shower room & every other extra, both practical & pampering. Neither a 1 night reservation nor triple occupancy of 1 room is available. **E-mail: gloriasplace@cableinet.co.uk**	£35.00 *see PHOTO over* CREDIT CARD VISA M'CARD	N	N	N
Mr & Mrs Andrew Hamilton **16, Lynedoch Place** **Edinburgh** **EH3 7PY** **Tel: (0131) 2255507** **Fax 0131 3320224** **Open: ALL YEAR** **Map Ref No. 16**	Nearest Road: A.9, A.1 A beautiful, listed Gerogian terraced house, built in 1821 & situated in the heart of the Georgian New Town. This elegantly furnished house, though modernised to the highest of standards, still retains all its original features including sash windows, cornices & marble fireplaces. 3 attractive & well-appointed en-suite bedrooms. Situated within 2 mins walk of Princes Street, this is the perfect spot from which to explore this vibrant city with shops, restaurants & places of historic interest.	£35.00 CREDIT CARD VISA M'CARD	Y	N	Y
Mrs Cecilia Leishman **Ellesmere House** **11 Glengyle Terrace** **Edinburgh EH3 9LN** **Tel: (0131) 229 4823** **Fax 0131 229 5285** **Open: ALL YEAR** **Map Ref No. 16**	Nearest Road: A.702 Guests are made welcome at this very elegant tastefully restored Victorian town house, quietly situated overlooking golf links in the centre of Edinburgh. Rooms are all en-suite & decorated to a very high standard & well-equipped with every comfort in mind. Delicious breakfasts are served. 'A home away from home.' Convenient for castle, Princes Street, Royal Mile, International Conference Centre, theatres & restaurants. Children over 10 years.	£23.00 *see PHOTO over*	Y	N	N

Ellesmere House. Edinburgh.

Elmview. Edinburgh.

Scotland
Edinburgh

		rate from £ per person	children taken	evening meals	animals taken
Marny Hill **Elmview** **15 Glengyle Terrace** **Edinburgh EH3 9LN** **Tel: (0131) 2281973** **Fax 0131 6223271** **Open: ALL YEAR** **Map Ref No. 16**	Nearest Road: A.702 Marny Hill's luxurious bed & breakfast is situated in the heart of Edinburgh within easy walking distance of Edinburgh Castle & Princes Street (1 km). Elmview is a wonderful base from which to enjoy your stay in Edinburgh. Each bedroom has been elegantly furnished & all are en-suite. Direct dial 'phones, fridges, fresh flowers are but a few of the thoughtful extras in each bedroom. **E-mail: elmview@cableinet.co.uk**	£35.00 🚭 *see PHOTO over* CREDIT CARD VISA M'CARD	N	N	N
Mr J.B. Stuart **Meadows Guest House** **17 Glengyle Terrace** **Edinburgh EH3 9LN** **Tel: (0131) 229 9559** **Fax 0131 229 2226** **Open: ALL YEAR** **Map Ref No. 16**	Nearest Road: A.702 Quietly situated overlooking a park, Meadows is warm, comfortable & spacious, with a friendly atmosphere. 5 attractive rooms, all with colour T.V. & tea/coffee-making facilities, 3 with an en-suite bathroom. Jon will welcome you, & help you with where to go, what to do & where to eat. Bookings of 3 nights or more taken in advance. Centrally located & within easy reach of the Castle, Princes St., shops, theatres & restaurants. **E-mail: meadows@web.13co.uk**	£27.00 CREDIT CARD VISA M'CARD AMEX	Y	N	Y
Mrs Moira Conway **Crannoch But & Ben** **467 Queensferry Road** **Edinburgh EH4 7ND** **Tel: (0131) 3365688** **Open: ALL YEAR** **Map Ref No. 16**	Nearest Road: A.90 Warm Scottish hospitality at this very pleasant private house. The two ground-floor guest rooms have private facilities & tea/coffee-making. The guest lounge has T.V., and evening tea or coffee is served whilst you digest the available information on all there is to do in Edinburgh. Private parking on site, and an excellent bus service to the heart of the city (just 3 miles to Princes Street).	£23.00 🚭	Y	N	N
Leonard & Suzanne Welch **Ravensdown Guest House** **248 Ferry Road** **Edinburgh** **EH5 3AN** **Tel: (0131) 5525438** **Fax 0131 5527559** **Open: ALL YEAR** **Map Ref No. 16**	Nearest Road: A.1, A.199 Built at the beginning of the 1900s, Ravensdown offers unsurpassed panoramic views of the Edinburgh skyline. Each of the 6 spacious, well-decorated bedrooms have modern amenities, colour T.V. & tea/coffee-making facilities. A warm lounge enables guests to socialise, with bar service on the premises. Your friendly hosts are always available to offer assistance with tours, etc. A delicious breakfast gets you off to a good start each morning. Private parking available. Only 3 kilometres from the city centre.	£17.00 🚭	Y	N	N
Rosalind Ritchie **Rosebank House** **190 Newhaven Road** **Edinburgh EH6 4QB** **Tel: (0131) 553 3223** **Fax 0131 555 0308** **Open: ALL YEAR** **Map Ref No. 16**	Nearest Road: A.90 Rosebank is a tranquil house of hidden delights. Walled gardens with thyme & camomile lawns surround this early-Georgian home. Bedrooms are elegant & comfortable, & all have private facilities. Situated 2 mins from the sea, Rosebank is only 10 mins from Princes St.. There is unrestricted street parking & frequent buses to the city centre. Your hosts enjoy spoiling their guests & providing delicious breakfasts. A delightful non-smoking house.	£35.00 🚭 *see PHOTO over* CREDIT CARD VISA M'CARD	N	N	Y

Rosebank House. Edinburgh.

		rate from £ per person	children taken	evening meals	animals taken
Mrs Nan Stark **Ben-Cruachan** **17 McDonald Road** **Edinburgh EH7 4LX** **Tel: (0131) 5563709** **Fax 0131 5563709** **Open: APR - OCT** **Map Ref No. 16**	Nearest Road: A.1 Guests are assured of a warm welcome & a friendly atmosphere at this attractive house, situated 1 km from Princes Street. Offering comfortable en-suite bedrooms, well-equipped with every comfort in mind & serving an excellent breakfast. Centrally situated within easy reach of the castle, Royal Mile, Holyrood Palace, shops, theatres & restaurants. Unrestricted parking & on all main bus routes. Children over 5 years.	£20.00	Y	N	N
Alan & Cathie MaGuire **Greenside Hotel** **9 Royal Terrace** **Edinburgh EH7 5AB** **Tel/Fax: (0131) 5570022** **Tel: (0131) 5570121** **Open: ALL YEAR** **Map Ref No. 16**	Nearest Road: A.1 Built in 1820, the Greenside Hotel is an elegant Georgian town-house hotel situated in the city centre & surrounded by peaceful garden settings in one of Edinburgh's most prestigious terraces. A few mins' walk from Waverly Station, Princes St., tourist attractions, local restaurants & theatre. 14 tastefully decorated rooms with all facilities. Large family rooms also available. Full Scottish Breakfast is served each morning.	£22.50 CREDIT CARD VISA M'CARD AMEX	Y	Y	N
Mrs Cathy Hamilton **Ailsa Craig Hotel** **24 Royal Terrace** **Edinburgh EH7 5AH** **Tel/Fax: (0131) 5566055** **Tel: (1031) 5561022** **Open: ALL YEAR** **Map Ref No. 16**	Nearest Road: A.1 Ailsa Craig Hotel is situated in the heart of Edinburgh near the city centre in one of the most prestigious terraces. This elegant Georgian town house hotel is situated only 10 mins walk from Princes Street, Waverly Station & many attractions. 18 tastefully furnished & decorated rooms, 15 with en-suite facilities, & all with 'phone, hairdryer, colour T.V. & tea/coffee-making facilities. A delicious breakfast & good evening meals are served. A perfect base for exploring Edinburgh.	£25.00 *see PHOTO over* CREDIT CARD VISA M'CARD AMEX	Y	Y	N
Dennis & Irene Robins **Sonas** **3 East Mayfield** **Newington** **Edinburgh EH9 1SD** **Tel: (0131) 6672781** **Fax 0131 6670454** **Open: ALL YEAR** **Map Ref No. 16**	Nearest Road: A.68, A.7, A.701 Guests are assured of a warm welcome & a memorable stay at Sonas (the old Gaelic word for peace & happiness). Built in 1876, & recently refurbished, it now provides 8 tastefully decorated bedrooms with en-suite facilities, & retains many of its original features, including a lovely sweeping staircase & ornate cornices. A delicious Scottish breakfast is served each morning. Private parking. Excellent bus service. An excellent base from which to explore Edinburgh.	£19.00	Y	N	N
Mrs Susan Berkengoff **Barony House** **4 Queens Crescent** **Edinburgh EH9 2AZ** **Tel: (0131) 6675806** **Fax 0131 6676833** **Open: ALL YEAR** **Map Ref No. 16**	Nearest Road: A.68, A.7, A.701 A fine, detached Victorian villa with beautiful garden - situated in a select residential area just off the main road. Queen's Crescent lies between the A.7/701 & A.68 main roads coming into the city from the south, & is only 1 1/2 miles from Princes Street. Private parking available. There are 8 guest bedrooms, 3 with en-suite facilities, & each with tea/coffee makers & T.V.. U.K. Freephone no. 0800 9804806.	£18.00	Y	N	N

Ailsa Craig Hotel. Edinburgh.

Teviotdale House. Edinburgh.

		rate from £ per person	children taken	evening meals	animals taken
David & Deborah Fraser **Glenalmond Guest House** **25 Mayfield Gardens** **Edinburgh EH9 2BX** **Tel/Fax: (0131) 6682392** **Open: ALL YEAR** **Map Ref No. 16**	Nearest Road: A.701 Glenalmond Guest House is an attractive home, conveniently situated on a main bus route, providing easy access to the city centre. Accommodation is in 8 comfortably furnished en-suite bedrooms, each with T.V. & tea/coffee-making facilities. (3 rooms are on the ground floor.) A lovely breakfast is served in the attractive dining room. Large car park. A warm welcome is assured from your hosts David & Deborah Fraser.	£23.00 (non-smoking)	Y	N	N
Mrs A. Helen Telfer **Ard-Thor** **10 Mentone Terrace** **Newington** **Edinburgh EH9 2DG** **Tel: (0131) 6671647** **Open: ALL YEAR** **Map Ref No. 16**	Nearest Road: A.7, A.68, A.701 A charming, 19th-century Victorian guest house situated only 10 mins from the city centre, castle & Princes Street by a good local bus service. The Ard-Thor is quiet & friendly, & your comfort is ensured by the personal attention of your host. Guests are offered a choice of 3 rooms, all with T.V. & tea/coffee-making facilities. Queens Park & Commonwealth Pool are nearby. This is an ideal place from which to explore Edinburgh.	£18.00 (non-smoking)	Y	N	N
Alan & Angela Vidler **Rowan Guest House** **13 Glenorchy Terrace** **Edinburgh EH9 2DQ** **Tel: (0131) 6672463** **Fax 0131 6672463** **Open: ALL YEAR** **Map Ref No. 16**	Nearest Road: A.701, A.7, A.68 Elegant Victorian home in one of the city's loveliest areas with free parking & only a 10 min bus ride to the centre. The castle, Royal Mile, restaurants & other amenities easily reached. The charmingly decorated bedrooms are comfortably & tastefully furnished with complimentary tea/coffee & biscuits. Breakfast including traditional porridge & freshly baked scones, will keep you going until dinner! Attentive friendly hosts. Partially non-smoking.	£20.00 CREDIT CARD VISA M'CARD	Y	N	Y
Mrs Jane E. Coville **Teviotdale House** **53 Grange Loan** **Edinburgh** **EH9 2ER** **Tel: (0131) 6674376** **Fax 0131 6674376** **Open: ALL YEAR** **Map Ref No. 16**	Nearest Road: A.7, A.702 Tastefully restored, elegant, Victorian gentleman's town house. Located in a quiet residential conservation area. Lovely original woodwork. All 8 spacious rooms have every modern facility, with private/en-suite bathrooms, colour T.V., radio & tea/coffee makers. Some rooms have a refrigerator. Breakfast is a banquet. Home-baked scones, jams & bread. Guaranteed to delight the most travelled of guests. Parking. 10 mins to town centre. A delightful home. **E-mail: teviotdale.house@btinternet.com**	£28.00 (non-smoking) *see PHOTO over* CREDIT CARD VISA M'CARD AMEX	Y	N	N
Maureen & Adolfo **Invernizzi** **Roselea House** **11 Mayfield Road** **Edinburgh EH9 2NG** **Tel: (0131) 6676115** **Fax 0131 6673556** **Open: ALL YEAR** **Map Ref No. 16**	Nearest Road: A.701 Always a warm welcome from Maureen & Adolfo at their elegant Victorian house. They have tastefully restored & refurbished their home to a high standard; whilst still retaining the original features. Each room has colour T.V., tea/coffee facilities &, of course, an en-suite or private bathroom. Whether on business or on holiday, this is an ideal oasis to return to & relax in. A delightful home, offering easy access to the many attractions & places of historic interest that Edinburgh has to offer. Children over 6 years.	£30.00 CREDIT CARD VISA M'CARD	Y	N	Y

Ardchoille Farmhouse. Auchtermuchty.

Forgan House. Newport-on-Tay.

Scotland
Fife & Inverness-shire

		rate from £ per person	children taken	evening meals	animals taken
Donald & Isobel Steven **Ardchoille Farmhouse** **Dunshalt** **Auchtermuchty KY14 7EY** Tel: (01337) 828414 Fax 01337 828414 Open: ALL YEAR Map Ref No. 19	Nearest Road: A.91, B.936 Relax & enjoy the warm comfort, delicious Taste of Scotland food & the excellent hospitality at Ardchoille Farmhouse. 3 en-suite twin-bedded rooms, tastefully furnished, with colour T.V. & tea/coffee trays offering home-made butter shortbread. Large comfortable lounge, & elegant dining room with fine china & crystal. Dinner is 4-course. Close by Royal Palace of Falkland, home of Mary Queen of Scots. 20 mins from St. Andrews, 1 hr.Edinburgh. Idea l base for golfing & touring.	£25.00 *see PHOTO over* CREDIT CARD VISA M'CARD AMEX	Y	Y	N
Mrs Patricia Scott **Forgan House** **Newport-on-Tay DD6 8RB** Tel: (01382) 542760 Fax 01382 542760 Open: ALL YEAR Map Ref No. 20	Nearest Road: A.92 Forgan House, the former manse of the area, is a listed Georgian country house situated in 5 acres of grounds & gardens (incl. a paddock & walled garden) in open countryside 6 miles from St. Andrews. The emphasis is on quality & comfort, & the spacious rooms provide panoramic views & private facilities.World-famous golf courses. 3 miles from one of Scotland's most secret & beautiful sandy beachesHoliday cottage available.	£25.00 *see PHOTO over* CREDIT CARD VISA M'CARD	Y	Y	N
Mrs Helen Black **Milton Farm** **Leuchars, St. Andrews** **KY16 0AB** Tel: (01334) 839281 Fax 01334 839281 Open: ALL YEAR Map Ref No. 21	Nearest Road: A.919, A.91 A warm & friendly welcome awaits you at Milton Farm. A spacious, tastefully modernised & peaceful Georgian farmhouse. 3 stylish & elegantly furnished bedrooms with very pretty linen. A full English breakfast is served, including home-made preserves & fresh farm eggs. Packed lunches are provided on request. Guest lounge with T.V. & delightful garden. Many excellent golf courses nearby. St. Andrews 5 miles. Children over 10. (This is a working farm.)	£25.00 *see PHOTO over* CREDIT CARD VISA M'CARD	Y	N	N

Inverness-shire

Peter & Penny Rawson **Feith Mhor Country Hse.** **Station Road** **Carrbridge,** **Inverness PH23 3AP** Tel: (01479) 841621 Open: Mid DEC - Mid NOV Map Ref No. 22	Nearest Road: A.9 A warm friendly atmosphere is found at this charming 19th-century house set in 1 1/2 acres of delightful garden, surrounded by peaceful, unspoilt countryside. Tastefully furnished, & full of character. 6 very comfortable en-suite bedrooms with tea/coffee & T.V.. Excellent views from each room. A pleasant dining room & spacious, comfortable lounge. Super home-cooking, using fresh produce in season. Vegetarian dishes provided, with prior notice. Children over 12 yrs.	£25.00	Y	Y	Y
Mrs Jenny Mackenzie **Old Pier House** **Fort Augustus** **PH32 4BX** Tel: (01320) 366418 Fax 01320 366770 Open: APR - OCT Map Ref No. 24	Nearest Road: A.82 Warm, friendly, Highland hospitality in this pretty farmhouse on the shores of Loch Ness, half a mile north of historic Fort Augustus & the famous Benedictine Abbey. Panoramic views over Loch Ness & surrounding mountains. 4 attractive en-suite bedrooms. Highland cattle, pony trekking, boats, fishing & a beautiful nature trail. Home-cooked meals with organic local produce used where possible. Log fires. Children over 5.	£20.00 CREDIT CARD VISA M'CARD	Y	Y	N

Milton Farm. St. Andrews.

Borlum Farmhouse. Drumnadrochit.

Scotland
Inverness-shire

		rate from £ per person	children taken	evening meals	animals taken
Duncan & Vanessa MacDonald-Haig **Borlum Farmhouse** Drumnadrochit IV3 6XN Tel: (01456) 450358 Fax (01456) 450358 Open: ALL YEAR Map Ref No. 23	Nearest Road: A.82 This 180-year-old farmhouse has a unique position overlooking Loch Ness. Each year, visitors world-wide are delighted with the fresh, tastefully furnished rooms, good food & friendly atmosphere. Borlum is an historic working hill farm, dating back to its service to Urquhart Castle in the 16th century. An excellent base for touring. The farm also has its own B.H.S.-approved riding centre, making it the ideal place to spend a riding holiday. *see PHOTO over* CREDIT CARD VISA M'CARD	£19.50	Y	N	N
Mrs Margaret Cairns **Invergloy House** **Spean Bridge** **Nr. Fort William** **PH34 4DY** Tel: (01397) 712681 Open: ALL YEAR Map Ref No. 29	Nearest Road: A.82 A really interesting Scottish coach house, dating back 110 years, offering 3 charming, comfortable twin-bedded rooms, with modern facilities, 2 with en-suite shower rooms & 1 with a private bathroom. 5 miles north of the village of Spean Bridge towards Inverness, it is signposted on the left, along a wooded drive. Guests have use of own sitting room, overlooking Loch Lochy in 50 acres of superb woodland of rhododendron & azaleas. Fishing from the private beach & rowing boats, & hard tennis court. Children over 8 welcome.	£19.00	Y	N	N
Mr & Mrs J. Campbell **The Grange** **Grange Road** **Fort William** **PH33 6JF** Tel: (01397) 705516 Open: MAR - OCT Map Ref No. 32	Nearest Road: A.82 Set in quiet gardens overlooking Loch Linnhe, yet only 10 mins from the town centre. The Grange offers superb accommodation in 3 en-suite rooms, each well-equipped & enhanced by a very relaxed atmosphere. The area is charming & the house is well-situated, only 1 1/2 hrs from Oban, Inverness & the Isles. An ideal base for touring the Highlands, & returning to a comfortable lounge log fire for chilly evenings. Vegetarians catered for. *see PHOTO over* CREDIT CARD VISA	£33.00	N	N	N
Mrs Vera G. Waugh **Cabana House** **Union Road** **Fort William PH33 6RB** Tel/Fax: (01397) 705991 Open: ALL YEAR Map Ref No. 32	Nearest Road: A.82 This elegant Victorian house has been renovated to an exceptional standard. 3 designer-decorated bedrooms, 2 en-suite, 1 with private bathroom. Situated in a prime position 5 mins from the town centre, with private parking & garden. An ideal holiday base for touring the spectacular Highlands & islands. Special interest courses in curtain design & paint effects held during spring & autumn.	£24.00	N	N	N
B.B. Henderson **Ashburn House** **1 Ashburn Lane** **Fort William** **PH33 6RQ** Tel: (01397) 706000 Fax 01397 706000 Open: MAR - NOV Map Ref No. 32	Nearest Road: A.82 Ashburn is a splendid Victorian house personally run by Highland hosts. Quietly situated by the shores of Loch Linhe only 600 yards from the town centre & among others the renowned Crannog Seafood Restaurant. An excellent base for touring the Highlands. Sample an imaginative & real Highland breakfast, served at your own individual table, complimented with freshly baked scones from the aga. There are 7 attractively furnished, en-suite bedrooms. Colour brochure & special weekly rates available. *see PHOTO over* CREDIT CARD VISA M'CARD	£30.00	Y	N	N

The Grange. Fort William.

Ashburn House. Fort William.

Scotland
Inverness-shire

	rate from £ per person	children taken	evening meals	animals taken
Michel & Barbara Bouchard **Ardconnel House** **Woodlands Terrace** **Grantown-on-Spey** **PH26 3JU** **Tel/Fax: (01479) 872104** **Open: MAR - OCT** **Map Ref No. 26**	Nearest Road: A.95, A.9 Built in 1890, during the Victorian era of elegance, Ardconnel House stands in its own spacious grounds overlooking a glorious pine forest, Lochan & Cromdale Hills. 6 bedrooms are en-suite, with quality beds, colour T.V., hairdryer & welcome tray, & are charmingly decorated. A superb 4-poster bedroom. Excellent home cooking is complemented by a well-selected, modestly priced wine list. Taste of Scotland selected member. Children over 10 yrs.	£25.00 (no smoking) *see PHOTO over* CREDIT CARD VISA M'CARD	Y	Y	N
Jim & Geraldine Reid **The Old Royal Guest House, 10 Union Street** **Inverness IV1 1PL** **Tel: (01463) 230551** **Fax 01463 711916** **Open: ALL YEAR** **Map Ref No. 27**	Nearest Road: A.9 Personally managed by the resident proprietors Jim & Geraldine, The Old Royal is conveniently situated in the centre of town, opposite the railway station. Accommodation is in 14 comfortable guest bedrooms, 5 with en-suite facilities. All have colour T.V. & tea/coffee makers. The Old Royal has a home from home atmosphere, & provides visitors with a comfortable holiday base from which to tour the locality. Children over 3. **E-mail: boss@jimr.demon.co.uk**	£20.00 CREDIT CARD VISA M'CARD	Y	N	N
Alison Parsons **Ballindarroch House** **Aldourie** **Inverness IV1 2DL** **Tel: (01463) 751348** **Fax 01463 751348** **Open: ALL YEAR** **Map Ref No. 27**	Nearest Road: A.9 Ballindarroch was originally built as a shooting lodge around 1870 & stands in 10 acres of woodland gardens above the Caledonian Canal. Decorated with hand-painted wallpaper & furnished with antiques & an eclectic selection of family pieces, the house offers a totally relaxing & peaceful environment only 10 mins from Inverness. Alison Parsons is an award-winning chef & can also offer gourmet dinners (on request). French, Italian, Spanish & German spoken.	£20.00	Y	Y	Y
Barbara Kinnear **Glenashdale** **Daviot East** **Inverness IV1 2EP** **Tel/Fax: (01463) 772221** **Open: ALL YEAR** **Map Ref No. 27**	Nearest Road: A.9 Glenashdale is a modern country house situated 7 miles south of Inverness in quiet countryside, with lovely views. All the comfortable bedrooms have en-suite facilities, central heating, T.V., radio & tea/coffee tray. Joe & Babs Kinnear invite you to escape the hustle & bustle of everyday living & join them in the beauty of the Scottish Highlands, where making all guests feel welcome is a top priority. Children over 6 years.	£20.00 (no smoking) CREDIT CARD VISA M'CARD	Y	N	N
Mrs Margaret Pottie **Easter Dalziel Farmhouse** **Dalcross** **Inverness IV1 2JL** **Tel: (01667) 462213** **Fax 01667 462213** **Open: ALL YEAR (Excl. Xmas & New Year)** **Map Ref No. 28**	Nearest Road: A.96, B.9039 This Scottish farming family offer the visitor a friendly Highland welcome on their 200-acre stock/arable farm. 3 charming bedrooms are available in the delightful early-Victorian farmhouse. The lounge has log fire & colour T.V.. Delicious home cooking & baking served, including a choice of breakfasts. Evening meals available summer only. Ideal base for exploring the scenic Highlands. Local attractions are Cawdor Castle, Culloden, Fort George, Loch Ness & nearby Castle Stuart. A delightful home.	£16.00 CREDIT CARD VISA M'CARD	Y	Y	Y

Ardconnel House. Grantown-on-Spey.

Scotland
Inverness-shire

		rate from £ per person	children taken	evening meals	animals taken
Mrs Sheila Hall **Talisker, 25 Ness Bank** **Inverness IV2 4SF** **Tel: (01463) 236221** **Fax 01463 234173** **Open: ALL YEAR** **Map Ref No. 27**	Nearest Road: A.9 Talisker was built over 150 years ago & is beautifully & quietly situated on the east bank of the River Ness, just minutes from the town centre & 10 mins walk from the train & bus stations, parks & theatre. Some of the 6 bedrooms overlook the river. All have central heating, remote colour T.V. & welcome tray, & there is ample private parking & storage for bicycles. E-mail:106735.2241@compuserve.com	£20.00 CREDIT CARD VISA M'CARD	Y	N	N

Isle of Bute

D. Cameron & B. Jeffery **Ardmory House Hotel** **Ardmory Road** **Ardbeg PA20 0PG** **Tel: (01700) 502346** **Fax 01700 505596** **Open: ALL YEAR** **Map Ref No. 25**	Nearest Road: A.844 Built in 1833, Ardmory House sits in its own grounds just over a mile from Rothesay town centre & commands an outstanding view over the bay, Firth of Clyde & Loch Striven. All bedrooms have en-suite facilities, colour T.V., 'phone, radio/alarm clock, hospitality tray, electric blankets & hairdryer. (Bedrooms & restaurant are non-smoking.) An ideal base for a relaxing break. E-mail: XGQ76@DIAL.PIPEX.COM	£30.00 CREDIT CARD VISA M'CARD AMEX	Y	Y	Y

Isle of Skye

Anthony & Jane Wilcken **Corry Lodge** **Liveras** **Broadford IV49 9AA** **Tel: (01471) 822235** **Fax 01471 822318** **Open: MAR - OCT** **Map Ref No. 30**	Nearest Road: A.850 Corry Lodge, on the Isle of Skye, is a most attractive period house dating from the late 18th century. It has a fine open outlook over Broadford bay, but with a sheltered location, & approximately 1,150 metres of unspoilt sea frontage. There are 4 comfortable & tastefully furnished bedrooms, each with en-suite bathroom, radio, colour T.V. & tea/coffee-making facilities. Corry Lodge forms an ideal base from which to tour the island either by car or bicycle, or on foot.	£25.00 CREDIT CARD VISA M'CARD	Y	Y	Y
Jon & Ros Wathen **Talisker House** **Talisker** **Carbost IV47 8SF** **Tel: (01478) 640245** **Fax 01478 640214** **Open: MAR - NOV** **Map Ref No. 36**	Nearest Road: A.863 Set on Skye's ruggedly beautiful west coast, Talisker House welcomes visitors today as it welcomed Johnson & Boswell during their historic Hebridean tour of 1773. With its fine trees & garden, it offers superb views to the sea & currently accommodates 4 couples in spacious & elegantly appointed comfort. Meals feature the best of local produce, & are complemented by carefully selected wines. E-mail: 106553.2053@compuserve.com	£32.00	Y	Y	N
Paul & Cathie Booth **Glenview Inn &** **Restaurant, Culnacnoc** **Staffin IV51 9JH** **Tel: (01470) 562248** **Fax 01470 562211** **Open: MAR - NOV** **Map Ref No. 31**	Nearest Road: A.855 A traditional island house lying between Trotternish Ridge & the sea & ideally situated for exploring North Skye. Bedrooms are individually decorated, warm & comfortable, with tea/coffee-making facilities. Glenview offers a relaxed & friendly atmosphere & the best of Scotland's varied larder. Only fresh food is used to create a menu including traditional, ethnic & vegetarian specialities. An excellent base for a relaxing break.	£25.00 CREDIT CARD VISA M'CARD	Y	Y	Y

Marlee House. Kinloch.

		rate from £ per person	children taken	evening meals	animals taken

Derek & Elizabeth Scott
Ashcroft Farmhouse
East Calder
Nr. Edinburgh EH53 0ET
Tel: (01506) 881810
Fax 01506 884327
Open: ALL YEAR
Map Ref No. 33

Nearest Road: A.71
Ashcroft is a new farmhouse, with all rooms on the ground floor. Surrounded by farmland, yet only 10 miles from Edinburgh city centre; 5 miles from the airport, A.720, M.8/M.9 motorways. Elizabeth provides early morning tea, before tempting guests with a full Scottish breakfast, incl. home-made sausage, local produce & Whisky marmalade. En-suite bedrooms, including 1 with a 4-poster. Parking. Regular bus service to city.

£26.00 | Y | N | N

(no smoking symbol)

CREDIT CARD
VISA
M'CARD

Misses E. & L. Stewart &
Mr D. Wimberley
Point Garry Hotel
20 West Bay Road
North Berwick EH39 4AW
Tel: (01620) 892380
Fax 01620 892848
Open: APR - OCT
Map Ref No. 34

Nearest Road: A.1
The Royal Burgh of North Berwick is situated between the historic castles of Tantallon & Dirleton. Point Garry, a Victorian listed building, overlooks both the 1st tee of the West Links Championship Golf Course & the sea. Accommodation is in 15 rooms, all en-suite, with colour T.V., central heating, tea/coffee-making facilities, 'phone & parking. 12 golf courses within 10 miles, including the world-famous Muirfield (4 miles). Free golf booking. Edinburgh 30 mins.

£27.50 | Y | Y | Y

CREDIT CARD
VISA
M'CARD

Mrs Gwen Scott
The Glebe House
Law Road
North Berwick EH39 4PL
Tel: (01620) 892608
Open: ALL YEAR (Excl. Xmas & New Year)
Map Ref No. 34

Nearest Road: A.198
A listed 18th-century manse situated in secluded grounds yet in the centre of the historic seaside town of North Berwick. It is elegantly furnished with many fine features. Bedrooms are decorated to the highest standard & have T.V. & tea/coffee facilities. (1 with 4-poster.) The beach is a 2 min walk as is the high street with shops & restaurants. Edinburgh is 30 mins by car. Many places of interest nearby including castles, museums & a distillery. 13 golf courses within 20 mins drive.

£20.00 | Y | N | N

Mr & Mrs K. Lumsden
Marlee House
Kinloch
Blairgowrie PH10 6SD
Tel: (01250) 884216
Open: ALL YEAR
Map Ref No. 41

Nearest Road: A.923
This pretty 16th-century manor house is set in extensive grounds by Marlee Loch which holds one of the largest wintering populations of Greylag geese in Britain. The house offers an informal country house atmosphere with log fires in winter. The charming bedrooms have central heating & en-suite bathrooms. An ideal base for golf, fishing & skiing or simply to rest on your way, in elegant & comfortable surroundings. Children over 12.

£25.00 | Y | N | N

see PHOTO over

Mr Iain H. Aitchison
Invertrossachs Country House
Invertrossachs Road
Invertrossachs
By Callander FK17 8HG
Tel: (01877) 331126
Fax 01877 331229
Open: ALL YEAR
Map Ref No. 38

Nearest Road: A.84, A.81
Escape for some privacy & comfort in the unforgettable setting of this Lochside Edwardian mansion with 33 acres, by the southern shores of Loch Venachar. Choose from the elegant Loch Room, the Victoria Suite or the Menteith Apartment. A king-size double or twin room; or a suite of rooms for 4/5 persons. Each has T.V., radio, 'phone, hairdryers, video & CD, & tea/coffee. A 5-course breakfast is served in the conservatory overlooking the Loch. The perfect break away from it all. Dinner by arrangement.
E-mail: IAIN_AITCHISON@COMPUSERVE.COM

£35.00 | Y | Y | Y

see PHOTO over

CREDIT CARD
VISA
M'CARD
AMEX

Invertrossachs. Callender.

Arran Lodge. Callander.

Scotland
Perthshire

		rate from £ per person	children taken	evening meals	animals taken
Robert & Pasqua Margarita Moore Arran Lodge Leny Road Callander FK17 8AJ Tel: (01877) 330976 Open: MAR - OCT Map Ref No. 37	Nearest Road: A.84, M.9 An enchanting Victorian bungalow, appointed to the highest standard. Enjoy tranquil riverside gardens, romantic 4-poster bedrooms, en-suite bathrooms & Robert's cooking. Altogether, sumptuous & scrumptious. Sink comfortably into champagne coloured sofas in the elegant lounge & delight in the surrounding river & country views. All bedrooms are centrally heated with colour T.V., hairdryers, hospitality tray etc. An utterly delightful home into which Robert & Pasqua bid you welcome. Children over 11 years.	£29.50 🚭 *see PHOTO over*	Y	Y	N
Mrs Daisy Ferries The Lodge House Crianlarich FK20 8RU Tel: (01838) 300276 Open: MAR - DEC Map Ref No. 39	Nearest Road: A.82 Although just by the roadside, The Lodge is secluded & all rooms enjoy an excellent view of the surrounding hills & glens. With only 6 rooms, your hosts aim to provide a personal service & compliment this with good Scottish home-cooking. In the small, informal bar, there is an extensive selection of malts for guests to enjoy both before & after dinner. The Lodge House is the perfect location for a relaxing break.	£25.00 CREDIT CARD VISA M'CARD	Y	Y	Y
Janice & Sandy Chisholm Tigh Na Struith Crianlarich FK20 8RU Tel: (01838) 300235 Open: MAR - OCT Map Ref No. 39	Nearest Road: A.82 Alongside the River Fillan, & 200 yds from the main road, this friendly family home guarantees a quiet night's sleep. In the same hands for 15 years, this guest house has earned itself high praise for realistic prices together with clean, smoke-free accommodation. Still the best value for money, as awarded in 1984 by the Guild of Travel Writers. All rooms with h/c, colour T.V., tea/coffee-making, central heating & superb views. Party-goers please note: no licence.	£20.00 🚭	Y	N	Y
Fiona Graham Mackeanston House Doune FK16 6AX Tel: (01786) 850213 Fax 01786 850414 Open: ALL YEAR Map Ref No. 40	Nearest Road: A.84 Here you will find a touch of luxury in a peaceful rural setting. A 17th-century family home with stylish en-suite bedrooms set in a mature garden looking south to Stirling Castle & the Wallace monument, within sight of Rob Roy country & the Trossachs. 1 hours' drive from Glasgow, Perth & Edinburgh & easy reach of airports. Home-baked bread, fresh fruit & vegetables from the garden feature in imaginative menus. A pretty traditional cottage is available as an annexe.	£28.00 🚭 *see PHOTO over*	Y	Y	Y
Pat & Peter Buxton Bheinne Mhor Perth Road Birnam Dunkeld PH8 0DH Tel: (01350) 727779 Open: ALL YEAR Map Ref No. 41	Nearest Road: A.9 A warm welcome awaits you at this comfortable, Victorian, detached house, with turret & private garden, ideally situated for lovely walks both in Macbeth's Birnam Woods & alongside the rivers Tay & Braan. Many places of historic interest & beauty nearby, including Dunkeld Cathedral, the Scottish N.T.'s 'The Hermitage' & the Loch of Lowes Wildlife Reserve. Boundless opportunities for anglers & golfers. 3 en-suite/private bedrooms with modern amenities. Dinner by arrangement.	£20.00 🚭	N	Y	N

Mackeanston House. Doune.

Allt-Chaorain House Hotel. Crianlarich.

Scotland
Perthshire

		rate from £ per person	children taken	evening meals	animals taken
Roger McDonald **Allt-Chaorain Country** **House, Inverhaggenie** **Crianlarich** **Nr. Loch Lomond** FK20 8RU **Tel: (01838) 300283** **Fax 01838 300238** **Open: APR - OCT** **Map Ref No. 39**	Nearest Road: A.82 Allt-Chaorain House is a small family hotel situated in an elevated position, with commanding views of Ben More & Strathfillian from the south-facing sun lounge. Accommodation is in 7 comfortable bedrooms, all with private facilities. 'Taste of Scotland' home cooking & packed lunches available on request. The friendly & relaxing atmosphere will unwind you as you sit by the log fire after walking, fishing or touring the central Highlands. Children over 5 years welcome.	£33.00 🚭 *see PHOTO over* CREDIT CARD VISA M'CARD AMEX	Y	Y	Y
Mrs Jean Lewis **Monachyle Mhor** **Balquhidder** **Lochearnhead FK19 8PQ** **Tel: (01877) 384622** **Fax 01877 384305** **Open: ALL YEAR** **Map Ref No. 42**	Nearest Road: A.84 Monachyle Mhor is a small, 18th-century, award-winning farmhouse hotel set in its own 2,000 acres, with magnificent views over 2 lochs. It is furnished with period furniture & fine pictures. All rooms have wonderful outlooks, & all 10 bedrooms are en-suite. The dining room & conservatory restaurant allow you to wine & dine on the very finest of Scottish food, including game from the Lewis' own estate. Stalking & fishing in season.	£30.00 CREDIT CARD VISA M'CARD	N	Y	N
Derek & Angela Straker **Dupplin Castle** **By Perth** **PH2 0PY** **Tel: (01738) 623224** **Fax 01738 444140** **Open: ALL YEAR** **Map Ref No. 35**	Nearest Road: A.9, M.90 Dupplin, a rare mid-20th-century Scottish mansion, stands in 30 acres of private parkland, with views over the River Earn valley to the hills beyond. Bedrooms are individually appointed with en-suite facilities. It is a country house of the highest quality, with all the sophistication & relaxed informality of an old-fashioned house party. Shooting, fishing & golf are all within easy reach, & available from Dupplin by prior arrangement. Perth 15 mins' drive. Edinburgh & Glasgow 1 hour. Children over 12. **E-mail: DUPPLIN@netcomuk.co.uk**	£50.00 CREDIT CARD VISA M'CARD	Y	Y	Y
Tricia & John Stiell **Kinnaird Guest House** **5 Marshall Place** **Perth PH2 8AH** **Tel: (01738) 628021** **Fax 01738 444056** **Open: ALL YEAR** **Map Ref No. 57**	Nearest Road: A.85, M.90 Would you like to relax in comfort? Then the warm, friendly atmosphere at Kinnaird is just the place. John & Tricia aim for high standards & traditional home comforts & cater for individual needs. Beautifully situated overlooking a leafy park to the south, & the charming town centre is within easy walking distance. Buses & trains are also within easy reach. An ideal base for exploring this beautiful region & many historical attractions.	£22.00 🚭 CREDIT CARD M'CARD	N	Y	N
Mrs Elizabeth Sanderson **Tigh Dornie** **Aldclune** **Killiecrankie** **Pitlochry PH16 5LR** **Tel/Fax: (01796) 473276** **Open: ALL YEAR** **Map Ref No. 44**	Nearest Road: A.9 Tigh Dornie is situated amid beautiful Perthshire scenery, approx. 5 miles north of Pitlochry. Offering attractive accommodation in 3 very comfortable & tastefully furnished guest bedrooms, each with an en-suite bathroom, T.V. & tea/coffee-making facilities. A warm & friendly welcome is assured from your hosts, who will ensure that your stay is a memorable one. An ideal spot for touring Scotland. Ample car parking.	£21.00 🚭	N	N	N

Gloagburn Farm. Tibbermore.

	rate from £ per person	children taken	evening meals	animals taken
Ian & Alison Niven **Gloagburn** **Tibbermore** **Perth** **PH1 1QL** **Tel: (01738) 840228** **Fax 01738 840228** **Open: ALL YEAR** **Map Ref No. 45**	Nearest Road: A.9 A spacious & attractively furnished family farmhouse set on a 450-acre working farm in beautiful open countryside. Accommodation is in 3 stylish bedrooms with pretty linens, 2 with excellent private bathrooms. Suppers available by prior arrangement. Full breakfast is served, including home-made preserves & home-produced fresh eggs. Within 3 miles of the A.9, & within easy reach of many golf courses & sites of historic interest. A relaxed & friendly home. Children over 8 years welcome. *see PHOTO over* CREDIT CARD VISA M'CARD AMEX	£24.00 🚭	Y	N	N

Renfrewshire

	rate from £ per person	children taken	evening meals	animals taken
Mrs Kate Bewick **Six Fathoms** **6 Polnoon Street** **Eaglesham** **Renfrewshire by** **Glasgow G76 0BH** **Tel/Fax: (01355) 302321** **Open: ALL YEAR** **Map Ref No. 48**	Nearest Road: A.77, A.726 Set in the picturesque village of Eaglesham, 10 miles from Glasgow. Guests can be sure of a warm, Scottish welcome at this delightful home, with a choice of 2 twin rooms - 1 with sitting room & private facilities - or 2 single rooms, 1 spacious, 1 cosy. All rooms are tastefully furnished & have colour T.V. & tea/coffee-making facilities. 3 pubs/restaurants, excellent & varied, within 5 mins' walk. Convenient for Glasgow & Prestwick International Airports, the M.74, Loch Lomond, Burns Country & the Burrell Collection.	£24.00 🚭	N	N	N

Ross-shire

	rate from £ per person	children taken	evening meals	animals taken
Ms A. Kempthorne **Duich House** **Letterfearn** **Glenshiel** **IV40 8HS** **Tel: (01599) 555259** **Fax 01599 555259** **Open: APR - OCT** **Map Ref No. 53**	Nearest Road: A.87 A warm welcome & personal service is assured from your hosts at Duich House. A finely furnished 1800s. home with beautifully appointed bedrooms & a log fire in the lounge. Nearby is Eilean Donan Castle, other historical sites, wild mammals, birds, seals & otters & all around there is superb walking. There are outstanding loch & mountain views. Duich House is a perfect base for exploring north-west Scotland & the Isle of Skye. Evening meals & animals by arrangement.	£35.00 🚭	N	Y	Y
John & Ariana Franchi **The Manse** **Innes Street** **Plockton** **IV52 8TW** **Tel: (01599) 544442** **Open: ALL YEAR** **Map Ref No. 54**	Nearest Road: A.87 Situated in the picturesque village of Plockton, called 'the Jewel of the Highlands'. The T.V. series 'Hamish Macbeth' was filmed in & around the village. The Manse was converted from the Free Church of Scotland Manse, & it now offers a range of accommodation - a large Victorian suite with bathroom & antiques/Chesterfield etc., a modern 4-poster room with en-suite shower room, & 2 smaller rooms with handbasins, tea/coffee & T.V.. All rooms have a view of Loch Carron. The speciality for evening meals is the local seafood.	£19.00	Y	Y	Y

Scotland
Roxburghshire

		rate from £ per person	children taken	evening meals	animals taken
Mrs H. Irvine **'Froylehurst'** **Friars** **Jedburgh** **TD8 6BN** **Tel: (01835) 862477** **Fax 01835 862477** **Open: MAR - NOV** **Map Ref No. 49**	Nearest Road: A.68 An attractive Grade 'B' listed late-Victorian sandstone townhouse retaining most original features, offering 4 comfortable guest bedrooms & residents lounge. All rooms have washbasins with h & c, tea/coffee-making facilities, colour T.V. & radio/alarms. Two shared bathrooms & toilets. Situated in a large garden overlooking the town in a quiet residential area but within 2 mins walking distance from many good pubs & restaurants. Ample parking. Children over 5 welcome. An ideal base from which to explore this region.	£16.00	Y	N	N
Mrs Jill Hensens **Ancrum Craig** **Ancrum** **Jedburgh TD8 6UN** **Tel: (01835) 830280** **Fax 01835 830259** **Open: JAN - SEPT** **Map Ref No. 49**	Nearest Road: A.68 Perfect peace. A country house boasting authentic Victorian features, standing in extensive grounds. Ancrum Craig has become widely known for exceptional tranquillity, quality & comfort. Only 2 miles from Ancrum village, enjoying magnificent views to the south & east to Cheviot. All rooms have en-suite facilities, colour T.V. & tea/coffee-making facilities. The elegant lounge, where you enjoy a welcoming cup of tea, has a log fire.	£19.00	Y	N	Y
Mrs Betty Smith **Whitehill Farm** **Nenthorn** **Kelso** **TD5 7RZ** **Tel/Fax: (01573) 470203** **Open: ALL YEAR (Excl. Xmas & New Year)** **Map Ref No. 50**	Nearest Road: A.6089 A comfortable & peaceful farmhouse with a large garden standing on a 455-acre, mixed farm 4 miles from Kelso. 4 attractive bedrooms - 2 single & 2 twin, 1 with en-suite shower room - have superb views over rolling countryside. All have central heating & washbasins. A pleasant sitting room with log fire is available to guests. An ideal base for touring this glorious region; maps available. Good home cooking. Dinner by arrangement. (Smoking restricted.)	£18.50	Y	Y	Y
Peter & Ann Mather **Belford on Bowmont** **Yetholm** **Kelso TD5 8PY** **Tel: (01573) 420362** **Open: ALL YEAR (Excl. Xmas & New Year)** **Map Ref No. 55**	Nearest Road: A.698 Built in 1794 & surrounded by the tranquil hills of the Scottish Borders, Belford on Bowmont stands in 1350 acres, providing a peaceful retreat from which to explore nearby historic castles, abbeys & towns. Guests are free to wander at will over the estate. Guests bedrooms, each with private bathroom & dressing room, have outstanding views of the Cheviot Hills. Warm welcome, home-cooking, local produce.	£20.00	N	Y	N
Marilyn Mackenzie **Paramount** **Main Street** **Town Yetholm** **Kelso TD5 8RF** **Tel: (01573) 420505** **Open: ALL YEAR** **Map Ref No. 55**	Nearest Road: A.68 Paramount is an elegant, comfortable Grade II listed town house, ideally placed for exploring the beautiful Borders countryside. Situated in the peaceful conservation village of Town Yetholm with fine views of the Cheviot Hills. The 3 guest rooms, all with private facilities, are fully equipped. Dinner is available by arrangement. Food is freshly prepared on the premises. Guests are welcome to bring their own wine. Children over 7.	£23.00	Y	Y	Y

Scotland
Roxburghshire

		rate from £ per person	children taken	evening meals	animals taken
Mrs P. M. Schofield **Torwood Lodge** **High Cross Avenue** **Melrose** **TD6 9SU** **Tel: (01896) 822220** **Open: ALL YEAR** **Map Ref No. 51**	Nearest Road: A.7, A.6091 Melrose, famous for its abbey, is located 37 miles south of Edinburgh at the heart of the beautiful border country, with its contrasting scenery & many stately homes. Torwood Lodge is a Victorian family house situated within easy walking distance of the town centre, & with superb views towards the River Tweed & hills beyond. There are 3 attractive bedrooms, each with en-suite bathrooms, tea/coffee-making facilities & colour T.V.. Private parking.	£23.00	Y	N	N

Stirlingshire

		rate from £ per person	children taken	evening meals	animals taken
Laird Andrew Haslam **Culcreuch Castle** **Fintry** **Loch Lomond** **Stirling** **G63 0LW** **Tel: (01360) 860555** **Fax 01360 860556** **Open: ALL YEAR** **Map Ref No. 52**	Nearest Road: A.811 Retreat to 700 years of history at magical Culcreuch, the ancestral fortalice & clan castle of the Galbraiths, home of the Barons of Culcreuch, & now a country house hotel where the Laird and his family extend an hospitable welcome. Set in 1,600 spectacular acres, yet only 19 miles from central Glasgow & 17 miles from Stirling. 8 handsome, well-appointed bedrooms with en-suite or private facilities, 4-poster bedroom supplement of £12 per person per night. Elegant period-style decor & antiques, log fires, the romance of dining by candlelight. Prices £43.00 Apr & Oct, £48.00 May - Sept p.p.p.n..	£36.00 *see PHOTO over* CREDIT CARD VISA M'CARD AMEX	Y	Y	Y

All the establishments mentioned in this guide are members of
The Worldwide Bed & Breakfast Association

When booking your accommodation please mention
The Best Bed & Breakfast

Culcreuch Castle.   Fintry.

Wales

Wales

Wales is a small country with landscapes of intense beauty. In the north are the massive mountains of the Snowdonia National Park, split by chasms & narrow passes, & bounded by quiet vales & moorland. The Lleyn peninsula & the Isle of Anglesey have lovely remote coastlines.

Forests, hills & lakeland form the scenery of Mid Wales, with the great arc of Cardigan Bay in the west.

To the south there is fertile farming land in the Vale of Glamorgan, mountains & high plateaux in the Brecon Beacons, & also the industrial valleys. The coastline forms two peninsulas, around Pembroke & the Gower.

Welsh, the oldest living language of Europe is spoken & used, most obviously in the north, & is enjoying a resurgence in the number of its speakers.

From Taliesin, the 6th century Celtic poet, to Dylan Thomas, Wales has inspired poetry & song. Every August, at the Royal National Eisteddfod, thousands gather to compete as singers, musicians & poets, or to listen & learn. In the small town of Llangollen, there is an International Music Eisteddfod for a week every July

North Wales.

North Wales is chiefly renowned for the 850 miles of the Snowdonia National Park. It is a land of mountains & lakes, rivers & waterfalls & deep

The Snowdon Mountain Railway.

glacier valleys. The scenery is justly popular with walkers & pony-trekkers, but the Snowdon Mountain Railway provides easy access to the summit of the highest mountain in the range with views over the "roof of Wales".

Within miles of this wild highland landscape is a coastline of smooth beaches & little fishing villages.

Barmouth has mountain scenery on its doorstep & miles of golden sands & estuary walks. Bangor & Llandudno are popular resort towns.

The Lleyn peninsula reaches west & is an area of great charm. Abersoch is a dinghy & windsurfing centre with safe sandy beaches. In the Middle Ages pilgrims would come to visit Bardsey, the Isle of 20,000 saints, just off Aberdaron, at the tip of the peninsula.

The Isle of Anglesey is linked to the mainland by the handsome Menai Straits Suspension Bridge. Beaumaris has a 13th century castle & many other fine buildings in its historic town centre.

Historically North Wales is a fiercely independent land where powerful local lords resisted first the Romans & later the armies of the English Kings.

The coastline is studded with 13th century castles. Dramatically sited Harlech Castle, famed in fable & song, commands the town, & wide sweep of the coastline.

The great citadel of Edward I at Caernarfon comprises the castle & the encircling town walls. In 1969 it was the scene of the investiture of His Royal Highness Prince Charles as Prince of Wales.

There are elegant stately homes like Plas Newydd in Anglesey & Eriddig House near Wrexham, but it is the variety of domestic architecture that is most charming. The timber-frame buildings of the Border country are seen at their best in historic Ruthin set in the

Wales

beautiful Vale of Clwyd. Further west, the stone cottages of Snowdonia are built of large stones & roofed with the distinctive blue & green local slate. The low, snow-white cottages of Anglesey & the Lleyn Peninsula are typical of the "Atlantic Coast" architecture that can be found on all the western coasts of Europe. The houses are constructed of huge boulders with tiny windows & doors.

By contrast there is the marvellous fantasy of Portmeirion village. On a wooded peninsula between Harlech & Porthmadog, Sir Clough Williams Ellis created a perfect Italianate village with pastel coloured buildings, a town hall & luxury hotel.

Mid Wales

Mid Wales is farming country where people are outnumbered three to one by sheep. A flock of ewes, a lone shepherd & a Border Collie are a common sight on these green hills. Country towns like Old Radnor, Knighton & Montgomery with its castle ruin, have a timeless quality. The market towns of Rhyader, Lampeter & Dolgellau have their weekly livestock sales & annual agricultural festivals, the largest of which is the Royal Welsh Show at Builth Wells in July.

This is the background to the craft of weaving practised here for centuries. In the valley of the River Tefi & on an upper tributary of the Wye & the Irfon, there are tiny riverbank mills which produce the colourful Welsh plaid cloth.

Towards the Snowdonia National Park in the North, the land rises to the scale of true mountains. Mighty Cader Idris & the expanses of Plynlimon, once inaccessible to all but the shepherd & the mountaineer, are now popular centres for walking & pony trekking with well-signposted trails.

The line of the border with England is followed by a huge earth work of bank & ditch. This is Offa's Dyke, built by the King of Mercia around 750 A.D. to deter the Welsh from their incessant raids into his kingdom. Later the border was guarded by the castles at Hay-on-Wye, Builth Wells, Welshpool, & Chirk which date from mediaeval times.

North from Rhayader, lies the Dovey estuary & the historic town of Machynlleth. This is where Owain Glyndwr's parliament is thought to have met in 1404, & there is an exhibition about the Welsh leader in the building, believed to have been Parliament House.

Wales lost many fine religious houses during the Dissolution of the Monasteries under Henry VIII. The ruins at Cymer near Dolgellau & at Strata Florida were abbeys of the Cistercian order. However, many remote Parish Churches show evidence of the skills of mediaeval craftsmen with soaring columns & fine rood screens.

The Cambrian Coast (Cardigan Bay) has sand dunes to the north & cliffs to the south with sandy coves & miles of cliff walks.

Llangrannog Headland.

Aberystwyth is the main town of the region with two beaches & a yachting harbour, a Camera Obscura on the cliff top & some fine walks in the area.

Water-skiing, windsurfing &

Wales

sailing are popular at Aberdovey, Aberaeron, New Quay, Tywyn & Barmouth & there are delightful little beaches further south at Aberporth, Tresaith or Llangrannog.

South Wales

South Wales is a region of scenic variety. The Pembrokeshire coastline has sheer cliffs, little coves & lovely beaches. Most of the area is National Park with an 80 mile foot path running along its length, passing pretty harbour villages like Solva & Broad Haven.

A great circle of Norman Castles stands guard over South Pembrokeshire, Roch, Haverfordwest, Tenby, Carew, Pembroke & Manorbier.

The northern headland of Saint

Tenby.

Brides Bay is the most westerly point in the country & at the centre of a tiny village stands the Cathedral of Saint David, the Patron Saint of Wales. At Bosherton near Saint Govans Head, there is a tiny chapel hidden in a cleft in the massive limestone cliffs.

The Preseli Hills hold the vast prehistoric burial chambers of Pentre Ifan, & the same mountains provided the great blue stones used at faraway Stonehenge.

Laugharne is the village where Dylan Thomas lived & worked in what was a boat-house & is now a museum.

In the valleys, towns like Merthyr Tydfil, Ebbw Vale & Treorchy were in the forefront of the boom years of the Industrial Revolution. Now the heavy industries are fast declining & the ravages of the indiscriminate mining & belching smoke of the blast furnaces are disappearing. The famous Male Voice Choirs & the love of rugby football survives.

The Vale of Glamorgan is a rural area with pretty villages. Beyond here the land rises steeply to the high wild moorlands & hill farms of the Brecon Beacons National Park & the Black Mountains, lovely areas for walking & pony trekking.

The Wye Valley leads down to Chepstow & here set amidst the beautiful woodlands is the ruin of the Great Abbey of Tintern, founded in 1131 by the Cistercian Order.

Swansea has a strong sea-faring tradition maintained by its new Marine Quarter - marina, waterfront village, restaurants, art gallery & theatre.

Cardiff, the capital of Wales, is a pleasant city with acres of parkland, the lovely River Taff, & a great castle, as well as a new civic centre, two theatres & the ultra-modern St. David's Concert Hall. It is the home of the Welsh National Opera & here also is the National Stadium where the singing of the rugby crowd on a Saturday afternoon is a treat.

Pony Trekking

Wales

Wales
Gazeteer

Areas of Outstanding Natural Beauty
The Pembrokeshire Coast. The Brecon Beacons. Snowdonia. Gower.'

Historic Houses & Castles

Cardiff Castle - Cardiff
Built on a Roman site in the 11th century.
Caerphilly Castle - Caerphilly
13th century fortress.
Chirk Castle - Nr. Wrexham
14th century Border Castle. Lovely gardens.
Coity Castle - Coity
Mediaeval stronghold - three storied round tower.
Gwydir Castle - Nr. Lanrwst
Royal residence in past days - wonderful Tudor furnishings. Gardens with peacocks.
Penrhyn Castle - Bangor
Neo-Norman architecture 19th century - large grounds with museum & exhibitions. Victorian garden.
Picton Castle - Haverfordwest
12th century - lived in by the same family continuously. Fine gardens.
Caernarfon Castle - Caernarfon
13th century - castle of great importance to Edward I.
Conway Castle - Conwy
13th century - one of Edward I's chain of castles.
Powis Castle - Welshpool
14th century - reconstruction work in 17th century.
Murals, furnishings, tapestries & paintings, terraced gardens.
Pembroke Castle - Pembroke
12th century Norman castle with huge keep & immense walls.
Birthplace of Henry VII.
Plas Newydd - Isle of Anglesey
18th century Gothic style house.
Home of the Marquis of Anglesey.
Stands on the edge of the Menai Strait looking across to the Snowdonia Range. Famous for the Rex Whistler murals.
The Tudor Merchant's House - Tenby
Built in 15th century.
Tretower Court & Castle - Crickhowell
Mediaeval - finest example in Wales.

Cathedrals & Churches

St. Asaph Cathedral
13th century - 19th century restoration. Smallest of Cathedrals in England & Wales.
Holywell (St. Winifred)
15th century well chapel & chamber - fine example.
St. Davids (St. David)
12th century Cathedral - splendid tower - oak roof to nave.
Gwent (St. Woolos)
Norman Cathedral - Gothic additions - 19th century restoration.
Abergavenny (St. Mary)
14th century church of 12th century Benedictine priory.
Llanengan (St. Engan)
Mediaeval church - very large with original roof & stalls 16th century tower.
Esyronen
17th century chapel, much original interior remaining.
Llangdegley (St. Tegla)
18th century Quaker meeting house - thatched roof - simple structure divided into schoolroom & meeting room.
Llandaff Cathedral (St. Peter & St. Paul)
Founded in 6th century - present building began in 12th century. Great damage suffered in bombing during war, restored with Epstein's famous figure of Christ.

Museums & Galleries

National Museum of Wales - Cardiff (also Turner House)
Geology, archaeology, zoology, botany, industry, & art exhibitions.
Welsh Folk Museum - St. Fagans Castle - Cardiff
13th century walls curtaining a 16th century house - now a most interesting & comprehensive folk museum.
County Museum - Carmarthen
Roman jewellery, gold, etc. Romano-British & Stone Age relics.
National Library of Wales - Aberystwyth
Records of Wales & Celtic areas. Great historical interest.
University College of Wales Gallery - AberystwythTravelling exhibitions of painting & sculpture.

Wales

Museum & Art Gallery - Newport
Specialist collection of English watercolours - natural history, Roman remains, etc.
Legionary Museum - Caerleon
Roman relics found on the site of legionary fortress at Risca.
Nelson Museum - Monmouth
Interesting relics of Admiral Lord Nelson & Lady Hamilton.
Bangor Art Gallery - Bangor
Exhibitions of contemporary paintings & sculpture.
Bangor Museum of Welsh Antiquities - Bangor
History of North Wales is shown. Splendid exhibits of furniture, clothing, domestic objects, etc. Also Roman antiquities.
Narrow Gauge Railway Museum - Tywyn
Rolling stock & exhibitions of narrow gauge railways of U.K.
Museum of Childhood - Menai Bridge
Charming museum of dolls & toys & children's things.

Brecknock Museum - Brecon
Natural history, archaeology, agriculture, local history, etc.
Glynn Vivian Art Gallery & Museum - Swansea
Ceramics, old & contemporary, British paintings & drawings, sculpture, loan exhibitions.
Stone Museum - Margam
Carved stones & crosses from pre-historic times.
Plas Mawr - Conwy
A beautiful Elizabethan town mansion house in its original condition. Now holds the Royal Cambrain Academy of Art.

Historic Monuments

Rhuddlan Castle - Rhuddlan
13th century castle - interesting diamond plan.
Valle Crucis Abbey - Llangollen
13th century Cistercian Abbey Church.

Cader Idris.

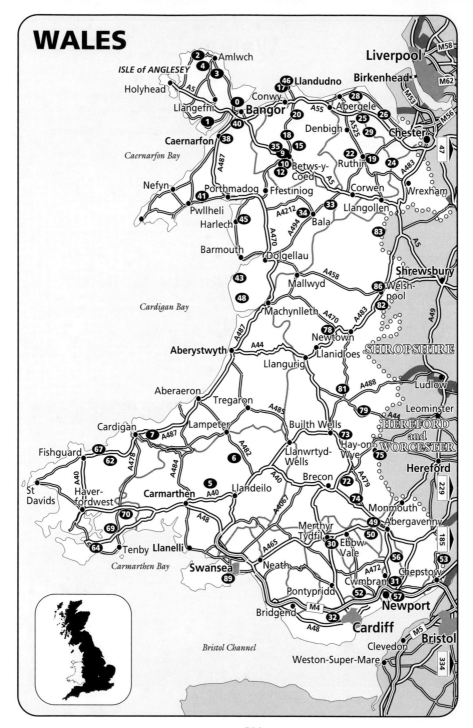

WALES

Liverpool

Birkenhead

M58

M62

M53

M56

ISLE of ANGLESEY

2 ● Amlwch

4

3

Holyhead

A5

Llangefni

46 ● Llandudno
17
28 ● Abergele

0 Conwy

Bangor

1

40

Caernarfon

38

20

A55

25 ● 26

Denbigh

29

Chester

47

Caernarfon Bay

35 9 15

18

10

12

Betws-y-Coed

A525

22

Ruthin

19 24

A483

Nefyn

Porthmadog ● Ffestiniog

A5

Corwen

Wrexham

41

Pwllheli

A4212

33

Llangollen

A494

34

45

Harlech

A5

Bala

83

Barmouth

A470

43

Dolgellau

A458

Shrewsbury

48

Mallwyd

86 Welsh-pool

Cardigan Bay

A470

A483

82

Machynlleth

A487

A44

78

Newtown

SHROPSHIRE

Aberystwyth

A44

Llanidloes

Llangurig

81

A488

Ludlow

Aberaeron

Tregaron

A485

79

Leominster

Lampeter

A44

HEREFORD

Cardigan

7 A487

Builth Wells

73

and

Fishguard

67

A482

6

Hay-on-Wye

75

WORCESTER

62

A478

Llanwrtyd-Wells

A40

Brecon

72

Hereford

St Davids

A484

5

Llandeilo

A40

229

Haver-fordwest

70

Carmarthen

A40

74

Monmouth

185

69

A48

A4067

49 ● Abergavenny

64 ● Tenby

Llanelli

A465

Merthyr Tydfil

50

Carmarthen Bay

Swansea

89

A472

56

53

30 Ebbw Vale

31

Chepstow

Neath

Cwmbran

52

57

Pontypridd

M4

Newport

Bristol Channel

Bridgend

32

A48

Cardiff

M5

Bristol

Clevedon

334

Weston-Super-Mare

WALES
Map references

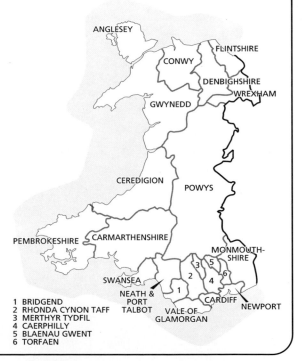

1 BRIDGEND
2 RHONDA CYNON TAFF
3 MERTHYR TYDFIL
4 CAERPHILLY
5 BLAENAU GWENT
6 TORFAEN

Llwydiarth Fawr Farm. Anglesey.

Wales
Isle of Anglesey

		rate from £ per person	children taken	evening meals	animals taken
Ms. Rosemary Ann Abas **Bwthyn** **Brynafon** **Menai Bridge** **Isle of Anglesey** **LL59 5HA** **Tel/Fax: (01248) 713119** **Open: ALL YEAR** **Map Ref No. 00**	Nearest Road: A.5, A.55 Bwthyn ('dear little house' in Welsh), offering character, comfort & genuine hospitality, is 1 minute from the beautiful Menai Strait, close by Telford's famous suspension bridge, 1 1/2 miles A.5/A.55, Irish Ferry 40 mins. Ideal base for coast, castles & Snowdonia. 2 warm, tastefully fitted en-suite double rooms, each with power shower (& 1 with a bath), colour T.V., tea/coffee makers etc. Scrumptious home-cooking. Over 45's Special - 3 nights Dinner, Bed & Breakfast £79.00 p.p.. Come as guests, leave as friends.	£15.00	N	Y	N
Marian Roberts **Plas Trefarthen** **Brynsiencyn** **Isle of Anglesey** **LL61 6SZ** **Tel: (01248) 430379** **Open: ALL YEAR (Excl. Xmas)** **Map Ref No. 01**	Nearest Road: A.4080 A beautiful Georgian house enjoying the most glorious position on the shore of the Menai Straits overlooking Snowdonia mountains & Carnarfon Castle. Only 6 miles from the Menai Bridge makes it ideal for touring Anglesey & the mainland, visiting local N.T. properties & beaches. Elegant bedrooms with en-suite bathrooms, colour T.V. & beverage facilities. Owned & run by well-known & international soprano Marian Roberts. Excellent self-catering for 6 available. CREDIT CARD VISA M'CARD	£21.00	Y	N	N
Tony & Gina Hirst **Hafod Country House** **Cemaes Bay** **Isle of Anglesey** **LL67 0DS** **Tel: (01407) 710500** **Open: MAR - OCT** **Map Ref No. 02**	Nearest Road: A.5025 A spacious Edwardian house standing in an acre of garden. Set in peaceful surroundings, with superb sea & mountain views. Only a 10-min. walk to the village, with its picturesque harbour & sandy beach. 3 delightful, en-suite bedrooms, with panoramic views, T.V. & tea/coffee facilities. Large, elegant lounge & separate dining room. Garden with tennis & croquet. Renowned for excellent food. Licensed. Nearby is golf, bird sanctuary, lake & sea fishing. Children over 8.	£22.50	Y	Y	N
Mrs Jane Bown **Drws Y Coed Farm** **Llannerch-Y-Medd** **Isle of Anglesey** **LL71 8AD** **Tel: (01248) 470473** **Open: ALL YEAR (Excl. Xmas)** **Map Ref No. 03**	Nearest Road: A.5025, A.5 Enjoy wonderful panoramic views of Snowdonia & countryside at this beautifully appointed farmhouse on a 550-acre working beef, sheep & arable farm. It's situated in peaceful, wooded countryside in the centre of Anglesey. Tastefully decorated & furnished, superb en-suite bedrooms with all facilities. Inviting spacious lounge with log fire. Delicious meals served. Games room. Historic farmstead. Lovely private walks. 25 mins to Holyhead. A warm welcome assured. CREDIT CARD VISA M'CARD	£20.00	Y	Y	N
Mrs Margaret Hughes **Llwydiarth Fawr Farm** **Llanerchymedd** **Isle of Anglesey** **LL71 8DF** **Tel: (01248) 470321/470540** **Open: ALL YEAR** **Map Ref No. 04**	Nearest Road: A.5 Secluded Georgian mansion set in 800 acres of woodland & farmland, with lovely open views. Ideal touring base for the island's coastline, Snowdonia & North Wales coast. 5 delightfully furnished bedrooms with en-suite facilities & T.V. & 2 cottage suites. Full central heating, log fires. Enjoy a taste of Wales with delicious country cooking using farm & local produce. Personal attention & a warm Welsh welcome to guests, who will enjoy the scenic walks & private fishing. Convenient for Holyhead-to-Ireland crossings. CREDIT CARD VISA M'CARD	£22.50 *see PHOTO over*	Y	Y	N

Glanrannell Park. Crugybar.

Penbontbren Farm Hotel. Glynarthen.

Wales
Carmarthenshire

		rate from £ per person	children taken	evening meals	animals taken
Mrs Charlotte Dent **Plas Alltyferin** **Pontargothi** **Nantgaredig** **Carmarthen SA32 7PF** **Tel/Fax: (01267) 290662** **Open: ALL YEAR (Excl. Xmas)** **Map Ref No. 05**	Nearest Road: A.40 A classic Georgian country house lying in the hills above the beautiful Towy Valley, overlooking a Norman hillfort & the River Cothi - famous for salmon & sea trout. There are 2 spacious twin bedrooms, each with private bathroom & stunning views, for guests who are welcomed as friends of the family. Antique furniture & log fires. Excellent local pubs & restaurants. Totally peaceful. Marvellous touring country for castles, beaches & rural Wales. Children over 10.	£20.00	Y	N	Y
David & Bronwen Davies **Glanrannell Park Country** **House Hotel, Crugybar** **Llanwrda SA19 8SA** **Tel: (01558) 685230** **Fax 01558 685784** **Open: APR - OCT** **Map Ref No. 06**	Nearest Road: A.482 In the lovely secluded Cothi Valley, this peaceful country house is 10 miles from the 3 Welsh market towns, Lampeter, Llandovery & Llandeilo. Within easy reach of the west coast & Brecon Beacons, it is a superb centre. Family-run by the Davies' for over 25 years, it has a reputation for excellent service, good food & fine wine. There are 8 attractive bedrooms, many en-suite. The colour brochure is a call away.	£30.00 *see PHOTO over* CREDIT CARD VISA M'CARD	Y	Y	Y

Ceredigion

G. B. Humphreys **Penbontbren Farm Hotel** **Glynarthen** **Cardigan** **SA44 6PE** **Tel: (01239) 810248** **Fax 01239 810248** **Open: ALL YEAR (Excl. Xmas)** **Map Ref No. 07**	Nearest Road: A.487 Penbontbren is a rare kind of place: a hotel which offers a genuine taste of Wales accompanied by all the modern comforts. Barrie & Nan Humphreys are your welcoming hosts - & you stay quite literally at their home, for the hotel has been in Nan's family for 4 generations. The accommodation is in a row of converted farmyard barns which have been transformed into rooms finished to extremely high standards, with the full range of facilities. Penbontbren is perfect for a relaxing holiday, tucked away down a country lane & yet only a few miles from the sandy coves & headlands of Cardigan Bay.	£34.00 *see PHOTO over* CREDIT CARD VISA M'CARD AMEX	Y	Y	Y

Conwy

Teresa & Keith Roobottom **The Ferns Guest House** **Holyhead Road** **Betws-Y-Coed** **LL24 0AN** **Tel: (01690) 710587** **Fax 01690 710587** **Open: ALL YEAR** **Map Ref No. 09**	Nearest Road: A.5, A.470 The Ferns Guest House is conveniently situated in the village of Betws-Y-Coed in the beautiful Snowdonia National Park. Offering 9 attractively furnished bedrooms, many en-suite, all with colour T.V. & tea/coffee-making facilities. Betws-Y-Coed is an ideal base for exploring this spectacular region, & is within easy reach of Llanrwst, Conwy, Caernarfon, Blaenau Ffestiniog & Portmeirion. Keith & Teresa Roobottom will make every effort to ensure that your stay at The Ferns is a pleasantly memorable one. Children over 4 years welcome.	£19.00 *see PHOTO over*	Y	N	N

The Ferns Guest House. Betws-y-Coed.

Tan Dinas. Betws-Y-Coed

		rate from £ per person	children taken	evening meals	animals taken
William & Marion Betteney **Bryn Afon Guest House** Pentre Felin Betws-Y-Coed LL24 0BB Tel: (01690) 710403 Open: ALL YEAR Map Ref No. 10	Nearest Road: A.5 A Victorian stone-built house situated on the banks of the River Llugwy overlooking the Pont-Y-Pair Bridge & waterfall. Well-appointed bedrooms with comfortable beds ensure a good night's sleep. Central for all tourist attractions & many local walks through the forests. Drying facilities available. Parking for all guests on the premises & a good choice of restaurants within 5-10 mins' walking distance.	£16.00	Y	N	N
Jean & Peter Whittingham **Fron Heulog Country House** Betws-Y-Coed LL24 0BL Tel: (01690) 710736 Fax 01690 710736 Open: ALL YEAR Map Ref No. 09	Nearest Road: A.5, A.470 The Country House in the Village! Enjoy the warmest welcome, a friendly atmosphere & real hospitality in this elegant Victorian stone-built house, located in quiet, peaceful, wooded, riverside scenery. Superb accommodation: comfortable bedrooms, full-facility en-suite bathrooms, spacious lounges, & a pleasant dining room. Parking. The heart of wonderfully picturesque Snowdonia - so much to see & do. More home than hotel! Croeso! - Welcome!	£20.00	N	N	N
Ann Howard **Tan Dinas** **Coed Cynhelier Road** Betws-Y-Coed LL24 0BL Tel: (01690) 710635 Fax 01690 710815 Open: ALL YEAR Map Ref No. 09	Nearest Road: A.5 A Victorian country house, offering peace, seclusion & a wonderful view. Surrounded by woodland yet only 500 yards from the village. Start with a delicious breakfast & finish your day with a candlelit dinner in the elegant dining room. Relax in the comfortable lounge or retire with a video or book to an attractive individually furnished bedroom which is appointed for your comfort. Forest walks from house. Ideal touring centre. Ample parking. A delightful home.	£18.00 *see PHOTO over*	Y	Y	N
Clive Muskus **Aberconwy House** **Llanrwst Road** Betws-Y-Coed LL24 0HD Tel: (01690) 710202 Fax 01690 710800 Open: ALL YEAR Map Ref No. 09	Nearest Road: A.470 A high standard of comfort & friendly, helpful hosts await you at Aberconwy. This large Victorian home, located in a lovely position above the picturesque village of Betws-Y-Coed, has panoramic views of the Llugney Valley, mountains & the River Conway. Accommodation is in a choice of 8 very comfortable en-suite bedrooms, with T.V. & tea/coffee makers. Most, also, have wonderful views. A residents' T.V. lounge & garden are also available. This is an ideal centre for touring, walking, fishing & golf. **E-mail: clive-muskus@celtic.co.uk**	£22.00 *see PHOTO over*	Y	N	Y
Modwena & Ian Cutler **Penmachno Hall** **Penmachno** Betws-Y-Coed LL24 0PU Tel: (01690) 760207 Open: ALL YEAR Map Ref No. 12	Nearest Road: A.5 Penmachno Hall was built as a rectory in 1862. Situated on the edge of the village in grounds of 2 1/2 acres, it is ideally located, being peaceful & secluded but enjoying easy access to all the various attractions of North Wales. The aim is to provide an informal, cosy atmosphere, with the very best of home cooking. Accommodation is in 4 delightful en-suite bedrooms. This is the perfect spot for a relaxing break.	£25.00 CREDIT CARD VISA M'CARD	Y	Y	N

Aberconwy House. Betws-Y-Coed.

Tan-y-Foel Country House. Capel Garmon.

Wales
Conwy

		rate from £ per person	children taken	evening meals	animals taken
Peter & Janet Pitman **Tan-Y-Foel Country** **House Hotel** **Nr. Betws-Y-Coed** **LL26 0RE** **Tel: (01690) 710507** **Fax 01690 710681** **Open: JAN - Mid DEC** **Map Ref No. 15**	Nearest Road: A.470, A.5 This unique award-winning family-run hotel is set high in the hills just outside Betws-Y-Coed, with beautiful scenery & an air of peacefulness & tranquillity. Accommodation is in 7 beautifully appointed en-suite bedrooms, each with its own 'Jewel Box' of colour. The 'Special 2 Day Breaks' are highly recommended. Children over 7 years welcome. A delightful base from which to explore this beautiful region. **E-mail: sjones@imaginet.co.uk** *see PHOTO over* CREDIT CARD VISA M'CARD AMEX	£45.00	Y	Y	N
Eileen & Peter Rigby **White Lodge Hotel** **9 Neville Crescent** **Central Promenade** **Llandudno LL30 1AT** **Tel: (01492) 877713** **Open: MAR - NOV** **Map Ref No. 17**	Nearest Road: A.55, A.470 Situated on the promenade of this beautiful Victorian holiday resort. All bedrooms are en-suite, & have tea/coffee-making facilities & colour T.V.s. There is a small bar & a pleasant lounge, facing the sea, for guests' use. 'White Lodge' offers an ideal touring centre for those day trips to Conway Castle, Caernarfon Castle, Chester or the mountains & valleys of Snowdonia. Children over 5 years welcome. CREDIT CARD AMEX	£25.00	Y	Y	N
Kate Aplin **Cae'r Berllan** **Betws Road** **Nr. Betws-Y-Coed** **Llanrwst LL26 0PP** **Tel: (01492) 640027** **Fax 01492 640027** **Open: MAR - OCT (& Dec)** **Map Ref No. 18**	Nearest Road: A.5, A.470 Tranquillity reigns in this magnificent 16th-century country house with massive oak beams & family antiques, set in beautiful private gardens in the Conwy Valley near Betws-Y-Coed. An ideal base for Snowdonia and North Wales. Luxurious beamed bedrooms, private facilities, T.V., etc. Wonderful views from every window. Renowned for high standards of international cuisine, served in the relaxed atmosphere of the inglenook dining room. The warmest of welcomes awaits you. *see PHOTO over* CREDIT CARD VISA M'CARD	£25.00	Y	Y	Y
Mary & Jack Marrow **Firs Cottage** **Maenan** **Llanrwst LL26 0YR** **Tel: (01492) 660244** **Open: ALL YEAR (Excl. Xmas)** **Map Ref No. 20**	Nearest Road: A.470 A 17th-century Welsh cottage & comfortable family home, situated in the beautiful Conway Valley, with excellent views to the hills. Firs Cottage offers 3 attractively furnished rooms, as well as a lovely garden in which to relax & plan visits to the many North Wales attractions, which are all within easy reach. Good food & a warm Welsh welcome will make for a memorable holiday.	£15.50	Y	N	Y
Ray & Barbara Valadini **Henllys (Old Court)** **Hotel** **Old Church Road** **Betws-Y-Coed** **Snowdonia LL24 0AL** **Tel/Fax: (01690) 710534** **Open: FEB - NOV** **Map Ref No. 09**	Nearest Road: A.5 No wonder our guests return time after time to this beautifully converted Victorian magistrate's court, set in peaceful riverside gardens. Choose from judges' chambers to the convicted felon's single cell. Each individually designed bedroom is fully equipped for your comfort. The police station houses the cosy fireside bar, & the magistrate's court the dining room, where superb food is imaginatively prepared from freshly grown produce. Non-smoking throughout. CREDIT CARD VISA M'CARD	£27.00	Y	Y	N

Cae'r Berllan. Betws-y-Coed.

Wales
Denbighshire

		rate from £ per person	children taken	evening meals	animals taken
Mrs Judith Mitchell **Castle Hotel** **St. Peters Square** **Ruthin LL15 1AA** **Tel: (01824) 702479** **Fax 01824 704924** **Open: ALL YEAR** **Map Ref No. 19**	Nearest Road: A.525, A.494 A happy hotel, with a friendly, informal atmosphere. Originally a 17th-century coaching inn - & latterly a favourite meeting place for King Edward VII & one of his paramours! Overlooking the market square of this pretty mediaeval town in the beautiful Vale of Clwyd. Freshly prepared local food, a comfortable bar & a lovely restaurant. En-suite bedrooms, colour T.V. & tea/coffee-making facilities. A short scenic drive to Llangollen. 5 mins' walk to a mediaeval banquet.	£22.00 CREDIT CARD VISA M'CARD AMEX	Y	Y	Y
Beryl J. Jones **Bryn Awel** **Bontuchel** **Ruthin LL15 2DE** **Tel: (01824) 702481** **Open: ALL YEAR (Excl. Xmas & New Year)** **Map Ref No. 22**	Nearest Road: B.5105 This 35-acre working farm is situated in the beautiful hamlet of Bontuchel, where you can relax in perfect peace & tranquillity & enjoy a wealth of wonderful walks, wild flowers & wildlife. Beryl has many cooking awards to her credit, & can oblige most requests for special diets. 1 room is en-suite & the other has a private bathroom. Each has colour T.V. & tea-making facilities. Heating throughout. A warm welcome & good food is top priority at this farmhouse.	£17.00 🚭	Y	Y	N
Jen & Bert Spencer **Eyarth Station** **Llanfair D. C.** **Ruthin** **LL15 2EE** **Tel: (01824) 703643** **Fax 01824 707464** **Open: ALL YEAR** **Map Ref No. 19**	Nearest Road: A.525 A warm & friendly reception awaits the visitor to Eyarth Station. A super, converted, former railway station located in the beautiful countryside of the Vale of Clwyd. 6 bedrooms, all en-suite. A comfortable T.V. lounge, & guests are welcome to use the garden, sun patio & outdoor heated pool. Conveniently located for the many historic towns in the region including Conwy, Caernarfon & Ruthin & their castles, with mediaeval banquet 2 minutes' drive away. The Roman town of Chester is also within driving distance. 1987 winner of Best Bed & Breakfast Award.	£21.50 *see PHOTO over* CREDIT CARD VISA M'CARD	Y	Y	Y
Mrs Elizabeth A. Parry **Llainwen Ucha** **Pentre Celyn** **Ruthin LL15 2HL** **Tel: (01978) 790253** **Open: ALL YEAR (Excl. Xmas & New Year)** **Map Ref No. 24**	Nearest Road: A.525 A working farm set in 130 acres overlooking the very beautiful Vale of Clwyd. Offering 3 pleasantly decorated rooms with modern amenities, & accommodating up to 5 persons. All rooms are centrally heated. Good home cooking made with fresh local produce; vegetarian meals on request. Conveniently situated for visiting Chester, Llangollen, Snowdonia & the coast. Offa's Dyke & fishing nearby. Mediaeval banquets are held at Ruthin Castle throughout the year.	£16.00 🚭	Y	Y	N

When booking your accommodation please mention
The Best Bed & Breakfast

Eyarth Station.   Llanfair D.C.

Wales
Denbighshire & Flintshire

	Nearest Road	rate from £ per person	children taken	evening meals	animals taken
Anwen Roberts **Bach-Y-Graig** **Tremeirchion** St. Asaph LL17 0UH Tel: (01745) 730627 Fax 01745 730627 Open: ALL YEAR (Excl. Xmas & New Year) Map Ref No. 25	Nearest Road: A.541, A.525 A super 16th-century farmhouse nestling at the foot of the Clwydian range, with undisturbed views of the surrounding countryside. Walk a 40-acre mediaeval woodland trail on the farm where the royal Black Prince once hunted, & enjoy the wealth of rare plants & flowers. All rooms are en-suite/private, with tea/coffee, radio/alarms & colour T.V.. A large lounge with colour T.V., an inglenook with log fires (during the colder part of the season) & central heating. Central for Chester, Snowdonia & coastal resorts.	£20.00 🚭	Y	N	N

Flintshire

	Nearest Road	rate from £ per person	children taken	evening meals	animals taken
Mrs Mary Jones **Greenhill Farm** **Bryn Celyn** **Holywell** CH8 7QF Tel: (01352) 713270 Open: MAR - OCT Map Ref No. 26	Nearest Road: A.55 A 16th-century working dairy farm, overlooking the Dee Estuary, which retains its old-world charm, with a beamed & panelled interior. Bedrooms are tastefully furnished, some having bathroom/shower en-suite. Relax & enjoy typical farmhouse food in the attractive dining room. (Dinner by prior arrangement.) Children's play area & utility/games room also available. A lovely home, within easy reach of both the coastal & mountain areas of North Wales.	£17.00	Y	Y	N
M. & N. Steele-Mortimer **Golden Grove** **Llanasa** **Holywell CH8 9NA** Tel: (01745) 854452 Fax 01745 854547 Open: Mid JAN - NOV Map Ref No. 28	Nearest Road: A.5151 Beautiful Elizabethan manor house set in 1,000 acres, close to Chester, Bodnant Gardens & Snowdonia, & en route to Holyhead. The Steele-Mortimer brothers & wives, having returned to the family home from Canada & Ireland, provide a warm welcome for their guests. The menu features home produce, including lamb & game, together with interesting wines & home baking. The atmosphere is friendly & informal. No smoking upstairs. Children over 12 yrs. Licensed.	£34.00 *see PHOTO over* CREDIT CARD VISA M'CARD	Y	Y	N
Susan & Neil Evans **The Old Mill Private Hotel** **Melin-Y-Wern** **Denbigh Road, Nannerch** **Mold CH7 5RH** Tel: (01352) 741542 Fax 01352 740254 Open: ALL YEAR (Excl. Xmas) Map Ref No. 29	Nearest Road: A.541 This small & friendly comfortable hotel has been created by the careful conversion of 19th-century stone-built stables. Now forming part of a watermill conservation area together with an adjacent wine bar, restaurant, gallery & traditional British Inn. The 6 fully equipped en-suite rooms are complemented by a residents' lounge in which to relax & read about 'places to visit & things to do'. Enjoy your first-class British breakfast in the spacious pine-furnished dining room. **E-mail: guest-services@old-mill.u-net.com**	£28.00 🚭 CREDIT CARD VISA M'CARD AMEX	Y	Y	Y

When booking your accommodation please mention
The Best Bed & Breakfast

Golden Grove. Llanasa.

Wales
Glamorgan & Gwent

		rate from £ per person	children taken	evening meals	animals taken
Paul & Monica Renwick **Sant-Y-Nyll** **St. Brides-Super-Ely** **Cardiff** **CF5 6EZ** **Tel: (01446) 760209** **Fax 01446 760897** **Open: ALL YEAR** **Map Ref No. 32**	Nearest Road: A.48 You can be assured of a friendly welcome to Sant-Y-Nyll, a charming Georgian country residence set in its own extensive grounds, with spectacular views over the Vale of Glamorgan. 6 guest rooms with modern facilities, T.V. & tea/coffee-making. Comfortable, warm & relaxing. Licensed. Children welcome. Cardiff just 7 miles. St. Fagans Welsh Folk Museum 2 miles. Paul & Monica look forward to meeting you. **E-mail: Sant-y-Nll@msn.com**	£17.50 CREDIT CARD AMEX	Y	N	Y
Michael & Kathleen Hurley **Tregenna Hotel** **Park Terrace** **Merthyr Tydfil CF47 8RF** **Tel: (01685) 723627** **Fax 01685 721951** **Open: ALL YEAR** **Map Ref No. 30**	Nearest Road: A.470, M.4 Family-run hotel with high level of comfort & class. 24 bedrooms with bathroom, 7 of which are designated for tourists & family use at special rates (50% reduction for children sharing). Telephone, tea/coffee service tray, colour T.V. in all rooms. Lunch, afternoon tea & dinner served 7 days a week. Brecon Beacons National Park 8 minutes' drive. 45 minutes Cardiff/Wales Airport, 2 1/4 hours London Heathrow Airport.	£26.00 CREDIT CARD VISA M'CARD AMEX	Y	Y	Y

Gwent

Mrs Beryl Watkins **The Glebe** **Croes-Y-Ceiliog** **Cwmbran** **Newport** **NP44 2DE** **Tel: (01633)450251** **Tel: (01633) 450242** **Open: ALL YEAR** **Map Ref No. 31**	Nearest Road: A.4042, M.4 A friendly & helpful host awaits you at Glebe Farm, a spacious, modern farmhouse overlooking a lovely corner of rural Wales where the family have farmed for generations. Accommodation is in 4 attractive & comfortable rooms, with modern amenities. A substantial breakfast is served in the morning, & in the evening, good pub fare can be found a pleasant walk away. The Glebe is the ideal spot for a relaxing break or for exploring this beautiful region. Convenient for the M.4/M.5.	£17.00 (no smoking)	Y	N	N

Gwynedd

Mrs Judy Cunningham **Abercelyn Country** **House** **Llanycil** **Bala LL23 7YF** **Tel: (01678) 521109** **Fax 01678 520556** **Open: ALL YEAR (Excl. Xmas)** **Map Ref No. 34**	Nearest Road: A.494 Set in landscaped gardens with its own mountain stream running alongside, this former rectory dates back to before 1721. Situated in the Snowdonia National Park, it is ideally located for walking or touring amongst the spectacular scenery. Bright & spacious en-suite bedrooms with views over Bala Lake, evenings relaxing before open log fires, & informal conversation over traditional breakfasts with hot home-baked bread, preserves & fresh coffee.	£20.50 (no smoking) *see PHOTO over* CREDIT CARD VISA M'CARD	Y	N	N

Abercelyn. Llanycil.

Wales
Gwynedd

	rate from £ per person	children taken	evening meals	animals taken
Richard Fullard & Beryl Gunn **Melin Meloch Water Mill** Nr. Bala LL23 7DP Tel: (01678) 520101 Mobile 0370 978790 Open: ALL YEAR Map Ref No. 33	Nearest Road: A.494 Just outside Bala, on the B.4401, close to the River Dee, stands this historic Water Mill, its stone walls draped in Virginia creeper. Set in lovely water gardens with a river running through the Victorian turbine. 5-ft wide doors lead into a unique galleried interior, filled with period furniture & bygones. Here, breakfast & dinner are served. Pretty en-suite rooms in the Mill cottage & granary offer comfort & privacy, with T.V. & hot-drinks trays. A secluded lodge is available. Animals & evening meals by arrangement. Children over 3.	£19.50 🚭 *see PHOTO over*	Y	Y	Y
Mrs Sue McGregor **Swn-Y-Dwr** Pentrefelin Betws-Y-Coed LL24 0BB Tel: (01690) 710648 Open: ALL YEAR Map Ref No. 35	Nearest Road: A.5 Swn-y-Dwr is a traditional Welsh stone cottage built 120 years ago. It is situated on the banks of the River Llugwy with private access from the garden to the river. 3 attractively furnished & well-equipped en-suite bedrooms, each with T.V. & tea/coffee facilities. An excellent breakfast is served. Although in a quiet location, it is only a 2 min walk from all amenities including shops & restaurants. A lovely family atmosphere prevails.	£17.00 🚭	Y	N	N
Beverley & Richard Bayles **The White House** Llanfaglan Caernarfon LL54 5RA Tel: (01286) 673003 Open: MAR - NOV Map Ref No. 38	Nearest Road: A.487 The White House is a large detached house set in its own grounds, overlooking Foryd Bay, & with the Snowdonia mountains behind. There are 4 tastefully decorated bedrooms, all with bath or shower, tea/coffee-making facilities & colour T.V.. Guests are welcome to use the residents' lounge, outdoor pool & gardens. Ideally situated for birdwatching, walking, windsurfing, golf & visiting the historic Welsh castles.	£17.50	Y	N	Y
Lynda & Nigel Kettle **Tyn Rhos Country House** Seion Llanddeiniolen Caernarfon LL55 3AE Tel: (01248) 670489 Fax 01248 670079 Open: ALL YEAR (Excl. Xmas) Map Ref No. 40	Nearest Road: B.4366 Tyn Rhos is a special place, set in a splendid location on the wide-open plain running between Snowdonia & the sea. Once a working farmhouse, it has now been transformed into a country house of great charm & comfort. Each individually designed bedroom has been furnished to the highest of standards. 2 delightful rooms, situated on the ground floor, have patio doors opening onto the garden. Award-winning Tyn Rhos serves super meals & the kitchen uses only the best local ingredients. Quality allied to exceptional value are the keynotes at Tyn Rhos. Children over 5.	£30.00 CREDIT CARD VISA M'CARD AMEX	Y	Y	N
Patricia Clayton **Trefaes Guest House** Y Maes Criccieth LL52 0AE Tel: (01766) 523204 Fax 01766 523013 Open: ALL YEAR (Excl. Xmas) Map Ref No. 41	Nearest Road: A.497 An elegant Edwardian house on the edge of Criccieth Green, with views of the sea and Castle. The 3 comfortable bedrooms have en-suite facilities, T.V., tea/coffee tray & central heating. Quiet lounge for reading, writing & cards, & secluded garden. Great Welsh breakfasts & 'Taste of Wales' evening meals with fish & vegetarian specialities. Parking in grounds. Excellent base for historic sites, sea and walking holidays. Children over 12 please.	£20.00	Y	Y	Y

Melin Meloch Water Mill. Llanfor.

Wales
Gwynedd

	rate from £ per person	children taken	evening meals	animals taken
Mrs Rita Murray **Min-Y-Gaer Hotel** **Porthmadog Road** **Criccieth LL52 OHP** **Tel: (01766) 522151** **Fax 01766 523540** **Open: MAR - OCT** **Map Ref No. 41** Nearest Road: A.497 A pleasant, licensed house in a quiet residential area, offering very good accommodation in 10 comfortable rooms, of which most have a bathroom en-suite. All have colour T.V. & tea/coffee-making facilities. The hotel enjoys commanding views of Criccieth Castle & the scenic Cardigan Bay coastline, & is only 2 mins' walk from the safe, sandy beach. Car parking on the premises. An ideal base for touring Snowdonia. **E-mail: minygaer.hotl@virgin.net**	£20.00 CREDIT CARD VISA M'CARD AMEX	Y	Y	N
Nick & Margaret Smyth **Pentre Bach** **Llwyngwril** **Nr. Dolgellau LL37 2JU** **Tel: (01341) 250294** **Fax 01341 250885** **Open: ALL YEAR (Excl. Xmas)** **Map Ref No. 43** Nearest Road: A.493 Large, warm, peaceful, award-winning farmhouse in pretty coastal village, with BR station. Delicious food prepared by Mid-Wales Cook of the Year 1994, including free-range eggs, organic produce & herbs. 3 attractive en-suite guest rooms, each with T.V. & easy chairs. In Snowdonia National Park, the adjacent mountains offer walks through history from Stone Age to present day. Also, sea, forests, rivers, steam railways, castles, pony trekking or relaxing on uncrowded beaches.	£20.00 *see PHOTO over* CREDIT CARD VISA M'CARD	N	Y	N
Gillian & Eric Newton **Davies, Noddfa Hotel** **Ffordd, Newydd** **Harlech LL46 2UB** **Tel: (01766) 780043** **Fax 01766 781105** **Open: ALL YEAR** **Map Ref No. 45** Nearest Road: A.496 A Victorian country house situated within the National Park, with superb views of Snowdon, Tremadog Bay & Harlech Castle. 4 comfortable rooms (2 en-suite, T.V.). Extensive menu, licensed. Gillian & Eric will be delighted to talk about both the medieval weaponry, displayed in the bar, & the history of Harlech Castle, & to give archery lessons in the hotel grounds. Very close to the Castle, beach, indoor swimming pool & theatre. Children over 4 years.	£18.00 CREDIT CARD VISA M'CARD	Y	Y	N
Antonio & Jennifer Fossi **Tan Lan Hotel** **Great Ormes Road** **West Shore** **Llandudno LL30 2AR** **Tel: (01492) 860221** **Fax 01492 870219** **Open: MAR - NOV** **Map Ref No. 46** Nearest Road: A.470, A.55 Tan Lan is an elegant hotel on the edge of town where you can enjoy your stay in delightful surroundings. Service is attentive & is combined with a friendly & comfortable atmosphere in which you may feel genuinely at home. Antonio & Jennifer offer extraordinarily good food in their charming dining room. Their welcome is as gracious as Llandudno, & the surrounding countryside is delightful. There are 17 comfortably furnished & well-equipped en-suite guest rooms.	£23.75 CREDIT CARD VISA M'CARD	Y	Y	Y

When booking your accommodation please mention
The Best Bed & Breakfast

Pentre Bach. Llwyngwril.

Ty Mawr. Llanegryn.

Wales
Gwynedd

		rate from £ per person	children taken	evening meals	animals taken
Lizzie & Richard Tregarthen **Ty Mawr** **Llanegryn** **Tywyn** **LL36 9SY** **Tel/Fax: (01654) 710507** **Open: ALL YEAR** **Map Ref No. 48**	Nearest Road: A.493 With mountains to the east & sea to the west, Ty Mawr snugs into the south-facing slope of the Dysnni Valley. Total peace & quiet. There are private entrances to each ground-floor, en-suite bedroom, which are very comfortable & also have tea/coffee-making facilities. Enjoy meals in the conservatory overlooking the garden & valley. Numerous venues of interest, & local heritage. Links golf at Aberdovey.	£20.00 *see PHOTO over*	N	N	N

Monmouthshire

Mr & Mrs B. L. Harris **The Wenallt** **Abergavenny** **NP7 0HP** **Tel: (01873) 830694** **Open: ALL YEAR** **Map Ref No. 49**	Nearest Road: A.465 A 16th-century Welsh longhouse set in 50 acres of farmland in the Brecon Beacons National Park & commanding magnificent views over the Usk Valley. Retaining all its old charm, with oak beams & inglenook fireplace, yet offering a high standard of accommodation, with en-suite bedrooms, good food & a warm welcome. An ideal base from which to see Wales & the surrounding areas. Licensed.	£16.50 *see PHOTO over*	Y	Y	Y
Bruce & Amanda Weatherill **Llanwenarth House** **Govilon** **Abergavenny** **NP7 9SF** **Tel: (01873) 830289** **Fax 01873 832199** **Open: Late FEB - Mid JAN** **Map Ref No. 50**	Nearest Road: A.465 A truly delightful 16th-century manor house, standing in its own beautiful grounds & surrounded by the tranquil scenic hills of the Brecon Beacons National Park. Elegantly furnished, tastefully decorated & with superb views, this house is a real pleasure to visit. Dinner, prepared by Amanda, a Cordon Bleu cook, is a delight. It is served by candlelight in the lovely dining room. 4 en-suite bedrooms. Fishing, golf, climbing, walking & shooting nearby. No smoking in dining room or bedrooms. Single supplement. Children over 10.	£36.00 *see PHOTO over*	Y	Y	Y

When booking your accommodation please mention
The Best Bed & Breakfast

The Wenallt. Gilwern.

Llanwenarth House. Govilon.

Wales
Monmouthshire

		rate from £ per person	children taken	evening meals	animals taken
Dinah L. Price **'Great House'** **Isca Road** **Old Village** **Caerleon** **NP6 1QG** **Tel: (01633) 420216** **Open: ALL YEAR** **Map Ref No. 52**	Nearest Road: B.4596 'Great House' is an attractive 16th-century house located on the banks of the River Usk. Retaining much of its original character (including beams & inglenook fireplaces), it offers 3 very pretty bedrooms with T.V. & tea/coffee-making facilities. A charming drawing room with T.V. & woodburner. Garden to rear leads to the riverbank. Within easy reach of superb golf course, fishing & forest trails. The ancient village of Caerleon is very near with its amphitheatre, museums & Roman Baths. Good pubs. Ideal as a stop-over for those on the way through Wales or onto Ireland. Children over 10.	£20.00	Y	N	N
Dereck & Vickie Stubbs M.H.C.I.M.A. **Parva Farmhouse Hotel &** **Restaurant** **Tintern** **Chepstow NP6 6SQ** **Tel: (01291) 689411** **Fax 01291 689557** **Open: ALL YEAR** **Map Ref No. 53**	Nearest Road: A.466, M.48 A delightful 17th-century stone farmhouse situated 50 yards from the River Wye. The quaint en-suite bedrooms, with their designer fabrics, are gorgeous, & some offer breathtaking views over the River Wye & woodland. The beamed lounge, with log fires, leather Chesterfields & 'Honesty Bar', is a tranquil haven in which to unwind. Mouth-watering dishes, served in the intimate, candlelit Inglenook Restaurant, reflect the owner's love of cooking. A super home, perfect for a relaxing break or for exploring beautiful Wales.	£27.00 *see PHOTO over* CREDIT CARD VISA M'CARD AMEX	Y	Y	Y
Mrs C. T. Park **Brick House Country** **Guest House, North Row** **Redwick, Magor** **Newport NP6 3DX** **Tel: (01633) 880230** **Fax 01633 882441** **Open: ALL YEAR** **Map Ref No. 57**	Nearest Road: M.4 Jt. 23 Brick House Farm is a listed Grade II Georgian farmhouse dating from about 1765, but with up-to-date conveniences. All double bedrooms have an en-suite bathroom. A pleasant T.V. lounge, dining room & bar. Full central heating. There is also a delightful garden where guests may take cream teas, weather permitting. Brick House is ideally placed for touring South Wales & the Wye Valley, or as a stopping-off point just over the Severn Bridge. Single room supplement. Children over 10 years welcome.	£21.00	Y	Y	N
Stuart & Ann Bradley **Pentwyn Farm** **Little Mill** **Pontypool NP4 0HQ** **Tel: (01495) 785249** **Fax 01495 785247** **Open: Mid JAN - Mid DEC** **Map Ref No. 56**	Nearest Road: A.472 Pentwyn is a 120-acre farm situated on the edge of the Brecon Beacons National Park. Good food and hospitality are of prime importance. The 16th-century, pink-washed longhouse has all the comforts of the 20th century without losing its charm. A large garden, with swimming pool. 4 pretty bedrooms (2 en-suite), with tea-making facilities. An attractive sitting room with open fire, piano & books. A restaurant licence. Rough shooting available. Children over 4 years.	£16.00	Y	Y	N

When booking your accommodation please mention
The Best Bed & Breakfast

Parva Farmhouse and Restaurant. Tintern.

Wales
Pembrokeshire

		rate from £ per person	children taken	evening meals	animals taken
Peter & Jane Heard **Tregynon Country** **Farmhouse Hotel** **Gwaun Valley** **Fishguard SA65 9TU** Tel: (01239) 820531 Fax 01239 820808 Open: ALL YEAR Map Ref No. 62	Nearest Road: B.4313 This is a traditional, beamed, award-winning, 16th-century, family-run farmhouse, standing in acres of grounds next to ancient oak woodlands & overlooking the glorious Gwaun Valley in the Pembrokeshire Coast National Park. It is unique, of great natural beauty & still quite unspoilt. 8 en-suite ground-floor rooms. Traditional & special diets, wholefood & vegetarian specialities, using fresh local produce when possible. A good range of wine is also available. Own trout ponds, 200ft waterfall & Iron Age fort, abundant wildlife. CREDIT CARD VISA M'CARD	£24.00	Y	Y	N
Nina & Hywel Williams **Bettws** **Parrog** **Newport SA42 0RX** Tel: (01239) 820559 Open: APR - OCT Map Ref No. 67	Nearest Road: A.40 Superbly renovated & refurbished Victorian house on spectacular Pembrokeshire coastal path. Breakfast in Victorian conservatory feet away from the sea with views across the estuary & bay. En-suite bedrooms including a family room, 50% reduction for children. Colour T.V., tea/coffee. Set in the Pembrokeshire National Park with facilities for walking, sailing, bird watching, golf & horse riding. A charming home.	£20.00	Y	N	N
L. E. & J. M. Fielder **Old Stable Cottage** **3 Picton Terrace** **Carew Village** **Tenby (Nr.) SA70 8SL** Tel: (01646) 651889 Open: APR - OCT Map Ref No. 69	Nearest Road: A.4075, A.477 The Cottage (Grade II listed), with inglenook fireplace & original bread oven, was once a stable & carthouse to 13th-century Carew Castle situated near the entrance & the creek of Carew River with its Tidal Mill. A spiral staircase leads to 3 charming, oak-beamed en-suite bedrooms with colour T.V., home-baked Welsh cakes & tea/coffee. Delicious food is prepared in the farmhouse kitchen on the Aga. Dinners by arrangement. A conservatory overlooks the garden.	£24.00	Y	Y	N
Mrs Jill McHugh **The Old Vicarage** **Manorbier** **Tenby** **SA70 7TN** Tel: (01834) 871452 Fax 01834 871452 Open: ALL YEAR Map Ref No. 64	Nearest Road: A.4139 Situated in the coastal village of Manorbier with its castle & beautiful beaches, The Old Vicarage offers gracious accommodation with glimpses of Barafundle Bay. Guests may enjoy the mature gardens or sit by a log fire in the drawing room. Both spacious bedrooms are furnished with antiques & have tea/coffee facilities. The renowned Pembrokeshire Coastal Path passes through the village. (2-bedroomed self-catering unit.) Irish ferries from Pembroke (20 mins) & Fishguard (50 mins). Beaches a 5-min. walk.	£19.00	Y	N	N
Peter & Margaret Gilder **Llangwm House** **Whitland** **SA34 0RB** Tel: (01994) 240621 Fax 01994 240621 Open: ALL YEAR Map Ref No. 70	Nearest Road: A.40 Llangwm House is a large, fully modernised farmhouse with panoramic views, ideally situated for the Pembrokeshire Coast, with its beautiful beaches, walks & abundant wildlife. The spacious bedrooms, all of which have private facilities, are tastefully furnished with comfort in mind. All have T.V. & tea/coffee-making facilities. Guests are assured of a warm welcome, & may find it interesting to watch Peter train his sheepdogs. Children over 5. Evening meals by prior arrangement. Licensed bar.	£20.00	Y	Y	Y

York House. Cusop.

Wales
Powys

	Nearest Road	rate from £ per person	children taken	evening meals	animals taken
Mrs Mary Cole 'Dolycoed' Talyllyn Brecon LD3 7SY Tel: (01874) 658666 Open: ALL YEAR Map Ref No. 72	Nearest Road: A.40 Dolycoed, built at the turn of the century, retains many of its interesting original features. Standing in a sheltered position in Brecon Beacons National Park, it offers a warm, friendly, homely welcome to all. Accommodation is in 2 comfortable guest bedrooms, with radio & tea/coffee makers, & a guests' lounge with colour T.V.. Many outdoor activities nearby: pony trekking, riding, fishing, watersports & walking.	£17.00	Y	N	Y
Nancy M. Jones Ty-Isaf Farm Erwood Builth Wells LD2 3SZ Tel: (01982) 560607 Open: ALL YEAR Map Ref No. 73	Nearest Road: A.470 Ty-Isaf Farm, situated in the attractive village of Erwood, offers accommodation in 3 comfortably furnished rooms with modern amenities & tea/coffee-making facilities. Plentiful English or Continental breakfasts are served. Special diets, & packed lunches provided by arrangement. Guests may relax in the cosy lounge, with T.V. throughout the day. An ideal base for touring.	£14.00	Y	Y	Y
Mrs Christina Jackson Glangrwyney Court Country Guest House Glangrwyney Crickhowell NP8 1ES Tel: (01873) 811288 Fax 01873 810317 Open: ALL YEAR Map Ref No. 74	Nearest Road: A.40 Glangrwyney Court is a Georgian mansion set in 4 acres of established gardens & surrounded by parkland. All rooms are comfortably furnished with antiques & fine porcelain & paintings & there is essentially a welcoming & homely atmosphere. Accommodation is in 5 attractive & well-appointed bedrooms, each with a private or en-suite bathroom. During the winter, log fires burn in all the sitting rooms & in the summer guests are able to relax with a drink in the gardens.	£18.50	Y	Y	Y
Mrs P. K. Cracroft Tretower House Tretower Crickhowell NP8 1RF Tel: (01874) 730225 Fax 01874 730225 Open: ALL YEAR Map Ref No. 74	Nearest Road: A.40 Charming old family house set in the beautiful Usk Valley, with views of the Black Mountains. A warm welcome awaits at Tretower House, where there are 2 comfortable rooms, 1 en-suite & 1 with private bathroom. Each has tea/coffee-making facilities. A delicious breakfast is sierved. Beautiful garden & plenty of walks, pony trekking, fishing & golf locally. A delightful home & an ideal first stop as you enter Wales.	£22.00	Y	N	N
Peter & Olwen Roberts York House Hardwicke Road Cusop Hay-on-Wye HR3 5QX Tel: (01497) 820705 Open: ALL YEAR Map Ref No. 75	Nearest Road: A.438 Peter and Olwen Roberts welcome you to their traditional Victorian guest house quietly situated in beautiful gardens on the edge of Hay. Sunny mountain views are enjoyed by all the well-appointed en-suite rooms. Ideal for a relaxing holiday spent browsing in the world-famous bookshops, exploring the National Park and Kilvert country, or just enjoying the freshly prepared home cooking. Private parking. Children over 8.	£22.00 *see PHOTO over* CREDIT CARD VISA M'CARD AMEX	Y	Y	Y

Trewythen. Llandinam.

Wales
Powys

	rate from £ per person	children taken	evening meals	animals taken
Mrs Ceinwen Davies **Trewythen Farm** **Llandinam** **SY17 5BQ** **Tel: (01686) 688444** Fax 01686 688444 **Open: MAY - OCT** **Map Ref No. 78**	£20.00 (no smoking) *see PHOTO over*	Y	Y	N
Leslie & Sylvia Knott **The Ffaldau Country House** **Llandegley** **Llandrindod Wells** **LD1 5UD** **Tel: (01597) 851421** Fax 01597 851421 **Open: ALL YEAR** **Map Ref No. 79**	£20.00 CREDIT CARD VISA M'CARD	Y	Y	Y
Anne & Tony Millan **Guidfa House** **Crossgates** **Llandrindod Wells** **LD1 6RF** **Tel: (01597) 851241** Fax 01597 851875 **Open: ALL YEAR** **Map Ref No. 81**	£21.00 *see PHOTO over* CREDIT CARD VISA M'CARD	N	Y	N
Mrs Gaynor Bright **Little Brompton Farm** **Montgomery** **SY15 6HY** **Tel: (01686) 668371** **Open: ALL YEAR** **Map Ref No. 82**	£19.00 (no smoking)	Y	Y	Y

Mrs Ceinwen Davies — Nearest Road: A.470. A warm Welsh welcome awaits at Trewythen, this mixed working farm which stands in quiet scenic surroundings, where an abundance of wildlife can be seen. The farmhouse offers superb bedrooms, with en-suite/private bathroom & tea-making facilities. A separate guests' dining room. The lounge (with its beams) has a log fire for the cooler evening as well as a colour T.V.. Evening meals by arrangement. Full central heating. Golf, fishing, pony trekking & lakes nearby.

Leslie & Sylvia Knott — Nearest Road: A.44. A picturesque, listed, c.1500 cruck house set in 1 1/2 acres of pretty garden. Country-cottage bedrooms with en-suite/private facilities & thoughtful extra touches. Relax in either the sitting room, a cosy smoker's bar, with a log fire, or a non-smoking room with books, T.V. & board games. Superb breakfasts, with an unequalled selection, & evening meals are served in the oak-beamed dining room full of romantic charm & family history. Meals are prepared from quality produce & home-grown vegetables. Irresistible desserts may tempt you. A selection of quality wines. Children over 10. Animals by arrangement.

Anne & Tony Millan — Nearest Road: A.483, A.44. Licensed Georgian guest house, situated in an ideal location for touring lakes, mountains, national parks & the coast. The bedrooms are all comfortable & spacious, most en-suite, all with colour T.V. & tea/coffee-making facilities. A ground-floor room is also available. Meals are prepared by Anne, who is Cordon-Bleu-trained. Dinner is a set menu, but special diets/requests can always be catered for with a little prior notice. **E-mail: guidfa@globalnet.co.uk**

Mrs Gaynor Bright — Nearest Road: B.4385. Robert & Gaynor welcome you to this charming 17th-century farmhouse, situated on this working farm. The house has much original character, with beautiful old oak beams. Furnished with traditional antiques. Pretty bedrooms, with en-suite bathrooms, enhanced by quality antiques. T.V.. Home-cooking is a speciality, although meals are by arrangement. Offa's Dyke runs through the farm. Situated on the B.4385, 2 miles east of the beautiful Georgian town of Montgomery. Come & relax in peaceful, stress-free countryside. Animals by arrangement.

When booking your accommodation please
mention
The Best Bed & Breakfast

598

Guidfa House. Llandrindod Wells.

Wales
Powys & Swansea

		rate from £ per person	children taken	evening meals	animals taken
Mr & Mrs Ben Howard-Baker **Glascoed Hall** **Llansilin** **Oswestry SY10 9BP** **Tel: (01691) 791334** **Open: ALL YEAR (Excl.** **Xmas & New Year)** **Map Ref No. 83**	Nearest Road: A.5 A delightful Grade II listed Elizabethan hall featuring a magnificent oak staircase & beams, & open log fires. Set within the beautiful foothills of the Welsh borders, it is an ideal spot for exploring many attractions & is within easy reach of Chester & Shrewsbury. There are 2 very attractive bedrooms, each with an en-suite/private bathroom. Also, a heated outdoor swimming pool & hard tennis court within the grounds. Children over 9 years. Animals by arrangement.	£32.00 CREDIT CARD VISA M'CARD	Y	Y	Y
Mrs Sue Jones **Lower Trelydan** **Farmhouse** **Guilsfield** **Welshpool** **SY21 9PH** **Tel: (01938) 553105** **Fax 01938 553105** **Open: ALL YEAR** **Map Ref No. 86**	Nearest Road: A.490 Graham & Sue welcome you to their wonderful, award-winning black-&-white farmhouse, set on their working farm & listed for its history & beauty. The bedrooms are tastefully furnished, with en-suite facilities & colour T.V. (on request). An oak-beamed lounge, & a dining room where home cooking is a speciality. Also, a licensed bar. Powis Castle & many beauty spots are nearby, as well as leisure activities & walks. Relax in this lovely home, & capture the atmosphere of 4 centuries of history in this outstanding house. Self-catering available in a new barn conversion.	£21.00 *see PHOTO over*	Y	Y	N

Swansea

Mrs Jan Maybery **Tides Reach** **388 Mumbles Road** **Mumbles** **Swansea SA3 5TN** **Tel: (01792) 404877** **Open: FEB - DEC** **Map Ref No. 89**	Nearest Road: A.4067 The warmest of welcomes awaits you at Tides Reach, where you will find a lovingly restored early Victorian town house elegantly furnished with antiques. 8 attractive bedrooms, 5 with en-suite facilities. Well situated on the seafront in the delightful village of Mumbles (the gateway to Gower), only 4 miles from the city centre. An ideal base for business or pleasure & convenient as a stop on your way to Ireland. Children over 7.	£17.50	Y	N	Y

When booking your accommodation please mention
The Best Bed & Breakfast

Lower Trelydan Farm. Guilsfield.

Towns & Counties Index

Towns & Counties Index

Town	County	Country	Town	County	Country
Crewkerne	Somerset	England	Harleston	Norfolk	England
Crianlarich	Perthshire	Scotland	Harrogate	Yorkshire	England
Criccieth	Gwynedd	Wales	Hartfield	Sussex	England
Crickhowell	Powys	Wales	Haslemere	Surrey	England
Darlington	Yorkshire	England	Hastings	Sussex	England
Dartmouth	Devon	England	Haverhill	Suffolk	England
Dereham	Norfolk	England	Hawes	Yorkshire	England
Devizes	Wiltshire	England	Hawkhurst	Kent	England
Didmarton	Gloucestershire	England	Hay-on-Wye	Powys	Wales
Diss	Norfolk	England	Hayling Island	Hampshire	England
Ditchling	Sussex	England	Haywards Heath	Sussex	England
Dolgellau	Gwynedd	Wales	Heathfield	Sussex	England
Dorchester	Dorset	England	Helston	Cornwall	England
Dorking	Surrey	England	Henfield	Sussex	England
Doune	Perthshire	Scotland	Henley-on-Thames	Buckinghamshire	England
Dover	Kent	England	Henley-on-Thames	Oxfordshire	England
Drumnadrochit	Inverness-shire	Scotland	Hereford	Herefordshire	England
Dunkeld	Perthshire	Scotland	Hexham	Northumberland	England
Dunoon	Argyll	Scotland	Holbeach	Lincolnshire	England
Duns	Berwickshire	Scotland	Holywell	Flintshire	Wales
Dunster	Somerset	England	Honiton	Devon	England
Durham	Durham	England	Hope Valley	Derbyshire	England
Duror in Appin	Argyll	Scotland	Horley	Surrey	England
Easingwold	Yorkshire	England	Horsham	Sussex	England
East Brent	Somerset	England	Hungerford	Berkshire	England
East Budleigh	Devon	England	Hunstanton	Norfolk	England
Edinburgh	Edinburgh	Scotland	Hurstpierpoint	Sussex	England
Edinburgh	Lothian	Scotland	Ilfracombe	Devon	England
Ely	Cambridgeshire	England	Inverness	Inverness-shire	Scotland
Emsworth	Hampshire	England	Ipswich	Suffolk	England
Etchingham	Sussex	England	Ironbridge	Shropshire	England
Exeter	Devon	England	Isle of Anglesey	Anglesey	Wales
Eyam	Derbyshire	England	Isle of Islay	Argyll	Scotland
Fakenham	Norfolk	England	Isle of Mull	Argyll	Scotland
Falmouth	Cornwall	England	Isle of Wight	Hampshire	England
Faringdon	Oxfordshire	England	Jedburgh	Roxburghshire	Scotland
Farnham	Hampshire	England	Kelso	Roxburghshire	Scotland
Faversham	Kent	England	Kendal	Cumbria	England
Fishguard	Pembrokeshire	Wales	Kenilworth	Warwickshire	England
Fordingbridge	Hampshire	England	Kentallen of Appin	Argyll	Scotland
Fort Augustus	Inverness-shire	Scotland	Keswick	Cumbria	England
Fort William	Inverness-shire	Scotland	Keswick-on-Derwentwater	Cumbria	England
Frensham	Surrey	England	Kettering	Northamptonshire	England
Garway	Herefordshire	England	Kingham	Oxfordshire	England
Girvan	Ayrshire	Scotland	Kingsbridge	Devon	England
Glastonbury	Somerset	England	Kington	Herefordshire	England
Glenshiel	Ross-shire	Scotland	Kirkbean-by-Dumfries	Dumfriesshire	Scotland
Glossop	Derbyshire	England	Kirkby Lonsdale	Cumbria	England
Grange-over-Sands	Cumbria	England	Kirkby Stephen	Cumbria	England
Grantham	Lincolnshire	England	Knutsford	Cheshire	England
Grantown-on-Spey	Inverness-shire	Scotland	Launceston	Cornwall	England
Grasmere	Cumbria	England	Leamington Spa	Warwickshire	England
Great Ayton	Yorkshire	England	Ledbury	Herefordshire	England
Great Yarmouth	Norfolk	England	Leek	Staffordshire	England
Grindon	Staffordshire	England	Leominster	Herefordshire	England
Guildford	Surrey	England	Lewes	Sussex	England
Hadleigh	Suffolk	England	Leyburn	Yorkshire	England
Halesworth	Suffolk	England	Lincoln	Lincolnshire	England
Harlech	Gwynedd	Wales	Liskeard	Cornwall	England

Towns & Counties Index

Towns & Counties Index

Recommendations / Complaints

Thank you for taking the trouble to supply this information .
We value your comments & will take appropriate action where necessary.
We regret that we are unable to reply to you individually.

Proprietors _____

House Name _____

Address _____

_____

_____

General Information about your
stay, the house & hosts etc.

_____

_____

_____

_____

_____

_____

_____

_____

Your Name _____

Address _____

_____

_____

**Reply to: W.W.B.B.A. P.O. Box 2070,
London. W12 8QW**

Recommendations / Complaints

Thank you for taking the trouble to supply this information .
We value your comments & will take appropriate action where necessary.
We regret that we are unable to reply to you individually.

Proprietors _____

House Name _____

Address _____

_____

_____

General information about your
stay, the house & hosts etc.

_____

_____

_____

_____

_____

_____

_____

Your Name _____

Address _____

_____

Reply to:W.W.B.B.A. P.O. Box 2070,
London. W12 8QW

Recommendations / Complaints

Thank you for taking the trouble to supply this information .
We value your comments & will take appropriate action where necessary.
We regret that we are unable to reply to you individually.

Proprietors _____

House Name _____

Address _____

_____

_____

**General information about your
stay, the house & hosts etc**.

_____

_____

_____

_____

_____

_____

_____

Your Name _____

Address _____

_____

**Reply to: W.W.B.B.A. P.O. Box 2070.
London. W12 8QW**